MARKETING RESEARCH
for Managerial Decision Making

Fifth Edition

Timothy R. Graeff
Middle Tennessee State University

Kendall Hunt
publishing company

www.kendallhunt.com
Send all inquiries to:
4050 Westmark Drive
Dubuque, IA 52004-1840

Dedication

To Myfanwy, Kathryn and Jori, for
their constant love and support;
and to the Lord, through whom
all things are possible.

—Tim

Contents

Introduction xiii

CHAPTER 1   What Is Marketing Research? 1

CHAPTER 2   Marketing Research as a Profession 11

CHAPTER 3   Marketing Research and the Decision-Making Process. 25

CHAPTER 4   Social Media and Emerging Technologies: Opportunities and Challenges 37

CHAPTER 5   Classes of Marketing Research 63

CHAPTER 6   The Marketing Research Process. 71

CHAPTER 7   Identifying Marketing Problems: Exploratory Research Techniques 83

CHAPTER 8   Secondary Data and Database Marketing. 101

CHAPTER 9   Focus Groups. 125

CHAPTER 10   Quantitative Research Objectives 171

CHAPTER 11   Survey Data Collection Methodologies 195

CHAPTER 12   Survey Error. 219

CHAPTER 13   Measurement. 251

CHAPTER 14   Reliability, Sensitivity, and Validity of Measurement Scales 275

CHAPTER 15   Scales Used in Marketing Research 287

CHAPTER 16   Writing Survey Questions and Organizing the Questionnaire 305

CHAPTER 17   Sampling Procedures 345

CHAPTER 18   Causal Research and Experimental Design 363

CHAPTER 19   Preparing and Analyzing Data 393

CHAPTER 20   Distributions and Statistics. 413

CHAPTER 21   Confidence Intervals. 425

CHAPTER 22   Hypothesis Testing 433

CHAPTER 23   Cross-Tabulating Survey Data 447

CHAPTER 24   Chi-Square Goodness of Fit Test 455

CHAPTER 25   One-Way Analysis of Variance (ANOVA) 469

CHAPTER 26   Correlation Analysis 479

CHAPTER 27   Two-Way ANOVA (Two Factors and Interaction) 485

CHAPTER 28   Multiple Regression Analysis. 495

CHAPTER 29   The Research Report 507

CASE 1   Strickland College Student Drinking Survey 527

CASE 2   The Red Hills Mall 539

CASE 3   Rockville Medical Center 547

Appendices 553

Index 571

Detailed Contents

INTRODUCTION   XIII

CHAPTER 1
. . . .

What Is Marketing Research?   1

What Is Marketing Research?   1
Who Uses Marketing Research?   2
When Is Marketing Research Necessary?   2
Basic and Applied Research   3
Marketing Information Systems   4
Who Makes Marketing Management Decisions?   5
Questions for Discussion   8
MINICASE 1.1 Tolmarck Inc.   9

CHAPTER 2
. . . .

Marketing Research as a Profession   11

Graduate Degrees in Marketing Research   13
Satisfaction with Marketing Careers   14
Marketing Research Certification   14
Marketing Research Contacts   15
Professional Ethics and Marketing Research   16
Questions for Discussion   20
MINICASE 2.1 Gold Coast Travel   22

CHAPTER 3
. . . .

Marketing Research and the Decision-Making Process   25

The IDO Model   26
Meeting with Clients and Developing Research
   Objectives   28
Consider the Marketing Objectives When Designing
   Research   31

Communicating Information to Decision
   Makers   34
Questions for Discussion   34
MINICASE 3.1 Winstrom Furniture Store   35

CHAPTER 4
. . . .

Social Media and Emerging Technologies: Opportunities and Challenges   37

Social Media and Marketing Research   39
Social Media Research Approaches and Methods   42
Online Communities   43
Mobile Surveys and Apps-Based Research   45
Social Media Monitoring and Analytics   46
Biometrics   51
Eye Tracking   51
Neuromarketing   53
The Promise of Emerging Technologies   54
Challenges Facing Marketing Research   55
Questions for Discussion   58
MINICASE 4.1 Precision Planting and
   Gardening   59

CHAPTER 5
. . . .

Classes of Marketing Research   63

Exploratory Research   63
Descriptive Research   65
Causal Research   66
Exploratory, Descriptive, and Causal Research   67
Questions for Discussion   68
MINICASE 5.1 Modern Styles Clothing Store   69
MINICASE 5.2 Good-to-Grow Gardening   69
MINICASE 5.3 Camp Fish   70

CHAPTER 6

The Marketing Research Process   **71**

The Marketing Research Process   71

The Most Important Stages in the Marketing Research Process   76

Sequence of Causes   77

Questions to Ask When Conducting Marketing Research   78

Questions for Discussion   81

MINICASE 6.1 Dalapatalio's Pizzeria   82

CHAPTER 7

Identifying Marketing Problems: Exploratory Research Techniques   **83**

Background Analysis   84

Employee Interviews and Employee Focus Groups   85

Mystery Shoppers   87

Observation   90

Ethnography   93

Focus Groups   97

Social Media Monitoring   98

Behavior, Behavior, Behavior   98

Questions for Discussion   98

MINICASE 7.1 College Bookstore   99

CHAPTER 8

Secondary Data and Database Marketing   **101**

Consumer Demographics   103

Consumer Psychographics and Lifestyles   103

Company Data   104

Industry Data and Market Intelligence   104

Consumer Panels   105

Store Audits   106

Evaluating Secondary Data   107

Database Marketing   108

Creating a Database   110

Databases and Marketing Performance   112

Loyalty Programs and Loyalty Cards   113

Store Credit Cards   114

Reward Credit Cards   115

Warranty Cards and Product Registration Cards   116

List Providers   116

RFM Analysis   118

Consumer Motivation and Reasons for Behaviors   119

Find, Make, Keep, Grow   120

Questions for Discussion   121

MINICASE 8.1 Parkersville Parks and Recreation Department   123

MINICASE 8.2 IsoFlex   123

CHAPTER 9

Focus Groups   **125**

Focus Groups and Marketing Objectives   129

Focus Group Facilities   131

Focus Group Composition   136

Designing a Focus Group Session   137

Moderating a Focus Group Session   141

Developing the Moderator's Guide   142

Sample Moderator's Guides   145

Use Broad Focus Group Questions   154

Do Not Express Your Opinions in a Focus Group   155

Laddering in a Focus Group Session   155

Projective Techniques in Focus Groups   160

Online Focus Groups   163

Post-Group Evaluation   165

Focus Groups and Conclusive Evidence   165

Questions for Discussion   165

MINICASE 9.1 Jack Daniel's Focus Group   168

MINICASE 9.2 King Pin Lanes   168

MINICASE 9.3 InTech Inline Skates   169

MINICASE 9.4 HealthSource   169

CHAPTER 10

Quantitative Research Objectives   **171**

Identifying Research Objectives   173

Research Objectives and the Decision-Making Process   174

The Consumer Purchase Process   175

Consumer Adoption Process Models   175

The Fundamental Questions for Marketers   176

If I Could Ask Only One Question, What Would
   I Ask?   177

Consider the Usefulness of Research
   Objectives   178

Do Not Rely Solely on Predictor Variables   178

Consider the Decision Maker   180

Do Not Forget to Survey Noncustomers   180

Do Not Confuse Customer Service with Customer
   Satisfaction   180

Consider Past, Present, and Future
   Behavior   183

Attitudes vs. Behavioral Intentions   184

When Designing Surveys, You Can Never Be Too
   Specific   189

Separate Primary from Secondary Data
   Objectives   190

Research Hypotheses   190

Questions for Discussion   191

MINICASE 10.1 Clayton Mark Hotel   192

MINICASE 10.2 Pennsylvania State Museum and
   Historical Society   193

CHAPTER 11

Survey Data Collection Methodologies   **195**

Personal Interviews   196

Telephone Surveys   199

Mail Surveys   201

Self-Administered Surveys   201

Online (Internet) Surveys   202

Mobile Surveys   204

Google Consumer Surveys   205

Omnibus Surveys   206

Syndicated Surveys (Studies)   206

Straw Polls   208

Computer-Based Interviewing   208

Global Survey Research   210

Avoid Cross-Cultural Marketing Mistakes   211

Unethical Survey Practices: Push Polls   213

Questions for Discussion   214

MINICASE 11.1 Johnathon Green, Real Estate
   Agent   216

CHAPTER 12

Survey Error   **219**

Random Sampling Error   221

Systematic Error and Bias   223

Types of Systematic Error and Bias in
   Surveys   225

Representative Sampling: A Two-Step Process   236

Cross-Sectional vs. Longitudinal Surveys   237

Interpreting Survey Results   241

Survey Error and the Decision-Making
   Process   245

Questions for Discussion   245

MINICASE 12.1 Reserved Parking Spaces   247

MINICASE 12.2 Marcony Grill   248

MINICASE 12.3 Virginia Woman Magazine   248

MINICASE 12.4 Student Express Bus   249

MINICASE 12.5 Pinky's BBQ Restaurant   249

CHAPTER 13

Measurement   **251**

Defining and Measuring Constructs   252

Levels of Measurement Scales   254

Allowable Scale Transformations   256

Nominal Scales   256

Ordinal Scales   257

Interval Scales   260

Ratio Scales   261

Zero on Nominal, Ordinal, and Interval
   Scales   262

Verbal Labels on Scales   262

Category Ranges and Ordinal Scales   263

Reporting the Median vs. the Mean   264

Interval Scales and Percentages   265

Measurement Scales and the Decision-Making
   Process   266

Questions for Discussion   268

MINICASE 13.1 MegaBucks Insurance
   Agency   273

MINICASE 13.2 America Reads   273

MINICASE 13.3 Miami Department of
   Tourism   274

CHAPTER 14

Reliability, Sensitivity and Validity of Measurement Scales **275**

    Reliability 276

    Sensitivity 279

    Validity 280

    Quality Scales and the Decision-Making Process 282

    Questions for Discussion 284

    MINICASE 14.1 Sweet Shop Ice Cream Parlor 285

CHAPTER 15

Scales Used in Marketing Research **287**

    Open-Ended Questions 288

    Closed-Ended Questions 289

    Likert Scales 293

    Semantic Differential Scales 294

    Stapel Scale 297

    Constant Sum Scale 297

    Index of Items 298

    Cautions with Ranking Questions 298

    Measurement Scales and the Decision-Making Process 301

    Questions for Discussion 302

    MINICASE 15.1 Grundy's Hardware Store 303

CHAPTER 16

Writing and Organizing Surveys **305**

    Avoid Ambiguous Questions 306

    Avoid Leading or Loaded Questions 309

    Avoid Double-Barreled Questions 311

    Avoid Taxing Questions 311

    Avoid Technical Language or Jargon 312

    Avoid Double Negatives 313

    Avoid False Comparisons 313

    Tips on Writing Survey Questions 314

    Organizing the Questionnaire 316

    Zero as a Separate Response Category 321

    Identifying Apathy Bias and Uninformed Response Bias 323

    Randomized Response Questions 325

    Increasing the Response Rates for Surveys 326

    Why Increase the Response Rates for Surveys? 327

    Guidelines for Interviewers 328

    Telephone Surveys and Do-Not-Call Lists 329

    Writing Survey Questions and the Decision-Making Process 330

    Sample Telephone Survey: Community Library 331

    Sample Telephone Survey: Consumer Outlook 334

    Questions for Discussion 338

    MINICASE 16.1 Wilson County School District 340

    MINICASE 16.2 Student Government Association 341

    MINICASE 16.3 Elect Janet Porter for Mayor Campaign 342

    MINICASE 16.4 The Bowlarama 342

    MINICASE 16.5 The Springfield Gazette Lifestyle Survey 343

CHAPTER 17

Sampling Procedures **345**

    The Goal and Means of Sampling 347

    Sampling Procedures 347

    Issues in Sampling 350

    Determining Sample Size 352

    Finite Population Correction Factor 356

    Sample Size and Margin of Error 356

    Population Variability and Sample Size 357

    Interpreting the Margin of Error 358

    Sampling and the Decision-Making Process 359

    Questions for Discussion 360

    MINICASE 17.1 George Saul for Governor Campaign 361

CHAPTER 18

Causal Research and Experimental Design **363**

    A Causal Relationship Is Impossible to Prove 365

    Increasing Confidence in a Causal Relationship 366

    Components of Experimental Designs 367

    Identifying Components of Experiments 368

    Controlling for Extraneous Variables (Confounds) 371

Designing an Advertising Experiment   373

Designing a Taste Testing Experiment   373

Factorial Designs   374

Internal and External Experimental Validity   376

Blind and Double-Blind Experiments   378

Test Marketing   379

Quasi- and True Experimental Designs   384

Causal Research and the Decision-Making
Process   389

Questions for Discussion   389

MINICASE 18.1 Palo Valley Wines   390

MINICASE 18.2 SharpCraft Bass Boats   391

CHAPTER 19

. . . .

Preparing and Analyzing Data   393

Developing the Coding Sheet   393

Coding Sheet for Credit Card Survey   394

Entering Data into a Data File   396

Coding Open-Ended Survey Questions   400

Developing Open-Ended Coding Schemes and
Categories   401

Reporting Open-Ended Responses in the Research
Report   404

Analyzing Quantitative Data   404

Note-Taking Surveys   408

Questions for Discussion   410

MINICASE 19.1 Mount Granite College Student
Health Services   410

MINICASE 19.2 Pine Tree Mobile Homes   411

CHAPTER 20

. . . .

Distributions and Statistics   413

Central Tendency   413

Dispersion   413

Statistics and Distributions   414

The Normal Distribution   415

The Standardized Normal Distribution   417

The Three Distributions of Statistical Inference   418

Central Limit Theorem   420

Questions for Discussion   421

MINICASE 20.1 Central Limit Theorem   421

CHAPTER 21

. . . .

Confidence Intervals   425

Confidence Interval for an Average   425

Confidence Intervals (Averages) for the
Note-Taking Survey   427

Confidence Interval for a Proportion   428

Confidence Intervals (Proportions) for the
Note-Taking Survey   429

Increasing Confidence in Estimates   430

Questions for Discussion   431

MINICASE 21.1 RazorCorp Heated Razor   432

CHAPTER 22

. . . .

Hypothesis Testing   433

Critical Values, Acceptance Regions, and Rejection
Regions   435

A Legal Example of Hypothesis Testing   436

Errors in Statistical Hypothesis Testing   437

Increasing Statistical Power by Increasing
Sample Size   438

Cautions with Hypothesizing No Effects   439

Hypothesis Test of an Average   442

Hypothesis Test of an Average: Note-Taking
Survey   443

Hypothesis Test of a Proportion   444

Hypothesis Test of a Proportion: Note-Taking
Survey   445

Questions for Discussion   445

MINICASE 22.1 Marvin's Neighborhood
Market   446

CHAPTER 23

. . . .

Cross-Tabulating Survey Data   447

Guidelines for Cross-Tabulating Survey Data   450

Cross-Tabs and Statistical Significance   451

Interpreting Cross-Tab Outputs from Statistical
Analysis Programs   451

Questions for Discussion   452

MINICASE 23.1 Treasure Box   453

CHAPTER 24

Chi-Square Goodness of Fit Test   **455**

Interpreting the Chi-Square Analysis Output   458

Chi-Square Goodness of Fit Test for the Note-Taking Survey   460

Questions for Discussion   464

MINICASE 24.1 Fur on the Floor Dog Grooming   464

MINICASE 24.2 Maple Street JazzFest   465

CHAPTER 25

Analysis of Variance (ANOVA)   **469**

Explaining Variability   471

ANOVA for the Note-Taking Survey   473

Multiple Comparison Procedures   474

Multiple Comparison Procedure for the Note-Taking Survey   475

Questions for Discussion   476

MINICASE 25.1 Super Speedway   477

CHAPTER 26

Correlation Analysis   **479**

Correlation Analysis for the Note-Taking Survey   481

Questions for Discussion   483

MINICASE 26.1 Super Speedway   483

CHAPTER 27

Two-Way ANOVA   **485**

Main Effects and Interactions   485

Identifying Main Effects and Interactions   486

Preference for Interactions Over Main Effects   489

Interpreting Margin Means   489

Two-Way ANOVA Hypotheses and Decision Rules   489

Two-Way ANOVA for the Note-Taking Survey   491

Questions for Discussion   492

MINICASE 27.1 The Caballero Grill   492

CHAPTER 28

Multiple Regression Analysis   **495**

Why Standardize Variables?   497

Standardized Regression Estimates (Beta Coefficients)   498

Multiple Regression Hypotheses and Decision Rules   499

Multiple Regression with Standardized Regression Estimates for the Note-Taking Survey   500

Model Building and Selection Procedures   501

Stepwise Regression for the Note-Taking Survey   502

Questions for Discussion   503

MINICASE 28.1 Super Speedway   504

CHAPTER 29

The Research Report   **507**

The Research Report and Marketing Objectives   507

Outline of a Research Report   508

The Research Presentation   513

Reporting Results with Charts   515

Survey Questions as Chart Titles   520

Keep Charts and Graphs Simple and Uncluttered   521

Interpreting Results in Charts and Tables   521

Marketing Research and Managerial Decision Making   524

Final Thoughts   524

Questions for Discussion   525

CASE 1   **Strickland College Student Drinking Survey**   **527**

CASE 2   **The Red Hills Mall**   **539**

CASE 3   **Rockville Medical Center**   **547**

APPENDICES

APPENDIX 1 **Table of Random Numbers**   **555**

APPENDIX 2 **Area under the Normal Curve (Z Values)**   **557**

APPENDIX 3 **Chi-Square (χ^2) Distribution**   **559**

APPENDIX 4 **The Group Research Project**   **561**

Index   **571**

Introduction

Marketing research is one of the most important business functions. The purpose of marketing research is to collect information that marketing managers need to make decisions. And, given that all managers, no matter what the business, industry, or service, must routinely make decisions, understanding marketing research and the processes involved in collecting information that managers use to make decisions is vitally important to any business student.

Marketing research is an exciting field of discovery that is relevant in almost any marketing situation. For example, some marketing research projects collect information about consumers, such as demographic characteristics, attitudes, beliefs, perceptions, intentions, and even purchase behavior. Some marketing research projects measure the potential effects of changing marketing variables such as price, product, place and promotion on consumers' attitudes and purchase intentions. Some marketing research projects identify new marketing opportunities and measure consumers' responses to new marketing ideas, products, services, or promotional campaigns. All areas of marketing use marketing research, including advertising, promotions, sales, distribution, logistics, pricing, manufacturing, and product design. This book examines the role of marketing research in helping marketing managers make marketing decisions.

In addition to describing important marketing research concepts, terms, techniques, and procedures, this book contains a number of MiniCases and Discussion Questions at the end of each chapter. These MiniCases and Discussion Questions supplement the material presented in the chapters to provide increased understanding of, and experience with, various aspects of a research project.

In addition to the MiniCases, there are three larger cases where students can interpret the results from marketing research to make marketing decisions and recommendations. These cases highlight how marketing research is used in varying industries and businesses, for example, education, retail, and health care services.

This book also contains a larger Group Project to be conducted throughout a semester. The material in the chapters, along with the MiniCases and Discussion Questions, are designed to provide marketing students with the information and skills needed to conduct the group research project, including developing research objectives, designing the data collection and sampling procedures, collecting the data, analyzing the data, and preparing a marketing research report. Groups of three to four students work on one small-business marketing research project. As students learn about marketing research topics and the stages in the research process throughout the semester, they work on their group project and review the projects from other groups. The purpose of the project is to give students hands on experience with using marketing research to deal with a small-business start-up decision.

Marketing researchers routinely update the methodologies that they use to gather information about consumers in response to changing technologies and cultural trends. Few could argue that one of the most significant trends in recent years has been the widespread acceptance of social media among consumers. Consumers have become very adept at communicating with each other via social media. Moreover, this new form of communication has opened up a wide array of new research techniques and approaches that marketers can use to listen to and communicate with consumers. One of the goals of this book is to highlight how such emerging technologies have shaped the research industry and are opening up exciting new areas of discovery into the world of consumers.

Marketing research is an exciting field with much to offer in the way of career opportunities. I hope that after reading this book you will come to appreciate the many benefits that marketing research has to offer. Even if you are not considering a career in marketing research, any marketing professional will undoubtedly be exposed to the results from marketing research when making marketing and business decisions. A basic understanding of the marketing research process, the techniques and methodologies used in marketing research, and even the limitations and possible sources of error associated with various research techniques will aid a marketing manager when making decisions. Not only must a marketing manager know the results of the research that he or she is using to make decisions, the manager must also fully understand the process by which that information was collected to be able to judge the usefulness of the information for making marketing decisions.

This book is designed to be used by:

- University students enrolled in an undergraduate marketing research course.
- Undergraduate university students seeking a career in marketing research.
- Undergraduate business students who do not intend to be professional marketing researchers, but who instead seek to be marketing/business managers who will use the results from marketing research to inform their decisions.
- Master's and doctoral level students seeking help in designing their thesis research.
- Marketing managers who wish to conduct their own marketing research projects.

CHAPTER 1

What is Marketing Research?

LEARNING OBJECTIVES

1 Define marketing research.

2 Identify the individuals and types of organizations that use marketing research.

3 Identify when marketing research is needed.

4 Describe the differences between primary and secondary data.

5 Describe the differences between basic and applied research.

6 Define marketing information system.

7 Define decision support system.

8 Explain the reasons why marketing decisions should be made by marketing managers, not marketing research.

9 Identify some of the most important questions that decision makers should ask researchers.

WHAT IS MARKETING RESEARCH?

Marketers and business managers need information to make decisions and to compete in the marketplace. For example, imagine that you own a company that manufactures and markets high-quality fishing equipment. What would you want to know about consumers and your target market? You might want to know how often consumers in your target market go fishing, why they go fishing, their satisfaction with current fishing equipment sold in retail stores and online, their desire or need for higher-quality fishing equipment, how much they currently spend on fishing equipment, and how much they would be willing to spend on higher-quality fishing equipment. Marketing research is the business function that collects this information in a systematic, unbiased, and objective manner and communicates it to decision makers so that decisions can be made to achieve marketing objectives.[1]

The information collected by marketing research is used to connect consumers and other publics to the marketer. This information is used to identify marketing problems and opportunities. It is also used to help marketing managers make and evaluate marketing decisions. And, it is also used to monitor marketing performance. More formally, the American Marketing Association defines **marketing research** as the function that links the consumer, customer, and public to the marketer through

> Marketing research is the business function that collects information in a systematic, unbiased, and objective manner and communicates that information to decision makers so that decisions can be made to achieve marketing objectives.

information used to identify and define marketing opportunities and problems; generate, refine, and evaluate marketing actions; monitor marketing performance; and improve understanding of marketing as a process. Marketing research specifies the information required to address these issues, designs the method for collecting information, manages and implements the data collection process, analyzes the results, and communicates the findings and their implications.[2]

By providing marketing managers with information obtained from marketing research, managers can hopefully make fewer risky and intuitive decisions that are often based on nothing more than gut feelings and hunches. Marketing research provides a means by which marketing managers can make decisions based on information obtained in a systematic, objective, and unbiased manner. Marketing research also provides managers with a means for quantifying their decisions. For example, you might choose to first enter the southeastern U.S. market with your high-quality fishing equipment because the quantitative data you received from marketing research indicates that this part of the country has the highest concentration of potential customers.

WHO USES MARKETING RESEARCH?

All organizations use marketing research. This includes for-profit and not-for-profit organizations. Anyone selling a physical product, an intangible service, an idea, a concept, a political candidate, or even themselves can benefit from using marketing research. At the extreme, you can even argue that individuals conduct marketing research when they ask their friends what they want to do on Friday night.

The purpose of marketing research is to collect information that marketing managers need to make decisions. And, given that all managers, no matter what the business, industry, or service, must routinely make decisions, understanding marketing research and the processes involved in collecting information that managers use to make decisions is vitally important to any manager or decision maker.

WHEN IS MARKETING RESEARCH NECESSARY?

Conducting marketing research is not necessary for making all decisions. Perhaps the first factor that most marketers consider when deciding to conduct marketing research is whether or not there is adequate time to collect, analyze, and implement the results from a research project. Marketing research can be time-consuming. A typical test market might last as long as one year. It might take two months to receive completed surveys that were sent to consumers in the mail. Further, ethnographic studies, where researchers observe consumers as they shop and interact with other consumers, might take months to complete. A second factor to consider is the cost to conduct the research. Marketing research can be very expensive. For example, research firms often charge between $15,000 and $20,000 to conduct relatively

Any individual or organization that sells anything, be it a physical product, an intangible service, or even an abstract idea or concept, can benefit from marketing research when making managerial decisions.

simple phone surveys of a few hundred consumers. Due to these costs, marketing research should be conducted only when the decision to be made is important enough to justify the expense. One way to decrease the cost of marketing research is to use existing data to make decisions. Data that already exists is called **secondary data**. And, marketing managers often use secondary data when making decisions.

Secondary Data. Secondary data is typically data that was collected for a purpose other than the specific managerial decision at hand. Examples of secondary data include previous surveys, customer sales records, census data, industry reports, and database lists of customers. Secondary data can usually be collected very quickly and is usually very inexpensive compared to collecting new and original data. A great deal of secondary data can be obtained from the Internet. Some websites require users to pay a subscription fee to gain access to the data on their site. But, many websites provide free access to existing research data. This makes obtaining secondary data very quick and easy. Secondary data will be discussed in more detail in a later chapter.

Primary Data. When the data that currently exists is not sufficient to help marketing managers make decisions, marketing researchers must collect new and original data. This new and original data is called **primary data**. Primary data can be collected using a variety of research techniques, such as focus groups, surveys, experiments, and even mystery shoppers. A fundamental purpose of this book is to outline these various research techniques and to discuss their relevance to the managerial decision-making process. Primary data can become secondary data later. Primary data has the advantage of being exactly what decision makers need for the particular decision. Primary data is also current, and the researcher has control over the quality of the data collection procedures and methodologies. However, primary data is usually more costly and time-consuming to collect compared to secondary data. As a result, researchers typically begin the research process by examining secondary data first, and then, if secondary data is neither available nor applicable to the decision at hand, researchers collect primary data.

Conduct marketing research when:
1 You have sufficient time.
2 You have sufficient money.
3 The decisions to be made are important enough to spend the time and money on research.
4 There is no existing (secondary) data that can be used to help make the managerial decisions.

BASIC AND APPLIED RESEARCH

Basic research is the term used to describe research that is conducted to increase our general understanding of a topic, phenomenon, or area of study. Its purpose is to increase our basic level of knowledge. Examples of this include basic medical research, archeological research, and basic physics or chemistry research. Basic research is usually not conducted to help solve a particular managerial problem. Rather, it is often conducted by academic researchers who hope to increase our understanding of the world around us. The results from basic research are often reported in academic journals. Examples of academic journals for marketing include the *Journal of Marketing*, *Journal of Marketing Research*, *Journal of Consumer Research*, and *Journal of Business Research*.

Applied research, on the other hand, is conducted to help solve a particular managerial problem and to help marketers make a particular managerial decision. The results of the research will be applied and used in the managerial decision-making process. Most of the research techniques discussed in this book are used to conduct applied research. Examples of applied research include focus groups, surveys, taste test experiments, test marketing, and advertising experiments.

MARKETING INFORMATION SYSTEMS

The entire system by which marketing research data and information is collected, analyzed, stored, and transformed into reports that can be used for making managerial decisions is referred to as a **marketing information system**. The marketing information system for an organization can be as simple as a single paper and pencil survey that is manually administered and analyzed, or as complex as a computerized customer loyalty program for automatically capturing customer purchase behavior by using scanner data. A marketing **decision support system** is a type of computerized information system that is designed to support day-to-day marketing management decisions. In many cases marketing decision support systems use interactive software allowing marketing managers to access, manipulate, and analyze marketing data. A single decision support system can perform multiple functions and analyses, and it can generate a variety of different reports to meet the varying needs of marketing managers. To be effective, a decision support system must be interactive and flexible. Marketing managers must be able to easily interact with the data and be able to access the data that they need, in the form that they need it. The system should allow managers to easily retrieve and manipulate the data and information that is most relevant to the particular situation and decision at hand. For some purposes, the system must also be portable, allowing managers to access data, perform predictive modeling analyses, and generate reports from a laptop computer or mobile device, such as a tablet or smartphone, so that they can make decisions while in the field, and not just in their offices.

To illustrate the use of a decision support system, consider a regional manager for a chain of grocery stores. As the manager travels from store to store, he or she can access current sales data for individual stores and compare those sales figures to nationwide sales data for grocery stores that was obtained from retail store audits. This analysis will allow the regional manager to adjust marketing strategies related to promotions, product placement, and inventories.

Improving Customer Relationship Management. Many businesses and organizations use marketing information systems and decision support systems for improving **customer relationship management**. Having easy access to timely data and information regarding individual customers allows a business to more effectively market to its customers. For example, a manufacturer's salesperson could provide better customer service by using a decision support system accessible from a laptop computer or tablet to customize product offerings, customize the order and delivery process, and even customize the terms of a sale, all based on previous sales and ordering data related to an individual customer. And all of these decisions could be made in real time, while talking with customers.

Decision support systems vary in complexity from marketer to marketer. For example, many hair salons keep relatively simple computerized customer records that can be accessed with the customer's phone number. A customer's previous history with the salon is retrieved from the system when that customer's phone number is entered. The customer history report tells the stylist how long it has been since the customer last had his or her hair cut or styled (indicating to the stylist the appropriate length of hair to cut), the type of cut or style the customer prefers, and any special needs that the customer might have. Accessing this information from the computer when a customer enters the salon makes the cutting and styling process more personal and individualized. Similarly, many hotels maintain computerized databases containing customer information. When guests check in at a hotel their history report can be called up on a computer screen. Based on this history report guests can be given coupons for their favorite stores, shows, and restaurants in the area of the hotel. Such personalized service can go a long way in improving guest satisfaction.

As another example, a sporting goods retailer might maintain a computerized customer loyalty program. When a customer scans his or her loyalty card at the time of purchase, all of the purchase data for that customer is automatically entered into a database. Managers at the store can then analyze the data in the database to identify relationships between product lines sold in their store. For example, managers might notice that customers who purchase tennis and golf equipment also tend to purchase higher-priced brands of clothing. This information could be used to make a variety of marketing decisions, including:

- The physical layout of the store could be rearranged so that higher-priced brands of clothing are located adjacent to the golf and tennis equipment.

- In-store salespeople could watch for customers who are shopping for golf or tennis equipment and then direct those customers to the higher-priced brands of clothing.

- Cross-promotional offers and sales could be designed, such as "Spend $100 on golf or tennis equipment, get $20 off your purchase of clothing."

- Personalized promotions and offers could be sent to a customer's home address or email address based on the products that the customer purchases.

WHO MAKES MARKETING MANAGEMENT DECISIONS?

Marketing research is a vital input into the marketing managerial decision-making process. However, marketing research should not be considered a replacement for marketing managers. Marketing decisions should be made by managers who use the results from marketing research as an input into their decision-making processes.

TAKE THIS SURVEY!

Before reading any further, please complete the following short survey that measures consumers' exercise behaviors and attitudes toward various brands of athletic shoes.

How often do you participate in the following athletic/exercise activities?	About once a week (or more often)	About once a month	About once every three months	About once every six months	About once a year	Never
Walking at least 1 mile for exercise.	○	○	○	○	○	○
Running or jogging at least 1 mile for exercise.	○	○	○	○	○	○
Bicycling at least 1 mile for exercise.	○	○	○	○	○	○
Swimming at least 20 minutes for exercise.	○	○	○	○	○	○

Circle the number that best represents your attitude toward the following brands of athletic shoes.	Dislike Very Much				Like Very Much
Converse	1	2	3	4	5
New Balance	1	2	3	4	5
Nike	1	2	3	4	5
Pontrey	1	2	3	4	5
Avia	1	2	3	4	5
Adidas	1	2	3	4	5

Marketing research should not be allowed to make decisions for managers. It is important to keep a clear distinction between the information-gathering function of marketing research and the decision-making function of marketing managers. The purpose of marketing research is therefore to serve as one of potentially many inputs into the decision-making process.

Administrative Error. There are a number of important reasons why marketing and business decisions should not be made based solely on the results of a single marketing research project. Many marketing managers mistakenly assume that the results from marketing research are always correct, accurate, and free from error or bias. Unfortunately, this is not always the case. There are numerous sources of error or bias that can be introduced into a research project at any of the stages in the marketing research process. Researchers can introduce error into research results based on the decisions that they make regarding the research process and how the research is administered. Error and bias can result from poorly designed data collection procedures and methods and even the way questions are worded and asked. This is referred to as **administrative error** because it is the result of something the researcher (administrator) did to cause the error. For example, imagine the potential error and bias associated with a survey in which consumers are asked "Would you ever consider purchasing a low-quality car such as a Kia?" This leading question will obviously underestimate purchase likelihood because the question implies that Kia is a low-quality car. Very few people would want to admit that they are considering purchasing a low-quality car. Researchers might also introduce error into the results due to a biased sampling plan or a biased sampling procedure.

Response Bias. Error and bias can also be introduced due to the way people tend to answer questions and how people sometimes censor their comments or even lie when asked questions by researchers. The information that is obtained from consumers and the answers that respondents give to survey questions might not represent consumers' true thoughts, beliefs, or feelings. This is referred to as **response bias**, because it is bias and error resulting from respondents censoring their answers or deliberately providing false answers. Respondents will sometimes give what they think is the socially acceptable answer. Other times, respondents might give false answers just to look good in the eyes of an interviewer, or to feel better about themselves. Consumers might overreport how often they participate in athletic activities for exercise because they are embarrassed to report that they do not exercise very often. Sometimes, respondents will even answer questions when they know nothing about the topic of the question. People do not want to appear ignorant, so they will sometimes give uninformed opinions about products or brands. If this happens, marketing managers will make decisions based on meaningless answers that respondents gave merely because they felt obligated to respond. This is called **uninformed response bias**. To illustrate how often this occurs and how easy it is for someone to provide such uninformed opinions, look at the exercise survey shown in the box titled "Take This Survey." If you completed this survey and you circled a number on the attitude scale for Pontrey athletic shoes, then you just gave an uninformed opinion. Pontrey is a fictitious brand—it does not exist!

Sampling (Statistical) Error. Unfortunately, many managers do not fully understand statistics and the concept of statistical error. Whenever researchers calculate statistical estimates, there can be error in the results due to simply sampling a subset of the population instead of surveying every member of the population. For example, when researchers calculate a 95 percent confidence interval for a proportion they must allow for a 5 percent chance that the true population proportion is not within the range of the calculated confidence interval.

Irrelevance of the Decision Maker. Perhaps the most important reason why decisions should not be based solely on the results from marketing research is that doing so reduces the relevance and importance of the human decision maker. If all decisions are made based solely on the results of marketing research there is no need for marketing managers. The marketing research department can run the company.

Marketing decision should be made by marketing managers, not by marketing research.

Marketing research is merely one of many inputs into the managerial decision-making process.

However, most people would agree that this is not an attractive strategy for running a business. People should make marketing decisions. Marketing researchers are paid to collect and provide useful information. And, marketing managers are paid to make marketing decisions. People have intuition, emotions, perceptions, and accumulated knowledge from past experiences that provide valuable guidance to decision making that research results alone do not provide. People understand right and wrong. They understand the ethical and moral implications of decisions. As such, marketing managers should make marketing decisions based on multiple sources of information, one of which is marketing research.

Making Informed Decisions. Given the numerous sources of error or bias that might possibly affect research results, it is incumbent upon researchers as well as marketing managers to fully understand how marketing research is conducted so that informed decisions can be made based on the results of research. A marketing research textbook and/or a course in marketing research methods would be beneficial to all marketing managers and decision makers. When dealing with marketing research, it is often assumed that the researchers are the ones who ask the questions (e.g., on surveys, in focus groups). However, when research results are presented to managers, decision makers must know what questions to ask of the researcher. For example, marketing decision makers should ask questions such as:

- Why was this particular methodology chosen?

- Are there characteristics of this methodology that might affect consumers' responses to questions? For example, did consumers in a focus group merely go along with an opinion leader? If using a mobile survey that consumers complete using their smartphone, did respondents give only cursory short answers simply to complete the survey and receive the incentive? If using online surveys, how can we be sure of the identity of the respondent?

- What questions were asked?

- How were the questions asked?

- Who asked the questions?

- How were the respondents/participants chosen?

- Who responded, and why?

- Who did not respond, and why not?

- Was there anything about the way the research was conducted that could influence consumers' responses?

QUESTIONS FOR DISCUSSION

1. Do you think that marketers and decision makers will come to rely more, or less, on marketing research in the next decade? Give specific reasons for your answer.

2. Use the Internet to identify as many local marketing research firms as you can. What types of research do these firms conduct?

3. Describe the differences between basic and applied research.

4. Describe the advantages and disadvantages of primary and secondary data.

5. How could each of the following organizations use marketing research? What information might these organizations want to collect, and from whom might they collect it? What marketing or managerial decisions might these organizations need to make? How could the results from marketing research help them make these decisions?
   a. Laundromat
   b. University
   c. Local police department
   d. Church
   e. The American Red Cross
   f. Politician
   g. Restaurant owner

6. Managers of a grocery store have used a decision support system to identify that consumers who purchase fresh fish also tend to purchase organic vegetables and items from the bakery. How could managers use this information to better market to their customers?

MINICASE 1.1

Tolmarck Inc.

Jack Tolens is the cofounder and CEO of Tolmarck Inc., which manufactures a variety of different products. Tolmarck sells a number of different brands within each of its product lines. And, each brand is overseen by a brand manager who is responsible for planning all aspects of the marketing strategy for that brand, including advertising, sales promotions, personal selling, distribution, and public relations. Jack has recently met with the Board of Directors who made it clear that they were concerned with Tolmarck's declining stock price. One strategy that was discussed at the Board meeting was to find ways to cut costs so that Tolmarck could better compete with its various competitors.

A few days after the Board meeting, Jack was talking with Steven Hostler, who was recently placed in charge of investigating the potential for a new brand. Steven Hostler began to discuss the marketing research that was being conducted for the potential new brand. Steven reviewed the plans to interview more than 500 randomly selected potential customers from the brand's target market using telephone surveys. Jack Tolens then asked about the timeline for this research and the decisions that Steven would be recommending. Steven told him that he knew this brand was a priority, and he also knew that Jack and the other senior managers were eager to introduce the brand. So, Steven mentioned that if the results from these surveys were favorable, he would go ahead and recommend manufacturing and marketing the brand. However, if the results from the surveys were not favorable, he would recommend that the brand not be introduced and marketed. He said that basing his decision on these surveys would speed up the decision-making process as well as the time it would take to start manufacturing and distributing the new brand.

1. If you were Jack Tolens, what would you say to Steven Hostler?

2. If you were Jack Tolens, and you were looking for ways to cut costs to remain competitive, what would you consider doing?

3. What is Steven Hostler's role in the decision-making process regarding this potential new brand (as it is described)?

4. What is the role of the research (the surveys) in the decision-making process regarding this potential new brand (as it is described)?

5. Would you ever allow the results of marketing research to make the decision for you? Why? Why not?

ENDNOTES

1   Adapted from the definition of research in American Marketing Association, Committee on Definitions, *Marketing Definition: A Glossary of Marketing Terms* (Chicago: American Marketing Association, 1960), 17.

2   American Marketing Association, "Definitions of Marketing Terms," **http://www.marketingpower.com/AboutAMA/Pages/DefinitionofMarketing.aspx**, May, 2013.

CHAPTER (2)

Marketing Research as a Profession

LEARNING OBJECTIVES

1 Describe the most common job titles for marketing researchers.

2 Describe the differences between research firms and corporate researchers/client side researchers.

3 Describe the job duties of a marketing research analyst.

4 Identify universities that offer graduate degree programs specializing in marketing research.

5 Identify and describe unethical practices associated with marketing research.

The marketing research industry is a growing and vibrant industry worldwide. In fact, according to a leading international research organization (ESOMAR, the World Association for Market, Social, and Opinion Research), marketing research is a $31.2 billion industry.[1] And, the industry is expected to continue growing.

Even though few students initially look favorably upon a career in marketing research, it should not be eliminated as a career option without first considering the possible careers that are available within the realm of marketing research and the many benefits of such careers. According to the United States Bureau of Labor Statistics (**www.BLS.gov**), employment opportunities in the marketing research industry are expected to grow by 41 percent from 2010 to 2020. This compares very favorably with a 14 percent growth rate expected for all occupations. This expected increase in employment is due in part to the large number of workers who plan to retire within the next 10 years as well as an increased use and reliance on data to make marketing decisions. In addition, marketing research has truly become a global industry. Research techniques that are commonplace for American marketers are becoming increasingly accepted and used by marketers all over the globe.

Many marketing researchers work for research firms that provide research services for clients; for example, such **full-service research firms** conduct surveys, focus groups, and other research projects for a fee. They provide their services to other businesses who hire them as contractors to perform research that the client does not want to perform or is unable to perform. Alternatively, some organizations are large enough to house their own marketing research departments and conduct their own research projects in-house. Many manufacturers, retailers, and service providers maintain their own marketing research departments. These researchers are often referred to as **corporate researchers**, or **client-side researchers**.

However, this does not exhaust the possible employers for marketing researchers. A single research project might be conducted by multiple research firms. Many research firms specialize in a particular aspect of the research process and then rely on partnering with other research firms to supply the additional expertise or abilities to complete other aspects of the project.[2] For example, there are many organizations that specialize in providing samples, such as lists of telephone numbers for conducting telephone surveys. There are many focus group facilities that specialize in qualitative research and maintain facilities for conducting focus groups. A growing number of research firms specialize in social media monitoring and provide services by which marketers can monitor what consumers are saying on social media. A growing number of research firms also specialize in ethnographic research, in which consumers are observed as they purchase and use products in their natural and native environments. There are also many firms that provide software for computer-based surveys (hosting surveys on servers or selling interviewing software to clients). Advertising agencies and PR firms also employ marketing researchers to conduct research when designing advertising or PR campaigns.

Most marketing research jobs require at least a bachelor's degree in marketing, research or quantitative methods, computer science, business administration, or a related field. Additionally, candidates for jobs in marketing research should be able to communicate effectively, be organized and detail oriented, be able to work with others effectively, and be willing to learn.

Project Director. Many marketing researchers begin as **project directors,** where they are responsible for conducting the fieldwork associated with a marketing research project. As a project director, one would work closely with the client on the day-to-day issues related to the project, for example, developing schedules for fieldwork and developing research instruments and materials.

Senior Project Director. With a few years' experience researchers often move into the position of **senior project director**. Senior project directors have greater responsibility for developing and fostering relationships with clients, and they often become involved in developing research proposals.

> Marketing research is an exciting field with much to offer in the way of career opportunities.

Marketing Research Analyst. The goal of many college graduates is to eventually become a **marketing research analyst**. Marketing research analysts are more involved in the strategic interpretation of marketing research results. They often formulate reports based on data that was collected by project directors, and they also make strategic marketing recommendations based on their interpretations of research results. As such, they often work closely with the client to better understand

FIGURE 2.1 Marketing Research Job Titles and Typical Salaries

Job Title	Typical Salary Range (excluding bonuses and other nonsalary compensation)[3]
Project Director	$30,000–$50,000
Senior Project Director	$40,000–$60,000
Marketing Research Analyst	$50,000–$80,000
Research Director/Manager	$50,000–$70,000
Senior Research Director/Manager	$60,000–$90,000
Statistician	$90,000–$110,000
Account Executive/Manager	$50,000–$70,000
Senior Account Executive	$70,000–$100,000
Vice President	$125,000+

the client's strategic marketing goals and objectives. And, research analysts are often the ones who make presentations to the client. As a result, marketing research analysts serve as the bridge between the research (data and results) and the implementation of marketing strategies based on the research.

Researchers who hope to become marketing research analysts need strong quantitative, analytical, and critical thinking skills. They also must possess excellent written and oral communication skills. Because they are the bridge between the client and the research results, they also need to be comfortable making presentations. In addition, many firms require that their research analysts possess a graduate degree in quantitative methods, marketing, or business administration.

The median pay for marketing research analysts for 2010 was $60,570.[4] Further, the top 10 percent earned more than $111,440. Thus, becoming a marketing research analyst can be an exciting, rewarding, and lucrative career choice. Figure 2.1 shows the typical job titles in marketing research and their associated pay levels.

GRADUATE DEGREES IN MARKETING RESEARCH

While not all marketing jobs require a graduate degree, there are a number of universities that offer graduate degree programs specifically for the marketing research industry and related fields. Some of these are one-year programs. In such cases, students can complete their course work in two semesters (e.g., fall and spring), and then finish their degree with a summer internship. These degree programs differ from the standard MBA in that they focus specifically on marketing research and research methods. Instead of taking courses in finance or economics that would be required for an MBA, students earning a **master's in marketing research (MMR)**, take courses in quantitative research methods, survey design and analysis, qualitative

FIGURE 2.2 Graduate Degree Programs in Marketing Research[5]

School	Graduate Degree Offered
Algonquin College	Accreditation as Certified Marketing Research Professional (CMRP)
Tilburg University	Master's in Marketing Research
DePaul University	Master of Science in Marketing Analysis
University of Georgia	Master's in Marketing Research (MMR)
University of Maryland	Master of Science in Survey Methodology
Hofstra University	Master of Science in Marketing Research
University of Nebraska–Lincoln	Master of Science in Survey Research and Methodology
University of Texas–Arlington	Master of Science in Marketing Research
Southern Illinois University	Master's in Marketing Research (MMR)
University of Connecticut	Master of Arts in Survey Research, Department of Public Policy
University of Wisconsin/A.C. Nielsen Center for Marketing Research	MBA with a Specialization in Marketing Research
University of Michigan—Institute for Social Research	Master of Science in Survey Methodology
Michigan State University	Master of Science in Marketing Research

research methods (e.g., focus groups and ethnography), and data analysis, interpretation, and presentation. The placement rate for students earning such degrees is usually very high. Universities that offer graduate degree programs in marketing research are shown in Figure 2.2.

> Marketing research professionals tend to be very satisfied with their career.

SATISFACTION WITH MARKETING CAREERS

Marketing research professionals tend to be very satisfied with their career. A recent survey of 1,287 full-time client-side researchers revealed that 73 percent of respondents were at least somewhat satisfied with their jobs.[6] Further, *U.S. News and World Report* recently ranked market research analyst as the number one best business job, followed by financial advisor, accountant, and compliance officer.[7] Not only is market research analyst seen as an excellent job within the realm of business, but **Money. CNN.com** recently ranked market research analyst as the seventh best job in their list of the top 10 best jobs in America.[8]

MARKETING RESEARCH CERFICATION

The Marketing Research Association (**www.MRA.org**) offers a **professional researcher certification (PRC)** for the marketing research industry. The goal of the professional researcher certification is to recognize the qualifications and expertise of marketing and opinion research professionals.[9] Most employers do not require that a researcher be certified, but obtaining the certification demonstrates a level of professional competence that can improve a job candidate's chances of obtaining a research-related job and furthering his or her career. To obtain the PRC, a candidate must have at least three years of experience in a research-related field and pass (with a score of at least 75 percent correct) a 100-question exam made up of multiple choice and true/false questions. Upon passing the exam and meeting all necessary requirements, applicants receive a professional researcher certificate.

MARKETING RESEARCH CONTACTS

As the field of marketing research has grown, so too has the number of professional organizations that are designed to help support the field of marketing research. Below is a list of some of these organizations. The easiest way to become familiar with these organizations is to visit their websites. Many of these sites include information about potential careers in marketing research, publications, conferences, codes of ethics, and even job postings. Become familiar with these organizations and their websites. They provide valuable information, guidance, training, and support to marketing researchers.

- Advertising Media Internet Community, **www.amic.com**
- Advertising Research Foundation, **www.thearf.org**
- American Advertising Federation, **www.aaf.org**
- American Association for Public Opinion Research, **www.aapor.org**
- American Association of Advertising Agencies, **www.aaaa.org**
- American Council on Consumer Interests, **www.consumerinterests.org**
- American Marketing Association, **www.marketingpower.com**
- Americas Research Industry Alliance, **www.ariaalliance.org**
- Belgian Association for Quantitative & Qualitative Marketing Research, **www.baqmar.eu**
- Business Marketing Association, **www.marketing.org**
- Council of American Survey Research Organizations, **www.casro.org**
- Direct Marketing Association, **www.the-dma.org**
- Federation of European Direct and Interactive Marketing, **www.fedma.org**
- International Market Research Society, **www.uniresearch.info**
- Marketing Research Association, **www.marketingresearch.org**
- Marketing Research and Intelligence Association, **www.mria-arim.ca**
- Marketing Science Institute, **www.msi.org**
- Professional Sales Association, **www.psamn.org**
- Public Relations Society of America, **www.prsa.org**

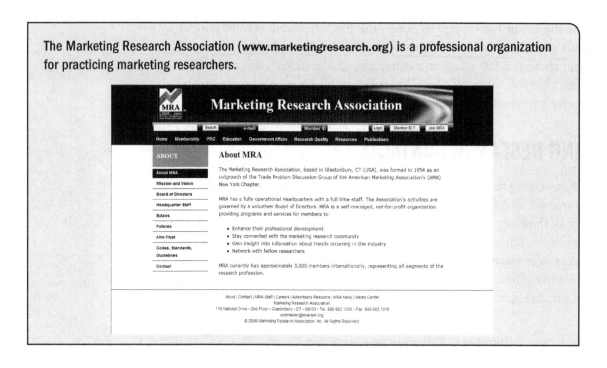

The Marketing Research Association (**www.marketingresearch.org**) is a professional organization for practicing marketing researchers.

- Qualitative Research Consultants Association, **www.qrca.org**

- The Research Club, **www.TheResearchClub.com**

- World Association for Market, Social, and Opinion Research, **www.esomar.org/**

PROFESSIONAL ETHICS AND MARKETING RESEARCH

As a profession, marketing researchers strive to maintain a high level of professional **ethics** when dealing with clients and conducting research projects. It is incumbent upon researchers to identify, understand, and avoid any **unethical practices** when conducting marketing research. Many professional organizations associated with the marketing research profession have adopted their own codes of ethics and statements regarding ethical best practices. Some of these codes of ethics are relatively short one-page descriptions. Others are lengthy documents. Most of them can be found on the Internet. For example, the **American Marketing Association** (**www.market-ingpower.com**) provides a code of ethical norms and values for marketers, including a preamble with general norms and specific values related to honesty, responsibility, fairness, respect, openness, and citizenship. The **Marketing Research Association** (**www.marketingresearch.org**) has adopted a very detailed 35-page code of marketing research standards. Ethical standards are given for designing and analyzing research projects, sampling, collecting data, tabulating and processing data, and conducting qualitative research.

Members of the **American Association for Public Opinion Research** (**www.aapor.org**) sign a Code of Professional Ethics and Practices, pledging to maintain high standards of scientific competence and integrity in conducting, analyzing, and reporting their work. Their code of professional ethics outlines best practices for dealing with the public, clients, and respondents. For example, members of AAPOR pledge to:

- Exercise due care in developing research designs and survey instruments, and in collecting, processing, and analyzing data, taking all reasonable steps to assure the reliability and validity of the results.

- Recommend that our clients use only those research methodologies that are well-suited for the particular problem at hand.

- Not knowingly recommend or use research methodologies that will yield misleading conclusions.

- Not knowingly form conclusions or make recommendations that are inconsistent with the data and results.

- Not knowingly imply that interpretations from the results should be accorded greater confidence than the data actually warrant.

- When working for a private client, keep confidential all proprietary information obtained about the client and about the conduct and findings of the research undertaken for the client.

- Be mindful of the limitations of our research techniques and capabilities and accept only those research assignments that we can reasonably expect to accomplish within these limitations.

- Not cite membership in the AAPOR as evidence of professional competence, since the AAPOR does not so certify any persons or organizations.

- Avoid practices or methods that may harm, humiliate, or seriously mislead survey respondents.

- Respect respondents' concerns about their privacy.

- Provide all persons selected for inclusion with a description of the survey sufficient to permit them to make an informed and free decision about their participation.

- Not misrepresent our research or conduct other activities (such as sales, fund-raising, or political campaigning) under the guise of conducting research.

- Hold as privileged and confidential all information that might identify a respondent with his or her responses, unless the respondent waives confidentiality for specific uses.

- Not disclose or use the names of respondents for nonresearch purposes unless the respondents grant us permission to do so.

- Include in any report of research results certain essential information about how the research was conducted. At a minimum the following items should be disclosed:

  - Who sponsored the survey, and who conducted it.

- The exact wording of questions asked, including the text of any preceding instruction or explanation to the interviewer or respondents that might reasonably be expected to affect the response.

- A definition of the population under study, and a description of the sampling frame used to identify this population.

- A description of the sample design, giving a clear indication of the method by which the respondents were selected by the researcher, or whether the respondents were entirely self-selected.

- Sample sizes and, where appropriate, eligibility criteria, screening procedures, and response rates computed according to AAPOR Standard Definitions.

- A discussion of the precision of the findings, including estimates of sampling error, and a description of any weighting or estimating procedures used.

- The results that are based on only parts of the sample, rather than on the total sample, and the size of such parts.

- The method, location, and dates of data collection.

Many professional organizations, such as the American Association for Public Opinion Research (www.aapor.org), provide guidelines for ethical practices related to conducting marketing research.

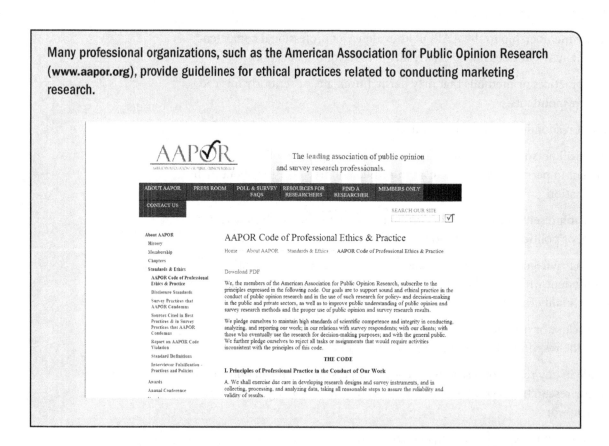

Additionally, the AAPOR condemns certain misleading practices that are sometimes performed in the name of research. These practices that are never considered to be legitimate or acceptable include:

- Requiring a monetary payment or soliciting monetary contributions from members of the public as part of a research process.

- Offering products or services for sale, or using participant contacts as a means of generating sales leads.

- Revealing the identity of individual respondents to a survey or participants in a research process without their permission.

- Representing the results of a 900 number or other type of self-selected "poll" as if they were the outcome of legitimate research.

- Conducting a so-called "push poll," a telemarketing technique in which telephone calls are used to canvass potential voters, feeding them false or misleading "information" about a candidate under the pretense of taking a poll to see how this "information" affects voter preferences.

Some of the codes of ethics that have been developed and adapted by research-related organizations provide only general references to unethical practices. Additional specific examples of unethical practices associated with researchers' interactions with focus group participants and survey respondents, and the collection and reporting of research data and results, are listed below.

- Using surveys or focus groups to promote or sell products.

- Purposely misleading a respondent.

- Purposely writing leading or loaded questions on a survey to obtain a desired response.

- Conducting a survey without the respondent's informed consent.

- Disclosing a person's personal information or responses without his or her prior consent.

- Using or selling consumers' personal information in a database for illegal activities.

- Misrepresenting the true purpose of a focus group, survey, or other research activity.

- Asking for a commitment of any kind during or immediately following a survey or focus group, for example, asking consumers to register for a political action committee, sign a petition, purchase a product, or cast a vote.

- Obtaining personal information such as credit card numbers or Social Security numbers during an interview or focus group.

- Making someone feel bad about his or her stated opinion.

Marketing researchers have an obligation to behave ethically in all matters dealing with clients, research respondents, marketing decision makers, and the general public. They also have an obligation to maintain high ethical standards when designing research, collecting data, analyzing data, and reporting research results.

- Purposely harming, humiliating, or seriously misleading a participant in a focus group or a survey respondent.

- Trying to change someone's mind or opinion during a focus group or interview.

- Altering or falsifying data and the results of a research report.

- Purposely excluding information about potential sources of error or bias in the results and data collection methodology or procedure.

- Not providing a complete reporting of the research methodologies, techniques, and procedures used in a research project.

Obtaining Accurate and Valid Measures. Besides being unethical, many of the practices listed above that deal with falsifying data, manipulating data, altering results, and leading consumers to respond in a desired manner, serve no useful purpose for the managerial decision-making process. It does a marketer no good to purposely and knowingly manipulate consumers' responses to survey questions or focus groups. Why would a marketer want to knowingly overestimate consumers' positive responses toward a product? The results from the research might change, but consumers' true attitudes, feelings, and perceptions will not change. A researcher can design a research project to make it seem as though consumers like a product, but this does not mean that consumers actually like the product. This gives decision makers a false sense of consumers' attitudes and feelings. Marketers need accurate information about consumers' true thoughts, feelings, and beliefs to make decisions. It is better to know that consumers honestly do not like a product than to fool oneself into thinking that consumers like a product. This is easily illustrated with a car-buying example. Imagine that you are considering purchasing a used car. Your friend is a mechanic who often inspects cars for people considering buying them. He is able to inspect the transmission, electrical system, brakes, suspension, and even the engine. It would make no sense to ask this mechanic to tell you that the car is in good working order, even if it is not, just because you like the car and want to hear a positive report. You want an honest assessment of the car. In fact, you want to be informed about as many potential problems with the car as possible. In general, marketing research is not intended to persuade, promote, manipulate, or alter consumers in any way. Rather, it is intended only to accurately measure consumers' opinions, thoughts, feelings, beliefs, and perceptions.

> As a profession, marketing researchers strive to maintain a high level of professional ethics when dealing with clients and conducting research projects.

QUESTIONS FOR DISCUSSION

1. Do you think that the demand for marketing researchers will increase or decrease in the next 10 years?

2. Would you ever consider a career in marketing research? Why? Why not?

3. Visit the website for the American Marketing Association (**www. marketingpower.com**) and search for available jobs in marketing research

using the AMA's Job Board. Click on Career Management, and then click on Resources for Job Seekers, and then click on AMA Job Board. You can search for specific job categories using the advanced search feature.

    a. Where are these marketing research jobs located?

    b. Are there any marketing research jobs in your area?

    c. What are the job duties and responsibilities?

    d. What is the minimum education requirement?

    e. What is the minimum experience requirement?

    f. What is the salary range?

4. What are some unethical practices that marketing researchers should avoid?

5. Which of the following situations illustrate unethical marketing research practices?

    a. You have recently been hired by a small research firm to be their focus group research coordinator. A potential client has inquired about having some customer satisfaction surveys conducted for their retail store. You try to persuade the client that they should use focus groups instead of surveys.

    b. A client working in the packaged foods industry has recently hired your research firm to conduct some focus groups to evaluate consumers' reactions to a new line of canned pastas. You have been named as the research project director. You inform the focus group moderator that if the results from the focus group are favorable the client might consider conducting even more research to further evaluate consumers' perceptions of the product. This would then lead to even more work for the focus group moderator and the research firm.

    c. You have been hired by a shopping mall to conduct a satisfaction survey of shoppers. Instead of hiring interviewers, you decide to save money by conducting a self-administered survey. Copies of the survey are placed on tables at various locations in the shopping mall and consumers can pick them up and fill them out on their own. A total of 48 surveys are completed. In your report, you state in the methodology section that "We interviewed 48 shoppers and found…"

    d. You have been hired to conduct some public opinion polls for a local political candidate. You are able to survey only 100 people for the telephone survey. In your report, you do not mention the sample size and you also do not report the margin of error for the survey.

    e. You have recently finished conducting some surveys that measured respondents' names, addresses, phone numbers, ages, incomes, and number and ages of children. A new client inquires about having some research done to help him identify potential customers for his insurance business. You inform him that you already have a list of names that he can use to identify potential customers based on age, income, and number of children.

f. You are working for a political candidate's campaign. You are asked to conduct some telephone surveys containing the following question: "If the opposition candidate were found guilty of raping a teenage girl, would that make you less likely to vote for that candidate?" The opposition candidate has never been charged with such a crime and there is no indication or evidence that he has ever committed such a crime.

MINICASE 2.1

Gold Coast Travel

Gold Coast Travel has been in business for over 12 years. Gold Coast offers travel-related services to residents of a medium-sized city near the eastern coast of the United States. Thomas Keltey has worked for Gold Coast ever since it opened for business. He has consistently been one of the best salespeople for Gold Coast Travel. In fact, he has won the employee of the year award on four different occasions. Cindy Haywood is the founder and owner of Gold Coast Travel. She has a very outgoing personality that she credits for her success. In fact, when interviewing potential employees, an outgoing personality is one thing that she considers essential for success in the travel services industry. She has grown her business based on repeat customers and referrals. However, two new travel agencies have opened in the last year, which has created intense competition for Gold Coast. She has decided to begin conducting more marketing research as a way to stay ahead of her competition. She has informed Thomas Keltey that she would like for him to be in charge of conducting these research projects. Thomas has agreed to conduct the surveys; however, he is concerned that he does not have much experience with marketing research and statistics.

One of the first research projects that Thomas was asked to conduct involved surveying recent customers about their satisfaction with Gold Coast Travel and its services. Cindy told Thomas that if the results from the survey were favorable, she would consider conducting even more research and possibly even give Thomas a raise and create a new position for him as marketing intelligence manager.

After the surveys were completed, Thomas prepared a report that he gave to Cindy Haywood. The results from the surveys were very favorable; however, the report that Thomas submitted did not provide any analysis related to sample size, sampling frame, data collection methodology and procedures, statistical margin of error, response rates, or any potential sources of error associated with the results.

Do you have any concerns about any unethical behaviors on the part of either Cindy or Thomas?

ENDNOTES

1   ESOMAR, "Global Market Research Report," 2011, **ESOMAR.org http://www.esomar.org/uploads/industry/ reports/global-market-research-2011/ESOMAR-GMR-2011_Preview.pdf**.
2   Dana Stanley, "Research Industry Taxonomy," July 2009, **www.Greenbook.org**

3 Marketing Research Careers, **http://www.marketresearchcareers.com**, June 2013.

4 Bureau of Labor Statistics Occupational Outlook Handbook, **http://www.bls.gov/ooh/**, June 2013.

5 Quirk's Marketing Research Media, "Degree Programs in Marketing Research and Market Research," **http://www .quirks.com/directory/Marketing_Research_Degrees.aspx**, June 2013

6 Emily Goon, "Happy (Mostly) To Be Here," *Quirk's Marketing Research Review*, June 2012, 56–61.

7 *U.S. News and World Report*, "Best Business Jobs," **http://money.usnews.com/careers/best-jobs/rankings/best-business-jobs**, June, 2013.

8 CNN Money, "Best Jobs in America," **http://money.cnn.com/pf/best-jobs/2012/snapshots/7.html**, June 2013.

9 Marketing Research Association Professional Researcher Certification Program, **www.MarketingResearchlorg/prc-faq**, June 2013.

CHAPTER ③

Marketing Research and The Decision-Making Process

LEARNING OBJECTIVES

1 Describe the relationship between marketing research and the managerial decision-making process.

2 Describe and explain the IDO model of marketing research and the decision-making process.

3 List and explain the types of questions that marketing researchers should ask when meeting with potential clients (managers, decision makers) to identify marketing objectives.

4 List and explain the types of questions that marketing researchers should ask when meeting with potential clients (managers, decision makers) to identify the types of decisions that managers must make.

5 List and explain the types of questions that marketing researchers should ask when meeting with potential clients (managers, decision makers) to identify the specific types of information that managers need to make decisions.

As previously stated, marketing managers need information to make decisions. Marketing research is the business function that collects this information and communicates it to decision makers. As such, researchers must have a clear understanding of the role that marketing research plays in the entire decision-making process. The purpose of marketing research is to collect information in a structured, systematic, and unbiased manner that will help marketing managers make decisions. It is those managerial decisions that will hopefully lead to improved marketing performance.

Researchers must be mindful of the performance results that marketing managers are hoping to achieve with their decisions. The marketing research process should begin by first determining the managerial objectives regarding marketing performance. Then, marketing managers must identify the decisions that are necessary to plan and implement marketing strategies designed to achieve those desired objectives. Then, working with marketing researchers, managers must identify the specific information that is needed for them to be able to make those decisions. Different types of decisions will require different types of information. And, researchers use a variety of methodologies and techniques for collecting information, each designed to collect different types of information. Sometimes the information needed to make decisions has already been collected and can be obtained from secondary data sources. Sometimes the information needed to make decisions must be collected from a survey. Other times the information needed to make decisions can be obtained only from a focus group, from a mystery shopper, or even from a controlled experiment.

The IDO Model

The purpose of marketing research is to collect the **information** that marketing managers need to help them make **decisions** to plan and implement marketing strategies that are designed to achieve marketing **objectives**. By working backwards from marketing performance objectives to the information that is needed to make decisions designed to achieve those performance objectives, marketing researchers can increase the quality, worth, and usefulness of the information generated from a research project. This is illustrated in Figure 3.1.

Planning Marketing Research Projects. This IDO model can be very useful in planning marketing research projects. For example, if the desired marketing objective is to increase the percentage of consumers in a market area who are aware of a store's location, marketing managers might have to decide which of three different advertising campaigns will hopefully lead to increased awareness. The purpose of the research will then be to measure which advertising campaign leads to greater awareness. This can be accomplished within the context of an advertising experiment where consumers view a number of different advertisements followed by measures of awareness for the advertised information at various time periods following exposure to the advertisements. As another example, if the desired objective is to increase distribution intensity by adding two new geographic regions to those in which a company sells their products, marketing managers might need to decide which geographic regions are the most attractive to enter. This would not require collecting any new primary data. Rather, this decision could be made by using information about the demographic characteristics of different market areas collected from secondary data sources such as the U.S. Census. As another example, if the desired objective is to improve product placement in existing retail outlets, this might not even require marketing research. Rather, it might require negotiations with channel partners to improve product placement by offering more attractive trade incentives. Marketing researchers should plan their projects by working backwards from the desired marketing objectives, to the decisions that need to be made to achieve those objectives, to the specific information required to make those decisions.

Reasons for Conducting Marketing Research. Marketing researchers can design effective and useful research projects if they know the managerial purpose motivating the desire to conduct the research project. For example, consider the case of a public library. Managers at the library approached a marketing researcher to ask for help in designing some focus groups. When asked about the reason for the focus

Marketing research efforts will be wasted if the results from the research do not help managers make decisions.

FIGURE 3.1 The IDO Model of Marketing Research and the Decision-Making Process

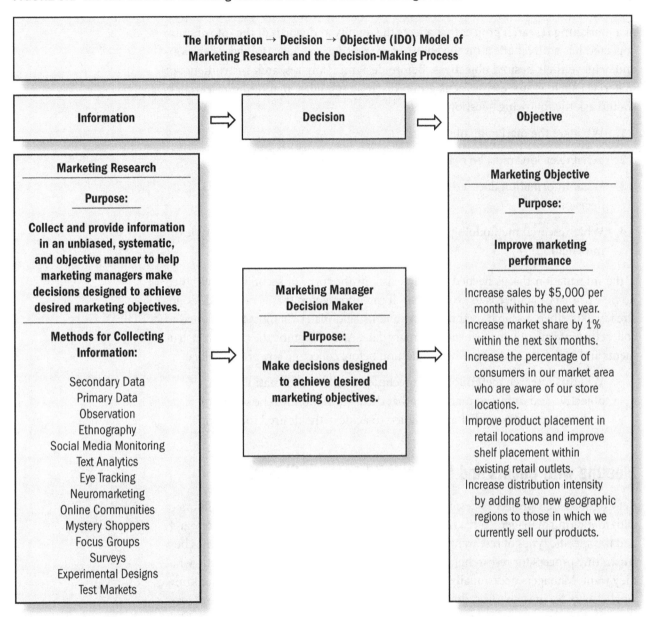

groups, the library managers indicated that they wanted to gather some information from local residents to see if the library's hours of operation needed to be extended. After a brief discussion about the advantages and disadvantages of focus groups, the researcher and the library managers agreed that they would be better served by conducting a phone survey of library users and nonusers who lived in the local area. The relatively small sample sizes associated with focus groups would not provide the type of information needed to make this type of decision. By learning about the purpose of the research and the role it would play in the managerial decision-making process, the researcher was able to design a research project that best fit with the information needs of the library managers.

Questions to Ask When Designing Research. Information collected from marketing research is a key input into the managerial decision-making process. Any aspect of a marketing research project that affects the quality and worth of the information collected has a direct effect on the ability of marketing managers to make decisions and achieve their desired objectives. Before designing any research instruments or materials, such as surveys or focus group discussion guides, marketing researchers should ask the following questions:

1. What are the marketing objectives?

2. What decisions must be made to achieve those desired objectives?

3. What information does a decision maker need to be able to make those decisions?

4. What research methodology or technique is best suited to collect that type of information?

If the information that is needed already exists in the form of secondary data, then no new primary data needs to be collected. If the information that is needed does not already exist, then research methods, instruments, and materials must be designed to collect that information in the form of primary data. After designing the research instruments and materials, ask the following question before collecting any primary data:

> Will this research methodology or technique collect information in an objective and unbiased manner so that the information will be useful in making the decisions that are designed to achieve the desired marketing objectives?

Meeting with Clients and Developing Research Objectives

Before a research project is designed and conducted, researchers will usually meet with marketing managers (often referred to as clients) to discuss the need for research and the specific types of research to be conducted. However, this can sometimes be a frustrating process for researchers because managers often do not know exactly what they want. Managers occasionally request research simply because they do not know what else to do. In such cases, doing research makes them feel better because at least they are doing something, instead of doing nothing. Still other times, managers think that they know what they want, and they have in mind a certain type of research that may or may not be appropriate for the decision task at hand. In such cases, it is helpful to use the IDO model as a structure for any conversations with managers (clients). Begin by identifying the overall marketing objectives, then identify the specific decisions that must be made to achieve those objectives, then determine the particular information that is needed to make those decisions, and then finally decide on the appropriate research technique or methodology for gathering that information.

Identifying Objectives. When researchers meet with mangers to discuss the need for research, they should guide the discussion and use it as an opportunity to help managers more clearly identify and refine their managerial and marketing objectives and the types of decisions that must be made to achieve those objectives. Use the IDO model to structure the conversation. For example, a manager might begin the conversation by saying, "Thank you for helping us with this project. We would like you to design some customer satisfaction surveys for us." Notice that the manager has already decided that a survey is the appropriate research methodology. However, a survey may or may not be the best methodology for collecting the information needed by the manager. The researcher should take the opportunity to help the manager identify the need for research and the need for a specific type of research before beginning to design a survey. Discuss the following (ask the following questions) when meeting with marketing managers:

- Before we even talk about a specific type of research, let's talk about your objectives so that we can make sure that any research we conduct will actually help you achieve your objectives.

- As you know, marketing research can be expensive. I want to make sure that you do not spend money on research that does not help you make effective decisions to achieve your marketing objectives.

- What is happening in your business that makes you think that you need to conduct some marketing research?

- What is the problem that you are trying to solve?

- What are your marketing objectives?

- Which objectives are you currently achieving, and which objectives are you currently not achieving?

- What is keeping you from achieving your marketing objectives?

These questions and discussions should be framed around the desire to use marketing resources in the most efficient and effective manner possible. Even though many managers do not fully understand the nuances of various research techniques and methodologies, they most certainly understand the value of money. Managers will appreciate that a marketing researcher understands the big picture and the need for limited research dollars to be spent wisely. Asking these questions forces managers to focus on the marketing objectives that are being met and those objectives that are not being met. In fact, most managers will be grateful that these questions are framed around the desire to help achieve marketing objectives rather than the desire to conduct research. The purpose of a research project is to increase the chances that marketing managers will be able to achieve their objectives.

Research Needs a Purpose. As a practical matter, is would be almost impossible to design a marketing research project without first determining the overall marketing objectives. Consider the case of a researcher who was asked to conduct some customer satisfaction surveys for a bank. However, there is no way of knowing what questions to ask on a survey without first determining the purpose of the survey

> A marketing researcher should not begin a research project without first identifying the desired marketing objective.

and the overall marketing objectives. The specific questions included on a survey will vary depending upon the marketing objectives. Consider the possible marketing objectives for a bank listed below:

- Identify new branch locations.

- Increase the number of customers doing online banking.

- Identify new online services that customers want.

- Identify new ATM locations.

- Increase branch traffic, that is, the number of customers coming into the branch.

- Identify customer complaints and areas for improvement in customer service.

- Develop new advertising themes.

- Identify the best media placement for new advertisements.

- Identify causes of high employee turnover.

Notice that for each of these objectives the decisions to be made will vary, as will the specific types of information needed to make those decisions, and also the research methodology or technique for collecting that information.

Identifying Decisions. After discussing the managerial objectives, turn the focus of the discussion toward the types of decisions that must be made to help the manager achieve those objectives. This can be accomplished by asking the following questions:

- What decisions must you make to achieve these objectives?

- What needs to happen for you to be able to solve these problems or achieve these objectives?

- Why are you currently not able to make decisions that can help you with this situation?

- What role do you play in making the decisions that will hopefully achieve these objectives?

- What do you need that you currently do not have?

Identifying Information. After determining the types of decisions that must be made to achieve the objectives, identify the specific information that is needed to help managers make decisions. This can be achieved by asking the following questions:

- Specifically, what pieces of information do you need to be able to make decisions that will hopefully achieve these marketing objectives?

- If you could design a research report that contained the specific information you needed to make your decisions, what information would be included in that report?

- What information would make you comfortable about making these decisions?

- Complete this sentence, "I could make a decision about this today if I knew _____."

- Complete this sentence, "I could take an action regarding this matter today if I knew _____."

Identifying Research Techniques. After identifying the specific types of information that are needed to make the decisions, the researcher can then determine the appropriate technique for obtaining that information. Researchers have a variety of research techniques and methodologies at their disposal, each designed to obtain different types of information for different purposes. Sometimes, the appropriate technique is not what the manager initially requested. A manager who initially wants to conduct a survey might discover that a focus group is a more appropriate technique for obtaining the information that is needed. Similarly, a manager who initially wants to conduct a focus group might discover that a survey better fits his or her information needs. Most managers will not be upset to learn that the type of research they initially wanted to conduct is actually not the best research for their situation if they can be shown that the final research technique and process agreed upon with the researcher will best help them make decisions, and in turn, best help them achieve their marketing objectives. Managers are very conscious of achieving marketing objectives. Discussions with a researcher that help managers achieve marketing objectives in the most cost-effective manner will be greatly appreciated.

> The information that is collected is useful to the decision-making process only when that information is communicated to decision makers in a way that is useful and informative to them.

Working Backwards through the IDO Model. Notice that initial discussions between a researcher and a manager (client) actually work backwards through the IDO model, initially focusing more on achieving marketing objectives and less on conducting research. Researchers should be hesitant to conduct research projects without first discussing the relationship between the results that can be expected from a project and the marketing objectives. Similarly, managers should be skeptical about any researcher who offers to begin work on a research project without first identifying the overall marketing objectives. Researchers should not sell a marketing research project (or a particular research methodology) without first identifying its appropriateness and usefulness to managers for achieving their marketing objectives.

Consider the Marketing Objectives When Designing Research

One of the most common mistakes people make when beginning a marketing research project is the failure to consider the entire relationship between marketing research, the decision maker, the decisions to be made, and the desired marketing objective. People often conduct marketing research without a clear understanding of how the results will help marketing managers make better decisions. As a result, they waste time, effort, and money collecting the wrong data, or they collect data that does not help decision makers make decisions. Such research is often easy to identify. The evidence is usually poorly worded survey questions or research instruments that contain ambiguous questions that provide very little input into the decision-making process. For example, consider the case of a university that provides a Student Express bus service for students. The Student Express bus has two routes that run between various parking lots adjacent to campus and various buildings on campus. The buses run between 7:30 a.m. and 4:30 p.m. During the past two years the number of students riding the Student Express has decreased and students have been heard complaining that the Student Express bus service needs to be expanded. So, in an effort to increase the number of students riding the bus the university conducted a survey. They asked questions about issues such as:

- How far away from campus do you live?

- In which lots do you most often park your car?

- How many times per week do you ride the Student Express bus?

- Do you like to ride the Student Express bus?

- How many people, including yourself, are usually on the Student Express bus when you ride it?

Unfortunately, while it might be nice to know how students respond to these types of questions, they do not provide any useful information. The problem is that the person who designed the survey did not fully understand that the desired marketing objective was to increase the number of students who ride the Student Express bus. And, that person did not fully understand the decisions that needed to be made to hopefully achieve that outcome. To make decisions that can impact the number of students riding the bus, decision makers needed information from questions such as:

Would you use the Student Express more often if:

- There were more buses?

- The buses ran longer hours?

- There were more bus stops on campus?

- The buses went to more parking lots?

- The buses went to more buildings on campus?

- The buses were larger?

- The buses were cleaner?

Notice how these are much more useful for making decisions about the bus service. They provide specific information that can easily be used to make specific decisions about the bus service. In sum, they are more actionable. If a large percentage of students reported that they would be more likely to ride the bus if the buses went to more buildings on campus, university administrators would know what changes needed to be made. Responses to these specific questions would help to define what students meant when they complained that the bus service needed to be expanded.

The four most important questions to ask when designing a marketing research project are:

1 What are the marketing objectives?
2 What decisions must be made to achieve those desired objectives?
3 What information does a decision maker need to be able to make those decisions?
4 What research methodology or technique is best suited to collect this information in an objective and unbiased manner?

As another example, consider the restaurant table-top comment card shown in Figure 3.2. The questions on this table-top comment card will not help the restaurant manager make any decisions designed to improve the restaurant or improve customer satisfaction. The questions on the survey are too broad and ambiguous to be useful and actionable. What if 90 percent of customers rated the menu as *Very Bad*? As a restaurant manager, what would you do? The answer is that you would not know what to do. What did customers not like about the menu? Did customers not like the layout of the menu? Did customers not like the prices on the menu? Did customers not like the selections on the menu? Did customers find the menu hard to read and understand? Unfortunately, we will never know. Thus, there is no way of identifying a managerial decision regarding changes to the menu that will lead to improved customer satisfaction. Similarly, if 90 percent of customers rated the interior of the restaurant as *Very Bad*, does this mean that they thought the temperature was too cold, that they did not like the colors on the walls, or that they thought the restaurant was too loud and noisy? Again, managers would not know what changes needed to be made to the restaurant interior. What if 90 percent of customers rated the servers as *Very Bad*? Would you replace the servers? Unfortunately, there is no way of knowing if customers were rating the attitude of the servers, the friendliness of the servers, the servers' knowledge of the menu, or the availability of the servers. If more specific questions were asked and the servers were rated very favorably on everything except availability, the correct managerial decision might be to hire more servers, not replace them. As these examples illustrate, researchers must always consider the desired marketing objectives and the decisions that need to be made to achieve those objectives. By doing this, researchers can provide actionable information and research results. If the research results do not provide useful input into the decision-making process, the research will be a waste of time, effort, and money.

FIGURE 3.2 Restaurant Table-Top Comment Card with Ambiguous Questions

Please evaluate our restaurant on the following:	Very Bad	Bad	Good	Very Good
Menu	☐	☐	☐	☐
Interior of restaurant	☐	☐	☐	☐
Exterior of restaurant	☐	☐	☐	☐
Server	☐	☐	☐	☐

Satisfying Clients. A recent survey conducted by **Greenbook.org** asked research buyers (i.e., clients who hire research firms to conduct marketing research) to rate the importance of various factors when selecting research suppliers (e.g., marketing research firms).[1] The results showed that a service mentality was of utmost importance. Research buyers (clients) seek marketing researchers who are able to listen to the client's needs and goals and can then develop an effective working relationship with the client. Listening and being familiar with the client's needs are of primary importance to research buyers. As highlighted in the IDO model, it is incumbent upon the marketing researcher to fully understand the needs and objectives of the marketing manager (client) before beginning any research project. It is the fit, or appropriateness, of a research technique for the particular needs of the marketing manager that determines the success of a research project and the satisfaction of the research client.

Pilot Testing. Often, researchers will conduct a **pilot test** of a survey in which a relatively small number of people are asked to complete the survey. In many cases the purpose of the pilot test is to determine if there are any problems with question wording or question interpretation that need to be corrected before sending the survey to a much larger sample. Additionally, pilot testing can also be very helpful for assessing the usefulness of surveys for managerial decision making. By looking at the results from the pilot test, managers can determine if all necessary information is obtainable from the questions that are asked on the survey. Also, pilot tests can reveal unexpected results. For example, managers might be surprised to learn that men in the pilot test rated a brand much more favorably than women did. Additional questions can then be added to the final survey to provide clarification or identify possible explanations for the difference.

Communicating Information to Decision Makers

Notice that the purpose of marketing research is to collect *and* provide information. It is not enough to merely collect information. The information that is collected is useful to the decision-making process only when that information is communicated to decision makers in a way that is useful and informative to them. A complete marketing research project involves more than merely collecting information. As such, an important consideration for researchers is how the results from a research project are communicated to marketing managers.

QUESTIONS FOR DISCUSSION

1. How does marketing research fit into the managerial decision-making process?

2. In your own words, describe the IDO model presented in this chapter.

3. What questions should marketing researchers ask when first meeting with potential clients?

4. What questions can marketing researchers ask to help identify managerial objectives?

5. What questions can marketing researchers ask to help identify the types of decisions that marketing managers need to make?

6. What questions can marketing researchers ask to help identify the specific information that is needed to make managerial decisions?

7. Does the marketing research process begin with the selection of a research methodology? Why? Why not?

8. When should marketing researchers select a technique or methodology for a research project?

9. Why should marketing researchers be familiar with many different research methodologies?

10. How can pilot tests of surveys be beneficial to the managerial decision-making process?

11. What are some of the potential limitations of marketing managers conducting their own research projects without any input or guidance from a professional marketing researcher?

12. In Lewis Carroll's classic novel *Alice in Wonderland*, there is a scene where Alice comes upon the Cheshire Cat and asks for his advice about which way she should go.

> Alice: Would you tell me, please, which way I ought to go from here?
>
> The Cat: That depends a good deal on where you want to get to.
>
> Alice: I don't much care where.
>
> The Cat: Then it doesn't much matter which way you go.
>
> Alice: …so long as I get somewhere.
>
> The Cat: Oh, you're sure to do that, if only you walk long enough.

What does this quote have to do with marketing research? How can marketing researchers use the lesson that is learned from this quote to help them design better marketing research projects?

MINICASE 3.1

Winstrom Furniture Store

You are a student majoring in marketing and you will graduate at the end of this semester. You recently received an email from Fred Winstrom, who is the president of Winstrom Furniture. Winstrom Furniture has been in business for 40 years. Albert Winstrom opened the furniture store and recently handed over the day-to-day operations to his son, Fred, two years ago. Winstrom Furniture currently has only one store, which is in the same location as when it opened 40 years ago. Fred comes from a background in biology and is still trying to learn the furniture business. He believes that to do this he needs to better understand his customers. Below is the text of the email from Fred Winstrom:

To:	You
From:	Fred Winstrom, President of Winstrom Furniture
Subject:	Marketing Research Survey
Date:	Today

It has come to my attention that you are a student majoring in marketing, so I was hoping that you could help us with some marketing issues. I would like to conduct a survey of my customers. However, I do not know much about survey research. Would you please write a draft of a survey that I can use? I would like to set up a meeting with you to discuss the survey and to talk about potential jobs in marketing here at Winstrom Furniture.

Thank you,

Fred Winstrom

President, Winstrom Furniture

You have set up a time to meet with Mr. Winstrom. You have also recently learned that Fred Winstrom is hoping to expand the Winstrom Furniture business and will soon hire a marketing director. Because you would like to apply for this position, you would like to impress Mr. Winstrom when you meet with him. When you meet with Mr. Winstrom:

1. What do you do?

2. What do you give him?

3. What do you tell him?

4. What do you discuss with him?

5. What words do you use when you discuss the survey that he wants to conduct?

ENDNOTE

1 "Greenbook Research Industry Trends Report," Winter 2013, **www.GRITreport.org**

CHAPTER 4

Social Media and Emerging Technologies: Opportunities and Challenges

LEARNING OBJECTIVES

1   Define consumer-generated media and discuss its relevance to marketers in today's business environment.

2   Discuss the impact of social media on marketing research.

3   Discuss some of the ways that marketers can use social media to conduct marketing research.

4   Define emerging technologies and discuss the impact of emerging technologies on marketing research.

5   Describe and then discuss the role of the following in conducting marketing research:

   a   Online communities

   b   Mobile surveys

   c   Social media monitoring

   d   Social media analytics

   e   Text analytics

   f   Eye tracking

   g   Neuromarketing

6   Describe some of the major benefits of emerging technologies for marketing research as well as for marketing decision making.

7   Discuss the following challenges/influences on marketing research:

   a   Do-it-yourself (DIY) research

   b   Decline of respondent cooperation

   c   Gamification of marketing research

   d   Big Data

The techniques and methodologies for conducting marketing research have changed and evolved over the years. Many of these changes result from advances in technologies that allow researchers to communicate with and collect information from consumers in ways that were previously impossible. The invention of the telephone improved the ability of marketing researchers to survey large groups of consumers without the need for travel. Similarly, when radio was introduced in the 1920s and television was introduced in the 1950s, these both opened up entirely new mediums through which marketers could communicate brand messages and advertising to consumers. Similarly, the invention of the computer and the use of retail scanner data have dramatically improved the quantity and quality of individual-level consumption data that marketing researchers are able to collect. Now, the growing use of social media has provided marketers and marketing researchers with an entirely new medium by which they can communicate with and collect information from consumers.

Brands as Social Objects. Marketers are coming to learn that brands are social objects. People purchase, use, and discuss brands in social environments. Further, consumers can establish deep and lasting social relationships with brands. Consumers can even form emotional bonds with brands that they have come to know and love. And, consumers often seek to share those emotions, experiences, perceptions, and attitudes with other consumers online via social media. For example, consumers have created online fan clubs for many brands. This is often referred to as consumer-generated media. **Consumer-generated media (CGM)** is any content that is created by consumers and is posted on the Internet for everyone in the general public to view. Such consumer-generated media can be in the form of text (e.g., product reviews, comments on forums or discussion boards, comments on Facebook pages), audio/video (e.g., videos on YouTube), or images (e.g., photos on Pinterest or Facebook pages). Given the social nature of brands and consumers' desire to share with other consumers through social media, it is becoming increasingly important for marketers to include social media in their set of techniques and methodologies for understanding consumers. Using social media as a marketing research tool allows marketing researchers to better understand the interactions between consumers as brands are consumed socially.

In the past, marketers had to actively seek out consumers and ask for their opinions and thoughts. Researchers contacted consumers by phone or in personal intercept interviews. And, for the most part, researchers drove the conversation and determined the topics to be discussed and the questions to be answered. Now, with social media, researchers can engage consumers in conversations via Twitter, Facebook pages, websites, and online forums. Researchers can also simply listen in on the conversations between consumers about brands, products, and services. In the past, these personal conversations between consumers occurred in relative privacy, for example over the backyard fence. Now, these personal conversations occur online for all to see and monitor. These conversations between consumers are an extremely valuable

> Consumers are becoming more and more willing and able to share their experiences with brands via social media. And, social media has opened up new ways for marketers to listen to, and communicate with, consumers.

source of information. They inform marketers of what consumers are thinking, how they talk and the language they use when referring to brands, products, or services, the issues or product features that are important to them, and how they respond to other types of comments and information that they might see in marketer-generated content, such as advertising.

To illustrate the impact that social media can have on marketers, consider the recent case of United Airlines. Musician Dave Carroll wrote a song and made a music video chronicling how his guitar was broken by United Airlines workers in 2008 and his dealings with the United Airlines customer service personnel. His song ("United Breaks Guitars") and YouTube video became instant hits, going viral and being viewed more than 12 million times. Such negative publicity about a brand can cause severe damage to a brand's image.

SOCIAL MEDIA AND MARKETING RESEARCH

The challenge for marketing researchers is to find ways for marketers to move from simply garnering Facebook fans and Twitter followers to using social media to communicate with customers and learn about them. Social media is becoming more than just a place for people to post funny pictures of themselves. It is becoming an important medium through which marketers are able to observe, listen in on, and communicate with consumers. For example, Macy's polled customers on social media sites when deciding to carry denim jeans in either bright neon colors or pastels. Wal-Mart even used social media when allowing customers to vote on which toys they wanted discounted.[1] By using social media, customers can feel like they are a part of the marketing decision-making process. They feel like they have a say in marketing decisions through their "likes" on Facebook, through their comments on online forums, and through their comments and complaints on Twitter.

Not only have marketers used social media to increase brand exposure and draw traffic to a company's website, but marketers are beginning to see the significant benefits of the marketing research insights that can come from using and monitoring social media for marketing research purposes. Perhaps the greatest benefit of using social media for marketing research is the increased communication between consumer and marketer. Marketers can observe and listen to consumers who are conversing in real time, using their own words, and responding to what is most important to them. Often, one of the most difficult aspects of marketing is identifying the important attributes, features, or issues associated with a product or service. Marketers can learn what is important to consumers by attending to their social media interactions and conversations. Similarly, by communicating with Twitter followers or Facebook fans, marketers can initiate dialogues and ask questions of consumers. Marketers can monitor Twitter conversations and respond in real time to tweets. Marketers can even post links to surveys on Facebook pages and include these links in Twitter responses.

Benefits of Social Media for Marketing Research. Incorporating social media as a research tool offers a number of benefits to marketers and marketing researchers. For example, by using social media, marketers can:

1. Measure the number of times a brand is mentioned in online conversations. A number of tools allow researchers to measure the number of tweets or Facebook mentions that contain a brand name or a keyword associated with a brand or company.

2. Listen in on consumers. By monitoring social media, researchers can better understand the terms and phrases that consumers use when talking about products or brands with other consumers online. This allows marketers to identify the words that might best resonate with consumers, thereby attracting their attention and drawing them in to their stores or to their websites.

> Marketers are coming to learn that brands are social objects that consumers purchase, use, and discuss in social environments.

3. Receive real-time analysis and feedback from consumers. The information garnered from monitoring social media allows marketers to better understand what is going through consumers' minds as they are involved in the purchase and consumption process, instead of waiting for hours, days, or even weeks to obtain this information from traditional research methods, such as focus groups or surveys. The more time that lapses between actual purchase and responding to questions about that purchase the greater the chance that consumers might forget the experience or even change their evaluations and feelings about that purchase experience. Consumers can even be asked to submit **SMS (short message service)** text diaries of their experiences while they are actually purchasing and using a product.[2] Consumers can tell researchers where they purchase the product, where they use the product, what they are doing when they use the product, and who they are with when using the product.

4. Examine historical trends. Social media research gives researchers access to historical data regarding consumers' attitudes, opinions, desires, likes, and dislikes. Social media analytics can access time-stamped data points from days, months, and even years ago.[3] This allows researchers to identify and match changes in consumers' social media comments with changes in marketing and promotional strategies in previous time periods.

5. Recruit participants for marketing research surveys. Marketers can conduct surveys of their Twitter followers or Facebook fans. Such fans and followers form a research panel of current and potential customers that can be used to recruit participants for a survey. Traditionally, finding a panel of such consumers would have been very difficult. Social media allows such panels to form on their own, driven by consumers' interests. A Facebook ad containing a link to a survey can be sent to groups of potential respondents targeted by age, sex, location, likes, and interests.

6. Communicate with customers. Marketers can regularly monitor Twitter to identify if any consumers are tweeting negative comments about a company, brand, or service. A personal message sent (tweeted) from a marketer to a customer can go a long way in developing long-term customer loyalty. Observing the topics that get re-tweeted can help identify the topics that are of most interest to consumers. Marketers can also respond to comments and questions from followers of a Facebook page.

7. Design better and more effective surveys. By monitoring social media sites such as Facebook and Twitter, marketing researchers can identify the terms, phrases, ideas, and issues that are most important to consumers, thereby helping them identify the topics that should be addressed on subsequent surveys. Social media can be used to help reduce the number of answer options on surveys by identifying the items that are most relevant to consumers and prospective customers.[4] For example, when designing a survey to measure where consumers purchase cups of coffee, a marketer could analyze social media sites looking for the number of times different stores, restaurants, gas stations, and even bookstores are mentioned. The locations mentioned most frequently are those that can be included as answer options on a survey of coffee purchasers.

8. Obtain more honest and sincere comments regarding brands. Because social media comments are often candid, blunt, and unfiltered, they can give marketers a sense of how involved and passionate consumers are about a brand, product, retailer, or service provider.

9. Identify product perceptions and brand positioning. The comments that consumers provide on social media sites can give marketers an understanding of how consumers perceive brands or products and identify the categories into which they place such brands or products. Marketers often seek to know how consumers perceive one brand in relation to other brands. Is a brand mentioned along with other brands? Is a brand being compared to other brands? If so, what topics are being discussed when a brand is mentioned? What problems or issues are being discussed when a brand is mentioned? Pinterest can be used as a tool for assessing a brand's true positioning relative to other brands in the minds of consumers. Researchers can simply examine the names of the boards on which Pinterest users have pinned photos of a brand.

10. Discover the questions that consumers are asking. With traditional research methods, such as surveys and focus groups, marketing researchers decide which questions to ask of consumers, and then consumers answer those questions. One interesting aspect of using social media for marketing research is that it flips this process around. When monitoring social media conversations, marketers are able to discover the questions that consumers

ask each other. Further, marketers are then able to respond to these questions. One of the best ways to identify consumers' needs, wants, concerns, and even hesitations is through the questions that they are asking each other in online forums, on Twitter, and on Facebook pages.

Why Monitor Social Media?. To illustrate the importance of monitoring social media, consider the case of Blockbuster Video and Best Buy. In the spring of 2009, Blockbuster Video retained the services of a law firm known for helping companies file for bankruptcy. Rumors that Blockbuster Video was going to file for bankruptcy spread via social media. One Twitter post used Blockbuster's stock symbol, BBI, when referring to the company. However, another Twitter user responded by asking if this was the symbol for Best Buy, whose stock symbol is BBY. A Best Buy employee who had been assigned to monitor social media immediately responded to the Twitter post to head off any mistaken assumptions that Best Buy was in financial trouble. Gina Debogovich, Best Buy's senior manager of communities said, "In a day when anyone can tweet, blog or post a video that may or may not be based in fact, brands have to be monitoring the conversations out there."[5]

By monitoring social media marketers can also begin to develop, foster, and even repair relationships with disgruntled customers. Many consumers still complain about products and services using relatively private communications, such as emails to the company, or by completing a comment box found on a "contact us" page. However, a growing number of consumers are complaining publicly via social media. How a marketer responds to these public complaints can go a long way to repairing relationships with customers. And, researchers have found that consumers who received responses to complaints that were aired publically (e.g., using social media) were much more delighted than were consumers who received responses to complaints that were sent via private forms of communication (e.g., email or phone call).[6]

> By monitoring social media, marketers can begin to develop, foster, and even repair relationships with disgruntled customers.

SOCIAL MEDIA RESEARCH APPROACHES AND METHODS

The acceptance of new and emerging technologies, such as social media for marketing research, provides additional avenues by which marketers can identify, contact, and engage with consumers. These new technologies are often referred to as **emerging technologies** because they are currently being developed and refined, and there is still much work to be done to increase their accuracy and usefulness when making managerial decisions. However, there can be no denying that social media is here to stay as a viable and valuable tool for marketing researchers. In fact, recent surveys of marketing research professionals indicate that emerging technologies such as online communities, mobile surveys, social media analytics, text analytics, eye tracking, and neuromarketing have already been adopted by many marketing researchers, or are currently under consideration for adoption. Figure 4.1 shows the percent of marketing researchers who have either adopted, or are considering adopting, these emerging technologies.[7]

FIGURE 4.1 Percent of Marketing Researchers Currently Using, or Considering Using, Emerging Technologies for Marketing Research

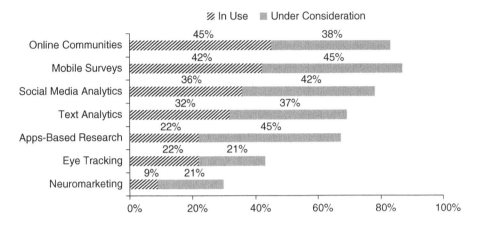

ONLINE COMMUNITIES

Online brand communities are essentially electronic versions of a group of consumers in a room talking about a brand, service, marketer, or usage situation, and freely offering opinions to each other. In an online environment, a **brand community** is often described as a group of like-minded consumers who identify with a brand and share significant rituals and traditions regarding a brand.[8] Online communities are becoming increasingly popular as a methodology for connecting with and interacting with consumers. Online brand communities can lead to enhanced relationships with a brand, hopefully leading community members to become advocates for a brand and encouraging them to act on this advocacy with increased purchasing behavior. In an online community, people come together virtually to share common interests, hobbies, activities, or goals, and interact online to socialize, share their opinions, work on projects, and voice their desires in order to receive rewards that can be either physical (actual) or virtual. For example, Mumsnet (**www.mumsnet .com**) is an online community of parents offering news, product reviews, and web chats dealing with parenting advice. World of Warcraft offers an online community of people who share an interest in the World of Warcraft games (**www.us.battle .net/wow/en/community**). Starbucks Coffee provides a forum for consumers to share, vote, and discuss issues related to Starbucks Coffee (**www.mystarbucksidea.force.com**). Huggies offers an online community (**www.huggies.com/answers**) where expectant mothers can come together virtually to ask and answer questions about such topics as signs of pregnancy, body changes during pregnancy, baby names, and baby gear. Of course, the online community is also used as a means of promoting Huggies brand diapers.

In an online brand community, people share their stories and experiences with a brand in a free and open exchange of ideas. An advantage of online brand communities is their ability to attract many varying constituents to a brand, for example customers, competitors, other organizations, reviewers, and even employees. As such, online brand communities provide marketers with an opportunity to develop and enhance relationships with large groups of people who are all interested in the particular brand. Additional examples of brands for which there are online communities include the Harley Owners' Group (HOG) for Harley-Davidson motorcycles, Kleenex, Ford (**www.syncmyride.com**, where consumers can interact and voice comments about the Sync product found in Ford automobiles), and Lego (**www.Lugnet .com**)—even Barbie has an online community (**www.Barbiecollector.com**).

Online brand communities provide marketers and marketing researchers with a new medium through which they can observe, listen to, interact with, and gain insights from their customers and potential customers. By listening to the conversations that consumers are having with each other, marketers can learn a great deal about consumers' likes, dislikes, needs, opinions, interests, passions, and concerns.

There are two main types of online brand communities: **open communities**, such as Facebook and online forums that can be accessed by marketers but are not managed by a specific marketer, and **managed communities** that are designed and moderated by the marketer.

Open Communities. There are numerous open online communities that form on Facebook and on online forums and discussion boards. There are online forums and communities for pretty much any product available to consumers. These online forums provide an outlet for consumers to start conversations and join in on existing conversations related to brands, products, and services. For example, there are online forums for:

- Canning and food storage (**http://canningpantryforum.yuku.com**)
- Acoustic guitars (**http://www.acousticguitar.com/ubb/Forum1/HTML/015923 .html**)
- Gardening and home products (**http://ths.gardenweb.com/forums/cookware**)
- Lawn care and maintenance (**http://www.lawnsite.com**)
- Hair care and hair care products (**http://forums.longhaircommunity.com**)
- Parenting and child care (**http://able2know.org/forum/childcare**)
- Pets and pet products (**http://www.petdiscussion.com**)
- Home repair and maintenance (**http://www.houserepairtalk.com/forum.php**)
- Dental care (**http://www.dentistry-forums.com**)

For each of the above product categories, marketers who are interesting in learning more about consumers of these products can gain a great deal of information and knowledge about consumers' interests, likes, dislikes, frustrations, and desires for new products by simply listening in on these conversations between consumers.

Managed Communities. Managed communities are developed and moderated by the marketer. Such communities designed for research purposes are often referred to as **marketing research online communities (MROC)**. MROCs are usually private and participants are invited to join after being screened and selected based on demographics and psychographic variables. Community members might be asked to engage in tasks, such as taking surveys or engaging in discussions about a product or service for which they are rewarded. Members can contribute via online chats and discussions, and they can submit audio or video files of themselves shopping, consuming the product, or just talking about the product or service. As marketers listen to and monitor the conversations that occur in the MROC they are able to react to those conversations. Many online communities include requests to complete customer satisfaction surveys regarding the brand and consumption experiences.

Online Community Managers. Many MROCs are managed and moderated by an **online community manager**. The community manager is responsible for setting the rules of the community, making personal connections with community members, making sure that all members feel engaged, and setting the overall tone of the community and discussions between members.[9]

Online Surveys and Online Communities. Online surveys can also be used as a launching point for inviting consumers to participate in an online community. For example, Rockbridge's OpinonPond™ combines online surveys with online communities. After completing an online survey and answering questions individually, respondents are each invited to "enter the pond" where they can comment on posted questions as well as see and respond to other people's comments. This gives consumers an opportunity to share with others who have recently participated in the same study. The text comments provided in OpinionPond™ can then be linked to the quantitative data that was obtained from the online survey to provide even greater understanding of consumers' survey responses. This allows researchers to go beyond mere numbers (e.g., a consumer circling a 4 on a 1–7 scale) to uncover the themes, topics, opinions, emotions, and even the relationships that underlie consumers' attitudes, perceptions, and beliefs.

> Online communities provide a means by which like-minded consumers who identify with a brand can come together to share common brand-related interests, hobbies, and activities.

MOBILE SURVEYS AND APPS-BASED RESEARCH

Mobile surveys give marketers even more flexibility in terms of how, when, and where consumers can complete surveys. Mobile surveys are completed using a cell phone or other mobile device. This gives consumers the ability to complete online surveys in any location at any time of day. For example, mobile surveys can be completed while waiting in line at a retail outlet to earn purchase discounts that can be redeemed immediately, at a concert, in a physician's waiting room, or even while traveling on a bus or other form of mass transit. This allows researchers to measure consumers' perceptions and opinions "in the moment." Guests relaxing by the pool at a resort can even complete mobile surveys to earn points that can be redeemed at the poolside bar.

Some mobile survey companies offer surveys that can be sent via a text message with a link to the online survey included in the message. However, most mobile surveys are administered through an app on the mobile device, thus requiring that consumers have access to the Internet and email via a data plan. For example, Research Now Mobile™ (**www.researchnow.com**) offers mobile surveys where respondents receive a push notification that lets the user know that they have received a survey to complete using the mobile survey app. Similarly, itracks Mobile (**www.itracks.com**) uses an app that allows respondents to submit text, video, or audio responses. Even without an Internet connection, respondents can complete the survey offline and their answers are automatically uploaded to a discussion board when there is an online connection.[10]

Quick response (QR) codes can also be used to initiate a survey that is completed on a mobile device. Such QR codes can be printed on packages, on in-store displays, in print advertising, and even on cash register receipts. Providing QR codes on receipts eliminates the need for consumers to type in phone numbers, URLs, or survey codes. Consumers simply use the QR code reader on their mobile device to quickly access the survey.

Mobile surveys also offer the ability to ask various types of questions, including short answer questions, multiple choice questions, and rating scales. Some mobile surveys ask respondents to take photos to be submitted with their survey responses. And, some mobile surveys even ask respondents to submit an audio response to questions. This can be very helpful if there are many open-ended questions on the survey and consumers have difficulty typing multiple responses on a small screen. Also, time and date stamps, along with GPS, can be used to identify when and where respondents completed the survey.

> The advantage of mobile surveys is that marketers can measure consumers' attitudes and perceptions at almost any time of day and in almost any location.

Mobile surveys are being used in many areas of research. Not only are consumers asked to complete mobile surveys, but researchers also use them. For example, mobile surveys can be incorporated into the mystery shopping process. Mystery shoppers can now access surveys and evaluation instruments via their mobile device and complete them during, or immediately following, their shopping trip.

By their nature, mobile surveys must be relatively short and easy for respondents to complete, with relatively few questions. This will require more focused and streamlined research objectives for a given project. As a result, mobile surveys might need to be conducted more frequently, with very specific goals for each survey.

SOCIAL MEDIA MONITORING AND ANALYTICS

One way that marketers can use the power of social media to garner valuable information about their customers and their brands is by using **media monitoring** services. Many firms provide services for monitoring the news and media coverage that relates to a company, brand, service, or even charity. Not only can they monitor traditional media such as newspaper, television, and radio, but they are also able to monitor online sources of information, such as blogs, Twitter, Facebook, LinkedIn, and online news sources. Media monitoring allows marketers to answer such questions as:

- What are consumers tweeting about our brands?

- Are these positive or negative comments?

- How are our brands being integrated into consumers' Facebook profiles?

- How do consumers view our brands compared to other brands?

- What are consumers saying about our brands to their friends?

- What are consumers sharing with the rest of the world via social media?

- What do consumers perceive to be our brand's strengths and weaknesses?

Today, marketers must be very mindful of what is being said about their company, their brands, their employees, and the services that they provide to their customers. A negative comment that spreads rapidly on social media can have a profound impact on a company's reputation. For instance, McDonald's has come to understand the benefits of monitoring social media after a hoax photograph was posted online claiming that McDonald's was charging African American customers an additional fee of $1.50 per transaction.[11] The hoax first appeared on Twitter, where the image went viral. The company's director of social media released a statement through Twitter declaring the photograph to be a hoax. McDonalds continued to reinforce this message through social media and even responded personally to concerned Twitter users. Fortunately, the number of people who believed the image to be authentic was eventually reduced.

> By monitoring social media marketers can learn what consumers are saying about brands to their friends. Such social media comments might be more valid measures of true attitudes than are responses to marketer-initiated surveys.

The 80 Percent Rule. Monitoring and analyzing social media content has become increasingly important for marketers. In fact, the content that is available on social media has become a major contributor to the wealth of data that marketers are able to collect about consumers. It has been estimated that 80 percent or more of business-relevant information is in the form of qualitative and unstructured text, such as emails, documents, audio, images, call center transcripts, service notes, SMS texts, blogs, Facebook posts, and Twitter postings.[12] Consider the types of information contained in communications between marketers and customers. When customers contact marketers, they usually do so in text form—sending an email or completing a comment box on a website. Further, when customers complain about products they often do so using social media outlets such as Twitter, Facebook, and YouTube. Most companies have massive amounts of text-based content and data related to conversations between the marketer and customers, and data related to conversations between employees at an organization that often goes unused when making managerial decisions. This is because most marketers are accustomed to analyzing and making decisions based on quantitative data. The challenge for marketing researchers is to develop tools and techniques for analyzing such unstructured information and integrating it with current information that is contained in relatively structured datasets, for example, responses from surveys that are stored in Excel spreadsheets.

Social Media Analytics. **Text mining** is the process of extracting data, information, and eventually meaning from text: from customer complaints, from customer service call center notes and logs, from emails, from salesperson entries, from open-ended comments to survey questions, and from text found online and on social media sites. **Social media analytics** refers to the process by which data from online sources, such as social media and blogs, is compiled and analyzed for marketing managerial decision making. A marketer might wish to assess how engaged consumers are with a brand by tracking the number of followers of the brand's Twitter account as well as the number of re-tweets and times that the brand name is mentioned in tweets.

In the past, this text would have been manually read and deciphered. Luckily, current advances in media monitoring and text analytics provide marketers with the means to scan, decipher, and use the massive amounts of information that are in text form online in social media. Text analytics software looks for keywords and topics and uses linguistic rules to evaluate the text and assign a sentiment score to indicate whether a comment is positive, negative, or neutral. Text analytics can complement traditional structured data by adding context, texture, richness, and emotions to the analysis. The result is a more complete understanding of consumers. This allows markets to make decisions based on all available information, not just numerical data from traditional marketing research surveys.

Social Media Monitoring. There are a number of social media monitoring tools available to marketers. For example, Google Alerts (**www.google.com/alerts**) is a tool that marketers can use to monitor online conversations regarding their company or brands. Using Google Alerts, a marketer can set up keyword searches using their brand name or company name and receive an email when the search engine indexes an instance of the keyword being used online.[13] SocialMention (**www.socialmention .com**) works in a similar manner but also reports mentions within Facebook and other social media. Similarly, Twitter Advanced Search (**www.twitter.com/search**) provides a search of tweets. Icerocket (**www.icerocket.com**) monitors Twitter, blogs, the web, news, and even images. HootSuite (**www.hootsuite.com**) can track mentions of brands found on Twitter, Facebook, MySpace, WordPress, Foursquare, and LinkedIn.

Social media monitoring services can identify when a brand is mentioned on consumer-generated media such as Twitter, Facebook, Pinterest, YouTube, MySpace, LinkedIn, and blogs.

Google Analytics. An especially popular monitoring tool is Google Analytics. **Google Analytics** is a service that tracks the number of people who visit a website and how they navigate through the website. It allows marketers to identify where their site visitors came from and the keywords they used in search engines to find a site. This type of analysis can be very useful when identifying the terms and phrases that consumers use to find websites, thereby providing a better understanding of what consumers are looking for when they search online. **External searches** refer to the keywords consumers use to find a website through search engines such as Google. Marketers can look for patterns, themes, and even the frequency with which certain words appear in these searches. This is important because it gives marketers a sense of how consumers perceive a product. Most importantly, this gives insight into what consumers want, what they need, what they are looking for, and what is most important to them—in their own words. Alternatively, **internal searches** refer to the keywords and phrases that consumers type into the search feature on a particular site. Both external and internal searches can be used by marketers to design and structure the information found on their company's website. This, in turn, will improve their sites as well as increase the quality of conversations with customers. Such searches tell marketers what potential customers are looking for, what terms they use, what is important to them, and what content keeps their attention.

In addition to tracking how visitors found a site, Google Analytics allows marketers to track page views, which pages consumers viewed per visit, and even how much time consumers spent on the site. This is important information for marketers. For example, it allows them to see the number of people who actually made it through the purchase process on a website, and if they did not, the last page they viewed before leaving the website. This helps marketers identify which pages are beneficial and which pages have a negative effect on consumers. For example, if a marketer developed a series of social media campaigns, they could identify which social media network most of their website visitors are coming from and how they each navigated through the website, including the specific pages they visited and which page was viewed last before exiting the site. Some of the most often used metrics that can be calculated by Google Analytics are:

- **Traffic**: Traffic refers to the total number of times a site is visited by consumers. This provides insight into how interested consumers are in a company or its brands.

- **Direct traffic**: Direct traffic refers to the number of consumers who enter a site by typing the site's URL directly into their browser address bar. This indicates whether or not consumers were previously aware of a site, or if they needed to find it using a search engine.

- **Landing page**: The landing page is the first page that a visitor sees when entering a site.

- **Page view**: Page view is a measure of how many times consumers view an individual page. This tells marketers which pages and content found on those pages are of most interest to consumers.

- **Bounce rate**: Bounce rate refers to the percent of visits to a site where the visitor views only one page and then leaves the site without viewing another page. A high bounce rate indicates that the pages on a site are not interesting to consumers, that the content on the landing page is not relevant to consumers, or that the landing page is confusing to consumers.

- **Conversion**: A conversion is when a consumer views a site and then completes a task, action, or goal. Purchasing a product and completing the transaction would be an example of a conversion goal.

- **Goal conversion rate**: The goal conversion rate is the percent of visitors who complete the task, action, or goal. This indicates how well a website and the content found on it are compelling consumers to action.

- **Loyalty**: Loyalty is a measure of the number of times that a visitor returns to a site in a specified time period. A high loyalty score indicates that consumers enjoy visiting the site and return to it often. A low loyalty score indicates that the content on the site does not attract repeat visits.

- **Time on site**: Time on site is a measure of how much time visitors stay on a site and view the pages. More time on site indicates that consumers view the pages and content as interesting or relevant.

- **Top exit pages**: The top exit pages record the pages that are most often the last page a visitor views before leaving the site. This indicates which pages are detrimental to marketing goals. However, if the top exit page is one that follows a conversion, such as a purchase, this is not a problem.

Text Analytics. Not only do marketers want to know about their own websites, but they also want to know what consumers are saying about their brands in the social media universe. **Text analytics** is the process of analyzing the qualitative text and comments found on social media, such as Facebook posts and tweets on Twitter. Text analytics sorts through, categorizes, and structures what is otherwise relatively unstructured qualitative data found on these social media sites.

Not only can marketers capture the comments that are being made about a brand, but they can also obtain an understanding of consumers' moods and emotions behind those comments. Most text analytics services are also able to use algorithms based on simple terms to assign a **sentiment score** by targeting emotionally charged words and phrases to determine whether a comment was positive, neutral, or negative. A sentiment score can be calculated for any text, including open-ended comments on surveys. However, assigning sentiment scores that accurately assess what is on consumers' minds is difficult to calculate with 100 percent accuracy.[14] It is difficult to translate a string of text and identify it as either a positive or negative sentiment. It is generally accepted that most sentiment scores that are automatically calculated are approximately 70 percent accurate. However, sentiment scores tend to be slightly less accurate when analyzing text from social media. The problem lies in the way that people talk and write and the various nuances associated with speech and text. It is often difficult to decipher the meaning behind a comment. For example, consider the famous quote from Groucho Marx, "Time flies like an arrow, fruit flies like a banana." This illustrates the problems with syntax and context. The same word can take on two completely different meanings in the same sentence. The most accurate way to classify the sentiment of a comment is to use human coders. However, this becomes almost impractical given the large amount of text that can be found online and through social media.

An additional problem is that comments made on social media sites tend to be brief and often contain slang language. For example, consider if a consumer tweets the following: "That new Corvette is one bad car." One must fully understand the context in which the word *bad* is being used. In a conventional sense, *bad* is often used to denote a negative attitude or evaluation. However, within the context of the tweet, the word *bad* is likely meant as a positive term. Similarly, consider the possible interpretations of a tweet sent about a new brand of shampoo: "It made my hair kinky."

In sum, a primary goal of text analytics is to be able to assign numerical values to the words or phrases that people post on social media sites so that researchers can then combine and integrate the results from traditional research, such as surveys, with the relatively unstructured data found from social media. However, text analytics and sentiment analysis have a long way to go before they can accurately deal with the many nuances of the English language and the manner in which consumers speak and write.

The Role of Social Media in Making Marketing Decisions. As social media monitoring tools become more accessible and become even more integrated into the marketing researcher's set of methodologies and tools, there might be a tendency to rely too much on them. One must recognize, however, that social media monitoring should be considered as an exploratory research technique. While it has many advantages and offers new ways to observe and communicate with consumers, it should not be considered a replacement for a complete marketing research project. Marketers must consider the possible sources of error or bias associated with making decisions based solely on social media monitoring. For example, are the consumers who comment via social media representative of the entire population of customers? Are certain types of people more likely to complain via social media?

BIOMETRICS

When it comes to innovative new technologies being used by marketing researchers, few can compare to those used in biometric research. **Biometric research** refers to any technique, apparatus, or data collection system designed to measure biological changes in the human body, such as body temperature, heart rate, breathing patterns, eye movements, facial expressions, and even brain activity in response to stimuli, such as advertisements, product displays, audio, and even movies.

EYE TRACKING

Eye tracking is the process of measuring eye activity, including where a person looks, what they ignore, when they blink, and even how the pupil reacts to different stimuli. Eye tracking data can be collected using an eye tracker that is mounted on a computer screen or other remote object, or by using a mobile eye tracker worn on a person's head just as they would wear a pair of eyeglasses. Many mobile eye tracker headsets use an infrared light that shines on the eyeball. Reflections of the light off of the eyeball are captured by a small camera and are used to determine the angle of the eyeball and a person's **gaze motion**, that is, where they are looking. With recent advances such headsets are becoming smaller and less cumbersome to wear.

In addition to asking consumers to answer questions on surveys, biometric analysis allows researchers to understand consumers' emotions and reactions to stimuli without having to ask them anything.

By having consumers wear the eye tracking headset researchers can measure how consumers look at pretty much any object in pretty much any situation. For example, researchers can track a person's gaze motion while viewing a computer screen, while walking down a shopping aisle, while walking through a store, or even while driving. By doing so, researchers can determine which visual elements are seen by consumers, which visual elements capture consumers' attention, and which elements are overlooked or ignored. Eye tracking has applications for designing web pages, advertisements, product packaging, billboards, store shelves, and any other aspect of marketing that can be viewed by consumers.

A **gaze plot** shows the order and duration of a person's gaze motion. This means that it can tell marketers what visual element a person's eyes are drawn to first as well as the pattern of their gaze over time as they view a stimulus such as a print advertisement. This is usually displayed as a web-like pattern of circles and lines, where the size of the circles indicates the amount of time spent looking at the various aspects of the stimulus. From this, marketers can track the order of a person's gaze motion. A heat map is similar, but it does not display lines tracking the order of gaze motion. Rather, a **heat map** measures the most attractive and interesting visual elements by displaying hot and cold spots of the stimulus. Hotter areas reveal where a person's gaze was concentrated and are often represented in red, whereas cooler areas reveal where a person's gaze was less concentrated and are often represented in green. A heat map gives a visual summary of a person's gaze motion. It displays the zones, or areas, of a visual stimulus that held the viewer's attention.

A major advantage of eye tracking is that it reveals what consumers are actually looking at, not just what they say they are looking at. Sometimes people will intentionally lie when asked to report what they were looking at, and for how long. Likewise, people often simply are not aware of how much time they spend looking at a stimulus or the order in which they view a stimulus. However, gaze plots and heat maps must always be interpreted within the context of the task the viewer was asked to perform. Was the person viewing the stimulus in a laboratory setting with a researcher nearby, or was the person viewing the stimulus in private at home? Similarly, a person's gaze motion will also be affected by the task at hand. Was the person viewing the stimulus in isolation, or within the context of viewing other stimuli? And, being told to simply look at a product package might lead to a different gaze pattern than being told to consider purchasing a product based on viewing the package design.

Facial Analysis. An extension of eye tracking research is the growing field of **facial analysis** measurement. Using web cameras attached to computers, researchers are able to detect facial expressions in consumers as they view a computer screen. For example, Realeyes (**www.realeyesit.com**) uses web cameras to read people's faces and to measure the emotions they are feeling. The system employed by Realeyes is able to assess a person's mood by plotting the position of facial features, such as eyebrows, mouth, and nostrils, and then employs algorithms to interpret changes in their alignment. For example, eyebrows are often raised when a person is surprised.[15] And, by tracking consumers' eyes researchers can determine which ads were viewed and attended to and the length of time to which they were attended.

This technology could soon allow marketers to customize online content based on consumers' emotional responses to such content as measured by their facial expressions. The ads you see online might soon be determined by your facial expressions as opposed to the ads on which you might click. To illustrate this, imagine browsing a website when an advertisement for a new car catches your eye. You do not click on it, but merely smile and go to another page. However, it follows you and displays even more pictures of the car and even offers an incentive to take a test drive. When you become irritated by the persistent advertisements for the same car you begin to frown. Detecting your frustration based on the changes in your facial expression, the ad then displays "Sorry for taking your time," and then discontinues showing any more ads for the car.[16] Such technology is already available for consumers to use. Philips has recently developed the Philips Vital Signs Camera App for the iPad2 and iPhone 4S that allows a user to measure his or her own heart rate and breathing rate simply by using the camera on an iPad2 or iPhone 4S. A person's heartbeat causes small changes in the color of the face. The camera detects micro-blushes to measure heart rate. Further, a person's chest moves up and down when breathing. The camera can detect such movements to measure breathing rate.[17]

NEUROMARKETING

A fast-growing area of biometric research is **neuromarketing**, where brain-tracking tools are used to monitor and measure neurological responses to stimuli.[18] Neuromarketing hopes to provide insight into why consumers prefer some products over others. Researchers track brain activity using either **electroencephalography (EEG)** or **functional magnetic resonance imaging (fMRI)** technology. By attaching electrodes to a consumer's head and monitoring the electrical patterns of his or her brain waves, researchers can measure responses such as excitement, anger, and even lust. Many neuromarketing researchers use a device that fits over the head and uses EEG technology to measure electrical activity directly below the scalp. By using such a device researchers can measure consumers' brain activity as they view stimuli in a laboratory setting as well as in the real world. For instance, NeuroFocus (**www.neurofocus.com**) has used such neuromarketing devices and found that people prefer in-store displays with rounded edges to those with sharper edges. And, in one instance, sales in a store rose 15 percent when sharp-edged displays were replaced by rounded displays.[19] To better understand how consumers respond to stimuli in the real world, NeuroFocus has recently unveiled Mynd™, which is a lightweight, dry (meaning there is no need for gel), mobile brain scanner that fits over the head. It can be linked to a wireless device and is even compatible with mobile devices such as an iPhone or iPad.[20]

> By examining brain waves, researchers are able to measure consumers' responses to stimuli without the threat of any bias that might accompany responses to survey questions.

Many well-known marketers have used neuromarketing to help them make decisions regarding advertising and product design. For instance, in 2008 Frito-Lay used neuromarketing to better understand consumers' perceptions of Cheetos. By studying the neurological responses of subjects, Frito-Lay was able to determine that consumers actually responded favorably to the fact that a person's fingers turn orange from eating Cheetos. Based on brain wave patterns researchers concluded that consumers' experienced a sense of giddy subversion over the messiness of the product. Using this insight, Frito-Lay developed an advertising campaign called "The Orange Underground" featuring 30-second television commercials where consumers were encouraged to commit subversive acts using Cheetos.[21] Frito-Lay also used neuromarketing to measure women's neurological responses when designing the packaging and advertising for its 100-calorie snacks targeted to women. CBS has even used neuromarketing to gauge viewers' responses to TV pilots and shows.[22]

THE PROMISE OF EMERGING TECHNOLOGIES

The promise of these emerging technologies is that they can provide additional insights into consumers' attitudes, perceptions, emotions, decisions, and behaviors. Although traditional techniques for conducting marketing research, such as surveys, focus groups, and in-depth interviews, have given marketers guidance when marketing products, there is still much that marketers do not know or understand about consumers. This is especially evident when one considers that most new products fail. In fact, the research agency AcuPoll estimates that 80 to 95 percent of new products introduced each year fail.[23] Obviously, traditional marketing research methods have been lacking in their ability to provide a complete picture of consumers and what drives their decisions and behaviors.

One problem could be that traditional marketing research methods tend to be very researcher driven. Surveys are designed by researchers and ask questions that the researcher believes will be informative. And, while the methods for delivering surveys have changed, the same basic approach to writing and asking survey questions has been used for decades. It is likely that researchers are simply asking the wrong questions, or are asking them in the wrong way. Similarly, the basic approach to structuring in-person focus groups has not changed significantly in the past few decades. Although focus groups allow for free-flow discussion, the direction of the discussion is still controlled for the most part by the moderator.

However, emerging technologies offer completely new approaches for researching consumers. Social media allows consumers to drive the conversation and identifies what consumers want to discuss. Neuromarketing and facial analysis allow marketers to better understand what is behind consumers' decisions and behaviors without the bias and censoring that often accompany self-reports of behaviors and attitudes. Consumers bias and censor their comments intentionally as well as unintentionally. However, neuromarketing, eye tracking, and facial analysis allow researchers to tap into the true drivers of consumers' behaviors and decisions without the need for self-reported behaviors. Such technologies allow researchers to measure what stimuli truly affect consumers and how they are being affected by it. Without the need for verbal responses, such biometric research approaches can offer a more valid measure of the influences on consumers even if consumers do not know when and how they are being influenced.

CHALLENGES FACING MARKETING RESEARCH

Even though the future of marketing research seems bright given the new technologies that are being developed for communicating with and understanding consumers, there are a number of challenges that face the marketing research industry. These challenges come from (1) the ever-growing means by which marketers can conduct marketing research on their own without the need to hire a professional researcher, (2) consumers' reluctance to participate in marketing research projects, and (3) problems associated with integrating new data with existing data sets.

Do-It-Yourself (DIY) Research. Do-it-yourself (DIY) research has grown in popularity and usage among marketers in recent years. As such, it is often seen as a challenge to the professional research industry because clients and other users of marketing research are able to formulate their own projects and collect their own data without the cost associated with hiring a professional researcher. For example, online survey sites such as **Surveymonkey.com**, **Qualtrics.com**, and **Surveygizmo.com** allow marketers to create and administer their own surveys. As previously discussed, online marketers are able to conduct their own online analytics using such tools as Google Analytics. This has obvious advantages for marketing managers. Beyond the reduced costs that would have been incurred to hire a research professional, such surveys and research projects can be created and conducted very quickly.

> Just because marketers can create and administer their own surveys, this does not mean that it would be best for them to do so.

However, while DIY online survey technology is accessible to anyone, such DIY research often lacks the knowledge, experience, and insights that accompany research projects conducted by professional marketing researchers. Just because marketers can create and administer their own surveys, this does not mean that it would be best for them to do so. Developing marketing research projects and surveys requires skills and expertise that many marketing managers simply do not possess. Managers who believe that anyone can create a survey often end up with useless data generated from vague, ambiguous, and misleading survey questions. Such DIY surveys often suffer from error and bias not easily identifiable by those with little research experience. In addition, marketing researchers are able to add value by providing guidance in analyzing and interpreting data. Many marketing managers are simply not proficient in statistical data analysis and interpretation.

> Consumers are becoming increasingly reluctant to freely provide information to marketing researchers, no matter how innocuous that information may be. More and more, marketing researchers will have to compensate consumers for any information they provide.

Decline of Respondent Cooperation. Marketing researchers will have to deal with consumers' growing **privacy concerns** and the decline of **respondent cooperation**. Researchers are discovering that consumers are becoming less willing to provide personal information about purchasing behaviors. More and more, researchers will have to compensate consumers for providing this personal information. This has already taken place for many retailers. Consumers often find 1-800 phone numbers printed on sales receipts and instructions directing them to call the number and complete a short phone survey. As compensation, consumers receive monetary discounts off their next store purchase, coupons sent to them in the mail, or even free meals at a restaurant. Sometimes, consumers are allowed to enter a drawing where they have a chance of winning a large monetary prize, such as a $1,000 shopping spree. But, they must complete the survey to be entered into the drawing. Many consumers will provide opinions and information about personal purchase behaviors only if they are compensated. Contact information about customers can also be very valuable when used for database marketing purposes. Marketers have even compensated consumers for nothing more than providing their email address (so that marketers can then communicate with their customers on an individual basis via email).

Gamification of Marketing Research. A recent strategy in the research industry to deal with the increasing reluctance of consumers to participate in marketing research is to introduce gamification into research projects. **Gamification** is the process by which researchers create activities (often online) with game-like features that collect information about consumers as they perform the activity. For example, Dunkin' Donuts allowed visitors to their Facebook page to enter SimCity Social, where they could receive virtual goodies, earn Facebook gifts, and play Dunkin' quests. Dunkin' Donuts also provided a game interface on their Facebook page where visitors pushed an image of a coffee cup along a coffee assembly line with stations where they could add flavors, sweeteners, and milk to fulfill a virtual customer's coffee order.[24] The player was given one minute to correctly fill the order. Players were given larger orders and less time to fill them as they moved up levels of the game. Ten players a day had the chance to each win $10 Dunkin' gift cards. This game was intended to be a research tool. Players began the game by entering their coffee preferences. This approach is much more enjoyable than traditional online surveys. It allows marketers to interact with customers and identify their preferences within the context of a fun game.

Big Data. The desire for new ways to learn about and understand consumers has increased in intensity. As the field of marketing research expands and the number of methodologies by which marketers can obtain information from and about consumers grows, the number of data sets from which marketers can extract information to make decisions has also grown. Marketers are now able to obtain data regarding consumers quicker and faster than ever before. In fact, IBM estimates that we now create 2.5 quintillion bytes of data every day. Further, they also estimate that 90 percent of the data that exists in the world today has been created in the last two years alone.[25] This huge increase in the number and size of such data sets is often referred to as **Big Data**. Not only are marketers able to obtain information about consumers from traditional methods, such as in-person focus groups, telephone surveys, paper-and-pencil surveys, and intercept surveys, but new technologies and the increasing acceptance of social media and mobile devices have given marketers even more methods by which they can communicate with consumers. And, the hope is that with enough data, marketers can predict consumers' attitudes, interests, and even behaviors with increased statistical confidence.

However, one potential downside to this massive increase in data is the potential negative effect that it can have on marketing decision makers. The term **analysis paralysis** is often used to describe situations where decision makers are faced with too much data when trying to make decisions. In effect, they simply become overwhelmed with data, so much so that they are not able to make a decision. The sheer amount of time that it can take to convert data into a usable form can have a debilitating effect on a decision maker's ability to make timely and effective decisions. As data sets become larger and more multifaceted, marketers are now being faced with challenges regarding the acquisition, storage, and analysis of such data.

A related limitation deals with the variety of data in such Big Data sets. Traditional data sets have contained **structured data** that can be obtained from quantitative data sources, such as surveys, and can be easily transformed, manipulated, and analyzed using traditional statistical procedures. However, many data sets now contain relatively **unstructured data**, such as open-ended responses, tweets, Internet searches, photos, videos, audio, and other qualitative data that is obtained from the Internet and social media. The problem for many researchers is how to integrate the existing structured data sets with the newer unstructured data sets. For example, the data sets from online surveys, computer assisted telephone interviewing (CATI) surveys, and even mobile surveys can be easily imported into Excel or another statistical analysis programs and then easily manipulated and analyzed. However, text, photos, video, and audio are not as easily integrated into existing data set formats.

New techniques, such as text analytics, enable researchers to analyze verbal comments, such as those from open-ended survey questions and text from online communications. The text analytics software uses **natural language processing algorithms** to sort through verbal comments and convert them to usable data; for example, identifying a person' attitude and emotions based on his or her written comments. The next few years will most likely see an increase in the number of firms developing technologies for integrating newer unstructured data with traditional structured data. For example, marketers may soon be able to easily integrate structured data about consumers' purchases, including what they buy, where they buy it, how often they buy it, and how much they spend, with unstructured data obtained from consumers' tweets, photos, videos, and even audio from social media sites. This combined data set would add incredible richness to the profiles that can be formed about consumers for predicting their future behaviors and purchases.

This massive amount of data is an asset to marketers only to the extent that they are able to use it to inform, guide, and assess managerial decisions. One of the primary functions of a marketing research analyst is to simplify large amounts of data into essential, useful, and managerial-relevant insights. In many ways, then, as the amount of data that is collected increases, the need for researchers who can synthesize, summarize, and condense the data will also increase.

Ethical Considerations. The massive amount of data being collected by marketing researchers also invites a number of ethical questions about its use. For example, consider the case of Target.[26] Target assigns every customer a guest ID number that is tied to their credit card, name, and/or email that is used to collect demographic information and a history of everything that customer buys. Using this database of

With the growing amount of data that can be collected about consumers comes increased awareness for the ethical use of that data.

information, Target sends coupons for baby products to customers who purchase products that indicate that they might be pregnant (e.g., calcium supplements, unscented lotions, large bags of cotton balls, hand sanitizers and washcloths). On one occasion an angry father complained to the manager of his local Target store about the coupons for baby products, such as maternity clothing and nursery furniture, being sent to his daughter who was still in high school. He was offended that Target would actually be trying to encourage her to become pregnant. The manager apologized and then called a few days later to apologize again. However, the second apology from the manager was accompanied by an apology from the father. It turned out that the daughter actually was pregnant but had not yet told her father. The father was still upset that Target knew more about his daughter's private life than he did.[27]

Emerging Technologies and the Decision-Making Process

It is clear that advances in technology can have significant effects on the marketing research industry. With new technologies come new methodologies and techniques for communicating with consumers, learning from them, listening to their conversations, and understanding their attitudes, perceptions, and motivations. The advent of social media offers a dramatic shift in the process by which marketing researchers can learn about consumers. Traditional research methods are very researcher driven. That is, researchers traditionally decide what questions to ask and it is the consumer who answers those questions. Now, with social media, that paradigm is shifting. Consumers are the ones driving the conversations and asking the questions. Through consumer-generated media they are able to offer opinions and initiate dialogues with other consumers, as well as with marketers, about the social aspect of consumption. Brands are social objects, and consumers are becoming more and more willing to talk about brands using social media. However, while social media and other emerging technologies offer exciting new ways to learn about consumers, such emerging technologies should not be considered as a replacement for traditional marketing research methodologies. There are still many unanswered questions about the quality of the data obtained from such emerging technologies and the potential biases and errors associated with them. As such, marketing managers would be wise to begin adopting and integrating these emerging technologies into their marketing research programs without allowing them to supplant and replace the time-tested, more traditional research methodologies.

QUESTIONS FOR DISCUSSION

1. View the YouTube video of the song "United Breaks Guitars." If you were responsible for monitoring social media for United Airlines, how would you respond to this video?

2. Have you ever used social media to comment about a product or service? What types of comments did you offer?

3. Have you ever complained publically about a product, service, or company via social media? Did you receive a response from the company/marketer? What type of response would you like to receive from the company or business about which you complained? How would you feel if you were to receive a response from a complaint that you made using social media?

4. How could your university use marketing research online communities (MROCs) to better identify students' needs and wants?

5. What are the main differences between open and managed online communities?

6. If you were using mobile surveys, what questions would you ask, and what incentive(s) would you offer to consumers:
   a. Waiting for a table at a restaurant
   b. Immediately after a concert or play
   c. Immediately after making a purchase at a department store
   d. Attending an NFL game
   e. Visiting a theme park
   f. Staying at a hotel/resort
   g. Using the services of a travel agency
   h. Visiting a museum/art gallery
   i. Waiting to check in and board an airline flight

7. Should marketers rely solely on the results from social media monitoring when attempting to learn how consumers perceive a brand or a product? Why? Why not?

8. What are the advantages and disadvantages of DIY research?

9. If you were designing the website for a local car dealership, how could you introduce the concept of gamification to the website? What activities could you ask visitors to the website to perform? What could you learn from this?

MINICASE 4.1

Precision Planting and Gardening

Cory Wood is a 21-year-old entrepreneur. Cory made money in high school by cutting lawns, mulching gardens, planting bushes and shrubs, trimming and maintaining landscaping, and other lawn and garden jobs. He loves working outdoors and he especially loves gardening. When he graduated from high school he decided to forgo college. Instead, he opened his own lawn and garden business, which he named Precision Planting and Gardening.

Business has been good, but not great. Most of his previous customers retained him to work on their lawn and gardens since he graduated from high school. However, Cory understands the need to grow his business. He recently created a website for his business, with photos of completed jobs, testimonials, phone numbers, and lists of services that he offers. His site also allows visitors to use search terms and phrases to find different pages and information on the site. He recently did some investigating and discovered that the most often used internal search term on his website was "lawn repair."

1. How could Cory use this information to better design his website?

2. How could Cory use this information to help him market and promote his business?

3. If you were searching online for this type of business (e.g., an external search using Google), what search terms would you use?

4. What do these terms indicate about how you view this service?

ENDNOTES

1 Candice Choi and Christina Rexrode, "Retailers Use Social Media for Market Research," *Associated Press*, December 23, 2012.

2 Annie Pettit, "Strength in Numbers: Using Social Media Research to Complement Traditional Methods," *Quirk's Marketing Research Review*, August 2011, 28–34.

3 Pettit, "Strength in Numbers: Using Social Media Research to Complement Traditional Methods," *Quirk's Marketing Research Review*, August 2011, 28–34.

4 Pettit, "Strength in Numbers: Using Social Media Research to Complement Traditional Methods," *Quirk's Marketing Research Review*, August 2011, 28–34.

5 Allison Enright, "Listen Up," **Internetretailer.com**, May 31, 2011.

6 Jim Stone and Eric Levy, "Are You Listening? Customer Service Expectations and Preferences in the Age of Facebook," *Quirks Marketing Research Review*, August 2012, 34–43.

7 "GreenBook Research Industry Trends Report (GRIT)," Winter 2013, **www.GRITreport.org**

8 A. M. Muniz and T. C. O'Guinn, "Brand Community," *Journal of Consumer Research*, March 2001, 412–432.

9 Job Muscroft, "Five Emerging Roles That Are Changing the Face of Marketing Research," **Facegroup.com**, January 23, 2012.

10 "Product and Service Updates: Smartphones Equipped for Qual," *Quirk's Marketing Research Review*, November 2012, 18.

11 V. Kanchana, "All Chatter's Not Good Chatter—Tips for Monitoring Negative Online Media," *Quirks Marketing Research Review*, November 2012.

12 Seth Grimes, "Structure, Models and Meaning," **InformationWeek.com**, March 1, 2005. Seth Grimes, "Unstructured Data and the 80 Percent Rule," Clarabridge Bridgepoints, 2008, Q3.

13 Enright, "Listen Up," **Internetretailer.com**, May 31, 2011.

14 Andy Beal, "Is Automated Sentiment Analysis Reliable?" **MarketingPilgrim.com**, August 24, 2009. Brian Tarran, "Automated Sentiment Analysis Gives Poor Showing in Accuracy Test," **Research-live.com**, June 2, 2010. Karin Kane, "Bracing for Impact: Understanding Social Media's Effect on Market Research," *Quirk's Marketing Research Review*, August 2011, 24–27. Jason Schubring, "12 Social Media Monitoring Tools Reviewed," **sixrevisions.com**, July 31, 2010.

15 "The All-Telling Eye: Webcams Can Now Spot Which Ads Catch Your Gaze, Read Your Mood and Check Your Vital Signs," *The Economist*, October 22, 2011, **http://www.economist.com/node/21533362**

16 "The All-Telling Eye: Webcams Can Now Spot Which Ads Catch Your Gaze, Read Your Mood and Check Your Vital Signs," *The Economist*, October 22, 2011 **http://www.economist.com/node/21533362**

17 James Mulroy, "App Uses Your Webcam to Detect Your Heart and Breathing Rates," *PC World*, November 18, 2011.

18 Carmen Nobel, "What Neuroscience Tells Us About Consumer Desire," *Harvard Business School: Working Knowledge*, March 26, 2012, **http://hbswk.hbs.edu/item/6950.html**

19 Adam Penenberg, "NeuroFocus Uses Neuromarketing to Hack Your Brain," August 8, 2011, **http://www.fastcompany.com/1769238/neurofocus-uses-neuromarketing-hack-your-brain**

20 David Zax, "Thinking Cap: 'Mynd' Is the First Dry, iPhone Compatible, Portable Brain Scanner," **http://neurofocus .com/pdfs/fastcompany_mynd_neuromarketing.pdf**, June 2013.

21 Nobel, "What Neuroscience Tells Us About Consumer Desire," *Harvard Business School: Working Knowledge*, March 26, 2012, **http://hbswk.hbs.edu/item/6950.html**

22 Penenberg, "NeuroFocus Uses Neuromarketing to Hack Your Brain", August 8, 2011, **http://www.fastcompany .com/1769238/neurofocus-uses-neuromarketing-hack-your-brain**

23 Laurie Burkitt and Ken Bruno, "New, Improved…and Failed," **Forbes.com**, March 24, 2012, **http://www.nbcnews .com/id/36005036/ns/business-forbes_com/t/new-improved-failed**

24 Leonard Murphy, "Five Companies That Are Using Big Data and Gamification to Disrupt Market Research," **www .Greenbook.org**, October 16, 2011.

25 Diane Liebenson, "Big Data: Opportunity or Threat for Market Research?" **www.Greenbookblog.org**, March 21, 2012. "Bringing Big Data to the Enterprise," IBM, **http://www-01.ibm.com/software/data/bigdata/**, June 2013.

26 Choi and Rexrode, "Retailers Use Social Media for Market Research," *Associated Press*, December 23, 2012.

27 Kashmir Hill, "How Target Figured Out a Teen Girl Was Pregnant Before Her Father Did," **Forbes.com**, February 16, 2012, **http://www.forbes.com/sites/kashmirhill/2012/02/16/how-target-figured-out-a-teen-girl-was-pregnant-before-her-father-did/**

CHAPTER 5

Classes of Marketing Research

LEARNING OBJECTIVES

1 Compare and contrast exploratory research, descriptive research, and causal research in terms of:

    a The purpose of the research.

    b When the research is typically conducted.

    c The type of data that the research yields.

    d The major techniques for conducting the research.

2 Describe how the marketing research process progresses from exploratory research to descriptive research, and finally to causal research.

There are many different ways of conducting marketing research, and there are a variety of techniques for collecting data and information. The most useful way to classify and describe the major techniques used in marketing research is to organize them in terms of their purpose and the stage of the research process in which they are typically conducted. The three major classes of marketing research are exploratory research, descriptive research, and causal research. Each major class of marketing research has its own general purpose and specific research techniques, as summarized in Figure 5.1.

EXPLORATORY RESEARCH

Exploratory research is typically conducted at very early stages in the research process. As its name implies, exploratory research is designed to explore. It is used to help clarify and classify the nature of problems. Exploratory research helps marketing researchers identify problems. Because problem identification is the first stage in the research process, exploratory research is often conducted early in the research process to help distinguish between observable symptoms and underlying problems. However, exploratory research is often not intended to provide conclusive evidence. Most exploratory research techniques rely on relatively small samples. In many cases exploratory research serves merely as the starting point in the research process. It often helps to identify information needed for subsequent research.

FIGURE 5.1 The Three Classes of Marketing Research

Exploratory Research	Descriptive Research	Causal Research
Identifies key marketing variables Identifies problems vs. symptoms Sets priorities for subsequent research	Describes consumers on key marketing variables	Identifies causal relationships between key marketing variables
Techniques Secondary Data Analysis Social Media Monitoring Mystery Shoppers Background Analysis Employee Interviews Observation Ethnography Focus Groups Projective Techniques	**Techniques** Personal Interviews Door-To-Door Surveys Mall Intercept Interviews Point-of-Purchase Surveys Telephone Surveys Mail Surveys Mobile Surveys Self-Administered Surveys Online Surveys	**Techniques** Experimental Design Laboratory Experiments Field Experiments Test Marketing

Conducted at early stages in the research process when marketing problems and questions are not well-defined.

- What do consumers think of this new product concept?
- Why are people not shopping at our stores?

Conducted at later stages in the research process when marketing problems and questions are well-defined.

- What effect will changing the package color from red to blue have on sales?
- Will a lower price lead to increased store traffic?

Exploratory research is used to:

- Define marketing problems and diagnose situations.

- Conduct a background analysis and identify background information to distinguish between problems and symptoms.

- Set priorities for future research by identifying variables that should be measured on subsequent surveys.

- Test new product concepts and measure consumers' perceptions of brand extensions.

- Discover new ideas and marketing opportunities.

- Identify new market segments and bases for segmenting markets.

- Gain insight into marketing problems from the consumer's perspective.

Exploratory research yields:

- Insight and understanding, not precise measurement. Because most exploratory research techniques rely on relatively small samples, the results are typically not presented with an accompanying statistical margin of error (± percent).

- Qualitative data. Even though some forms of exploratory research yield quantitative data to which we can assign a number, such as income, age, or even the number of times consumers visit a supermarket each week, many forms of exploratory research yield **qualitative data**, to which we cannot assign a number, such as the nature of a respondent's smile during a focus group, or a person's awkwardly formed face when taste testing a new food product that he or she does not like.

DESCRIPTIVE RESEARCH

Descriptive research is conducted to discover, identify, and describe important characteristics of a segment, target market, or population. Descriptive research is often used to describe large groups of people on important variables that have been identified from exploratory research. It is designed to answer questions such as "Who are our customers? What products do our customers purchase? Where are our customers shopping? When do our customers purchase our products? How do our customers purchase our products?" The information obtained from descriptive research is often considered conclusive and is often used to make managerial decisions. It usually involves a representative sample with a relatively large sample size and an accompanying small statistical margin of error. Thus, it is important that descriptive research be designed and conducted with as little bias and error as possible. Descriptive data is most often collected with surveys.

Descriptive research is used to:

- Forecast demand for a new product or business.

- Measure customers' satisfaction with products or retail outlets.

- Measure customers' awareness for marketing efforts and promotions.

- Measure customers' attitudes and purchase intentions.

- Identify potential customers and create customer databases for future promotional and direct marketing efforts.

Without first conducting exploratory research, researchers will often not know what variables need to be measured with descriptive research (surveys) or manipulated in causal research.

Due to small sample sizes, the results from exploratory research are often not considered to be conclusive.

- Measure consumers' behaviors.

- Measure consumers' demographics.

Descriptive research yields:

- Precise measurement if questions are asked in an unbiased manner of a representative sample of sufficient size and characteristics.

- Conclusive evidence.

- Quantitative data that can be tabulated and analyzed statistically.

- Multiple responses from a single respondent so that relationships between variables can be examined.

Because of their larger and more representative samples, descriptive research surveys are often used to confirm, or validate, the conclusions from previous exploratory research.

CAUSAL RESEARCH

Causal research is designed to identify causal relationships between important marketing variables. It usually involves experimentation and experimental design. It can be used to help predict the effects of changes in the marketing mix, such as changes in price, changes in product design, changes in promotion, and changes in channels of distribution on key performance variables, such as sales, purchase frequency, consumers' brand attitudes, and consumers' purchase intentions. Causal research often involves experimental designs that control for **extraneous variables**, thus allowing the researcher to examine the effects of **independent variables** on **dependent variables**.

Causal research is used to:

- Measure and predict consumers' brand attitudes toward new products.

- Identify marketing mix decisions that will lead to the most favorable brand attitudes and purchase intentions.

- Identify the effects of changes in marketing mix elements on sales and market share.

- Examine the causal effects of marketer-controlled variables on key dependent variables.

Causal research yields:

- Precise measurement about the relationships between key marketing variables.

- Conclusive evidence.

- Quantitative data that can be analyzed statistically.

To summarize, the results from exploratory research help to identify key variables to be measured on subsequent surveys. Descriptive research describes the target market on these key variables and identifies marketing mix variables to be manipulated in a subsequent experiment. Causal research identifies the causal relationships between key marketing mix variables and performance variables, such as sales or number of customer complaints.

EXPLORATORY, DESCRIPTIVE, AND CAUSAL RESEARCH

To illustrate the relationship between these three general classes of research techniques, consider the case of a food products manufacturer that noticed sales of its prepackaged lunchmeat were declining. Recognizing that declining sales were merely the visible result of some underlying problem, they determined that the true problem could be related to any of a number of marketing variables. It could be a problem with price (perhaps their price was too high), distribution (perhaps they were not selling their products in stores convenient to customers), advertising (perhaps there were not enough promotions to create consumer awareness), product features (perhaps there was something about the lunchmeats that customers did not like), or even the product's image. To narrow down the possibilities they conducted some focus groups (exploratory research) of approximately 40 consumers. They conducted five group sessions of eight consumers each.

The results from the focus groups helped researchers identify that the problem was most likely with the product's features. Focus group participants did not mention issues related to distribution, lack of advertising, high price, or other possible causes for low sales. Most of their comments were directed at the product itself. The next step was to identify the specific product features that customers did not like. Possible problems could exist with the size of the lunchmeat, the shape of the lunchmeat, the color of the lunchmeat, the packaging for the lunchmeat, or even the thickness of the lunchmeat. They used surveys (descriptive research) of 500 people to identify that most consumers did not like the package. The lunchmeat was not sold in a resealable package. Thus, the next step would be to change the package. But, before making a nationwide change they decided to conduct some test markets (causal research) in three different cities where they introduced their new resealable package. Results from the test markets were favorable. So, based on all of the research information and data available, they decided to change the package of their lunchmeat to a resealable package.

Notice that the focus groups helped to identify the issues about which they needed to ask on the survey. The survey was used to identify the specific product feature that most likely needed to be changed to have a positive effect on sales. Finally, the causal research confirmed that changing the package to a resealable package would lead to increased sales. Without conducting the exploratory research (focus groups), they would have needed to ask an enormous number of questions on the survey dealing with all possible causes of low sales. And, without doing the surveys, they would not have known which product feature needed to be changed to increase sales. Even if focus group participants mentioned the resealable package, the survey of a much larger representative sample was needed to confirm that the majority of customers felt the same way about the lack of a resealable package.

> The purpose of causal research is to examine the cause and effect relationship between variables.

> Exploratory research identifies important variables. Descriptive research measures large groups of people on those variables. Causal research identifies cause-and-effect relationships between those variables.

QUESTIONS FOR DISCUSSION

1. What type of research, exploratory, descriptive, or causal, would you recommend to help answer the following questions?
    a. Is there a need for our product?
    b. What markets are there for our product? Where are the markets? How large are the markets?
    c. What package color (either blue or green) will lead to more favorable purchase intentions?
    d. What effect will reducing the price have on our sales?
    e. Which advertisement (either A or B) will lead to more favorable brand attitudes?
    f. Why are people not shopping at our stores?
    g. What motivates consumers to purchase our products?
    h. Where are our customers shopping?
    i. What are the demographic characteristics of our customers?

2. Identify the type(s) of marketing research that yield the following:

	Exploratory Research	Descriptive Research	Causal Research
Insight, rather than precise measurement			
Qualitative data			
Quantitative data			
Precise measurement			
Information about causal relationships between marketing variables			
Conclusive evidence			
Results accompanied by a statistical margin of error			
Results from a large sample			

3. Which type of research, exploratory, descriptive, or causal, would be best for the following situations?
    a. A researcher wants to know if requiring salespeople to spend more time in training will lead to an increase in their productivity.
    b. A researcher wants to know the demographics of a target market for a new product.
    c. A researcher wants to know consumers' reactions to a new drink sweetener that also helps to control seasonal allergies.

4. In your own words, describe the differences between exploratory research, descriptive research, and causal research.

Modern Styles Clothing Store

You are the manager of Modern Styles, which is a retail store that sells higher-priced women's clothing. Susan Rodan, the store owner, opened Modern Styles 12 years ago. At that time Susan was employed by a packaged foods manufacturer, but she had always been interested in clothing and fashion. So, when a retail space opened up in one of the shopping malls located near the center of one of the oldest neighborhoods in the city, she jumped at the opportunity and opened Modern Styles. Because the retail space was relatively small, she decided to focus on selling higher-priced fashions so that her profit margins would make up for lower sales volume. Susan has just called you and asked you to meet with her in her office. She tells you:

> I don't know what is going on. Our sales used to be much better. But, in the last year our sales have really fallen off. I want you to conduct a customer satisfaction survey to find out what our customers think. Come up with a survey by the end of this week and then we can begin to hand it out to our customers when they are in our store. My best friend owns a research firm and she offered to enter and analyze the data at no charge. So, this research will cost us nothing.

What do you tell Susan Rodan? What words or terms do you use? What phrases do you use? What role do you take in the conversation?

Good-to-Grow Gardening

Three years ago, Bill Martin opened Good-to-Grow, which manufactures and markets home gardening products. You were recently hired as the marketing and promotions manager. Bill Martin is an avid gardener who had always wanted to be in business for himself. So, when he was laid off from his previous job he decided to follow his passion and start his gardening products business. The business has done very well. Sales have steadily grown each of the last three years. Bill has just called you on the phone and tells you:

> For a long time now we have known that our customers do not like our distribution channels. They wish that they could buy our products in a greater variety of stores that are closer and more convenient to them. And we see how this is a problem. I have heard that focus groups are the "hot" thing in customer research. Some have even said that if you are not doing focus groups you don't really know your customers. So, I want you to design and conduct some focus groups to identify the stores in which we should sell our products. Here is a list of potential retail outlets where we could sell our products. Count the number of people who say that they would like to be able to buy our products in each of these stores. The stores that are mentioned the most frequently will be the ones that we approach first about selling our products in their stores.

What do you tell Bill Martin? What words or terms do you use? What phrases do you use? What role do you take in the conversation?

Camp Fish

Jack Johnston is the owner of Camp Fish, which is a retail store that sells fishing and camping supplies. Camp Fish is located in an outdoor lifestyle shopping center. Jack Johnston has recently contacted you about conducting some customer satisfaction surveys for him. He has offered to pay you to develop a survey that he can use to measure where his customers live, where they like to fish and camp, how often they go fishing and camping, and the type of fishing that they most enjoy. He would like to survey his current customers, so he plans to offer an incentive to his customers to complete the survey while they are in his store. After completing the survey, the customer will be allowed to enter his or her name and email address into a drawing to win a $100 shopping spree at Camp Fish.

What do you tell Jack Johnston?

CHAPTER 6

The Marketing Research Process

LEARNING OBJECTIVES

1 Describe and explain the 10 major steps in the marketing research process.

2 Describe the differences between marketing problems and marketing symptoms.

3 Describe the differences between managerial objectives and marketing research objectives.

4 Describe what is meant by a sequence of causes.

5 Identify the most important stages in the marketing research process.

THE MARKETING RESEARCH PROCESS

It is helpful to think of marketing research as a process, or as a series of activities that must be performed. Marketing researchers must make decisions at each of the stages in the research process regarding the objectives of the research project, the specific data collection techniques and procedures that will be used, the research instruments and the manner in which information is to be collected, the sampling procedures, the data analysis techniques, and the manner in which the results from the project will be communicated to marketing managers and decision makers. A generic model of the marketing research process is shown in Figure 6.1.

Define the Problem

As shown in Figure 6.1, the marketing research process begins with defining the problem. It is very important that researchers properly define the problem and clearly distinguish the problem from the observable symptoms of the problem before beginning any research project. Marketing research is conducted to gather information to solve problems, not to solve symptoms. For example, decreasing sales and decreasing store traffic might stimulate the need to conduct a marketing research project. However, even though it is a negative situation, decreasing sales is not a problem. Similarly, decreasing store traffic is not a problem. Decreasing

FIGURE 6.1 The Marketing Research Process

1	Define the problem.
2	Identify management objectives.
3	Develop research objectives.
4	Decide on the data collection techniques and procedures.
5	Develop all research instruments and materials.
6	Plan the sampling procedure.
7	Collect the data.
8	Analyze the data.
9	Prepare and present the research report.
10	Identify needs for subsequent research.

sales and decreasing store traffic are most likely the observable symptoms of some underlying unobservable problem related to the marketing mix or other external factors. For example, the problem could be that the prices of the products sold in a store are too expensive for customers to afford. Or, the problem could be that the location of a store is not convenient for customers. Or, the problem could be that a store's sales force is poorly trained, resulting in poor customer satisfaction. There are any number of problems that could lead to decreasing sales and decreasing store traffic.

> Problems are different from symptoms. Symptoms are the visually identifiable and measurable result of problems. Marketing researchers seek to identify and solve problems, not symptoms.

The difference between marketing problems and marketing symptoms is illustrated in Figure 6.2. **Marketing symptoms** are the visually identifiable result of marketing problems. **Managerial objectives** are usually framed within the context of marketing symptoms, which are the visually identifiable means by which marketing performance is measured and evaluated. Alternatively, **research objectives** are usually framed within the context of identifying **marketing problems** by collecting and providing information about internal and external influences on marketing strategies.

Must the Research Process Always Begin with a Problem? No. Research is often conducted on an ongoing basis to identify new ideas, new opportunities, new markets, new bases for segmentation, and even new product positioning strategies. If a company does not continually conduct marketing research to identify new ideas and opportunities, their competitors will. In fact, success in marketing usually leads to competition entering a market. Many marketers will conduct marketing research to identify new ideas for staying ahead of competition. As such, many marketing research projects do not begin with a stated problem to be solved. If, however, the research process does begin with a problem, the purpose of marketing research is to gather information to help managers solve the problem, not the symptom. And, there are numerous exploratory research techniques that can be used to identify marketing problems. In such a case, the marketing problem should be well-defined and identified before conducting any subsequent descriptive or causal marketing research.

FIGURE 6.2 Marketing Problems vs. Marketing Symptoms

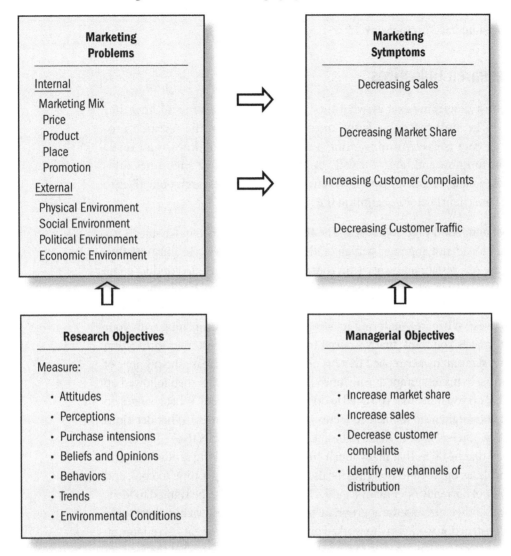

Identify Management Objectives

Before starting a research project and collecting data, researchers must first identify the managerial objectives. What does management want the marketing research to help them achieve? What are the marketing performance objectives? Unfortunately, managerial objectives are rarely stated in measurable terms that are specific for research purposes. For example, managers often want to conduct research to help them increase sales by $100,000 a month, or to increase market share by 2 percent within the next year. While these outcomes can be measured, they do not tell the researcher what to measure and how to measure it. Managerial objectives are often stated in terms of changing observable symptoms, such as increasing sales. Alternatively, research objectives must be related to measuring and identifying the underlying problems, such as consumers' perceptions of price, consumers' awareness of advertising, consumers' perceptions of brand image, or consumers' perceptions of product positioning that are the potential causes of the observable symptoms. Managerial objectives are often stated as "To increase...," "To decrease..." Research objectives should be stated as, "To measure..."

Develop Research Objectives

Researchers must determine exactly what they are going to measure and how they will measure it. In most cases this is the most difficult stage in the research process. Collecting data is easy. Administering a survey is easy. But, knowing exactly what you want to know and how you will get that information is sometimes difficult. Once completed, it is often helpful to communicate these research objectives to management (the client) before beginning the research.

The IDO Model and Identifying Objectives. The IDO model described in Chapter 3 is a very useful tool for identifying management and research objectives. To illustrate this, consider the case of a restaurant owner who contacted a research firm to conduct some customer satisfaction surveys of his customers. When the researcher met with the restaurant owner, the researcher began the discussion by asking the following questions: "What are your objectives? What are you trying to accomplish? What is happening with your restaurant that makes you think that you need to conduct some customer satisfaction surveys?" The restaurant owner replied that his objective was to increase the number of customers coming to his restaurant during lunch hours. The researcher then followed up by asking, "What do you think that you need to do to make this happen? What changes do you think that you might need to make to increase your lunch business? What decisions do you think that you will have to make to be able to achieve this objective?" The owner then mentioned that he knew that many lunch customers were seeking sandwiches and other quick meals, as opposed to ordering meals that required longer time to cook and prepare. He did not currently offer many sandwiches on his menu, so he wanted to identify the types of sandwiches, and the appropriate prices for these sandwiches, that would appeal to the construction workers who worked on construction sites near his restaurant. Given this, the researcher then knew the research objectives, including what the focus of the survey should be, the types of questions that needed to be asked, and the population to be surveyed. Notice that the restaurant owner had already identified the problem and that his decisions would center on the menu and the introduction of new menu items that would appeal to lunch customers who had only limited time to eat. If, on the other hand, the owner did not know specifically what his information needs were, and he did not know what course of action would help to increase his lunch business, exploratory research techniques such as focus groups, mystery shoppers, or observational research might have been needed to identify the problem and potential courses of action.

Decide on the Data Collection Techniques and Procedures

After researchers and managers have agreed on the objectives of the research project, researchers must decide on the appropriate data collection techniques and procedures. What research technique is best suited for collecting the specific types of information that decision makers need? How will the data and information be collected?

How will surveys be given to customers? How will the information outlined in the list of research objectives be collected? The selection of research techniques and procedures follows directly from the research objectives and the type of information needed by managers to make decisions. For example, will it be necessary to conduct focus groups? Will it be necessary to send out surveys in the mail to consumers? Are personal interviews required? Are experiments required?

Develop All Research Instruments and Materials

After deciding on the techniques and procedures to be used, researchers must develop all of the materials necessary to collect the data and information. This could include the focus group moderator's guide, the questionnaire, the cover letter to accompany the survey, and even detailed instructions for interviewers.

> The IDO model can be a very useful tool for identifying both managerial objectives and research objectives.

Plan the Sampling Procedure

If a sample is to be taken, researchers must decide who will be in the sample and how these people will be chosen. Will the sampling procedure have only one stage of sampling, or will there be multiple stages of sampling (e.g., choosing five stores in a state, then choosing customers who have recently purchased from those five stores)? Will a random selection process, such as a simple random sampling procedure be used? Or, will a different sampling procedure be used, such as a cluster sampling procedure, or a systematic sampling procedure? How many people will be in the sample?

After developing all of the data collection techniques, instruments, and sampling procedures, the researcher should have these approved by management (the client) before beginning the research. This creates a contract, or agreement, between the client and the researcher. Both know exactly what will be researched, what data will be collected, and how it will be collected. Notice that it is very important to keep management (the client) informed about the research and the specific types of information that will be collected. The last thing that a researcher wants to hear from a manager (client) is "That's not what I needed."

Collect the Data

Researchers must also make decisions regarding the specific data collection methodologies and procedures that will be used. How will the data be collected in an unbiased and systematic manner? What will the researcher do? When will the researcher do it? How will the researcher do it? How can the possibility of error or bias associated with the data collection procedures be reduced?

Enter and Analyze the Data

After the data and information have been collected it must be entered into a data file or other type of database so that it can be analyzed. At this stage in the research process the researcher must perform all statistical analyses necessary to satisfy the research objectives.

Prepare and Present the Research Report

A marketing research project is complete only after the results from the research are communicated to decision makers. Prepare the report and present it to management (the client). What is the best format for the research report? How familiar is the reader with statistics and research methodology? Will the reader be able to understand the report and use the information contained in it to help him or her make decisions?

Identify Needs for Subsequent Research

Rarely is one research project able to provide all information necessary to make decisions regarding complex marketing problems. Often, the results from one research project prompt the need for additional research projects. Good research frequently raises more questions than it answers. The results from a research project might be unexpected or need further clarification that can only be provided from additional research projects. Additional research projects might be needed to further investigate certain variables, or the relationships between variables, that were not considered in an earlier research project. In many ways, the marketing research process never ends. There will always be a need for information to make managerial decisions.

THE MOST IMPORTANT STAGES IN THE MARKETING RESEARCH PROCESS

Even though all 10 of the stages in the marketing research process are important, the first three—define the problem, identify management objectives, and develop research objectives—are by far the most important in terms of producing research results that will be useful to decision makers. Recall the IDO model of marketing research and the decision-making process shown in Figure 6.3.

Most marketing symptoms are the result of a chain of multiple cause-and-effect relationships, that is, a sequence of causes.

If marketing researchers are not able to clearly differentiate between marketing problems and marketing symptoms, they will likely end up solving the symptom,

FIGURE 6.3 The IDO Model of Marketing Research and the Decision-Making Process

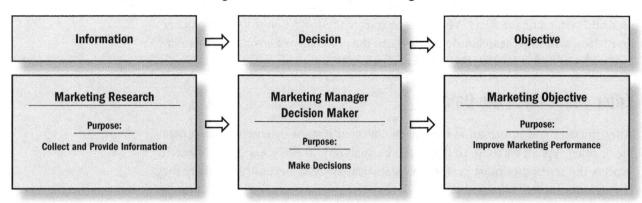

FIGURE 6.4 A Sequence of Causes

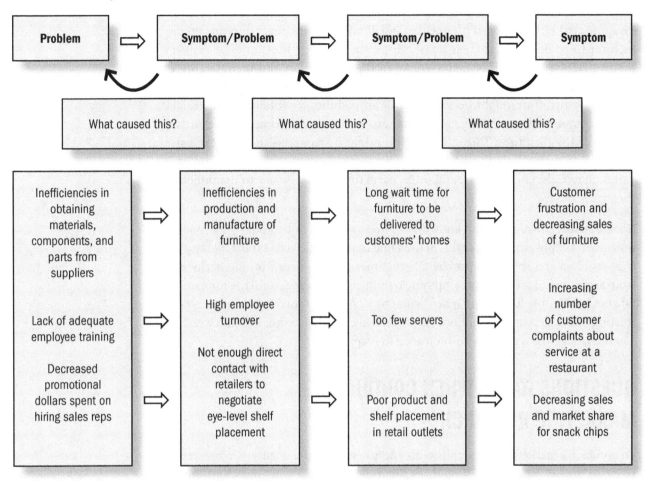

or solving a different problem than the one for which the research was intended. Further, if marketing researchers do not fully understand the marketing manager's objectives and the decisions they must make, it is likely that the research objectives will be misguided. This can lead to a research project that will not generate information that is useful to the decision-making process. Some of the mistakes that researchers make in conducting research projects can be fixed relatively easily. For example, poorly worded survey questions can be changed and surveys readministered. Likewise, biased sampling plans can be corrected and additional samples taken. But, if the researcher has not correctly identified the problem to be solved and the research objectives that will help managers fulfill their marketing objectives, it is very likely that the research will be a waste of significant time, effort, and money.

SEQUENCE OF CAUSES

In many business and marketing situations there is not just one problem and one symptom. Often, there is a sequence of multiple problems and symptoms. A problem that is identified as the cause of poor marketing performance might actually be the result of some other underlying problem. This is illustrated in Figure 6.4.

For example, decreasing sales of furniture might be the result of slow delivery times, that is, when customers inquire about potential delivery dates they are disappointed by the amount of time that it will take for furniture from this manufacturer to be delivered to their home. However, this long wait time for delivery might itself be the result of inefficiencies in the production and manufacture of the furniture at the factory. And, inefficiencies in the production and manufacture of the furniture might be the result of an inability to obtain raw materials, wood, components, and other parts that are necessary to complete the manufacture of the furniture. Thus, the solution might be to establish more exclusive distribution networks with suppliers, or even to consider purchasing a supplier of wood, materials, components, and other parts that are necessary to manufacture furniture.

Root Causes. Most gardeners know that a weed must be pulled out by its roots. If not, it will simply grow back again. In the same manner, marketers must identify the root problem and solve that problem. Sometimes this requires working backwards from symptom, to problem, to symptom, to problem, and so on, until the fundamental root problem is identified. When marketers do not do this they run the risk of treating only the symptom and not the underlying problem. And, just like weeds in a garden, negative symptoms will continue to reappear.

QUESTIONS TO ASK WHEN CONDUCTING MARKETING RESEARCH

To conduct a marketing research project and to evaluate the quality of a marketing research project, researchers should ask themselves the following questions during the research process.

Define the Problem

- Have we identified the true problem, or just a symptom of that problem?
- What problem(s) will hopefully be solved with the input of marketing research results?

Identify Management Objectives

- What does management want to do with the results of the research?
- Is the research being done to support a decision that has already been made?
- What are the managerial objectives and can these be translated into measurable research objectives?
- What decisions must marketing managers make?

Develop Research Objectives

- What information is needed for management to make decisions to achieve their marketing objectives?

- Will these research objectives yield results that will help marketing managers make decisions?

- Are the research objectives stated in specific and measurable terms?

- Which objectives can be met with secondary data, and which objectives must be met with primary data?

- What is to be measured and how will it be measured?

- Can a research project be designed and developed to achieve the objectives?

- Are there other important research objectives not yet identified, or are there other relevant variables to be measured?

- Can these research objectives be met with just one research project, or are two or more research projects needed?

Decide on the Data Collection Techniques and Procedures

- What research technique or methodology is best suited to colleting the specific types of information needed by decision makers?

- Are multiple research methods required?

- Are the techniques and procedures for collecting the data appropriate to the research objectives?

- Are the procedures for collecting the data complete?

- How will the research instruments and materials be administered, and how will the data be collected?

- Are there any sources of error or bias associated with the data collection procedures?

- Is there a chance for nonresponse error or self-selection bias?

- Who will complete the survey (respondents), and why?

- Who will not complete the survey (nonrespondents), and why not?

Develop All Research Instruments and Materials

- Does the focus group moderator's guide identify all important issues to be discussed during the focus group?

- Does the survey include a cover letter or scripted introduction?

The three most important stages in the marketing research process are:
1 Define the problem.
2 Identify management objectives.
3 Develop research objectives.
If marketing problems and objectives are not correctly identified at beginning stages in the research process, it will not matter how well the research is conducted and analyzed because marketers run the risk of wasting a great deal of time and money researching and solving the wrong problem.

- Does the cover letter or scripted introduction answer the following questions: What is this? Who wants to know? Why do they want to know this? Why was I chosen? How important is this? Will this be difficult? How long will this take? Will this cost me anything? What do I get out of this? Will I be identified with my answers? How will this be used? When should I do this?

- What questions are needed to satisfy the research objectives?

- Do the research instruments have any biased or poorly worded questions that are loaded, leading, ambiguous, vague, taxing, or double-barreled?

- Is the ordering of questions on the research instruments appropriate?

- Do the research instruments require any skip, filter, or branching questions? If so, are they placed in the appropriate location in the survey?

- Do the research instruments measure all variables and issues identified in the list of research objectives?

- Do the research instruments use the appropriate scales for measuring the issues and variables as they are stated in the list of research objectives?

- Do the research instruments provide a means for determining the representativeness of the respondents?

Plan the Sampling Procedure

- How will the research participants (respondents) be selected?

- Is a sample selection procedure based on random selection required (probability sampling procedure)?

- What will be used as a sampling frame?

- Will the sampling frame systematically eliminate any members of the population from being included in the sample (sampling frame error)?

- What sample size is needed?

- What will be the specific sampling procedures?

- Will the sampling procedure yield a representative sample of the population?

- Are any members of the population systematically eliminated from being included in the sample?

- Will any members of the population be either overrepresented or underrepresented in the sample?

Collect the Data

- Will the data be collected in a systematic, objective, and unbiased manner?

- How long will the data collection take?

- Who will collect the data?

Analyze the Data

- What analyses need to be performed on the data to satisfy the research objectives?
- What variables are being analyzed?
- What level scales are used to measure these variables?
- What analysis techniques are appropriate for analyzing variables measured on these scales?

Prepare and Present the Research Report

- Who will receive the report?
- What will they do with the report?
- Is the report well-organized and easy to read?
- What is the level of statistical knowledge or understanding of the person reading the report?
- What information, issues, or results are of most interest to the reader?
- Does the report present the results of the marketing research project in a way that will help marketing managers make decisions?

QUESTIONS FOR DISCUSSION

1. In general, what are the differences between marketing problems and marketing symptoms?

2. It is often said that the most dangerous part of an iceberg is the part below the water. How does this relate to the differences between marketing problems and marketing symptoms?

3. What are some negative symptoms that might be observed in managing and marketing a restaurant? What are some problems that could cause these observable negative symptoms?

4. From a marketing research perspective, identify which of the following are problems, and which are symptoms:
   a. Decreasing sales
   b. Advertisements that convey the wrong image about a brand
   c. Poorly trained sales force
   d. Decreasing market share
   e. A price that is too high for customers in a target market to afford
   f. Product packaging that does not properly contain the product
   g. Too few product installation instructions included in the package

5. A farm implement manufacturer employs you as a marketing research consultant. They tell you that their objective is to maximize their product-line profits. Have they adequately defined their research objective?

6. Why do marketing managers tend to focus on marketing symptoms, and why are their managerial objectives often stated in terms of marketing symptoms?

7. Which of the stages in the marketing research process do you think are the most important, and why?

8. What is meant by a sequence of causes? Identify a possible sequence of causes leading to an increase in customer complaints about the produce section of a grocery store.

MINICASE 6.1

Dalapatalio's Pizzeria

You are the manager of Dalapatalio's Pizzeria, which is a pizza restaurant located in the suburban part of a large city. Dalapatalio's Pizzeria has seating for 120 customers and also offers delivery service. One day, Vinnie Dalapatalio, the owner of the restaurant, begins to discuss with you the declining business that he has noticed over the last four months. He is concerned that fewer and fewer people are coming to Dalapatalio's Pizzeria to eat. He then tells you that he has decided to do something about it. He has decided to offer a "Buy One Pizza, Get Two Free" promotion. He thinks that this will have a significant positive effect on his business and the number of customers. He plans to offer the "Buy One Pizza, Get Two Free" promotion for about two months. Then, if business has picked up, he will discontinue the promotion and return to his regular pricing.

What do you tell Vinnie Dalapatalio? What words or phrases do you use?

CHAPTER $\bigodot$ **7**

Identifying Marketing Problems: Exploratory Research Techniques

LEARNING OBJECTIVES

1 Define background analysis and identify the types of information collected in a background analysis.

2 Describe employee interviews and discuss the advantages and disadvantages of employee interviews.

3 Describe mystery shoppers and discuss the uses and benefits of mystery shoppers to marketers.

4 Describe observation research and describe the unique characteristics, advantages, and disadvantages of observation research techniques.

5 Compare and contrast human observation with mechanical observation.

6 Describe ethnography and the uses of ethnographic observation techniques by marketers.

7 Describe what is meant by a participant observer.

8 Discuss the use of online and mobile ethnography.

As discussed previously, it is very important to identify and understand the difference between observable marketing symptoms and their underlying problems. However, marketing problems are often difficult to identify. For example, consider the following situation.

> PrintMax makes computer printers and other peripherals. Marketing managers at PrintMax have noticed a steady decrease in sales over the past two years. During this time, PrintMax has been selling their printers in larger discount stores such as Wal-Mart. From in-store interviews of customers shopping for printers in these stores, marketing managers have repeatedly heard customers mention that they were not going to buy a PrintMax printer because it was too expensive.

What was the problem? An immediate reaction to this situation would have been to consider lowering the price for PrintMax printers. But, this would have been a mistake. The consumers who shopped for printers in large discount stores were not very knowledgeable about computer equipment and peripherals. As such, they relied on retail salespeople to inform them about the relative merits of competing printers. In fact, it actually turned out that the true problem was with the retail sales force that PrintMax was relying on to promote and sell their printers. The employees of the discount stores were not adequately knowledgeable to communicate the printer's true value. Also, in-store promotions were not compensating for this lack of knowledge among the employees. Thus, what seemed like a problem with pricing was really a problem with promotion, sales messages, and channels of distribution. Selling through independent retailers forced PrintMax to rely on the employees of those retailers to sell their printers. Consider another situation.

> Music Source is a small, independently owned music store located in a suburban part of a large city. Music Source sells and rents musical instruments and also offers music lessons. The owners of Music Source noticed a steady decline in all aspects of their business. They also noticed that larger music stores had been opening in other parts of town and their business had actually been growing. These larger music stores sold a wider selection of musical instruments and frequently offered in-store concerts and clinics by famous musicians to promote their music lessons.

What was the problem? An immediate reaction to this situation would have been for Music Source to consider expanding their product line to include a greater variety of musical instruments and to also offer in-store clinics similar to those offered by the larger stores. But, this would have been a mistake. As it turned out, the true problem was the demographics of the market that Music Source was serving. The people living in this suburban area of town had grown older and no longer had school-age children, which is the prime market for instrument sales, rentals, and lessons. Thus, what seemed like a problem with the product line (the limited variety of instruments and lack of in-store clinics) was really a problem of changing market demographics. Expanding their product line would not have solved the problem.

Exploratory research techniques are often used to identify marketing problems and clearly differentiate between marketing problems and marketing symptoms. Some of the most often used techniques for identifying marketing problems are background analysis, employee interviews, mystery shoppers, observation, ethnography, focus groups, and social media monitoring.

BACKGROUND ANALYSIS

How could PrintMax and Music Source have identified their true problems? Many marketing problems can be identified by first conducting a **background analysis**. In conducting a background analysis, marketers gather as much information as possible related to the background of a situation (sometimes, this is referred to as a **situation analysis**). This includes gathering information about demographic changes, general economic changes, changes in the nature and amount of competition, and even changing market and environmental conditions. Much of this information can be collected with secondary data. In many ways a background analysis is similar to conducting a SWOT analysis for strategic planning where a manager identifies *strengths*, *weaknesses*, *opportunities*, and *threats* to a company or organization.

To illustrate the usefulness of a background analysis, consider the case of a private university where the student enrollment has been declining steadily for the last two years. Before surveying prospective students about their attitudes and perceptions of the university (which would require time and money), officials at the university should examine:

- Changes in demographics. Perhaps there have been fewer graduating high school seniors over the last few years.

- Changes in the economy. Perhaps a weaker economy means that fewer students can afford to attend college.

- Changes in federal student loan programs. Perhaps student loans are more difficult to obtain or are more expensive than in previous years.

- The presence of other alternatives for students. Perhaps other universities are offering expanded online degree programs allowing students to attend those universities without traveling.

As another example, consider the case of a coin-operated laundromat where sales have been declining steadily over the past two years. Before surveying customers about their attitudes and perceptions of the laundromat, managers should examine:

- Mortgage rates. Perhaps lower mortgage rates make it cheaper to own a home, so people do not need to rent apartments and do laundry at a laundromat.

- Interest rates and attractive financing. Perhaps low interest rates and attractive financing offers from manufacturers and retailers allow more consumers to purchase big-ticket items for their homes, such as washing machines and dryers.

- New competition. Perhaps newer laundromats have opened in town.

- Crime. Perhaps there has been an increase in crime near the laundromat.

- Road construction. Perhaps there has been recurring road construction near the laundromat that many consumers seek to avoid.

EMPLOYEE INTERVIEWS AND EMPLOYEE FOCUS GROUPS

In most cases, the purpose of marketing research is to obtain information about consumers. However, this does not mean that the information must always come directly from consumers. Not all marketing problems can be identified by

> Exploratory research techniques for identifying marketing problems include:
> · Background Analysis
> · Employee Interviews
> · Mystery Shoppers
> · Observation
> · Ethnography
> · Focus Groups
> · Social Media Monitoring

researching consumers. Consumers can provide information only from their perspective about what they see and directly experience. Information needed to identify marketing problems can also be collected from employees, salespeople, suppliers, buyers, or from other members within the channel of distribution. **Employee interviews**, employee surveys, and employee focus groups can be used to identify marketing problems. For example, PrintMax could have conducted some focus groups involving the retail sales employees. By conducting a focus group session where sales employees act out a sales situation in the context of a role-playing exercise, researchers could have quickly identified the true problem. If researchers surveyed only customers, they would have repeatedly heard comments dealing only with the high price.

It is often beneficial to survey or interview employees, such as front-line customer service representatives, salespeople, sales managers, checkout clerks, and even store managers. These people are in direct contact with consumers on a daily basis. They hear the concerns, criticisms, complaints, suggestions, and compliments from consumers. They are a valuable resource to the marketing researcher. They can be surveyed or interviewed on a formal or informal basis.

Ask employees/customer service personnel:

- What do you hear consumers saying?

- What do consumers tell you about the products or services?

Advantages of employee interviews and focus groups include:

- They can be cheaper than surveying consumers. Employees are already being paid so there is no need to offer financial incentives that might be required to survey customers. This is part of an employee's job.

- By speaking to one customer service employee you are speaking to hundreds of consumers.

- Employees can summarize and translate consumers' comments into terms management can understand (industry lingo).

- This lets employees feel like they have an input into managerial decisions. Don't just ask employees what they hear consumers saying, but also ask employees what they think.

Disadvantages of employee interviews and focus groups include:

- Employees might have vested interests and report only those comments that further their interests. They might censor or bias their comments.

- The telephone game. Comments and words tend to change when they are repeated from one person to another. The information employees report might not be exactly what they heard from consumers.

Mystery shopping is an ideal marketing research tool for identifying marketing problems by observing customer service from the perspective of a consumer.

MYSTERY SHOPPERS

A **mystery shopper** could have also helped PrintMax identify the true problem. Mystery shoppers are becoming a very popular research technique for identifying marketing problems, improving customer service, and uncovering consumers' perceptions from the customer's point of view.[1] Mystery shoppers are especially useful in retail settings where there is a high degree of customer contact with employees. However, while mystery shopping is typically considered to be a technique used only in the traditional retail environment (e.g., grocery store, hotel, department store), mystery shoppers can also be effectively used to evaluate other industries, such as state and local government agencies and even health care providers. Mystery shoppers look and act like ordinary customers. Their primary function is to evaluate customer service from a customer's perspective. Mystery shoppers can be used to evaluate customer service inside the store and outside the store. Mystery shoppers will visit a store, call a retailer on the phone, or even visit a retailer's website. When a mystery shopper visits a retail store, he or she will carefully notice everything that customers might experience in the store. They look around. They shop for predetermined items. They record the amount of time that it takes for a salesperson to approach them. They ask questions to create problems so that they can observe how the customer service employee solves the problem. Sometimes, they even complain to see how employees react.

When their shopping trip is finished, they will then complete a detailed report on their personal experiences. Sometimes the reports involve answering as many as 200 questions about their experiences. Often, the mystery shopper reports and questionnaires can be completed online. Mobile surveys have now made it possible to complete mystery shopping reports using a mobile device, which helps to reduce the amount of time between the shopping experience and the shopper's reported evaluations of that experience. Mobile surveying also allows shoppers to record audio comments and take photos or videos that can be added to the report along with the results from the evaluation survey and any text comments. These reports provide a detailed evaluation of customer service, from the cleanliness of the store, to whether or not the employee at a fast food restaurant tried to up-sell them to a value size meal, to whether or not customer service employees smiled or said "Thank you." Examples of the items on which a restaurant hostess or server might be evaluated include:

- Was your initial greeting friendly and enthusiastic?

- Were you quoted a wait time?

- Was the table clean?

- Was the silverware clean?

- Was the music level appropriate?

- Was your server well-groomed?

- Was your server wearing a neat and clean uniform?

- Did you server converse with you on a personal level?

- Were your beverages refilled promptly when requested?

- Were you offered a specific dessert or after-dinner drink from the bar?

- Did anyone engage with you as you left the restaurant?

The purpose of a mystery shopper is to collect data about a store or company in an objective, dispassionate, and unobtrusive manner. Mystery shoppers are often employed by outside research firms. This provides them with an objective and unbiased frame of reference when evaluating the store. However, sometimes mystery shoppers are employees of the organization being evaluated. You can learn more about mystery shoppers by visiting the following websites: **www.mysteryshopperjobs. com**, **www.mystery-shoppers.com**, and **www.mysteryshop.org**.

Mystery shoppers evaluate everything that customers might experience. This includes everything customers might see, smell, hear, touch, or feel. They evaluate:

- The physical environment.

- The cleanliness of the store.

- Customer service.

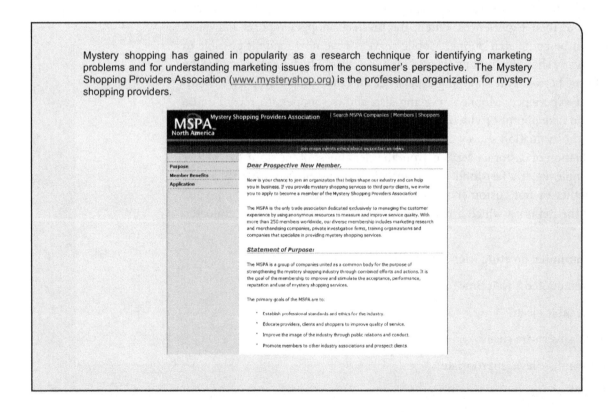

Mystery shopping has gained in popularity as a research technique for identifying marketing problems and for understanding marketing issues from the consumer's perspective. The Mystery Shopping Providers Association (www.mysteryshop.org) is the professional organization for mystery shopping providers.

- Employee performance.

- Whether or not employees are courteous.

- Whether or not employees are knowledgeable.

- Displays of merchandise.

- Patterns of employee behaviors.

- Employee integrity.

They do this by:

- Trying out some of the merchandise.

- Asking questions.

- Asking for help.

- Voicing some complaints.

Mystery shoppers provide information about:

- Why customers do or do not come back.

- Variables that might negatively affect customer satisfaction and employee performance.

- Consistency of quality and service across multiple store locations.

- Possible areas for employee training.

Possible limitations of mystery shoppers include:

- Mystery shoppers should be trained to make accurate and objective observations.

- Mystery shoppers provide information about only one point in time.

Mystery shopping has become increasingly accepted as a valid research tool for improving marketing performance and gaining insight into marketing problems from the customer's perspective. In 2002, the Mystery Shopping Providers Association (MSPA; **www.mysteryshop.org**) developed a two-level certification program for educating shoppers in the processes and techniques of mystery shopping. The Silver Certification program provides shoppers with a fundamental understanding of the mystery shopping industry and assures that the shopper has the basic skills to read, comprehend, and follow directions. Shoppers can complete this training online. The Gold Certification program involves attending a day-long series of workshops covering the mystery shopping industry in more detail. In 2008, the MSPA began offering the Gold Certification training via DVD, so shoppers can become certified without having to travel to attend the workshops. The certification is not required to be employed as a mystery shopper. However, the certification is an indication to a company looking to employ a mystery shopper that the shopper is knowledgeable in the procedures, policies, methods, ethics, and standards of the mystery shopping industry.

OBSERVATION

Observational research techniques have become increasingly popular among marketing researchers as a means of better understanding consumers and identifying marketing problems. **Observation research** allows researchers to record patterns in consumers' behaviors as they interact with products, people, and their physical surroundings in a natural environment.[2] Whereas focus groups and surveys rely on measuring consumers' self-reported responses to questions, observation research allows marketers to measure what people actually do and how they actually interact with their surrounding environment. For example, observation researchers might be stationed in the convenience store of a gas station to observe and record how much time consumers spend in the store and in specific aisles, the direction in which consumers travel through the store, whether or not consumers initiate conversations with other consumers, and whether or not they pick up and examine any products near the cashier's counter. Observation in retail stores allows marketers to study how consumers browse through stores, how they locate products and brands in stores, the amount of time they spend reading package labels, and their queuing behaviors when forming lines to pay for products.

The main advantage of observation research techniques is that they allow marketers to directly measure actual behaviors, instead of self-reports of behavior, which can be easily biased or censored. For example, self-reports of behaviors, such as the amount of time consumers spend engaging in a behavior, can be very inaccurate. Consumers can deliberately overestimate or underestimate the amount of time they spend performing certain activities. Additionally, self-reports of behaviors can be inaccurate due to consumers simply forgetting or not paying attention to what they are doing. In such cases, consumers might report behaviors that are socially acceptable.

> Marketers can learn a great deal about customers merely by observing them.

Traditional research methods, such as focus groups and surveys, rely on consumers' self-reports of behaviors and memories for events. And, the situational contexts in which these self-reports are provided can be very artificial and contrived. For example, most focus groups are conducted in professional focus group facilities, not in the environments in which the behaviors being discussed are performed. It is difficult for consumers to accurately remember and report the nuances of their behaviors, thoughts, and emotions regarding washing their car when they are seated around a conference table in a focus group room. Observation techniques solve this problem by studying consumers within the context of their daily lives.

The main disadvantage of observation research is that only behaviors and physical characteristics of consumers can be recorded. Observation does not allow researchers to measure and record psychological and attitudinal constructs such as attitudes, intentions, emotions, motivations, and reasons for behaviors. Additionally, many private behaviors cannot be recorded via observation. Marketers of personal care products might have a difficult time observing consumers' behaviors regarding toothpaste, deodorant, toilet tissues, and foot powder.

Human vs. Mechanical Observers. The two main types of observation research are those that use **human observers** and those that use **mechanical observers**. In many situations it is desirable to have a human researcher as the observer. Humans are able to observe and form immediate interpretations of consumers' behaviors. Examples of human observation in marketing include:

1. Observing consumers as they shop in retail stores.

2. Observing consumers as they use and consume products.

3. Observing consumers as they interact with other consumers in retail environments.

4. Observing consumers as they examine products and make in-store purchase decisions.

5. Observing consumers as they interact with other consumers in nonretail environments, such as social gatherings.

6. Recording the license plates of cars parked in a store parking lot.

One might think that human observers are always preferable to mechanical observers. However, in some situations it is easier and more efficient to observe consumers using mechanical observation. Video cameras and audio recorders can sometimes record behaviors more accurately than humans can. Video cameras do not get tired, they do not get distracted, and they have no inherent biases in recording consumers' behaviors. Machines are often preferable to humans when observing large numbers of consumers over long time periods. Machines are also preferable to humans when the behavior of interest is rare, infrequent, unpredictable or erratic. It is far cheaper to run a video camera nonstop than it is to pay a human observer to wait for an infrequent behavior to occur, for example, a consumer picking up a bottle of $100 wine in a liquor store. Marketers have used many different types of mechanical observation of consumers, including:

- Video and audio recorders.

- Electronic checkout scanners.

- Nielsen television boxes for measuring which family members are watching television.

- Arbitron's Portable People Meters for recording the radio stations that people listen to.

- Retailers' loyalty cards and rewards programs for tracking customers' purchases.

> Marketing researchers need not be present to observe the behaviors of consumers. Consumers' behaviors can be monitored and recorded using mechanical observation.

- Proprietary (store) credit cards for recording customers' purchases.

- Turnstiles for measuring traffic flow and traffic patterns.

- Web-based tracking of consumers viewing Internet sites.

Many of these mechanical observation devices are **covert** in that consumers are often less likely to notice the presence of the recording device than they are to notice the **overt** presence of a human observer. In many cases mechanical observation devices become invisible to consumers because consumers are either not aware of their presence, or they are not aware that the device is recording their behaviors. This has the advantage of reducing biases because consumers are less likely to know that they are being watched, and as such, are less likely to alter their behaviors. However, many researchers have ethical concerns regarding the level of deceit associated with covert observation where consumers are not aware that their behaviors are being recorded.

Geolocation. Most smartphones today have a GPS chip inside of them which uses satellite data to calculate a user's exact location. **Geolocation** is the process of locating the exact geographic position of an object, such as a mobile phone or computer. Such geolocation applications can be used by marketing researchers to observe consumers and track their exact movements. To illustrate how geolocation can be used by marketing researchers to observe consumers, consider the following possible situations:[3]

- To better understand traffic patterns in a city, a government agency studies driving patterns by collecting geolocation pings from a sample of drivers.

- A marketer collects geolocation data instead of self-reported behaviors to better understand how frequently a sample of shoppers visits different grocery stores.

- A car manufacturer collects geolocation data from a sample of women who drive minivans to better understand how minivans are used.

Observation in Simulated Shopping Environments

One of the main advantages of observation research techniques is that they allow researchers to track consumers' behaviors in natural, real-life environments. However, when it is not feasible to conduct such observation research in real-life environments (often due to privacy issues), **simulated shopping environments** can be used. For example, The PreTesting Group (**www.pretesting.com**) has developed multiple techniques and technologies for recording consumers' behaviors in simulated environments. Some of these techniques are described below.

Print Advertising Viewing. Consumers are led to believe that publishers want their opinions on newly proposed magazines. Unknown to consumers, a marketer's target advertisement is placed in each of two different magazines that consumers are to read. As consumers read through the magazines, two cameras hidden in a nearby table lamp record how much time they spend looking at each page of the magazine, and they also record consumers' eye movements. The patented PeopleReader™

> Even if researchers are not able to observe consumers in real-life environments, consumers can be observed and tested in simulated shopping environments.

technology measures consumers' level of involvement with each page. The patented Eye Tracking System™ also measures the specific places on the pages that consumers are looking at. This helps marketers identify the most attention-getting elements of print advertisements.

Direct Mail. Consumers are asked to sort through a day's mail as if they have just come home from work. They are also given the opportunity to discard any pieces of mail that they do not want, or do not want to open. The two hidden cameras in a nearby table lamp record consumers' level of involvement with each piece of mail and the movement of their eyes as they read through a piece of mail.

Packaging. Consumers are seated in front of a five-foot screen that shows a life-size image of retail store shelves through which consumers can browse. Consumers can navigate through the shelves using a control panel. As a product package catches their attention, consumers can zoom in to examine it more closely. Consumers make purchase decisions revealing the ability of selected package designs to grab consumers' attention.

Billboard Advertising. Consumers are seated in front of a five-foot screen and asked to "drive" down a road at 45 mph. They are instructed to look for specific road signs to determine their visibility. This keeps them from artificially paying increased attention to billboards for target advertisements that are included in the images that are shown on the screen. Following their simulated drive, consumers are asked to recall the billboards they remember seeing during the drive. PreTesting's Eye Tracking System also records which visual elements of the billboards were examined, and which visual elements were ignored.

ETHNOGRAPHY

Ethnography is the study of human behavior in natural and native settings—where people live, work, play, socialize, shop, relax, and entertain themselves. Ethnographers observe how people behave and interact with each other and their physical and social environment.[4] Ethnography is a specialized form of observation that is relatively new to marketing and business disciplines, but has a long and rich history with origins in anthropology. Ethnography usually involves well-trained researchers who observe and study consumers in the diverse environments in which consumers are influenced by, and interact with, goods and services.[5]

In many cases, ethnographers are **participant observers** who directly intermingle with the people they are observing. Marketing researchers who are participant observers immerse themselves into social groups and settings and overtly interact with consumers by listening to them and engaging them in conversations, participating in activities, and even conducting interviews. Ethnographers record and collect photographs, audio and video tapes of activities and interviews, and detailed field notes of their experiences. Instead of searching for specific information gleaned from a single consumer's behaviors, ethnographers often seek to find and

Observation and ethnographic research approaches have gained wide acceptance among business decision makers as tools for identifying the actual behaviors of consumers in natural and native environments, as opposed to self-reports of behaviors that are often biased or censored by consumers.

understand the common themes, meanings, and interpretations of the behaviors of groups of consumers. The advantage of being a participant observer is that it allows the researcher to obtain a greater appreciation for the phenomenon, issue, topic, or people being studied. However, a disadvantage is that whenever a researcher directly participates with subjects for extended periods of time there is the possibility of decreased objectivity because the researcher becomes part of the phenomenon being studied.

The theory behind ethnography is that researchers must fully experience something before they can fully understand it. This is one of the main reasons behind the increased acceptance of ethnography as a form of marketing research to better understand how consumers interact with products. In most cases the researcher is not as familiar with the product or service being researched as is the marketer and consumer. Observation and ethnography can help increase researchers' familiarity with, and understanding of, the products, services, people, situations, and behaviors they are researching.

Ethnography has become well-accepted by many of today's best and most successful businesses. Business and marketing decision makers have come to recognize the value of ethnographic research methods. For example, Hyundai has used ethnography when designing their cars. Hyundai CEO John Krafcik recently described this process: "We'll send a couple of product planners and market researchers out with

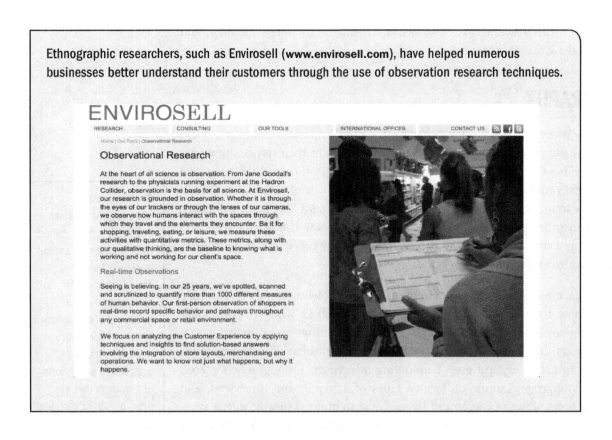

Ethnographic researchers, such as Envirosell (www.envirosell.com), have helped numerous businesses better understand their customers through the use of observation research techniques.

consumers and just literally spend a day or two with them, looking at their cars, seeing how they live their lives around their cars. When they go to Costco, where do they put those big, huge things of toilet paper? It gives us insights. We're trying to find what we call unmet needs."[6] Envirosell (**www.envirosell.com**), started by Paco Underhill more than 25 years ago, has been a leader in the use of observation research techniques to help businesses better understand their customers.[7] They boast a long list of clients who have benefited from the use of observation research and ethnography, including Burger King, Cracker Barrel, Starbucks Coffee, Gap, Old Navy, Sam's Club, Walgreen's, Johnson & Johnson, and Sony Music.

Whereas some observational research studies can be completed in a relatively short time (i.e., a few hours to a few days), true ethnographic studies with participant observers often require more time, as long as a few weeks to a few months. This longer time horizon highlights a key advantage of ethnography—the longer a participant observer interacts with the subjects, the more familiar and accustomed the subjects become with the observer, and the less likely subjects are to bias or censor their comments, or to alter their behaviors in response to the observer's presence. Thus, longer ethnographic studies can lead to data that is less likely to be influenced by respondent bias. However, the longer an ethnographer directly interacts with the people he or she is attempting to study, the less objective the ethnographer can become.

As research tools, observation and ethnography provide marketing researchers with the ability to learn much more about consumers than could be learned from secondary accounts of consumers' behaviors. Specifically, observation and ethnography allow marketing researchers to:

- Measure actual behavior, instead of self-reports of behavior.

- Uncover the unspoken cultural and social patterns of behavior surrounding product use.

- Understand product purchase, consumption, and disposal from the consumer's point of view.

- Gain a holistic view of consumers as they behave and interact with each other and with products in their daily lives.

- Observe usage patterns and usage situations.

- Measure the amount of time that consumers spend performing product-related behaviors.

- Observe how consumers interact with their physical environment and physical spaces.

- Learn the terminology and language that consumers use when discussing products with friends.

- Experience what the consumer experiences.

- Understand the social context of group interactions involving products or services.

- Understand the cultural aspects of behavior and decision making.

Ethnography and Multicultural Research. Ethnography can also be used very effectively for marketers conducting multicultural research. For example, many marketers have become increasingly interested in Hispanic consumers. The U.S. Census Bureau reports that the Hispanic population in the United States has grown by 35 percent from 2000 to 2010. And, the number of Hispanic consumers in the United States is expected to increase by another 12 million by 2020. Ethnography can be a very useful tool for better understanding such markets, especially for marketers with little knowledge of Hispanic culture. When conducting ethnography, a lack of knowledge of the consumers being studied is actually an advantage. One of the fundamental principles of ethnography is that the researcher should observe without any prior knowledge or preconceived notions about the people being studied.[8]

Online/Mobile Ethnography. Observing consumers in their natural and native habitats, for example at home, at a shopping mall, in a grocery store, and so on, can yield valuable insights into consumers' behaviors, attitudes, perceptions, and beliefs. However, traditional ethnographic studies can be somewhat intrusive and imposing upon consumers' time and privacy. Further, there can also be considerable costs associated with finding and recruiting consumers to participate in an ethnographic study, in addition to the expenses for traveling to visit multiple consumers in multiple locations. In response to these costs, marketing researchers have recently begun to conduct online ethnographic studies. With **online ethnography**, consumers are asked to record their own behaviors and provide photos, videos, and even keep online diaries about their purchasing habits.

> With online and mobile ethnography, consumers can record their own behaviors and even submit photos and videos of themselves purchasing, using, and interacting with brands and other consumers.

Instead of interviewing and/or videotaping a consumer for a number of hours on a single day, online ethnographic studies often span a week or more. Participating consumers are asked to devote a few hours during this time period to recording and reflecting on their behaviors. Consumers are often asked to take photos or videos of their surroundings, their shopping trips, and even their homes. They are also asked to record online diaries of behaviors, including written reflections of their own behaviors. Smartphones with cameras have significantly aided in this process. Using mobile devices to collect such qualitative data is referred to as **mobile ethnography**. For example, consumers might be asked to photograph their kitchens, including the inside of their pantries. They might even be asked to videotape themselves, or have another family member videotape them, putting away groceries following a trip to the grocery store. These photos and videos are then submitted to a moderator who can then respond to them with follow-up questions for the consumer to answer. By viewing these photos and videos, marketers could learn how consumers tend to store groceries in their homes and how consumers categorize different food products. Do consumers store food products based on shape and type of packaging, by similarity to other food products, or by meal combinations (i.e., food products that tend to be eaten together)? By examining how certain food packages are stored alongside other food packages in consumers' homes, marketers might gain insight into better placement of products in grocery stores.

Mobile ethnography can give researchers access to deep contextual data regarding consumers' purchases that occur at times and locations that would otherwise not be accessible to a researcher performing a traditional in-person ethnographic study. For example, mobile ethnographic studies have been conducted:[9]

- In the bathroom. Women were asked to use their smartphones to conduct a photographic tour of their bathrooms to provide greater contextual understanding of leg care products.

- At the gas pump. Consumers were asked to record their reactions when using a credit card to pay for gasoline.

- At a fast food restaurant. Consumers were asked to photograph their fast food dinners and provide detailed explanations about their purchases and their consumption experience. This afforded access to consumers' opinions and perceptions even during late night trips to a restaurant.

One obvious advantage of online and mobile ethnography is that they are not intrusive. Consumers' daily lives are not interrupted by an outsider coming into their homes or following them around as they shop. Another advantage is that consumers are able to participate and submit their materials at their convenience. Additionally, a greater number of consumers can participate in an online ethnography than in a traditional ethnographic study. There are less time demands on the moderator or observer because consumers record their own behaviors. And, as people become more and more accustomed to posting information about themselves online, the amount and richness of data obtained from online ethnographies will likely increase in the future. Finally, identifying and recruiting participants is much easier with online ethnography. This is often done via an online panel with members who are accustomed to being asked to participate in marketing research studies and surveys. For example, Decision Analyst (**www.Decisionanalyst.com**) claims to have over 8 million members in their online America Consumer Opinion® panel. And, the fact that no outside researcher will need to enter the home often makes members of these online consumer panels more likely to participate.

FOCUS GROUPS

Focus groups have been a mainstay of marketing researchers for many years. In fact, many marketers claim that if you are not doing focus groups you do not really understand your customers. Focus groups allow marketing researchers to probe for the underlying motivations, beliefs, concerns, and emotions that accompany purchase decisions and product use. Focus groups are often used at early stages in the research process when problems are not well-defined or even known. Many marketing problems can be identified by simply having a conversation among consumers in the context of a focus group. More will be said about focus groups in a later chapter.

> As marketers get closer to measuring the actual behaviors of customers, the more useful and predictive their research results become.

SOCIAL MEDIA MONITORING

As described in previous chapters, social media monitoring is an effective technique for monitoring the online conversations between consumers. By listening in on such conversations, social media monitoring is essentially a form of observation in an online environment. Monitoring what consumers post on Facebook or tweet via Twitter can greatly aid in identifying problems. If sales are declining, or if the number of product returns has increased dramatically, the words and phrases that consumers use when talking about products on social media can provide valuable clues as to potential marketing problems.

BEHAVIOR, BEHAVIOR, BEHAVIOR

A key advantage of observation, ethnography, and mystery shoppers is that they allow marketing researchers to measure actual behaviors, instead of merely measuring self-reports of behaviors. The closer that marketing researchers can get to measuring actual behaviors, the more useful and predictive their research results will become. While consumers often bias and censor their answers on surveys and their comments in a focus group session, behaviors do not lie. Marketing researchers often care less about what consumers say they do and more about what consumers actually do. Focus groups and surveys tell us only what people say they do, or what they say they did. Observation, ethnography, mystery shoppers, and database marketing with purchase tracking capabilities can tell marketers what consumers actually do, as well as what they actually did.

QUESTIONS FOR DISCUSSION

1. The Metro Transit Authority (MTA) is the public transportation provider for a large city. The MTA has noticed a steady decrease in the number of people riding buses to and from downtown. This decline began in the late 2000s and has continued to the present day. What information could the MTA obtain from a background analysis to help it identify the true problem? What would they want to know to help them identify the true problem?

2. If you entered a Target store and noticed someone standing near the door with a clipboard and making notes as they observed shoppers in the store, how would this affect your behaviors as you shopped?

3. If you were designing a mobile ethnography study of students at your university to learn how they purchase food from on-campus vendors or cafeterias, what would you ask the students who were participating in the mobile ethnography to do?

4. If you were designing some mystery shopping research for a hotel, what would you observe and/or measure?

5. What are the advantages and disadvantages of both mechanical observation and human observation techniques?

6. If researchers invited you to attend an employee focus group to discuss consumers' perceptions of the products or services that are sold at the store, company, or organization where you work, what would you tell them?

7. Why do you think that observation and ethnography are gaining in popularity as research techniques?

8. What are the advantages and disadvantages of mobile ethnography compared to traditional ethnography?

9. Go to a local retailer (e.g., Wal-Mart, Target) and observe consumers as they enter the store and as they leave the store. What behaviors do you notice? What do people tend to do as they enter the store (e.g., search for a cart, put items such as keys or umbrellas away, look for the weekly advertisement)? What do people tend to do as they leave the store (e.g., check their receipt for errors, check to make sure that all of their purchases are in the bags)? Do different types of people tend to behave in different ways? How could marketers use this information from your observations?

10. Go to a local fast food restaurant and observe consumers as they purchase and eat their meal. What do consumers do when they are waiting in line (e.g., look up at the menu, look at the food preparation areas behind the counter)? What do consumers do at the drink station (e.g., do they put ice in their cup before or after filling their cup with a drink, do they mix drinks, do they put ice in their cup and then pour out some of the ice before filling their cup with a drink)? How could marketers use this information from your observations?

11. If you were the owner of a business, would you rather measure consumers' responses to survey questions, or measure their actual behaviors? Why?

12. Compare and contrast surveys and observation research in terms of the types of information that can be measured.

MINICASE 7.1

College Bookstore

The bookstore on your college campus has recently employed you as a marketing research consultant. George Cousins, the manager of the bookstore, wants to better understand the process by which students purchase and wear university logo apparel. Specifically, George has asked for your help in designing some research to answer the following questions: What influences students' decision to purchase university logo apparel? When do students purchase university logo apparel? Where and when do students wear university logo apparel? What factors influence where and when students wear university logo apparel? George has recently heard about some other colleges using observation research to better understand the behaviors of students.

What type(s) of observation research do you recommend? Who would you observe? What would you observe? Where would you observe it?

ENDNOTES

1   Al Goldsmith, "Mystery Shopping 101," *Quirk's Marketing Research Review*, January 1997, 33–34.

2   Michael Quinn Patton, *Qualitative Research & Evaluation Methods*, 3rd ed. (Thousand Oaks, CA: Sage Publications, 2002).

3   Dana Stanley, "10 Use Cases for Geolocation in Market Research," April 5, 2012, **http://researchaccess. com/2012/04/10-use-cases-for-geolocation-in-market-research/**

4   Eric J. Arnould and Melanie Wallendorf, "Market-Oriented Ethnography: Interpretation Building and Marketing Strategy Formulation," *Journal of Marketing Research* 31, no. 4: 484–504.

5   Jennifer McFarland, "Margaret Mead Meets Consumer Fieldwork," *Harvard Management Review*, September 2001.

6   Tom Krisher, "Under CEO John Krafcik, Hyundai Goes from Joke to Contender," *Associated Press*, April 15, 2012.

7   Paco Underhill, *Why We Buy: The Science of Shopping* (New York: Touchstone Publishers, 1999).

8   Pablo Flores and Jennifer Karsh, "Getting to Know You: Conducting Ethnographic Research with Hispanic Consumers," *Quirk's Marketing Research Review*, February 2012, 36–39.

9   Dana Slaughter, "Oh, The Places You Can Go (With Mobile!)," Newqualitative.org, February 11, 2013, **www.newqualitative.org/blog/oh-the-places-you-can-go-with-mobile**

CHAPTER 8

Secondary Data and Database Marketing

LEARNING OBJECTIVES

1 Define secondary data and describe the advantages and disadvantages of secondary data.

2 Locate sources of secondary data available on the Internet.

3 List and explain the criteria that marketers should use to evaluate the quality and worth of secondary data.

4 List and describe the types of secondary data available to marketers.

5 Define consumer demographics and identify sources of demographic secondary data on the Internet.

6 Locate sources of company data, industry data, and market intelligence on the Internet.

7 Define consumer panels and describe the differences between consumer purchase panels and consumer media panels.

8 Define store audits and discuss their relevance to marketers.

9 Define database marketing and discuss the purpose of database marketing.

10 Describe procedures that marketers can use to create databases of customers.

11 Describe how databases can be obtained via:

    a Loyalty programs and loyalty cards.

    b Store (proprietary) credit cards.

    c Reward credit cards.

    d Warranty cards and product registration cards.

    e List providers on the Internet.

12 Define RFM analysis and describe how it is used to identify a marketer's best customers.

13 Discuss the role of database marketing in helping marketers to make new customers, keep current customers, and grow the value of customers.

As stated previously, marketing research can be very expensive. It is therefore recommended that marketers first seek out any usable data and information that currently exists that can be used to make decisions, before incurring the expense of collecting new and original data. Such data that is already available in some form is referred to as **secondary data**. It is most often data that was collected for a purpose other than the current research purpose. For instance, the U.S. Census measures numerous demographic characteristics of Americans. Marketers can use this data to make decisions about locations for new stores and the choice of new target markets. Marketers can even use this data to identify new marketing opportunities and new product concepts based on changes in the demographics of the American population. An aging population might indicate the potential for new products targeted toward the elderly. An increase in the birth rate might similarly indicate the potential for new products targeted toward children.

Before spending money and time on collecting new and original primary data, researchers should begin a research project with secondary data that is already available from internal sources as well as from external sources. Internal sources of secondary data include sales invoices, accounts receivable reports, quarterly sales reports, sales activity reports, and previous marketing research reports. Secondary data can also be obtained from external sources. The Internet has made this form of marketing research very cheap, easy, and accessible. Below is a list of websites often used for secondary data relevant to marketing.[1]

- CIA World Factbook (economic and demographic information about foreign countries): **www.cia.gov**

- Federal Trade Commission: **http://www.ftc.gov**

- Housing and Urban Development: **http://www.hud.gov**

- PollingReport.com (a resource on trends in American public opinion): **www.pollingreport.com**

- Sales & Marketing Management (publications including the *Survey of Buying Power*): **www.salesandmarketing.com**

- SecondaryData.com (marketing resources links provided by Decision Analyst, Inc.): **www.secondarydata.com**

- National Retail Federation: **www.nrf.com**

- U.S. Bureau of Economic Analysis, Survey of Current Businesses: **www.bea.gov**

- U.S. Bureau of Labor Statistics: **www.bls.gov**

- Consumer Expenditure Survey: **www.bls.gov/cex/home.htm**

- The Conference Board: **www.conference-board.com**

- U.S. Department of Commerce: **www.commerce.gov**

- Board of Governors of the Federal Reserve System: **www.federalreserve.gov**

- U.S. White House Economic Briefing Room: **www.whitehouse.gov/briefing-room**

> Before beginning any primary data collection, first determine if there is any usable data that can be obtained from secondary data sources.

- U.S. Census Bureau (demographic statistics of the United States): **www.census.gov**
- ShopperTrak: **www.shoppertrak.com/news-resources**
- International Council of Shopping Centers: **www.icsc.org**
- Consumer Federation of America: **www.consumerfed.org**
- Credit Union National Association: **www.cuna.org**

Variety of Data Available from Secondary Sources

Even though many people think that secondary data contains only demographic data, there is actually a wide variety of secondary data that can be obtained from the Internet. In addition to demographic data, marketers can obtain secondary data on consumers' attitudes, consumers' interests, consumers' lifestyles and psychographics, company data, industry data and market intelligence, and even consumers' purchase behaviors.

CONSUMER DEMOGRAPHICS

The best source for secondary data on consumer **demographics** is the U.S. Census (**www.census.gov**). Here, marketers can easily obtain data on demographic variables such as income, age, sex, occupation, housing, birth rate, population changes and trends, and even origins and ethnicity. Data can be compiled by a number of different geographical areas and populations, from the national population, to state and county populations, to metropolitan statistical area and zip code populations, all the way down to the individual block level. This is a valuable and easy to use resource for marketers. And, the demographic data obtained from the U.S. Census is often more reliable and accurate than data obtained from any individual survey conducted by an independent researcher. It is very difficult to survey large groups of the American population more efficiently than how they are surveyed by the U.S. Census.

CONSUMER PSYCHOGRAPHICS AND LIFESTYLES

There are many sources of secondary data on consumer **psychographics** and **lifestyles**. Many marketing research firms regularly conduct public opinion surveys and publish the results from these surveys on their web sites. For example, Maritz Marketing Research Inc. (**www.maritz.com**) offers free access to the results from their Maritz Poll. They have surveyed the American population on a number of lifestyle topics, including automobiles, the economy, education, entertainment and leisure, food and restaurants, health and fitness, love, shopping, social issues, sports, and the workplace. This information can be very valuable to many marketers. For instance, fast food marketers would want to know what American's favorite fast food item is. Outdoor grill marketers would want to know the percentage of Americans who plan to cook with a barbecue grill on the Fourth of July. And, greeting card marketers would want to know the percentage of Americans who describe themselves as romantic.

The U.S. Census website (**www.census.gov**) is perhaps the marketing researcher's best source of secondary data related to demographics of the American population.

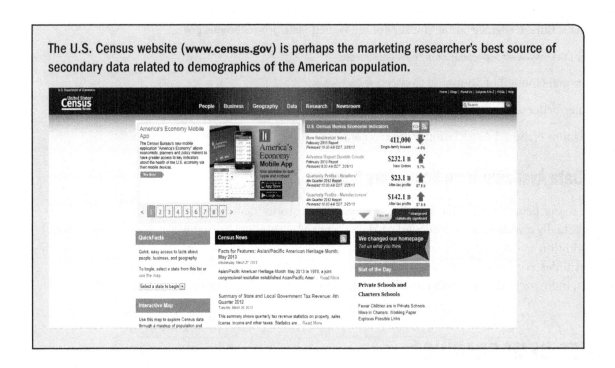

Another well-known source for psychographic, attitudinal, and lifestyle data is Gallup Inc. (**www.gallup.com**). Gallup offers free access to the results from their public opinion surveys on such varied topics as alcohol and drinking, baseball, consumers' views of the economy, nutrition and food, personal health issues, and consumers' satisfaction with their personal lives.

COMPANY DATA

Information about individual companies can also be obtained from secondary data. For example, Hoovers Inc. (**www.hoovers.com**) offers comprehensive company and industry intelligence. They have a database of more than 32 million private and public companies. Marketers can purchase reports containing information on a company's history, their products and operations, executive biographies, historical financial statements, and their competitive landscape. Information in these reports can be used for business-to-business sales prospecting. It can also be used to analyze competitors and research potential corporate partnerships.

INDUSTRY DATA AND MARKET INTELLIGENCE

In addition to data specific to individual companies, marketers can also obtain secondary data on entire industries. Not only does the U.S. Census Bureau (**www.census. gov**) measure demographics of people, but it also conducts research on American businesses. The **economic census** profiles American business every five years, from the national to the local level. It includes a survey of business owners and a report on business expenses. It also reports on specific industries, including manufacturing, wholesale trade, retail trade, transportation and warehousing, entertainment and recreation, and food services.

In addition to the economic census that is conducted every five years, the U.S. Census Bureau conducts more than 100 economic surveys on an annual, quarterly, and monthly basis for numerous sectors of the American economy. The **Annual Survey of Manufacturers (ASM)** provides estimates of statistics for commercial manufacturing establishments with paid employees. The **County Business Patterns (CBP)** survey provides data on changing economic activities at various geographic levels: national, state, county, and even metropolitan statistical areas. Marketers can use this data to analyze the market potential of small geographical areas.

Another governmental agency, the **Bureau of Labor Statistics (www.bls.gov)**, provides statistics by industry. The BLS Industry At-A-Glance consists of profiles of 12 industry supersectors. Each profile contains a variety of facts about the industry supersector and includes links to additional statistics. The 12 industry supersectors are construction, education and health services, financial activities, government, information, leisure and hospitality, manufacturing, natural resources and mining, other services, professional and business services, transportation and utilities, and wholesale and retail trade.

In addition to governmental agencies, there are many companies that provide marketing research reports on industries. MarketResearch.com (**www.marketresearch .com**) offers global business intelligence on industries as well as specific product categories. For example, a marketer can purchase a research report on market trends related to pet clean-up and odor control products. They also offer reports on very specific product categories, such as the U.S. market for footwear, the market for swimwear, the market for recreational vehicles, the market for in-car entertainment, the market for hay farming, the market for salad dressing, and even the worldwide market for pickles. At a typical price of $500 to $4,000 for each, these reports provide a relatively inexpensive alternative to primary data collection. Other sources of this type of secondary data on industries include U.S. Business Reporter (**www .activemedia-guide.com**) and BizMiner (**www.bizminer.com**).

Marketers are not limited to only demographic data from secondary sources. Secondary data can also be obtained regarding consumer psychographics and lifestyles, information about individual companies, industry data and market intelligence, and consumers' purchase patterns from consumer panels and store audits.

CONSUMER PANELS

A **consumer panel** is a large sample of consumers who have agreed to provide marketing research firms with information regarding their purchasing and media habits.[2] Consumers participating in a **diary purchase panel** record detailed information about their daily purchases. This information is collected at the time of purchase or at home immediately following the purchase. Many research firms require consumers to complete detailed questionnaires regarding their purchases. Some research firms, such as The Nielsen Company (**www.nielsen.com**), provide consumers with handheld scanners to make recording product purchases easier. Consumers use handheld scanners in the convenience of their home to easily scan all of their purchases just as they would at the checkout counter.[3] Consumer panels are often used to track sales of products in the **consumer packaged goods (CPG)** industry, such as foods and pharmaceuticals. Consumers agree to participate for an extended period of time and submit reports detailing their purchases either once a week or once a month. Panel members are also surveyed to measure attitudes and opinions related to the products they buy. In exchange, consumers receive money, coupons, gifts, and information back from the research firm. The data from such consumer panels can then be sold to other marketers as secondary data. Nielsen also allows marketers to obtain data from subset panels that focus on the Hispanic market, beauty products, and products for babies and children. An advantage of consumer panels is the ability to measure actual purchases as opposed to only stated purchase intentions that would be measured on a survey.

Consumers participating in a **diary media panel** allow electronic devices to automatically record their media viewing and listening behaviors. The **Nielsen Television Index** (**www.nielsen.com**) is the most widely recognized diary media panel. The results from such panels are used to help marketers measure the effectiveness of promotional messages and also select appropriate programs in which to place their advertising. In larger markets, the television viewing habits of panel members are measured electronically with **People Meters™**. The People Meter™ is a small box that is connected to a television set. Each member of a household is assigned a button on the box that they are to press indicating whether or not they are present in the room when the television set is turned on. The People Meter™ records not only what channel is being watched, but also which members of the household are watching it. The viewing habits of residents in smaller markets are measured with paper and pencil in seven-day diaries, in which family members record what they watched and how long they watched it. Approximately 2 million paper diaries are measured during a year by Nielsen. For more information about consumer panels, see **www.npd.com** (NPD Group, Inc., formerly National Purchase Diary).

Arbitron Inc. (**www.arbitron.com**) offers consumer diary media panels for measuring consumers' radio listening behaviors. Traditionally, listeners were required to keep a diary of the radio stations they listened to during the course of a day. However, you can imagine how difficult this would be given that people listen to the radio in their kitchen, in their car as they drive to and from work, at work, in their garage, and even in their shower. Fortunately, advances in technology have reduced the need for such paper and pencil diaries. Arbitron has recently introduced the **Portable People Meter (PPM™)**. The PPM™ is a device about the size of a cell phone that a person wears throughout the day. It works by detecting embedded codes that identify the source of a broadcast transmission. As a person changes the station on the radio, the PPM™ automatically detects the station that is being listened to.

STORE AUDITS

A **store audit** is the process by which physical records of product movement and inventory are examined, analyzed, and verified. **Retail audits** are used to measure the amount of product sales from the retailer (drugstore, grocery store, discount retailer) to the consumer. **Wholesale audits** are used to measure products that are moved from wholesalers to retailers.[4]

Retailers (and wholesalers involved in a wholesale audit) who participate in the audit allow the auditor into their stores, stockrooms, and warehouses to record and examine company records regarding sales, orders, and product movement. In exchange, the retailer (or wholesaler) receives monetary payments and audit reports from the audit service. These audit reports are a source of valuable secondary data on product sales and movement, relative market shares for different brands, and industry trends and competition. Audits can be used to:

- Determine the total size of a market (in terms of sales) by type of retail outlet, type of product, geographic area, or size of market.

- Measure relative market (brand) share for competing brands in a market.

- Identify and analyze problems related to distribution and inventory.

- Measure the effects of promotions, point of purchase (POP) displays, and shelf space on product sales.

- Measure the effects of varying prices on product sales.

- Measure the effects of sales promotions such as coupons, multi-packs, premiums, and in-store displays on product sales.

- Forecast potential sales for new or existing products within a market.

- Assess the effectiveness of promotions on sales and market (brand) share.

- Measure consumers' acceptance of new products and features.

- Identify trends in the retail environment for a particular product class.

Compared to consumer diary panels, the advantage of store audits is their timeliness and accuracy. Store audits measure product sales at the point of sale. There are no biases associated with consumers failing to record or report their purchases. For more information about store audits, see **www.nielsen.com** (Nielsen—Scantrack), and **www.infores.com** (Information Resources—InfoScan).

EVALUATING SECONDARY DATA

There are clearly advantages to using secondary data as opposed to relying solely on primary data for marketing decisions. Secondary data is readily available and is often very inexpensive. Sometimes secondary data is free. The Internet has made secondary data even easier to obtain and use. Anyone with a computer and an Internet connection can easily access large amounts of data on Americans and American consumers. Sometimes, secondary data is even more reliable and accurate than primary data. This is often the case when obtaining secondary data from reputable sources and governmental agencies. The samples used by governmental agencies, such as the U.S. Census, are often larger than those that can be generated

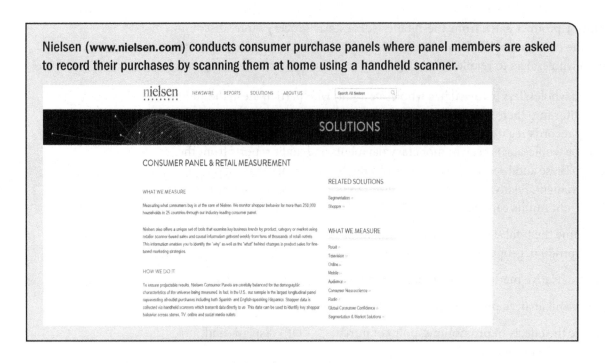

Nielsen (www.nielsen.com) conducts consumer purchase panels where panel members are asked to record their purchases by scanning them at home using a handheld scanner.

by an independent researcher designing a single study. Governmental agencies also tend to have larger budgets and longer time frames for conducting their studies. As a result, they can collect data from very large samples that are highly representative of the population.

However, it is important to carefully evaluate the quality of the data that is obtained from secondary data sources (see Figure 8.1). Conventional wisdom tells us that we often get what we pay for. Secondary data, and the research that collected the data, should be evaluated on a number of important factors, including the purpose of the research, the accuracy of the results, the consistency of the results and research methodologies across different sources and time periods, the credibility of the source of the data, the methodology used to collect the data, the presence of any errors or biases in the methodology and results, the timeliness of the data, and the sample characteristics and sampling procedures.

Even though secondary data has many advantages, it is necessary to evaluate the worth of the data to the managerial decision making process. Recall the IDO model of marketing research and the decision-making process presented Figure 8.2. To make decisions, marketing managers need information that is accurate, reliable, consistent, credible, and timely. A deficiency in any one of these areas can severely limit the ability of secondary data to provide useful inputs into the decision-making process.

DATABASE MARKETING

A database is a computerized list of past, current, and potential customers compiled from either a company's internal sources or purchased from external sources. The purpose of **database marketing** is to allow marketers to identify very small segments,

FIGURE 8.1 Questions to Ask When Evaluating Secondary Data

- What was the purpose of the research?
- How accurate are the results?
- How consistent are the results and research methodologies across sources and time periods?
- How credible is the secondary source?
- What research methodology was used to collect the data?
- Was there any potential bias in the way that the data was collected or reported?
- How timely is the data?
- What was the sample size, and what were the sample characteristics?
- How was the sample chosen?
- What was the population from which the sample was taken?
- What units of measurement were used?

FIGURE 8.2 The IDO Model

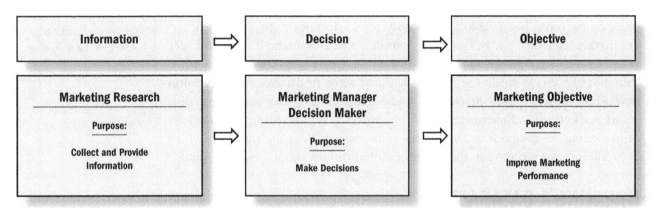

even as small as one person. This allows for very efficient personalized marketing communication between the company and the customer. This type of marketing is often referred to as **direct marketing** because the marketer communicates directly with an individual customer. Examples of direct marketing include mailing catalogs to consumers, mailing free samples to consumers, phone calls from telemarketers, and email campaigns. Most of the consumers who receive such direct marketing efforts are identified from a customer list. Such customer lists are generated from database marketing efforts, which in turn, are the result of marketing research.

Efficiency of Database Marketing. Database marketing is designed to increase the efficiency of marketing and promotional efforts. Imagine how much money is wasted on television advertising when a company pays for an advertisement knowing that a potentially large percentage of consumers who see the advertisement are not even in the marketer's target market. For example, consider how much money would be wasted if Pampers decided to advertise infant diapers during the Super Bowl. Only a small percentage of Super Bowl viewers would be in the market for infant diapers. Even still, Pampers would have to pay for advertising time based on the total number of viewers watching the Super Bowl. A more efficient marketing approach would be to mail free samples to parents of newborn children. By doing so, they would spend their money on promotions targeted directly toward potential customers. There would be very little money wasted on promoting to consumers who are not in the market for infant diapers.

Marketers often refer to the **80/20 rule**. This means that 80 percent of a company's sales come from 20 percent of their customers. A small group of very loyal repeat customers often sustains a company's sales. If the 80/20 rule applies to a particular business, database marketing provides a means for identifying the 20 percent. Generally, promotions generated from databases of customers have higher response rates (e.g., redeemed coupons, orders from websites) than those sent from mass marketing.

Evolution of Marketing. Marketing has changed and evolved over the years. Early in the 20th century many businesses relied on mass marketing. The emphasis was on production and distribution efficiency. To achieve this, customers were given very few product choices. Consumers in the early 1900s were told that they could purchase a new Ford Model T in any color they wanted, as long as it was black. Later, businesses saw the value in identifying and targeting individual segments. Automobile manufacturers began making various styles and sizes of cars to appeal to different market segments. Today, marketing is undergoing a dramatic shift toward very focused target marketing and database marketing. Other terms used to described this shift of focus to smaller segments identified through databases are **precision marketing**, **synchronized marketing**, **niche marketing**, **micro marketing**, **pinpoint marketing**, and **narrowcasting** (as opposed to **broadcasting**). These views of marketing are designed to identify the right consumers at the right time when they will be most receptive to marketing communications about a specific brand.

CREATING A DATABASE

One way in which marketers can obtain a customer database is to create it themselves. And, creating a customer database need not be a difficult task. Marketers simply need to ask three questions:

1. How can I get a list of my current and potential customers' names, addresses, phone numbers, and email addresses?

2. How can I use that list of names to communicate directly with my customers on an individual basis?

3. How can I use that list to identify my best customers?

In most cases, marketers simply need to offer an incentive for which consumers will provide their names, addresses, phone numbers, and email addresses. Many consumers will freely give their names, addresses, and phone numbers when they enter a drawing or a contest to win a prize, or even when they request that they be included in a mailing list to receive monthly coupons, online newsletters, emails, or special offers from a store. Below are some other examples of how marketers can create their own database of customers.

Creating a customer database need not be difficult. Sometimes it is merely a matter of offering an incentive in the form of a prize, giveaway, or coupon in exchange for customers' names, email addresses, and other contact information. Even though consumers do not like giving out their name and contact information, they will willingly write their name, address, phone number, and email address on a piece of paper to enter a drawing to win a prize.

Many marketers believe that the future of marketing lies in databases which allow marketers to identify who their customers are, record their customers' purchase patterns, communicate directly with their customers individually, and identify their best customers.

- Jerry's Pizza restaurant places a fish bowl on its cashier counter where customers place their business cards in hopes of winning a free lunch. The restaurant manager can track who their customers are and what part of town they are coming from. They also have a weekly drawing to win a free meal up to $50. Customers write their name, phone number, address, and email address on the contest entry form. Using the email addresses, the restaurant owner sends an electronic newsletter to his customers. The newsletter contains pizza trivia (world's largest pizza, pizza toppings from around the world, etc.), information about weekly specials, and a coupon for their next visit.

- The hostess at a busy restaurant asks for a guest's cell phone number when waiting for a table. Instead of using buzzers or pagers, the hostess sends a text message to the cell phone number when that guest's table is ready. The restaurant manager can now send text messages to guests asking them to complete mobile surveys using their cell phone. A guest might even be asked to complete a mobile survey while they are waiting for their table, in exchange for a free appetizer or a free dessert.

- A local fabric store has a drawing to give away a trip to Hawaii. Customers must write their name, phone number, and email address on the entry form. Instead of newspaper advertisements to promote upcoming sales, customers in the database receive an electronic newsletter sent to their email address. The electronic newsletter also contains a coupon for their next visit.

- A local photographer identifies the names of people who are engaged to be married and records the dates of the weddings. Before important dates, such as the anniversaries for each couple, he mails coupons for portraits. In addition to the coupons, he includes promotional materials detailing his expertise in photography, and he even describes how professional-quality portraits can be a wonderful gift to give a loved one for a special occasion, such as a wedding anniversary. This is an example of **synchronized marketing** because he is identifying the people who will likely want to purchase portraits, and he is identifying the time when these people will most likely want to purchase portraits. Thus, he is sending his promotional materials to the right people at the right time.

- When children purchase a stuffed animal from Build-A-Bear Workshop, they sit down at a computer screen to enter their name, birth date, email address, and even the name of the animal they just purchased. Many children go to Build-A-Bear Workshop for birthday parties or as a birthday present. A few weeks before the child's next birthday, an email is sent to that child containing a $5 coupon good for products in the store. The email is also an attempt to encourage the child to have his or her birthday party at Build-A-Bear Workshop.

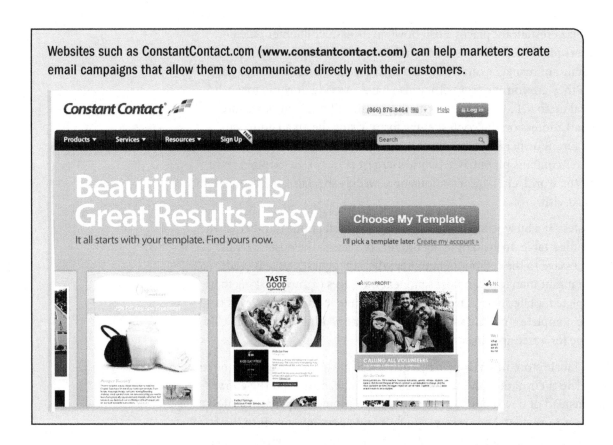

Websites such as ConstantContact.com (www.constantcontact.com) can help marketers create email campaigns that allow them to communicate directly with their customers.

An interesting note regarding the incentives offered to consumers is that the word *free* is the most powerful word in the direct marketing lexicon. Of the three ways to say the same thing—"50 percent off," "half-price," or "buy one, get one free"—tests show that "buy one, get one free" draws a 40 percent higher response than the other two.[5]

If a marketer is unable to create his or her own database of customers, there are many database marketing firms that will help merchants develop lists of their customers and use these lists for email marketing campaigns, electronic newsletters, and even text messaging. SuddenValues (**www.suddenvalues.com**) offers email and text messaging services as well as providing websites for participating merchants. ConstantContact (**www.constantcontact.com**) specializes in developing customized emails and electronic newsletters that can be sent to a list of customers.

To develop and implement database marketing, ask the following questions:
1 How can I get a list of my customers?
2 How can I use the list to communicate directly with my customers as individuals?
3 How can I identify my best customers?

DATABASES AND MARKETING PERFORMANCE

Marketing researchers can have a direct and significant effect on marketing performance by using databases to develop direct marketing campaigns. To illustrate this, consider the case of a small, independently owned gas station. The station owner sold gas and also performed minor car repairs, such as oil changes and repairing flat tires. The station owner knew that oil changes led to a very high profit margin. As such, he wanted to sell more oil changes. The question was, how could he encourage more customers to purchase an oil change at his gas station? He decided to have a drawing. Every time a customer came to his station to purchase gas, he asked them if they would like to enter their name and contact information into a weekly drawing to win a free tank of gas. Most of his customers did this. And, every week he posted the name of the winner for that week. He also used the list of names and addresses for direct marketing purposes. He emailed coupons for oil changes at a reduced price to customers on the list. As a result of using the database, the number of oil changes he sold per month increased from 15 to 50. He tripled his oil change business simply by identifying his customers and then sending them coupons in the mail.

Using customer databases to develop direct marketing campaigns offers significant benefits to marketers. Direct marketing campaigns, such as email campaigns, provide instant feedback to marketers about what marketing strategies work and what strategies do not work. As a result, marketers can continually refine their marketing strategies and campaigns.

LOYALTY PROGRAMS AND LOYALTY CARDS

Loyalty programs are becoming increasingly popular as tools for marketing research and database marketing. The fundamental purpose of a loyalty program is to identify customers by name, and then offer them an incentive to continue purchasing from the marketer. Many retailers, such as bookstores and music stores, have created customer loyalty programs. Customers join a points club where they receive points every time they make a purchase. Accumulated points can be redeemed for merchandise. Information about consumers' purchases is captured in the database when customers use the loyalty card at the time of purchase. Consumers' personal information that was provided whey they completed the application for the loyalty card can then be matched in the database with their personal purchase information.

Perhaps the most visible loyalty programs used by marketers are the discount cards offered by most supermarkets and grocery stores. When consumers scan their loyalty card at the time of purchasing groceries their purchase data is recorded in the database. The incentive that is offered to consumers is the reduced price on items when they use their discount card at the time of purchase. This encourages customers to use their cards, which increases the amount of data collected in the database. Retailers can then use the information in the database to identify their best customers and even send targeted promotions and coupons to individual customers.

Positioning Data Collection Efforts. Loyalty programs and discount cards are good examples of how marketing researchers often need to position their data collection efforts so that they are perceived as providing a benefit to consumers. Very few consumers would sign up for the "So We Can Track What You Are Buying Card." But, millions of consumers have already signed up for the "Kroger Plus Card." The words and phrases that are often used to name loyalty cards are listed in Figure 8.3. Notice that these card names suggest benefits to consumers. There is no mention of their use as a data collection tool.

FIGURE 8.3 Frequently Used Names for Loyalty Cards

Bonus Card	Plus Card
Bonus Savings Club	Points Club
Coupon Plus Card	Preferred Customer Card
Customer Choice Card	Reward Card
Discount Card	Savings Club
Fan Card	Super Card
Kid's Club Card	Ultimate Card
Loyalty Card	Value Card
Maximum Savings Card	Valued Customer Card
Membership Card	VIP Card

Variations on traditional loyalty cards are even used in nonretail environments. For example, some churches now provide their members with keychain cards that are very similar in appearance to traditional retail loyalty cards. A church member swipes his or her card through a card reader when entering the church to attend worship services, meetings, rehearsals, or other special events. These cards have dramatically improved the ability of such organizations to keep better records of membership and attendance at various functions.

STORE CREDIT CARDS

Proprietary store credit cards are another tool that marketers can use to create customer databases. There are two main reasons why store credit cards have grown in popularity. First, possessing a store credit card makes consumers more likely to purchase products from that store. Consumers are less likely to purchase products from stores for which they do not have a credit card. Second, these proprietary store credit cards serve as a way to collect purchase information about individual consumers. When a customer purchases goods or services using the store credit card, information about that customer (obtained from the credit card application) and information about that customer's purchases are matched in the database. This allows retailers to track the specific products their customers buy, how often their customers buy the products, and how much of the products their customers buy. Retailers encourage consumers to obtain a store credit card by offering a purchase discount for completing an application.

The customer-specific purchase data in the database can easily be used to target promotional messages to individual customers. For instance, many retailers have begun using smaller, more specialized catalogs. A department store might have a catalog for men's big and tall clothing, another catalog for women's plus size clothing, and yet another catalog for maternity clothing. If a customer is identified as a frequent purchaser of men's big and tall clothing they are targeted to receive the men's big and tall clothing catalog. It makes little sense to send the men's big and tall clothing catalog to a woman who buys only women's petite-size clothing. Further, the database can also be used for **predictive targeting**. Customers who currently buy maternity clothing will be targeted to receive the baby clothing catalog, the nursery furniture and accessories catalog, and even the children's toys catalog. Pregnant women will soon need to buy products for infants and toddlers. Marketers can also employ predictive targeting based on information that has been accumulated over many years. Customers who currently purchase infant and toddler clothing can be targeted to receive the preteen clothing catalog 10 years in the future.

REWARD CREDIT CARDS

Credit cards can also serve as **reward cards** for customers. For example, GM joined with MasterCard to offer the GM MasterCard. When cardholders use their GM MasterCard for purchases they earn a 5 percent rebate toward the purchase or lease of an eligible new GM car, truck, or SUV. When a consumer uses his or her GM MasterCard to pay for $100 in groceries, that consumer earns $5 toward the purchase of a GM car or truck. Reward money can be accumulated over a number of years. This provides cardholders with an incentive to purchase a GM car because they will earn a reduction in the price based on their accumulated rewards. But more importantly, GM now has a database of millions of potential customers. The only reason for having and using a GM MasterCard is if you intend to purchase a GM automobile. And, by encouraging consumers to use their GM MasterCard for as many purchases as possible, GM can also identify the lifestyles of various consumer groups within their database. A consumer's lifestyle can be inferred from the products that person purchases. GM also surveys cardholders about driving and car preferences.

GM is not alone in their use of such reward cards. Even though reward credit cards are often associated with the travel industry, many other retailers have begun using them for marketing purposes. In each case, the marketer can create a database of potential customers and their purchase behaviors. A marketer knows that consumers who have their card are potential customers. Why would a consumer have a Disney Visa card if they did not intend to redeem their accumulated Disney Dream Reward Dollars sometime in the future? Examples of reward credit cards include:

> Most consumers have no idea of the amount of private purchase data that marketers can obtain from database marketing efforts.

- The Universal Entertainment MasterCard, where consumers earn points that can be redeemed for movies and concert tickets, theme park tickets, CDs, DVDs, and other entertainment merchandise.

- The Toys "R" Us Visa, where consumers earn points that can be redeemed at Toys "R" Us and Babies "R" Us.

- The Disney Premier Visa, where consumers earn Disney Dream Reward Dollars that can be redeemed for a variety of Disney merchandise and vacations.

- The Starbucks Visa, where consumers earn Duetto™ Dollars.

- The L.L. Bean Visa, where consumers earn coupon dollars that can be redeemed for purchases made at L.L. Bean.

- The Grand Ole Opry Visa, where consumers earn points that can be redeemed for Grand Ole Opry tickets and merchandise.

- The Ann Taylor Visa, where consumers can earn Ann Taylor Rewards certificates.

- The Harley-Davidson Visa, where consumers earn gift certificates that can be used for Harley-Davidson products and accessories.

WARRANTY CARDS AND PRODUCT REGISTRATION CARDS

Databases can also be created from the information consumers provide on product **warranty cards** and **product registration cards**. Most of these cards include surveys that measure consumer demographics as well as numerous aspects of consumers' lifestyles, activities, interests and hobbies. For instance, some of the questions on warranty cards measure consumers' intentions for the next 12 months, including their intentions to purchase a home, their intentions to purchase a car, their intentions to get married, and even whether or not they plan to have a baby. Warranty cards and product registration cards from a variety of different products can then be aggregated into a large database of information regarding consumers' actual purchases, as well as their responses to various survey questions (see **www.equifax .com**). A marketer who wants to open a wedding planning service could purchase a list of consumers in a particular geographic area who reported that they intend to get married within the next 12 months. A small company that makes high-quality fishing equipment might purchase a list of people who live in the southeastern United States, who have annual incomes greater than $90,000, who have a credit card, and who like outdoor activities, such as hunting, camping, and fishing. All of this information would have been obtained from consumers' answers to the surveys on the warranty cards.

LIST PROVIDERS

A database is essentially a list of customers. There are many businesses that specialize in selling lists of consumers as well as lists of other businesses. Such **list providers** usually have websites where marketers can review their lists and purchase them online. For example, **www.bestmailing.com**, **www.directoriesUSA.com**, **www.HDML.com**, **www.listbazaar.com**, and **www.americanbusinesslists.com** sell lists of businesses as well as lists of consumers. Most of these lists are relatively inexpensive. For example, the

Database marketing can help marketers answer the questions:
- Who are our customers?
- What are our customers buying?

However, database marketing cannot answer the question:
- Why are they buying it?

Focus groups, projective techniques, and laddering interviews (discussed in the next chapter) can help to answer such questions regarding consumers' motivations.

cost for a basic list, including names and addresses, might be $60 per 1,000 names. This can be a very inexpensive and efficient way to obtain the names and addresses of potential customers.

The lists purchased from these providers can be either compiled lists or response lists. **Compiled lists** are those that are compiled from phone books, zip codes, or other aggregate directories of the American population. The cost for these lists is typically between $25 and $75 per 1,000 names. **Response lists** are those that are the result of consumers responding in some way that results in their name being added to the list. For instance, when a consumer submits a warranty card for a new SLR digital camera, that person is placed on a list of people interested in photography. We know that this person is interested in photography because he or she recently purchased a camera. When consumers redeem a coupon for Healthy Choice Entrées, they might be placed on a list of people interested in healthy foods. Typically, prices for response lists are higher than prices for compiled lists. This is because response lists are better indicators of consumers' actual behaviors. The price for a response list can range from $50 to $150 per 1,000 names. Responsivelists.com (**www.responsivelists.com**) sells such response lists. They offer lists based on consumers' levels of interest in various product categories as well as consumers' lifestyles. For instance, a marketer can purchase a list of consumers who are interested in exercise and fitness, pets, gardening, outdoor sports, home decorating, automobiles, and even weight loss and dieting.

Marketers can also purchase lists of email addresses of consumers who have agreed to participate in **opt-in email** marketing programs. For example, Postmaster Direct (**www.postmasterdirect.com**) sells lists of email addresses that belong to consumers who have visited their website or their partner sites and voluntarily enlisted to receive commercial emails about topics of interest.

Other types of databases are also available for purchase. For instance, ClusterPlus provides breakdowns of the American population based on demographics (see **www .knowledgefactory.co.za**). And, PRIZM (Potential Rating Index by Zip Code Market) provides breakdowns of the American population based on demographics and lifestyles (see **www.claritas.com**).

Mailed Regression. The more specific the list, the more useful it will be in identifying potential customers. But, even if marketers have only a general list of consumers, they can still perform a mailed regression analysis as a prospecting tool.[6] With **mailed regression**, a marketer sends direct marketing materials (such as email campaigns) to a small random sample generated from a general list. The marketer keeps a record of those customers who responded by making a purchase. Then, the marketer purchases a larger list of customers matching the characteristics of those original customers who responded. The second list should contain better prospects. In this way, marketers can continually refine their databases and customer lists.

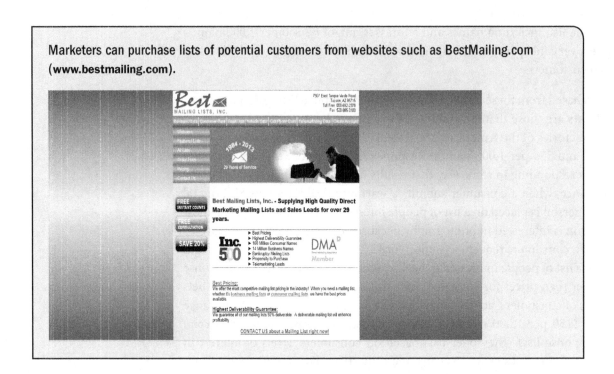

Marketers can purchase lists of potential customers from websites such as BestMailing.com (www.bestmailing.com).

RFM ANALYSIS

Once a marketer has a database, how do they sort through it to identify their best customers or best prospective new customers? **Recency, frequency, monetary (RFM) analysis** is one technique that can be used to identify the best customers from a database. RFM analysis is a powerful tool that markers can use to grow the value of customers by more aggressively marketing to their best customers. One of the purposes of RFM analysis is to identify those customers who are most likely to respond to direct marketing campaigns, and thus, increase the response rate for these campaigns. A direct marketing campaign costs money, so marketers want to maximize the sales-to-cost ratio.

RFM analysis is a procedure for sorting the customers in a database into 125 segments. This is done by sorting the database into **quintiles**: the top 20 percent, the second 20 percent, the third 20 percent, the fourth 20 percent, and finally the bottom 20 percent (see Figure 8.4). Smaller databases can be sorted into fewer segments, and larger databases can be sorted into more segments.

Recency. The first step is to sort the database based on the date of the most recent purchase. The 20 percent of customers who made the most recent purchases are assigned an R value of 5. The 20 percent of customers who made the next most recent purchases are assigned an R value of 4, and so on. All customers are assigned an R value of 5, 4, 3, 2, or 1. The theory behind this is that the customers who purchased from a marketer most recently are more likely to respond to a direct marketing campaign than customers who purchased from a marketer in the distant past.

FIGURE 8.4 Recency, Frequency, Monetary Analysis

Relative Rank in the Database	Recency Score	Frequency Score	Monetary Score
Top Quintile	5	5	5
Second Quintile	4	4	4
Third Quintile	3	3	3
Fourth Quintile	2	2	2
Bottom Quintile	1	1	1

Frequency. In a similar manner, customers are then assigned an F value indicating their quintile rank based on how frequently they purchase. The 20 percent of customers who purchase the most frequently are assigned an F value of 5. The 20 percent of customers who purchase the next most frequently are assigned an F value of 4, and so on. All customers are assigned an F value of 5, 4, 3, 2, or 1.

Monetary. Customers are then assigned an M value indicating their quintile rank based on how much money they spend when they make a purchase. The 20 percent of customers who spend the most when they make a purchase are assigned an M value of 5. The 20 percent of customers who spend the next most when they make a purchase are assigned an M value of 4, and so on. All customers are assigned an M value of 5, 4, 3, 2, or 1.

The Combined RFM Score. By combining the three values, each customer now has an RFM score. Those customers with RFM scores 555 are in one segment, those customers with RFM scores 435 are in a different segment, and so on. There are 125 possible segments (5 R values × 5 F values × 5 M values = 125). The theory is that customers in segment 555 are the most likely to respond to direct marketing campaigns. Recency tends to be the best predictor of response, followed by frequency, and finally monetary.[7] Thus, customers in segment 555 are the best customers, followed by customers in segment 554, followed by customers in segment 553, and so on. RFM analysis also tends to be a better predictor of response than demographic variables such as age, income, and sex. Demographic variables tell marketers who their customers are—their customers' income, age, and even whether or not they own their own home. Alternatively, RFM analysis tells marketers when their customers buy a product, how often they buy it, and how much of it they buy. The more actual purchase behaviors that marketers can measure, the more successful they will be in identifying their best current customers, as well as their best prospective customers.

> Marketers can use RFM analysis to identify their best customers who have purchased the most recently, the most frequently, and who spent the most.

CONSUMER MOTIVATION AND REASONS FOR BEHAVIORS

Database marketing allows marketers to measure distinctly different types of information compared to that which can be measured from surveys. Surveys can measure only consumers' characteristics and consumers' stated purchase behaviors and intentions. Alternatively, database marketing allows marketers to measure actual purchase behavior. The closer marketers can get to measuring behaviors, the better off they will be. Surveys can measure only who customers are and what customers say. Database marketing can measure what customers are doing and what customers are buying. However, database marketing cannot measure consumers' motivations or the reasons for consumers' behaviors. With a loyalty card, a grocery store can measure that a customer purchased a family size can of soup, but it cannot measure why that customer bought it. Focus groups, projective techniques, and laddering interviews (discussed in the next chapter) are designed to collect data to help marketers answer questions related to motivations and reasons for behaviors. Marketers gain increasing insight and understanding into consumers as they move from measuring only characteristics and stated intentions, to measuring actual behaviors, to measuring the motivations and reasons for those behaviors.

> Knowing who your customers are is nice. Knowing what your customers buy is better. And, knowing why your customers buy it (or don't buy it) is even better.

FIND, MAKE, KEEP, GROW

While there are many benefits of adopting a database marketing view of marketing, perhaps the greatest benefit of database marketing is that it focuses a marketer's attention directly toward customers—finding and making new customers, keeping current customers, and identifying the best customers to grow the value of a customer base. Adopting a database marketing philosophy focuses attention on three key questions:

1. How can I get a list of my current and potential customers' names, addresses, phone numbers, and email addresses?

2. How can I use that list of names to communicate directly with my customers on an individual basis?

3. How can I use that list to identify my best customers?

Database marketing focuses attention away from the process of marketing, and toward the desired results of marketing activities: finding and making new customers, keeping current customers, and growing the value of a customer base through the use of RFM analysis. The focus of a business should be on finding new customers, keeping customers, and growing the value of customers.[8] This is important to understand when dealing with business owners. If a business owner gives a marketing manager a $200,000 budget, the owner does not want to hear the marketing manager say, "With our $200,000 promotion budget we were able to buy three new 30-second television advertisements, we sponsored a NASCAR team, and we sponsored a community music festival." Instead, the owner wants to hear, "With our $200,000 promotion budget we developed a database of our customers, we made 120 new customers (find, make), we increased the repeat purchase rate among our customers from 50 percent to 57 percent (keep), and we increased the average purchase order amount by $110 per customer (grow)."

> One of the most significant benefits of adopting a database marketing philosophy is that it focuses marketers' attention directly on customers—finding potential customers, making new customers, keeping current customers, and growing the value of customers.

QUESTIONS FOR DISCUSSION

1. What is secondary data?

2. What are the advantages and disadvantages of secondary data?

3. When is secondary data used?

4. What are some of the criteria that marketers should use when evaluating the quality and worth of secondary data?

5. Are there any situations where marketers would be better off relying on the results from secondary data, as opposed to primary data?

6. What types of consumer- and market-related data is available to marketers from secondary sources?

7. How (why) do supermarket discount cards represent the future of marketing?

8. Is it cheaper to make a new customer or keep an existing customer? How does your answer relate to the use of databases by marketers?

9. Rank the following questions in terms of their importance to marketers. That is, if you could know the answer to only one of these questions, what question would you most want answered? Then, if you could know the answer to a second question, what question would that be, and so on.

    Who are our customers?

    What are our customers doing (buying)?

    Why are our customers doing (buying) it?

10. What types of marketing research can help marketers answer each of the following questions?
    a. Who are our customers?
    b. What are our customers doing (buying)?
    c. Why are our customers doing (buying) it?

11. What is a database (as it relates to marketing) and what is the purpose of database marketing?

12. Why do retailers offer you 10 percent off of your current purchase if you sign up for their store credit card?

13. Why do grocery stores offer discount cards and loyalty cards to their customers (e.g., Kroger Plus Card)?

14. Is the use of database marketing more or less efficient than traditional advertising media (TV, print, radio, outdoor, etc.) at achieving marketing goals?

15. What is the 80/20 rule and what does it have to do with database marketing?

16. Compare and contrast the use of database marketing efforts with the use of surveys (phone, mail, mall intercept, etc.) in terms of the types and worth of data that marketing researchers can measure.

17. How do decisions that marketing researchers make regarding the collection and use of secondary data and the use of database marketing influence the managerial decision-making process?

18. Visit the website for the U.S. Census Bureau (**www.census.gov**) to see how easy it is to obtain detailed demographic data about states, counties, and even individual cities. Find *Quick Facts*, and then select your home state.
    a. What is the median household income for your home state?
    b. Is this higher or lower than for the United States as a whole?

    Click on *Browse Data Sets*. Click *Social Characteristics* (under *American Community Survey*.)
    a. What is the average family size in your home state?
    b. What percent of males in your home state have been divorced?
    c. Who is more likely to have been divorced, males or females?
    d. What percent have a bachelor's degree or higher?
    e. What percent were born in the United States?
    f. Are residents of your home state more likely to be of Polish, German, Dutch, Russian, or Greek heritage?

    To answer the above questions for your home county, go back to the table that listed the demographics for your home state. Then, use the boxes at the top of the page to select your home county.

19. Visit the websites for Maritz Marketing Research (**www.maritz.com**) and find the Maritz Poll (click on *Our Companies*, then click on *Maritz Research*, then click on *Insights*). Find an interesting result from one of their polls and discuss how a marketer might be able to use the information from this poll to help them market their product or service.

20. Visit the websites for Gallup (**www.gallup.com**) and then click on *Trends A–Z* found at the bottom of the page. Find an interesting result from one of their polls and discuss how a marketer might be able to use the information from this poll to help them market their product or service.

21. Visit the website for Hoovers (**www.Hoovers.com**). Locate a company you are familiar with and then see what information about that company is available.

22. Visit the website for MarketResearch.com (**www.marketresearch.com**). Imagine that you wanted to start a business manufacturing your own line of children's clothing. Before investing in this new business you might want to obtain information about this market. Click on *Consumer Goods*, and then click on *Consumer Goods and Retailing*. Sort through the research reports that are available for the apparel category.

MINICASE 8.1

Parkersville Parks and Recreation Department

You have recently been hired as the marketing and promotions manager for the Parkersville Parks and Recreation Department. Your job is to promote the various parks and recreation facilities to city residents. Your boss, Kaye Muntzing, is the executive director of the Parks and Recreation Department. She calls you into her office one day to inform you of her desire to increase your marketing and promotional efforts. She tells you:

> I think we need to promote our city's parks and recreation facilities more aggressively to all residents, not just the younger residents. But, to do this we need to know more about the demographic makeup of the people who live here in Parkersville. I want you to design a telephone survey that we can use to get a better sense of the ages and demographics of all the people who live in Parkersville. I don't want to have anyone else do this survey for us. Quite frankly, I don't trust anyone else to do this for us. I want to make sure that we get good and accurate data about who lives here in Parkersville.

What do you do? What do you tell Kaye Muntzing? What do you discuss with her?

MINICASE 8.2

IsoFlex

Johnny Nakamora owns a small karate studio. He recently developed a stretching aid called IsoFlex made out of vinyl straps that can be used to help his students stretch before karate lessons. He has noticed that his students who use the IsoFlex prior to their karate lessons experience significantly fewer injuries and pulled muscles. Johnny currently attends many karate trade shows across the country where he sells the IsoFlex to other karate studios. However, he believes that this market is about "tapped out." He has requested a meeting with you to discuss ways that he can identify new markets and customers. By looking at the following websites, what would you recommend to Johnny Nakamora? How could he use these websites to increase sales by identifying new markets and customers?

www.bestmailing.com
www.directoriesUSA.com
www.listbazaar.com

ENDNOTES

1   John W. Ellis, "Third-Party Vendors Deliver First-Class Sales," *Marketing News*, April 27, 1998, 2; J. D. Mosley-Matchett, "Marketers: There's a Feminine Side to the Web."*Marketing News*, Feb. 16, 1998, 6; D. A. Aaker, V. Kumar, and G. S. Day, *Marketing Research*, 6th ed. (New York: John Wiley & Sons, Inc., 1998); B. G. Yovovich, "Browsers Get Peek at Rivals' Secrets," *Marketing News*, Nov. 10, 1997; R. D. Frost and J. Strauss, *The Internet: A New Marketing Tool* (Upper Saddle River, NJ: Prentice Hall, Inc., 1998).

2 Seymour Sudman and Robert Ferber, *Consumer Panels* (Chicago: American Marketing Association, 1979).

3 Leon Winters, "Home Scan vs. Store Scan Panels: Single Source Options for the 1990s," *Marketing Research*, December 1989.

4 Susan Caminiti, "What the Scanner Knows about You," *Fortune*, December 3, 1990; see also James Sinkula, "Status of Company Usage of Scanner Based Research," *Journal of the Academy of Marketing Science*, Spring 1986.

5 Susan Headden, "The Junk Mail Deluge," *U.S. News and World Report*, December 8, 1997, 40–48.

6 Headden, "The Junk Mail Deluge," *U.S. News and World Report*, December 8, 1997, 40–48.

7 Arthur Middleton Hughes, *Marketing Tools* (May 1996): 4–10.

8 Peter F. Drucker, *The Essential Drucker* (New York: Harper Collins, 2001).

CHAPTER 9

Focus Groups

LEARNING OBJECTIVES

1 Define focus groups and discuss the advantages and disadvantages of focus groups.

2 Compare and contrast focus groups with surveys in terms of the types of information and data that can be measured.

3 Describe the major characteristics of professionally managed focus group facilities.

4 Discuss the relationship between marketers, focus group facilities, focus group moderators, and consumers.

5 Discuss the role of a focus group moderator.

6 Describe the process by which marketing researchers locate and recruit potential focus group participants.

7 Define screening surveys and discuss the importance of screening surveys for recruiting potential focus group participants.

8 Discuss new trends in online focus groups and video streaming of live focus groups.

9 Explain the importance of the moderator's guide and write a moderator's guide for a focus group.

10 Define funneling and discuss the role of funneling in developing the moderator's guide and moderating a focus group.

11 Define a laddering interview and explain how laddering interviews are used in the context of a focus group session.

12 Describe the major projective techniques used in focus group sessions.

Focus groups remain one of the most popular exploratory research techniques used by marketers today. In fact, recent surveys of marketing researchers reveal that traditional in-person focus groups are the most often used qualitative research technique (used by 60 percent of researchers), followed by traditional in-person in-depth interviews (IDIs, used by 45 percent of researchers).[1] A **focus group** is an unstructured, free flow interview with 6 to 10 people. It is not a rigid question and answer session. Participants are typically seated around a conference table and encouraged to discuss their intentions, attitudes, lifestyles, usage experiences, and so on. The session is often lead by a professional moderator who has been trained to organize, lead, and control focus groups.[2] Focus groups have become so popular that some marketers argue that if you are not doing focus groups you do not fully understand your customers.

Advantages of Focus Groups. Besides being flexible and easy to conduct, focus groups offer a number of advantages over other research techniques. The inherent group dynamics of focus groups can often yield insights not obtained from an in-depth interview of a single consumer or a paper and pencil questionnaire. This is because focus groups are much less researcher driven. One participant might say something that triggers other thoughts in another participant, who then says something that triggers other thoughts in yet another participant, and so on. Another advantage of focus groups is the ability to measure nonverbal communication, body language, facial expressions, tone of voice, and social interactions.

Uses of Focus Groups. Focus groups are a very flexible and versatile means of conducting marketing research and collecting information about customers. Focus groups can be used to:

- Obtain general background information about a topic of interest.
- Generate research hypotheses to be tested in subsequent quantitative research.
- Identify new product ideas and creative concepts.
- Obtain consumers' impressions of products, programs, services, institutions, or other objects of interest.
- Identify the source of marketing problems.
- Identify how products are purchased and used.
- Find new uses for products.
- Identify new advertising or promotional themes.
- Identify new target markets.
- Test alternative marketing campaigns and promotional offers.
- Determine your competitor's strengths and weaknesses.
- Identify and streamline a product's positioning.
- Identify potential usage situations for a brand.
- Identify potential competitive advantages.
- Identify the benefits and personal goals that consumers seek from products.
- Better understand consumers' purchase behaviors and purchase motivations.
- Better understand consumers' decision-making processes.

- Perform usability tests for new or modified products.

- Generate ideas in a brainstorming session.

- Learn how consumers talk about a product. This can facilitate the design of questionnaires, survey instruments, or other research tools to be used in quantitative research.

- Pretest surveys by getting feedback on question wording, clarity of instructions, and multiple interpretations of survey questions.

Focus groups have even extended their usefulness beyond that of typical consumer products. Focus groups are often used for mock trials and movie testing. Movie studios screen test movies before they are released. Reactions from test audiences can lead to changes in the story, plot development, characters, and even movie endings.

When Focus Groups are Not Appropriate. Even though focus groups have a wide variety of uses, there are some purposes for which focus groups are not intended. Focus groups involve a relatively small number of consumers. Sample sizes for focus groups tend to be much smaller than for descriptive research, such as surveys. As such, they are not a statistically valid measure of a much larger population of consumers. They do not provide precise measurement, and the results from one focus group might not generalize to a much larger population. For example, just because 75 percent of focus group participants (six out of eight) say that they intend to purchase a product, marketers cannot conclude that 75 percent of all consumers in this market intend to purchase the product.

Focus groups have become so popular that some marketers argue that if you are not using focus groups you do not fully understand your customers.

Potential Disadvantages of Focus Groups. The social component of focus groups makes them very different from surveys. When completing a survey, consumers' answers are anonymous, or at least no one other than the researcher knows an individual consumer's responses. However, with a focus group, responses are public and any comment is open to discussion. This social component often makes interpreting the results from focus groups difficult. Sometimes it is not clear whether participants are giving their honest opinions and thoughts, or if they are merely being influenced by the other people in the group. Decisions that are made in a group can be very different from the decisions that are made by separate individuals. Decisions that are made in groups can be more polarized and extreme than decisions made by individuals. This can lead to a **bandwagon effect**, where a person says something merely because other people are also saying the same thing, especially when discussing issues for which individual decision makers have very little involvement, their individual feelings are relatively moderate, or their attitudes are not strongly held. Unfortunately, this describes many typical consumer purchases. In such situations, participants might just go along with an opinion leader, go along with the person who holds the strongest opinion, or even go along with the person who first voices his or her opinion.

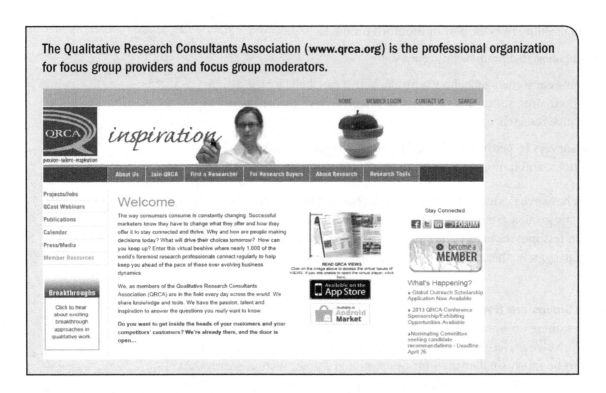

The Qualitative Research Consultants Association (www.qrca.org) is the professional organization for focus group providers and focus group moderators.

Opinion Leaders in Focus Groups. Another potential disadvantage of focus groups is that an **opinion leader** can dominate the group. Sometimes a very vocal and opinionated person can have an overbearing influence on the discussion. They will try to be the first person to answer a question. They will vocally disagree with other participants. And, they will sometimes try to persuade other participants to agree with their views and opinions. Fortunately, such opinion leaders can be controlled by an experienced focus group moderator who has been trained to encourage all participants to talk and share their thoughts.

Focused Focus Groups. Focus groups have a variety of uses. But, it is best to limit the number of objectives for a focus group. Do not try to do too much in one group session. Do not try to taste test a new product, test a variety of new advertising campaigns, and examine consumers' reactions to a number of new positioning strategies all in one session. Respondents might become confused. Results could also become diluted if there is not enough time to fully explore the multiple dimensions of a single topic. It is best to identify a single overall goal for one group session. If there are other objectives, address these by using more than one focus group.

The **Qualitative Research Consultants Association** is a not-for-profit organization that promotes excellence in all aspects of qualitative research and focus groups. By visiting their website (**www.qrca.org**) you can locate other members, find focus group facilities, and even post and view projects and jobs.

FOCUS GROUPS AND MARKETING OBJECTIVES

As discussed previously, the IDO model (shown in Figure 9.1) highlights the importance of understanding the role of marketing research in the overall marketing decision-making process.

The purpose of marketing research is to collect the information that marketing managers need to help make decisions. By working backwards from the marketing objective to the information that is needed to make a decision that is designed to achieve that performance objective, marketing researchers can increase the quality, worth, and usefulness of the information generated from a research project.

Is a Focus Group Appropriate? Before designing and conducting a focus group, researchers must fully understand the role that the information generated from a focus group will play in helping marketing managers make decisions. Any aspect of a marketing research project that affects the quality and worth of the information collected has a direct effect on the ability of marketing managers to make decisions and achieve their desired objectives. To increase the quality, worth, and usefulness of information that focus groups can provide to marketing managers, researchers should carefully consider the following questions:

- Will a focus group yield the type of information needed to make the managerial decision?

- Does the managerial decision require quantitative data from large groups of consumers? If so, focus groups are not the appropriate research methodology.

- Does the managerial decision require numerical responses to questions, such as percentages or means? If so, focus groups are not the appropriate research methodology.

FIGURE 9.1 The IDO Model of Marketing Research and the Decision-Making Process

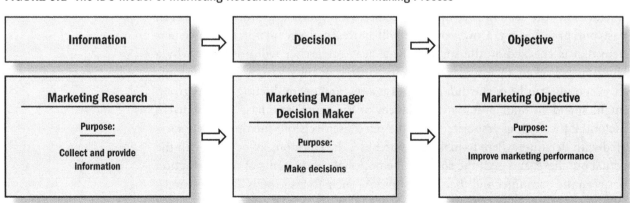

- Is the purpose of the focus group to obtain results that are statistically valid and results that can be generalized to a larger population? If so, focus groups are not the appropriate research methodology.

- Is the focus group meant to be a quick replacement for a survey? If so, a focus group is not the appropriate research methodology.

- Is there any bias in the focus group process that could lead to error in the results generated from the focus group session?

- Will the screening process generate a pool of potential focus group participants who are adequately representative of the population of consumers from whom marketing managers need to obtain information?

Focus Groups and Surveys Compared. Focus groups and surveys differ in many important ways, including their purpose, scope, approach, methodology, uses and benefits. Surveys are very efficient at measuring opinions and responses to questions across a broad range of individuals. They provide descriptive information, but at a relatively shallow level. Because they tend to be relatively standardized, surveys can provide only a surface level understanding of consumers. They do not provide much opportunity to probe individual responses to explore the beliefs, perceptions, attitudes, feelings, and motivations behind responses to individual questions. In contrast, focus groups allow for depth of understanding of consumers. They allow researchers to follow up questions and probe deeply into the beliefs, attitudes, feelings, and motivations behind responses to questions. However, their small sample size yields only a narrow understanding of consumers, as opposed to the broad descriptions that result from surveys of much larger samples of consumers. A researcher conducting a focus group is limited to the small sample of consumers participating in the focus group. Whereas surveys provide breadth of understanding, focus groups provide depth of understanding.

To further illustrate the differences between surveys and focus groups, consider a researcher interested in the purchase process for digital televisions. A survey will allow the researcher to measure factors such as where consumers purchase a television, the factors that are important in the purchase process, and even past purchase history. However, little will be learned except for the particular item that is checked on the survey. The survey researcher will not know why a consumer checked a particular box on the survey, or the consumer's motivations for responding as he or she did. In contrast, a researcher conducting a focus group might spend an hour probing the nuances of the actual purchase process itself, including the feelings associated with the purchase decision, the thoughts associated with deciding where to make the purchase, the emotions associated with the actual purchase, and even the social and emotional components of the interaction between the consumer and the salesperson. As such, focus groups allow researchers to better understand the beliefs, perceptions, feelings, and motivations behind responses to questions.

FOCUS GROUP FACILITIES

Before discussing the details of developing, organizing, and conducting focus groups, it is beneficial to describe the role that **focus group facilities** play in the marketing research industry. There are many tasks that must be performed before conducting a successful focus group. Sometimes it is best to leave these tasks to an experienced professional focus group facility. There are many professionally managed focus group facilities in the United States. In fact, most large cities have at least one professionally managed focus group facility operating in that city. These facilities can handle all of the duties associated with developing, organizing, and conducting focus groups. A marketing research project might include many phases and components, such as focus groups, surveys, and experiments. The focus group facility serves as a subcontractor responsible for the focus group component of the research.

> Most large cities have at least one professionally managed focus group facility.

Finding a Focus Group Facility. Finding a focus group facility is usually an easy task. There are a number of sources for locating facilities across the country, and even outside the United States. Most notably, *The Impulse Survey* of focus group facilities is published annually by the Impulse Research Corporation (**www.impulsesurvey.com**). The survey contains ratings of focus group discussion and viewing facilities based on input from over 5,000 moderators and researchers worldwide. Facilities are rated based on their performance in seven different areas: (1) recruiting, (2) personnel and the service they provide, (3) the physical facility, including conference and viewing rooms, (4) location, (5) food service, (6) value, and (7) an overall score which is a weighted average of the other six individual ratings. Marketers can visit the Impulse Survey website to locate facilities in different markets and then compare the facilities based on their Impulse Survey ratings.

Online Directories. There are also a number of online directories that marketers can use to find focus group facilities. However, these directories do not provide the comparative rating assessments that the Impulse Survey provides. Some of the most well-known directories are *The Green Book* (**www.greenbook.org**), *Quirk's Marketing Research Source Book* (**www.quirks.com**), and **FocusGroups.com**(**www.focusgroups.com**). All of these directories provide listings of focus group facilities by market, and they also provide direct links to the websites for the facilities they list. These directories are also good sources for locating other types of research providers, such as test kitchens, telephone interviewing facilities, mystery shoppers, and shopping mall facilities.

The Key Players in Focus Groups. In most cases, the focus group facility operates as a subcontractor to the marketer or to the lead research firm that is coordinating the research project. Very rarely does the marketer or lead research firm have direct contact with consumers in terms of finding consumers and screening consumers to participate in the group session. The local facility usually handles such recruiting tasks. The relationship between a focus group facility, the marketer, the professional focus group moderator, and consumers is shown in Figure 9.2.

FIGURE 9.2 Key Players in Focus Groups

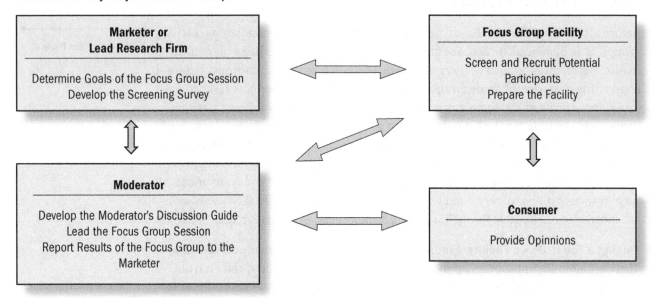

To illustrate these relationships assume that a marketer, such as Proctor & Gamble (P&G), has developed a new oatmeal breakfast cereal that contains caffeine. They have decided to target college students who are interested in quick and healthy breakfasts. Further, the caffeine in the oatmeal replaces the caffeine in a cup of coffee, making this a quick, healthy, and affordable breakfast for college students.

P&G might want to conduct some focus groups of college students to gauge their reaction to this new product. They might choose to conduct these groups in Kansas City, Portland, Cleveland, and Atlanta. To begin arranging these focus groups, P&G will first contact facilities in each of these cities to see if their facilities are available on the dates needed. If the facilities are available, P&G will reserve them for those days. Each of the focus group facilities will then be in contact with marketing managers from P&G (or the lead research firm, now referred to as the focus group facility's client) to discuss their goals for the research project. The facility and the marketer will agree on a moderator for the group session(s). The moderator will then be in contact with both the marketer and the facility to develop the moderator's guide and goals for the session. The facility will also obtain a detailed description of the type of consumer that the marketer wants to participate in the focus group. The marketer will likely supply the facility with a screening survey to be used in identifying and recruiting consumers for the focus group. After recruiting the necessary number of consumers the facility will handle all other aspects of preparing the facility for the focus group session, including setting up the room in an appropriate manner, preparing food, compensating participants, providing for videotaping, and any other requirements the marketer might have.

One of the most important skills for a focus group moderator to have is the ability to make a group of strangers feel so comfortable with each other that they are willing to freely express their innermost thoughts, feelings, and beliefs. An effective moderator must truly be a "people person."

The Moderator

In the situation just described, the facility will ask if P&G has their own **moderator** whom they want to use, or if P&G wants the facility to locate a local moderator. The advantage of using the same moderator for all groups is that it provides for consistency across groups in terms of the questions that are asked, how questions are asked, and the moderator's understanding of the objectives of the focus group research. However, this adds costs associated with travel, hotels, and meals for the moderator. Often, the marketer will ask the facility to find a local moderator for the project. The main advantage of this is that the moderator comes from the same market area as the consumers. As such, the moderator and consumers will likely speak the same language, use the same phrases in describing things or expressing their opinions, and share common experiences and activities. This can greatly improve communication between the moderator and consumers. The last thing a researcher wants is a moderator who cannot communicate effectively with consumers in the group. In addition, a local moderator will be able to approach the focus group objectively. A moderator employed by the marketer for whom the research is being conducted might have inherent biases that could manifest themselves in the way they ask questions, the way they respond to comments from participants, and even the way they interpret the results from the group.

Moderator Training. Moderating a focus group requires skill and training. Professional focus group moderators have received extensive training and have experience in controlling and leading a discussion among a group of strangers.[3] There are many sources for obtaining moderator training. For example, training sessions are available through the Burke Institute (**www.burkeinstitute.com**) and through the American Marketing Association (**www.marketingpower.com**).

Finding a Moderator. Moderators can be found by using the online directories previously mentioned. Most moderators choose to specialize in a particular product class, market type, or consumer demographic. For example, some moderators specialize in conducting focus groups of children. Some moderators specialize in conducting focus groups of elderly consumers. Some moderators specialize in conducting focus groups on very specific topics, even as specific as equine products. Some moderators specialize in conducting focus groups dealing with healthcare issues and healthcare products. Some moderators even specialize in conducting focus groups for products marketed through particular channels of distribution, such as products marketed online.

The more experience a moderator has with a particular issue, product, or type of consumer, the better that moderator will be at leading the discussion and identifying key pieces of information that are important for the group. Often, a moderator with a specialty is required. For example, if AutoZone wanted to conduct focus groups of men who change their own oil, the moderator must know about cars and the language associated with car repairs and maintenance to effectively communicate with participants.

Once selected, the moderator will communicate with the marketer regarding the objectives of the session and the moderator's guide to be used. Many marketers will allow the moderator to provide input into developing the moderator's guide, including the specific questions that are to be asked and question wording. Following the session, the moderator will prepare a report to be given to the marketer. They might also meet with the marketer to discuss the group, discuss their observations from the group, and offer any recommendations they might have for the marketer.

The Screening Survey

The facility will also ask if the marketer has a screening survey that they want to use for recruiting potential participants. The selection of participants for a focus group is an especially important step in organizing a focus group. The marketer knows exactly what type of consumer they want in the group. The **screening survey** is used to identify and recruit participants to a focus group who match the desired profile as defined by the marketer. For example, P&G might specify that they want eight college students who regularly exercise to stay in shape, who are interested in healthy foods and activities, and who have a difficult time "getting going" in the morning. The selection process for a focus group is not random. It is very purposeful. The purpose of the screener survey is to identify precisely the type of consumer to invite to the focus group.

Once they have the screener survey, the facility will begin searching for consumers in the local area to identify those who meet the specific requirements for that group. Sometimes the screening surveys are conducted in shopping malls. Most times, however, the screening surveys are conducted over the phone. Many facilities have separate phone rooms where telephone screening surveys are conducted. Sometimes they will have to randomly call phone numbers in hopes of identifying appropriate consumers. But, this can often be very inefficient. To avoid the inefficiencies of randomly calling consumers, many facilities maintain a database of consumers and phone numbers that is continually updated. If you look on the website for a focus group facility you will probably see "Become a Respondent" or "Join Our Panel." By clicking on this, consumers can complete a survey and enter their name and phone number into the database in hopes of being contacted to participate in a group. Some of these surveys can be very long, requiring potential participants to provide information about demographics, home ownership, employment, whether or not they smoke, occupation, types and brands of alcohol consumed, model and year of cars owned, sex and date of birth of children, ownership of various products, radio stations they listen to, health conditions, travel and vacation plans, political party affiliation, investments they own, clothing size, and hobbies and interests. The more detailed the database, the easier it is for the facility to locate very specific types of consumers and hard-to-find groups of people. After identifying the appropriate consumers, the facility will usually invite 10 to 12 of these consumers to attend the focus group. It is best to invite more than needed. Rarely do all of the consumers who are invited to attend the session end up attending. Notice that the marketer has no contact with consumers. Rather, the focus group facility is in direct contact with consumers.

The Focus Group Facility

If you were to visit the website of a focus group facility, you will likely see a layout of the entire facility along with pictures of individual rooms. The three main rooms in a facility are the focus group room, the viewing room, and the client lounge. The **focus group room** is where the moderator and the consumers are seated around a table and the focus group takes place. The **viewing room** is where the client sits and observes the focus group from behind the **one-way mirror**. Most viewing rooms will have data ports and phone lines so that the client can prepare reports and communicate with others while viewing the group session. Many facilities will also have **client lounges** where clients can relax between sessions, take a nap, talk on the phone, or even watch television. Facilities will take great care in making their clients comfortable. This is because the client is the facility's customer. The facility is marketing their services to the client. Anything that helps to make the client more comfortable and makes his or her experience more enjoyable increases the chance that the client will use the facility again in the future. It also increases the chance that the client and moderator will rate the facility favorably on the Impulse Survey.

Most focus group facilities have **test kitchens** for cooking and preparing foods. This is very important if the focus group involves consumers taste-testing various food products that need to be freshly prepared. A frozen food manufacturer might even want to conduct part of a focus group session in the test kitchen to observe how consumers open the package, heat the meal, and subsequently eat the meal. Sometimes marketers will even take very detailed measurements of food before it is served to focus group participants. They often weigh the food, measure the temperature of the food, measure the size of the food, and even take pictures of the food before serving it. The appearance of food items can have a significant effect on consumers' evaluations. Pizza manufacturers will take pictures of pizzas as they are removed from the oven to determine if the amount of burned spots on the cheese is related to consumers' taste preferences.

Some facilities also have focus group rooms that are large enough to set up **simulated shopping environments**. For example, greeting card marketers will often place a number of pyramid-shaped card racks in a room that contain numerous greeting cards. They will then ask consumers to shop for a card for a particular occasion, such as Mother's Day. They will observe consumers' behaviors, including where they begin looking for cards (at the top of the rack, or at the bottom of the rack), the way they move around the rack (starting at the left and moving to the right, starting at the right and moving left, or starting in the middle of the rack), the amount of time they spend looking at the cards, and even what they do when they have made a choice.

Sometimes, physical interaction with a product is required to adequately evaluate it. For instance, to evaluate consumers' perceptions of a new laundry detergent, a focus group facility might set up simulated laundry rooms were consumers actually wash a load of laundry with the new detergent. In some situations, a focus group might need to be conducted off-site. Marketers of motor oil might require that the group session be held at a local garage where consumers can actually change the oil in their own car. As consumers change the oil in their cars, they can talk about what they are doing, why they are doing it, any problems they are having, and even offer suggestions for improving motor oil or the oil change process.

Many facilities also have entrance doors that are in discreet locations away from the main entrance to the facility. These discreet entrances are for politicians, celebrities, and other high-profile individuals who might want to observe a focus group. Political candidates often like to be inconspicuous when they observe firsthand the reactions and opinions of potential voters.

Video Streaming Focus Groups. One of the disadvantages of focus groups is the cost associated with traveling to numerous facilities across the country to view group sessions in person. Recent advances in technology have made focus groups even more attractive and convenient. Focus Vision Worldwide Inc. (**www.focusvision.com**) provides a service that allows subscribers to view live focus groups online from anywhere in the world. By using a password, users can view their focus group as well as participate in an online chat with other observers of the same group session. This means that managers at the corporate headquarters in Seattle do not need to be physically present to view their focus group that is being conducted in Miami. As of 2013, Focus Vision reported that their services were available in nearly 1,000 focus group facilities worldwide. Focus Vision is not the only supplier of such services. For example, Active Group (**www.activegroup.net**) has also developed a long list of facilities that are connected into its network to provide **video streaming services**. Such video streaming capabilities are very appealing to marketers and any other organizations that seek to conduct focus groups. As such, the logos (and links to websites) for these video streaming services will usually be displayed in a conspicuous location on a focus group facility's website. This makes their facility more attractive than competing facilities that are not connected to a video streaming service provider.

FOCUS GROUP COMPOSITION

Individual focus group sessions should be small, with 6 to 10 people each. If you want to include more people, you should conduct multiple focus groups each with 6 to 10 participants. Within a focus group, participants should be relatively similar to each other. Homogeneous groups work best. For example, conduct a focus group consisting of only women with children (no women without children), a focus group with only single women (no married women), or a focus group with only elderly men (no young men). There are two major reasons for keeping focus groups homogenous. First, it helps to avoid arguments and disagreements that could result from consumers with different viewpoints and different backgrounds. For example, a focus group with four women who have children between the ages of 8 and 10, and four women without children, would not be a good idea for testing reactions to a new laundry detergent designed to remove tough food stains. The women without children might defer to the judgment of the women with children. They might believe that the mothers of young children have had more experience removing food stains from clothing. Secondly, keeping focus groups homogenous helps to identify individual segments, each with their own opinions, desires, and needs. The distinction between segments can become blurred and overlooked if the focus group contains very heterogeneous participants.

Participant Familiarity. Another issue with the composition of focus groups deals with participants referring friends and family members to also participate in the focus group. Try to avoid recruiting focus group participants who are familiar with each other for the same focus group session. This familiarity can sometimes inhibit honest comments about potentially sensitive or embarrassing issues.[4]

> The participants in a focus group session should be very similar to each other. Homogeneous focus groups work best.

Mini-Groups. A variation on the traditional focus group is a **mini-group**, which includes only four to five participants. A group with three respondents is called a **triad**. In fact, any group of two or more consumers and a moderator formed for the purpose of research can be considered a form of focus group. Mini-groups work especially well when the session will last for one hour or less. When there is limited time, groups with more than five participants do not work well because not everyone has ample time to say everything they want to say. Smaller groups also allow marketers to understand consumers at a more intimate level. Participants can explain their feelings, thoughts, and preferences at a deeper and more detailed level. As such, they are especially useful for dealing with specialized audiences in which the intent is to get more in-depth insights and when participants are difficult to find and recruit.[5] However, the downside to this is that with fewer people there will be fewer experiences to discuss. Mini-groups can lead to increased depth of understanding while sacrificing breadth of understanding.

> Often, the most difficult stage in setting up a focus group session is finding enough consumers who fulfill the screening criteria.

Even though mini-groups are becoming more popular, some professional focus group moderators are not sold on them. Mini-groups are not universally accepted among marketing researchers. Many moderators prefer the more traditional focus group with eight participants.

DESIGNING A FOCUS GROUP SESSION
Identify the Goals and Objectives of the Focus Group Session

Perhaps the most important step in designing a focus group session is determining what you want to learn from the focus group. Developing a list of goals and objectives acts as a safeguard against irrelevant and time-consuming lines of questioning. Make sure that a focus group is the appropriate research technique for achieving the managerial objectives.

Develop the Moderator's Guide

The focus group **moderator's guide** (also called the **discussion guide**) is an outline of the focus group session. It lists the questions to be asked by the moderator, and it lists any activities that are to be performed during the session. The moderator's guide also provides a timeline for the session, listing the amount of time to be spent on each major issue or activity. This keeps the session moving and helps to avoid spending too much time on any one issue. The list of questions should flow directly from the list of goals and objectives for the focus group session. It provides a logical framework for the discussion. It keeps the moderator and the participants on the subject. It should contain all relevant and important questions, allowing the moderator to concentrate on the discussion at hand rather than having to formulate new questions. It also allows for consistency and comparability of results from several different sessions (e.g., sessions conducted in different geographical regions). Have the moderator's guide approved by both the researcher and the client (the marketer, or the lead research firm). However, recognize that a focus group moderator's guide should not limit the questions that are asked. Often, new questions are formulated during a focus group in response to comments made by participants. Try to ask all of the questions that were developed for the moderator's guide, but allow for new questions as well. Some focus group facilities allow clients viewing the session from behind the one-way mirror to interject new questions during the course of a focus group session.

Select the Location

Choose a location that is convenient and comfortable for the participants. Participants who are comfortable, at ease, and relaxed will provide much better information than those who are uncomfortable and tense. As previously mentioned, there are many professionally managed focus group facilities across the country that offer many important advantages and services, such as databases of consumer names and phone numbers, telephone recruiting capabilities, food preparation, video and audio recording equipment, and client lounges and viewing rooms from which the focus group can be observed. However, a focus group can also be conducted very effectively in a hotel conference room, and even in the back room of a retail store. If conducting national research, try to conduct focus groups in three to four different geographic locations across the country—at least one session in the southeast, southwest, northeast, and northwest.

Select the Participants

Screening and identifying participants is often the most difficult step in setting up a focus group. Choose participants from the current and potential target market. Screen potential participants with phone interviews or intercept interviews to identify relevant characteristics. For example, a pet food manufacturer might be interested in researching single women between the ages of 20 and 30 who own a cat.

As previously mentioned, many focus group facilities and marketing research firms have databases of potential participants that can be sorted by such important characteristics. You will usually have to provide an incentive for participating. Often this incentive is money (e.g., $75 for a 90 minute session). Try to confirm 10 to 12 participants, knowing that only 8 or 9 will actually show up. Be prepared for difficulty. You might have to call 50 consumers to identify and confirm 8 for your focus group. Beware of consumers who frequently participate in focus groups just to receive the monetary compensation. Most researchers do not allow consumers to participate in a focus group if they have already participated in another group within the last six months. This helps to eliminate "professional" focus group participants.

Screening Surveys. **Screening surveys** are usually very detailed and contain at least 5 to 10 questions designed to identify a specific type of consumer. Not only are participants screened on important demographic characteristics, but they can also be screened based on product use, product familiarity, purchase history, and other psychographic and lifestyle variables. Participants can even be screened based on purchase patterns and purchase motivations for various products—what they buy, where they buy it, how they buy it, when they buy it, and why they buy it. For example, researchers might be interested in consumers who buy a particular style of shoe, and who tend to make shoe purchase decisions based primarily on price, versus style or brand name. Consumers who do not meet the exact criteria spelled out by the screening questionnaire are not invited to attend the focus group.

Articulation Questions. Many researchers also use articulation questions in their screening interviews. **Articulation questions** are designed to identify participants who will be willing and able to share their thoughts, opinions, and beliefs with a group of other consumers. In essence, articulation questions are used to identify talkative people. If participants are being paid, the last thing a research wants is a group of eight consumers who are not willing to speak up and provide input into the discussion. As part of the screening interview, researchers can ask potential participants, "Describe five things that are red," "Describe your last family vacation," or even "What would you do if the won the lottery?" Although these seem like unusual and irrelevant questions, they allow the researcher to identify consumers who can think quickly and who are able to easily verbalize their thoughts. More structured articulation questions can also be asked. For example, a researcher might ask some of the following questions during the screening interview.

Now I will read a number of statements. For each statement please indicate the degree to which it describes you on a 1–10 scale where 1 means that it does not describe you at all, and 10 means that it describes you perfectly.

- I am usually able to describe things in great detail.
- I am a creative person.
- I often like to think about things in order to discover new things about myself.

- I am very articulate.

- I am very comfortable talking with people I have recently met.

- I find it easy to strike up a conversation with people I have just met.

- I have very good verbal communication skills.

- I have a very outgoing personality.

Strict criteria are often set for such questions. If five of the above questions are used, a consumer might be required to answer all five with a score of seven or greater to be considered for the focus group.

Prepare the Facility

A focus group session should assume the nature of a round table discussion. Tape record or videotape the session so that you do not need to take many notes during the session. Most focus group facilities have focus group rooms that are equipped with recording equipment and one-way mirrors. Try to keep the focus group session less than two hours long. Tired, bored, irritated and hungry people are not good focus group participants.

Brand Sensitivities. To avoid biasing respondents' comments during a focus group session, it is important to consider the potential for brand sensitivities prior to conducting the session. **Brand sensitivities** refer to stimuli in the focus group's physical environment that might impact respondents' thoughts or comments. For example, if a focus group is designed to identify the magazines that adult women read, there should not be any magazines available in the waiting room of the focus group facility. If copies of *Cosmopolitan* are available for female participants to read prior to the session, this could significantly affect their responses to questions such as "What are some of the women's magazines that you can think of?" If the session deals with soft drinks, do not offer respondents a Coca-Cola product as they wait for the session to begin. If the session deals with snack foods, do not offer respondents Ruffle's brand potato chips before or during the session. In any of these instances, the products or brands that are available to respondents can artificially increase their attention to these products or brands during the session.

> Be aware that stimuli in the physical environment within which a focus group is being conducted can influence participants' thoughts and comments.

In addition, the color of the clothing that a moderator wears can also impact respondents' comments. In a focus group on clothing choices and preferred brands, researchers should avoid wearing clothing that prominently displays brand names or logos, such as Tommy Hilfiger. If the focus group deals with soft drinks, a bright red shirt worn by the moderator might cause respondents to unconsciously think about Coca-Cola products. A brown shirt worn by a moderator might cause respondents to think about UPS when discussing how they ship packages. An orange shirt or an orange dress worn by a moderator might cause respondents to think about Home Depot when discussing home improvement projects and stores for buying home improvement products and materials.

MODERATING A FOCUS GROUP SESSION

When consumers arrive for the focus group, it is generally a good idea to rescreen them before the actual group begins. This will confirm that the person attending the focus group is indeed the same person who was screened on the phone. By mingling informally with participants in a waiting room, researchers can also try to identify any participants who might be drunk, who might seem overly tired, who might have had a very bad day (they were in a car accident), who might have had a very good day (just got engaged), who might be otherwise distracted during the focus group, or who are extreme introverts or extroverts. Consider removing any of these people. Researchers want participants who can concentrate on the topic at hand and who are not going to be easily distracted by other thoughts.

During the session, one participant might try to dominate the discussion. Avoid letting one person lead and dominate the discussion. This can inhibit comments and suggestions from other members of the group. There are some simple techniques that moderators can use to control an extreme talker or an **opinion leader**. Stand immediately next to them. Stand directly behind them. Lightly touch the person's shoulder. Create and maintain eye contact with other people in the group. Call on other participants by name. Usually, the talker will get the hint and begin to reduce their verbal dominance. But, do not publicly embarrass or humiliate any member of the group. Consumers in a group will often form a bond with each other. As such, they might come to the aid of any other member who is embarrassed or publicly humiliated. Avoid creating any antagonistic situation between the moderator and participants.[6]

When moderating a focus group session, you should try to:

- Have fun and keep the session enjoyable for all participants.

- Keep the discussion on topic.

- Ask all questions that were identified prior to the session. However, questions need not always be asked in the exact order they appear in the moderator's guide.

- Encourage all participants to talk, participate, and become involved in the discussion. If someone has not spoken for a while, ask that person a question that will require them to become involved.

- Play devil's advocate if none are present.

- Follow up and investigate interesting and worthwhile comments or ideas from participants.

- Structure the questions by asking broad questions first, then specific questions later.

- Clearly repeat comments if a participant is soft-spoken so that people in the viewing room know what is being said, and so that all comments can be heard on the video.

When moderating a focus group session, you should avoid:

- Mentioning the company or brand name for which you are working (unless it is necessary).

- Wasteful topics, useless excursions, or verbal arguments between participants.

- Letting one person dominate the discussion.

- Letting more than one person talk at a time.

- Letting a comment that you do not fully understand go unexplained (unprobed).

- Asking questions that can be answered with a single word. Do not ask, "Is there anything else?" Instead, ask questions such as, "What else can you tell me about that?" and "Tell me more about that."

- Standing in the way of the camera.

DEVELOPING THE MODERATOR'S GUIDE

The **moderator's guide** is the list of general questions to be asked during the focus group. It provides a guide for the discussion. The list of questions should flow directly from the list of goals and objectives for the focus group session. The questions in a moderator's guide should be general and broad. They should allow the participants a great deal of freedom in answering. You should not restrict participants' thoughts. A participant might suggest something important that was not previously considered. The moderator's guide should do the following:

1. Identify the composition of participants for the group. Who will be in the group? The list of questions and issues to be discussed might vary by group.

2. Contain an introduction. Participants will want to know what they are doing and what this group is all about.

3. List the amount of time to be spent on each topic during the session. This will help to keep the moderator from running out of time before all questions or issues have been discussed.

4. Use the **funneling technique**. The order of questions or issues should go from broad to specific. Answers to specific questions might influence answers to later questions. For example, discuss what people like to do and where they like to go for fun and recreation first. Then ask them for their impressions of the city parks in a neighborhood.

5. Allow and encourage respondent-generated ideas. The moderator's guide should not contain any ideas that are offered (suggested or implied) by the moderator before respondents have had a chance to present and discuss them on their own. For example, do not ask, "Do you like the number of water fountains available in the city parks?" before asking, "Tell me, what do

you like and dislike about the city parks?" If the number of water fountains in the city parks is important to residents, they will mention it before you specifically ask about it.

6. Provide relevant information that marketing managers need to make decisions. The moderator's guide should contain questions that are designed to provide answers and insights that are relevant to the particular marketing problem at hand.

Below is a list of some of general topics and issues that could be included in a focus group moderator's guide for a physical product. Similar issues would be considered in developing a moderator's guide for examining consumers' experiences with a retail store or a service provider.

Introduction. Introduce yourself and explain the purpose of the group session and the use of any recording equipment.

Warm-Up/Ice Breaker. Do you own a product of the type being discussed? What brand is it? When was it purchased? Who uses it?

Product/Brand Awareness. How did you first become aware of this product? What type of information about this product caught your attention? What type of information about this product did you like (need), and what type of information did you not like (not need)?

Individual/Personal Factors. How would you describe yourself? What are your interests? What past experiences have you had with this type of product? What do you think of this type of product? How do you plan on using this product?

Need Identification. When did you discover you had a need for this type of product? What happened to cause you to want (or need) a product of this type? Was your desire to purchase this product based on a need, or based on a want? What kind of product is this to you: convenience good, necessity, shopping good, staple (and so on)?

Purchase Motivation. What caused you to buy this product? Why did you buy one brand over another? Probe for details about specific influences such as:

- Where the product was purchased, including the specific location.
- Sales personnel.
- Friends, relatives, or other significant individuals.
- Prior experiences with similar products.
- Type of product desired and when it will be used.
- Warranty expectations.
- Deals (special prices or discounts).
- Price.
- Advertising.

> The moderator's guide shows the general plan for the group session, including the general issues to be discussed, the specific questions to be asked, and the amount of time to be spent on each topic.

Information Search. Did you actively look for information before making up your mind? Did you do any comparisons among the available products? Did you check any product reviews or other research reports? What sort of information was persuasive in your purchase decision?

Decision-Making/Purchase Process. Did you make the purchase decision by yourself? Did you consult with anyone? Was it a group decision? What is your relationship with the person(s) who gave you advice regarding this product?

Actual Purchase. Where did you buy this product? Were you alone or did others come along? What were your positive and negative experiences when purchasing the product? If you were selling this product, how would you sell it? Would you do anything differently than the salesperson who sold you the product? Discuss how you feel about the purchase experience. Was it a pleasant or unpleasant experience? What factors were important in making the experience positive or negative? If you could change the purchase experience in any way, what would you change? How would this change make a difference? What did you expect of the salesperson during and after the sale? Did the salesperson meet these expectations?

Use/Consumption Situations. How do you use this product? In what situations or in what ways do you use this product? Do you use it for a variety of different purposes?

Evaluation. Will you buy the product again? Have you recommended it to others? Do you plan to recommend the product to others? Do you feel you got a good deal? Why, or why not? What makes you think this? Have you had contact with the store or salespeople since you bought the product? What kind of contact? Was this contact pleasant or unpleasant? Why?

Ideal/Expectations. Describe your ideal product. What would you ideally like? If you could design this product, what would it look like? How is this different from the current product? What do you expect from this product? What do you expect it to be? What do you expect it to do for you?

Additional Comments. What else about the purchase experience would you like to share with the group that we have not yet discussed?

Establishing the Ground Rules for a Focus Group Session

A focus group is almost always a one-time occurrence that will last for at most only two hours. There is very little (if any) opportunity to follow up with a participant after the session has concluded. As such, it is critical that all focus group participants be at ease and feel comfortable enough to willingly participate in the discussion. Participants can be made to feel comfortable from the very outset of a focus group session with the help of a few simple **ground rules**. When a moderator introduces participants to the focus group process they will usually mention at least a few of the following ground rules for the session that are designed to make all participants feel at ease, feel comfortable sharing with others, and feel motivated to participate.

Before we begin, I want to go over a few ground rules that we will follow for this session:

- We want to hear what you have to say.

- All opinions are important and should be shared.

- There are no right or wrong answers.

- Please talk one at a time. Do not speak while someone else is speaking.

- Speak clearly and loud enough for all to hear.

- Avoid side comments or side discussions while someone else is speaking. This could be seen as rude. And, I do not want to miss any important comments.

- We will not criticize or critique anyone else's opinion.

- Please turn off all cell phones and other portable communication devices.

- Do not feel bad if there might be some topics we discuss about which you know very little. Do not feel like you have to know everything about all of the topics that we will discuss today.

- Please be candid, but also cordial with your comments.

SAMPLE MODERATOR'S GUIDES

Below are four sample moderator's guides for focus groups. However, it is important to remember that no two focus group moderator's guides need to be exactly the same. By their nature, focus groups allow for great flexibility in the types of questions that participants are to answer and discuss and the activities that participants are asked to perform. So, do not feel compelled to design a moderator's guide that conforms exactly to another moderator's guide that you might have seen before. The best strategy is to design a guide that best fits the needs of the particular situation.

Pine Tree Mobile Homes

As an example of a moderator's guide, consider the following situation. Pine Tree Mobile Homes has just recently opened a branch sales office in a city that is home to a university with 20,000 students. Relatively few of the students at the university live on campus. Most live in apartments or houses and commute to campus on a daily basis. Pine Tree would like to market their mobile homes to college students as an affordable housing option. However, they do not know much about college students and their preferences in housing options. They would like to conduct a focus group of some college students. Below is an outline of a moderator's guide that could be used in this situation.

Group Composition: College students.

Welcome/Introduction/Overview of Focus Group Process (10 minutes)

General Information Regarding Housing Options (20 minutes)

Where do you currently live?

Why do you live there?

What are the advantages and disadvantages of living there?

List all of the possible housing options for college students. [List on large paper taped to walls.]

What are the advantages and disadvantages of each housing option?

Ideal Housing (20 minutes)

Where would you ideally like to live as a college student?

Draw a picture of your ideal housing option.

Describe your walk/drive home after classes to your ideal housing.

Mobile Homes (20 minutes)

What do you know about mobile homes? Probe if subjects do not mention price, size, neighbors, location.

Draw a picture of a mobile home.

Draw a picture of a person who lives in a mobile home.

Chris lives in a mobile home. Describe Chris. What does Chris look like? What type of person is Chris? Describe Chris's friends. What does Chris do for fun? Does Chris have a job? if so, what job?

Consider a Mobile Home (20 minutes)

Would you ever consider living in a mobile home? Why? Why not?

What would it take for you to consider living in a mobile home? Probe if subjects do not mention price, size, neighbors, and location.

If you would consider living in a mobile home, would you rather rent or buy a mobile home?

Notice that these questions are open-ended. Rather than being specific survey questions, they are intended to be discussion starters. They address broad issues that are important to understanding the attitudes of college students toward mobile homes. Also, notice that there are a number of activities planned for the session. Participants are asked to draw pictures of people, draw a picture of their ideal housing, and even draw a picture of a mobile home. Participants are asked to describe a fictitious walk home to their ideal housing situation. And, participants are even asked to describe a fictitious person who lives in a mobile home. These activities are examples of **projective techniques**, which will be discussed in more detail later in this chapter. Many focus group participants often find these activities to be more interesting and fun than participating in a traditional small-group question and answer session.

Minchberg Library

As another example of a moderator's guide, consider the case of Minchberg Library, located in the center of a city with a population of 80,000 people. Library managers wanted to examine issues regarding library usage, patron's perceptions of the library services that are offered, and preferred locations for new library branches.

Group Composition: Adult residents with at least one child still in school (K–12).

Introduction (10 minutes)

Welcome. Thank you for coming to this group session tonight. Please write your name on the table tent that you see in front of you. We have provided some light snacks and drinks so that you can relax and enjoy yourselves while we are talking with each other tonight. Also, I want you to notice that we will be videotaping this session. You can see the video camera in the corner of the room. We are videotaping this session so that I can use it to help me put together my research report. So, please try not to have side conversations with other group members during this session. This will allow me to be able to hear all of your comments when I go back and review the tape to compile my research report.

First, let's introduce ourselves. My name is Janet, and I am here to lead this group discussion. This is my job. I am a professional moderator and I lead these types of groups all over the country. Today I am very fortunate to be able to lead this group with all of you. Now, let's go around the table and let each of you introduce yourself.

Library Services (20 minutes)

What services do you expect to be available at a local public library? [List on paper taped on walls around the room.]

Which of these services are available to you at this library?

How does this library (the Minchberg Library) compare to what you expect in a library? Better or worse?

Library Usage (20 minutes)

How many of you regularly use this library? [How often?]

Users: Why do you use this library regularly?

Nonusers: Why do you not use this library regularly?

What would make you want to use this library more often/more regularly? [If not mentioned, probe for library hours, wireless Internet access, DVD/CD/game check out, coffee shop/snack bar.]

Please complete the following sentence: "If the Minchberg Library offered _____, I would probably use the Minchberg Library more often."

Library Locations (20 minutes)

Complete the following sentence: "The location of a public library should be _____."

If you were in charge of selecting a new branch location, where would you build it? Why there?

Is having a public library close to your home important to you? Why? Why not?

How close to your home would a public library branch need to be to make you more likely to use it?

Library's Effect on Quality of Life in Our City (20 minutes)

If you were moving to a new city, would the public library have any effect on your decision to move? Why? Why not?

Complete the following sentence: "Having a top-notch public library in town makes me _____."

Does a public library have an effect on a city's image? How?

Does a public library have an effect on the overall quality of life for people who live in that city? How?

Katori's Camera Shop

As another example of a moderator's guide, consider the case of Katori's Camera Shop. The owner of the camera store wanted to learn about consumers' perceptions of, and experiences with, purchasing a new camera from her store.

Group Composition: Consumers who have recently purchased a camera from Katori's Camera Shop.

Introduction and Purchase Decision (25 minutes)

All of you here recently purchased a new digital camera from Katori's Camera Shop. As a way to get started, let's talk about the factors that influenced (1) your decision to buy the digital camera that you purchased, and (2) your decision to purchase it from Katori's Camera Shop (if not raised by the group, probe for the importance of each of the following):

- Location of the store.

- Sales personnel.

- Recommendations from friends, relatives, or other significant individuals.

- Prior experience with Katori's Camera Shop.

- Type of camera desired and how it is to be used.

- Warranty.

- Price.

- Special price discounts or rebates.
- Advertising for Katori's Camera Shop.

Purchase Experience (10 minutes)

Now, let's talk about the actual purchase experience. Was it a pleasant or an unpleasant experience? What did you like about it? What did you not like about it? (Probe: Why? What factors were important in making the experience positive or negative?)

If you could change the purchase experience in any way, what would you change? (Probe: Why? How would this change make a difference?)

Consumer Regret (25 minutes)

How do you feel about your purchase? Are you happy with it? Are you unhappy with it? Do you feel that you got a good deal on your camera purchase? (Probe: Why or why not? What makes you think this?) Would you purchase another camera from Katori's Camera Shop in the future? Would you recommend Katori's Camera Shop to a friend?

Post-Purchase Contact (20 minutes)

Have you had any contact with, or communication from, the store or salespeople since you bought your camera? (Probe: What kind of contact? Was this contact pleasant or unpleasant? Why?)

What do you expect of a camera salesperson during and after the sale? (Probe: How many of you feel these expectations were met by your salesperson?)

Additional Comments (20 minutes)

Is there anything else about your purchase experience that you would like to share that we have not yet discussed?

> Researchers should avoid influencing consumers' thoughts and opinions. Focus group moderators can unintentionally influence participants' thoughts by the clothing the moderator wears, comments the moderator makes, and any brand sensitivities in the focus group facility.

ClarkTown Mall

As another example of a moderator's guide, consider the case of ClarkTown Mall, which is a shopping mall located near a university in a large city. Marketing managers for the mall noticed a growing enrollment at the local university and they wanted to identify new ways to market to the local college students in an effort to increase the amount of shopping that students do at the mall. Marketing managers for the mall wanted to learn more about students' shopping habits and their perceptions of ClarkTown Mall compared to other malls and shopping centers in the area.

Group Composition: Local college students selected from the general population, each participating for the incentive of a $30 gas card. Free pizzas, drinks, and cookies will also be served during the focus group session.

Introduction (5 minutes)

Discuss video and audio recording equipment.

Rules of the session:

- No wrong answers.

- We want to hear your opinions on a number of issues.

- Do not hesitate to tell us everything that you are thinking.

- Talk one at a time.

- Speak into the table microphone.

Introduce participants—name, year in school, where they live, major.

General Shopping Perceptions (10 minutes)

Today we are here to talk about shopping and where you like to go shopping.

What comes to mind when I say "mall/shopping center/lifestyle center"?

What comes to mind when I say "shopping?" Are these positive or negative thoughts?

What do you like about shopping? What do you NOT like about shopping?

Shopping Profile (15 minutes)

What kind of shopper are you (e.g., shopaholic, shop for fun, necessity)?

How often do you go shopping?

What do you go shopping for?

How fashion conscious are you? [(Not) 1 → 10 (Very)]

- Unconcerned with fashion.

- Aware of fashion trends but unmoved by them.

- Mainstream.

- Trendy/fashion forward.

- On the cutting edge.

Where is your favorite place to shop (store, shopping center, mall)? Why?

Does your level of fashion consciousness impact where you like to shop?

What do they have/offer (stores, food, activities, location, parking, etc.)?

What experiences do you like/not like when you are shopping?

When you go shopping, what sorts of experiences are you looking for (ideal shopping experience)?

Identifying Shopping Centers/Malls (15 minutes)

Please tell me all of the shopping centers/malls that you can think of in this local area. What are your perceptions of each of these?

What do they have/not have, provide/not provide?

How often do you shop at these shopping centers/malls? Why? Why not?

What sorts of experiences do you have when you shop there?

Ideal Shopping Center/Mall (15 minutes)

If you could design the ideal shopping center/mall for you (as a college student) what would it look like? What would it have?

- Indoor/outdoor shopping?
- Types (specific) stores?
- Food court/restaurants?
- Activities?

What would you be able to do there?

What types of experiences would you be able to have there?

ClarkTown Mall (CTM) Perceptions (15 minutes)

Have you ever shopped at the CTM? Why? Why not?

If not, why do you shop at other malls/shopping centers? Is transportation an issue?

Stores that you like? Stores you wish they had at CTM?

Food/restaurants you wish they had at CTM?

How is CTM different from other malls/shopping centers?

What would you change about CTM to make you more likely to visit and shop at the CTM?

Advertising (5 minutes)

How do you hear about malls/shopping centers? Advertising? Facebook? Twitter?

What would be the best way for you to hear (learn) about malls/shopping centers?

Advice to ClarkTown Mall Management (10 minutes)

If the marketing manager for the CTM were seated with us today, and he/she wanted college students to shop at CTM more often, what would you tell him/her?

Complete this sentence: "I would shop at the ClarkTown Mall more often if
_____"

Introducing the Focus Group

It is very important that the focus group moderator not influence respondents' answers and comments. Sometimes even the slightest slip of the tongue can have a significant impact on respondents' thoughts. If a moderator accidentally mentions a brand name or mentions a store name, respondents will likely become more aware of that name, and thus pay more attention to it than they otherwise would. If a moderator mentions the brand name Budweiser, consumers will be more likely to mention Budweiser when asked to list the brands of beer that they can think of. As another example, if a moderator mentions the word tennis, respondents might be more likely to mention tennis when asked about the types of sports that they like to play, or even the types of activities that they like to participate in for fun.

Funneling Technique. When introducing respondents to the focus group, moderators should try to be as broad or abstract as possible. For example, if a moderator introduces the focus group by saying, "Today we are here to talk about tennis," this will focus respondents' attention on tennis for the rest of the session. Alternatively, if a moderator introduces the focus group by saying, "Today we are here to talk about the things you like to do for fun," this will not artificially focus respondents' attention on any one activity from the beginning of the session. Use the **funneling technique** by asking very broad questions first, followed by more specific questions later in the session. The moderator might begin by asking, "First, let's talk about the things you like to do for fun." Let respondents mention all activities they consider when seeking to have fun. Take note if tennis is mentioned. If not, this might indicate that respondents do not consider tennis to be in the category of "things I like to do for fun." Manufacturers of tennis equipment would see this as valuable information when designing promotional campaigns to sell tennis equipment and when seeking to increase primary demand for tennis in general. Should tennis be promoted as something people do for fun, or should it be promoted as an exercise?

Frosty Curl Moderator's Guide. To illustrate the use of the funneling technique, consider the case of Frosty Curl ice cream shop. One of Frosty Curl's highest profit margin products is ice cream cakes. They would like to sell more ice cream cakes, but they have noticed that most customers purchase them only for birthdays. They designed some focus groups to identify additional consumption situations for which customers would be willing to purchase a Frosty Curl ice cream cake. Below is the moderator's guide that was developed for these group sessions.

Group Composition: Married women with at least one child (any age).

Introduction (5–10 minutes)

Welcome. Thank you for coming to this group session tonight. Please write your name on the table tent that you see in front of you. We have provided some soft drinks so that you can relax and enjoy yourselves while we are talking with each other tonight. Also, I want you to notice that we will be videotaping this session. You can see the video camera in the corner of the room. We are videotaping this session so that I can use it to help me put together my research report. So, please try not to have side conversations with other group members during this session. This will allow me to be able to hear all of your comments when I go back and review the tape to compile my research report.

First, let's introduce ourselves. My name is Terry and I am here to lead this group discussion. This is my job. I am a professional moderator and I lead these types of groups all over the country. Today I am very fortunate to be able to lead this group with all of you. Now, let's go around the table and let each of you introduce yourself.

Special Occasions (20–30 minutes)

Today we are here to talk about special occasions and celebrations and the types of food that you would expect to serve or eat at such special occasions. So, let's start by first identifying some special occasions or celebrations for which you might expect food to be present.

- List special occasions/celebrations on white board.
- If not listed, add graduations, weddings, anniversaries, birth of baby, Valentine's Day, Christmas Day, New Year's Day, divorce, mortgage "burning."

What types of food would you serve at these occasions?

- List types of food. Probe: Why these foods?

Special Occasion Foods (20 minutes)

Now I will mention some foods and I want you to give me your first reaction to them as a food that could be served for a special occasion/celebration. What special occasion(s) would each be served at and why?

- Chocolate cake, cupcakes, cookies, ice cream cakes.

Frosty Curl Ice Cream Cakes (20–30 minutes)

Now, let's talk more specifically about Frosty Curl ice cream cakes.

- For what special occasions would you buy and serve a Frosty Curl ice cream cake?
- Why? Why not?
- What would make you more likely to purchase a Frosty Curl ice cream cake for some of the previously mentioned special occasions?
- If you were designing an advertisement to sell Frosty Curl ice cream cakes, what would you show/say in the ad?

Focus groups are very different from surveys. Good results from focus groups are obtained by asking very broad questions. In contrast, good results from surveys are obtained by asking very specific, structured, and detailed questions.

Notice that this moderator's guide uses the funneling technique by going from broad to specific, and it also introduces the purpose of the focus group at a very broad level (identifying special occasions) by not mentioning Frosty Curl ice cream cakes until later in the session. It also encourages respondents to generate their own ideas without any ideas being suggested or implied by the moderator before respondents can mention them on their own. Also, by framing the discussion around special occasions, it provides relevant information that marketing managers at Frosty Curl can use to make decisions to market their ice cream cakes.

USE BROAD FOCUS GROUP QUESTIONS

Given their purpose, focus group questions should be relatively broad. For example, "What are some important characteristics that you use in deciding where and how often you go out to eat in the evenings?" is a relatively broad question. Alternatively, "How satisfied are you with the taste of the deli subs at McAllister's Deli?" is a much more specific question. If you ask specific questions about specific brands, stores, or attributes, these questions should be asked at the end of the focus group session. Or, they should be asked only after broader questions have been asked. Specific questions allow you to probe participants' responses to earlier broad questions.

Focus group questions should not provide too many cues about suggested types of responses. For example, imagine that you are interested in opening a new nightclub and you want to know the characteristics of nightclubs that college students perceive to be important. You want to know this so that you can design the nightclub with those characteristics that are important to college students.

Do NOT ask:

How important is it for a nightclub to have each of the following:	Not Important	Somewhat Important	Very Important
Pool tables	☐	☐	☐
Dart boards	☐	☐	☐
Video games	☐	☐	☐
Big screen TVs	☐	☐	☐
Live music	☐	☐	☐

The problem with this highly structured and specific question format is that it can give consumers ideas that they might not have considered on their own. College students might indicate that all of the characteristics you have listed are important. More is usually better than less. Even if students would not have thought about it themselves, they might indicate that video games are important. Another problem with this is that there is no way of determining which of the above characteristics is most important. A person could indicate that both pool tables and dart boards are very important. But, there is no way of knowing which of these two is more important to them.

A better way to ask the question in a focus group is, "What characteristics are important to you in determining the nightclubs you visit?" This broader question forces students to generate only those factors that truly are important to them. And, researchers can infer that the first characteristic a student mentions is most important to them. Thus, this broader question not only measures what students think is important, but also measures the order in which they report these characteristics. After students have been forced to generate their own list of important factors, then more specific questions about a previously identified list of factors can be asked.

This also applies when asking about competition or potential competitors. Ask the focus group question so that subjects must generate their own list of competitors. For instance, ask, "Name all of the nightclubs near campus catering to students." Then ask, "What are your impressions of each of the following nightclubs?"

DO NOT EXPRESS YOUR OPINION IN A FOCUS GROUP

Focus groups are well-suited for measuring consumers' opinions, thoughts, beliefs, and feelings. Avoid expressing the opinion of the researcher or marketer during a focus group. For example, a campus bookstore was conducting some focus groups on students. The moderator asked, "Would you be interested in being able to rent computer software from the bookstore?" A student responded with, "What do you mean? Could we take the software home to use, or would there be space available in the bookstore to use the computers there?" The best response would be for the moderator to say, "Which would you prefer? What would you like to be able to do? And, why?" This allows students to express their opinions without revealing what the bookstore management was considering prior to the focus group. Do not respond with, "We were thinking about providing space in the bookstore for you to use the computers and software there. Would you like that?" This limits students' responses and also limits researchers' ability to identify new marketing opportunities. As another example, a moderator was conducting a focus group dealing with bottled vitamins. At one point during the focus group a consumer asked, "Would these bottles have a screw-top lid, or would they have a flip-top lid?" The best response from the moderator would have been, "Which would you prefer, and why?" Revealing the researcher's opinion during a focus group can cause respondents to alter, bias, and even censor their comments, and thus fail to reveal their true opinions.

Focus groups should not be used as a promotional tool. The purpose of a focus group is to discover consumers' true feelings and thoughts, not to influence them.

LADDERING IN A FOCUS GROUP SESSION

A basic principle of marketing is that marketers sell personal benefits and satisfied values, not products. Consumers do not buy a lawn mower because they want a lawn mower. They buy it because they want their grass cut. Cutting their grass is the benefit of owning a lawn mower. And, even more importantly, they want the best-looking lawn in the neighborhood. Consumers do not buy ¼ inch drill bits. They buy ¼ inch holes. The ability to make a ¼ inch hole is the benefit of purchasing and owning a ¼ inch drill bit.[7]

Means-End Chains. A **means-end chain (MEC)** is a generic framework for analyzing the personal benefits that consumers want from products. The basic idea behind MEC theory is that products are not ends in themselves. Rather, products are merely the means to achieving a desired end. Concrete product attributes and features are the means by which consumers achieve more abstract product benefits and consequences, which in turn are the means by which consumers achieve even more abstract personal goals and values. A generic MEC is of the form shown in Figure 9.3.

Marketers use the concept of a means-end chain when developing marketing campaigns and promotional messages. Often, marketers will promote the personal goals and values associated with product use as opposed to promoting a product's attributes and features. Promotional messages that make connections between concrete product features and more abstract personal goals and values can lead to increased involvement on the part of consumers.[8] When consumers see and comprehend the connection between a product's features and their own personal goals and values, the product becomes more personally relevant to them. As such, they pay more attention to it and the messages that promote it. As an example of promoting abstract personal goals and values, BMW introduced their "Story of Joy" campaign that aired during the 2010 Winter Olympics. The "Story of Joy" television campaign was designed to show images of BMW drivers and their joyful experiences with the car and the brand. The television advertisement contained the following narration, "We realized a long time ago that what you make people feel is just as important as what you make. And at BMW we don't just make cars, we make joy."

FIGURE 9.3 Means-End Chains

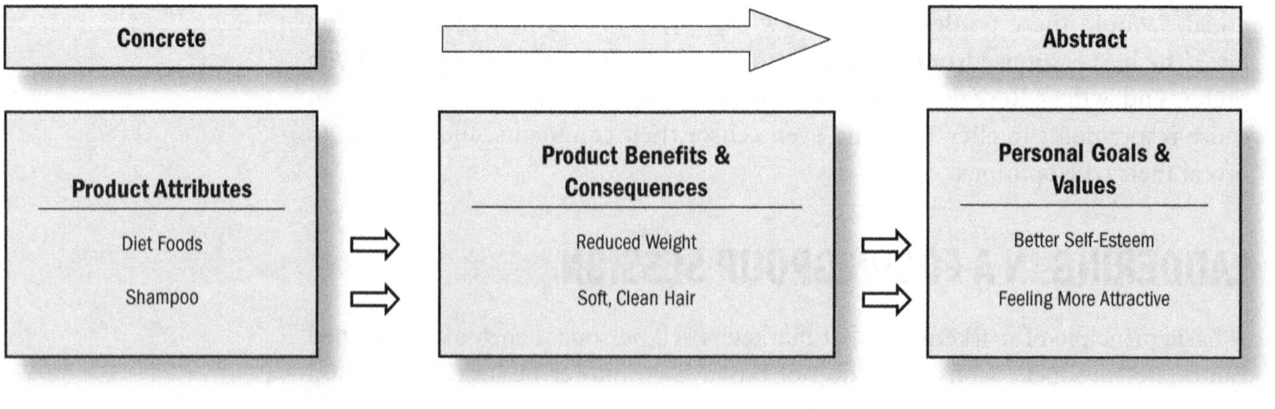

The Laddering Interview. The benefits that consumers are seeking from products can be identified in the context of a focus group by using a **laddering interview** technique.[9] The purpose of a laddering interview is to move consumers up the ladder of abstraction from very concrete **product attributes**, to more abstract **product benefits**, and finally, to highly abstract **personal goals or values**. This is done by continually asking *why* questions. As an example, you might discover that older consumers are very interested in purchasing smartphones so they can communicate with distant relatives and friends, and so they can feel like they are participating more in the lives of their grandchildren who live in a different state. As another example, consider the following partial transcript from a focus group laddering interview:

Researcher: I noticed that you said you prefer AquaFlora Brand laundry detergent. *Why* is that?

Consumer: Because I like the way it smells.

R: What is it about the smell that you like?

C: I like the flowery smell.

R: *Why* do you like the flowery smell?

C: Because it makes me think the clothing is really fresh after being washed.

R: *Why* do you like thinking that your clothes are really fresh?

C: I want my children and husband to feel good in their clothes after I wash them.

R: *Why* do you like that?

C: Because it makes me feel like a better mother.

R: *Why* do you like to feel like a better mother?

C: Because I do.

After conducting this laddering interview the marketer has identified that this particular consumer is looking for a detergent that will make her family's clothing fresh and clean, as well as help her feel like a better mother. The marketer might use these themes in their advertising and use it as a way to position their brand relative to competition.

Notice how the following excerpts from laddering interviews begin with attribute related comments and are then followed up with very personal, self-relevant comments.[10]

- "I buy Maybelline cosmetics because it is a good brand name at a reasonable price." *Why is it being reasonably priced so important to you?* "Well, buying a quality product that isn't high-priced makes me feel good about myself because I am spending my money wisely."

> Perhaps the most important question that a moderator can ask during a focus group session is "Why?"

- "I like to eat Honey Bunches because it tastes good and it fills me up in the morning, so I'm not hungry an hour later." *Why is it important that you are not hungry an hour later?* "First of all, I have more energy and tend to get more accomplished at my job. And, not having to stop work to eat something keeps me working and I get more done at work."

- "Johnson & Johnson's nonallergenic soap is really gentle on my skin and I can buy it almost anywhere I go." *Why should soap be gentle on your skin?* "Since its gentle on my skin, my skin doesn't dry up. I have this self-image of having very soft and delicate skin."

A laddering interview begins by identifying important concrete product attributes or features, and then continues by asking consumers to describe the more abstract benefits and personal goals and values that are associated with these attributes. Identify these important product attributes or features by beginning the laddering interview with the following types of questions:

- What do you like about this product (brand)?

- Why do you think that this product (brand) is a good value for the price?

- What other products (brands) would you consider and why?

- How is this product (brand) similar or dissimilar to other products (brands)?

- What are the important characteristics of this product (brand)?

- What features of this product (brand) do you like best?

- What would it take for you to switch products (brands)?

Subsequent questions should then link back to the attributes or features identified from these questions.

FIGURE 9.4 Dos and Don'ts of Conducting a Laddering Interview

Do	Do Not
Ask questions that will reveal personal reasons for behaviors.	Rush.
Ask questions that cause a person to think and respond with a sentence, not a yes or no.	Ask questions that can be answered with a single word.
Keep asking "Why?"	Force the interviewee to answer the question in a certain way.
Question a person's reasons for his or her responses.	Expect to get to a value in one or two questions.
Allow the questioning to flow, even if the questions are not directly brand related.	Assume that people mean something other than what they say.
Ask questions that give the interviewees freedom to answer the question as they see fit.	Force the issue. Some of the consequences may not lead to where you want to go. Change topics and start again.
Be aware of facial expressions, tone of voice, and gestures as participants answer the questions.	Get discouraged.

Reasons for Attitudes. Researchers should not be content with knowing only consumers' preferences and attitudes. Researchers want to know the reasons behind those preferences and attitudes. Laddering is a way of identifying the desired benefits, goals, and values that determine consumers' preferences and attitudes. Identifying these desired benefits can be very useful in identifying market segments. For example, two consumers might evaluate the same product very differently for very different reasons. A construction foreman might evaluate a new truck with a large eight-cylinder engine very favorably because it would be helpful for hauling heavy equipment. Alternatively, a college student might evaluate the same truck very negatively because it would mean higher gas bills (see Figure 9.5).

Laddering Interviews for Identifying Competitors. It is also important to realize that many different products can lead to the same desired benefit. A laddering interview technique can help marketers identify potential competitors. However, do not think that your competitors are only those other products that are similar to yours. Recognize that consumers buy benefits, not products. As such, marketers sell benefits, not products. Thus, you are competing with other marketers selling the same benefits. For example, a consumer participating in a focus group was asked why he recently purchased a family vacation on a cruise line. He said it was for the purpose of entertainment, recreation, and relaxation. Marketers selling family vacations on cruise lines (competing for consumers' discretionary dollars) should realize that they are competing not only with other cruise lines, but they are also competing with any other products that could also lead to the same benefit. In a broader sense, they are also competing with marketers selling home theater systems and boats because they both provide the same benefit (see Figure 9.6).

FIGURE 9.5 Multiple Benefits from a Single Product

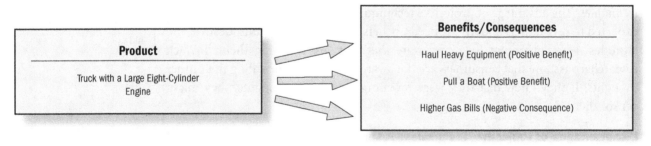

FIGURE 9.6 Multiple Products Providing the Same Benefit

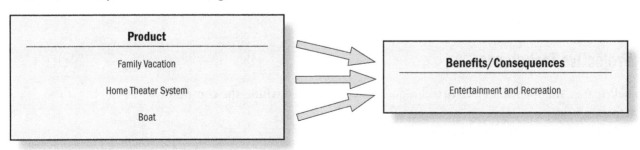

Reverse Laddering Interviews. After identifying the benefits and values that consumers are seeking from a particular product, ask them to identify any other products that can potentially lead to that same benefit. This amounts to a reverse laddering interview. A **reverse laddering interview** works backwards from benefits to identify other products or services that also lead to those same benefits.

PROJECTIVE TECHNIQUES IN FOCUS GROUPS

Projective techniques are a variety of disguised tests that contain ambiguous stimuli such as words, incomplete sentences, pictures, and inkblots.[11] They are designed to measure the underlying motives, opinions, emotions, and beliefs that would normally be concealed or censored. Projective techniques are often used within the context of a focus group. They are very popular because consumers find them to be more enjoyable than traditional surveys. Many researchers find that traditional surveys are too limited in the types of variables that can be measured. For instance, it is very difficult to measure brand personality with paper and pencil surveys. However, projective techniques are very useful for measuring hard to quantify constructs such as purchase motivation, brand image, self-image, perceptions, and product symbolism. Be creative and have fun when designing and conducting projective technique exercises for focus groups. Projective techniques can also be used as a diversion or activity break during a focus group.

Theoretical Basis for Projective Techniques. The theoretical basis for most projective techniques is that a person's inner feelings influence how they perceive ambiguous stimuli. The words people use, the sentences they complete, and even the pictures they draw are projections of their inner thoughts, hence the name *projective techniques*. The advantage of projective techniques is that consumers' responses are expected to reveal their underlying needs, beliefs, motives, fears, wants, desires, and attitudes, whether or not they are aware that they are exposing them. In fact, researchers assume that consumers are not aware that they are revealing their inner thoughts. If they knew that they were revealing their inner thoughts, they might censor them.[12]

> Projective techniques are very useful for uncovering thoughts, feelings, and beliefs that consumers might otherwise try to hide.

Disadvantages of Projective Techniques. A shortcoming of projective techniques is that they are often hard to quantify and analyze. Because of this, the results from most projective techniques are not meant to be quantified. Rather, the results from projective techniques are typically analyzed by looking for common themes that appear in consumers' responses.

Projective Techniques

Below are a number of projective techniques that can be used within the context of a focus group.

Word Association. A **word association** task is very good for identifying brand image and the feasibility of a proposed brand extension. Do not have consumers dwell on a name for a long time. Measure their first responses because consumers do not have much time to dwell on names in most shopping environments (e.g., grocery stores).

What is the first thing that comes to mind when you hear the following:

- Pepsi _____
- Diet Coke _____
- RC Cola _____

Story/Sentence Completion. A **story or sentence completion** exercise is similar to a word association except that consumers complete sentences or stories.

- A person would go to The Comedy Club when they _____.
- People who shop at Miller's Grocery Store are _____.
- The local Channel 5 News broadcast is most liked by _____.

Third Person Technique. A **third person technique** is when consumers are asked to respond for a third person. They are asked to describe why another consumer thinks, feels, believes, or behaves in a certain way. People tend to be more honest when discussing why someone else purchased a product than when discussing why they purchased a product. For example, a consumer who tells a researcher "I bought my BMW because of its performance and resale value, but my neighbor bought his just to impress people," might be revealing that impressing people also played a role in his purchase decision.

- Why do you think other people purchase BMWs?
- Why did that lady in the advertisement decide to shop at Wal-Mart?
- Why do other consumers shop at Sophisticated Fashions?

Role Playing. **Role playing** is a way for consumers to reveal their true feelings without actually expressing them verbally. For example, consumers might not want to tell researchers that they think Wal-Mart employees are stupid and arrogant, but they might act stupid and arrogant during a role-playing exercise.

- Act out the role of a McDonald's drive-thru order taker.
- Act out the role of a Wal-Mart sales clerk.
- Act out the role of a Honda salesperson.

Brand Personality. A **brand personality** exercise is another good technique for measuring **brand image**. Consumers are asked to describe a brand as a person, object, or animal. Researchers look for the characteristics of animals or objects that seem to be manifest in the brand being described. For example, it is less important to know that respondents described Honda as a dog, than it is to know that they perceive dogs as possessing the qualities of loyalty, faithfulness, and reliability.

- If Budweiser were an animal, it would be a _____.

- If Porsche were an animal, it would be a _____.

- If Honda were an animal, it would be a _____.

- Describe a day in the life of Pepsi.

- If NASCAR were here in this room, describe him or her.

Collages and Photo Sorts. Making **collages** and **photo sort** exercises are fun research techniques designed to measure perceptions of brands. Consumers cut out pictures that represent a particular brand and then paste the pictures onto a collage representing brand images, product symbolism, or even consumption situations. Consumers then discuss why they chose those images and how they relate to the brand. In a photo sort, consumers are given photographs of people showing various demographics, moods, situations, lifestyles, and settings. They are then asked to select and explain why (and how) certain photographs represent a brand and the meaning of that brand.

Psycho Drawings. A **psycho drawing** is a fun exercise where consumers are asked to draw pictures that represent brands, consumers, and even purchase and usage situations. Consumers often have difficulty describing brands or stores using adjectives. However, a picture is worth a thousand words. Look for common elements or themes that appear in the drawings.

- Draw a picture of the typical BMW owner.

- Draw a picture of the typical Honda Civic owner.

- Draw a picture of a consumer entering the First American Bank.

Thematic Apperception Test. In a **thematic apperception test (TAT)**, consumers are given a picture and must interpret what is happening in the picture, describe what the characters in the picture are thinking or saying, or tell a story about the picture. These pictures can be in the form of comics where the text bubble leading from a person's mouth is empty. Consumers must fill in what the person is saying or thinking.

- Interpret what is happening in this picture.

- Write down what the person in this picture is saying.

The picture in Figure 9.7 could be used as a thematic apperception test in a focus group for a restaurant. It could be used to measure business executives' perceptions of a restaurant. Focus group participants could be instructed to write down what the other two people in this picture are saying if one of these three people says, "Let's celebrate this deal by going out to dinner at The Prince Manor Restaurant."

FIGURE 9.7 Thematic Apperception Test to Measure Perceptions of a Restaurant

Debate Sessions. A **debate session** can be used for products as well as organizations. Divide participants into groups and assign each group one side of an issue. The moderator asks questions and directs the debate. Listen for each group's arguments and messages to assess what they understand about the issue.

ONLINE FOCUS GROUPS

Online focus groups have been a growing trend in the last few years. For example, **itracks.com** (**www.itracks.com**) provides online focus group services. Invoke Solutions (**www.invokesolutions.com**) also provides online focus group sessions. Their **Invoke Engage** platform allows marketers to conduct online focus groups of up to 500 participants who can log on at their convenience. During the online group session participants interact with other participants as well as with the session moderator. They respond to open-ended and closed-ended questions dealing with concepts, new product ideas, and even multimedia stimuli, including pictures, videos, audio, and websites. As with a traditional focus group, a session can last for up to 90 minutes.

Concerns that online research will be able to study only the most technically minded consumers (techies) have declined over the years as more and more consumers and business people become accustomed to working and interacting via the Internet. However, the obvious advantages of online focus groups, such as no geographical limitations and ease of use, are accompanied by a number of unanswered questions about online qualitative research that deserve further study. These include:[13]

- Are respondents who they really say they are?

- Is the information they provide when signing up on the database or at the time of screening for a particular focus group true?

- How can we be sure that someone else hasn't substituted for them?

- How often should online respondents participate?

- Are participants signing up regularly because they enjoy the experience or are they merely seeking the incentive?

- Are online focus groups less likely to experience bias resulting from group dynamics? Or, do they merely have different group dynamics and biases compared to in-person focus groups?

- Does the anonymity of a screen name make online respondents more honest, saying what's really on their minds rather than being polite?

- Does the anonymity of being online make respondents more open and honest about sensitive subjects?

- Is the bluntness in chat rooms true candor, or is it just rudeness?

- Are focus groups in this interactive medium truly interactive?

- How much moderator–respondent and respondent–respondent interaction really takes place if respondents are busy typing?

- Can researchers and observers gain a clear sense of individual respondents the way they can in physical observation?

- What ways can be found to encourage respondents to give longer answers?

- How much is lost by the absence of body language and vocal inflection?

Online focus groups, such as those conducted by Invoke Solutions (www.invokesolutions.com) are an effective means of obtaining feedback and opinions from a large number of consumers in a short period of time.

POST-GROUP EVALUATION

After conducting a focus group, it is important to evaluate the session and the information that was obtained from it. This can be done by asking the following questions:

- What did we see in this session?

- What did we hear in this session?

- What can we conclude from this session?

- What questions did this focus group session answer for us?

- What questions did this focus group session not answer for us?

- What do we know now that we did not know before the focus group session?

- What questions do we have now that we did not have prior to this focus group session?

- Are there additional focus groups that must be conducted to further explore any issues?

FOCUS GROUPS AND CONCLUSIVE EVIDENCE

Interpreting the results from a focus group can be tricky. Given their nature, the small sample size for focus groups suggests that they are not designed to provide conclusive evidence regarding marketing management decisions. One should not overstate the importance of comments made by only a handful of customers. On the other hand, one should not understate the importance of comments made by focus group participants if these views are shared by the majority of customers. The results from a focus group should be subsequently confirmed with a survey of a much larger sample.

QUESTIONS FOR DISCUSSION

1. What are some characteristics of consumers that marketers can measure using focus groups that they cannot measure using surveys?

2. Why do you think that focus groups are popular as a method of conducting marketing research?

3. Lois wants to conduct some focus groups to identify the issues and features that are most important to consumers when they purchase a new camera. But, she can't decide how to ask the question. Which of the following questions (either a or b) would you suggest she use in the focus group, and why?
   a. How important is each of the following features to you in deciding which camera to purchase: price, warranty, top shutter speed, exposure compensation, spot-metering capability?
   b. What features are important to you in deciding which camera to purchase?

4. In your own words, describe projective techniques. Why do you think that they are popular with marketing researchers as a way to gather information from, and about, consumers?

5. If you were calling consumers on the phone to recruit them for a focus group, would it be a good idea to ask them, "Describe your last vacation" as part of the screening survey?

6. A consumer participating in one of your focus groups mentions that he hates your product and would never use it. Would it be a good idea to try to change his mind and convince him that your product is a good product worthy of being purchased?

7. Find an advertisement for a product that shows how purchasing a product will help consumers achieve a very personal goal or value. How could marketing researchers identify these types of personal goals or values that consumers are seeking from purchasing products?

8. Should focus groups be used as a promotional tool for selling products? What are the potential advantages and disadvantages of using focus groups to sell products? What are the potential ethical issues involved in using focus groups to sell products?

9. Haggar is considering introducing a new line of men's clothing. They decide to conduct a focus group interview to measure possible reactions to the new clothing line. Haggar invites 25 men, and tries to make the group as heterogeneous as possible (i.e., they try to invite men who have unique backgrounds and characteristics). Is this a good idea?

10. Describe how decisions regarding focus groups (setting up a focus group, screening participants, types of questions asked during a focus group, composition of the focus group) can affect the managerial decision-making process.

11. The chapter identified a number of articulation questions that could be asked during a telephone screening survey. Identify at least two other open-ended articulation questions that could be used in a focus group telephone screening survey.

12. Identify and describe some projective techniques, exercises, or activities that can be conducted within the context of a focus group to address each of the following situations.
    a. Quaker Oats would like to extend the brand name Quaker into the fresh vegetable category. But, they must first learn what the brand name Quaker means to consumers.
    b. Hyundai wants to better identify the personality of its car buyers and the perceived image of Hyundai among consumers.
    c. Shoney's wants to better understand consumers' positive and negative perceptions of their customer service personnel, such as hostesses and servers.

d. Colgate wants to better understand the tooth brushing experience and the images and feelings associated with brushing one's teeth.

e. O'Charley's wants to better understand consumers' perceptions of its restaurant and identify the situations when consumer would, and would not, consider eating at an O'Charley's restaurant.

13. For each of the brands referred to below in laddering interviews (Maybelline, Honey Bunches, and Johnson & Johnson's):

a. Develop a 30-second television commercial promoting the brand using the themes identified from the laddering interview. What is the main theme of the commercial? What information do you want consumers to "take away" from the commercial? What is the main benefit you are selling in the commercial? How does the commercial help position the brand, create an image for the brand, or create a personality for the brand?

b. Develop a web page for the brand. What information will you place on the web page? What is the main benefit you are selling on the web page? What graphics or links to other websites will you place on the web page? How does the web page help position the brand, create an image for the brand, or create a personality for the brand?

- "I buy Maybelline cosmetics because it is a good brand name at a reasonable price." *Why is it being reasonably priced so important to you?* "Well, buying a quality product that isn't high-priced makes me feel good about myself because I am spending my money wisely."

- "I like to eat Honey Bunches because it tastes good and it fills me up in the morning, so I'm not hungry an hour later." *Why is it important that you are not hungry an hour later?* "First of all, I have more energy and tend to get more accomplished at my job. And, not having to stop work to eat something keeps me working and I get more done at work."

- "Johnson & Johnson's nonallergenic soap is really gentle on my skin and I can buy it almost anywhere I go." *Why should soap be gentle on your skin?* "Since its gentle on my skin, my skin doesn't dry up. I have this self-image of having very soft and delicate skin."

MINICASE 9.1

Jack Daniel's Focus Group

You have recently been hired by Jack Daniel's to coordinate their marketing research efforts related to sponsoring NASCAR teams and NASCAR events. One of your first duties is to oversee the focus groups that were developed and planned by your predecessor. While becoming acquainted with the research project you are able to meet with the moderator that your predecessor hired to conduct all of the focus group sessions that will be conducted at various cities across the country. The moderator's name is Kyle Heusen, and he has lived in southern California all of his life. Kyle informs you that he likes to take a few minutes before every focus group session to "get into his karma." He also likes to wear flowery shirts and sandals during a session. He believes that this projects a "positive energy throughout the room." He never wears a tie or jeans. You have also noticed that the first focus group is scheduled for Birmingham, Alabama. The focus group is scheduled to include eight men between the ages of 35 and 50 who are regular drinkers of whiskey and who are avid NASCAR fans.

What do you do, if anything? Are you concerned about anything related to these group sessions?

MINICASE 9.2

King Pin Lanes

King Pin Lanes has been in business for 17 years. King Pin Lanes is a bowling alley located near the downtown business district of a city with a population of 200,000 people. King Pin Lanes offers 16 bowling lanes and a concession stand that sells candy, snacks, pizza slices, and soft drinks. There is also a small game room with 12 video game machines. Managers at King Pin Lanes have noticed that sales have declined steadily during the last few years. Fewer and fewer people are coming to King Pin Lanes to bowl. Managers at King Pin Lanes have contacted you about conducting some focus groups to identify potential problems that could be the causes for decreasing sales at King Pin Lanes and potential solutions to these problems. Specifically, they have asked for your help with the following:

1. Designing the screener questionnaire to identify the appropriate participants.

2. Developing the moderator's guide, including the questions to be asked and any exercises to be conducted during the focus group.

3. Determining if there is a need for multiple focus groups. If so, determining if a different moderator's guide is needed for each group.

4. Deciding where the focus group(s) will be conducted.

5. Deciding if participants will be compensated for attending. If so, how much?

MINICASE 9.3

InTech Inline Skates

InTech is a relatively small marketer of inline skates. As a way to differentiate themselves from competition and to gain market share, they have developed a strategy to market a brand of inline skates specifically to older Americans (50 and older) as a means of staying healthy and physically fit, even in older years. However, they do not know if this strategy will be successful. They have hired you as a marketing research consultant. They want you to develop a moderator's guide that they can use for a focus group. They do not know much about the older market. They would like to assess the potential success of this new marketing strategy and identify specific marketing approaches that would be best for marketing a line of inline skates to older Americans.

1. Design the screener questionnaire to identify the appropriate participants.

2. Design the moderator's (discussion) guide for the focus group.

MINICASE 9.4

HealthSource

HealthSource would like to investigate the potential success of a new chain of health clubs targeted specifically to older Americans (50 and older). HealthSource has noticed the success of other marketers who target specific groups of consumers, thereby gaining a competitive advantage as a niche marketer. For example, Curves is a health club targeted specifically to women. Sport Clips is a hair salon/barber shop targeted specifically to men who like sports. Unfortunately, HealthSource does not know much about the older market. They have hired you as a marketing research consultant to develop a moderator's guide for a focus group. The purpose of the focus group is to measure the potential success of this new chain of health clubs targeted toward older Americans and identify marketing strategies for promoting it to older Americans.

a. Design the screener questionnaire to identify the appropriate participants.

b. Design the moderator's (discussion) guide for the focus group.

ENDNOTES

1 "GreenBook Research Industry Trends Report," Winter 2013, **www.GRITreport.org**

2 For a more complete discussion of focus groups, see Richard A. Krueger, *Focus Groups: A Practical Guide for Applied Research*, 2nd ed. (Thousand Oaks, CA: Sage Publications, 1994).

3 Naomi R. Henderson, "Trained Moderators Boost the Value of Qualitative Research," *Marketing Research*, June 1992, 20.

4 Nelson E. James and Nancy Frontczak, "How Acquaintanceship and Analyst Can Influence Focus Group Results," *Journal of Advertising*, 17 (1988): 41–48.

5 Krueger, *Focus Groups: A Practical Guide for Applied Research*, 2nd ed. (Thousand Oaks, CA: Sage Publications, 1994).

6 Thomas L. Greenbaum, *Moderating Focus Groups: A Practical Guide for Group Facilitation* (Thousand Oaks, CA: Sage Publications, 2000).

7 Timothy R. Graeff, "Product Comprehension and Promotional Strategies," *Journal of Consumer Marketing*, 12 no. 2 (1995): 28–39.

8 Graeff, "Product Comprehension and Promotional Strategies," *Journal of Consumer Marketing*, 12 no. 2 (1995): 28–39; Timothy R. Graeff, "Comprehending Product Attributes and Benefits: The Role of Product Knowledge and Means-End Chain Inferences," *Psychology & Marketing*, 14 no. 2 (1997): 163–183.

9 Thomas L. Greenbaum, *The Handbook for Focus Group Research*, 2nd ed. (Thousand Oaks, CA: Sage Publications, 1998).

10 Brian Wansink, "New Techniques To Generate Key Marketing Insights," *Marketing Research*, Summer 2000, 28–36.

11 Harold H. Kassarjian, "Projective Methods," in Robert Ferber, ed., *Handbook of Marketing Research* (New York: McGraw-Hill, 1974), 3–87; Sidney J. Levy, "Dreams, Fairy Tales, Animals, and Cars," *Psychology and Marketing*, 2 (Summer 1985): 67–82.

12 Robert K. Schnee, "Quality Research: Going Beyond the Obvious," *Journal of Advertising Research*, 28 (February–March 1988, 9-12.

13 Judith Langer, "On and Offline Focus Groups: Claims, Questions," *Marketing News*, June 5, 2000, H38; see **www .langerassc.com**

CHAPTER 10

Quantitative Research Objectives

LEARNING OBJECTIVES

1 Discus why measurable quantitative research objectives are important to marketing researchers when designing surveys.

2 Describe the characteristics of measurable research objectives.

3 Define categorical variable and continuous variable.

4 Define independent variable and dependent variable.

5 Discuss how models of the consumer purchase and adoption process can be used to identify research objectives.

6 Define gap analysis and describe how a gap analysis can help to identify marketing problems and opportunities.

7 Compare and contrast customer service with customer satisfaction.

8 Describe a customer contact (service) audit.

9 Describe when marketing researchers should measure past behavior, when they should measure present behavior, and when they should measure future (expected) behavior on surveys.

10 Compare and contrast attitudes and behavioral intentions.

11 Describe the process by which marketing researchers can measure behavioral intentions on surveys.

12 Describe the characteristics of good research hypotheses.

As previously discussed, the three main classes of marketing research are exploratory research, descriptive research, and causal research. Marketing research projects often progress by first using the qualitative results from exploratory research to identify key variables that are of interest to marketers. Then, descriptive research is used to describe target markets on those key variables. Thus, the results from exploratory research are often used to develop subsequent quantitative research objectives that can be measured using surveys. The results from a focus group are often very helpful in determining what information needs to be obtained from a survey. But, this need for information must be translated into specific and measurable quantitative research objectives for surveys. Before designing and administering a survey, researchers must know exactly what information they want to obtain from a survey and the form in which they want the information.

Measurable Research Objectives. **Quantitative research objectives** and **hypotheses** must be stated in clear and measurable terms. However, stating research objectives in clear and measurable terms is not as easy as it might appear. For example, stating that the objective of a survey is to measure the effectiveness of two different advertisements is not a good research objective. The problem with this research objective is that it does not specify how effectiveness is to be measured. Effectiveness can be measured in many different ways. It can be measured in terms of day-after recall, consumers' attitudes toward the advertisements, consumers' attitudes toward the brands, or even consumers' purchase intentions. A research objective is measurable only after it specifies what is to be measured. This means that an objective must specify how it will be **operationalized**. Quantitative research objectives should specify who you are researching, the relevant variables you are measuring, and what will be calculated from the data. By specifying this, researchers then know how to ask the question on a survey and the type, or level, or scale to use when asking the survey question.

Who Are the Subjects of the Research?. Research objectives should clearly identify the specific people who are the subjects of the research. For example, do you want to measure the attitudes of all consumers, or the attitudes of only female consumers between the ages of 18 and 35? Do you want to measure the attitudes of everyone on your college campus, or the attitudes of only freshman and sophomore students? Identifying the specific subjects for a survey helps in later stages of the research process when researchers develop sampling plans and procedures and develop specific data collection procedures and methodologies.

What Relevant Variables Are to Be Measured?. A **variable** is anything that varies or changes in value, or that can assume different numerical or categorical values. As such, a consumer is not a variable. But, a consumer's income is a variable because it can change or take on different values. Similarly, a university student is not a variable. But, a university student's attitude toward a new business is a variable.

Categorical variables are those that can take on only a small, limited number of values. A person's sex, a person's occupation, a person's year in school, and even the brand of car a person owns are categorical variables. Usually, closed-ended survey questions that offer a choice of categories from which to choose measure categorical variables. For example, measuring age by forming categories, such as *Less than 18*, *18–25*, *26–30*, and so on, yields a categorical variable.

Conversely, **continuous variables** are those that can take on many values that represent a relative placement along a single continuum or a single dimension. In some cases continuous variables can take on an almost unlimited number of values. A person's age, a person's income, the time it takes someone to drive to work, and the distance someone lives from a retail store can be measured as continuous variables. Usually, numerical open-ended survey questions that provide only a blank space on which respondents are to enter a number, or enter an amount, measure continuous variables. Measuring age by allowing respondents to write in their age ("What is your age? _____") yields a continuous variable. Note, however, that while continuous variables can be measured as categorical variables (e.g., measuring age by forming categories such as *Less than 18, 18–25, 26–30*, and so on), categorical variables cannot be measured as continuous variables. You cannot measure a person's sex as a continuous variable.

Independent variables are those variables that the researcher can manipulate independently of other variables. Independent variables are thought to have causal effects on other dependent variables. The four Ps of the marketing mix (price, product, promotion, and place) are independent variables because they can be manipulated independently of other variables to have a causal effect on sales. Other independent variables include income, age, occupation, and where consumers live.

Dependent variables are those variables for which their value, or level, is dependent upon the manipulation of other independent variables. Sales and market share are considered dependent variables because they change, or vary, based on changes in other variables. The value of a dependent variable is dependent upon the causal effect of at least one independent variable. Attitudes, purchase frequency, and number of customer complaints are also considered dependent variables.

What Will Be Calculated from the Data? How will the variable be measured and what analysis will be performed on the resulting data? Is the researcher interested in measuring the average age of consumers, or the percentage of consumers who say that they are very likely to purchase a new product? Specifying what is to be calculated, either an average or a percentage, determines the type of measurement scale needed to measure the variable and to allow that type of analysis to be performed on the data. A more detailed discussion of measurement scales is provided in chapter 13.

> Research objectives should state:
> 1 The subjects of the research.
> 2 The relevant variables to be measured.
> 3 The calculations to be performed on the data.

IDENTIFYING RESEARCH OBJECTIVES

It is usually more difficult to decide what questions to ask than it is to get answers to those questions. Gathering information is often easy. Deciding what information needs to be gathered is usually more difficult. Be specific about what you want to know before you ask for it. Otherwise, you might just measure the wrong thing. You might spend a significant amount of money, time, and effort gathering information to solve the wrong problem. Be careful what you say you want to measure in your objectives, because you just might get it. Vague objectives usually result in vague results. Specific research objectives yield more useful information for decision making. For example, discovering that 90 percent of students rent DVDs tells you very little about students' DVD rental behaviors. How often do students rent DVDs? How many DVDs do students rent? When was the last time students rented

DVDs? Notice that the vague objective does not provide answers to these questions. Alternatively, discovering that 90 percent of students rent at least two DVDs every week tells you much more about students' DVD rental behaviors.

The primary purpose of this chapter is to present some helpful hints and suggestions for identifying quantitative research objectives. Of course, the objectives for any survey will vary according to the specific situation. But, there are a number of general guides, frameworks, and models that marketing researchers can use to help them identify important research objectives.

RESEARCH OBJECTIVES AND THE DECISION-MAKING PROCESS

Perhaps the most important consideration in determining quantitative research objectives is the overall marketing objective. Recall the IDO model of marketing research and the decision-making process shown in Figure 10.1. Be aware of the marketing objectives and the specific decisions that need to be made to achieve these marketing objectives. What information do marketing managers need to be able to make the decisions designed to achieve these marketing objectives?

Always keep in mind that the purpose of marketing research is to collect and provide information that marketing managers can use when making marketing decisions. Always keep these marketing decisions in mind when designing marketing research. Ask yourself:

- What is the purpose of this research?

- What decision(s) will be made as a result of this research?

- What decision(s) will be guided by this research?

- How will the information from this particular research objective help make these marketing decisions?

FIGURE 10.1 The IDO Model

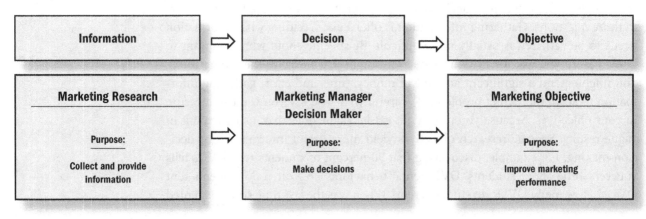

Try to keep your research **goal-directed** and **decision-oriented**. If a research objective does not help achieve the goal of making a particular decision, then it should not be asked on a survey.

THE CONSUMER PURCHASE PROCESS

A generic model of the **consumer purchase process** can be used as a helpful framework for identifying quantitative research objectives.

Prepurchase. Analyze consumers' prepurchase behaviors for products including various aspects of problem recognition and search behavior. Identify consumers' knowledge and preference for various brands. Where do consumers search for information? How do consumers learn about various purchase alternatives? What do they know about various brands, stores, or services?

Purchase. Focus on how consumers evaluate various alternatives. Where do they buy their products? What criteria do they use in evaluating different brands? How do they pay for these brands? How often do they buy these brands? How much are they willing to pay for different brands? Why do they buy different brands?

Consumption. Explore how consumers use your products. How and when do they use your products? In what consumption situations do they use your products? Are different products or brands purchased for different usage situations?

Postpurchase. Explore consumers' postpurchase behaviors including various behaviors unique to your market. How satisfied are consumers with different brands? What are consumers' future purchase intentions? How do consumers communicate their level of satisfaction or dissatisfaction?

Marketing Problems and Opportunities. Identify marketing problems and opportunities facing you as a marketer. Identify what implications these problems or opportunities have for you in developing a strategic marketing plan. How does your brand compare to the competitor's brand? How is your brand different from other brands? Are there any consumer needs and desires that are not being fulfilled by existing brands?

Customer Characteristics. Identify the important characteristics of consumers in your market. These characteristics might include demographic, psychographic, lifestyle, personality, or behavioral dimensions. Identify potential segments and bases for segmenting markets.

CONSUMER ADOPTION PROCESS MODELS

Another way to identify important research objectives is to consider models of the **consumer adoption process**. Such models describe the process by which consumers try new products, use products, adopt new products, and eventually become brand-loyal consumers.

- **Exposure**: Are consumers exposed to your product information?

- **Awareness**: Are consumers aware of your product information? Do they pay attention to your product information?

- **Interest**: Are consumers interested in trying and purchasing your product?

- **Trial**: Is product trial easy? How much financial risk is involved in purchasing your product for the first time?

- **Desire**: Do consumers want your product?

- **Intention**: Have consumers built up an intention to purchase your product?

- **Ability**: Do consumers have the financial ability to purchase your product?

- **Action**: Is it easy for consumers to purchase your product? Is it readily available and easily obtained?

Poor marketing performance, such as low sales or low store traffic, can result from problems at any of the above stages in the adoption process. For example, consumers might want a product (desire), but not have enough money to purchase the product (ability). Consumers might not buy a product because they never pay attention to advertising for that product (awareness) even though they are exposed to the advertising (exposure). Alternatively, consumers might want to buy a product (intention), and have enough money to buy the product (ability), but cannot buy the product because it is not sold in stores that are convenient to them (action). Also, consider the attitudes, beliefs, behaviors, opinions, perceptions, buyer demographic characteristics, and marketer-controlled variables such as the marketing mix elements that might affect each of the above stages.

> One of the best ways to identify important research objectives is to consider the process by which consumers try, purchase, consume, adopt, and dispose of products.

THE FUNDAMENTAL QUESTIONS FOR MARKETERS

Below are some of the fundamental questions that marketers might want to have answered. Consider these questions when developing research objectives.

- Who are our customers?

- Where are our customers?

- What do our customers want?

- What are our customers buying?

- When do our customers want it?

- When are our customers buying it?

- Where are our customers buying it?

- Why are our customers buying it?

- Why are consumers not buying it?

- How are our customers buying it?

- How often are our customers buying it?

- Who is buying the product?

- Who is using the product?

- Who disposes of the product after use?

- Who makes the decision to purchase the product?

- Who initiates the purchase decision process?

- How are our customers using the product?

- In what situations do our customers purchase and use the product?

- Who are our loyal customers?

- Why would customers buy our product again?

- Why would customers not buy our product again?

- How do consumers communicate their purchase and use experiences to us?

- How do consumers communicate their purchase and use experiences to other consumers?

- What other similar or competing products do customers buy?

IF I COULD ASK ONLY ONE QUESTION, WHAT WOULD I ASK?

A useful exercise for identifying research objectives is to ask the following series of questions.

- If I were allowed to ask only one question on the survey, what would I ask?

- If I were allowed to ask one more question, what would I ask?

- If I were allowed to ask a third question, what would I ask?

- And so on.

Answering these questions will help to identify and prioritize the research objectives that are most important. This can be very helpful when trying to limit the length of your survey. If you have 20 research objectives, but you determine that you can ask only five questions (corresponding to five research objectives), this helps identify the five questions you should ask (corresponding to the five most important research objectives).

CONSIDER THE USEFULNESS OF RESEARCH OBJECTIVES

To shorten a list of research objectives, try to predict the usefulness of the information that each objective will yield. For example, consider a marketer who is interested in opening a new bagel shop in a small town. She wants to conduct some surveys of local townspeople to estimate demand for this new bagel shop. Thus, the purpose of the research is to help her make a business investment decision: "Should I open this new business?" As part of her research objectives she states that she wants to know consumers' preferred flavor of bagel. Although interesting, this information will not help her make her business investment decision. Thus, it should not be asked at this stage in developing her new business. Note, however, that this information will probably become very important after she decides to open the bagel shop. Thus, it can become an important objective for subsequent research.

DO NOT RELY SOLELY ON PREDICTOR VARIABLES

Marketers often find themselves trying to measure **predictor variables** (independent variables) of a key variable (dependent variable) rather than directly measuring that key variable. For example, consider a marketer who was interested in starting a computer dating service on a college campus. He decided that one of his main objectives was to measure the percentage of students from out of state. He reasoned that students from out of state probably know very few other people on campus, and therefore, they would be likely to use a computerized dating service. The problem with this is that the key variable of interest was actually the percentage of students who know fewer than 10 other students on campus, regardless of whether or not they were from out of state. Do not dance around the issue trying to measure indicators of key variables of interest when you can directly measure those key variables of interest. Think about what a survey question will tell you. Then, if a more direct question can be asked, go ahead and ask that more direct question. Think about the key aspect of consumers' attitudes or behaviors that a survey question is designed to predict. Then, if that aspect of consumers' attitudes or behaviors can be measured more directly, go ahead and ask the more direct question. The only time that researchers should measure only predictors of key variables is when those key variables cannot be measured directly.

As another example, consider a marketer who was deciding whether or not to open a bicycle rental service near a university. Students could rent a bicycle for a semester and ride it to and from campus. She decided to measure only three variables on her survey: (1) the percentage of students who live less than two miles from campus, (2) the percentage of students who have difficulty finding parking on campus, and (3) the percentage of students who like to ride bicycles. She reasoned that those students who live close to campus, who have trouble finding a parking space, and who like to ride bicycles would be likely to use her bicycle rental service. Thus, these three variables were designed to predict students' willingness to rent a bicycle. This is illustrated Figure 10.2.

Questions 1, 2, and 3 in Figure 10.2 were designed to predict whether or not students would rent a bicycle. However, the key variable of interest was actually whether or not a student would rent a bicycle. If she could ask only one question on the survey, she should ask the question, "Would you be willing to rent a bicycle?" However, it is often useful to ask questions 1, 2, and 3 because they can help explain the results from other questions on the survey. For example, consider the results shown in Table 10.1 for situation A. If only 5 percent of students surveyed said that they would be willing to rent a bicycle, the answers to questions 1, 2, and 3 can help explain this low percentage. If only 9 percent of students live within two miles of campus, only 3 percent of students have difficulty finding a parking space, and only 4 percent of students like to ride a bicycle, this explains the low percentage of students willing to rent a bicycle.

Now, consider the results shown for situation B. In situation B, 5 percent of students would rent a bicycle. But, 70 percent of students live within two miles of campus, 85 percent of students have difficulty finding a parking space, and 80 percent of students like to ride a bicycle. This indicates that there might be some aspect of the marketing mix that is leading to this low level of interest. All of the indicator variables suggest potential demand for the bicycle rental business. Therefore, the low willingness to rent a bicycle might be due to problems with specific aspects of her

FIGURE 10.2 Independent Variables that Predict a Dependent Variable

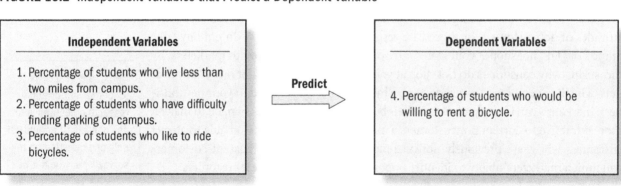

TABLE 10.1 Results from the Bicycle Rental Service Survey

Survey Question	Situation A	Situation B
1. Percentage of students who live less than two miles from campus.	9%	70%
2. Percentage of students who have difficulty finding parking on campus.	3%	85%
3. Percentage of students who like to ride bicycles.	4%	80%
4. Percentage of students who would be willing to rent a bicycle.	5%	5%

marketing plan, such as a price that is too expensive, an inconvenient location for picking up the bicycles, or even the wrong style of bicycles.

CONSIDER THE DECISION MAKER

Keep in mind how the decision maker will use the results from the research. This can affect whether you measure categorical variables or continuous variables. For example, consider the difference between measuring consumers' attitudes toward a restaurant on a continuous 7-point attitude scale, where 1 = dislike and 7 = like, compared to a simple categorical scale which asks, "Will you eat at this restaurant again?" Many managers will have difficulty understanding that the average rating on the 7-point scale was a 3.2. What does a 3.2 mean? Alternatively, they most certainly will understand if you report that only 12 percent of customers said that they would eat at this restaurant again. Even though attitudes can be measured as continuous variables, it is sometimes better to measure attitudes as a categorical variable using a simple yes or no question. The decision to measure variables as categorical or continuous variables will depend on how the measurements are to be analyzed and used in the decision-making process.

DO NOT FORGET TO SURVEY NONCUSTOMERS

Marketing researchers are very interested in measuring the attitudes and perceptions of their current customers. Customer satisfaction surveys can be effectively used for this purpose. However, do not forget about consumers who are not your customers. The attitudes of noncustomers, or those who respond to a survey with, "I do not buy your brand," or "I do not shop at your stores" are sometimes of most interest to marketers. By measuring why consumers do not shop at your stores, why they do not buy your products, why they do not use your service, or why they are not interested in your new business, marketers can identify aspects of their business that need to be changed to make it more attractive to current noncustomers. Growth can come from being able to attract customers who were previously noncustomers. Researching only current customers will limit a marketers' ability to identify opportunities for making new customers.

One of the best ways to identify important research objectives is to ask oneself, "If I could ask only one question on the survey, what would it be?"

DO NOT CONFUSE CUSTOMER SERVICE WITH CUSTOMER SATISFACTION

Marketers frequently conduct **customer satisfaction surveys**.[1] This is especially true of businesses with a high degree of customer contact, such as retail businesses. However, many marketers fall into the trap of confusing **customer service**, which is the actual service provided by the business to the customer, with **customer satisfaction**, which is the level of customers' satisfaction with the service provided by the marketer. In reality, customer service and customer satisfaction are distinctly different variables that should be measured separately.

Marketers should never confuse customer service with customer satisfaction.

Customer Service vs. Customer Satisfaction. To illustrate the difference between customer service and customer satisfaction, consider the case of a woman who called a local car dealer to inquire about getting an oil change for her car. On the phone she asked, "Can I come in and get my car's oil changed?" The response she received was, "Sure, come on in, we should be able to take you right away." But, when she arrived she had to wait 18 minutes before they began the oil change on her car. After paying for the oil change she was given a customer satisfaction survey. One of the questions asked, "How long did you have to wait before we began servicing your vehicle?" The response options were *Less than 20 minutes, 20–30 minutes, 31–40 minutes, 41–50 minutes, 51–60 minutes,* and *More than one hour.* Even if she checked the first category (less than 20 minutes), which indicated the best customer service with respect to wait time, does this mean that she was satisfied? No. She expected that the dealership would begin work on her oil change "right away." Realize that customer service does not always equate to customer satisfaction. Rather, customer satisfaction is a function of customer service in relation to customer expectations. Consumers are satisfied when service exceeds their expectations, and they are dissatisfied when service falls short of their expectations.

So, what should marketing researchers measure? Obviously, measuring only customer service ("How long did you actually wait?") is not enough. Researchers should also measure consumers' **expectations** ("How long did you expect to wait?"), consumers' perceived **importance** ("How important is wait time to you?"), and customer **satisfaction** ("Were you happy with the amount of time you had to wait?").

Gap Analysis

Measuring customer service along with customer expectations allows marketers to perform a gap analysis. A **gap analysis** is a research and analysis technique for directly comparing the results of two or more survey questions. In this case, the gap analysis would compare service to expectations. This comparison allows marketers to identify the specific service features that are exceeding expectations and the specific service features that are falling short of expectations. For example, the chart in Figure 10.3 shows the results from a gap analysis where consumers rated their perceptions of marketer performance on five different customer service features as well as their expectations for those service features, where 7 = greater performance and greater expectations. Clearly, there are gaps in performance and expectations for service features 1 and 2. Situations where performance falls short of expectations are referred to as **negative gaps**. Even though consumers rated the marketer's performance on feature 1 relatively favorably, performance still fell short of expectations. Similarly, there appears to be a wide negative gap between performance and expectations for feature 2. Service feature 4 illustrates a **positive gap** where performance exceeds expectations. Notice that a gap analysis could also be performed comparing any combination of performance, expectations, satisfaction, and importance.

FIGURE 10.3 Gap Analysis Comparing Customers' Expectations and Performance Ratings

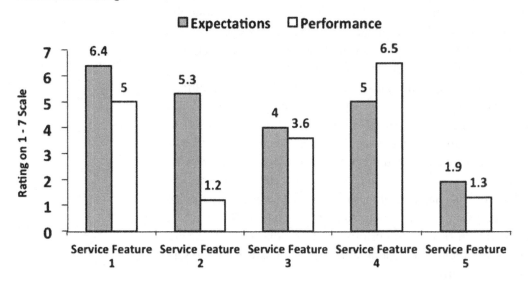

Marketers can create a false sense of security for themselves if they do not ask questions about expectations or importance. If the marketer had not measured customers' expectations regarding service feature one (as shown in Figure 10.3), they might have falsely assumed that customers were satisfied, since the performance rating was relatively favorable. Similarly, apparent problems might not really exist. If the performance for a service feature is rated relatively negatively, this might not necessarily be a problem if the service feature is not important to customers, or if customers have relatively low expectations for it. Such could be the case for service feature 5 in the above example.

Customer Contact (Service) Audit. There are many variables for which a gap analysis can be conducted. Marketers working in service industries often conduct **customer contact (service) audits** where they measure customers' perceptions of service quality as well as management's perceptions of service quality. The variables that are often measured in customer contact (service) audits include:

- Consumers' perception of service quality.

- Consumers' expectations regarding service quality.

- Management's perceptions of service quality.

- Management's perceptions of customer satisfaction.

- Management's perceptions of customer expectations.

- Management's perceptions of standards for service quality.

- Actual service standards.

- Actual service provided.

- Consumers' perceptions of what is promised.

- Management's perceptions of what is promised.

- What is actually promised.

By performing a gap analysis on any combination of these variables, marketers can gain valuable insight into their service quality, how consumers perceive their service quality, and how consumer perceptions compare to management's perceptions. Sometimes, marketing problems arise because perceptions differ between consumers and management. It can be an eye-opening experience for management to learn that the service they think is being provided is completely different from either the service that is actually being provided or from the service that consumers perceive is being provided.

> In many cases, measuring past and current behavior is of less importance than measuring future (expected) behavior.

CONSIDER PAST, PRESENT, AND FUTURE BEHAVIOR

Be aware of the differences between past, present, and future behavior. Past behavior does not always predict future behavior. Consider all potential reasons for consumers' past behaviors and why their actions in the past might not predict their future behaviors. To illustrate this, imagine that a national pizza delivery chain was considering opening a new pizza delivery restaurant in a very small town. They surveyed local residents about their pizza purchasing habits. They discovered that none of this town's residents had ever ordered a pizza to be delivered to their home. Does this mean that there is very little demand for a pizza delivery business in this small town? Does this mean that people in this town would never order a pizza to be delivered to their home? No. It could be that residents never ordered a pizza to be delivered to their home because there had never been a pizza delivery business in the town. Beware of trying to predict future behaviors based only on information about consumers' past behaviors. There might be valid reasons why past behaviors will not predict future behaviors.

As another example, consider a student who wanted to open a massage therapy service on a college campus. He surveyed students and found that only 4 percent of students had ever paid for professional massage therapy. Does this mean that there is very little demand for this type of business? Not necessarily. Consider all of the possible explanations for these students' past behaviors. It could be that very few students had ever been to a massage therapist because very few students had ever had an interest in it. But, it could also be that very few students had ever been to a massage therapist because there had never been one convenient to them. When measuring past behavior, always consider the possible reasons for that past behavior.

When marketers introduce new or improved products that previously did not exist, open new stores that previously did not exist, or offer new services that previously did not exist, they are, by definition, changing the marketing and retail environment. Consumers' behaviors in the previous marketing and retail environment (where a newly developed product had not previously existed, or where a new store had not previously existed) cannot be expected to predict their behaviors in the new marketing and retail environment.

ATTITUDES VS. BEHAVIORAL INTENTIONS

When designing surveys it is important to consider the type of information that will be most useful to a decision maker. Regrettably, many researchers often measure **attitudes** without measuring **behavioral intentions**. They ask if consumers like a brand. They even ask consumers if a retail store should begin to offer certain new products or services. Unfortunately, measures of attitudes are often of limited use to marketing managers. Conversely, measures of behavioral intentions are often more useful and informative to the decision-making process. Just because consumers say that they like a product, brand, or service does not mean that they intend to purchase it. For example, just because consumers answer *yes* to the survey question "Should the Gringo Grill begin to accept phone-in orders so that customers can call ahead with their order before they arrive to eat at the Gringo Grill?" does not mean that these consumers would ever consider using such a "phone-in" order service themselves. Sometimes consumers answer survey questions based on what they think other consumers might like, or might want to purchase. A consumer might never consider phoning in a restaurant order prior to arriving at a restaurant, but they might respond favorably to it on the survey thinking that other consumers might want to use the service. It is then possible that many consumers will respond favorably to the idea of a new product or service, without any of them actually intending to use it themselves. As another example, consumers might respond *yes* to the question "Should the Johnstown Utility District offer online bill paying as an option for paying your monthly utility bills?" However, answering *yes* to this question does not necessarily mean that a consumer would use online bill paying themselves.

Instead of measuring only attitudes, researchers should also measure behavioral intentions. Measures of behavioral intentions are much more useful and informative to the decision-making process. To illustrate this, consider these two conclusions found in a research report:

- 60 percent of respondents said that we should offer online bill paying.
- 60 percent of respondents said that they, personally, would use online bill paying, if it were available.

The first conclusion reports only the percentage of consumers who hold positive attitudes toward the possibility of using online bill paying. However, the second conclusion is much more informative in that it reports the percentage of respondents who would actually use online bill paying. A marketing manager would be much more comfortable making decisions based on the second conclusion.

Measuring Behavioral Intentions

An easy and effective way to measure behavioral intentions is by using the following question forms:

If _____, would you _____?

Would you _____, if _____?

These question forms present respondents with a possibility (e.g., "If _____") and ask them to indicate their behavioral intentions with respect to that possibility. This can be very useful when predicting future behaviors. To illustrate, consider the text of a phone survey that is shown below. This telephone survey was conducted as part of an economic development study to identify the types of new commercial businesses and community improvements that residents of a small town would like to see in their town. Notice how the questions measure personal behavioral intentions and even measure expected frequency of use, not just attitudes.

> Hello. My name is _____ and I am working with Insight Marketing Research. We conduct public opinion polls of local residents on a number of important topics. Tonight we are conducting a telephone survey of Clearville residents to measure the types of retail and commercial businesses that you would like to see in the Clearville area. This survey has been developed by the Economic Development Committee of Clearville and has been approved by Mayor Bill Bethers. He and the town planners would like your input into the types of businesses that will be a part of Clearville in the future.
>
> I want to assure you that we are not selling anything. This survey is very short and will take only a few minutes to complete. Your participation is completely voluntary. If we should come to a question that you do not want to answer, simply tell me and we will go on to the next question. Also, you may quit the survey at any time.

May I begin?

> First, I will read a list of different types of businesses. For each, please tell me whether or not you would like to see that type of business in Clearville, and then tell me whether or not you would probably be a "regular" customer of that type of business. Please keep in mind that all new retail businesses must meet the architectural design standards for Clearville that were passed in 2012.
>
> Let's start with fast food restaurants. Is this a type of business that you would like to see more of in Clearville, and if so, would you probably be a regular customer of this type of business if it were in Clearville?
>
> 1   NO, I would NOT like to see this type of business in Clearville
> 2   YES, I would like to see this type of business in Clearville, but I probably would NOT be a regular customer
> 3   YES, I would like to see this type of business in Clearville, and I probably WOULD be a regular customer

How about food markets or grocery stores?

   1   NO, I would NOT like to see this type of business in Clearville

   2   YES, I would like to see this type of business in Clearville, but I probably would NOT be a regular customer

   3   YES, I would like to see this type of business in Clearville, and I probably WOULD be a regular customer

How about professional services, such as legal, accounting, or tax services?

   1   NO, I would NOT like to see this type of business in Clearville

   2   YES, I would like to see this type of business in Clearville, but I probably would NOT be a regular customer

   3   YES, I would like to see this type of business in Clearville, and I probably WOULD be a regular customer

If a greater number of new retail business were opened near the center of town (near the library and the statue of General Greyton), but there were no parking spaces immediately adjacent to those businesses, would you be willing to park your car in a parking lot and walk to the businesses that were near the center of town (assuming the parking lot were within a short walking distance to the businesses)?

   1   YES

   2   NO

Do you believe that the town of Clearville should build walking and bicycle paths that connect the current businesses with any new retail businesses near the center of town?

   1   YES

   2   NO

If walking and bicycle paths were built that connected the current businesses with any new retail businesses near the center of town, approximately how often would you use those paths?

   1   Every day

   2   A few days a week

   3   A few days a month

   4   A few days a year

   5   Never

Do you believe that the town of Clearville should build walking and bicycle paths that connect the various neighborhoods with the parks in Clearville?

   1   YES

   2   NO

If walking and bicycle paths were built that connected the various neighborhoods with the parks in Clearville, approximately how often would you use those paths?

1 Every day
2 A few days a week
3 A few days a month
4 A few days a year
5 Never

Now we would like to ask you about retirement living centers. If town planners were considering allowing a retirement living center to be built in Clearville, is this something that you would be in FAVOR of, would you be indifferent toward it, or would you actively OPPOSE a retirement living center in Clearville?

1 I would FAVOR (support) retirement living centers in Clearville
2 I would be indifferent—neither favor nor oppose them
3 I would OPPOSE retirement living centers in Clearville

If there were a retirement living center in Clearville, would you consider living there when you are retirement age (or now, if you are already retirement age)?

1 YES
2 NO

Measuring Attitudes vs. Measuring Behavioral Intentions. To further illustrate the difference between measuring attitudes and measuring behavioral intentions, consider the case of the Wilcox Memorial Library located on the campus of a large university. The dean of the Wilcox Memorial Library wanted to increase the number of students who visit the library and use the services of the library. He identified a number of changes that could be made to the library and the library's policies and he wanted to examine the potential effects of these changes on students' use of the library. Specifically, he was considering:

- Allowing students to bring food and drinks into the library.

- Providing more places for students to meet and work on group projects.

- Allowing students to reserve meeting rooms.

- Designating more "quiet areas."

One approach to examining these issues on a survey would be to ask questions such as:

- Would you like to be able to bring food and drinks into the Wilcox Memorial Library?

- Do you think that the Wilcox Memorial Library should provide more places for students to meet and work on group projects?

- Would it be a good idea for the Wilcox Memorial Library to allow students to reserve meeting rooms?

- Would it be better if the Wilcox Memorial Library designated more "quiet areas?"

Notice, however, that these questions measure attitudes but do not measure specific behavioral intentions with respect to students visiting the library more often if these changes were implemented. Questions that measure behavioral intentions with respect to visiting the library are shown below.

Which of the following would make you, personally, want to <u>come to the library more often</u>?

☐ If I could bring food and drinks into the library.

☐ If there were more places to meet with student groups.

☐ If I could reserve a student meeting room.

☐ If there were more designated "quiet" areas.

Which of the following would make you, personally, want to <u>stay longer at the library</u>?

☐ If I could bring food and drinks into the library.

☐ If there were more places to meet with student groups.

☐ If I could reserve a student meeting room.

☐ If there were more designated "quiet" areas.

As another example, consider the case of the Fredericksburg City Zoo. The zoo director recently announced an initiative to increase attendance at the zoo. She was considering a number of changes to the zoo to hopefully increase zoo attendance. Among these potential changes were:

- Lowering the admission price from $8 to $6.

- Increasing the number of educational animal shows and demonstrations.

- Building a picnic area and allowing guests to bring their own food and drinks into the zoo for picnics.

- Increasing the size of the petting zoo area and adding more animals to the petting zoo.

"If ___, would you ___?" This is one of the most useful and effective means of measuring behavioral intentions on surveys. Marketing managers often find that measuring behavioral intentions is more useful to the decision-making process than merely measuring attitudes.

The questions shown in Figure 10.4 illustrate the difference between asking survey questions that measure only attitudes toward these new changes and asking questions that measure behavioral intentions related to these new changes. Obviously, the questions that measure behavioral intentions will be more useful to the zoo director in identifying those changes that will have the greatest effect on increasing attendance at the zoo.

FIGURE 10.4 Measuring Attitudes vs. Measuring Behavioral Intentions

Question That Measures Only Attitudes	Question That Measures Behavioral Intentions
Should the Fredericksburg City Zoo lower the admission price from $8 to $6?	If the Fredericksburg City Zoo lowered the admission price from $8 to $6, would you, personally, visit the zoo more often?
Should the Fredericksburg City Zoo increase the number of educational animal shows and demonstrations?	Would you, personally, visit the Fredericksburg City Zoo more often if they increased the number of educational animal shows and demonstrations?
Would you like to see a picnic area at the Fredericksburg City Zoo where people could bring their own food and drinks into the zoo for picnics?	If the Fredericksburg City Zoo built a picnic area where you could bring your own food and drinks into the zoo for picnics, how often would you, personally, visit the zoo?
Would it be a good idea for the Fredericksburg City Zoo to increase the size of the petting zoo area and add more animals to the petting zoo?	If the Fredericksburg City Zoo increased the size of the petting zoo area and added more animals to the petting zoo, would that make you, personally, want to visit the zoo more often?

WHEN DESIGNING SURVEYS, YOU CAN NEVER BE TOO SPECIFIC

Be very specific when developing research objectives and consider how the results from a survey question will help managers make a decision. For example, consider the following questions taken from a customer satisfaction survey for a retail store:

	Poor	Below Average	Average	Above Average	Excellent
Invoice	☐	☐	☐	☐	☐
Interior of Store	☐	☐	☐	☐	☐
Exterior of Store	☐	☐	☐	☐	☐
Customer Service Personnel	☐	☐	☐	☐	☐
Salespeople	☐	☐	☐	☐	☐

None of these will provide actionable results. What if all of the customers who completed this survey rated the invoice as *poor*? What does that mean? How should the invoice be changed? A marketing manager would not know. To provide actionable results, these questions should be much more specific. For example, the survey questions should measure customers' perceptions of the amount of the invoice, the time it takes to receive the invoice, the ability of consumers to understand the invoice, and even the accuracy of the invoice. Then, if all customers rate the time to receive the invoice as *poor*, a marketing manager would know what to change. The same can be said for all five of the issues listed above. What is it about the interior of the store, the exterior of the store, the customer service personnel, and the salespeople that customers do or do not like? It could be that customers think salespeople are knowledgeable, pleasant, and helpful, but also think that it is difficult to communicate with salespeople. Measuring these specific aspects of salespeople will allow managers to identify the specific actions that need to be taken to improve marketing performance.

Never Too Specific. The fundamental principle to keep in mind when developing quantitative research objectives and designing surveys is that research objectives for a survey can never be too specific. If you think that a quantitative research objective or a survey question is too specific, do not worry. Survey questions can never be too specific. In fact, the more specific the quantitative research objective and the survey question, the more useful it will be to the researcher and the decision maker. Knowing that 60 percent of students at a university rent at least two science fiction DVDs every week is more useful and informative than knowing only that 60 percent of students rent DVDs. And, the more specific a survey question is, the easier it is for respondents to answer it. For instance, asking consumers, "How likely are you to buy a pair of running shoes?" is not a very specific question. Because it is somewhat vague, it is actually very difficult to answer. Consumers must try to figure out what the researcher is asking. Alternatively, asking consumers, "How likely are you to buy a pair of Nike brand running shoes that cost more than $100 from a retailer on the Internet within the next two weeks?" is a very specific question. As such, it is very easy to answer because consumers know exactly what is being asked. Always remember, survey questions can never be too specific.

SEPARATE PRIMARY FROM SECONDARY DATA OBJECTIVES

One way to keep marketing research surveys short is to identify those objectives that can be met with secondary data. Separate those objectives that can be met with secondary data from those objectives that must be met with primary data. Only those objectives that require primary data should be used to develop a survey. This can help to keep surveys as short as possible, and only as long as necessary.

> When designing survey questions, you can never be too specific.

RESEARCH HYPOTHESES

Research objectives are sometimes stated as hypotheses. **Hypotheses** are statements about what a researcher expects to find. They are statements about possible solutions to problems. Hypotheses often make assertions about possible answers to research questions. In many cases, hypotheses are simply educated guesses. The following are examples of research hypotheses.

- A salesperson's productivity is positively related to their level of job satisfaction.

- Increased advertising expenditures lead to increased sales.

- Males have more favorable attitudes toward our product than females.

Good research hypotheses contain two key components: (1) they state the variables that are to be measured, and (2) they state a comparison between two or more alternatives. These two key components are critical to being able to test the hypothesis.

Without them, researchers do not know how to test the hypothesis. For example, the following is a poorly written hypothesis:

Bad Hypothesis: Advertisement A is effective.

The problem with this hypothesis is that it cannot be tested. It does not specify what is to be measured to determine the advertisement's effectiveness. Is advertising effectiveness to be measured in terms of day-after recall, attitude toward the advertisement itself, or purchase intentions after viewing the advertisement? Even if the hypothesis stated that advertising effectiveness is to be measured in terms of day-after recall, it still provides no means of determining the level of day-after recall that is to be considered effective. A better hypothesis would state the variable that is to be measured as well as a comparison by which the hypothesis is to be tested.

Better Hypothesis: Advertisement A leads to higher day-after recall scores than advertisement B.

Notice that this hypothesis can be easily tested. It specifies that day-after recall is to be used as the measure of effectiveness. And, it also states a comparison between day-after recall scores for advertisement A and advertisement B. As another example, consider the following hypothesis:

Bad Hypothesis: Consumers like our product.

This hypothesis suffers from the same problems as the previous hypothesis. A better hypothesis would be:

Better Hypothesis: Consumers have more favorable purchase intentions toward our new product, compared to our competitor's product.

QUESTIONS FOR DISCUSSION

1. Why is it important for research objectives to specify the subjects of the research, the variables that are to be measured, and the calculations that will be performed on the data?

2. Robert owns a local restaurant and he has hired you to conduct some customer satisfaction surveys. He has designed a survey with four questions. What would you do to make this survey and the results from it more useful to Robert?

Please evaluate our restaurant on the following:	Poor	Below Average	Average	Above Average	Excellent
Evaluate the food.	☐	☐	☐	☐	☐
Evaluate the service.	☐	☐	☐	☐	☐
Evaluate the interior of the restaurant.	☐	☐	☐	☐	☐
Evaluate the exterior of the restaurant.	☐	☐	☐	☐	☐

3. Think back to the last time you purchased a car. How would you model the adoption process that you went through as a consumer before you purchased the car? Identify important research objectives for measuring various aspects of this adoption process.

4. Why is annual income often measured as a categorical variable on surveys? Why is age often measured as a continuous variable on surveys?

5. What are some independent variables and dependent variables associated with a restaurant?

6. Describe the steps in the consumer purchase and adoption process for a new computer.

7. How could a gap analysis or customer contact audit be used by the following marketers? What could be measured?
   a. A car dealership.
   b. An auto parts store.
   c. A truck and van rental business.
   d. An apartment building.
   e. A health club.
   f. A pediatrician.

8. Should marketing researchers measure past behavior, present behavior, or future (expected) behavior?

9. Describe the relationship between quantitative research objectives and the managerial decision-making process.

MINICASE 10.1

Clayton Mark Hotel

The Clayton Mark Hotel is a 10-story hotel located on the beach in Panama City, Florida. The hotel is 30 years old and could use some remodeling. Phil Deblaker, the owner of the Clayton Mark, feels that the hotel has become a bit "stale." He would like to give the hotel a complete makeover, not just in terms of physical remodeling, but also in terms of the services that the hotel offers and the quality of those services. Currently, the hotel has an outside pool, indoor exercise room, a bar with access to both the lobby and an outdoor deck, and a restaurant with indoor and outdoor seating. He recently attended a conference where some hospitality industry experts were discussing the value of customer contact audits for improving customer service and customer satisfaction. If you were hired by Phil Deblaker to conduct a customer contact (service) audit:

1. What questions would you ask?

2. Of whom would you ask these questions?

3. How would you ask these questions?

4. When would you ask these questions?

5. What would you measure on the audit, and how would you measure it?

6. How would you report the results from the audit?

Pennsylvania State Museum and Historical Society

Sarah Travis is the director of the Pennsylvania State Museum and Historical Society. Her duties include managing the daily operations of the museum and promoting the museum to visitors. She is also in charge of all fundraisers and community events that are associated with the Museum and Historical Society. As she was reviewing the attendance records for the past year she noticed a slight decrease in attendance. This is a concern for her because one of the major sources of revenue for the Museum and Historical Society is from admission fees. She believes that an increase in the number of visitors will result in increased revenue, even if the admission price is lowered slightly. She has noticed that other museums have been able to recoup lost revenue from a lower admission price through an increased number of visitors. She has also identified a number of other potential changes that could be made to the Museum and Historical Society that might possibly lead to increased attendance, including:

- Lowering the admission price from $12 to $10.

- Offering free admission on Saturdays.

- Offering free admission to children under the age of 10 every day of the week.

- Providing more live demonstrations and lectures.

- Dressing museum educators in period costumes.

- Allowing hands-on interaction with a greater number of exhibits.

- Extending the hours of the museum (opening earlier and closing later).

- Adding more lights to brighten the lighting in the museum.

She would like you to help her write some survey questions that:

1. Measure guests' attitudes toward each of these changes.

2. Measure guests' behavioral intentions related to each of these changes

ENDNOTE

1   A. Dutka, *AMA Handbook for Customer Satisfaction* (Lincolnwood, IL: NTC Business Books, 1994).

CHAPTER (11)

Survey Data Collection Methodologies

LEARNING OBJECTIVES

1 Compare and contrast telephone surveying with telemarketing.

2 Define and explain sugging and frugging.

3 Define and explain omnibus surveys.

4 Define and explain syndicated surveys.

5 Define and explain straw polls.

6 Discuss unethical practices associated with survey research.

7 Compare and contrast:

    a Personal interviews.

    b Telephone surveys.

    c Mail surveys.

    d Self-administered surveys.

    e Online surveys.

    f Mobile surveys.

After conducting exploratory research to help define the problem, and after developing specific quantitative research objectives to be measured on a survey, the researcher must decide how to administer the survey and how to collect the survey data.[1] The most often used methods for collecting survey data are personal interviews, telephone surveys, mail surveys, self-administered surveys, online surveys, and mobile surveys. A number of factors will influence the choice of methodology, including the number of questions to be asked, the need for visual aids, the speed with which the data must be collected, the characteristics of a population and the sample, and the amount of flexibility required for the survey. The major factors influencing the choice of a particular methodology for collecting survey data are shown in Figure 11.1.

FIGURE 11.1 Factors Influencing the Choice of Survey Methodology

Survey Methodologies	Factors to Consider
Personal Interviews Door-to-Door/In-Home Mail Intercept Point-of-Sale	How many questions will be asked?
	Are the questions potentially embarrassing or sensitive in any way?
	Are visual aids, such as advertisements or product packages, needed?
Telephone Surveys	How geographically disperse is the population and the sample?
	How quickly are the results needed?
Mail Surveys	Will it be necessary to probe consumers' responses and ask for further clarification?
Self-Administered Surveys	Will the survey need to be customized or adapted to individual consumers?
Online Surveys	How technologically literate are the people to be surveyed?
Mobile Surveys	Does an interviewer need to be present to conduct the interview?

PERSONAL INTERVIEWS

With **personal interviews**, an interviewer is in direct face-to-face communication with a respondent. The interviewer asks the survey questions and records the respondent's answers. In most cases, the respondent does nothing more than speak his or her answer to the questions. Personal interviews consist of door-to-door and in-home interviews, mall intercept interviews, and point-of-sale intercept interviews.

Advantages of Personal Interviews

- Provide for two-way communication between the researcher and the respondent.

- Personal interviews are versatile and flexible. Questions and surveys can easily be changed or adapted to different situations or different people.

- Can be conducted almost anywhere—in a house, in a shopping mall, or on a college campus.

- Provide for immediate feedback. Respondents' answers, as well as information about the survey itself ("Are the questions clear and easy to understand?"), can be obtained immediately.

- Very low chance that consumers will misunderstand the survey questions because interviewers can repeat or clarify the wording of questions for respondents.

- Interviewers can probe respondents' answers for greater understanding and richer data ("Why did you say that?" "What does that mean?" "Were you thinking anything else when you said that?").

- Fairly high **completion rate**. Once respondents agree to begin the survey, they tend to complete the interview. It is more difficult to walk away from an interviewer in the middle of a personal interview than it is to simply hang up a phone in the middle of a telephone interview.

- High individual **item response rates** because it is difficult for respondents to refuse to answer a question in a personal interview.

- Allow for visual aids such as advertisements, product sketches, and even product prototypes.

- Good for pretesting surveys to be sent to a larger sample of consumers because you can identify problems with question wording and confusion.

- Do not require that respondents are able to read and write.

- Do not require that respondents be technologically literate.

Disadvantages of Personal Interviews

- Because respondents are not anonymous, they might bias or censor their responses.

- Characteristics of the interviewer can lead respondents to bias or censor their responses.

- Different interviewer techniques can lead respondents to bias or censor their responses.

- Can be expensive and time-consuming.

> A survey is a very efficient methodology for discovering the thoughts, beliefs, perceptions, and attitudes of large groups of people. And, there are many different means by which surveys can be conducted.

Door-To-Door/In-Home Interviews

Even though personal interviews can be conducted at a consumer's home, very few **door-to-door interviews** or **in-home interviews** are conducted these days. In most cases, the potential disadvantages of these interviews outweigh their advantages.

Disadvantages of Door-to-Door and In-Home Interviews

- Possibly exclude people who live in apartments or condominiums where solicitation or door-to-door surveying is not allowed.

- The sample can be biased by the type of people who stay at home. But, this bias can be reduced by callbacks, where researchers call again at a different time, or on a different day.

- Potentially very high refusal rate that could lead to nonresponse bias and an unrepresentative sample.

- Expensive and time-consuming.

- Security concerns of respondents as well as interviewers. Many people are reluctant to open their front door to strangers. Similarly, many interviewers are uncomfortable approaching a stranger's front door.

Mall Intercept Interviews

Mall intercept interviews, where researchers stop consumers as they walk through a shopping mall and ask them to participate in the survey, have become a very popular means of collecting survey data from consumers. The safety issues that are associated with door-to-door and in-home interviews are eliminated. Consumers feel relatively safe in a shopping mall with hundreds of other people present.

Advantages of Mall Intercept Interviews

- Consumers are more willing to participate in a mall than at home because there is more security in a crowded mall than at home.

- Very good if seeking a particular type of person who can be identified visually (e.g., parents of young children, elderly), which can reduce the cost and time of sampling.

- When consumers are in a shopping mall, products and purchasing issues are salient to them. They are in the role of a consumer and their minds are on shopping-related issues.

A key advantage of conducting personal interviews in shopping malls is that consumers can be surveyed while they are in the "mode" of a shopper. Because they are currently shopping, they are thinking about products and purchase-related issues.

Disadvantages of Mall Intercept Interviews

- Relatively low participation rate.

- Potential sample bias associated with a high refusal rate.

- Potential sample bias due to sampling consumers at only one shopping mall. Different shopping malls tend to attract different types of consumers in terms of demographics, socioeconomic status, lifestyle, and culture.[2]

Point-of-Sale Intercept Interviews

Consumers can be surveyed while they are still in a store or immediately after they make a purchase.[3] This is called a **point-of-sale interview**. Researchers can observe customers in a store and intercept them as they are shopping or as they are leaving the store.

Advantages of Point-of-Sale Intercept Interviews

- Actual purchase behavior can be observed and recorded.

- Short time interval between actual purchase and interview, so there is less bias or error in responses due to forgetting or due to consumers' evaluations changing over time.

Disadvantages of Point-of-Sale Interviews

- Some stores might be reluctant to allow such interviews of customers.

- Inherent bias toward positive responses. Point-of-sale interviews include only those consumers who shop in a store, or those consumers who purchase products from a store. People who are not currently customers or people who are potential customers are usually excluded from the survey.

- Do not allow you to ask, "Why did you not shop at this store?"

TELEPHONE SURVEYS

Telephone surveys are one of the most frequently used methods for collecting survey research data from a large group of respondents who are representative of all consumers in a target market.[4] In most cases, researchers randomly select phone numbers to call and ask consumers to participate in the survey.

Advantages of Telephone Surveys

- Relatively willing subjects lead to a higher response rate and a larger sample.

- Data can be collected and analyzed very quickly. Data can be analyzed immediately if answers are entered directly into a computer database using **computer assisted telephone interviewing (CATI)** software.

- Relatively inexpensive compared to personal interviews and mail surveys. Often, the only expenses are employees (interviewers) and phone lines.

- Respondents are often more willing to answer personal questions over the phone where there is no face-to-face contact. Telephone survey respondents are anonymous.

- Relatively high cooperation rate. Respondents do not need to open their door or let a stranger into their house.

- Callbacks are easy.

- Geographic flexibility. It is just as easy to call someone in your hometown as it is to call someone two time zones away.

> Telephone surveys are popular due to the efficiency with which a large sample can be surveyed in a very short time period, for example, one evening.

Disadvantages of Telephone Surveys

- Interviews and surveys are not easily adapted to individual consumers. Most CATI-based surveys are highly standardized. All respondents typically answer the same survey with exactly the same questions. This limits the opportunity for probing responses and individualized questions.

- Surveys must be short (15 minutes or less) because completion rates tend to decrease with longer interviews.

- A disadvantage of **random digit dialing (RDD)** is that businesses and organizations (not just individual households) are also called, which wastes time and money.

- No chance for using visual aids such as advertisements, products, or even display boards.

- Limited types of survey questions that can be used. Some scales are visual, in that respondents need to be able to see the scale to answer the question.

Marketing Research vs. Telemarketing. It is very important to understand the difference between **telemarketing**, which refers to selling a product over the phone, and **telephone research**, which refers to surveying consumers over the phone. The **Telemarketing and Consumer Fraud and Abuse Prevention Act (1995)** and the **1991 Telephone Consumer Protection Act (TCPA)** are federal laws that restrict unsolicited telephone calls for the purpose of selling goods and services. Under these laws, all calls made for the purpose of selling something (either telemarketing or telephone soliciting) must comply with a person's request not to be called. However, telephone surveys are not bound by such **do-not-call** requests. As such, legitimate survey researchers are not bound by do-not-call lists.

Unfortunately, many people equate telephone surveying with telemarketing. They both involve marketers using telephones. However, there are clear distinctions between the two. Telemarketers are attempting to sell (solicit) something, whereas telephone surveyors are merely attempting to ascertain (elicit) the public's opinions. Confusion about the difference between telemarketing and telephone survey research has made many consumers reluctant to participate in legitimate telephone surveys and has led to an increase in the number of complaints that researchers receive regarding violations of do-not-call laws.

Sugging and Frugging. Additionally, it is illegal to identify the purpose of a telephone call as research and then attempt to sell goods or services under the guise of conducting a poll, survey, or other type of marketing research. This is referred to as **sugging**.[5] Some telemarketers have intentionally developed questions to establish a respondent's susceptibility to sales pressure or their level of interest in some product or service. Once a person has been identified as a potential customer, a follow-up sales call is made. Laws regulating sugging have been passed due to increased consumer reluctance to participate in telephone surveys because consumers often believe that the researcher will also attempt to sell them something. If the telemarketer or researcher plans to sell goods or services, this disclosure must be made promptly in the first part of the call before the non–sales portion of the call takes place. Similarly, **frugging** refers to fund-raising under the guise of marketing research.

Telephone surveying is NOT telemarketing!

MAIL SURVEYS

Often, surveys are sent to consumers through the **mail** (postal service).

Advantages of Mail Surveys

- Geographic flexibility. You can mail a survey anywhere.

- Relatively inexpensive compared to personal interviews. However, efforts to increase response rates for mail surveys, such as providing financial incentives for completing and returning the survey, tend to increase the cost.

- The consumer can complete the survey at their convenience, so there are fewer errors due to time constraints.

- High respondent anonymity that can reduce social desirability bias and many other response biases.

- Respondents have time to carefully consider their responses.

- Good if questions require a considerable amount of thinking or calculating.

Disadvantages of Mail Surveys

- Little control over the personal meaning of questions. The same question can mean different things to different people. And, a researcher would never know this with a mail survey. Pretesting the survey in a personal interview can reduce these problems.

- Usually highly standardized and not adaptive. Every respondent receives the same survey with exactly the same questions. There is virtually no opportunity to probe people's responses, and there is no way to adapt individualized questions to individual respondents based on their answers to previous questions.

- Potentially very long lag period between mailing out the surveys and having them returned (potentially six to eight weeks).

- Must be relatively short to increase response rates.

- Very low response rates if not designed well.

- Little control over who completes the survey.

- High chance for self-selection bias and nonresponse error.

SELF-ADMINISTERED SURVEYS

A **self-administered survey** is one that is made available to consumers and allows them to self-select whether or not they will complete the survey. For example, a survey could be placed on a table in a retail store and consumers can complete the survey if they wish. Completed surveys are then placed in a box, returned to a central location, or even mailed at the consumer's convenience. Self-administered surveys share many of the same advantages and disadvantages of mail surveys.

Advantages of Self-Administered Surveys

- Cheaper than mail surveys. You might only need postage on the return envelope.

- Consumers can complete them at their own pace.

- Give consumers time to consider their answers.

Disadvantages of Self-Administered Surveys

- Sample selection bias. Only those people who are very interested in the topic or those people who feel very strongly about a topic will choose to complete the survey. This could lead to self-selection bias and nonresponse error. These errors are discussed in the next chapter dealing with survey error.

Self-administered surveys are highly susceptible to biases due to differences between respondents and nonrespondents. Often, only those people who feel strongly about an issue choose to take the time to complete the survey.

ONLINE (INTERNET) SURVEYS

The advent of the Internet has opened up a completely new methodology for survey researchers to gain access to potential respondents. And, creating an online survey is becoming easier and easier, even for people with very little knowledge of the Internet and how to create web pages. Many websites offer survey authoring software that is easy to use, even for computer novices (see **www.surveymonkey.com** and **www.zoomerang.com**). Invitations to complete an online survey can be sent via email to a list of consumers provided by the marketer. However, if the marketer does not have a list of consumers, many of these online survey providers also offer panels of consumers to whom surveys can be sent. For example, SurveyMonkey Audience is a panel of more than 1 million consumers to whom a survey can be sent. Similarly, Ask Your Target Market (**www.AYTM.com**) allows marketers to create their own survey, incorporate video or images, and then send the survey to consumers who are members of AYTM's online panel of more than 4.5 million consumers in five different countries. Marketers can even target panel members based on demographics. The price for such surveys starts at 95 cents per completed survey.

Even though there are a variety of survey research techniques that marketing researchers use, each with unique advantages and disadvantages, online surveys have become the technique of choice for marketing researchers (see Figure 11.2). However, not all surveys are conducted online. While many surveys are still conducted over the phone, in face-to-face personal interviews, on mobile devices, and through the mail, online surveys have quickly become the technique used most often by survey researchers.[6]

Advantages of Online Surveys

- Very low cost per completed survey.

- Can incorporate visual and audio stimuli into the survey.

- No chance for interviewer error or interviewer bias.

- Can collect large amounts of data in very little time.

- Eliminates the need for researchers to enter the data.

- Reduced data entry errors. Errors on the part of respondents can be automatically identified by the web-based survey program. If a respondent enters a value outside of an acceptable range, the program will respond with an error message and request that the respondent re-enter his or her answer.

- Complicated skip patterns can be easily incorporated into the survey.

- Worldwide geographic flexibility. Respondents can access the survey from anywhere around the world.

- Privacy and anonymity allows researchers to ask potentially embarrassing, sensitive, or potentially threatening questions.

Disadvantages of Online Surveys

- Potential sample bias. Internet surveys exclude respondents or populations that do not have access to a computer or the Internet. However, this disadvantage diminishes as more and more people around the world gain access to the Internet.

- Technical computer problems can keep a respondent from being able to complete the survey.

- Little control over who actually completes the survey.

- High chance for self-selection bias and potentially low response rates.

- Require that respondents can read and that respondents are at least somewhat computer literate.

FIGURE 11.2 Survey Techniques Used Most Often by Survey Researchers

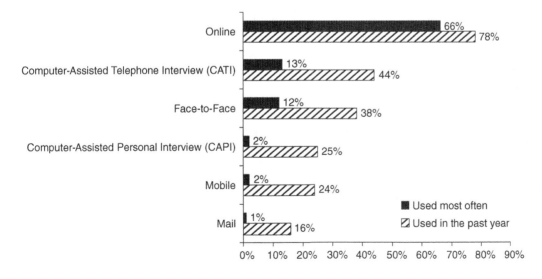

Many websites, such as **www.surveymonkey.com**, offer online survey authoring software that is very easy to use, even for people with very little familiarity with the Internet and how to create a web page.

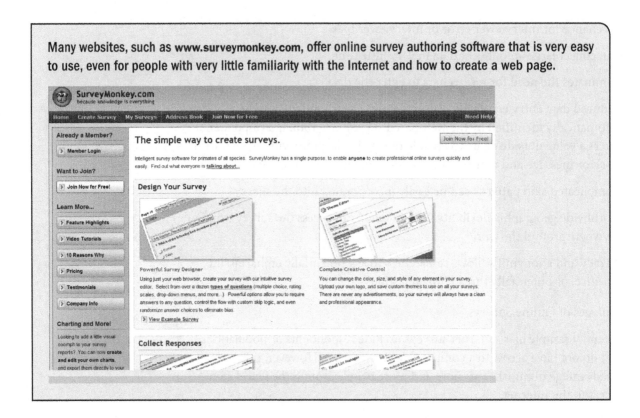

MOBILE SURVEYS

Mobile surveys give marketers even more flexibility in terms of how, when, and where consumers can complete surveys. **Mobile surveys** are completed using a cell phone or other mobile device. This gives consumers the ability to complete online surveys in almost any location at any time of day.

Advantages of Mobile Surveys

- Can be completed almost anywhere and at any time of day.

- Allow researchers to measure consumers' perceptions and opinions "in the moment."

- Great variety in types of responses—respondents can submit text, photo, video, or audio responses.

- If no connection to the Internet, consumers can complete the survey offline and their answers are automatically uploaded when there is an online connection.[7]

- Can use quick response (QR) codes to easily access and activate a survey in a retail setting or at home. Such QR codes can be printed on packages, on in-store displays, in print advertising, and even on cash register receipts.

- Providing QR codes on receipts eliminates the need for consumers to type in phone numbers, URLs, or survey codes.

- Can use a variety of question types, including short answer questions, multiple choice questions, and rating scales.

- Time and date stamps, along with GPS, can be used to identify when and where respondents completed the survey.

Disadvantages of Mobile Surveys

- The surveys must be very short with relatively few questions.

- Questions must be easy for respondents to answer.

- Fewer issues can be addressed on any one mobile survey.

- Must be conducted more frequently to compensate for the limited number of questions that can be asked.

- Some consumers might have difficulty typing in responses to open-ended questions on a small screen.

- Not all consumers have smartphones or other such mobile devices.

GOOGLE CONSUMER SURVEYS

Google recently launched a service that provides researchers with an alternative method for conducting online surveys. **Google Consumer Surveys** presents an Internet user with a survey question as a means of gaining access to online content found on affiliated websites.[8] For example, a website might erect a **surveywall** and allow access to certain content only if the user answers a survey question. The surveywall is similar to a **paywall** used by online publishers to charge viewers who want to view the premium content on the website. However, in this case, the website is not charging for access to the content, it is merely requiring viewers to answer a survey question. If the user agrees to answer the survey question, he or she is given access to the online content and the website erecting the surveywall is compensated for each completed response. This provides marketers with relatively low-cost research and access to a large number of potential respondents from everyday people browsing the web in a very short amount of time. Researchers can survey the general population for only 10 cents per response. Alternatively, researchers can target a subpopulation using inferred demographic data for 50 cents per response. Demographic data (age, sex, geographic region) is inferred based on a respondent's IP address and browsing history.

The website on which a Google Consumer Survey question is placed is referred to as a **publisher**. Marketing researchers pay to have their survey questions placed on publisher websites. The publisher is then paid by Google to host the survey on their site. This provides benefits to everyone involved. Researchers gain access to a large group

There is not any one best methodology for conducting a survey. Each type of survey methodology has its advantages and disadvantages. The best survey methodology is the one that best fits the needs of the researcher for that particular situation.

of potential respondents. Website publishers are able to monetize their premium online content. And, consumers can support their favorite publisher websites.[9]

Although Google Consumer Surveys provide many benefits, there are a number of limitations to this type of surveying. A respondent answers only one or two questions. As such, there is no opportunity for follow-up questions. If the researcher wants to ask a list of multiple questions, each question will be answered by a different set of respondents. This limits the ability to gain deeper insights in consumers' perceptions, beliefs, feelings, and behaviors. Cross-tabulating responses must be performed across subjects, not within subjects. There is no way to compare how one respondent answered multiple questions. As such, many researchers view Google Consumer Surveys as more similar to a quick polling tool as opposed to being a replacement for a complete survey. However, Google Consumer Surveys can be used to help prepare and pretest survey questions to be included in a larger subsequent survey.

OMNIBUS SURVEYS

Many research and public opinion polling firms conduct surveys on a regular basis to which marketers can add questions piggyback style. Such surveys are called **omnibus surveys**. Omnibus surveys include questions from a variety of clients that deal with a wide range of topics and issues. For example, Harris Interactive (**www .harrisinteractive.com**) conducts nationwide omnibus telephone surveys as well as nationwide omnibus online surveys of young consumers. These surveys are efficient means of combining a number of relatively short surveys (i.e., less than 20 questions each) into one survey. The Harris Interactive omnibus telephone survey usually consists of responses from 1,000 people, and their online omnibus survey usually consists of responses from 2,000 people. Using an omnibus survey can also save time. These surveys can be conducted in less than one week. The cost for adding questions to the Harris Interactive omnibus survey ranges from $1,000 to $1,500 per closed-ended question. The cost for adding open-ended questions ranges from $2,000 to $3,000 per question. Kelton Research and The Omnibus Company (**www.omnibus .com**) also conduct omnibus surveys on a regular basis.

SYNDICATED SURVEYS (STUDIES)

A **syndicated survey** (study) is one in which multiple companies or organizations join together to create (or fund) a survey to be conducted on a topic in which they all share a common interest. The survey is then administered to a large sample of respondents repeatedly at set intervals over time, for example, every six months. The main advantage of a syndicated survey is that the cost of conducting the survey is spread over all participating companies or organizations. The companies or organizations participating in a syndicated survey are often referred to as **subscribers**. Think of the participating companies and organizations as subscribing to the research reports that are produced on a regular basis, much like subscribing to a magazine or other periodical. All subscribing organizations receive a common research report that contains information of relevance to all of them. Many syndicated surveys also allow subscribers to add proprietary questions to the core set of questions. The results from these proprietary questions are released only to the company or organization requesting them. Of course, these additional proprietary questions are added at an additional cost.

As an example of a syndicated survey, IPSOS Public Affairs (**www.ipsos-pa.com**) conducts various syndicated surveys. One such survey, Illinois Pulse, is a quarterly tracking survey of residents of Illinois. Subscribers receive quarterly reports from surveys that measure residents' satisfaction with public services in Illinois. Another well-known provider of syndicated surveys is J.D. Power and Associates (**www.jdpower .com**). J.D. Power and Associates conducts nationwide surveys of consumers by mail, telephone, and email on a variety of topics, most notably the automotive industry. LiveContact (**www.livecontact.com**) provides syndicated surveys on the healthcare industry and patient issues. These surveys allow subscribing organizations to better understand changes in patient behavior and also yield insight into how patients use pharmaceuticals and other health-related products. Argus Information and Advisory Services LLC (**www.argusinformation.com**) conduct regular syndicated surveys for financial services institutions, such as the U.S. Credit Card Payments Study. Foresight Research (**www.foresightresearch.com**) conducts a syndicated survey of consumers who purchase pickup truck accessories, examining what truck accessories are purchased and the various factors that influence such purchases.

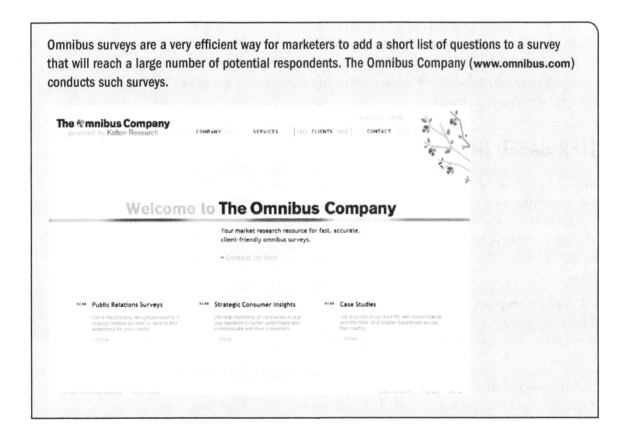

Omnibus surveys are a very efficient way for marketers to add a short list of questions to a survey that will reach a large number of potential respondents. The Omnibus Company (www.omnibus.com) conducts such surveys.

STRAW POLLS

People often hear about the results from straw polls and wonder how these polls differ from other forms of public opinion polls and marketing research surveys. The name *straw poll* is generally considered to have originated from the process by which a farmer would determine the wind direction and speed by throwing a few pieces of straw into the air. **Straw polls** are often used as a quick and nonscientific method of gauging trends, predicting changes in the political winds, or quickly measuring people's opinions. Straw polls are often considered to be nonscientific polls because they do not rely on representative sampling (sometimes referred to as statistical sampling) and, as such, often fall prey to many forms of error and bias. A straw poll is actually an informal public opinion survey. They are often used for political polling, where the results from a straw poll are unofficial and the results are not binding. In such cases, they are used to predict the results of a later official vote or election. They are also becoming more and more common as daily public opinion questions on websites (**virtual straw polls**). A website might post a daily question to which visitors to the website can respond if they so desire. Most straw polls can be characterized as ad hoc, informal, unofficial, and impromptu.

Straw polls often fall prey to a number of errors and biases due to the lack of control over the sample and the sampling procedure. Given the often impromptu nature of straw polls, their samples are often not representative of the larger population. In many cases straw polls rely on convenience sampling procedures. For example, only those members present at a meeting are included in the sample, or only those people who happen to visit a website on a given day are asked to vote in an online *poll of the day*. Straw polls are especially susceptible to nonresponse error and self-selection. Often, the topic of the survey can have significant effects on a person's desire to respond to the poll question. As such, the results of the poll reflect the opinions of only those people who choose to respond.

COMPUTER-BASED INTERVIEWING

A recent trend has been the increased use of computer-based interviewing. The primary goal of computer-based interviewing is to eliminate the sources of error associated with human interviewers (e.g., forgetting to ask a question, phrasing a question differently when asking it of different respondents, or deliberately falsifying research results). Below are the acronyms for various computer-based interviewing methodologies.[10]

- **ACASI, Audio Computer–Aided Self-Administered Interviewing.** Self-administered survey where the respondent uses a computer-based questionnaire, but the computer reads questions to the respondent over headphones.

- **Audio SAQ, Audio Self-Administered Questionnaire.** Respondents use a paper questionnaire, but questions are read to respondents over headphones.

- **CAPI, Computer-Assisted Personal Interviewing**. The researcher reads questions to respondents from a computer screen (computer-based questionnaire) and keys in the respondent's answers.

- **CASI, Computer-Assisted Self-Administered Interviewing**. Self-administered survey using a computer-based questionnaire. The researcher directs selected respondents to a computer where respondents key in their own answers.

- **CATI, Computer-Assisted Telephone Interviewing**. Researchers call potential respondents, ask questions as directed by the computer, and key data directly into the database.

- **EMS, Electronic Mail Survey**. Surveys are sent online to respondents, who complete them and send them back via email. Or, participants respond to an email query by accessing a website and completing the interactive survey on the site.

- **FASI, Fully Automated Self-Interviewing**. Respondents approach independent stations, such as kiosks, read questions on the screen, and then key in their own responses.

- **FATI, Fully Automated Telephone Interviewing**. An automated voice asks questions by telephone, and respondents key in their own answers using the touch-tone keypad on their phone.

- **MCAPI, Mobile Computer–Assisted Personal Interview**. An online survey is accessed and completed using a smartphone or other mobile device.

- **TATI, Touch-Tone-Aided Telephone Interviewing**. An interviewer-administered telephone survey where respondents use the touch-tone buttons on their phone to answer questions.

Advantages of computerized interviewing include:

- Improves response rates.

- Reduces data input errors.

- Allows for more complex surveys by using automated skip patterns and sequences.

- Reduces analytic time.

- Reduces the opportunity for human error, making the survey more efficient and accurate.

- Allows the researcher to incorporate video, music, pictures, and sounds into surveys.

- Reduces social desirability bias. The anonymity of a computer reduces the discomfort of answering sensitive or embarrassing questions in the presence of a human interviewer.

GLOBAL SURVEY RESEARCH

Researchers often conduct survey research in other countries and cultures. They also conduct research on consumers who are from foreign cultures, but who are living in the United States. When doing this, researchers must recognize that not all countries and cultures are the same as the United States. There are a number of factors one must consider before conducting survey research in other countries, or when surveying American consumers who are from foreign cultures.[11] Such factors include:

- Social/culture environment.
- Competitive environment.
- Demographics of consumers.
- Political environment.
- Legal environment and policy structures.
- Technological environment and consumers' access to technology.
- Economic conditions and trends.
- Religious beliefs and customs.
- Language and terminology differences.
- Familiarity with company and brand names.
- The nature of products (e.g., many Americans consider cell phones a necessity, but they might be considered luxuries in some other countries).
- Availability of sampling frames and lists from which samples can be generated.

Mail Surveys

When conducting mail surveys of consumers from varying cultures, researchers should consider:

- Availability of postal services.
- Literacy rates and the ability of respondents to read the survey questions.
- Responses to different types of survey questions and familiarity with different types of rating scales.
- Willingness to participate.
- Interpretations of questions and meanings of words.
- Responses to the physical layout of survey instruments, such as instructions, headings, and colors.
- Legality of mail surveys.

Phone Surveys

When conducting phone surveys of consumers from varying cultures, researchers should consider:

- Availability of phones.
- Responses to different types of survey questions and familiarity with different types of rating scales.
- Willingness to participate and reveal personal information without a personal relationship.
- Legality of phone surveys.

Personal Interviews

When conducting personal interviews of consumers from varying cultures, researchers should consider:

- Willingness to reveal personal information to a stranger.
- Availability of shopping centers for mall intercept interviews.

Online and Mobile Surveys

When conducting online and mobile surveys of consumers from varying cultures, researchers should consider:

- Availability of computers and access to the Internet.
- Availability of smartphones or other mobile devices.
- Literacy rates and the ability of respondents to read the survey questions.
- Computer literacy rates and ability of respondents to successfully execute the computer operations required to complete the survey.
- Degree to which different cultures are willing to provide answers to personal questions via the Internet or using their phone.

AVOID CROSS-CULTURAL MARKETING MISTAKES

Even if marketing research is not being conducted in foreign countries, researchers should be aware of any cultural differences among consumers living in the United States. There are many examples of marketers who did not fully understanding the potential differences in cultures and languages. Such differences can cause significant problems when it comes to reading and understanding survey questions. Below are a number of examples where marketers failed to fully understand cultural and language differences between consumers of varying cultures.[12]

- The name of a new detergent meant *dainty* in English, *song* in Gaelic, *horse* in an African language, *dimwitted* in the Mideast, *out of one's mind* in Korean, and was obscene and offensive in Slavic languages.

- Ford Fiera translated to *ugly women* in Spanish.

- The Caliente model translated into *streetwalker* in Mexico.

- In Brazil, the Pinto model translated into *small male appendage*, but was later changed to Corcel, which means *horse*.

- Evitol shampoo translated to *dandruff contraceptive* in Brazil.

- Pet Milk translated as *to break wind* in French.

- In Mexico, Fresca soft drinks translated to *lesbian*.

- A new airline trying to enter the Australian market used the emu as its symbol; unfortunately, the emu is an Australian bird that cannot fly.

- The group of Chinese characters that sounded like Coca-Cola when spoken aloud translated to *bite the wax tadpole*.

- When Hunt-Wesson attempted to introduce its Big John brand into French-speaking Canada, the translation Gros Jos turned out to be slang for *a woman with large breasts*.

- Belgian consumers translated GM's *body by Fisher* into *corpse by Fisher*.

- The famous Pepsi slogan "Come alive with Pepsi" translated in Germany as *come out of the grave*, and in Taiwan as *bring your ancestors back from the dead*.

- Oregon-based Taco Time learned that in Japan, *tako* translated to either *octopus* or *idiot*.

- When Gerber started selling baby food in Africa, they used the same packaging as in the United States, with the beautiful baby on the label. Later, they learned that in Africa companies routinely put pictures on the label of what is inside, since most people cannot read English.

- A popular chocolate candy in Europe did not sell well in the United States. Its name was *ZIT*.

- To attract American tourists, a dress shop in Paris featured the sign, "Come in and have a fit."

- John Deere discovered that in many South American cultures, the deer is a symbol for homosexuality.

- Mist Stick (a curling iron) translated to *manure wand* in Germany.

- An airline trying to enter the Australian market promoted their *rendezvous lounges*, which translated to *room for lovemaking*.

- Coors put its slogan "Turn it loose" into Spanish, where it was read as *suffer from diarrhea*.

- Scandinavian vacuum manufacturer Electrolux used the following in an American campaign: "Nothing sucks like an Electrolux."

- An American T-shirt maker in Miami printed shirts for the Spanish market that promoted the Pope's visit. Instead of "I saw the Pope" (*el Papa*), the shirts read "I saw the potato" (*la papa*).

- In Italy, a campaign for Schweppes tonic water translated the name into *Schweppes toilet water*.

- Frank Perdue's chicken slogan "It takes a strong man to make a tender chicken," was translated into Spanish as, *it takes an aroused man to make a chicken affectionate.*

- When Parker Pen marketed a ballpoint pen in Mexico, its advertisement was supposed to read, "It won't leak in your pocket and embarrass you." The company thought that the word *embarazar* meant *to embarrass*. Unfortunately, it actually means *to impregnate*. So, the advertisement read, "It won't leak in your pocket and make you pregnant."

- In a Mexican hotel, a sign read, "The manager has personally passed all of the water here."

- In Thailand, a dry cleaners' advertisement read, "Drop your trousers here for best results."

- In a Japanese hotel, a sign read, "You are invited to take advantage of the chambermaid."

UNETHICAL SURVEY PRACTICES: PUSH POLLS

A **push poll** is not even a poll at all. It is a form of political telemarketing where the intent is to manipulate public opinion regarding a political candidate by relying on innuendo. In most cases the questions contained in the push poll contain misleading, false, or deceptive information designed to push public opinion toward one candidate and away from another. The questions often have no basis in fact. Push polls often contact large numbers of respondents (potential voters) and there is often little or no effort made to record and analyze respondents' answers to questions. For example, a political campaign might survey potential voters and ask the following question about the opposition candidate, "Would you be less likely to vote for Bill Bontworth if you knew that he had been found guilty of tax evasion and cheating on his federal tax returns?" even though Bill Bontworth had never been suspected of tax evasion and there was no indication that he had ever cheated on his taxes. The purpose of the question is to plant the idea that he cheated on his taxes in the mind of voters. This unethical type of political telemarketing is not legitimate survey research and can severely damage the reputation of legitimate telephone survey researchers, thus causing respondents to be less willing to respond to telephone surveys.

The American Association for Public Opinion Researchers (**www.aapor.org**) has identified the following characteristics that will usually indicate to a respondent that the telephone call is not a legitimate survey:

- One or only a few questions are asked, all about a single candidate or a single issue. This small number of questions allows the push poll to contact as many people as possible.

- The questions are uniformly strongly negative (or sometimes uniformly positive) descriptions of the candidate or issue.

- The organization conducting the calls is not named, or a phony name is used.

- Evasive answers are given in response to requests for more information about the survey.

In addition, the AAPOR also offers the following characteristics that will often indicate to a journalist, reporter, or survey professional that a telephone call is not a legitimate survey:

- The number of people called is very large, sometimes many thousands. In contrast, legitimate surveys usually rely on smaller representative samples, for example, between 500 and 1,000 respondents.

- The calls are not based on a random sample.

- It is difficult to find out which organization conducted the interviews.

However, the AAPOR also cautions that not all polls containing negative information about one or more candidates are push polls. Political campaigns often conduct legitimate "message testing" surveys where they measure voters' reactions to potential campaign messages or advertising content designed to sway voter sentiment from one candidate to another. And, many messages tested during political campaigns contain negative information.

QUESTIONS FOR DISCUSSION

1. What are the main advantages and disadvantages of personal interviews, mail surveys, telephone surveys, self-administered surveys, online surveys, and mobile surveys?

2. If the results from a survey were needed very quickly, what type of survey would you recommend (personal interview, telephone, mail, self-administered, online, or mobile)?

3. If you were designing a survey to measure various aspects of domestic violence, what type of survey would you recommend (personal interview, telephone, mail, self-administered, online, or mobile)?

4. Describe the relationship between a researcher's choice of survey data collection methodology and the managerial decision-making process. How could the choice of methodology affect a manager's ability to make marketing decisions?

5. Is telemarketing the same thing as telephone survey research?

6. Which survey research methodology is most often used by marketing researchers? Why?

7. What is the difference between omnibus surveys, syndicated surveys, and straw polls?

8. Find a virtual straw poll on a website (e.g., **www.espn.com**, **www.si.com**). Who will likely respond to this poll? What potential sources of error are associated with the poll and the results from it?

9. Which type of survey methodology would be best for the following situations?
   a. You work for a company that markets barbecue grills and outdoor cooking equipment. You want to know the percentage of Americans who use a barbecue grill at least once during the summer.
   b. You work for a shoe manufacturer and you want to learn the issues that are most important to consumers when they choose to buy shoes.

10. Evaluate the following survey methodologies:
    a. Personal interviews (door-to-door, mall intercept, point of sale)
    b. Telephone
    c. Mail
    d. Self-administered
    e. Online
    f. Mobile

    on each of the following characteristics/factors:
    1. Data from all respondents can be collected and analyzed very quickly.
    2. A large number of questions can be asked.
    3. Allows for asking questions about embarrassing or sensitive issues.
    4. Can use visual aids.
    5. Is geographically flexible.
    6. Respondents' answers can be probed for additional comments.
    7. High chance that the respondent might misunderstand the questions.
    8. Easy for respondents to skip an individual question that they do not want to answer.

9. Interviewer characteristics or interviewer techniques can bias responses.

10. Short time interval between behavior and answering questions about that behavior.

11. Callbacks are easy.

12. Questions can be easily adapted to individual consumers.

13. Immediate two-way communication between researcher and consumer.

14. Good for asking questions that require much thought, time, or mental calculations.

15. High control over who actually completes the survey.

16. Open-ended questions can be easily asked and answered.

17. Ability to read and write is required.

18. Requires access to a computer or mobile device and the Internet.

19. Requires respondents who are computer literate.

20. Surveys can be completed at respondents' convenience.

21. Shopping and product-related issues are fresh on consumers' minds during the interview.

MINICASE 11.1

Johnathon Green, Real Estate Agent

Johnathon Green has worked in real estate sales for his entire professional life. He has been able to form numerous friendships with other real estate agents in the area. Even though they are all in direct competition with each other, they all seem to be able to work together with an understanding that the goal is to help a potential home buyer find the home that is best for him or her. Recently, Johnathon has been seeking a way to better assess local residents' perceptions of the economy, residents' perceptions of the local real estate market, and residents' desire to buy a home. He has contacted a number of local research firms about this, but the prices that they quote him for conducting this type of public opinion polling are more than he can afford. He understands the need to conduct marketing research and the benefits that it could provide to someone in his situation. However, he is starting to think that he will never be able to know the answers to these questions.

1. What do you tell Johnathon Green?

2. What type of research do you recommend for him?

ENDNOTES

1 P. H. Rossi, J. D. Wright, and A. B. Anderson, *Handbook of Survey Research* (New York: Academic Press, 1983).

2 Seymour Sudman, "Improving the Quality of Shopping Center Sampling," *Journal of Marketing Research* 17 (November 1980): 423–431.

3 S. M. McIntyre and S. D. F. G. Bender, "The Purchase Intercept Technique in Comparison to Telephone and Mail Surveys," *Journal of Retailing* 62 (Winter 1986): 364–383.

4 D. A. Dillman, *Mail and Telephone Surveys: The Total Design Method* (New York: Wiley, 1978).

5 Diane K. Bowers, "Sugging Banned, At Last," *Marketing Research* 7 no. 4 (Fall 1995): 40.

6 "Greenbook Research Industry Trends Report," Winter 2013, **www.GRITreport.org**, based on sample size of n = 1,372 (technique used last year) and n = 1,026 (technique used most often).

7 "Product and Service Updates: Smartphones Equipped for Qual," *Quirk's Marketing Research Review*, November 2012, 18.

8 Paul Christ, "The Marketing Value of Google Consumer Surveys," **KnowThis.com**, April 7, 2012, **http://www .knowthis.com/blog/postings/the-marketing-value-of-google-consumer-surveys**

9 Paul McDonald, Matt Mohebbi and Brett Slatkin, "Comparing Google Consumer Surveys to Existing Probability and Non-Probability Based Internet Surveys," **Google.com**, June, 2013, **http://www.google.com/insights/ consumersurveys/static/consumer_surveys_whitepaper.pdf**

10 Rebecca Piirto Heath, "The Digital Interviewer," *Marketing Tools*, August 1997, 28–31.

11 Michael Quinn Patton, *Culture and Evaluation: New Directions for Program Evaluation* (San Francisco: Jossey-Bass, 1985); see also, Walter J. Lonner and John W. Berry, *Field Methods in Cross-Cultural Research* (Newbury Park, CA: Sage, 1986); E. D. Jaffe and I. D. Nebenzahl, "Alternative Questionnaire Formats for Country Image Studies," *Journal of Marketing Research* (November 1984): 463–471.

12 David A. Ricks, *Big Business Blunders: Mistakes in Multinational Marketing* (Homewood, IL: Dow Jones-Irwin, 1983); Syed H. Akhter, *Global Marketing* (Cincinnati: South-Western College, 1994), 49–50; Mike Kelly, "Side-Splitting Translations: These Phrases Will Tickle Your Funny Bone," *Milwaukee Journal*, November 25, 1990, H5.

Survey Error

LEARNING OBJECTIVES

1 Define survey error, population parameter, and sample statistic.

2 Compare and contrast random sampling error and systematic error (bias) in terms of:

    a The cause of each type of error.

    b The effect of each type of error on sample statistics.

    c Whether or not each type of error can be estimated statistically.

    d How each type of error can be reduced.

    e Whether or not each type of error can be eliminated.

3 Define and explain standard error of the mean and standard error of the proportion.

4 Describe nonresponse error and the effect of nonresponse error on survey results.

5 Explain the procedures that researchers can use to estimate nonresponse error.

6 Describe and explain the major types of response bias.

7 Describe some strategies for reducing response bias.

8 Describe and explain the major types of administrative error.

9 Compare and contrast cross-sectional surveys with longitudinal surveys.

10 Describe the sources of error associated with cross-sectional surveys and longitudinal surveys.

11 Explain the difference between a tracking study and a panel study.

12 Describe the sources of error associated with tracking studies and panel studies.

13 Explain the process by which researchers should interpret the results from surveys.

The purpose of a survey is to measure important characteristics of a population of people. These characteristics of a population are called **population parameters**. For instance, the population parameter of interest might be the average age of consumers in a market area. Unfortunately, marketers rarely know the exact value of a population parameter. The only way to know the exact value of a population parameter would be to survey every member of the population. This would be called taking a **census**. But, in most cases, taking a census is not feasible. Therefore, we usually can only estimate population parameters with the statistics calculated from samples. The **sample statistics** serve as our best estimate, or best guess, of the true population parameter. The sample average is used to estimate the

FIGURE 12.1 Population Parameters and Sample Statistics Used to Estimate Them

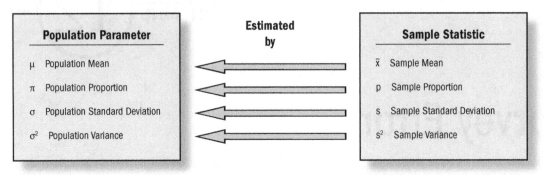

population average. The sample proportion is used to estimate the population proportion. The sample standard deviation is used to estimate the population standard deviation. And, the sample variance is used to estimate the population variance. This is illustrated in Figure 12.1.

Whenever a subgroup (sample) of people is sampled from a much larger population, the sample statistic that is calculated will probably be slightly different from the actual (true) population parameter. For example, the average age of the people in a sample will likely be slightly different from the true average age of all people in the population from which the sample was taken. This difference between the calculated sample statistic and the population parameter is called **survey error**.

Imagine that the true average age of consumers in a market area is 39, but we do not know this. From a sample of 1,000 consumers randomly drawn from the population of all people who live in this market area, we might calculate a sample average age of 36. If we were to take a second sample of 1,000 consumers from the same population we might calculate a second sample average age of 41. Every time we take a sample of different consumers we are likely to calculate a slightly different sample average. This is because each sample includes different people (even though all of the samples are taken from the same population). And, we rarely survey every member of the population. Therefore, we must assume that every sample will include some survey error. Researchers try to design data collection procedures that reduce the total amount of survey error. To do this, researchers must be aware of the possible causes of survey error. The two major types of survey error are random sampling error and systematic error (often referred to as bias). Researchers should be able to answer five questions related to each type of error.

> Survey error refers to the difference between the calculated sample statistic and the true population parameter.

1. What caused the error?

2. What is the effect of the error on sample statistics?

3. Can the error be estimated statistically?

4. How can the error be reduced?

5. Can the error ever be eliminated?

FIGURE 12.2 Comparing Random Sampling Error to Systematic Error

	Random Sampling Error	**Systematic Error & Bias**
What causes the error?	Randomly selecting a subset of people from the population. Each time a sample is taken, different people will be included in the sample, and thus, a different sample statistic will be calculated.	Problems with data collection procedures, including question wording, the nature of the survey procedures, characteristics of the interviewer, respondents wanting to please the interviewer, etc.
What is the effect of the error on sample statistics?	Random. The sample statistic is just as likely to overestimate the population parameter as it is to underestimate the population parameter.	Systematic. Because of bias, the sample statistic tends to either overestimate or underestimate the true population parameter consistently and systematically across all respondents.
Can the error be estimated statistically?	Yes. The amount of random sampling error can be estimated as the standard error of the mean when calculating an average, and the standard error of the proportion when calculating a percentage.	No. The amount of systematic error and bias cannot be estimated statistically.
How can the error be reduced?	Increasing the sample size (the denominator in the standard error equations) will reduce the amount of random sampling error in the estimates.	Change the data collection procedures and methodology to reduce or eliminate the source of the bias. Increasing the sample size has no effect on reducing the amount of bias.
Can the error ever be eliminated?	No. Whenever a sample is used to estimate a population we must always assume that there is some random sampling error. The only way to eliminate random sampling error is to take a census.	Probably not. Even though researchers design data collection methodologies to reduce as much systematic error and bias as possible, it is unlikely that all sources of systematic error and bias can be eliminated.

Answers to these five questions are summarized in Figure 12.2 and are discussed in detail in the next sections of this chapter.

RANDOM SAMPLING ERROR

What Causes Random Sampling Error?

With **random sampling error**, the difference between the population parameter, which is the characteristic of the population we are trying to estimate, and the sample statistic, which is calculated from the sample data, is a result of taking a sample of only a subset of the population, rather than taking a census of every member of the population. This type of error is often referred to simply as sampling error. Each time a different sample is taken from the same population the sample statistic will be slightly different because there will be different people in each sample. Because of this, researchers must always assume that there will be some random sampling error in a survey whenever they sample a subset of the population. For example, imagine that a

> Random sampling error is error that occurs in both directions—sometimes the sample statistic underestimates the population parameter, and sometimes it overestimates the population parameter.

researcher sampled 1,000 students at a university to measure their average age. Assuming that no student lies about his or her age, the average age from the sample will probably be slightly different from the true average age of all students. This is simply the result of taking a random sample from the population and not measuring every person in the population. Random sampling error is sometimes referred to as **pure sampling error** because it is the result of taking a random sample, and nothing more.

What is the Effect of Random Sampling Error on Sample Statistics?

Random sampling error occurs whenever researchers survey a random sample of people from a population, instead of surveying every member of the population. Random sampling error is the result of taking a random sample, and nothing more. Because of random sampling error, a sample result is just as likely to underestimate the true population parameter as it is to overestimate the true population parameter. Sometimes the sample statistic will be less than the true population parameter. Sometimes the sample statistic will be greater than the true population parameter. There is no consistency in terms of the direction of the error. The direction of the error is random. Random sampling error is error that can occur in both directions. This is illustrated in Figure 12.3. The statistics calculated from sample 1 and sample 4 underestimate the population parameter, whereas the statistics calculated from sample 2 and sample 3 overestimate the population parameter.

FIGURE 12.3 Random Error Occurs in Both Directions

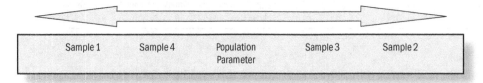

Can Random Sampling Error be Estimated Statistically?

Yes, the amount of random sampling error for a survey can be estimated by calculating the **standard error of the mean** (when calculating and estimating a mean) and the **standard error of the proportion** (when calculating and estimating a proportion). The formulas for calculating the standard error of the mean and the standard error of the proportion are shown below.

$$SE_{mean} = S/\sqrt{n} \qquad\qquad SE_{prop} = \sqrt{p(1-p)/n}$$

The SE_{mean} is the statistical estimate of how much random sampling error is associated with a sample average. The SE_{prop} is the statistical estimate of how much random sampling error is associated with a sample proportion.

Estimating Random Sampling Error. The amount of random sampling error for a survey can only be estimated. The exact amount of random sampling error (or any type of error) can never be calculated. Since survey error is the difference between the sample statistic and the population parameter, and since the value of the population parameter is usually not known, researchers never know exactly how much error is associated with a survey. If researchers already knew the value of the population parameter, there would be no need for a survey.

How Can Random Sampling Error be Reduced?

Increasing the sample size reduces random sampling error. Notice in the above formulas that increasing the sample size (the denominator) reduces the standard error. As more people are included in the sample, the sample estimate should become closer and closer to the population parameter.

Can Random Sampling Error Ever be Eliminated?

No. The only way to eliminate random sampling error is to conduct a census and survey every member of the population. But, this is rarely done. Thus, whenever we take a sample of a subset of the population we must always assume that there will be some random sampling error.

SYSTEMATIC ERROR AND BIAS

What Causes Systematic Error and Bias?

With **systematic error** and **bias**, the difference between the population parameter and the sample statistic is due to characteristics of the data collection methodologies or surveying procedures. In some cases, systematic error is due to subjects not telling the truth or misrepresenting their responses. For example, imagine that 1,000 male students at a university are randomly selected to participate in a survey measuring the average number of days per week that they exercise for more than 20 minutes. This is done by having these male students come individually to a designated interview room where they are greeted by a very attractive female interviewer who asks them how often they exercise. These male students will most likely overestimate how often they exercise to impress the interviewer. Imagine that the interviewer also asks questions about their expected income five years after graduation. Again, male students will probably overestimate this.

What is the Effect of Systematic Error and Bias on Sample Statistics?

Recall that random sampling error is often called pure sampling error because it is the result of taking a random sample, and nothing more. Because of random sampling error, sample results are just as likely to be less than the true population parameter as they are to be greater than the true population parameter. However, bias is a special type of error that is consistently in one direction. The population parameter is either overestimated or it is underestimated. The direction of the error is systematically the same for all respondents (thus the name systematic error). Bias often occurs when people are asked questions about sensitive or potentially embarrassing issues, such as income, weight, or age. If people consistently underreport their answers to survey questions, the sample statistic will be consistently less than the true population parameter and the sample statistic will underestimate the parameter. This is illustrated in Figure 12.4.

Bias refers to error that is in one direction.

If people consistently overreport their answers to survey questions, the sample statistic will be consistently greater than the true population parameter and the sample statistic will overestimate the parameter. This is illustrated in Figure 12.5.

Can Systematic Error and Bias be Estimated Statistically?

No. There is no statistical procedure for estimating the amount of systematic error or bias in a survey. There is no way to statistically estimate how much male respondents are overestimating how often they exercise if they are trying to impress an attractive female interviewer.

How Can Systematic Error and Bias be Reduced?

Systematic error and bias can be reduced by changing the data collection procedures and methodologies. For example, more anonymous survey methods might be better-suited for measuring how often male students exercise. The physical presence of another person is most likely what is causing males to overestimate how often they exercise. Notice that increasing the sample size will have no effect on reducing

FIGURE 12.4 Bias That Underestimates the Population Parameter

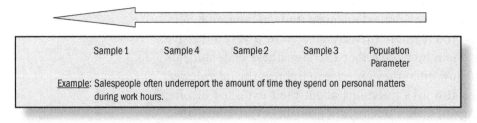

| Sample 1 | Sample 4 | Sample 2 | Sample 3 | Population Parameter |

Example: Salespeople often underreport the amount of time they spend on personal matters during work hours.

FIGURE 12.5 Bias That Overestimates the Population Parameter

| Population Parameter | Sample 4 | Sample 3 | Sample 2 | Sample 1 |

Example: Salespeople often overreport the amount of time they spend on job-related activities during work hours.

systematic error and bias. Unless the biasing effect of the attractive female interviewer is removed, males will tend to overestimate how often they exercise. Therefore, before collecting survey data, researchers should try to identify (or predict) any potential sources of bias and then design the research methodologies and survey procedures to reduce these sources of bias.

Can Systematic Error and Bias Ever be Eliminated?

It is unlikely that researchers can eliminate all sources of systematic error and bias from a survey. However, by understanding the sources of systematic error and bias, researchers can design data collection methodologies and surveying procedures in such a way as to eliminate as many sources of systematic error and bias as possible.

TYPES OF SYSTEMATIC ERROR AND BIAS IN SURVEYS

By definition, there will always be some random sampling error when sampling only a subset of the population. The only way to reduce random sampling error is to increase the sample size. But, there are steps that can be taken to reduce, and hopefully eliminate, at least some sources of systematic error. Thus, by understanding the following types (sources) of error, data collection procedures can be designed to reduce these errors. The major types of systematic error and bias are nonresponse error, response bias, and administrative error. These are shown in Figure 12.6.

Nonresponse Error

Nonresponse error occurs when:

- Respondents who complete the survey are not representative of the larger population.

- Respondents who complete the survey are different from nonrespondents who do not complete the survey (on an important dimension).

- The conclusions from the research would change with a higher response rate.

Nonresponse error occurs when respondents are different from nonrespondents.

Nonresponse error can also result from a **self-selection bias** among respondents. Self-selection bias occurs when only those people who care very strongly about an issue choose to complete the survey. As a result, extreme positions are overrepresented in the results. Nonresponse error also occurs when respondents' desire to complete the survey is related to the topic of the survey.

To illustrate the potential problems associated with nonresponse error, consider the comment cards often found on restaurant tables. Who typically completes these comment cards? Usually, only those customers who feel very dissatisfied or unhappy about their dining experience take the time to complete a comment card. And, these dissatisfied customers might not be representative of all customers who have eaten

FIGURE 12.6 Sources of Error in Surveys

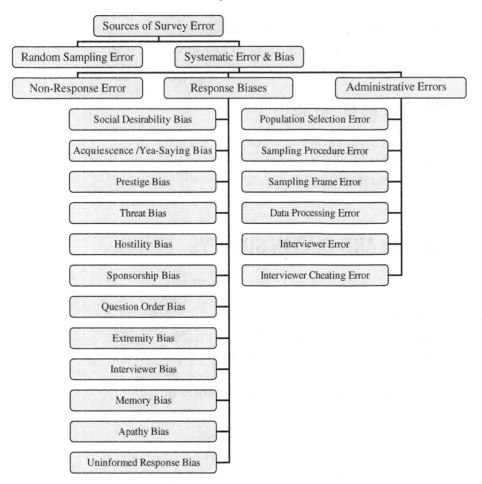

at a restaurant. Imagine that a restaurant has 10 comment cards returned for the month of January. If 90 percent of these cards (9 out of 10) have negative comments, should the restaurant manager be concerned? Based on only the percentage of negative comments on the completed cards, you might conclude that the restaurant is doing a poor job. But, is there any potential source of error in these results? Is it possible that less than 1 percent of all customers filled out these cards? If so, are the 10 customers who filled out the comment cards different in any way from the other customers who did not fill out the cards? If all of the restaurant's customers for a month filled out the cards, would the conclusion be different? Are the respondents similar to the nonrespondents?

There is a potential for nonresponse error in this situation because the customers who typically complete restaurant comment cards are those who are very dissatisfied with their dining experience. As a result, respondents are not representative of all customers. Respondents are different from nonrespondents. Moreover, the conclusions from the research would likely change with a higher response rate that included a greater number of customers who were satisfied with their dining experience.

TABLE 12.1 Results from Respondents to the Sewage Treatment Survey

	Number of Respondents	Percentage of Respondents
Favor the sewage treatment plant	50	20%
Oppose the sewage treatment plant	200	80%
Total	250	

Consider another example of nonresponse error. The planning commission for a city mailed 1,000 surveys to residents evenly distributed across the city. The survey asked residents about their feelings toward a proposed sewage treatment plant to be located in the southeast part of town. A mail survey was used because they wanted to give residents time to think about the issue before responding. Of the 1,000 mailed surveys, 250 surveys were returned. The response rate for the survey was 25 percent (a very high response rate for a mail survey) and the results are shown in Table 12.1.

Based on these results, researchers concluded that the residents of this city generally opposed the plant. But, was this the correct conclusion? What if the 25 percent of residents who responded to the survey lived mainly in the southeast part of town? And, what if the other 75 percent of residents of the city generally favored the plant because it would not be in the part of town where they lived? But, they were not motivated to complete the survey because the sewage treatment plant would not have any direct effect on them. If this were the case, and if everyone who received a survey returned it, the results might have looked like those in Table 12.2.

The conclusion with a 100 percent response rate would be that residents generally favored the plant. Notice that the conclusion would have changed with a higher response rate. This is because the sample would now include additional respondents whose opinions were different from the opinions of the initial respondents.

Identifying Nonresponse Error

To identify potential errors in survey research, especially when respondents can self-select whether or not they will complete the survey, researchers should ask themselves the following questions:

- Who will complete the survey (be the respondents)? And, why?

- Who will not complete the survey (be the nonrespondents)? And, why won't they complete the survey?

TABLE 12.2 Results from Respondents and Nonrespondents

	Original Respondents	Original Nonrespondents	Total (based on 100% response rate)
Favor the plant	50 (20%)	600 (80%)	650 (65%)
Oppose the plant	200 (80%)	150 (20%)	350 (35%)
Total	250	750	1,000

If respondents are different from nonrespondents on a dimension that is important to, or related to the main variable of interest, there is a chance for nonresponse error. Not only must the sample of people receiving the survey be representative, but the respondents who complete the survey must also be representative of the population.

Estimating Nonresponse Error

Fortunately, there are a number of methods that researchers can use to estimate whether or not nonresponse error is present in their results.[1]

Comparing Sample Characteristics to Population Characteristics. If researchers know important characteristics of the population, they can compare the characteristics of the sample to the characteristics of the population. For example, the researcher can compare demographics of the survey respondents to demographic data about the population (e.g., age, income, sex, occupation). For the sewage treatment plant survey mentioned previously, researchers should have measured the part of town where respondents lived. If 25 percent of the city's residents lived in the southeast part of town, a representative sample would include approximately 25 percent of the completed surveys from this part of town. Caution is advised, however, when the values for the population were themselves obtained from a previous survey. There might have been some nonresponse error in the original survey results that are being used as a measure of the population. Perhaps the same people responded, or did not respond, to both surveys.

To identify the potential for nonresponse error (especially when respondents can self-select whether or not they will complete a survey), researchers should ask themselves:

1 Who will respond, and why?

2 Who will not respond, and why not?

Extrapolation. Even if researchers do not know important characteristics of the population, they can still estimate nonresponse error by extrapolating.[2] **Extrapolating** is based on the assumption that people who respond less readily, people who respond later, or people who need additional incentives to respond are more similar to nonrespondents than respondents. Researchers can extrapolate based on successive waves or time trends.

Extrapolating Based on Successive Waves. As an example of extrapolating based on **successive waves**, consider a researcher who emailed a survey to 1,000 consumers (wave one). Two hundred respondents completed the survey. Three weeks later, the researcher emailed a reminder note encouraging people to complete the survey (wave two). An additional 100 respondents completed the survey. If the email reminder was used to encourage people to complete the survey, the 100 people who responded later, during wave two, are assumed to have responded because of the additional incentive and are thus assumed to be more similar to the original nonrespondents. A researcher could compare characteristics of the group of 100 respondents who needed an additional incentive from wave two to the group of 200 initial respondents from wave one. If the respondents from wave two are found to be significantly different than respondents from wave one, this indicates the possibility of nonresponse error. Remember, the respondents in wave two came from the set of original nonrespondents.

Extrapolating Based on Time Trends. If no incentive other than the survey itself is sent to consumers, the people responding later are assumed to be more similar to nonrespondents than they are to respondents who responded early. Researchers can then extrapolate based on **time trends**. For example, if the last 10 percent of surveys received are from people who are significantly different from the people who completed the first 90 percent of surveys received, this indicates the possibility of nonresponse error.

Response Bias

Response bias occurs when respondents do not answer survey questions truthfully, or when their answers are not representative of how they truly behave, think, or feel. Sometimes, people intentionally or unintentionally misrepresent their true state. To identify potential response bias, ask yourself, "Why would someone lie, misrepresent, bias, or censor their answers?" There are many potential answers to this question. Sometimes, response bias is simply due to the topic of the question. Other times, response bias occurs because of the data collection procedures and the characteristics of interviewers. Response bias is also caused by the order of questions on a survey and the wording of survey questions. And, response bias can also result from people simply forgetting, wanting to be nice, wanting to appear informed and not ignorant, and even from people wanting to please the interviewer. The major types of response bias are discussed below.[3]

Social Desirability Bias. People naturally want others to view them favorably with respect to **socially acceptable** values, behaviors, beliefs, and opinions. Thus, answers to survey questions are often guided by what is perceived as being socially acceptable. For example, even if a person has never donated money to charity, they might report that they have donated when asked on a survey. Donating money to charity is a socially acceptable behavior, whereas not donating money to charity is a socially unacceptable behavior. Social desirability bias can influence responses to questions about whether or not people spank their children, whether or not they recently purchased any fur coats, or even whether or not they voted in recent elections. Research on topics about which there are socially acceptable behaviors, views, and opinions is very susceptible to social desirability bias. Social desirability bias can result from the nature of the data collection procedures or settings, the degree to which a respondent seeks to present themselves in a favorable light, the degree to which the topic of the survey and the survey questions refer to socially value–laden topics, the degree to which respondents' answers will be viewed publicly versus privately (anonymously), respondents' expectations regarding the use of the research and their individual answers, and the extent to which respondents can guess what types of responses will please the interviewer or sponsor of the researcher.

Acquiescence/Yea-Saying Bias. With **acquiescence bias**, a response is based on respondents' perceptions of how they think the researcher wants them to respond. Respondents might acquiesce and respond favorably toward the idea of a new product because they think that is what a marketing researcher wants to hear. The manner in which interviewers react to respondents' answers can also give respondents cues regarding what the interviewer wants to hear. The way interviewers provide encouragement to respondents can affect their perception of what they are supposed to do and how they are to respond. Some respondents can also be biased by a natural tendency toward positive responses. This is called a **yea-saying bias**. People often rely on the time-tested rule "If you can't say anything nice, don't say anything at all." Such tendencies toward positive responses can even vary across cultures.

Prestige Bias. Many people will bias their responses to make themselves appear more prestigious in the eyes of others. Males might overestimate their income if the interviewer is an attractive female. People naturally overestimate social status and occupation, and underestimate their weight, age, and the extent to which they suffer from embarrassing medical problems.

Threat Bias. With **threat bias**, a response is influenced by the extent to which respondents feel threatened by negative consequences associated with certain answers. People might lie about whether or not they have ever shoplifted because of the potential legal ramifications of admitting to shoplifting. If people believe that they might be punished for admitting that they behave in a certain manner, they will not admit to that behavior.

Hostility Bias. With **hostility bias**, a response is biased due to feelings of anger on the part of the respondent. If respondents feel forced to complete a long survey, or if the interviewer or data collection procedures make respondents mad, they might deliberately fabricate answers to retaliate against the researcher. Any negative emotional reactions to the research or the data collection procedures themselves can introduce confounding variables and additional sources of bias into the research results.

Sponsorship Bias. With **sponsorship bias**, a response is influenced by respondents' perceptions of the person or organization sponsoring the research. If respondents know who is sponsoring the research they can often figure out how the research sponsor wants them to respond, leading to demand effects. A **demand effect** is when people change their behaviors, self-reports of behaviors, or answers to survey questions to meet the expectations of an observer or interviewer. People might underestimate the amount of red meat they eat on a survey conducted by the American Heart Association. Alternatively, people might overestimate the amount of red meat they eat on a survey conducted by the National Cattlemen's Beef Association. This is similar to acquiescence bias in that people often answer survey questions based on how they think the researcher wants them to respond. Sponsorship bias is often associated with surveys measuring low-involvement situations or behaviors.

Question Order Bias. Beliefs, feelings, or attitudes that are made salient because of questions asked early in a survey can influence responses to subsequent questions. Questions about teenage delinquency and other social problems associated with

Whereas nonresponse error refers to the difference between respondents and nonrespondents, response bias refers only to respondents and the reasons why they might bias, censor, or otherwise alter their responses to survey questions.

It is unlikely that researchers can ever eliminate all sources of systematic error and bias. There might be factors biasing respondents' answers that researchers are not aware of. Even still, researchers should design data collection methodologies and procedures to eliminate as many sources of systematic error and bias as possible.

young people asked early in a survey can influence responses to subsequent questions about spanking, child discipline, and corporal punishment. If consumers are first asked to evaluate Budweiser beer, and are then asked to list all brands of beer that they can think of, they will most likely include Budweiser in their list because it was just mentioned in a previous question. Also, the order in which a series of questions are asked on a survey can affect responses to the items. Extreme evaluations (e.g., strongly positive or strongly negative) of the first few items in a list might influence evaluations about subsequent items in the list. Some respondents will use answers to earlier questions as anchors against which answers to later questions are compared. Such a process is often referred to as **anchoring and adjusting**.

Extremity Bias. Many people do not like using the extreme ends of scales and do not like feeling that they are at the extreme, compared to others. For example, if income categories are set up as *Less than $20,000*, *$20,000–$30,000*, *$30,001–$40,000*, and so on, a person who earns $19,000 might bias their response by choosing the second category so that they are not in the bottom income category. When asked about the amount of time spent on personal matters while at work, people will naturally not want to be in the top category. One solution to this problem is to include additional response categories that are at the extreme ends of the scale, even if you do not expect anyone to use them.[4] For example, make the income categories *Less than $10,000*, *$10,000–$15,000*, *$15,001–$20,000*, *$20,001–$25,000*, and so on. This way, someone earning $19,000 is more likely to honestly report their income by checking the third income category without having to be in the bottom income category.

Interviewer Bias. Characteristics of an interviewer can cause people to bias their responses. An attractive interviewer might cause males to bias their responses related to income, weight, or frequency of exercising. However, the effects of interviewer characteristics are minimized in telephone interviews compared to in-person interviews simply because the respondent cannot observe the interviewer. An interviewer's reactions to a respondent's answers can actually encourage certain types of responses and inhibit others. Based on an interviewer's smile, frown, or even the raise of an eyebrow, people can determine what the interviewer wants to hear (what would please him or her), and then give them those answers. If a person gives an opinion on a controversial topic and the interviewer responds with, "Hmmm…that's interesting," the respondent can quickly determine that the answer was not expected, or somehow out of line with normal responses. The respondent might censor, bias, or otherwise alter subsequent answers. Interviewer training can reduce this problem.

Memory Bias. People forget things over long periods of time, and evaluations and opinions can easily change over time. Memory for events can be biased by **telescoping errors**. **Backward telescoping** occurs when respondents report that recent events occurred further back in time. **Forward telescoping** occurs when respondents report that distant events occurred more recently than they really did.[5] Further, evaluations can also change over time. A person might not feel as strongly about the quality of a restaurant meal (either positively or negatively) the more time that lapses between when they ate the meal and when they are asked about it. Evaluations (both positive and negative) can become more moderate as more and more time lapses. What is terrific today might be evaluated as only pretty good a week from now. Similarly, what is terrible today might be evaluated as not that bad a week from now. If asking for evaluations, beliefs, perceptions, or attitudes toward events, try to minimize the amount of time between the person's experience of the event and when they are asked questions about it.

Apathy Bias. This results from respondents who do not care about the survey or who decide to respond quickly or randomly simply to finish the survey. This can happen with very long surveys and with surveys for which respondents have not developed a commitment to complete the survey.

Uninformed Response Bias. Respondents often answer questions about which they have no knowledge or experience simply because they feel obligated to respond. They do this because they do not want to appear uninformed or ignorant. Offering, and making sure that respondents are aware of, a *Don't Know* or *No Opinion* option on the survey tends to reduce this bias. However, many people will still answer questions about which they are uninformed even when they are told it is acceptable to respond with *Don't Know*.

Uninformed responses are especially troublesome in that efforts to increase response rates can actually have unintended negative effects on the validity of research results. Stimulus factors designed to increase item response rates can lead to higher uninformed response rates.[6] Uninformed respondents can be encouraged to provide meaningless answers to survey questions. Further, if the purpose of the research is to measure beliefs, attitudes, or perceptions, respondents' familiarity with similar-sounding attitude objects can also guide their responses. Thus, respondents often unintentionally give uninformed responses simply because they are mistaken about the object being evaluated.[7]

Reducing Response Bias

As listed above, there are many sources of response bias. By being aware of these, researchers can design survey data collection procedures to minimize the likelihood that these sources of response bias will have significant effects on the survey results. Some strategies for reducing these types of response bias are listed below.

- To reduce *social desirability bias* and *threat bias*, assure respondents of anonymity of responses and privacy with respect to data related to their individual responses.

- To reduce *social desirability bias*, *prestige bias*, and *interviewer bias*, use anonymous survey data collection procedures whenever possible, and consider using procedures that do not require an interviewer.

- To reduce *acquiescence bias* and *yea-saying bias*, avoid revealing the purpose of the research, the sponsor of the research, or the source of the survey.

- To reduce *hostility bias* and *apathy bias*, make the survey short, interesting, and easy to complete. Try to get respondents committed to completing the entire survey. Use **prompters** to help respondents work their way through the survey, such as, "The next section will be easier," "Thank you for your help with those questions, please answer a few more questions," or "There are only a few more questions remaining to answer."

- To reduce *question order bias* and *extremity bias*, carefully consider the order of the survey questions and the possible response categories. Try to ask more general questions earlier in the survey, and ask questions about more specific issues, people, events, places, or ideas later in the survey. This process of asking general questions prior to more specific questions is referred to as **funneling**.

- To reduce *memory bias*, decrease the amount of time between a respondents' experience of an event and their responses to questions about that event.

- To identify and reduce *uninformed response bias*, make respondents aware that they can answer any question with *Don't Know* or *No Opinion*. Include questions that measure respondents' level of knowledge about a topic in addition to their attitudes and opinions about a topic.

Reverse-Scored Items. One commonly used survey technique is to include **reverse-scored** items on the survey. Most survey questions are phrased positively. However, researchers will sometimes purposely reverse the phrasing of some items so that they are phrased negatively to increase the chance that respondents will read all of the questions, decreasing the likelihood of acquiescence bias, apathy bias, and **straight line (column) responding** (e.g., apathetically circling a column of the same answers for every question). For example, questions 1, 2, and 4 below are phrased positively, whereas question 3 is phrased negatively. If respondents answer *strongly agree* (*SA*) to all four questions, this indicates that they did not carefully read all four questions. They might have assumed that all four questions were phrased positively, leading to a straight line (column) of *strongly agree* answers.

1. I am very articulate.	SD D N A SA
2. I am very comfortable talking with people I have recently met.	SD D N A SA
3. I often have difficulty striking up a conversation with people I have just met.	SD D N A SA
4. I have very good verbal communication skills.	SD D N A SA

A respondent's answer to a reverse-scored question must be converted by subtracting the answer's scale value (X) from the total number of scale values plus one. In this example, if *SD* were coded as 1, and *SA* were coded as 5, a respondent's answer to question three would be converted as (6 – X) to place all four scales in the same direction. Reverse-scored items should always be converted before performing any statistical analysis on the data.

Response Bias and Question Wording

The wording of survey questions themselves can also lead to response bias.[8] **Leading questions** are those that contain words or phrases that suggest or imply a certain answer. They lead people to respond in a biased manner. Such response bias is not due to respondents purposely biasing their answers, but rather to the particular way in which a survey question is worded. Consider the following question:

> More and more, people are coming to accept text messaging in social situations as socially acceptable behavior. Do you feel that text messaging in social situations is socially acceptable behavior?

Many respondents will respond with *yes*, because the question implies that many other people feel that it is acceptable behavior. Some strategies for avoiding response bias due to question wording are listed below.

- Avoid suggestions and implications in the question. Asking, "How pleased were you with the efficient manner in which the governor dealt with the state's financial problems?" will lead to biased responses because the question implies that the governor dealt with the problems efficiently.

- Avoid emotionally charged words. Asking about possible solutions to the terrorism *crisis* will result in different responses than asking about solutions to the terrorism *problem*, which in turn will lead to different responses than asking about solutions to the terrorism *situation*. Compared to a *situation*, a *crisis* usually demands quicker and greater attention.

- Do not provide reasons or justifications for responses in the question. Let respondents come up with their own reasons for how they answer. Asking, "Do you support an increase in the state income tax to raise money to help fund education so that the children in our state will be better prepared to succeed in life?" encourages positive responses because of the justification given in the question—to help children be better prepared to succeed in life.

- Use a counter-biasing statement. A **counter-biasing statement** is given at the beginning of a question and assures respondents that all responses are acceptable and appropriate. Students might naturally overestimate the amount of time they spend studying. However, including a counter-biasing statement such as, "Some students spend very little time studying, others spend a great deal of time studying. How many hours do you study in a typical week?" lets respondents know that all answers are acceptable, even those that indicate very little studying.

Administrative Error and Bias

Administrative error and bias occurs when the researcher designs the data collection methodology in a way that leads to error. The major types of administrative error are listed below.

Population Selection Error. This occurs when the researcher identifies the wrong population of interest for the research, or the researcher does not include all possible consumers in the population. For example, a researcher might incorrectly identify only men as the population of interest when conducting research on men's cologne. A significant percentage of men's cologne is purchased by women. Because of this, conclusions from the research will not generalize to the entire correct population of male and female purchasers of men's cologne.

Sample Selection Error. This occurs when the researcher selects a sample that is not representative of the population, the sample systematically excludes certain population elements from being included in the sample, or the sample systematically overrepresents or underrepresents some segment of the population. This can occur from errors in the way the sample is chosen (the sampling procedures) as well as errors associated with an unrepresentative sampling frame.

Sampling Procedure Error. The purpose of random sampling is to assure that all population members have an equal, nonzero chance of being selected in the sample, leading to a representative sample. Some nonprobability sampling procedures that are not based on random selection procedures can lead to biased and unrepresentative samples. For example, university students employed to conduct personal intercept interviews at a shopping mall might interview only young shoppers. This could lead to a biased sample in terms of age. As another example, researchers might intercept and survey only those shoppers who look like they will respond in ways that the researcher wants them to respond. This will also lead to an unrepresentative sample and sample selection error.

> Population selection error and sample selection error are particularly problematic. It does not matter how well the research is conducted if the researcher has sampled from the wrong population or selected a biased sample from the correct population.

Sampling Frame Error. Sample selection error can also arise from errors associated with the sampling frame used for the research. The **sampling frame** is the list of population elements from which the sample is chosen. It is often referred to as the **working population** because it is the list of population elements with which the researcher is working. For example, a researcher interested in the fashion opinions of American women might purchase a subscription list from *Cosmopolitan* magazine and randomly call the women on the list. Unfortunately, the list of women who subscribe to *Cosmopolitan* magazine might not be representative of the entire American female population. Even though the sampling procedure for selecting women from the list might be completely random, leading to a representative sample of women from the sampling frame, the sampling frame itself is not representative of the entire population. For samples of the general population, phone directories are sometimes used as sampling frames and generally lead to representative samples. However, phone directories exclude people with unlisted phone numbers, exclude new residents who recently moved to an area after the directories were printed, and exclude people who use only cell phones.

Data Processing Error. This occurs when the researcher enters the wrong data, enters the wrong number, or even enters data for the wrong subject. The purpose of computer-based interviewing is to eliminate as many of these human errors as possible.

Interviewer Error. This occurs when an interviewer forgets to ask a question, purposely avoids asking a question, or even asks the wrong question. Interviewers might feel uncomfortable when asking respondents for their age. If so, they might not ask this question.

Interviewer Cheating Error. This occurs when researchers purposely fill in an answer because they did not ask the question during the interview, or when researchers purposely fill in an answer they want. If interviewers fail to ask respondents for their age, they might simply enter their best guess of the respondent's age.

Of these administrative errors, population selection error and sample selection error are by far the most important and can cause the most problems with respect to survey results and conclusions. Data processing error, interviewer error, and interviewer cheating error will occur simply because researchers deal with people, and people often make mistakes. However, data processing error, interviewer error, and interviewer cheating error do not usually cause significant problems with survey results and conclusions.

REPRESENTATIVE SAMPLING: A TWO-STEP PROCESS

The goal of sampling is to generate a representative sample of the population. If the sample is not representative, valid conclusions cannot be made about the population based on the sample results. There are two steps to obtaining a representative sample. Errors at either step can result in an unrepresentative sample.

Step One: The Sample of People Receiving the Survey Must be Representative

The sample of people who are selected to receive the survey must be representative of the entire population. If the people in the sample who are selected to receive the survey are not representative of the entire population, increasing the response rate will not significantly increase the representativeness of the final sample of respondents who complete the survey. To achieve a representative sample, a researcher must know the characteristics of the population (e.g., demographics) and identify all variables that could possibly be related to the key variable of interest, or identify variables that could be related to consumers' desire to complete the survey. For example, where people live might be related to their desire to complete a survey measuring attitudes toward a new sewage treatment plant. As another example, if

> Not only should the sample of potential respondents who receive the survey (are asked to complete the survey, are asked to participate in the research) be representative of the population, but the sample of respondents who complete the survey should also be representative of the population.

researchers were interested in measuring the attitudes of American women toward recent fashions, purchasing a list of women who subscribe to *Cosmopolitan* magazine would be considered a biased sampling frame. Increasing the number of women from this list who respond to the survey will not make the sample more representative and the results more accurate (with less survey error), because the sampling frame itself is not representative of the population.

Step Two: The Sample of People Responding Must be Representative

The final sample of respondents who complete the survey and return it to the researcher must be representative of the population. If the sample selected to receive the survey is representative (step one), then increasing the response rate will help to ensure a representative final sample by reducing the chance for self-selection bias and nonresponse error. To accomplish this, the researcher (i.e., the survey) must have a means of measuring characteristics of the respondents (e.g., demographics) to compare to the larger population. Measuring demographics on a survey allows researchers to determine whether or not the sample of respondents is representative of the larger population. This will help to identify potential nonresponse error and aid in determining whether or not more surveys need to be sent to certain types of people. For example, if people living in only the southeast part of a town respond to a survey on a proposed sewage treatment plant located in the southeast part of town, more respondents must be obtained from the other areas of town to achieve a representative sample. However, increasing the sample size will lead to a more representative sample, more accurate results, and less survey error only if the respondents who received the survey are representative of the larger population.

CROSS-SECTIONAL VS. LONGITUDINAL SURVEYS

Sometimes the purpose of a survey is to measure one variable, or the relationships between more than one variable at only one point in time. Such surveys are called cross-sectional surveys because they are designed to measure a cross section of a population at one point in time. In contrast, some surveys are designed to measure the changes in one variable, or the changes in the relationships between more than one variable over time. Such surveys are called longitudinal surveys because they are designed to measure changes in a population over time.

Cross-Sectional Surveys

A **cross-sectional survey** is one in which the sample is made up of a cross section of the population. A cross-sectional survey is designed to measure one variable, or the relationships between two or more variables at one point in time. All respondents to the survey are measured at the same time.

Sources of Error with Cross-Sectional Surveys. Cross-sectional surveys are susceptible to all of the types of error described so far in this chapter, such as random sampling error, nonresponse error, response bias, and administrative error.

Longitudinal Surveys

A **longitudinal survey** is one in which multiple samples are taken over time to measure the changes in one variable, or the changes in the relationships between two or more variables over time. Longitudinal surveys are actually a series of individual cross-sectional surveys conducted over time. An example of a longitudinal survey is when researchers measure consumers' confidence in the local and national economy. Such surveys are longitudinal surveys in that they track the relative increase or decrease in consumer confidence over time. When multiple samples are taken over time the researcher must decide whether to conduct a longitudinal survey as a tracking study or as a panel study.

Tracking Study. A **tracking study** is a longitudinal study in which the multiple samples each consist of different respondents. For example, group A is sampled at time period one (t_1), group B is sampled at time period two (t_2), group C is sampled at time period three (t_3), and so on. The consumers surveyed at t_1 are different from the consumers surveyed at t_2, and so on.

Panel Study. In a **panel study**, the same consumers are surveyed over time. For example, the same group of consumers is surveyed at t_1, t_2, t_3, and so on. The differences between the samples for tracking studies and panel studies are illustrated in Figure 12.7.

Sources of Error with Longitudinal Studies. Even though longitudinal surveys are conducted over time, the surveys conducted at each point in time can be considered as individual cross-sectional surveys. Thus, longitudinal surveys are susceptible to all of the types of error described so far in this chapter. However, because multiple surveys are conducted over time, longitudinal surveys are susceptible to additional sources of error, as shown in Figure 12.8. These sources of error will depend upon whether the longitudinal survey is conducted as a tracking study or a panel study.

FIGURE 12.7 Tracking Studies vs. Panel Studies

	Time Period		
	t_1	t_2	t_3
Tracking Study (samples)	A	B	C
Panel Study (samples)	A	A	A

FIGURE 12.8 Sources of Error for Cross-Sectional and Longitudinal Surveys

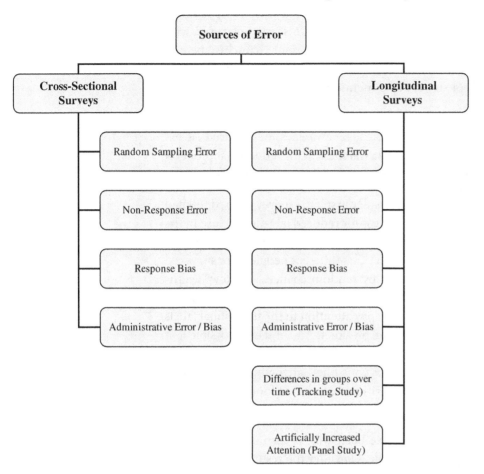

A potential source of error when conducting tracking studies is that the researcher often does not know if the differences in measures across time are due to actual changes in the variable, or if they are simply due to differences in the subjects selected for each sample. Alternatively, a potential source of error when conducting panel studies is that the researcher does not know if the differences in measures across time are due to actual changes in the variable, or if they are due to artificial effects of the measurement methodology.

To illustrate these sources of error, consider the case of Peanut Butter, Inc., a company that makes and markets Crunchity brand peanut butter. An advertisement for Crunchity peanut butter was aired on television from January through March. The advertisement emphasized the reduced-fat properties of Crunchity peanut

TABLE 12.3 Awareness for "Reduced Fat"

	Time Period		
	January	**February**	**March**
Percentage of consumers who mentioned reduced fat	10%	15%	20%

butter. The marketers wanted to measure the percentage of consumers who were aware of the reduced-fat property at three different times: at the end of January, at the end of February, and again at the end of March. This was measured with a phone survey asking consumers, "What do you know about Crunchity peanut butter?" They recorded the percent of consumers who mentioned the reduced-fat property. The percentages of consumers who mentioned reduced fat are shown in Table 12.3.

What effect did the advertisement have on increasing awareness of "reduced fat"? It appears that the advertisement led to increased awareness of the reduced-fat property over the three months. But, could there be other explanations for the observed results?

Errors Associated with Tracking Studies. Consider first if the survey were conducted as a tracking study. Did the increase in awareness for reduced fat (the increase in the percent of people mentioning reduced fat) result from the advertisement, or was the increase in awareness simply due to the fact that different people were surveyed each time? Is it possible that in January, just by random chance, very few health-conscious consumers were included in the sample? Health-conscious consumers are those who read the ingredient labels on foods, pay attention to the nutritional labels on foods, who choose healthy foods, or who are on a diet. And, is it also possible that in February and March, just by random chance, more health-conscious consumers were included in the sample? Health-conscious consumers are naturally more likely to pay attention to information about the nutritional aspects of food. Thus, the differences in the sample, and not the advertisement, could explain the results.

In anticipation of this problem, it would have been wise to also measure health-consciousness among consumers in the sample. Consider the results in Table 12.4, showing both the percentage of consumers who mentioned reduced fat, as well as the percentage of consumers who reported that they were health-conscious. In

TABLE 12.4 Awareness of "Reduced Fat," Controlling for Health-Consciousness

Situation A	Jan.	Feb.	March	Conclusion
Percentage of consumers who mentioned reduced fat	10%	15%	20%	
Percentage of consumers who reported being health-conscious	30%	40%	50%	Increased awareness due to differences in the samples

Situation B	Jan.	Feb.	March	Conclusion
Percentage of consumers who mentioned reduced fat	10%	15%	20%	
Percentage of consumers who reported being health-conscious	30%	30%	30%	Increased awareness due to advertisement

situation A, the increased awareness most likely resulted from differences in the samples (including more health-conscious consumers in February and March). However, in situation B, the increased awareness could be attributed to the advertisement because the percentage of health-conscious consumers was the same for each sample.

Errors Associated with Panel Studies. Now, consider if the survey were conducted as a panel study. In a panel study, the same consumers would have been surveyed in January, February, and again in March. Did the increase in awareness of reduced fat (the increase in the percent of people mentioning reduced fat) result from the advertisement, or did it result from consumers' increased attention to advertisements for Crunchity peanut butter because they were repeatedly asked questions about it? It is very difficult to measure the amount of increased attention that consumers pay to an advertisement because a researcher continues to ask them questions about that brand. Thus, many researchers prefer to conduct longitudinal studies as tracking studies because the differences in samples at each time the survey is conducted are relatively easy to measure.

Additional Errors in Longitudinal Studies. Additional sources of error can be introduced if there are seasonal effects involved with the topic of a survey. For example, it is possible that consumers might begin to pay more attention to the fat and calorie content of foods as the summer months approach. Many people begin diets early in the spring to get in shape for the summer and outdoor activities. This seasonal effect could also explain the increased attention that consumers gave to the reduced-fat properties of the peanut butter. And, this source of error would be present regardless of whether the survey was conducted as a tracking study or a panel study.

INTERPRETING SURVEY RESULTS

All that researchers ever really know is what they measure—the box a consumer checks on a survey or the numbers and words they write on a survey. Therefore, there are two important questions that researchers must answer when interpreting research results.

1. What did we observe?

2. Why did we observe it?

These two questions and the possible answers to them are shown in Figure 12.9.

What Did We Observe?

The first of these two questions seems relatively straightforward. However, it is important to consider the manner in which researchers answer the question "What did we observe?" Many researchers inadvertently misrepresent the results of research by

FIGURE 12.9 Interpreting Research Results

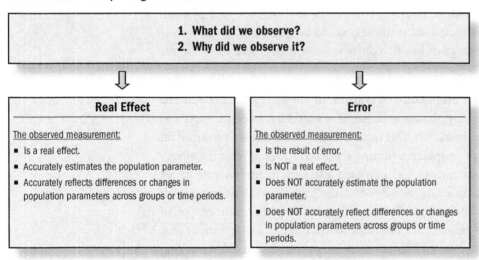

| **CHAPTER 12** SURVEY ERROR

overstating what was found in the results. They say more than they should say about the observed results and they overinterpret the observed results. For example, imagine that college students completed an online survey containing the following question:

Do you spend at least four hours per week studying for tests in your classes?
☐ Yes   ☐ No

What if 80 percent of respondents answered *yes* to this question? How should this be reported? Many researchers might mistakenly report that:

Eighty percent of students spend at least four hours per week studying for tests in their classes.

Although this sounds like a reasonable and accurate reporting of the result, it is not. It actually overstates the result. In actuality, all that can be said is:

Eighty percent of those students who responded to the survey and completed it reported that they spend at least four hours per week studying for tests in their classes.

Notice the difference between these two statements. The first statement assumes that the results are accurate and are free from error. Implicit in the first statement is the conclusion that 80 percent of all students in the population behave this way with respect to studying. Researchers should never assume that their results are free from error. Researchers should never imply conclusions about a larger population when such conclusions are still in doubt. The second statement retreats from these assumptions and implications by adding the phrase, "who *responded* to the survey and *completed* it, *reported* that they…" This type of wording is important when reporting research results because researchers do not want to give decision makers a false sense of confidence, or certainty, about the research result. Perhaps only those students who spend a great deal of time studying completed the survey, leading to nonresponse error. Further, even if all students completed the survey, there is a high probability that many of them lied by overreporting the amount of time they spend studying, resulting from social desirability bias. Researchers can report only what respondents said that they think, feel, do, or intend to do. Researchers never know what respondents actually think, feel, do, or intend to do. Researchers should report only what they found, or observed. They should not overreport or overinterpret the research result.

Why Did We Observe it?

The second important question that researcher must answer is, "Why did we observe it?" That is, why did we observe this particular measurement or this particular difference in measurements across groups or time periods? There are two possible answers to this question. Each answer refers to a possible explanation for the observed measurements.

1. The observed measurement is a real effect. The observed measurement is an accurate estimate of the population parameter. The observed measurements reflect accurate differences or changes in population parameters across groups or time periods.

2. The observed measurement is the result of error. The observed measurement is not a real effect. The observed measurement is not an accurate estimate of the population parameter. The observed measurements do not reflect accurate differences or changes in population parameters across groups or time periods.

To illustrate these two possible explanations for observed measurements, consider the case of an elementary school district. A survey was designed to measure the amount of time that parents of elementary school children spend reading to their children and working with their children on homework and schoolwork. Surveys were given to the schoolchildren to take home to their parents. Participating in the survey was not mandatory and parents were to return completed surveys in the mail.

The results from the survey of parents revealed that parents spend an average of two hours each night reading to their children and working with them on school-work. What could explain this finding? One possibility is that the survey result is an accurate estimate of the population parameter. In other words, parents in this school district really do spend an average of two hours each night reading to their children and working with them on schoolwork. However, a second possibility is that the survey result is due to error. The survey result could overestimate the true amount of time that parents spend working with their children simply because of random sampling error. The fewer parents who respond, the more random sampling error will be associated with the estimate. Of course, the survey result is also just as likely to underestimate the true amount of time that parents spend working with their children because of random sampling error. However, it is more likely that parents will naturally want to overreport the amount of time they spend reading to their children and working with them on schoolwork on a survey administered by the school district. This could result from social desirability bias, prestige bias, or even acquiescence bias. Equally likely is the possibility that only those parents who spend much time reading to their children and working with them on schoolwork will be willing to complete and return the survey. This important difference between respondents and nonrespondents will lead to nonresponse error. Further, it is also possible that children who do not spend much time on schoolwork simply failed to give the survey to their parents.

In the previous Crunchity peanut butter example, the observed increase in awareness over time could be due to the advertisements (a real effect, an accurate estimate of the population parameter). Alternatively, the observed measurements could be due to (biased by) error. In a cross-sectional survey, such error could include random sampling error, systematic error or bias, nonresponse error, response bias, and even administrative error. In a longitudinal survey, these same sources of error could bias results at any given time when a measurement is taken. In addition, longitudinal surveys can suffer from errors related to differences in samples across time (tracking studies), and the artificial increases in attention given to the topics of survey questions that are repeatedly asked of the same consumers (panel studies).

P Values and Survey Error. Unfortunately, as researchers we can be certain of only what we observe. We cannot be certain of why we observed it. Researchers might never know why a consumer checked a particular box, or why a consumer wrote down a particular answer to a survey question. As will be discussed in later chapters, statistical tests allow for the possibility that observed measurements are due to either real effects or error. The *p value* of a statistical test indicates the probability that the observed measurement is due to error, and not due to a real effect. However, such *p values* indicate only the probability that the observed measurements are due to random sampling error and not systematic error or bias. Even if a statistical test reveals a very low *p value*, for example, $p < .01$, indicating that there is less than 1 percent chance that the observed results are due to random sampling error, the observed measurements could still be the result of systematic error or bias that cannot be estimated statistically (e.g., response bias, sample bias, nonresponse error). This is why it is important that researchers understand all sources and types or error.

Reporting the Margin of Error for a Survey. When reporting the margin of error for a survey, it is important to clearly state that the ± percent margin of error refers only to random sampling error and does not account for the possibility of systematic error or bias in the results. This is illustrated below in an excerpt from a marketing research report.

> The results reported here are based on telephone interviews with 495 randomly selected adult residents, 18 years and older. With a sample of 495 people, we can say with 95 percent confidence that the amount of survey error due to taking a random sample instead of surveying all members of the population is ± 4.4 percent. Other factors such as problems with question wording and question interpretation can also introduce additional bias or error into the results.

SURVEY ERROR AND THE DECISION-MAKING PROCESS

It is very important that marketing researchers and marketing managers understand the concept of error and the many different sources of survey error. Whether random sampling error or systematic error, any source of error means that the results from marketing research might be incorrect. And, marketing decisions should not be made based on such incorrect results. As discussed in this chapter, it is unlikely that all sources of error can be completely eliminated from research results. Therefore, decision makers must be fully informed about the potential sources of error in the research results that they are using to make their decisions. A researcher would be negligent if he or she reported the results from a research project but did not also discuss the potential sources or error associated with the results. Not only do decision makers need to know the results from a research project ("What did we observe?"), but more importantly, they also need to know the possible explanations for the research results ("Why did we observe it?").

QUESTIONS FOR DISCUSSION

1. Compare and contrast random sampling error and systematic error (bias) in terms of:
   a. What causes the error?
   b. What is the effect of the error on sample statistics?
   c. Can the error be estimated statistically?
   d. How can the error be reduced?
   e. Can the error ever be eliminated?

2. The VP for student affairs at a university would like to survey students regarding their preferred location for a new parking garage located on campus. Using the terms nonresponse error, self-selection bias, and biased sample, describe the advantages and disadvantages of each of the following data collection procedures.
   a. A mail survey sent to students' post office boxes.
   b. An online survey posted to the university's website.
   c. An online survey where the link to access the survey is sent to students via their email address.
   d. Handing out surveys in selected classes and having students complete the survey during a class.

3. Describe what is meant by nonresponse error and what causes nonresponse error. Does a low response rate necessarily cause nonresponse error? How does asking demographic questions on surveys help identify the potential for nonresponse error?

4. What response biases might be associated with the following situations?

    a. A company's sales representatives are asked to report the percentage of time they spend making presentations to prospects, traveling, talking on the phone to customers, participating in meetings, working on the computer, and other on-the-job activities.

    b. A survey printed on letterhead from the National Education Association asked, "Should the U.S. government increase funding for education?"

5. A survey was administered in 30 randomly selected elementary schools across the country. It asked children to rate the importance of various factors when deciding which breakfast cereal they eat. Only 5 percent of the children checked off price as the most important consideration in determining their cereal selections. Further, 80 percent rated price as unimportant in determining their cereal selections. Based on these results, researchers concluded that price is of very little concern when marketing children's cereal. Do you agree with the conclusion? Why or why not?

6. A mail survey dealing with gun control was sent to a sample of 1,000 residents of Alabama. Half of the surveys were completed and returned. Two hundred (40 percent) of the respondents favored stricter gun control laws, whereas 300 (60 percent) opposed stricter gun control laws. Based on these results, and given that the survey was conducted to measure the attitudes of all people in this state, what do you conclude about the attitudes of people in this state toward gun control? What potential sources of error are associated with this research methodology?

7. In an effort to attract more customers to their store, the managers of a retail store decided to conduct some point-of-sale interviews of customers. They interviewed customers immediately after they made a purchase. The survey asked questions about what customers liked and disliked about the store and the merchandise sold in the store. Describe any potential problems or disadvantages associated with this research and the research methodology.

8. Burger King places little comment cards on their tables. Last month, a manager compiled the results from these cards. The results showed that this Burger King restaurant was doing very poorly in service quality. Out of 60 completed comment cards, 50 had negative comments. Should this Burger King be concerned with trying to improve their service quality?

9. What is a demand effect? For which survey methodologies might demand effects be present?

10. What role does survey error play in the managerial decision-making process? Why is it important for marketing managers to fully understand the various types of survey error?

11. Identify whether each of the following types of error are likely to be present for personal (intercept) interviews, mail surveys, telephone surveys, self-administered surveys, online surveys, and mobile surveys.

Type (Source) of Error	Personal (Intercept) Interviews	Mail Surveys	Telephone Surveys	Self-Administered Surveys	Online Surveys	Mobile Surveys
Nonresponse/Self-Selection Error						
Social Desirability Bias						
Acquiescence/Yea-Saying Bias						
Prestige Bias						
Threat Bias						
Hostility Bias						
Sponsorship Bias						
Question Order Bias						
Extremity Bias						
Interviewer Bias						
Memory Bias						
Apathy Bias						
Uninformed Response Bias						
Population Selection Error						
Sample Selection Error						
Data Processing Error						
Interviewer Error						
Interviewer Cheating Error						

MINICASE 12.1

Reserved Parking Spaces

The following email was sent to employees of a large company. The purpose of the email was to identify potential demand among employees for reserved parking spaces.

Date:	October 27
To:	All Employees
From:	Joe Smith, VP, Human Resources
Re:	Reserved parking spaces

A few employees have asked about acquiring a reserved parking space as a convenience. We would like to determine the percentage of employees who would be in favor of our company making reserved parking spaces available for employees to purchase. The cost for a reserved space would probably be from $50 to $100 a year.

I WOULD BE INTERESTED IN PURCHASING A RESERVED PARKING SPACE ___ Yes ___ No

Name _____ Email _____

Please reply to this email with your response, or print this survey and return it to Human Resources, Box 100.

The email was intended to serve as a survey measuring the percent of employees who favored allowing employees to purchase reserved parking spaces. Mr. Smith received 50 completed surveys, and 45 (90 percent) of those surveys were marked yes.

1. What does this tell Mr. Smith about the level of demand for all employees?

2. Do 90 percent of all employees want reserved spaces?

3. Which employees are more likely to complete the survey?

4. Which employees are more likely to disregard the email and not complete and return the survey?

MINICASE **12.2**

Marcony Grill

The Marcony Grill is a restaurant that serves steak, fish, pasta, and salads. The Grill is open seven days a week for both lunch and dinner. Gil and Robert Marcony are co-owners of the Grill. They each inherited half ownership of the Grill following their father's death four years ago. Gil and Robert Marcony have recently employed you as a marketing research consultant. They inform you that the number of customers eating at the Marcony Grill has steadily decreased over the past two years. They believe that this is due to a problem with the restaurant's image. No significant changes have been made to either the interior or exterior of the restaurant, or to the advertising that is used to promote the restaurant in the last three years. Two months ago they decided to conduct some marketing research on their own. They decided to evaluate the image of the Marcony Grill and consumers' perceptions of the Grill. A survey was placed on each table in the restaurant that diners could complete the survey if they wished. They inform you that even after analyzing the data they are still totally confused. Results from the survey indicated that their customers liked the restaurant and also had very favorable perceptions of the restaurant's image. They are considering replicating the same survey again to obtain a larger sample. What do you tell them?

MINICASE **12.3**

Virginia Woman Magazine

A new magazine, *Virginia Woman*, was recently introduced in January of this year. Advertisements promoting the new magazine were placed in every major newspaper in Virginia from March to July. To determine the effectiveness of their newspaper advertisements in creating awareness for the magazine, the magazine publisher employed the research firm Data Analytics to conduct a telephone tracking poll of 500 randomly selected Virginia residents in each of three months: March, May, and July. The results from the tracking poll showed that only 20 percent of those people surveyed in March were aware of the magazine, 30 percent of those surveyed in May were aware of the magazine, and 40 percent of those surveyed were aware of the magazine in July. The publishers were very impressed with these results and attributed the increased awareness to the newspaper ads.

What questions would you ask of the researchers from Data Analytics before you accept their conclusion that the newspaper advertisements were a significant factor in increasing awareness for the new magazine?

MINICASE 12.4

Student Express Bus

Administrators at a large university recently decided to move some of the student parking spaces to more remote parking lots around campus. In conjunction with this, they also added one more Student Express bus to help students get to classes from these remote parking lots. These changes were made in February. To measure students' reactions to these changes, they randomly selected students to complete an online survey containing 15 questions dealing with various aspects of parking on campus and potential difficulties associated with parking on campus. The survey was administered in early February, then again in March, and then again in April. The survey was emailed to 1,000 students each time it was conducted. Administrators hoped to measure the change in students' perceptions as a result of relocating the student parking spaces and adding one Student Express bus. The results showed that in February, 10 percent of the students reported that there were significant difficulties with respect to parking on campus. In March, 20 percent of students reported difficulties in parking. And, in April, 30 percent of students reported difficulties in parking. They concluded that relocating the student parking spaces was associated with an increase in students' perceived parking problems on campus.

1. In detail, describe why you either agree or disagree with their conclusion, and the questions you would need to ask about their research procedures and methodology to better evaluate their conclusion if the survey were conducted as a *tracking study*.

2. In detail, describe why you either agree or disagree with their conclusion, and the questions you would need to ask about their research procedures and methodology to better evaluate their conclusion if the survey were conducted as a *panel study*.

MINICASE 12.5

Pinky's BBQ Restaurant

The owners of Pinky's BBQ Restaurant want to better understand customers' attitudes and perceptions related to their restaurant. They approach you about helping them conduct a customer satisfaction survey. They have developed a draft of a survey and some ideas for administering the survey. They tell you that they would like to print the survey on small cards that can be left on the restaurant tables. Customers can complete the survey if they wish. When you ask them about this they tell you that they do not want to ask customers to complete the survey because they do not want to seem "imposing" or "pushy."

1. What do you tell them about their plans for conducting the survey?

2. What recommendations do you have for the restaurant owners?

3. What could be done to increase the percent of restaurant customers who complete the survey?

4. What incentives could be offered to customers as well as to servers to reduce error?

ENDNOTES

1   For a more detailed discussion of these techniques see J. Scott Armstrong and Terry S. Overton, "Estimating Nonresponse Bias in Mail Surveys," *Journal of Marketing Research* 14 (August 1977): 396–402.

2   Armstrong and Overton, "Estimating Nonresponse Bias in Mail Surveys," *Journal of Marketing Research* 14 (August 1977): 396–402.

3   Timothy R. Graeff, "Response Bias," in *Encyclopedia of Social Measurement* (New York: Elsevier, 2005).

4   Robert A. Peterson, *Constructing Effective Questionnaires* (Thousand Oaks, CA: Sage Publications, 2000).

5   Vicki G. Morwitz, "It Seems Like Only Yesterday: The Nature and Consequences of Telescoping Errors in Marketing Research," *Journal of Consumer Psychology* 6 (1997): 1–29.

6   Timothy R. Graeff, "Uninformed Response Bias in Telephone Surveys," *Journal of Business Research*, 55 no. 3 (2002): 251–259; Timothy, R. Graeff, "Reducing Uninformed Responses: The Effects of Product-Class Familiarity and Measuring Brand Knowledge on Surveys," *Psychology & Marketing* 24 no. 8 (2007): 681–702.

7   Timothy R. Graeff, "Exploring Consumers' Answers to Survey Questions: Are Uninformed Responses Truly Uninformed?" *Psychology & Marketing* 20 no. 7 (2003): 643-667.

8   Jean M. Converse and Stanley Presser, *Survey Questions: Handcrafting the Standardized Questionnaire* (Thousand Oaks, CA: Sage Publications, 1986).

CHAPTER $\bigcirc$ **13**

Measurement

LEARNING OBJECTIVES

1 Discuss the importance of measurement to marketing research.

2 Compare and contrast abstract constructs and concrete constructs.

3 Describe the difference between a conceptual definition and an operational definition.

4 Define measurement scale.

5 Compare and contrast the four levels of quantitative measurement scales—nominal scales, ordinal scales, interval scales, and ratio scales—in terms of what the scales measure and what can be calculated from the data.

6 Describe the allowable transformations for nominal scales, ordinal scales, interval scales, and ratio scales.

7 Identify the significance and meaning of "zero" on the four different levels of quantitative measurement scales.

8 Discuss the impact of verbal labels on measurement scales.

9 Discuss how using category ranges to measure continuous variables can impact the level of a measurement scale.

Measurement is one of the most important functions of marketing research. One could say that the fundamental purpose of marketing research is to measure things. The things that marketing researchers measure are called **constructs**, or concepts. Marketing researchers measure **demographic constructs**, **psychographics constructs**, and **behavioral constructs** (see Figure 13.1).

FIGURE 13.1 Constructs that Marketing Researchers Measure

Demographic Constructs	Psychographic Constructs	Behavioral Constructs
Age	Attitudes	Purchase Amount
Income	Interests	Purchase Frequency
Number of Children	Opinions	Brand Choice
Occupation	Beliefs	Store Patronage
Home Ownership	Intentions	Complaining Behaviors
Marital Status	Perceptions	
	Feelings	

DEFINING AND MEASURING CONSTRUCTS

Abstract and Concrete Constructs. Marketers measure a variety of different constructs, from very abstract constructs to very concrete constructs. **Abstract constructs** are typically not tangible. They cannot be seen and they are typically hard to define and measure. Such abstract constructs include brand loyalty, brand personality, involvement, channel power, and attitudes. Constructs such as attitudes, beliefs, and opinions are neither visible nor observable. To measure such abstract constructs, researchers must assume that the constructs exist based on their observable (theoretical) effects on other constructs. For example, if a consumer always buys brand X, researchers can assume that this consumer has a positive attitude toward brand X, even though the attitude that (theoretically) is causing the purchase behavior can be neither seen nor observed. On the other hand, **concrete constructs** are more tangible. Concrete constructs can often be seen and they are typically easier to define and measure. Such concrete constructs include age, sex, marital status, income, height, and number of children. Concrete constructs are easier to measure because they are easier to define.

To measure constructs in marketing, researchers need to know three things.[1]

1. What is the construct?

2. What will be measured to indicate the presence or absence of the construct?

3. What scale will be used to measure the construct?

What is the Construct?

Conceptual Definitions. Researchers must first define what they are attempting to measure. A **conceptual definition** tells researchers what the construct is. It defines what the construct is, usually in terms of other constructs. For example, speed is often defined in terms of two other constructs: distance and time (e.g., miles per hour). In marketing, the construct *level of interest in an advertisement* can be defined as the degree to which an advertisement is perceived to be personally relevant and the degree to which consumers perceive associations between the advertised information and their own personal goals or values. While this conceptual definition tells researchers what the construct is, it does little to tell them exactly how to measure "level of interest in an advertisement."

> The level of scale used to measure a construct determines what can and cannot be said about the construct being measured.

What will be Measured to Indicate the Construct?

Operational Definitions. Whereas a conceptual definition tells researchers what a construct is, an **operational definition** tells researchers what to measure to indicate the presence or absence of the construct.[2] It gives meaning to the construct by specifying how researchers should measure it, or what researchers should measure. For example, *level of interest in an advertisement* can be **operationalized** (operationally defined) in terms of (indicated by) pupil dilation, the number of thoughts a consumer forms about an advertisement while viewing it, or even the amount of time a consumer spends looking at an advertisement. Even though an operational definition does not tell researchers what the construct is, it does tell researchers that they can determine which of two advertisements is more interesting by measuring the amount of time a consumer spends looking at each advertisement. Operational definitions indicate the construct, they operationalize a construct, and they tell researchers what to measure. But, they do not tell researchers what the construct is. The conceptual definition tells researchers what the construct is.

What Scale will be Used to Measure the Construct?

A **measurement scale** is a systematic way of assigning numbers, or scale values, to those things being measured. Quantifying constructs by assigning numerical scale values conveys information about the variable or construct being measured. For instance, we usually quantify temperature. Which is more informative, "It is sort of cold," or "It is 47° F"? The quantified measurement, 47° F, is more informative because most people will know exactly what it means on the Fahrenheit scale. However, "It is sort of cold" has little meaning because it could mean different things to different people.

Multiple Scales to Measure a Single Construct. The difficult part of measurement in marketing is that a single construct can be measured on a number of different scales. And, different scales can lead to different conclusions about the constructs being measured. For example, consider two consumers, Bill and Mary. We can operationalize these two consumers' brand loyalty to Pepsi as the percentage of their total number of soft drink purchases that are Pepsi (see Table 13.1).

If we measured (operationalized) loyalty in terms of the percentage of soft drink purchases that are Pepsi, we would conclude that Mary is more loyal. Alternatively, if we measured (operationalized) loyalty in terms of the total number of Pepsi soft drinks purchased, we would conclude that Bill is more loyal. Notice that two different measures of the same construct can lead to two completely different conclusions. Further, consider that loyalty can also be measured (operationalized) in terms of:

- Time interval between purchases of Pepsi.

- Rating on a 7-point attitude scale, where 1 = dislike Pepsi and 7 = like Pepsi.

- Answer to the question, "I am a loyal Pepsi drinker."

- Number of other brands purchased.

Each scale might lead to a different conclusion about which consumer is more loyal to Pepsi.

> One of the most difficult aspects of measurement in marketing is that a single construct can be measured on a number of different scale, each leading to a different conclusion.

TABLE 13.1 Scales for Measuring Loyalty to Pepsi

	Number of Pepsi Soft Drinks Purchased per Month	Total Number of Soft Drinks Purchased per Month	Percentage of Soft Drink Purchases per Month That Are Pepsi
Bill	5	50	10%
Mary	3	10	30%

What do the Numerical Scale Values Mean?

All quantitative measurement scales assign numerical values to those things being measured. The question that researchers must answer is, "What do the numerical scale values mean?" The interpretation and meaning of numerical scale values will vary according to the type of scale used and the properties of the scale. The next section outlines the four major levels of quantitative measurement scales and the meaning of the numerical scale values associated with each.

> All quantitative measurement scales assign numbers to those things being measured. The question is, "What do those numbers mean?"

LEVELS OF MEASUREMENT SCALES

There are four major **levels of quantitative scales**: nominal scales, ordinal scales, interval scales, and ratio scales. Each scale has unique properties associated with it. As such, the meaning of the numerical scale values will vary by level of scale. A nominal scale is the lowest-level scale, having the fewest properties and containing the least information. An ordinal scale has all the properties of a nominal scale, plus one additional property. An interval scale has all the properties of an ordinal scale and a nominal scale, plus one additional property. And, a ratio scale has all the properties of an interval scale, an ordinal scale, and a nominal scale, plus one additional property.

Measures of Central Tendency. It is important to understand the differences between these types of measurement scales because the level of scale determines the **measure of central tendency** that can be used to summarize the measurements (results). Figure 13.2 shows the measures of central tendency that can be calculated for each level of scale.

The **mode** of a distribution is the value that occurs most frequently. The **median** indicates the middle of a distribution, meaning that half the observations are less than it, and half are greater than it. The **mean** of a distribution is the arithmetic average (the sum of all observations divided by the number of observations). To illustrate these measures of central tendency, imagine that there are 15 children in a classroom and their ages are distributed as shown in Figure 13.3.

FIGURE 13.2 Measures of Central Tendency and Level of Scale

Scale	Measure of Central Tendency
Nominal	Mode
Ordinal	Mode, Median
Interval	Mode, Median, Mean
Ratio	Mode, Median, Mean

FIGURE 13.3 Age of Children in a Classroom (X = One Child)

```
                                                        X
                        X                               X
                        X                               X
                X       X               X               X
        X       X       X       X       X               X
Age     1       2       3       4       5       6       7
```

The mode of this distribution of ages is 7 because there are more children 7 years old than any other age. The median is 4, because there are seven children younger than 4, and there are seven children older than 4. The mean is 4.4. Notice that the mode, median, and mean for a single distribution can be very different from each other. This is important because interval scales and ratio scales allow us to calculate the mode, median, and mean. However, an ordinal scale allows us to calculate only the median and the mode. And, a nominal scale allows us to calculate only the mode. The properties of nominal scales, ordinal scales, interval scales, and ratio scales are summarized in Figure 13.4.

FIGURE 13.4 Levels of Measurement Scales

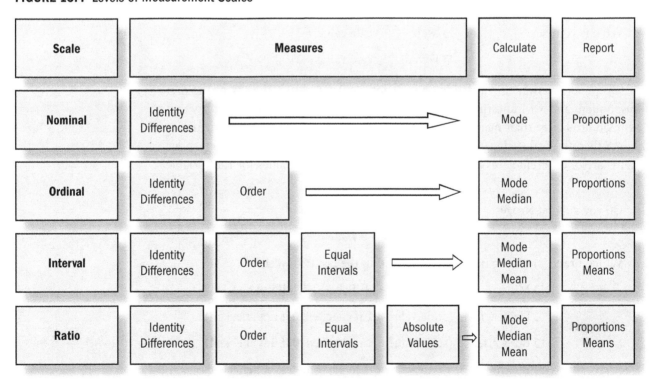

FIGURE 13.5 Allowable Transformations for Scales

Scale	Allowable Transformations
Nominal	Identity-preserving transformations
Ordinal	Order-preserving transformations
Interval	Interval-preserving (linear) transformations
Ratio	Ratio-preserving transformations

ALLOWABLE SCALE TRANSFORMATIONS

A **scale transformation** changes the values of a scale from the units of one scale to the units of another scale. **Allowable transformations** retain the information content of the original scale. Figure 13.5 shows the allowable transformations for nominal scales, ordinal scales, interval scales, and ratio scales.

NOMINAL SCALES

A **nominal scale** is the simplest type of measurement scale. The numbers or letters that make up the scale serve as labels only. These labels allow us to classify and identify differences in those things being measured. For nominal scales we can calculate the mode. The scales below are nominal scales.

What is your sex? ☐ Male (scale value = 1)

☐ Female (scale value = 2)

If two people answer this question and we enter a 2 indicating the sex of the first respondent and a 1 indicating the sex of the second respondent, we cannot say that women are better than men simply because they have a scale value of 2, which is larger than the scale value for men (1). All that we can say is that these two respondents are of different sexes because they have different scale values for the variable sex.

Do you shop at Kroger? ☐ Yes (scale value = 1)

☐ No (scale value = 2)

Which brand(s) of beer have you purchased in the last two weeks:

☐ Miller (scale value = 1 if checked, 0 if not checked)

☐ Heineken (scale value = 1 if checked, 0 if not checked)

☐ Budweiser (scale value = 1 if checked, 0 if not checked)

☐ Busch (scale value = 1 if checked, 0 if not checked)

☐ Bud Light (scale value = 1 if checked, 0 if not checked)

Allowable Transformations for Nominal Scales

Identity-preserving transformations can be performed on nominal scales. For instance, in a sample of 60 men and 40 women we can assign the scale value of 1 for *male* and 2 for *female* (these would be the values entered into the computer). We can also reverse these scale values and assign the scale value of 2 for *male* and 1 for *female*. This is allowable because the transformation retains the informational property of the original scale—different numbers indicate different sex of respondents.

Reporting the Results from Nominal Scales

The results from nominal scales can be summarized by reporting percentages as well as the mode, which is the most frequently occurring observation. For example, we can make statements such as:

- Sixty percent of the sample respondents were male, and 40 percent were female.

- The majority of the respondents were male.

- Most of the respondents were male.

- There were more males than females in the sample.

ORDINAL SCALES

An **ordinal scale** has all the properties of a nominal scale, plus it measures constructs in terms of an ordered relationship, such as big to small, best to worst, first to last, and even longest to shortest. For ordinal scales we can calculate the mode and the median. The most common method for assigning scale values to the categories in an ordinal scale is to simply assign a 1 to the lowest category, a 2 to the next highest category, a 3 to the next highest category, and so on. This is illustrated below.

What is your class standing?	☐ Freshman	(scale value = 1)
	☐ Sophomore	(scale value = 2)
	☐ Junior	(scale value = 3)
	☐ Senior	(scale value = 4)
Evaluate this product:	☐ Excellent	(scale value = 5)
	☐ Above Average	(scale value = 4)
	☐ Average	(scale value = 3)
	☐ Below Average	(scale value = 2)
	☐ Terrible	(scale value = 1)

Notice that these numerical scale values indicate the relative order, rank, or placement of each category in relation to the other categories. On this scale, larger scale values indicate evaluations that are more favorable. Compared to *above average*, *excellent* is a more favorable evaluation of a product. This is reflected in the larger numerical scale value for *excellent* compared to the numerical scale value for *above average*. However, the numerical scale values do not convey any information beyond order, or relative rank. It makes no sense to say that one product rated as *excellent* (5 on the scale) is five times better than a second product rated as *terrible* (1 on the scale). Similarly, it makes no sense to say that one product rated *above average* (4 on the scale) is twice as good as a second product rated *below average* (2 on the scale). Such ratio comparisons cannot be made with an ordinal scale. All that can be said is that products rated as *excellent* are perceived by the respondent to be better than products rated as *above average*. A ranking task also produces an ordinal scale:

> Rank order your preference for the following (1 for your favorite, 2 for your next most favorite, etc.)
>
> _____ Coke
>
> _____ Pepsi
>
> _____ RC Cola
>
> _____ Mountain Dew

Allowable Transformations for Ordinal Scales

Order-preserving transformations can be performed on ordinal scales. To illustrate this, Figure 13.6 presents the results from a survey of 100 consumers who evaluated a brand. Twenty consumers rated the brand *excellent*, 30 consumers rated the brand *above average*, and so on. The original scale values assigned to these categories were 5 for *excellent*, 4 for *above average*, 3 for *average*, 2 for *below average*, and 1 for *poor*.

The first transformation (assigning the value of 20 for *excellent*, 16 for *above average*, and so on) is allowable because it retains the ordinal property (ordinal information) of the original scale. However, the second transformation (assigning the value of 18

> Ordinal scales can identify if two measurements differ in terms of relative rank, or placement along a scale, but not by how much they differ.

FIGURE 13.6 Transformations for an Ordinal Scale

Number of Consumers	Scale	Original Scale Value	Allowable Transformation	Not Allowable Transformation
20	Excellent	5	20	18
30	Above Average	4	16	20
25	Average	3	12	45
15	Below Average	2	9	13
10	Poor	1	2	5
Total = 100				

for *excellent*, 20 for *above average*, and so on) is not allowable because it does not retain the ordinal property of the original scale.

Reporting the Results from Ordinal Scales

The results from ordinal scales can be summarized by reporting percentages, the mode, and also the median. The median makes sense because there is order to what is being measured. For example, we can make statements such as:

- Twenty percent of respondents rated the brand as *excellent*, 30 percent rated the brand as *above average*, and so on.

- The median rating was *above average*.

Combining Categories. The results from ordinal scales can also be reported by combining the results from more than one scale category by using the phrase "at least." However, researchers must be careful about the order in which they say *at least*, the *percent*, and the *scale value*. Report the results from ordinal scales with the following convention: *percent, at least, scale value*. For example:

- Seventy-five *percent* of consumers rated the brand *at least* *average, or better*.

- Forty *percent* of students in this class are *at least juniors*.

- Ninety-five *percent* of people said that this year's fair was *at least* *somewhat better than* last year's fair.

Ordinal Scales and the Mean

Means cannot be calculated for data measured on ordinal scales. This is because ordinal scales do not measure in equal intervals. The equal intervals property of a measurement scale refers to the intervals between the scale categories themselves, not the numerical scale values that are assigned to the different scale categories. To illustrate this, consider the scale shown below:

Please rate this product: ☐ Excellent   (scale value = 3)

☐ Very Good   (scale value = 2)

☐ Terrible   (scale value = 1)

Notice that the numerical scale values convey the ordinal property of the scale: *excellent* is better than *very good*, which is better than *terrible*. In addition, the numerical scale values seem to imply that the scale categories are in equal values. In numerical terms, the difference between 3 and 2 is the same as the difference between 2 and 1. However, the scale categories are not in equal intervals. Perceptually, the difference between *excellent* and *very good* is relatively small. Conversely, the perceptual difference between *very good* and *terrible* is relatively large. As such, the numerical scale values do not accurately reflect the perceptual differences in the scale categories and cannot be used to calculate a mean.

INTERVAL SCALES

An **interval scale** has all the properties of an ordinal scale plus it measures constructs in **equal intervals**. For interval scales we can calculate the mode, median, and mean. The scales below are interval scales.

How well do you like this class?	Dislike	1 2 3 4 5 6 7	Like
Evaluate this product:	Terrible	1 2 3 4 5 6 7	Excellent
How likely are you to purchase this product?	Very Unlikely	1 2 3 4 5 6 7	Very Likely

These scales merely identify two endpoints of a continuum on which consumers are to report their answer. There are seven equally spaced intervals on the continuum. The individual scale categories along the continuum are not named or labeled.

Allowable Transformations for Interval Scales

Interval-preserving (linear) transformations can be performed on interval scales. Consider the following scale:

Rate this brand: Poor   1   2   3   4   5   Excellent

If 100 men and 100 women evaluated a brand by circling one of the numbers on the scale that best represented their evaluation, we can calculate the mean rating for men and for women. If the mean rating for men = 4.0 and the mean rating for women = 2.0, can we claim that men liked the brand twice as much as women liked the brand? The answer is no. The reason is because this scale could be transformed to the following:

Rate this brand: Poor   11   12   13   14   15   Excellent

And, if respondents circled the number corresponding to the same position on the scale, the mean rating for men would now be 14, and the mean rating for women would now be 12. It is obvious that 14 is not twice as large as 12. Any transformation of an interval scale that retains the equal interval properties is allowable. However, ratio comparisons (e.g., men like it *twice* as much) cannot be made with interval scales. Consider the two transformed scales below.

Allowable transformation:	Poor	21	22	23	24	25	Excellent
Not allowable transformation:	Poor	20	25	26	27	30	Excellent

Even though the second transformed scale retains the ordinal property of the scale, it does not retain the equal intervals property of the scale.

Reporting the Results from Interval Scales

The results from interval scales are most often summarized by reporting the mean with statements such as, "The average rating was 4.0, on a 5-point scale, where

5 = excellent, 1 = poor." However, the results from interval scales cannot be reported by making ratio comparisons. To make ratio comparisons requires a ratio scale.

RATIO SCALES

A **ratio scale** has all the properties of an interval scale plus it has an absolute zero point. An **absolute zero point** on the scale indicates the absence of the construct being measured. A ratio scale measures constructs in terms of their absolute value. With ratio scales, we can calculate the mode, median, and mean. Constructs such as age, income, distance, time, and weight can be measured on a ratio scale because each has an absolute zero point. Most "count" questions (where consumers write in a number indicating the number of things) are ratio scales. The scales below are ratio scales.

What is your annual income? (Write in a dollar amount.) $_____

How many miles do you live from campus? _____ miles.

How many pets do you currently own? _____

Allowable Transformations for Ratio Scales

The only allowable transformations of ratio scales are those that preserve the ratio properties of the original scale. As such, ratio scales are not often transformed because they already measure in absolute values.

Reporting the Results from Ratio Scales

The results from a ratio scale can be summarized by reporting the mean with statements such as:

- The average age of respondents in the sample was 45.7 years.
- Respondents reported renting an average of 1.5 DVDs every week.

Zero on a Ratio Scale

A ratio scale has an absolute zero point indicating the absence of the construct being measured. However, this does not mean that we would ever expect anyone to respond with a zero on the scale. For instance, the survey question, "I am _____ years old" is a ratio scale. It makes sense to say that a 10-year-old child is twice as old as a 5-year-old child. Even though we would never expect anyone to respond by entering a zero for this question (this would mean they had not been born yet), a zero still has meaning. It indicates a lack of age. As another example, we can ask, "How many miles do you live from our store in Greenhills?" We would not expect anyone to respond with a zero. This would indicate they lived on the very same spot as the store. However, it is still a ratio scale. It makes sense to say that someone who lives 10 miles from the store lives twice as far as someone who lives 5 miles from the

All quantitative measurement scales can include a zero as part of the scale. But, only on ratio scales does zero mean the absence of the construct being measured.

store. The absolute zero point indicates a lack of distance. In fact, for most constructs that can be measured on ratio scales, we would not expect consumers to ever enter a zero (e.g., age, income, time, distance, weight, height, or even the amount of money spent on groceries).

ZERO ON NOMINAL, ORDINAL, AND INTERVAL SCALES

A ratio scale is not the only scale that can have a zero as one of its scale values. However, a ratio scale is the only scale for which a zero indicates the absence of the construct being measured. Zero can be a scale value for nominal scales, ordinal scales, and interval scales. For instance, a zero can be easily incorporated into a nominal scale. Instead of assigning a scale value of 1 for males and 2 for females, a researcher can assign a scale value of 0 for males and 1 for females. This does not change the properties of the scale in any way. Different scale values indicate different sex.

What is your sex?	☐ Male	(scale value = 1)
	☐ Female	(scale value = 2)
What is your sex?	☐ Male	(scale value = 0)
	☐ Female	(scale value = 1)

But what does the zero mean on a nominal scale? It means the same thing that any other number means on a nominal scale. It indicates differences, and nothing more. It does not indicate the absence of the construct being measured. Similarly, zero can be a scale value on an interval scale. Consider the two interval scales shown below:

Rate this brand: Poor   0   1   2   3   4   Excellent

Rate this brand: Poor   1   2   3   4   5   Excellent

Both scales are essentially equivalent. They both identify a continuum from poor to excellent, and they both identify five equally spaced intervals along that continuum. But, what does the zero mean on the first scale? It means the same thing that any other number means on an interval scale. It indicates a relative place along the continuum, and nothing more. The zero on the first scale does not indicate a lack of attitude, or the absence of an attitude toward the brand. The numbers on an interval scale are arbitrary. As such, adding a zero as one of the numbers along the continuum does not make the scale a ratio scale.

VERBAL LABELS ON SCALES

Whenever **verbal labels** are assigned to the internal categories of a scale (as opposed to the scale endpoints), the scale should be treated as an ordinal scale instead of an interval scale. For example, the scale shown below is an interval scale:

Very Bad   1   2   3   4   5   6   7   Very Good

This scale merely identifies two endpoints on the continuum from *Very Bad* to *Very Good*, and seven equally spaced intervals along the continuum. In contrast, the scale shown below should be treated as an ordinal scale.

Very Bad	Bad	Somewhat Bad	Neither Good Nor Bad	Somewhat Good	Good	Very Good
1	2	3	4	5	6	7

Even though this scale has the same number of scale places as the previous scale (seven), and the same numerical scale values, we cannot be sure that the differences in the meaning of the verbal labels are in equal intervals. We cannot be sure that the difference in meaning between *Very Good* and *Good* is the same as the difference in meaning between *Good* and *Somewhat Good*. Thus, we cannot be sure that it measures in equal intervals.

The equal intervals property of an interval scale refers to the intervals between the meanings of the scale points themselves, not the intervals between the numerical scale values that are assigned to the different scale points. In the above example, the difference between 7 and 6 (the numerical scale values assigned to the scale points) is the same as the difference between 6 and 5, in purely mathematical terms. However, the difference in meaning, or the difference in perception between *Very Good* and *Good*, might not be the same as the difference in meaning, or the difference in perception, between *Good* and *Somewhat Good*.

CATEGORY RANGES AND ORDINAL SCALES

Sometimes, consumers are not able to provide an exact numerical answer to a question. This is often the case when measuring annual income. Most consumers do not know their exact annual income. However, most consumers can probably report their annual income if it is measured on a scale that provides $10,000 ranges of incomes. This is illustrated with the survey question below:

What was your personal annual income last year?
- ☐ Less than $10,000
- ☐ $10,000–$20,000
- ☐ $20,001–$30,000
- ☐ $30,001–$40,000
- ☐ $40,001 or more

Income is a construct that can be measured on a ratio scale. Zero income means that a person has no income. So, is the scale shown above a ratio scale, or is it an ordinal scale? It is an ordinal scale. This is because there is a range of values for each category response. If a consumer selected the $20,001–$30,000 category, what was their income? There is no way to know. Since we do not know consumers' exact income,

FIGURE 13.7 Income Measured on an Ordinal Scale

Consumer	Personal Annual Income	Income Categories	Survey Response
Bill	$22,000	☐ Less than $10,000	
Tom	$34,000	☐ $10,000–$20,000	
Carol	$39,000	☐ $20,001–$30,000	Bill
		☐ $30,001–$40,000	Tom, Carol
		☐ $40,001 or more	

the scale cannot measure in equal intervals and an average cannot be calculated. To further illustrate this, consider the three consumers described in Figure 13.7.

If each of these three consumers answered the income question as shown in Figure 13.7, Bill would select the *$20,001–$30,000* income category, whereas Tom and Carol would both select the *$30,001–$40,000* income category. Is the difference between Bill's income and Tom's income the same as the difference between Bill's income and Carol's income? No. In absolute values, there is a $12,000 difference between Bill's income and Tom's income, whereas there is a $17,000 difference between Bill's income and Carol's income. Unfortunately, we would never know these actual differences if income were measured in $10,000 ranges of income. Because of this, the income categories do not measure in equal intervals. Thus, whenever there is a range of values for scale categories, the scale should be treated as an ordinal scale, and neither an interval scale nor a ratio scale.

REPORTING THE MEDIAN VS. THE MEAN

The mean is a higher level measure of central tendency than the median. The mean contains more information about the distribution. If a scale allows researchers to calculate the mean, should they always report the mean? Or, should they ever report the median? To help answer these questions, consider the two samples in which consumers reported their annual income shown in Figure 13.8. Notice that the samples are the same except for the outlier in sample two (consumer L) whose income is very different than the other consumers' incomes.

For sample one, the median income = $35,000, and the mean income = $35,000. In sample two, the median income = $35,000, and the mean income = $58,333. In sample one, half of the incomes are less than the average income, and half of the incomes are greater than the average income. However, in sample two, 83.3 percent of the incomes are less than the average income, whereas only 16.6 percent are greater than the average income. Reporting the mean for sample two could be misleading. It would not make sense to most people that almost all of the consumers in sample two had incomes less than the average. Including the income for consumer L greatly

FIGURE 13.8 Outliers and Measures of Central Tendency

Sample One		Sample Two	
Consumer	Annual Income	Consumer	Annual Income
A	$10,000	G	$10,000
B	$20,000	H	$20,000
C	$30,000	I	$30,000
D	$40,000	J	$40,000
E	$50,000	K	$50,000
F	$60,000	L	$200,000

increased the average in sample two. Whenever there is a potential for **extreme outliers**, the median is often reported instead of the mean. This is because outliers have no effect on the median, whereas outliers can have a significant effect on the mean.

INTERVAL SCALES AND PERCENTAGES

Because interval scales measure in equal intervals, both percentages and averages can be calculated from the data. However, be careful when trying to interpret the results from interval scales. Because interval scales measure variables on a continuum, it is often difficult, if not impossible, to determine where sections of the continuum begin and end. For example, consider the interval scale below that can be used to measure consumers' liking for brand X.

How well do you like brand X?   Dislike   1 2 3 4 5 6 7   Like

What number on this scale indicates *liking*? Where does *dislike* end on this scale? Where does *like* begin on this scale? How would a researcher report the percentage of respondents who *like* the brand? The answer is that they would not be able to. There is no way to know where *dislike* ends and know where *like* begins on this scale. Does a 4 on this scale indicate that a consumer likes the brand? There is no way to know. Does a 2 on this scale indicate that a consumer has only a very small liking for the brand? Does only a 1 indicate disliking? Again, there is no way to know.

Differences in Scale Value Interpretation. Another issue that compounds these interpretation problems is that different people might use the scale values differently. Some consumers might consider anything less than the midpoint (4) to indicate disliking. Alternatively, other consumers might consider scale values below the midpoint to indicate a small amount of liking, but not disliking. Without verbal labels for each numerical scale value, a researcher would not know how consumers interpreted and used the numerical scale values.

Measurement Scales and Decision Making. Because of this characteristic of interval scales, researchers sometimes measure such constructs as attitudes, liking, preferences, and even intentions to purchase products with simple *yes* or *no* questions. Even though a *yes* or *no* question is measured on only a nominal scale, it might actually provide more useful information for decision makers in certain situations. If marketing managers need to know the percentage of consumers who intend to purchase a brand, they would benefit more from using the following question, compared to using an interval level scale:

Do you intend to purchase our brand within the next month?   ☐ Yes   ☐ No

With this scale, there is no question about the meaning of a *yes* response, or about the meaning of a *no* response. There is no need to guess or infer about the meaning of a numerical scale value.

Researchers should always consider the decision maker when designing surveys and other research instruments. By knowing how the data is to be used by decision makers, researchers can use the appropriate scales for the decision-making situation. In fact, people often use simple *yes* or *no* questions for making some of the most important decisions in their lives. When a man asks a woman to marry him, he does not ask, "On a scale from 0 to 10, how much would you like to marry me?" Instead, he asks, "Will you marry me, yes, or no?" Compared to a 0–10 scale, a simple *yes* or *no* question actually does a better job of measuring the woman's willingness to marry him. Similarly, simple *yes* or *no* questions do an excellent job of measuring constructs such as consumers' intentions to purchase products and consumers' desire to own products.

MEASUREMENT SCALES AND THE DECISION-MAKING PROCESS

Knowing the differences in the levels of measurement scales is not a trivial matter. On the contrary, it plays a key role in the decision-making process and can have a direct effect on the quality of marketing decisions. Recall the IDO model of marketing research and the decision-making process, shown in Figure 13.9.

Marketing researchers must understand the properties of nominal scales, ordinal scales, interval scales, and ratio scales. The level of scale used on a survey, or other research instrument, determines the type of calculations that can be performed on the data, and it also determines the manner in which the research results can be analyzed and reported. For example, if marketing managers need to know the average age of different target markets, an ordinal scale cannot be used to measure age. If marketing managers need to be able to make ratio comparisons of specific variables related to a target market, ratio scales must be used to measure these variables.

FIGURE 13.9 The IDO Model of Marketing Research and the Decision-Making Process

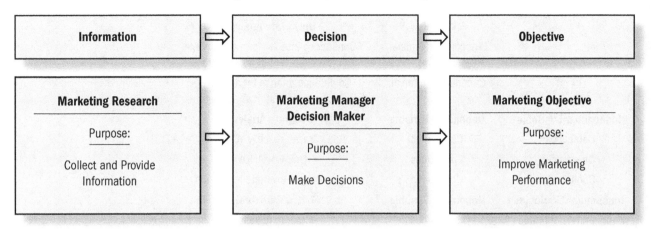

Therefore, levels of measurement scales can have a direct effect on the quality of marketing decisions and the ability of marketing managers to make decisions that are designed to achieve marketing objectives.

Measurement Scales and Types of Statistical Analysis. Additionally, the level of scale on which a variable is measured determines the types of statistical analyses that can and cannot be performed on the data related to that variable. Many students often wonder why there are so many different statistical tests that they must learn in their statistics and marketing research courses. They might ask, "Why can't we simply perform a t-test for everything?" Well, the answer lies in the level of scale with which the data is measured. The choice of the appropriate statistical procedure for analyzing one, two, or even three or more variables depends upon the level of scale on which the variables are measured. Different statistical tests have been developed to analyze data for all of the possible combinations of measurement scales. For example, if researchers wished to examine the difference in mean incomes (measured on a ratio scale yielding a continuous variable) for men and women (measured on a nominal scale yielding a categorical variable), the appropriate test for that combination of variables would be an analysis of variance (ANOVA). If researchers wished to examine the relationship between consumers' annual incomes (measured on a ratio scale yielding a continuous variable) and the amount of money consumers donate to charity annually (also measured on a ratio scale yielding a continuous variable), the appropriate analysis for that combination of variables would by either regression or correlation analysis. The reason there are so many different statistical tests is because there are multiple combinations of nominal, ordinal, interval, and ratio scaled variables. The statistical analyses appropriate for the various combinations of variables are shown in Figure 13.10.

FIGURE 13.10 Statistical Analyses for Various Combinations of Variables

	Variable	Univariate Analysis
	Categorical (Nominal, Ordinal)	Confidence interval for a percentage, hypothesis test of a proportion
	Continuous (Interval, Ratio)	Confidence interval for an average, hypothesis test of an average
Independent Variable	**Dependent Variable**	**Bivariate Analysis**
Categorical	Categorical	Cross-tab, chi-square
Categorical	Continuous	One-way ANOVA
Continuous	Continuous	Correlation, bivariate regression
Independent Variables	**Dependent Variable**	**Multivariate Analysis**
Continuous, Continuous	Continuous	Multiple regression
Continuous, Categorical	Continuous	Multiple regression
Categorical, Categorical	Continuous	Two-way ANOVA

QUESTIONS FOR DISCUSSION

1. Describe the differences between nominal scales, ordinal scales, interval scales, and ratio scales.

2. If you wanted to measure the average age of students at your university, what level scale would you need to use?

3. Shaquille O'Neal wore uniform number 34. Michael Jordan wore uniform number 23. Because 34 is larger than 23, does this mean that Shaquille O'Neal was a better basketball player? Discuss why or why not.

4. If it is 40° Fahrenheit in Nashville, Tennessee, and it is 80° Fahrenheit in Miami, Florida, is it twice as hot in Miami as it is in Nashville? What if it were 40° Kelvin in Nashville and 80° Kelvin in Miami?

5. Why is it important for marketing managers to fully understand the various levels of measurement scales? How does the level of a measurement scale affect the managerial decision-making process?

6. Researchers measured consumers' attitudes toward a new product with the following scale:

   Evaluate this product: ☐ Excellent   (scale value = 5)

   ☐ Above Average   (scale value = 4)

   ☐ Average   (scale value = 3)

   ☐ Below Average   (scale value = 2)

   ☐ Terrible   (scale value = 1)

a. Betty rated the product *Above Average*, whereas Tom rated the product *Below Average*. Can you say that Betty liked the product twice as much as Tom did, since 4 is twice as large as 2?

b. Vern rated the product *Excellent*, whereas Danny rated the product *Terrible*. Can you say that Vern liked the product five times as much as Danny did?

7. Researchers measured consumers' attitudes toward a new brand of beer with the following scale:

How well do you like this brand of beer?   Dislike 1 2 3 4 5 6 7 Like

John circled a 6 on the scale. Stan circled a 2 on the scale. Can you say that John liked the beer three times as much as Stan?

8. Researchers measured the distance that students live from campus with the following scale:

How many miles do you live from campus? _____ miles.

Jane entered "10 miles," whereas Stacey entered "5 miles." Can you say that Jane lives twice as far from campus as Stacey?

9. Researchers asked consumers to indicate on the following scale how often they visit the Glenview Mall:

☐ Very often   (scale value = 5)

☐ Often   (scale value = 4)

☐ Sometimes   (scale value = 3)

☐ Rarely   (scale value = 2)

☐ Never   (scale value = 1)

To test whether there is a difference in how often men and women visit the mall, researchers averaged the scores (scale values) for each sex and then made a statistical comparison of these averages (using a t-test comparing two means). Is this appropriate?

10. Researchers measured men's and women's attitudes toward a new brand of beer on the following scale:

Dislike   0 1 2 3 4 5 6   Like

The average rating for the men was 4.2, whereas the average rating for the women was 2.0.

a. Is it appropriate to calculate averages for men and women?

b. Does it appear that men liked the beer more than women did?

c. Can you conclude that men liked the beer twice (two times) as much?

11. Researchers asked consumers the following two survey questions:

How many days do you drink Diet Coke during a typical week?

☐ None   ☐ 1   ☐ 2   ☐ 3   ☐ 4   ☐ 5   ☐ 6   ☐ 7

What is your age?   ☐ Younger than 35   ☐ 35 or older

For consumers younger than 35 years old, the average number of days that they drink Diet Coke in a typical week was 2.2. For consumers 35 and older the average was 4.8. Researchers concluded that older consumers (35 years and older) drink more than twice as much Diet Coke, compared to younger consumers (34 or younger). Do you agree?

12. Researchers asked consumers the following two survey questions:

How much do you spend on groceries in a typical week? I spend $ _____ on groceries in a typical week.

How many children under the age of 18 do you have living in your household? _____

The average amount of grocery expenditures for consumers with one or no children living in the household was $145.34. The average amount of grocery expenditures for consumers with two or more children living in the household was $320.60. Researchers concluded that households with two or more children spend more than twice as much on groceries than households with one or no children. Do you agree?

13. Researchers asked college students the following two survey questions:

How much do you currently pay for rent (per month)? (If none, leave this question blank.)

☐ Less than $100   ☐ $300–$399

☐ $100–$199   ☐ $400–$499

☐ $200–$299   ☐ $500 or more

Do you earn more than $1,000 per month in income? ☐ Yes   ☐ No

Based on the results, researchers concluded that college students who earn more than $1,000 per month in income pay on average more than twice as much as college students who earn less than $1,000 per month in income. Evaluate this conclusion.

14. Male and female college students were asked the following survey question:

How many days per week do you rent movies?

☐ None   ☐ 1   ☐ 2   ☐ 3   ☐ 4   ☐ 5   ☐ 6   ☐ 7

Researchers averaged the responses separately for male and female students and found that the average for male students was 4.2, whereas the average for the female students was 1.8. Researchers concluded that male students rent more than twice as many movies per week as female students. Do you agree?

15. For the credit card survey shown below:
    a. Identify the level of scale for each survey question (nominal, ordinal, interval, or ratio).
    b. Describe how the results from each survey question should be reported in a research report.

Do you currently have any credit cards in your name? ☐ Yes ☐ No

I have at least one of the following credit cards (check all that apply):

☐ Visa	☐ Department Store Card
☐ MasterCard	☐ Gas Company Card
☐ American Express	☐ Other _____

How many bank credit cards (Visa or MasterCard) do you currently have?

☐ None

☐ 1–2

☐ 3–4

☐ 5–6

☐ 7 or more

Within the last year, how many months did you have an outstanding balance on your credit card, meaning that you did not pay the full balance at the end of the month? (If none write in zero.) _____ months.

What do you typically purchase using your credit card? (Check all that apply.)

☐ Clothing	☐ Food/drinks at restaurants, bars, etc.
☐ Music (CDs, tapes, etc.)	☐ Gas for your car
☐ Groceries	☐ Other _____

Today, what is the approximate amount of your outstanding balance (the amount that you will still owe after you pay your monthly payment) on all of your credit cards combined? Write in the dollar amount. (If no outstanding balance, write in zero.) $ _____

A credit card is a
symbol of success.   Strongly Disagree   1 2 3 4 5 6 7   Strongly Agree

What is your age (in years)? I am _____ years old.

What is your approximate personal annual income? $_____

What is your sex?   ☐ Male   ☐ Female

16. For the car owner survey shown below:
    a. Identify the level of scale for each survey question (nominal, ordinal, interval, or ratio).
    b. Describe how the results from each survey question should be reported in a research report.

Do you own a car?   □ Yes   □ No

How much did you pay for your current car?   □ Less than $1,000

                                               □ $1,000–$5,000

                                               □ More than $5,000

How much is your car currently worth?   □ Less than $1,000

                                               □ $1,000–$5,000

                                               □ More than $5,000

Did you take out a loan to purchase your current car?   □ Yes   □ No

What is the current balance on your car loan? $_____

What are your monthly car payments?   □ Less than $200

                                               □ $200–$400

                                               □ $401–$600

                                               □ $601 or more

Do you think you will buy a car within the next year?

    □ Yes, probably a new car.

    □ Yes, probably a used car.

    □ No, I will not buy a car within the next year.

Indicate your level of agreement with each of the following statements, where 1 = Strongly Disagree and 5 = Strongly Agree.

    A car is something to be used.   1 2 3 4 5

    A car is something to be taken care of.   1 2 3 4 5

    A car should always be bought with cash, not with a loan.   1 2 3 4 5

    A person should get a new car every 2–3 years.   1 2 3 4 5

What is your sex?   □ Male   □ Female

What is your marital status?

    □ Married   □ Single   □ Divorced   □ Widowed   □ Other _____

What is your age (in years)? _____

MegaBucks Insurance Agency

You recently attended a job fair sponsored by your university. While at the job fair you spoke to a woman from MegaBucks Insurance Agency. She gave you the following information about careers in life insurance sales:

> Insurance sales is a career with unlimited income potential and flexible hours. In fact, *Careers 2013* recently reported that insurance sales compensation averaged $70,000 per year, increasing to $100,000 after 10 years. And, 20 percent of all insurance sales agents earned over $150,000 in 2012. Compensation for insurance sales is higher than for many other sales professions. According to *Careers 2013*, the median income for a manufacturing salesperson is only $56,000, and is $62,000 for a real estate or advertising sales representative. The table below outlines the average yearly earnings of the insurance agents working at MegaBucks Insurance Agency:

Based on Gross Commissions

Top 25 agents	$388,620
Top 100 agents	$289,752

1. Are you convinced by this information?

2. What measure of central tendency was reported for insurance sales?

3. What measure of central tendency was reported for other sales positions?

4. Is there anything misleading about this information?

5. What does the information in the table tell you about potential outliers in the distribution of sales incomes?

America Reads

America Reads is a not-for-profit organization committed to promoting reading among Americans. A recent study found that Europeans read an average of five fiction novels per year. Researchers working for America Reads wanted to compare this number to the average number of fiction novels that Americans read per year. So, they decided to include the following question on a survey of Americans.

How many fiction novels do you read in a year?
☐ None   ☐ 1–3   ☐ 4–6   ☐ 7–9   ☐ 10–12   ☐ 13 or more

What do you tell the researchers working for America Reads?

MINICASE 13.3

Miami Department of Tourism

You work for a public relations firm that has been hired by the Miami Department of Tourism to develop promotional materials designed to attract tourists to the Miami area during the winter months. One of the brochures states:

> Looking for a warm Christmas? The average temperature in Miami during December is 80° F, twice as warm as the average December temperature in Wisconsin (40° F).

What do you do?

What do you tell the person who wrote this?

ENDNOTES

1 Fred N. Kerlinger, *Foundations of Behavioral Research* (New York: Holt, Rinehart and Winston, 1973).
2 Barry F. Anderson, *The Psychology Experiment* (Montery, CA: Brooks/Cole, 1971).

CHAPTER 14

Reliability, Sensitivity, and Validity of Measurement Scales

LEARNING OBJECTIVES

1 Define reliability and explain the importance of reliability to measurement scales in marketing research.

2 Define sensitivity and explain the importance of sensitivity to measurement scales in marketing research.

3 Define validity and explain the importance of validity to measurement scales in marketing research.

4 Compare and contrast how reliability can be estimated using measures of repeatability and measures of internal consistency.

5 Describe the measurement dilemmas associated with the test-retest method for estimating the reliability of a measurement scale.

6 Describe the relationship between the reliability and the sensitivity of a measurement scale.

7 Discuss the effects of *Don't Know* or *No Opinion* options on the validity of measurement scales in marketing research.

8 Describe the physical characteristics that can reduce the validity of measurement scales used in marketing research.

Imagine that you wake up one morning and step onto your bathroom scale. It reads 178.3 pounds. You step off of the scale and then immediately step back on it again. But this time it reads 179.1 pounds. You step off of the scale and then immediately step back on it for a third time. This time it reads 177.2 pounds. Imagine your frustration about not being able to determine your actual weight. How can you determine whether you are losing weight or gaining weight?

Now, imagine that you have decided to build some bookshelves for your home. Unfortunately, the only tool you have for measuring is a warped yardstick. You are concerned about how well you can build the bookshelves, given that the warped yardstick will not yield accurate measurements. So, you go to the local hardware store. You purchase the least expensive tape measure that you can find in the store. You take it home, only to be disappointed when you remove it from the package.

FIGURE 14.1 Three Qualities of Good Measurement Scales

Reliability	**Sensitivity**	**Validity**
Similar results are obtained over time and across varying situations. The measurement instrument is free of measurement error. The measurement scale always measures the same thing.	The measurement scale is able to measure slight changes, differences, or variability in the stimuli or responses being measured.	The measurement scale measures what it is supposed to measure, or what it claims to measure.

The tape measure measures only in ½ inches. It does not have any tick marks on the tape indicating ¼ inch, 1/8 inch, or 1/16 inch measurements. You are concerned about not being able to make very exact, or precise, measurements.

Qualities of Good Measurement Scales. None of the measurement scales described above possesses the qualities that are required of a good measurement scale. The bathroom scale is neither dependable nor reliable because it does not provide the same measurement of weight on a repeated basis. The warped yardstick does not provide an accurate measure of length. And, the tape measure does not provide very sensitive or exact measurements of length.

The three major qualities of good measurement in marketing, and any other social science, are reliability, sensitivity, and validity. Researchers want to use measurement scales that are reliable, sensitive, and valid. These three qualities of measurement scales are summarized in Figure 14.1.

RELIABILITY

A **reliable** scale is one that is dependable. It always measures the same thing every time it is used. To illustrate this quality of measurement scales, imagine that your shift at work ends at 3 p.m. Every day, your roommate arrives to give you a ride home at exactly 3:25 p.m. You would like your roommate to pick you up at 3:05, but you must wait an extra 20 minutes every day. Even though you might describe your roommate as always being late, at least your roommate is dependable in terms of when he or she will arrive. Your roommate is dependably late. If you have to meet with your supervisor after work, you know that you will always have an extra 20 minutes. This quality of being dependable is the same quality as reliability. Reliability of a measurement scale means that:

- Similar results are obtained over time and across varying situations.

- The measurement instrument is free of measurement error.

- The measurement scale always measures the same thing.

For example, a metal ruler is generally considered to be a more reliable measure of length than a wooden ruler. This is because a metal ruler is less likely to change shape and size with varying environmental and atmospheric conditions.

Reliability and Measurement Theory. Classical measurement theory starts with the assumption that a person's observed score (x_i) on a test item (e.g., survey question) is equal to the sum of their true score (τ_i) plus an error score (ε_i).

In equation form: $x_i = \tau_i + \varepsilon_i$.

Note that Greek letters (τ, ε_i) represent unobservable scores, similar to the way Greek letters represent population parameters which we never know. The reliability of a measurement scale, or test item i, is defined as the squared correlation between the observed scores and the true scores, $\rho^2(x_i, \tau_i)$, which equals the ratio of true score variance to observed score variance:

$$\rho^2(x_i, \tau_i) = \text{Var}(\tau_i)/\text{Var}(x_i)$$

Therefore, reliability is the percentage of the variance in observed scores accounted for by true scores. If true scores were observed, we could easily use statistical regression techniques to regress the observed scores on the true scores, and then use the resulting R^2 as an estimate of a scale's reliability. However, true scores are generally unknown, in the same way that true population parameters are unknown. Therefore, researchers must estimate the reliability of a measurement scale. Reliability can be estimated based on the repeatability and internal consistency of a measurement scale.[1]

Estimating Reliability: Repeatability

Test-Retest Method. The **test-retest method** is when the same item (survey question) is administered repeatedly to the same sample of people. The test-retest method is thus a longitudinal measure of reliability. The correlation of the observed scores across two administrations is an estimate of reliability. However, in practice the assumptions required for this measure are not likely to hold for the following reasons:

1. **Instability of true scores**. True scores can change over time. Decreasing the time interval between measurements can reduce such instability of true scores across time.

2. **Memory effects**. When people answer a question for the second time, they sometimes answer based only on their memory of how they answered the first time. Increasing the time interval between measurements can reduce such memory effects.

Notice the measurement dilemma that is associated with estimating reliability based on repeatability and the test-retest method. Decreasing the time interval between measurements reduces problems with instability of true scores across time, but also increases the likelihood of memory effects. And, increasing the time interval between measurements reduces problems with memory effects, but also increases the likelihood of instability of true scores across time.

Estimating Reliability: Internal Consistency

Reliability can also be estimated based on **internal consistency** using the split half method, equivalent forms method, or coefficient alpha.

Split Half Method. The **split half method** can be used to assess the internal consistency of a survey that contains a large number of questions, such as a **multi-item index**. Researchers can compare the results from one-half of the scaled items (e.g., odd-numbered items) to the results from the other half (e.g., even-numbered items). This offers advantages over the test-retest method because it eliminates problems with instability of true scores over time and problems with memory effects. However, the researcher must assume that the items in both halves of the test are equivalent. Different split halves can lead to different estimates of reliability. Note, however, that this is not a problem with a two-item scale. To illustrate the split half method, imagine that teacher effectiveness is measured with the following six items:

	SD	D	N	A	SA
1. The instructor is well-prepared.	☐	☐	☐	☐	☐
2. The instructor is knowledgeable about the topic.	☐	☐	☐	☐	☐
3. The instructor presents material clearly.	☐	☐	☐	☐	☐
4. The instructor is good-looking.	☐	☐	☐	☐	☐
5. The instructor wears nice clothes.	☐	☐	☐	☐	☐
6. The instructor likes the same sports that I like.	☐	☐	☐	☐	☐

Imagine what would happen if this scale were split into two halves, with items 1 through 3 in one half, and items 4 through 6 in the other half. Obviously, these two halves are not equivalent. Sometimes it is difficult to show that two halves are equivalent.

Equivalent Forms Method. The **equivalent forms method** is when two sets of questions are designed to be as similar as possible. Subjects complete both sets of questions. The correlation between the two question sets is then used as the measure of reliability. However, it must be assumed that the two question sets are actually equivalent. If researchers find a low correlation between the question sets, they are faced with the question, "Is the low correlation due to low reliability, or due to using two question sets that are not equivalent?" What if question set A contains items 1 through 3 from the previous example, and question set B contains items 4

> To make decisions, marketing managers need information that has been measured on scales that are reliable, sensitive, and valid.

> A reliable scale is one that consistently measures the same thing every time it is used. However, that does not necessarily mean that it measures the right thing. A measurement scale can be reliable, but not valid. A scale can consistently measure the wrong thing.

through 6 from the previous example? Note that the split half method and the equivalent forms method both estimate reliability at one point in time. They do not measure reliability over time. They also assume that the construct being measured is one-dimensional.

Coefficient Alpha. The **coefficient alpha** (**Cronbach's Alpha**) is often used to measure the internal consistency of a linear composite of items (meaning more than two items in a scale, such as an index of items). Alphas close to 1.0 (0.70 and greater) indicate high internal consistency. Researchers typically prefer scales with very high alphas (0.80 and above).

SENSITIVITY

Sensitivity refers to a measurement scale's ability to measure slight changes, differences, or variability in the stimuli or responses being measured. Imagine that you decide to purchase a new bathroom scale to replace the unreliable one described at the beginning of this chapter. When you arrive at the store you see that there are three scales on display. You step on the first scale and it displays 171 pounds. You step on the second scale and it displays 171.3 pounds. You then step on the third scale and it displays 171.32 pounds. The first scale is the least sensitive, displaying weight to the nearest pound. The second scale is more sensitive, displaying weight to the nearest tenth of a pound. The third scale is the most sensitive, displaying weight to the nearest hundredth of a pound.

As another example, consider the following three scales to measure liking for a product:

A. Rate our product. ☐ Bad ☐ Good

B. Rate our product. Bad   Good

                       ①   ②   ③   ④   ⑤

C. Rate our product [Place a mark on the line that best indicates your answer.]

               Bad ———————— Good

Scale A is probably the most reliable of these three scales. It offers the best chance that consumers will mark the exact same answer every time they use the scale (assuming that their attitude toward the object being evaluated does not change). Scale C is the most sensitive of the three scales. It allows for many possible response options. Scale B allows for only five different responses. Scale A allows for only two different responses. Even though reliability and sensitivity are both desirable, researchers typically have to give up one to get more of the other. Very reliable scales tend to be relatively insensitive. Alternatively, very sensitive scales tend to be relatively unreliable. Thus, while scale A is very reliable, it is not very sensitive. Alternatively, while scale C is very sensitive, it is not very reliable. Scale B offers an acceptable amount of both reliability and sensitivity.

VALIDITY

Validity refers to a measurement scale's ability to measure what it is supposed to measure, or what it claims to measure. If a scale measures what it says it is measuring, then it has high validity. If a scale does not measure what it says it is measuring, then it has low validity. A warped yardstick is not a valid measure of length because it does not measure the true, or accurate, length of an object. As another example, a five-item spelling test that contained the words *bat, run, hit, umpire,* and *out* would not be a valid measure of general spelling ability. The problem is that it contains mostly short words that pertain to one domain—baseball. It is possible that a child who follows baseball religiously could be a terrible speller, yet perform very well on this test. As another example, asking consumers to indicate how likely they would be to purchase a product might not be a valid measure of actual purchase intention. Consumers might say that they intend to buy the product just to please the researcher (acquiescence bias or yea-saying bias). As another example, a three-item scale to measure teacher effectiveness made up of items 4 through 6 from the previous example would not be a valid measure of teacher effectiveness.

Validity is by far the most important quality of a measurement scale. A valid scale measures what it is supposed to measure. Further, by definition, if a scale is valid, it is also reliable. If a scale measures what it is supposed to measure, it must always measure that same thing. Unfortunately, validity is also the most difficult quality of a measurement scale to assess and demonstrate. For example, how do we know if a survey question accurately measures consumers' true attitudes or intentions? Because of this, reliability is sometimes used as a surrogate measure of validity. That is, even if a researcher cannot assess the validity of a scale, at least the researcher can demonstrate that the scale is reliable. However, reliability does not guarantee validity. A scale can be reliable, but not valid. It is possible for a scale to consistently measure the wrong thing.

Face (Content) Validity

Face (content) validity means that there is general agreement from professionals and people working in a field that a scale will accurately measure what it claims to measure. From the previous teacher effectiveness example, items 1, 2, and 3 would have more face validity than items 4, 5, and 6.

Criterion Validity

Criterion validity refers to the ability of a measurement scale to correlate highly with previously developed standard measures of the same construct. For example, a new measure of customer satisfaction should correlate highly with current and previous scales used to measure customer satisfaction.

Concurrent and Predictive Validity

Concurrent validity can be established when a new measurement scale is used at the same time as a previously established measure. **Predictive validity** can be established when the new measurement scale is used before a previously established measure.

Convergent and Discriminant Validity

Concurrent and predictive validity can be used to establish the **convergent validity** of a measurement scale. Convergent validity refers to the ability of a measurement scale to correlate highly with other measures of that same construct. Conversely, **discriminant validity** can be established through low correlations between a measurement scale and other scales that are supposedly not measuring the same construct. That is, a measurement scale should be able to discriminate among a construct and other different constructs.

With respect to the teacher effectiveness example, convergent validity can be established if the scale correlates positively with end-of-the-semester standardized test scores (the better the teacher, the better the students should perform on standardized tests covering the course material), and negatively with the number of complaints about the teacher received by the department chair (the better the teacher, the fewer the complaints). However, a question could exist about the validity of standardized test scores and number of complaints as valid measures themselves.

Construct Validity

Construct validity refers to the ability of a measure to provide empirical evidence consistent with a theory based on the construct that it is designed to measure.[2]

Don't Know Options and Validity

Some researchers are reluctant to include a *Don't Know* or *No Opinion* (*DK/NO*) option on their surveys. They argue that *DK/NO* options only reduce individual item response rates. Respondents can easily avoid answering a question by simply checking the *DK/NO* box. In effect, *DK/NO* options can lead to smaller samples and lower response rates. However, the potential advantages of including a *DK/NO* option far outweigh any disadvantages associated with reduced item response rates.

DK/NO options increase the validity of a measurement scale. *DK/NO* options allow respondents who truly are uninformed, and respondents who truly have no opinion about a topic, to indicate this lack of knowledge or opinion. Forcing respondents to answer a question when they really have no knowledge or opinion introduces uninformed response bias into the results. It forces people to guess, answer randomly, or even provide the answer they believe the researcher wants to hear. Such answers are not valid measures of respondents' true thoughts, feelings, or beliefs. Most

> Adding a Don't Know option to a survey question increases that question's validity. It allows consumers who truly are uninformed to respond as such without forcing them to mark an answer or report an opinion that does not accurately represent them.

researchers would rather have a smaller sample of responses that accurately reflect respondents' true thoughts, feelings, or beliefs than a larger sample of responses that contain error and bias. Even though including a *DK/NO* option might decrease the quantity of responses, it increases the quality of responses.

This can have significant effects on the usefulness and accuracy of information provided to decision makers, especially for surveys designed to measure consumers' attitudes toward lesser-known brands, products, or stores. To illustrate, consider the case of The Clearwater Café. The Clearwater Café had been in business for almost one year and was developing a very strong base of loyal and repeat customers. It seemed that everyone who ate at the café liked it. The owner of the café decided to conduct some surveys to measure attitudes of local residents toward the café. Attitude questions were written without *DK/NO* options, as shown below.

What is your overall attitude toward The Clearwater Café?

Very Negative   1 2 3 4 5 6 7   Very Positive

As it turned out, only about half of those people surveyed were aware of the café. And, of those people who were aware of the café, almost all of them had very positive evaluations of the café, that is, they circled "7" on the scale. However, the other half of respondents were unaware of the café. Most of these people circled the midpoint on the scale, that is, they circled "4." Responses from those people who were unaware of the café were combined with the responses from those people who were aware of the café. When the average rating was calculated, the large number of moderate responses caused the average rating to be less positive than it should have been. As a result, the owner received a false measure of consumers' attitudes toward his café. The lack of a *DK/NO* option led to a biased result that was not a valid measure of consumers' attitudes.

As this situation illustrates, not providing a *DK/NO* option can greatly reduce the validity of a measurement scale. When forced to answer a question for which they are uninformed or have no opinion, many consumers will choose the midpoint of a scale. This way, they are rating the object neither negatively nor positively. Unfortunately, if no *DK/NO* option is provided, these uninformed moderate ratings are then combined with the other informed ratings when calculating the mean for a rating scale. This forces the average rating toward the middle of the scale. Mean ratings of objects for which informed consumers hold very positive evaluations become more negative, and mean ratings of objects for which informed consumers hold very negative evaluations become more positive. In either case, the mean rating is not a valid measure of consumers' true evaluations.

QUALITY SCALES AND THE DECISION-MAKING PROCESS

Decision makers must have information to be able to make decisions. The measurement scales that are used to obtain that information should be reliable, sensitive, and

FIGURE 14.2 The IDO Model of Marketing Research and the Decision-Making Process

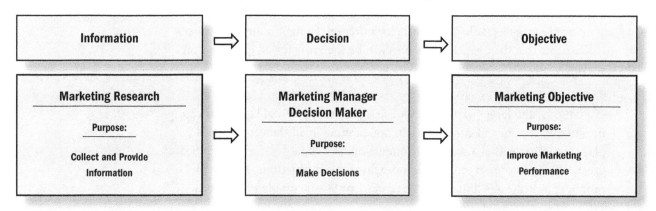

valid. For example, to be able to make informed decisions regarding changes in a patient's diet and exercise program, a doctor must have reliable and valid measures of the patient's weight and changes in weight over time. The same applies to marketing decision makers, who need information to make their decisions. Recall the IDO model of marketing research and the decision-making process, shown in Figure 14.2.

Marketing managers need information to be able to make decisions that are designed to achieve desired marketing objectives. The measurement scales that are used to obtain that information should be reliable, sensitive, and valid. Marketing managers need information obtained from measurement scales that reliably measure the same construct every time they are used, and that accurately measure what they are supposed to measure.

Threats to the Validity of Measurement Scales

As discussed previously, consumers often lie, censor, or otherwise alter their responses when answering survey questions. The most common types of response bias are listed in Figure 14.3. These response biases lower the validity of survey questions and measurement scales.

In addition, the physical characteristics of measurement scales can also threaten the validity of survey questions. Survey questions will tend to have lower validity when:

FIGURE 14.3 Response Bias

Response Bias	
Social Desirability Bias	Question Order Bias
Acquiescence/Yea-Saying Bias	Extremity Bias
Prestige Bias	Interviewer Bias
Threat Bias	Memory Bias
Hostility Bias	Apathy Bias
Sponsorship Bias	Uninformed Response Bias

- The direction of scales is not consistent throughout the survey (i.e., positive evaluations are placed on the right side of the scale for some questions, but are placed on the left side of the scale for other questions). Many consumers will assume that the direction of scales will be the same for all questions on a survey.

- Smaller scale values are assigned to the verbal labels indicating positive evaluations, and larger scale values are assigned to the verbal labels indicating negative evaluations. If consumers do not carefully read the verbal labels placed at either end of a scale, they often assume that larger numbers indicate greater liking, more agreement, or more favorable evaluations, and smaller numbers indicate less liking, less agreement, or less favorable evaluations.

- There is an even number of scale points with no midpoint on the scale. This forces people to provide a response that is either on the positive end of the scale or on the negative end of the scale. When forced to choose, many people will choose the positive end of the scale. This leads to results that overestimate positive evaluations.

- There is no *DK/NO* option provided. This will force people who are uninformed, or who have no opinion, to report an opinion. Uninformed respondents often choose the midpoint on the scale, causing the mean rating from the scale to be more moderate than it should be.

- A scale does not provide enough response options, or is not sensitive enough to adequately measure small differences or changes in respondents' thoughts, feelings, perceptions, or beliefs.

QUESTIONS FOR DISCUSSION

1. In your own words, compare and contrast reliability, sensitivity, and validity.

2. Margaret wants your opinion about some survey questions to be included on a customer satisfaction survey for FloamyFeet brand shoe insoles. She wants to measure consumers' attitudes using the following scale:

   How much do you like FloamyFeet brand shoe insoles?

   Like very much   1 2 3 4 5 6   Do not like at all

   Describe how you would change this scale to increase its validity.

3. What effect does adding a *Don't Know* response option have on the validity of a scale?

4. Describe the relationship between reliability and sensitivity.

5. Discuss the reliability, sensitivity, and validity of the scales used to measure teacher effectiveness at your university.

6. Can a measurement scale be reliable but not valid?

7. Can a measurement scale be valid but not reliable?

8. Which survey question (either a or b) would be a more reliable measure of consumers' attitudes toward a product?

    a. Rate our product.   ☐ Bad   ☐ Good

    b. Rate our product.   Bad 1 2 3 4 5 Good

9. Is measuring a consumer's purchase intention during a focus group a valid measure of actual purchase intention? What types of response bias might reduce the validity of these measures of purchase intentions in the context of a focus group?

10. Describe the difficulties associated with estimating reliability using the test-retest method.

11. What role does the reliability, sensitivity, and validity of measurement scales play in the managerial decision-making process?

12. Why must marketing managers know the reliability, sensitivity, and validity of the measurement scales used to measure the information on which they are basing their decisions?

MINICASE **14.1**

Sweet Shop Ice Cream Parlor

You are the manager of the Sweet Shop Ice Cream Parlor. The Sweet Shop is located in a densely populated residential area of town and has a relatively loyal following, even though it opened for business only one year ago. All of the customers of the Sweet Shop say great things about the ice cream and the service. The owner of the Sweet Shop wants to conduct some telephone surveys to measure residents' attitudes toward the Sweet Shop. He has developed the following question to be asked during a phone interview of 300 randomly selected residents from all areas of the town.

> On a five-point scale, where 5 = positive, and 1 = negative, how would you rate your overall feelings toward the Sweet Shop Ice Cream Parlor?

The owner has decided to base your annual bonus on the results from the survey. If the average rating from this question is ≥ 4.0, you will receive a $10,000 bonus. However, if the average rating from this scale is < 4.0, you will receive only a $1,000 bonus. The surveys will be conducted by an independent research firm. Further, the owner does not want to include a *DK/NO* option because he believes that it only leads to a lower response rate (people can simply answer *DK/NO* without giving an opinion), and he wants to get his money's worth from the surveys.

What do you tell the owner of the Sweet Shop Ice Cream Parlor?

ENDNOTES

1 J. Paul Peter, "Reliability: A Review of Psychometric Basis and Recent Marketing Practices," *Journal of Marketing Research* 16 (February 1979): 6–17.

2 F. M. Andrews, "Construct Validity and Error Components of Survey Measures," *Public Opinion Quarterly* (Summer 1984): 432.

CHAPTER 15

Scales Used in Marketing Research

LEARNING OBJECTIVES

1 Compare and contrast the use of open-ended questions and closed-ended questions on marketing research surveys.

2 Discuss the reasons for caution when using open-ended questions on marketing research surveys.

3 Define restricted choice questions.

4 Explain why the response options for restricted choice questions should be mutually exclusive and collectively exhaustive.

5 Describe the difference between monadic rating scales and comparative rating scales.

6 Discuss the use of checklist questions on marketing research surveys.

7 Describe Likert scales and semantic differential scales.

8 Describe Stapel scales and constant sum scales.

9 Discuss the effect that the number of scale points has on the validity of semantic differential scales.

10 Define an index of items and describe how an index of items can be used in marketing research.

11 Describe and explain the potential problems associated with using ranking tasks on marketing research surveys.

Marketing researchers have many choices available to them regarding the types of questions that can be asked on surveys. There are many different measurement scales that marketing researchers can use. Among the most often used scales are verbal open-ended scales, numerical open-ended scales, restricted choice closed-ended scales, checklist questions, Likert scales, semantic differential scales, Stapel scales, and constant sum scales. Each type of scale has its own unique characteristics, making it more suitable for some situations and less suitable for other situations.

OPEN-ENDED QUESTIONS

Open-ended questions give respondents complete freedom in responding. They allow respondents to answer a question by writing in (or speaking) whatever they want. Respondents might answer the question by filling in the blank space (or speaking) with words, phrases, complete sentences, or even numbers. The most often used open-ended scales are verbal open-ended scales and numerical open-ended scales.

Verbal Open-Ended Questions

Consumers respond to **verbal open-ended questions** by providing a verbal response, either a word, phrase, or sentence. Below are some examples of verbal open-ended scales.

Why did you buy Reebok running shoes instead of any other brand of running shoes? _____

What could we do to improve our service? _____

Do you have any other comments or suggestions about our company's products? _____

Numerical Open-Ended Questions

Consumers respond to **numerical open-ended questions** by providing a numerical response. Below are some examples of numerical open-ended scales.

What is your annual (personal) income? $_____

What is your age (in years)? _____

How many children do you have? _____

How many DVDs do you rent in a typical month? _____

Open-ended questions are often used in exploratory research when the researcher does not know the range of all possible responses to a question. They can be used to identify the category answers that will be used on a later survey. In addition, open-ended questions are often asked at the end of a survey. Asking, "Do you have any other comments?" makes the entire survey **collectively exhaustive**. It allows consumers to respond about a topic or issue that might not have been asked on the survey.

> Researchers should be cautious when using open-ended questions on surveys; especially when surveys are self-administered.

Cautions with Open-Ended Questions. A disadvantage of open-ended scales is that consumers might not know how to respond. If a survey asks, "What is your age?" consumers might respond with "middle-aged" or "young." In such cases, consumers are most likely not trying to be funny or cute with their answer. Instead, they probably do not realize that they are supposed to answer the question by entering a number. Whenever using open-ended questions, make sure that respondents

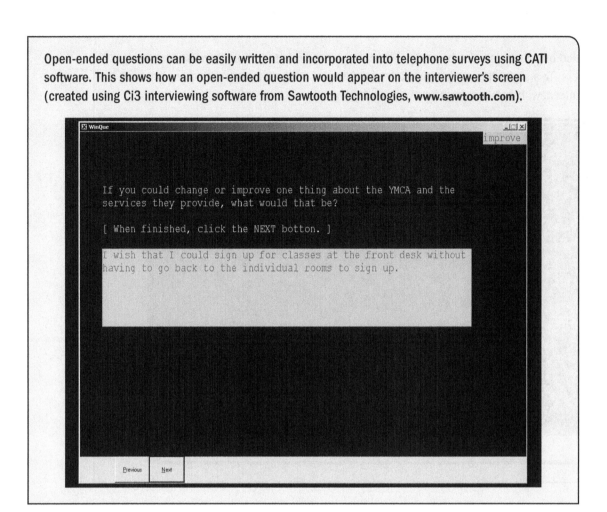

Open-ended questions can be easily written and incorporated into telephone surveys using CATI software. This shows how an open-ended question would appear on the interviewer's screen (created using Ci3 interviewing software from Sawtooth Technologies, **www.sawtooth.com**).

understand exactly how they are supposed to respond. Do not be afraid to tell them to "write in a number," "enter a dollar amount," or "write a verbal description." Do not tell respondents what their answer should be, but feel free to tell respondents the form, or manner, in which they are to respond. An additional disadvantage of open-ended questions is the cost associated with coding and analyzing them. The words or phrases that respondents provide cannot be analyzed with traditional statistical techniques because they are not quantitative. Thus, verbal open-ended scales do not have a level of scale. However, if verbal open-ended responses are coded into categories representing the content of the responses, and numerical values are assigned to these categories, this would constitute a nominal scale. The numerical open-ended scales shown above, where consumers answer the question by writing in a number, are ratio scales.

CLOSED-ENDED QUESTIONS

Closed-ended questions allow respondents to answer by choosing one of multiple response categories. The advantage of this is that there are no problems with two

Closed-ended questions can also be easily written and incorporated into telephone surveys using CATI software. This shows how such a question would appear on the interviewer's screen (created using Ci3 interviewing software from Sawtooth Technologies, **www.sawtooth.com**).

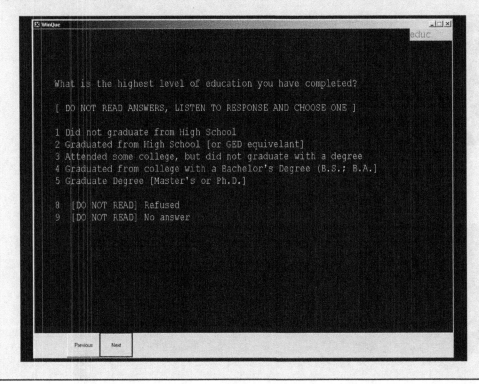

different respondents answering the question two different ways, as might be the case with an open-ended question. An additional advantage of closed-ended questions is that they do not force consumers to come up with an appropriate answer on their own. Consumers merely choose from the list of provided responses. As a result, they are less effortful than open-ended questions. Some people are intimidated by a blank line or a blank text box for an online survey in which they are to write an answer. Most closed-ended questions are either restricted choice questions (where consumers choose only one category when answering the question) or checklist questions (where consumers can choose more than one category when answering the question).

Restricted Choice Questions

With **a restricted choice question**, respondents are to select only one of the response categories provided to them. Restricted choice questions should be **mutually exclusive**, meaning that the respondent should not be able to choose more than one category. Additionally, restricted choice questions should be **collectively exhaustive**, meaning that all possible answers are included in the list of response alternatives.

The questions below are examples of restricted choice questions. Notice that respondents should select only one of the categories provided. Notice also that the income scale shown below is mutually exclusive (the categories do not overlap) and collectively exhaustive (everyone, regardless of their income, can choose a category that describes their income).

What is your sex?   ☐ Male   ☐ Female

Do you shop for groceries at Kroger?   ☐ Yes   ☐ No

What year are you in school?   ☐ Freshman   ☐ Sophomore
                               ☐ Junior   ☐ Senior

What is your annual (personal) income?

  ☐ Less than $10,000

  ☐ $10,000–$19,999

  ☐ $20,000–$29,999

  ☐ $30,000 or more

The two restricted choice scales shown below are also referred to as **monadic rating scales** because they each ask about only one concept.

How important is price in deciding which car to buy?

  ☐ Very Important

  ☐ Fairly Important

  ☐ Neutral

  ☐ Not So Important

  ☐ Not At All Important

How satisfied were you with your last car?

  ☐ Very Satisfied

  ☐ Somewhat Satisfied

  ☐ Neither

  ☐ Somewhat Dissatisfied

  ☐ Very Dissatisfied

> Be careful when intermixing restricted choice questions with checklist questions on surveys. Respondents can easily become confused about whether to choose only one response or to choose more than one response.

In contrast to a monadic rating scale that asks about a single concept, a **comparative rating scale** asks respondents to answer by comparing two or more objects or concepts. They might compare two or more brands, ideas, advertisements, stores, or restaurants. The question below is an example of a comparative rating scale.

Compared to Billy Bob's Burger Joint, Betty's Burger Palace is:

☐ Much Worse   ☐ Worse   ☐ Same   ☐ Better   ☐ Much Better

When using comparative rating scales, make sure that respondents are adequately familiar with both of the concepts that they are comparing. For example, a survey question might ask, "Compared to a Cadillac XTS, how would you rate the acceleration of a Honda Accord?" If respondents are not familiar with the acceleration of both Cadillac and Honda automobiles, they will not be able to answer this question.

Checklist Questions

Checklist questions allow consumers to select more than one response category. The scales below are examples of checklist questions. Notice that including the *other* category makes the list of response categories collectively exhaustive. It allows for all possible responses, even those that were not identified as an option on the survey. However, when asking checklist questions, make sure that respondents know that they can choose more than one answer. Many researchers will include the phrase, "Check all that apply," or an equivalent phrase, at the end of a checklist question.

What classes have you taken at this university? (Check all that you have taken.)

☐ Promotions

☐ Marketing Research

☐ Personal Selling

☐ Retail Management

☐ Marketing Management

☐ Other (please specify) _____

What type of music do you like to listen to? (Check all that apply.)

☐ Country   ☐ Rock   ☐ Jazz   ☐ Other (please specify)_____

The "Other" Category. When using closed-ended questions is advisable to include *other* as one of the choices available to respondents. This is especially true when asking about topics for which there are a large number of possible answers. For instance, when asking which brands of beer a consumer purchases, it would be impossible to list all brands. In this case it would be best to list the most likely brands that a consumer might purchase and then include *other* as the final option. Doing so makes the checklist question collectively exhaustive. That is, it allows for all possible brands to be captured by the survey without having to list every possible brand. Also, it is advisable to include *please specify* along with the word *other*. This encourages respondents to also write in the other brand name instead of merely checking the box for *other*.

Checklist questions can also be written for telephone surveys using CATI software. This shows how a checklist question would appear on the interviewer's screen (created using Ci3 interviewing software from Sawtooth Technologies, www.sawtooth.com).

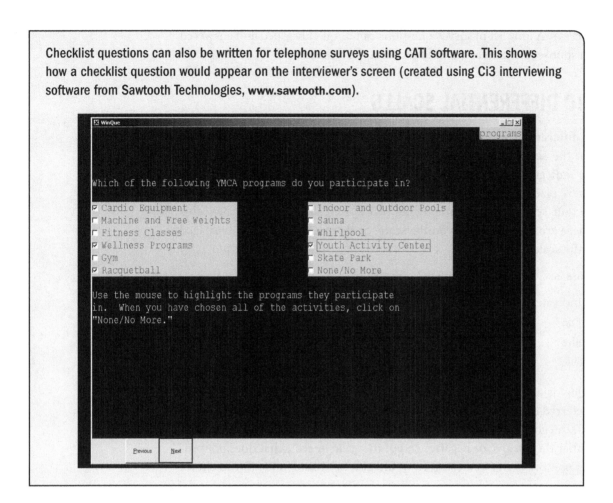

LIKERT SCALES

A **Likert scale** is a special form of restricted choice closed-ended scale where the researcher provides a statement, not a question, and respondents indicate their level of agreement with the statement on a scale where *SA = Strongly Agree, A = Agree, N = Neither, D = Disagree*, and *SD = Strongly Disagree*. This scale was developed by Rensis Likert, for whom it is named.[1]

Please answer the following questions:	SD	D	N	A	SA
This class is interesting.	☐	☐	☐	☐	☐
I enjoy fishing.	☐	☐	☐	☐	☐
I am a loyal Pepsi drinker.	☐	☐	☐	☐	☐
I was very satisfied with my last car.	☐	☐	☐	☐	☐

Likert scales are very useful when there is a large number of questions (statements) that can all be answered with *Strongly Agree, Agree, Neither, Disagree*, or *Strongly Disagree*. Most consumers are very familiar with these answers and they find this type of question relatively easy to answer. Likert scales are very good when conducting telephone surveys. A long list of survey questions can be quickly asked and answered if the same response alternatives are used for all of the questions.

SEMANTIC DIFFERENTIAL SCALES

A **semantic differential scale** provides **bipolar adjectives** or phrases that anchor either end of the scale. This scale format was developed by Charles E. Osgood.[2] Respondents indicate where their feelings, beliefs, or perceptions lie on the scale. They do this by placing their answer closer to one end or the other end of a continuum. The four semantic differential scales below are called 7-point scales. This is because there are seven numbers on the scale, or there are seven equally spaced intervals on the scale.

This class is: Boring   1 2 3 4 5 6 7   Exciting

Please indicate your feelings about this coffee cake on the following scales:

Bad	1 2 3 4 5 6 7	Good
Negative	1 2 3 4 5 6 7	Positive
Unfavorable	1 2 3 4 5 6 7	Favorable

The scale below is a 6-point scale. A scale with an even number of scale points is sometimes referred to as a **forced choice scale** because it does not provide a neutral, or indifferent, category at the middle of the scale. It forces respondents to choose an answer on either the positive or negative end of the scale. A scale that does not provide a *Don't Know* or *No Opinion* category would also be considered a forced choice scale.

How likely are you to purchase this product?

Not at all likely   1 2 3 4 5 6   Very Likely

Semantic differential scales can also be designed with spaces instead of numbers. Here, consumers place a check mark, or an X, in one of the spaces.

The image of Mercedes-Benz is:

Old-Fashioned   ___ ___ ___ ___ ___ ___ ___   Modern

Unattractive   ___ ___ ___ ___ ___ ___ ___   Attractive

Semantic differential scales can also be designed to allow respondents to place a slash mark anywhere along a line (continuum) to indicate their response. Researchers must then measure the distance from one end of the scale to the slash mark. This is typically measured in millimeters. These scales are called **graphic rating scales** or **continuous rating scales**.[3] These scales can be positioned horizontally or vertically.

As a spokesperson for Pepsi, Madonna would be:

Terrible   _____   Excellent

Improper   _____   Proper

Opposite Endpoints of the Same Dimension. The bipolar adjectives or phrases used for a semantic differential scale must represent opposite ends of the same dimension. The scales shown below would be almost impossible for consumers to answer because the bipolar adjectives do not represent opposite ends of the same dimension.

Please rate Toyota automobiles on the following scales:

Inexpensive ___ ___ ___ ___ ___ ___ ___ Modern

Attractive ___ ___ ___ ___ ___ ___ ___ Unreliable

Image Profiles

An advantage of using Likert scales and semantic differential scales is the ability to easily display results for numerous items. When the same scale is used for multiple survey items the results can be presented in the form of an **image profile**, sometimes called a **snake diagram**. This is helpful when a brand or store is evaluated on a number of different dimensions. The image profiles shown in Figure 15.1 and Figure 15.2 demonstrate how overall differences and similarities between attitude objects can be represented.

FIGURE 15.1 Likert Scale Image Profile

The employees at this store:	Strongly Disagree	Disagree	Undecided	Agree	Strongly Agree
Are helpful					
Are knowledgeable about the merchandise					
Answer my questions effectively					
Are available when I need them					
Seem to like working here					
Have a positive attitude toward customers					

Bill's Grocery ———————   Jane's Quick Mart – – – – – –

FIGURE 15.2 Semantic Differential Scale Image Profile

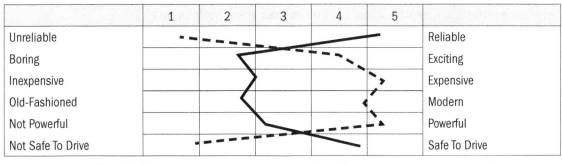

	1	2	3	4	5	
Unreliable						Reliable
Boring						Exciting
Inexpensive						Expensive
Old-Fashioned						Modern
Not Powerful						Powerful
Not Safe To Drive						Safe To Drive

Chevrolet Corvette – – – – – –   Honda Accord ———————

Number of Scale Points

The number of scale points is an important decision when designing semantic differential scales. Most semantic differential scales used for marketing research surveys are 5-point scales or 7-point scales. As previously mentioned, a semantic differential scale that uses an even number of scale points forces respondents to choose an answer on either the positive end or the negative end of the scale. As such, scales with an even number of scale points can have less validity than similar scales with an odd number of scale points. There are many topics (brands, products, stores) about which people honestly have neither a positive nor a negative opinion. With an odd number of scale points, there is a midpoint that people can use to indicate a moderate opinion.

Most of the semantic differential scales shown in this book use either five or seven scale points. In fact, 5-point scales and 7-point scales are well-accepted industry standards. A scale with fewer than five scale points, for example a 3-point scale, is generally not considered to be sensitive enough to accurately measure the variations in consumers' opinions. It is very difficult to evaluate brands on a 3-point scale, where, 1 = *Bad*, 2 = *Neutral*, and 3 = *Good*. Most people would like at least two more scale points to be able to evaluate brands as either *Somewhat Bad* or *Somewhat Good*.

Natural Divisions of a Continuum. When asked to evaluate things on a continuum, most people naturally divide a continuum into five segments. This is illustrated in Figure 15.3. Most people recognize that there is a middle range on the continuum, with two extreme ranges at either end. Additionally, they perceive that there are moderate ranges between the middle and the two extreme ranges. As a result, 5-point semantic differential scales accurately reflect the naturally manner in which people mentally divide a continuum.

Too Many Scale Points. A semantic differential scale with more than seven scale points becomes almost too sensitive. The more scale points on a scale, the greater the assumption that respondents can make very small (and meaningful) distinctions between the scale points. For instance, a 21-point scale assumes that respondents can make meaningful distinctions between a 17 and an 18 on the scale. However, this assumption is often difficult to support, especially for low-involvement issues or products. Therefore, semantic differential scales with more than seven scale points are seldom used.

> The verbal labels used as the endpoints of semantic differential scales must represent opposite ends of the same dimension.

FIGURE 15.3 Natural Division of a Continuum into Five Segments

1	2	3	4	5
Extreme Negative Range	Moderately Negative Range	Middle Range	Moderately Positive Range	Extreme Positive Range

STAPEL SCALE

The **Stapel scale** (developed by Jan Stapel) is a unique scale where respondents are asked to rate an attitude object (brand, store, service) on a single characteristic or dimension that is usually represented by a single word or phrase. Each item has 10 response categories that are displayed vertically. However, notice that there is no midpoint for this scale, which forces respondents to choose a response on either end of the scale. For example, consumers might be asked to rate the degree to which the word *reliable* describes a car, from −5 to +5, where positive numbers indicate that the word describes the car and negative numbers indicate that the word does not describe the car.

+5 Describes very accurately

+4

+3

+2

+1

Reliable

−1

−2

−3

−4

−5 Does not describe

CONSTANT SUM SCALE

With a **constant sum scale**, respondents are asked to allocate 100 points between a set of response options indicating the relative importance of each option. More important options receive a greater number of points and less important options receive fewer points. However, constant sum scales can be difficult for some consumers to complete. This is especially true when the 100 points must be allocated between a large number of response options.

Thinking back to when you bought your most recent car, please distribute 100 points among the following reasons according to their relative importance to you when deciding where to buy your car.

Location of dealership	
Friendliness of sales staff	
Service department hours	
Recommendations from friends	
Total	100 points

INDEX OF ITEMS

Sometimes, the constructs that marketing researchers want to measure cannot be measured with a single question. In such cases, researchers can measure a **multidimensional construct** with more than one question or item. This is called creating an **index of items**. An index refers to measuring a single construct with multiple items. For instance, the consumer price index is a measure of relative price increases and decreases based on the prices for a variety of different goods and services. A stock market index is a measure of the stock market based on multiple stocks. Increasing the number of items in an index will tend to increase the reliability (and sometimes the validity) of the scale.

Below is an example of four questions combined to form an index of consumers' attitudes toward an automotive service center. Each item represents one aspect, or dimension, of the common attitudinal domain. The scores for the items are then combined (either summed or averaged) to obtain an overall measure of the multidimensional construct.

This service center takes a personal interest in me.	SD	D	N	A	SA
The employees are friendly and courteous.	SD	D	N	A	SA
This service center is more interested in making money than in treating me fairly.	SD	D	N	A	SA
Customer service employees act in a professional manner.	SD	D	N	A	SA

The scores on each question are combined to arrive at an overall attitude toward the service center. Notice that the third question must be **reverse scored**. The answer to this question must be converted using the formula $(6 - X)$ to place all four scales in the same direction (e.g., $6 - 1 = 5$). To reverse score an answer, subtract the answer's scale value from the total number of scale values, plus one.

Sometimes, indices are calculated to estimate more whimsical aspects of consumption. For the past 29 years economists at PNC Financial Services Group have calculated the Christmas Price Index. This index is a measure of the total cost of all 364 items that are repeated throughout "The Twelve Days of Christmas" carol. For December 2012, the total price for all 364 items was $107,300.[4] As another example, **Amazon.com** calculates an index of the most romantic cities in America. The cities are ranked by compiling data on the sales of romance novels, relationship books, romantic comedy movies, romantic music (by such artists as Dean Martin, Barry White, and Luther Vandross), and sexual wellness products.[5]

CAUTIONS WITH RANKING QUESTIONS

Sometimes, ranking questions are asked on surveys to measure consumers' attitudes, importance, intentions, or preferences. With a **ranking question**, respondents are asked to rank order a series of alternatives. For example, consumers might be asked the following question:

> Please rank the following factors in terms of their importance to you in deciding where you purchased your new car. Rank these from 1 to 5, with 1 being the most important factor and 5 being the least important factor.
>
> _____ Low price
>
> _____ Large selection of cars to choose from
>
> _____ Convenient location of the dealership
>
> _____ Trust I have in the dealership
>
> _____ Service department

Cautions with Ranking Tasks. There are a number of problems associated with ranking questions that researchers must be aware of before deciding to use them on surveys. First, a ranking task artificially forces respondents to identify one of the response options as the most important (or, the one that they like the best if they are ranking items in terms of their preference or liking for them). Similarly, it artificially forces respondents to identify one of the response options as the least important (or, the one that they like the least if they are ranking items in terms of their preference or liking for them). This introduces error into the results and reduces the validity of survey results when respondents feel equally toward two or more items on the list. What if consumers think that all of the factors are important? Conversely, what if consumers think that none of the factors are important? Allowing respondents to evaluate multiple items individually and independently (e.g., rate each item on a 7-point scale, where 1 = not important, and 7 = very important) increases the validity of survey results by allowing for equal ratings of multiple items.

Consumers might find it difficult to rank the items shown above if all items were equally important, and if all items had equally positive effects on deciding where they bought their new car. If a consumer ranked *service department* as the least important of the items given, researchers cannot conclude that *service department* was not important in making that person's purchase decision. It might have been ranked last because the ranking task artificially forced the consumer to rank one of the items last. If allowed to rate each item individually and independently, all of the factors might have been rated as relatively important, as shown in Figure 15.4.

Similarly, consider the individual ratings shown in Figure 15.5. If a consumer ranked *low price* as the most important factor, this does not mean that *low price* was necessarily important to this consumer's purchase decision. It might have been ranked first because the ranking task artificially forced the consumer to rank one of the items first.

Further, if two consumers each ranked *low price* as the most important factor, researchers cannot conclude that *low price* was equally important to both consumers.

This is illustrated in Figures 15.4 and 15.5. However, individual and independent ratings would allow greater insight into the relative importance of *low price* across consumers.

In addition to not allowing for relative comparisons across consumers, ranking tasks also do not allow for relative comparisons of differences within an individual consumer. This is because ranking questions yield only ordinal-level data. In both examples shown in Figures 15.4 and 15.5, the independent ratings of each factor indicate that the difference in importance between *large selection* and *convenient location* is not the same as the difference in importance between *convenient location* and *trust in the dealership*. However, with just a ranking there is no way of measuring the relative difference in importance of various factors to an individual consumer. Individual and independent ratings of each factor would allow for such relative comparisons for consumers because ratings on a 7-point scale as shown above yield interval-level data.

Ranking Tasks and Mental Burdens. An additional drawback to ranking questions is the mental burden they place on consumers. Most people have a difficult time wranking more than five items in a list. Moreover, as the number of items in the list

FIGURE 15.4 Ratings vs. Rankings: All Factors Important

	Not Important						Very Important	Rank
	1	2	3	4	5	6	7	
Low price							x	1
Large selection of cars to choose from							x	2
Convenient location of the dealership							x	3
Trust I have in the dealership						x		4
Service department						x		5

FIGURE 15.5 Ratings vs. Rankings: All Factors Unimportant

	Not Important						Very Important	Rank
	1	2	3	4	5	6	7	
Low price		x						1
Large selection of cars to choose from		x						2
Convenient location of the dealership		x						3
Trust I have in the dealership	x							4
Service department	x							5

increases, so too does the difficulty associated with ranking them. A list that contains 10 or more items requires a great deal of time and mental effort on the part of respondents, making it almost impossible to generate a meaningful ranking. After ranking a few of the items, most people will finish ranking the remaining items by simply choosing them randomly without much, if any, thought in an effort to quickly and easily complete the task. To demonstrate the difficulty associated with a ranking task, think about 10 of your friends. Now, try to rank them from 1 to 10, with 1 being the friend you like the most, and 10 being the friend you like the least. It is almost impossible to rank them. It would even be very difficult to rank only five of your friends. In sum, ranking questions might seem like valid measures of consumers' perceptions, beliefs, feelings, attitudes, and preferences. However, the multiple concerns associated with the validity of ranking questions make them unattractive to many survey researchers.

Be careful when using ranking tasks on surveys. A ranking task forces respondents to rank one alternative first and rank one alternative last. Ranking tasks do not allow respondents to indicate that two or more alternatives are equal in evaluation.

MEASUREMENT SCALES AND THE DECISION-MAKING PROCESS

Marketing managers need information to be able to make decisions that are designed to achieve desired marketing objectives. As discussed in the previous chapter, measurement scales should be reliable, sensitive, and valid. Marketing managers need information obtained from measurement scales that reliably measure the same construct every time they are used and that accurately measure what they are supposed to measure. The characteristics of measurement scales can affect the validity of survey questions and impact their usefulness to decision makers. Survey questions will tend to have lower validity when:

- Restricted choice categories are not mutually exclusive. A person's true response appears in more than one response category.

- Restricted choice categories are not collectively exhaustive. A respondent's true response is not included in the set of response options.

- Respondents are not aware that they can select more than one category on a checklist question. All of a person's true responses are not measured by the research.

- Checklist questions are not collectively exhaustive. A respondent's true response is not included in the set of response options.

- There is an even number of scale places on a semantic differential scale. This forces people to provide a response that is either on the positive end of the scale or on the negative end of the scale.

- A multidimensional construct is measured with only a single item instead of multiple items (an index). All aspects, or dimensions, of a person's true thoughts, feelings, perceptions, or beliefs are not measured by the research.

- Consumers are forced to rank a list of items when they feel equally toward two or more of the items on the list. A ranking task artificially forces consumers to rank one of the items first, and it artificially forces consumers to rank one of the items last.

QUESTIONS FOR DISCUSSION

1. Which would be easier for consumers to answer during a telephone survey, a Likert scale or a semantic differential scale? Why?

2. Would you ever use a 6-point semantic differential scale? Why or why not?

3. How many scale points would you recommend using on a semantic differential scale for an online survey?

4. Are three scale points ever too few for a scale?

5. Would a 21-point scale ever have too many scale points?

6. What assumptions must you make about consumers when designing a question with 21 scale points?

7. What are some of the physical characteristics of scales that can have an effect on the ability of marketing managers to make marketing decisions?

8. Write a verbal open-ended survey question to measure the reason(s) why consumers shop for groceries at Kroger.

9. Write a numerical open-ended survey question to measure how far consumers live from an airport.

10. Write a restricted choice (category scale) survey question to measure how far consumers live from an airport, making sure that the categories are mutually exclusive.

11. Write a checklist survey question to measure all of the grocery stores at which consumers shop, making sure that the categories are collectively exhaustive.

12. Write a survey question to measure consumers' liking for Burger King, using a Likert scale.

13. Write a survey question to measure consumers' liking for McDonald's, using a semantic differential scale.

14. Write a survey question to measure the degree to which consumers perceive that their personal financial advisor is knowledgeable about investments, using a Stapel scale.

15. Write a survey question to measure the relative importance of five separate factors in determining consumers' level of satisfaction with a restaurant, using a constant sum scale.

16. Create a four-item index to measure consumers' attitudes toward a multiscreen movie theater, using either Likert scales or semantic differential scales.

17. Create a five-item index of survey questions to measure consumers' attitudes toward a hospital emergency room.

MINICASE 15.1

Grundy's Hardware Store

Grundy's Hardware Store has been in business for nearly 20 years. Grundy's is an independent hardware store that prides itself on offering quality products and exceptional customer service that is more personal than consumers could receive from national home improvement warehouses, such as Home Depot and Lowe's. One area in which Grundy's takes particular pride is their personal and prompt delivery service. When customers purchase a large item from Grundy's Hardware Store, the customer can pretty much name their own delivery date and time. And, delivery is free.

You have recently been hired as the customer service manager for Grundy's Hardware Store. You would like to measure customers' perceptions of your delivery service. The owner informs you that three years ago, the previous customer service manager used simple surveys that were mailed to all customers immediately after they received delivery of their purchased item(s). A copy of this survey is shown below. The owner has asked you to use the same survey to allow for direct comparisons to the results that were obtained three years ago.

> Dear Grundy's Customer:
>
> Our records show that we recently made a delivery to your home. As part of our continuing efforts to see how we are doing, would you please tell us if the delivery service you received was:
>
> Below Expectations   1   2   3   4   Above Expectations
>
> Detach this card and drop it in any mail box, postage free.
>
> Thank you,
> Denny Grundy
> Owner, Grundy's Hardware Store

What do you do?

What do you tell the owner of Grundy's Hardware Store?

ENDNOTES

1   Rensis Likert, "A Technique for the Measurement of Attitudes," *Archives of Psychology* 19 (1931): 44–53.
2   Charles Osgood, George Suci, and Percy Tannenbaum, *The Measurement of Meaning* (Urbana: University of Illinois Press, 1957); Naresh K. Malhotra, "A Scale to Measure Self-Concepts, Person Concepts and Product Concepts," *Journal of Marketing Research* 18 (November 1981): 456–464.

3   C. L. Narayana, "Graphic Positioning Scale: An Economical Instrument for Surveys," *Journal of Marketing Research* 14 (February 1977): 18–122; S. I. Lampert, "The Attitude Pollimeter: A New Attitude Scaling Device," *Journal of Marketing Research* (November 1979): 578–585.

4   Adam O'Daniel, "PNC Index Says Price of Christmas is up 4.8%," *Charlotte Business Journal*, November 26, 2012.

5   Aubrey Cohen, "Amazon's 20 Most Romantic Cities," **http://www.seattlepi.com/lifestyle/article/Amazon-s -20-most-romantic-cities**, February 5, 2013.

CHAPTER (16)

Writing and Organizing Surveys

LEARNING OBJECTIVES

1 Identify, describe, and discuss how marketing researchers can avoid:

   a Ambiguous questions.

   b Leading questions.

   c Loaded questions.

   d Double-barreled questions.

   e Taxing questions.

   f Questions containing technical language or jargon.

   g Questions containing double negatives.

   h Questions containing false comparisons.

2 Identify strategies and suggestions for writing questions and organizing surveys.

3 Discuss the importance of a cover letter or scripted introduction to a survey.

4 Explain how funneling can be used to help organize surveys.

5 Discuss where difficult questions and demographic questions should be placed on surveys.

6 Describe how filter questions and skip (branching) questions can be used on marketing research surveys.

7 Explain the importance of "zero" as a separate response category for survey questions.

8 Define reverse-scored questions and discuss how they are used on surveys.

9 Explain how randomized response questions are used to measure potentially embarrassing or sensitive issues on marketing research surveys.

10 Describe strategies for increasing response rates for surveys.

11 Describe the general guidelines for interviewers when conducting marketing research interviews.

12 Discuss the role of do-not-call laws on telephone survey research.

After identifying the goals and objectives for a survey research project, survey questions should be written to achieve those specific research objectives. A good survey is one that achieves the research objectives. Even though there are many ways to phrase and ask questions, and there are very few strict rules regarding survey questions, there are a number of guidelines that researchers should follow to increase

FIGURE 16.1 Questions to Avoid on Surveys

Ambiguous Questions	Taxing Questions
Leading Questions	Technical Language or Jargon
Loaded Questions	Double Negatives
Double-Barreled Questions	False Comparisons

the likelihood that the survey will achieve the research objectives.[1] Writing survey questions is not difficult, as long as you avoid making some common errors.[2] Eight types of questions that researchers should avoid asking on surveys are listed in Figure 16.1.

AVOID AMBIGUOUS QUESTIONS

Ambiguous questions are those for which the wording of the question, or the wording of the response alternatives, can have multiple interpretations or meanings. For example, the following question is ambiguous:

How often do you go bowling?
☐ Never ☐ Rarely ☐ Sometimes ☐ Often

The words *never, rarely, sometimes*, and *often* can have different meanings for different consumers. One person might consider *often* to mean going bowling every week, whereas someone else might consider *often* to mean going bowling once a month. The question below is also ambiguous:

Do you live close to Billy Bob's BBQ? ☐ Yes ☐ No

This can have different meanings for different consumers. One person might think that living 10 miles from the BBQ is far away, whereas someone else might think that living 10 miles from the BBQ is close. Consider another ambiguous question. The words *many* and *extracurricular* can have different meanings to different people.

Do you attend many extracurricular events on campus? ☐ Yes ☐ No

Identifying Respondents' Intent. Ambiguous questions are also those that do not clearly identify respondents' intent when answering a question. For example, consider the survey question below.

	Strongly Disagree	Disagree	Neither	Agree	Strongly Agree
I like the amount of icing on Grandma Powell's frozen cinnamon buns.	☐	☐	☐	☐	☐

If a respondent checks *Strongly Disagree*, what does that mean? Does the respondent think that there is too much icing on the cinnamon buns, or not enough icing on the cinnamon buns? A researcher would not know. More importantly, marketing managers for Grandma Powell's frozen cinnamon buns would not know how to change their product. Better ways of asking the question are shown below.

	Strongly Disagree	Disagree	Neither	Agree	Strongly Agree
There is <u>not enough</u> icing on Grandma Powell's frozen cinnamon buns.	☐	☐	☐	☐	☐
I wish that there were <u>more</u> icing on Grandma Powell's frozen cinnamon buns.	☐	☐	☐	☐	☐

Notice that the response alternatives to these questions clearly indicate respondents' intent when answering the question. If a respondent checks *Strongly Agree* to either of these two questions, there is no question about their intent, or their desire for more icing on the frozen cinnamon buns.

As another example of an ambiguous question that does not clearly identify a respondent's intent, consider the following question:

	Strongly Disagree	Disagree	Neither	Agree	Strongly Agree
I am in favor of tougher gun laws.	☐	☐	☐	☐	☐

Notice that even though a *Strongly Agree* response indicates that the respondent is in favor of tougher gun laws, it does not give decision makers any idea about what aspect of gun laws that this respondent thinks should be tougher. Does this mean that the respondent wants to make it more difficult for someone to purchase a hand gun? Does this mean that the respondent wants longer jail sentences for someone convicted of a crime using a gun? Does this mean that the respondent wants greater monetary penalties for the illegal use of a hand gun? We would not know. More specific questions are needed, such as:

	Strongly Disagree	Disagree	Neither	Agree	Strongly Agree
I am in favor of laws that make it <u>more difficult for someone to purchase</u> a hand gun.	☐	☐	☐	☐	☐
I am in favor of <u>longer jail sentences</u> for someone convicted of a crime using a hand gun.	☐	☐	☐	☐	☐

(continued)

Marketing researchers have a great deal of freedom in the types of questions that can be asked on a survey. There are no strict rules about how a survey question must be asked. However, researchers should avoid asking questions that are ambiguous, leading, double-barreled, taxing, that contain technical language or jargon, use double negatives, or ask for false comparisons.

	Strongly Disagree	Disagree	Neither	Agree	Strongly Agree
I am in favor of <u>greater monetary penalties</u> for the illegal use of a hand gun.	☐	☐	☐	☐	☐

To avoid ambiguous questions:

- Specify the units of measurement. This includes amounts, time frames, locations, and types of products. Do not ask consumers how much beer they drink. Be more specific in the question. Ask consumers how many 12-ounce bottles of imported beer they drink in a typical week.

- Be very specific when asking about behavioral intentions. Specify the brand, store, or time frame of interest.

- Avoid using the word *ever*, especially for low-involvement behaviors. Do not ask, "Have you ever eaten a Nestlé Crunch bar?" Even if consumers cannot recall ever eating the candy bar, they might respond with, "I guess I have eaten a Nestlé Crunch bar because ever implies such a long time." An exception to this is when questions are asked about relatively high-involvement behaviors that people are likely to remember. For example, "Have you ever traveled to China for business or job-related reasons?" is an acceptable question. Most people should be able to remember doing this.

- Pretest the questions to make sure that the survey questions and the possible answers (response alternatives) mean the same thing to all respondents, as well as the researcher who will interpret the answers and results.

- Avoid using words that are open to multiple interpretations and are very ambiguous because they do not specify a specific measurement scale. The questions shown below suffer from this problem.

  How many *times* do you study during the week?

  What *type* of car do you own?

  How *often* do you play tennis?

  If a researcher wants to know the *brand* and *model* of the car a consumer owns, that should be specified and asked in the question.

- As a general rule for designing surveys and writing survey questions, you can never be too specific. If you think that the survey question is too specific, don't worry, it probably isn't.

- Be aware that *times* does not mean the same thing as *amount, number,* or *duration.* For example:

Asking:	Does Not Measure:
How many *times* do you make photocopies per semester?	*Number of copies* made per semester.
How many *times* do you do laundry in a typical month?	*Number of loads* of laundry done per month.
How many *times* do you play tennis per month?	*Number of hours* playing tennis per month.
How many *times* do you study during a typical week?	*Number of hours* spent studying per week.

Defining Categories for Respondents

Researchers should not take for granted that respondents know what certain words mean, or that respondents will interpret a word or response category as it was intended by the researcher. Sometimes, words or response categories should be defined for respondents. For example, a survey might ask consumers to report the number of portable communication devices they own. Defining what portable communication devices means can greatly aid in reducing error and respondent frustration. This can be easily accomplished by listing a few examples of portable communication devices in parentheses within the question (e.g., mobile phone, tablet). As another example, respondents might find it helpful if the researcher were to define different types of stores, such as department stores (e.g., JCPenney, Macy's) and discount stores (e.g., Wal-Mart, Target). However, one needs to be aware that such definitions can focus respondents attention on just those items listed.

AVOID LEADING OR LOADED QUESTIONS

Leading or **loaded questions** are those that contain words or phrases that suggest or imply a certain answer. They lead consumers to respond in a biased manner that does not reflect their true feelings, thoughts, behaviors, or beliefs. They often contain reasons, or justifications, for a particular answer within the question. For example, the following questions are leading:

> Do you think that you would ever purchase a low-quality car like a Kia?
> ☐ Yes   ☐ No

Consumers will not want to admit that they would ever consider purchasing a *low-quality car*.

> More and more people are deciding to shop at the Green Banks Mall. Are you likely to shop at the Green Banks Mall sometime within the next month?
> ☐ Yes   ☐ No

Consumers might be led to respond with *yes* because they are told in the question that many other consumers are shopping at the mall.

Do you support a state income tax that would raise money to help fund education so that the children in our state will be better prepared to succeed in life?   ☐ Yes   ☐ No

People are more likely to respond with *yes* because most people want children to be better prepared to succeed in life. Notice that this question includes a reason for answering *yes*—so that children will be better prepared to succeed in life.

To avoid leading or loaded questions:

- Avoid emotionally charged words. For example, asking about possible solutions to a *crisis* will result in different responses than asking about solutions to a *problem*, which in turn will lead to different responses than asking about solutions to a *situation*.

- Avoid making assumptions that are implicit in your questions. For example, do not ask, "How much do you like the efficient manner in which the student shuttle works on campus?" This implies that the shuttle is efficient. The only question is whether or not the student likes the efficient service. Instead, ask, "Is the student shuttle efficient?" or "Do you like the student shuttle?"

- Avoid using extreme terminology, such as *all, always, every, never, nobody,* or *none.* There are always exceptions. Very few things are ever *all* we expect them to be. The service at a restaurant might not have been *all* that a consumer expected, but it might have been good enough to make that consumer want to come back. Was your trip to Disney World when you were a child everything you thought it would be? Probably not. But, chances are that you still wanted to go back to Disney World again.

- Use a **counter-biasing statement** to reduce the embarrassment of emotionally charged questions. A counter-biasing statement gives acceptable ranges and tells respondents that either extreme is acceptable. For example, change, "How many hours do you study in a typical week?" to "Some students spend very little time studying, others spend a great deal of time studying. How many hours do you study in a typical week?" This should not cause bias in responses because it tells respondents that both extremes are acceptable.

- Do not provide reasons or justifications for responses in the question. For example, do not ask, "Should Congress pass tougher gun laws making it illegal to possess a gun within one mile of a school *so that you can feel more comfortable about the safety of your children while they are at school*?" Instead ask, "Should Congress pass tougher gun laws making it illegal to possess a gun within one mile of a school?" Let the respondent come up with his or her own reason for responding with either *yes* or *no.*

AVOID DOUBLE-BARRELED QUESTIONS

Double-barreled questions are those that ask two questions in one. For example, the following questions are double-barreled:

> Do you think that faculty and students are responsible for students'
> learning?   □ Yes   □ No

What if someone thinks that only students are responsible for their own learning? They have no way of answering this question so that their true beliefs are represented in their answer. If they select *yes*, this implies that they believe that faculty are also responsible for student learning. Alternatively, if they select *no*, this implies that they do not think that either faculty or students are responsible for student learning.

> Do you drink fruit juice because it tastes good and is good for you?
> □ Yes   □ No

What if someone drinks fruit juice because it is good for them, but not because of the taste? Again, they have no way of answering this question so that their true beliefs are represented in their answer.

To avoid double-barreled questions:

- Avoid using the word *and* in a question. This creates two questions.

- Never confuse consumers' attitudes (liking) for a product with their intention to purchase the product. Ask about attitudes and intentions by using two separate questions. Consumers might like your product (e.g., Ferrari automobiles), but have no intention of buying one, and vice versa. Consumers often do not buy products that they like. Perhaps they did not have enough money, or maybe the product wasn't available when they went to buy it. The opposite also holds true. Consumers often buy products that they do not like. Very few consumers will admit that they really like McDonald's hamburgers. But, many of these same consumers often buy McDonald's hamburgers because they are inexpensive and convenient.

> The word "and" should never be used in a survey question.

AVOID TAXING QUESTIONS

Taxing questions ask consumers to engage in an excessive amount of thinking or mental calculating. Such questions might overly tax the respondent's memory. Because they are so mentally taxing, consumers often skip these questions, or consumers might even decide to end the survey. The following are examples of taxing questions:

> How much did you spend each of the last five times you shopped for
> groceries at the grocery store? _____

> How many trips to the bank did you make this past year? _____

These questions are almost impossible to answer. Consumers cannot remember how much they spent on groceries each of the last five times they shopped at the grocery store. And, consumers cannot remember how many trips they made to the bank during the past year.

To avoid taxing questions:

- When measuring behaviors that can span long periods of time, ask for estimates of behaviors for short time periods. Rather than asking, "How often do you shop at the supermarket?" ask, "How many shopping trips did you make to the supermarket in the past two weeks?" Then, project this to monthly or annual figures. If no seasonal or holiday patterns are involved, the results should be more accurate than forcing consumers to estimate over long time periods. As another example, do not ask, "How much money did you spend on groceries last year?" Instead, ask, "How much money do you spend on groceries in a typical two-week period?"

- If consumers are not able to freely recall information, use an easier memory task like recognition that consumers are better able to perform (even though an unaided recall task is a stronger test of memory).

- Do not ask a question that you do not think consumers can answer because they cannot remember the answer. An overly taxing or difficult question will lead to resentful and angry respondents, making them less likely to complete and return the survey.

AVOID TECHNICAL LANGUAGE OR JARGON

Marketers are accustomed to speaking in the language of marketing and business. Unfortunately, the typical consumer is unfamiliar with this language and the terms that marketers often use. For example, consumers will not understand questions about channels of distribution, merchandising techniques, or even the marketing mix. Avoid using such **jargon** or **technical language** in writing survey questions. The following examples contain technical language or jargon that respondents might not understand.

> Would you be willing to pay more for this product if you knew that the price was below the retailer's break-even point?   ☐ Yes   ☐ No

> Do you think that six months from now, the unemployment rate will be higher or lower?   ☐ Higher   ☐ Lower

To avoid technical language or jargon:

- Pretest the survey questions to make sure that all respondents can fully and correctly understand the questions.

- Use common everyday language, even if it is not proper grammar.

- Use words and response options that the respondent understands. Instead of asking whether the unemployment rate will be higher or lower, ask, "In the next six months, do you expect that there will be more job openings, or fewer job openings?" Try to rephrase complicated concepts or technical terms using everyday language.

AVOID DOUBLE NEGATIVES

It is best to phrase survey questions positively. For example, "This product is good," "I would consider purchasing this product," and "The information in the brochure was informative" are phrased positively. Positively phrased questions are much easier to read, understand, and answer than negatively phrased questions, such as, "This product is bad," "I would not consider purchasing this product," and "The information in the brochure was not informative." If a question is phrased negatively and the consumer has positive feelings or opinions, the consumer must disagree with a negatively phrased statement. This can be very confusing. However, if the question is phrased positively and the consumer has positive feelings or opinions, they simply agree with the positive statement, which is much less confusing.

Note that you might want to phrase a few survey questions negatively just to make sure that people are actually reading the questions. This is called **reverse scoring** a question and can be used to identify apathy and uninformed response bias. However, a question with a **double negative** becomes almost impossible to understand and answer. The following questions contain multiple negatives.

- Do you not like bicycles that do not have hand brakes?

- Would you never eat at a restaurant that did not have a no-smoking section?

- I would never not buy a product that did not have the features that I wanted.

- I would never not go back to a store where I did not receive good service.

To avoid double negatives:

- Pretest the survey questions to make sure that all respondents can fully and correctly understand the questions.

- Try to phrase survey questions in a positive frame. Instead of asking, "Which of these movies did you not like?" ask, "Which of these movies did you like?"

AVOID FALSE COMPARISONS

False comparisons force respondents to make a comparison or choice when they cannot. The survey questions below force consumers to choose between two options, when in fact they might want to choose both options, or choose neither option.

Do you drink fruit juice because it tastes good, or do you drink it because it is good for you? ☐ Tastes good ☐ Good for you

This false comparison does not allow for the possibility that a consumer drinks fruit juice for both of the stated reasons. As another example, the following question suffers from the same problem.

Did you purchase your Honda because you got a good deal on the financing, or because you really like the style of the car?
☐ Got Good Deal on the Financing   ☐ Really Like the Style

To avoid false comparisons:

- Pretest the survey questions to make sure that all respondents can fully and correctly understand the questions.

- Write survey questions so that each question asks about a single concept. Use multiple questions to measure multiple issues, brands, attributes, criteria, justifications, or beliefs.

TIPS ON WRITING SURVEY QUESTIONS
Always Remember Your Research Objectives

If research objectives are stated in specific and measurable terms, the task of writing survey questions simply becomes one of restating the objectives in question form. Consider the example below.

Objective: To measure the percentage of students who would be willing to rent at least three DVDs from our DVD rental and delivery service every month.

Survey Question: Would you be willing to rent at least three DVDs from our DVD rental and delivery service every month?

Keep Things Simple

Do not make the survey overly complicated. For example, if the objective is to measure the percentage of consumers who intend to shop for flowers at a new florist within the next month, simply ask, "Do you intend to shop for flowers at this florist within the next month?" Researchers do not always need complicated or high-level scales. Often, simple *yes* or *no* questions are adequate.

How many questions should be asked on a survey? A survey should be as long as necessary, and as short as possible.

Use Everyday Language

Even though survey questions should be written using correct grammar and English, they should also be written in the language that people use in everyday speech. If you are having trouble deciding on the best wording for a question, you should stop writing and ask yourself, "What do I really want to know?" Then, answer the question out loud by saying, "What I really want to know is _____." And then fill in the blank. Often the best way to write is to say out loud what you want to write, and then write down what you have just said. Writing a survey question just as you would ask someone a question in a face-to-face conversation is often the best way to eliminate confusing language and jargon.

A good survey is one that does what the researcher wants it to do. A good survey fulfills the research objectives and measures all necessary variables in a way that provides useful information for decision-making purposes.

Consider the Possible Responses

Consider all possible responses to a survey question and then ask yourself, "If people respond a certain way, what does this tell me?" For example, if you are considering opening a new florist and you want to measure how often people purchase flowers from a florist, you should not ask the following question:

When was the last time you purchased flowers from a florist?

Within the last: ☐ Day   ☐   Week   ☐ More Than One Week

If all respondents answer that they have purchased flowers within the last day, what does that mean? Does this mean that everyone in the sample purchases flowers every day? Is it possible that everyone in the sample purchases flowers only once a year and they all happened to purchase flowers yesterday? There is no way to know. It would be better to ask consumers how often they purchase flowers in a typical month. Then, if all of the respondents answer that they purchase flowers twice in a typical month, this would be a better indicator of their purchasing behaviors.

Ask Only What Needs to be Asked

Ask only those questions that need to be asked. Keep the survey as short as possible. If a question is not important to the managerial decision that needs to be made, do not ask it. If a question will not provide useful information for making decisions, do not ask it.

Caution When Using Open-Ended Questions

Be careful when using open-ended questions on surveys. Use open-ended questions on surveys only when it is absolutely necessary. Consumers often do not know how they are to respond when no response categories are provided for them. As a result, you might receive answers that seem very strange and odd. For example, asking consumers, "How often do you purchase gas for your car?" might result in the following responses: "Whenever I need to," "When the tank is empty," or even, "Whenever my wife doesn't want to fill up the car herself." If researchers are interested in specific time periods, such as once a week or twice a week, these should be provided as response alternatives on the survey. Strange responses to open-ended questions most often result from consumers not knowing how they should respond, or not knowing the type of response that the researcher is seeking. When using open-ended questions, do not be afraid to give consumers specific instructions and directions regarding the type of response they are to give. For example, tell them to "write in a number" or "write in a dollar amount." Most consumers want to be helpful and they will not be offended by very detailed instructions as to how they should respond.

ORGANIZING THE QUESTIONNAIRE

As the previous section highlighted, the way a question is phrased and asked is very important. Additionally, the manner in which a survey is structured and organized is also very important. Below are some guidelines for organizing the questionnaire.

Have a Cover Letter or Scripted Introduction

Every survey should have an **introduction** that describes the nature of the survey and describes why respondents should complete the survey. Mail surveys should include a written **cover letter**. Telephone surveys and personal interviews should include a scripted **oral introduction** to the survey. Online surveys need an introduction included in the email asking respondents to participate as well as on the first page of the survey.

The introduction is a vital component to obtaining respondents' interest and cooperation. The introduction provides the researcher with an opportunity to capture the respondents' attention and interest, garner cooperation and commitment from the respondent, establish trust in the survey process, and establish the credibility of the researcher. And, this should all be done with as few words as possible.

For situations where there is an interviewer (e.g., telephone and personal interviews), the introduction should always begin by identifying the name of the interviewer. Usually, giving the interviewer's first name will suffice when conducting random anonymous surveys of consumers. However, providing both the first and last name of the interviewer is recommended when surveying professionals, such as doctors or lawyers, or when surveying business professionals for business-to-business studies.

The introduction should also:

- Provide the name of the firm or organization conducting the research.

- Reassure respondents that the purpose of the survey is to measure opinions and that you are not selling anything.

- Politely ask the respondent to participate in the survey, and not make the respondent feel pressured to respond in any way.

- Describe the nature of the survey and the purpose of the survey.

- Give an estimate of the amount of time that the survey will take to complete.

- Describe any incentive that is being offered and how respondents can receive the incentive.

When conducting a mail survey, the introduction can be in included in a cover letter or written on the front page of the survey. Because of this, the introduction can be somewhat lengthy, including details regarding the survey. However, for phone surveys and online surveys, the introduction should be relatively short and concise. Below is an example of an introduction to a telephone survey conducted to identify the types of new commercial businesses that residents would like to see in their town.

> Hello. My name is _____ and I am working with Insight Marketing Research. We conduct public opinion polls of local residents on a number of important topics. Tonight we are conducting a telephone survey of Clearville residents to measure the types of retail and commercial businesses that you would like to see in the Clearville area. This survey has been developed by the Economic Development Committee of Clearville and has been approved by Mayor Bill Bethers. He and the town planners would like your input regarding the types of businesses that will be a part of Clearville in the future.

> I want to assure you that we are not selling anything. This survey is very short and will take only a few minutes to complete. Your participation is completely voluntary. If we should come to a question that you do not want to answer, simply tell me and we will go on to the next question. Also, you may quit the survey at any time. May I begin?

Notice that this introduction:

- Clearly identifies the interviewer and the organization conducting the survey.
- Identifies the purpose of the survey.
- Assures respondents that the interviewer is not selling anything.
- Establishes trust and credibility by notifying respondents that the survey was approved by the town's mayor and economic development committee.
- Informs respondents that the survey is short.
- Assures respondents that their participation is voluntary and that they can skip any question that they do not want to answer.

Whenever interviewers conduct intercept interviews or telephone surveys, they should be prepared to answer the following types of questions that respondents might ask about the survey and their participation in the survey.

- What is this survey about?
- Is this a survey, or are you going to sell me something?
- Will this survey be difficult and time-consuming?
- Who is conducting this survey?
- Who wants this information?
- Why do they want this information?

- Why was I selected to complete this survey?

- Will it cost me anything to complete this survey?

- How will I benefit from completing this survey?

- How important is this survey and the information that I will provide?

- How long will it take for me to complete this survey?

- How will the results from this survey be used?

- Will I have to answer questions about potentially sensitive or embarrassing issues?

- Will my name be associated with any of my answers to the survey questions?

Telephone Surveys and Female Respondents. An interesting phenomenon that often occurs with telephone surveys is that women are generally more likely to answer the phone than are men. This can lead to a biased sample that overrepresents women and underrepresents men when the purpose of the survey is to examine the general population, including men and women. Of course, this will not be a problem if the interviewer specifically asks to speak to either a male or to a female when the population of interest is either men or women.

So, how does an interviewer conducting surveys of the general public attempt to even out the percentage of male and female respondents without specifically asking to speak to a male or to a female? One technique is to include a question such as the following in the introduction to a phone survey:

> May I speak with the person age 18 or older living at this address whose birthday is coming up next?

By random chance there is a 50 percent probability that the person in the household whose birthday is coming up next is a male, and a 50 percent probability that the person is a female. As such, this type of question will help to increase the percentage of males in the sample without having to specifically ask to speak to a male. This will help to ensure a more representative sample based on sex.

Begin with Easy and Interesting Questions

Begin the questionnaire with questions that are easy to answer and that obtain the respondent's interest.[3] You might begin the survey with filter questions or skip questions that are easy to answer. Titles of questionnaires are also important. Use a title to make the survey sound important. For example, a "Nationwide Survey," or a "Survey of Top Students" sounds like an interesting and important survey that should be completed.

Go from General to Specific

If possible, ask general questions first. Use some warm-up questions to get the respondent thinking about the concept. Then, ask more specific questions later. This is often referred to as **funneling**, because the order of questions goes from broad to specific. Answers to specific questions can influence answers to later questions. For example, if you ask, "How well do you like Budweiser beer?" and then ask, "List all those brands of beer that you can think of," most people will list Budweiser beer because it was just mentioned in the previous question. Ask general listing (recall) questions first, and then ask respondents to evaluate specific brands later.

Ask Difficult Questions Later

Ask questions that require work or a significant amount of cognitive effort in the middle or at the end of the survey. Allow respondents to build up some motivation, momentum, interest, and commitment to the survey. Once respondents have answered a few questions they are much more likely to continue answering the remaining questions.

Use Prompters for Long Surveys

Insert **prompters** at strategic points in the survey if the survey is relatively long (e.g., more than two pages). For example, use prompters such as:

- You only have a few more questions to answer.

- This next section will be easier.

- Now that you have helped us with those comments, we would like to ask a few more questions.

These simple comments on a survey can greatly affect a respondent's desire to complete the survey. However, prompters are typically not needed for relatively short questionnaires (one to two pages). When completing a short survey, respondents can see that the survey has only a few questions.

Labeling the sections of the survey also helps consumers work through the survey. It helps to break up a long survey. It gives respondents a sense of the types of questions they are answering as well as a sense of the types of questions that they will answer in later sections of the survey.

Progress bars for online surveys are also very helpful when respondents cannot see how long the survey is or how many questions remain to be answered. A progress bar displays the percent of the survey that has been completed. These are especially helpful if survey questions are displayed one page at a time.

Ask Demographics Last

Ask potentially sensitive or threatening demographic questions last. This keeps respondents from becoming defensive or embarrassed. Imagine beginning an online survey where the first four questions are "How old are you? How much money do you make? How much do you weigh? What is your sex?" If these are asked later in the survey (preferably at the end of the survey), respondents are already conditioned to respond. Often, demographic and classificatory questions are not of primary

> Unless they are required for filtering respondents, questions measuring demographics should be placed at the end of the survey.

interest to the researcher and are used to measure sample characteristics to assess the representativeness of a sample. Demographic questions can even be identified by telling the respondent, "The next few questions are for classification purposes only." Demographic questions can be asked at the beginning of a survey if they are needed to filter respondents or to be used in a skip pattern.

Use Filter Questions

Filter questions are often used at the beginning of surveys to screen out those respondents who are not qualified to answer a second question because it is outside of their knowledge or experience. For example, the question below should be asked with a filter:

Where do you generally have check-cashing problems in Nashville?

Notice that this question assumes that respondents have problems cashing checks in Nashville. The question should be asked with a filter, such as:

Do you ever have problems cashing a check in Nashville?

☐ No   ☐ Yes (If yes, where? _____)

Use Skip or Branching Questions

Skip or **branching questions** are used to direct respondents to different parts of the survey. They are often used at the beginning of a survey to lead respondents to appropriate questions or sections of the survey. For example, the question below uses a **skip pattern** to direct respondents to different parts of the survey.

Have you purchased a used car in the past year?

☐ Yes (go to question #2)   ☐ No (go to question #8)

Realize, however, that using too many skip questions can make the survey very confusing. As such, multiple skip patterns should be avoided on self-administered surveys and mail surveys. Consumers can easily become lost on a survey if there are too many skip patterns. When this happens, they usually terminate the survey. Avoid using more than two separate skip patterns on a single survey. An advantage of online surveys is the ability to program even very complicated skip patterns into the survey. Consumers do not need to be responsible for knowing where they should go on the survey based on their answers to the survey questions. The programmed skip pattern automatically takes them to the correct question. Telephone surveys using computer-assisted telephone interviewing (CATI) software can also program skip patterns into the survey that will automatically direct the interviewer to the appropriate questions based on consumers' answers to previous questions.

Be Consistent with the Direction of Scales

Avoid changing the direction of the scales used on a survey. As previously mentioned, it is best to write survey questions that are phrased positively. And, it is sometimes useful to include some reverse-scored items to check whether or not respondents are reading the questions and to assess if respondents' answers are internally consistent. However, the direction of scales should remain consistent throughout a survey. For example, do not have respondents answer the first 10 questions on Likert scales where *Strongly Agree* is on the right-hand position of the scale and then have respondents answer a second set of questions where *Strongly Agree* is on the left-hand position of the scale. In general, the positive position of scales should be consistently on either the right-hand side or the left-hand side of the scale throughout the entire survey. If not, this can create confusion on the part of the respondent. Further, it threatens the validity of the results. For example, if the first set of questions uses scales where the positive ends of the scales are on the right, respondents might assume that all of the remaining scales also have the positive ends of the scales on the right.

Close with a Thank You

Every survey should conclude by thanking the respondent for their time, effort, and cooperation. For intercept surveys and telephone surveys, interviewers can also remind respondents of the purpose of the survey. For example, tell respondents:

> Thank you for taking the time to complete this survey. You opinions are valuable and they will help us to design new products that best satisfy the needs and wants of our customers. I hope that you will consider participating in future surveys if asked to do so.

Improving Survey Quality

Researchers can also include questions at the end of the survey that allow respondents to evaluate the survey itself. Answers to such questions can allow the researcher to identify survey questions that were confusing, determine if the survey needs to be shortened, identify additional questions that can be added to the survey, and assess respondents' overall satisfaction with taking the survey.

ZERO AS A SEPARATE RESPONSE CATEGORY

When measuring variables for which zero is a reasonable and meaningful answer, zero should always be separated out as its own response category. For example, consider the two survey questions below.

> How may DVDs do you rent in a typical week?
> ☐ 0–1   ☐ 2–3   ☐ 4–5   ☐ 6 or more

> How may DVDs do you rent in a typical week?
> ☐ 0   ☐ 1–2   ☐ 3–4   ☐ 5 or more

Notice that the first question includes zero in the same category as one. If a consumer checks this *0–1* category, does that mean that this consumer rents no

DVDs per week, or does it mean that this consumer rents one DVD per week? We would not know. And, there is an important difference between renting no DVDs per week and renting one DVD per week. This can cause a significant problem for decision makers if a large percentage of respondents check this *0–1* category. Decision makers might be faced with a situation where most consumers rent no DVDs per week. Or, they might be faced with a situation where most consumers rent one DVD per week. Unfortunately, they would not know the true situation. This would make managerial decision making almost impossible. The second question avoids this problem by making *zero* its own response category. If most consumers check the *zero* category there is no question about the meaning of this result.

As another example, consider the potential problems with measuring the number of dependent children living with a consumer. There is a major difference between having zero dependent children living with you and having one dependent child living with you. As such, zero should not be included with other response options. In sum, when zero is a reasonable and meaningful answer to a question, response categories such as *zero*, *none*, *nobody*, and *never* should always be separated out as their own response categories.

Including Zero with Other Response Options. The exception to this general rule is when measuring variables for which zero is not an expected response, or for which zero is not a reasonable or distinctly meaningful answer. In such cases, zero can be included with other response alternatives. This is the case for measuring variables such as height, weight, time, and distance. It would be perfectly acceptable to ask a question such as:

How much time does it take you to drive to work in the morning?

☐ 0–10 minutes

☐ 11–20 minutes

☐ 21–30 minutes

☐ 31 minutes or more

There is very little meaningful difference between zero minutes driving time and one minute driving time. In fact, researchers would never expect someone to answer zero to such a question. This would imply that they lived at the same location as their place of employment. Of course, this assumes that the question is being asked of consumers who all drive to work, as opposed to consumers who use a different form of transportation. This same line of reasoning also applies when measuring income. Even though it is possible for someone to have zero income, very few consumers have zero income. And, even if they did have zero income, they would probably be of little interest to marketers. As such, zero is very rarely separated out as its own category for measuring income.

IDENTIFYING APATHY BIAS AND UNINFORMED RESPONSE BIAS

One possible source of error in surveys (especially for long surveys) is that respondents become bored or apathetic about answering the questions. They might decide to answer randomly so that they can finish the survey quickly (**apathy bias**). They might even provide an answer to a question about which they are uninformed simply because they believe that they are supposed to answer all questions (**uninformed response bias**). Respondents might even become angry with the researcher for making them complete a long survey (**hostility bias**).

How can researchers identify such apathetic or uninformed responses? There are two strategies that are often employed in survey research to identify the extent to which respondents are reading the questions and answering them conscientiously. These two strategies are called reverse scoring and repeating. Reverse scoring and repeating questions are both designed to check for internal consistency within a respondent's answers.

Reverse-Scored Questions

Most survey questions will be phrased positively. However, some survey questions are purposely phrased negatively. These negatively phrased questions are called **reverse-scored questions**. For example, consider the following four questions found on a teacher evaluation form.

1. This teacher is organized.	SD	D	N	A	SA
2. This teacher answers questions effectively.	SD	D	N	A	SA
3. This teacher does not care about students' learning.	SD	D	N	A	SA
4. This teacher wants me to learn.	SD	D	N	A	SA

Notice that the third question is reverse-scored. All of the other questions are phrased positively, but question 3 is phrased negatively. If respondents answer *Strongly Agree* (*SA*) to all questions, including question 3, this might indicate that they did not carefully read all of the questions. They might have assumed that all of the questions were phrased positively. If they generally liked the teacher, a general **halo effect** might have caused them to answer *Strongly Agree* to all questions. If respondents considered the teacher to be good in one area, they might have assumed (or perceived) that the teacher was good in all other areas. This will often result in **straight line responding** because respondents' answers are all the same and they form a straight line. Even though it is possible for a consumer to carefully read and consider the survey questions and end up answering every question with the same answer, it is not very likely. We expect to see at least some variation in consumers' responses to survey questions. As a result, some researchers will discard the data from respondents who provide only straight line responses.

Repeated Questions

The same question can be asked more than once on longer surveys. These are called **repeated questions**. This can be done by paraphrasing, or stating the question slightly differently the second time it is asked. If answers to the same question vary greatly, this indicates low internal consistency in a respondent's answers. This could result from a respondent not reading all of the questions. It could also indicate that respondents were answering randomly each time they answered the question. However, it is very important that essentially the same question be asked each time on the survey. Realize that slight changes in wording can greatly affect the content and meaning of a question.

Be aware, however, that it is unreasonable to expect consumers to respond exactly the same way each and every time they answer a question. For example, if a consumer circled a 5 on a 7-point scale (1 = Dislike; 7 = Like) the first time they answered a question, and then circled a 6 the second time they answered the same question, this difference is not large enough to conclude that their answers were internally inconsistent. At least they responded on the positive end of the scale both times. Alternatively, if this same consumer circled a 2 the second time they answered the question, this discrepancy is large enough to indicate low internal consistency. The first response was on the positive end of the scale, whereas the second response was on the negative end of the scale.

Incomplete Surveys. Also, be aware that apparently inconsistent answers do not always indicate that a respondent was actually inconsistent. To illustrate this, consider the case of a survey used by a hospital. Patients completed the survey as they were being discharged from the emergency room. The purpose of the survey was to measure patients' level of satisfaction with the hospital care they received from the emergency room. The four questions from the survey are shown below.

1. I was admitted quickly.	SD	D	N	A	SA
2. I had one nurse attend to me my entire stay.	SD	D	N	A	SA
3. The doctor saw me quickly.	SD	D	N	A	SA
4. Overall, I would evaluate my stay very favorably.	SD	D	N	A	SA

A patient responded with *Strongly Agree* (*SA*) to the first three questions, but *Strongly Disagree* (*SD*) to the last question. This apparent inconsistency between the individual questions (questions 1, 2, and 3) and their overall rating of their stay in the hospital (question 4) could be due to an incomplete survey. Perhaps the negative overall rating was due to factors not measured on the survey. Such factors could include that the doctor did not explain things well, the nurse was rude, or even the temperature in the room was too cold. If these questions had been asked, the apparent inconsistency could easily be explained. Including an "Any other comments?" or "Is there anything else you want to tell us?" question at the end of the survey will help to identify this and make the entire survey collectively exhaustive.

RANDOMIZED RESPONSE QUESTIONS

People sometimes lie about their true feelings, attitudes, behaviors, and intentions when answering survey questions. They lie because they are embarrassed to answer truthfully, or because they want to avoid any negative consequences associated with answering honestly. It is likely that few people will admit to cheating on their federal income taxes. A strategy that survey researchers can use to increase the likelihood of someone answering honestly, even to potentially embarrassing or sensitive questions, is to use randomized response questions.[4]

Randomized response questions consist of two questions where the answer to the first question (known only to the respondent) determines which of two subsequent questions the respondent answers—either an innocuous question or a potentially sensitive question. Randomized response questions are used when asking about potentially embarrassing, threatening, or otherwise sensitive issues. They reduce response bias by allowing the respondent to answer potentially sensitive questions honestly because the researcher does not know which of two questions the respondent is answering.[5]

To illustrate randomized response questions, all respondents are asked an initial question similar to the one shown below. Respondents do not reveal their answer to this initial question.

> Is the last digit in your Social Security number odd or even?
>
> > If odd, answer question A below.
> >
> > If even, answer question B below.

If the last digit is an odd number, they answer question A. Alternatively, if the last digit is an even number, they answer question B.

> A. Is the last digit in your home phone number between 5 and 9?
>
> B. Have you ever shoplifted?   ☐ Yes   ☐ No

After reading question A or B, respondents write down either *yes* or *no*, or they answer orally either *yes* or *no*. Respondents are assured anonymity and are likely to answer truthfully because only they know which of the two second questions (A or B) they are answering. If they answer *yes*, they could always say that they were answering question A, even if they really answered question B. Based on simple probability theory, the percentage of respondents who have ever shoplifted can be determined as follows:

$$P(yes) = [P(question\ A) \times P(yes\ to\ A)] + [P(question\ B) \times P(yes\ to\ B)]$$

The probability of a *yes* response is equal to the probability of answering question A multiplied by the probability of answering *yes* to question A, plus the probability of answering question B multiplied by the probability of answering *yes* to question B. To illustrate, 35 percent of the respondents answered *yes* to the second question. Since the probability of having to answer question A is 50 percent, and the probability of having to answer question B is 50 percent, and the probability of having a phone number that ends in a digit between 5 and 9 is also 50 percent, the percentage of respondents who have ever shoplifted (X) can be calculated as:

$$0.35 = [0.5 \, (0.5)] + [0.5 \, (X)]$$

$$0.35 = 0.25 + 0.5 \, (X)$$

$$0.10 = 0.5 \, (X)$$

$$0.20 = X$$

Therefore, 20 percent of the respondents have shoplifted.

Such randomized response questions can be used during a personal interview, for mail surveys, for online surveys, and on self-administered surveys. If they are being used in a mail survey, researchers sometimes include a coin, such as a half dollar, with the survey. Respondents flip the coin to determine which of the two subsequent questions they answer. They also get to keep the coin.

Any question that results in a 50/50 chance of answering one of two possible answers can be used as the initial question. For example, instead of asking if the last digit in their Social Security number is odd or even, researchers could ask:

- Is the last digit in your home address odd or even?
- Was the last digit in the street address of the home in which you lived as a child odd or even?
- Is the last digit in your age odd or even?
- Is the last digit on your car's license plate odd or even?

However, to be able to calculate probabilities and solve for the percentage of respondents who answered the question of interest, the probabilities associated with both the initial question and the innocuous second question must be known. This is why questions that have a 50/50 probability associated with them are most often used.

INCREASING THE RESPONSE RATES FOR SURVEYS

A high response rate is always a principal goal for survey researchers. There are a number of techniques that researchers can use to increase the response rates for their surveys.

Personalized Introduction or Cover Letter. Every survey should have a cover letter or introduction. Even personal intercept surveys and phone surveys should have a scripted oral introduction that describes why the study is being conducted and why the respondent should complete the survey. This helps motivate respondents to complete the survey. A personalized introduction to the survey will generally lead to higher response rates than a generic "Dear Consumer" introduction.

Financial Incentives or Premiums. Financial incentives are probably the most effective way of increasing response rates. Offering money for completing a survey works effectively for all income levels. Everyone likes receiving money. Receiving money or other gifts can also create guilt in the respondent, who is then motivated to complete the survey to relieve the guilt.

Survey Importance. Make the survey sound important and interesting. Do not lie, but make the survey appealing. Try to make the survey seem large in scope and importance.

Follow Up Letters, Emails, or Postcard Reminders. These can increase response rates by encouraging nonrespondents to respond. Those who would normally not respond can be encouraged to respond with additional incentives.

Stamped Return Envelope. All mail surveys should have a postage-paid return envelope provided for the respondent. Very few people will pay the postage to return a survey.

Cutoff Dates. Including a cutoff date, or deadline date, by which the survey should be returned can increase the speed with which surveys are returned. However, cutoff dates and deadline dates usually have little effect on the number of surveys that are completed and returned.

WHY INCREASE THE RESPONSE RATES FOR SURVEYS?

There are a number of reasons why researchers are interested in higher response rates for surveys.

Get Your Money's Worth. Conducting survey research can be expensive in terms of money, time, and effort. Researchers must pay for the cost of printing, the cost of phone service and phone lines, the cost of salaries for interviewers, and even the cost of postage for mailing and return envelopes. A nonrespondent who receives the survey but who does not complete the survey means wasted money, time, and effort. Researchers are concerned with the cost per respondent, not just the cost per survey (or cost per contact). Increasing the response rate decreases the cost per respondent for the research.

Decrease the Margin of Error. Increasing the sample size leads to decreases in the margin of error for statistical estimates. The standard errors of the mean and proportion are calculated as:

$$SE_{mean} = S/\sqrt{n} \qquad\qquad SE_{prop} = \sqrt{p(1-p)/n}$$

For both, the sample size is the denominator in the equation. Thus, increasing the sample size reduces the standard error of the estimates. Results can then be reported with greater accuracy and confidence. For example, the margins of error for various sample sizes are shown in Table 16.1.

A smaller margin of error (resulting from a larger sample size) also leads to a narrower confidence interval for statistical estimates. Confidence intervals for means and proportions are calculated as:

$$\mu = \overline{X} \pm Z\,(SE_{mean}) \qquad \pi = p \pm Z\,(SE_{prop})$$

TABLE 16.1 Sample Size and Margin of Error

Sample Size	Margin of Error (± %) (based on a 95% confidence level)
n = 100	± 10%
n = 250	± 6%
n = 500	± 4%
n = 1,000	± 3%

At the same confidence level (Z), a narrower confidence interval can be reported due to the smaller standard error of the estimate.

Increased Statistical Power. With an increased response rate and a larger sample, there is increased **statistical power** to reject null hypotheses when in fact they should be rejected (when they are false). For example, there would be very little statistical power to conclude that males and females have different attitudes toward a product with only 10 male and 10 female respondents. However, there would be much greater statistical power to conclude that males and females have different attitudes toward a product with 1,000 male and 1,000 female respondents.

More Representative Sample. An increased response rate increases the chance that the sample is representative of the population. Of course, this is based on the assumption that the consumers who receive the survey are in fact representative of the population.

Decreased Chance for Nonresponse Error. A low response rate does not necessarily mean that there will be nonresponse error resulting from a difference between respondents and nonrespondents. But, a high response rate reduces the chance of nonresponse error. This is because there will be more respondents and fewer nonrespondents. Again, this is based on the assumption that a representative sample of consumers received the survey.

GUIDELINES FOR INTERVIEWERS

The purpose of any legitimate survey or interview is to accurately measure respondents' thoughts, opinions, feelings, and beliefs. Questions should be asked in an unbiased, systematic, and objective manner. The interviewer should avoid at all costs exerting any undue influence on respondents' answers or responses to survey questions.

Many interviewers do not realize that even the most subtle factors can significantly affect how a respondent answers survey questions. Respondents' answers to personal interviews where there is direct and visual two-way communication between an interviewer and respondent are highly susceptible to being influenced by an interviewer. And, even though respondents cannot see telephone interviewers, responses to telephone surveys can also be influenced by the actions of the interviewer. When conducting an interview, either in a home, in a shopping mall, in a store, in a one-on-one interviewing room, or over the phone, interviewers should be aware of the following guidelines for their conduct and the manner in which they ask questions.

- Be familiar with the questions before you begin the first interview.

- Be aware of your personal appearance. Look and act professionally. For interviews in shopping malls or at interviewing facilities, interviewers should wear professional-looking attire. However, interviewers must also dress appropriately for the interviewing situation. Interviewers can wear more casual clothing when interviewing people at an outdoor jazz festival or sporting event.

- Be aware of your nonverbal communication. The way an interviewer nods his or her head in agreement with a respondent's answer, or the way an interviewer smiles in response to an answer, can give respondents subtle cues about expected answers to survey questions.

- Be aware that changes in voice tone and vocal inflections can affect respondents' answers.

- Remain neutral. Be careful to neither agree nor disagree with respondents' answers.

- Be upbeat and pleasant throughout the entire interview and try to maintain the same mood during the entire interview. If not, respondents can sense that certain answers make the interviewer angry, uncomfortable, or uneasy. Respondents can also sense if an answer is what the interviewer wanted to hear.

- Avoid changing the wording of questions too much. Even slight changes to the wording of a question can dramatically change the meaning of the question.

- Read the questions in the order that they appear on the survey. Do not jump around.

- Speak slowly and calmly. Make sure that all respondents understand what is being asked.

- Do not give your opinion. If a consumer responds to a question by asking, "I don't know, what do you think?" do not give your opinion. Instead, say, "Well, today were are hoping to find out what you think," or "Actually, we are very interested in hearing what you have to say about this."

- Record what respondents say verbatim. Do not try to paraphrase respondents' answers during the interview.

- When necessary, keep respondents on task and do not allow respondents to stray off topic for too long.

- Thank the respondent at the end of the interview.

TELEPHONE SURVEYS AND DO-NOT-CALL LISTS

Telephone survey researchers sometimes find that consumers are reluctant to participate in telephone surveys due to confusion about the difference between telemarketing calls and survey research calls. Many consumers think that telephone surveying is the same thing as telemarketing. A consumer might respond by saying, "You can't call me. I'm on the do-not-call list. You have just violated federal laws and I am going to report you." It is important that survey researchers deal with such comments in a polite, civil, and explanatory tone. Simply inform the respondent that, "Yes, you are right that some telemarketing calls are limited by the federal government and telemarketers are not allowed to call consumers who have placed their names on a do-not-call list. However, this is not a telemarketing call and we are not trying to sell you anything. We are merely conducting a survey of consumers' opinions, and telephone surveys are not limited by the do-not-call laws. We are not trying to sell you anything or ask for money. We are merely asking for your opinions." Even though telephone survey research is not limited by the do-not-call laws, many marketers and marketing research firms will maintain an internal do-not-call list as a courtesy to consumers and their potential customers. If consumers want to learn more about the do-not-call laws and the differences between telemarketing and telephone surveys, they can contact the Federal Communications Commission (FCC) at Federal Communications Commission, 1919 M Street NW, Room 254, Washington, DC 20554; phone: (202) 418-0200; online: **www.fcc.gov**.

WRITING SURVEY QUESTIONS AND THE DECISION-MAKING PROCESS

Marketing managers need information to be able to make decisions that are designed to achieve desired marketing objectives. Marketing managers need information obtained from survey questions that accurately measure what they are supposed to measure. The wording of survey questions and the manner in which survey questions are organized on a questionnaire are important factors in determining the worth, quality, and usefulness of the results from a marketing research survey. Survey questions will tend to have lower validity when:

- The survey questions contain ambiguous words, phrases, or response categories.

- The survey questions contain leading or loaded words or phrases that cause people to bias their responses.

- The survey questions are double-barreled and ask respondents to answer two questions in one.

- The survey questions contain technical language or jargon that respondents do not understand.

- The survey questions contain double negatives which confuse respondents.

- The survey questions contain false comparisons which force respondents to choose between two or more options when in fact they are not able to choose between them.

- The order of questions on the survey influences respondents' answers to the questions. Questions asked early in the survey can cause respondents to think about issues or topics that influence their answers to later questions.

- Respondents answer questions they are not supposed to answer because appropriate skip or filter questions are not used.

- Too many skip or filter questions are used, causing respondents to become confused and even lost on the survey.

SAMPLE TELEPHONE SURVEY: COMMUNITY LIBRARY

Below is the text from a portion of a telephone survey using CATI interviewing software. Notice how the questions are asked in a conversational tone. Each question appears on a separate screen. The numbers to the left of each response option indicate the number to be entered on the computer keyboard indicating a respondent's answer. When a number is entered for a question, the interviewing software automatically shows the next question. These numbers are for the interviewer's use only. They are not mentioned along with the response options. Doing so would only confuse respondents.

> Hello, my name is _____ and I am working with Market Insights Research here in town. Tonight we are surveying local residents on a number of important issues related to the Mortimer Library here in Glockton County. May I speak with the person age 18 or older living at this address whose birthday is coming up next?
>
> [IF NOT A HOME ADDRESS] "Sorry, I got the wrong place." [PRESS 2]
>
> [WHEN RIGHT PERSON IS ON THE LINE] I am working with Market Insights Research. We are not selling anything. We are conducting a telephone survey of Glockton County residents for the Mortimer Library. The survey is short and will take only a few minutes to complete. Also, this interview is completely anonymous and completely voluntary. If we should come to any question that you don't want to answer, just let me know and we'll go on to the next question. May I begin?
>
> > 1 Yes [GO TO FIRST QUESTION]
> >
> > 2 No [STOP INTERVIEW]

1. If all other things were equal and a political candidate described himself or herself as the "library candidate," meaning that they would devote much effort and attention to improving the Mortimer Library, would this make you more likely to vote for the candidate, less likely to vote for the candidate, or have no effect on your vote?

   1 More likely to vote for the candidate

   2 No effect on voting for the candidate

3 Less likely to vote for the candidate

9 [DO NOT READ] Don't know/refused

2. With respect to the number of library locations (branches), would you say that the Mortimer Library currently has enough branches, too many branches, or too few branches?

1 Too many branches

2 Enough branches

3 Too few branches

9 [DO NOT READ] Don't know/refused

3. How important is it to have a branch of the Mortimer Library within five miles of where you live?

1 Very important

2 Somewhat important

3 Neither

4 Somewhat unimportant

5 Not at all important

9 [DO NOT READ] Don't know/refused

4. Do you know where the main branch of the Mortimer Library is located?

1 Yes

2 No

9 [DO NOT READ] Don't know/refused

5. If there were more signs placed around town directing people to the Mortimer Library, would that make you more likely to go to the library, less likely to go to the library, or have no effect on how often you visited the library?

1 More likely to visit the library

2 No effect

3 Less likely to visit the library

9 [DO NOT READ] Don't know/refused

6. If there were a coffee shop or snack shop similar to Starbucks in the Mortimer Library, would this make you more likely to go to the library, less likely to go to the library, or have no effect on how often you visited the Mortimer Library?

1 More likely to visit the library

2 No effect

3 Less likely to visit the library

9 [DO NOT READ] Don't know/refused

7. How important is it to integrate library branches into new community centers that are currently being built around town?

     1 Very important

     2 Somewhat important

     3 Neither

     4 Somewhat unimportant

     5 Not at all important

     9 [DO NOT READ] Don't know/refused

8. If a library branch were placed in a community center close to where you live, how often do you think you would visit such a library branch?

     1 Every day

     2 About two to three days a week

     3 About once a week

     4 About once every two weeks

     5 About once a month

     6 About once every two months

     7 About once every six months

     8 Less than once every six months

     9 Never

     9 [DO NOT READ] Don't know/refused

9. If the Mortimer Library had an auditorium for meetings, lectures, shows, and other types of performances, would this make you more likely to visit the library, less likely to visit the library, or have no effect?

     1 More likely to visit the library

     2 No effect

     3 Less likely to visit the library

     9 [DO NOT READ] Don't know/refused

10. How often do you currently visit the Mortimer Library?

     1 Every day

     2 About two to three days a week

     3 About once a week

4 About once every two weeks

5 About once a month

6 About once every two months

7 About once every six months

8 Less than once every six months

9 Never

9 [DO NOT READ] Don't know/refused

SAMPLE TELEPHONE SURVEY: CONSUMER OUTLOOK

Below is the text from a portion of another telephone survey using CATI interviewing software. Notice that the questions are phrased in everyday language and every effort has been taken to make certain that the respondent understands the questions.

Hello, my name is _____ and I am working with New Vision Research. We are surveying local residents on a number of important consumer issues. May I speak with the person age 18 or older living at this address whose birthday is coming up next?

[IF NOT A HOME ADDRESS] "Sorry, I got the wrong place." [PRESS 2]

[WHEN RIGHT PERSON IS ON THE LINE] I am working with New Vision Research. We are conducting a public opinion poll to measure consumers' outlook on the national and local economy. The survey is short, and will take only a few minutes to complete. Also, this interview is completely anonymous and completely voluntary. If we should come to any question that you don't want to answer, just let me know and we'll go on to the next question. May I begin?

1 Yes [GO TO FIRST QUESTION]

2 No [STOP INTERVIEW]

[PRESS 1 OR 2]

[PRESS CTRL/END TO TERMINATE AN INTERVIEW]

1. Turning first to business conditions in the country as a whole, would you say that business conditions in the country as a whole are good, bad, or somewhere in between?

1 Good

2 In between (good/bad)

3 Bad

8 [DO NOT READ] Refused

9 [DO NOT READ] Don't know

2. And how about six months from now, do you expect that in the country as a whole business conditions will be better than they are today, worse than they are today, or just about the same?

    1 Better six months from now

    2 About the same

    3 Worse six months from now

    8 [DO NOT READ] Refused

    9 [DO NOT READ] Don't know

3. Now turning to business conditions in the local area, would you say that business conditions in the local area are good, bad, or somewhere in between?

    1 Good

    2 In between (good/bad)

    3 Bad

    8 [DO NOT READ] Refused

    9 [DO NOT READ] Don't know

4. And how about six months from now, do you expect that in the local area, business conditions will be better than they are today, worse than they are today, or just about the same?

    1 Better six months from now

    2 About the same

    3 Worse six months from now

    8 [DO NOT READ] Refused

    9 [DO NOT READ] Don't know

5. Now turning to the availability of jobs in the local area, would you say that jobs are easy to find, can be found with effort, or hard to find?

    1 Easy to find

    2 Can be found with effort

    3 Hard to find

    8 [DO NOT READ] Refused

    9 [DO NOT READ] Don't know

6. How about in the next six months, do you expect that in the local area there will be more job openings than there are now, fewer job openings than there are now, or about the same number of job openings?

    1 More job openings

    2 About the same

    3 Fewer job openings

8 [DO NOT READ] Refused

9 [DO NOT READ] Don't know

7. We are interested in how people are getting along financially these days. Would you say that you, and any family members living with you, are better off financially than you were a year ago, worse off financially than you were a year ago, or about the same?

    1 Better off

    2 About the same

    3 Worse off

    8 [DO NOT READ] Refused

    9 [DO NOT READ] Don't know

8. Now looking ahead, do you think that 12 months from now you, and any family members living with you, will be better off financially, worse off financially, or about the same?

    1 Better off

    2 About the same

    3 Worse off

    8 [DO NOT READ] Refused

    9 [DO NOT READ] Don't know

9. About the big things people buy for their homes, such as furniture, a refrigerator, stove, television, and things like that, generally speaking, do you think now is a good time for people to buy major household items, a bad time, or somewhere in between?

    1 Good time

    2 In between (good/bad)

    3 Bad time

    8 [DO NOT READ] Refused

    9 [DO NOT READ] Don't know

10. How about buying a house? Is now a good time to buy a house, a bad time to buy a house, or somewhere in between?

    1 Good time

    2 In between (good/bad)

    3 Bad time

    8 [DO NOT READ] Refused

    9 [DO NOT READ] Don't know

11. How about buying a car? Is now a good time to buy a car, a bad time to buy a car, or somewhere in between?

> 1 Good time
>
> 2 In between (good/bad)
>
> 3 Bad time
>
> 8 [DO NOT READ] Refused
>
> 9 [DO NOT READ] Don't know

The next few questions are for classification purposes only.

12. In what year were you born? [ENTER THE YEAR THEN PRESS ENTER]

[IF PERSON REFUSES, TYPE IN A SINGLE ZERO]

13. Which of the following best describes your racial background?

> 1 White
>
> 2 Black/African American
>
> 3 Hispanic
>
> 4 Asian/Pacific Islander
>
> 5 Other
>
> 8 [DO NOT READ] Refused
>
> 9 [DO NOT READ] No answer

14. Which of the following income categories best describes your total household annual income for the previous calendar year? Was it:

> 1 Less than $10,000
>
> 2 Between $10,000 and $30,000
>
> 3 Between $30,001 and $50,000
>
> 4 Between $50,001 and $70,000
>
> 5 More than $70,000
>
> 8 [DO NOT READ] Refused
>
> 9 [DO NOT READ] No answer

15. In which county do you live?

> 1 Dickson
>
> 2 Randall
>
> 3 Wilcox
>
> 4 Other

8 [DO NOT READ] Refused

9 [DO NOT READ] No answer

16. This completes the interview. Thank you for participating in the survey.

[HANG UP, THEN, WITHOUT ASKING, RECORD WHAT YOU PERCEIVE TO BE THE RESPONDENT'S SEX]

1 [DO NOT READ] Male

2 [DO NOT READ] Female

9 Could not tell

QUESTIONS FOR DISCUSSION

1. Why is it important for marketing researchers to carefully write their survey questions?

2. Find a survey that includes an ambiguous question. Discuss how this ambiguous question can cause problems in terms of analyzing the data and interpreting the results from the survey.

3. Write an introduction for a phone survey designed to measure consumers' perceptions of a minor league baseball team. What would you say in the introduction? How would you introduce the survey?

4. Discuss what effect the visual layout or visual appeal of a survey can have on consumers' desire to complete the survey.

5. What are some of the issues associated with designing surveys that can have an effect on the managerial decision-making process?

6. If we are trying to measure consumers' attitudes and purchase intentions toward our product, would the following be a good survey question?

   I like this product and would consider buying it.   ☐ Yes   ☐ No

7. Are the following good questions to ask on a survey of customers at a restaurant?

Evaluate the following:	Very Bad	Bad	Good	Very Good
Menu	☐	☐	☐	☐
Interior of restaurant	☐	☐	☐	☐
Exterior of restaurant	☐	☐	☐	☐
Server	☐	☐	☐	☐

8. For each of the survey questions below:
   - Identify if it is ambiguous, leading, loaded, double-barreled, taxing, uses jargon, uses a double negative, or asks for a false comparison.

- Rewrite each question.
  1. How often do you eat cereal for breakfast?
     ☐ Never ☐ Sometimes ☐ Occasionally ☐ Often
  2. Do you like the friendly attitude of Wal-Mart employees?
     ☐ Yes ☐ No
  3. What media do you rely on most?
     ☐ Television ☐ Radio ☐ Internet ☐ Newspapers
  4. What did you eat for lunch each of the last seven days? _____
     _____
  5. Do you feel that tougher gun laws will reduce the number of senseless murders in America?
     ☐ Yes ☐ No
  6. Do you often shop at lower-class discount stores like Dollar General? ☐ Yes ☐ No
  7. Which is not a brand of laundry detergent that does not control for static cling?
     ☐ Downy ☐ Tide ☐ Cheer
  8. Do you live within 10 minutes of the new Wal-Mart Super Center store? ☐ Yes ☐ No
  9. Do you like "Chock o' Nuts" coffees and would you consider buying them? ☐ Yes ☐ No
  10. Where do you usually shop for clothes? _____
      _____
  11. What are your annual expenditures for groceries? _____
      _____
  12. How many bottles of beer do you drink in a normal week? _____
      _____
  13. How many times did you brush your teeth this week? _____
      _____
  14. Did you purchase your BMW because of its performance, or its image?
      ☐ Performance ☐ Image
  15. Are you married or single? ☐ Yes ☐ No
  16. More and more people are coming to accept texting in social situations as acceptable behavior. Do you feel that texting in social situations is acceptable behavior?
      ☐ Yes ☐ No
  17. Do you think that musicians and music retailers are responsible for the high cost of music CDs?
      ☐ Yes ☐ No
  18. Are you likely to buy a tablet? ☐ Yes ☐ No
  19. Did you notice the new merchandising techniques used by Wal-Mart this week? ☐ Yes ☐ No

20. Are you likely to purchase a pair of running shoes?   ☐ Yes   ☐ No
21. Giving this professor a favorable evaluation will greatly enhance her chances of receiving tenure and being able to provide a secure future for her family. Please evaluate this professor.
22. How often do you go to the supermarket? _____
_____
23. Have you ever eaten a Snickers candy bar?   ☐ Yes   ☐ No
24. Have you eaten at any lower-class restaurants (like Buffy Bill's) in the past month?
    ☐ Yes   ☐ No
25. How much milk do you typically drink for breakfast?
    ☐ Very Little   ☐ Not Much   ☐ A Good Deal   ☐ A Lot
26. Weren't you pleased with the good service you received last night at the Clayton Mark Hotel?
    ☐ Yes   ☐ No
27. In light of the recent crisis with terrorism, should the U.S. increase its missile defenses?
    ☐ Yes   ☐ No
28. Was the service at Logan's Steakhouse all you could expect?
    ☐ Yes   ☐ No
29. Did you like the taste and texture of the coffee cake?   ☐ Yes   ☐ No
30. Do you like the distribution channels that have been established for Rockport shoes?
    ☐ Yes   ☐ No
31. Which of the following would you not purchase if it did not contain caffeine?
    ☐ Diet Coke   ☐ Coke   ☐ Sprite
32. Did you choose this school for its academics or its convenience?
    ☐ Academics   ☐ Convenience

MINICASE 16.1

Wilson County School District

You have recently been hired by the Wilson County school district as a marketing consultant. The school district asks parents to complete an online survey at the end of every school year. The purpose of the survey is to identify any potential problem areas and to gauge parents' perceptions of the education that their child is receiving from his or her school. Three of the questions from the online survey are shown below.

	Strongly Disagree	Disagree	Neither	Agree	Strongly Agree
The focus on <u>athletics</u> at my child's school is appropriate.	SD	D	N	A	SA
The focus on <u>academics</u> at my child's school is appropriate.	SD	D	N	A	SA
The focus on <u>the arts</u> at my child's school is appropriate.	SD	D	N	A	SA

What do you do? What do you tell administrators at the Wilson County school district?

MINICASE 16.2

Student Government Association

Gachenberg University is a small private university. The Student Government Association at Gachenberg University has been working toward making some changes in the way that students' grades are determined and calculated. Many students have complained about the plus/minus grading scale that many professors use when calculating and determining grades. The plus/minus grading scale is optional for faculty members, and students have complained that the scale actually hurts their overall grade point average more than it helps it. Also, a large percent of students at Gachenberg University are involved in service learning projects for many of their classes. This means that they sometimes miss classes to participate in the service learning projects for other classes. As a result, the Student Government Association has developed two referendums for which students are to vote online. An email containing a link to the online ballot was sent to every student. Below is the text of the referendums and the online ballot.

Referendum: 001 – SGA Referendum

Should Gachenberg University eliminate the plus/minus grading scale?

Vote <u>For</u> or <u>Against</u>

For ⊙ Against ⊙

Referendum: 002 – SGA Referendum

Should Gachenberg University professors penalize a student's final grade based upon attendance in that class?

Vote <u>For</u> or <u>Against</u>

For ⊙ Against ⊙

What do you tell the Student Government Association about these referendum questions?

What does "For" mean? What does "Against" mean?

MINICASE 16.3

Elect Janet Porter for Mayor Campaign

You have been hired by the Elect Janet Porter for Mayor campaign as a marketing research consultant. The campaign manager shows you the text of a telephone survey that is being developed to help the candidate better understand the perceptions of voters. To save money and time, the survey will be conducted as a fully automated telephone interview (FATI). A computer-generated voice will ask the questions and respondents will enter their answers by using the touchtone keypad on their phone. Below is one of the questions they plan to ask on the survey.

What is the number one problem facing Johnson County today?

If <u>Taxes</u>, press 1

If <u>Growth</u>, press 2

If <u>Education</u>, press 3

If <u>The Number of Commercial Businesses</u>, press 4

If <u>Roads</u>, press 5

If <u>Other</u>, press 6

What do you tell the campaign manager about this survey question and its ability to accurately measure what voters are thinking?

MINICASE 16.4

The Bowlarama

The Bowlarama is a bowling alley located between two large neighborhoods in a large Midwest city. Gil Blanton, the marketing manager for The Bowlarama, has developed the following survey questions to measure local residents' perceptions and attitudes regarding bowling. He has developed a very good working relationship with Frank Stanhof, who is the marketing manager for one of the local shopping malls. Frank Stanhof has agreed to allow Gil to conduct his survey using intercept interviews of consumers at the shopping mall. What do you tell Gil Blanton about these survey questions?

1. What is your age?

   ☐ 20–25   ☐ 46–55

   ☐ 26–35   ☐ 56–65

   ☐ 36–45   ☐ Over 65

2. What is your sex?

   ☐ Male   ☐ Female

3. What is your marital status?

   ☐ Single   ☐ Married

4. What is your income?

   ☐ $0–$2,000   ☐ $10,000–$20,000   ☐ $50,000 and above

   ☐ $2,000–$5,000   ☐ $20,000–$30,000

   ☐ $5,000–$10,000   ☐ $30,000–$50,000

5. Have you ever bowled?   ☐ Yes   ☐ No

6. If yes, do you bowl for: ☐ Fun   ☐ Exercise

7. How often do you bowl for the above?

   ☐ 0–1 times per month   ☐ 0–1 times per year

   ☐ 2–3 times per month   ☐ 2–3 times per year

   ☐ 4–5 times per month   ☐ 4–5 times per year

   ☐ 6 or more times per month   ☐ 6 or more times per year

8. Did you know that bowling has been shown to be a very good exercise that can strengthen back and arm muscles?

   ☐ Yes   ☐ No

9. How far do you live from the Bowlarama on Park Street? _____

MINICASE 16.5

The Springfield Gazette Lifestyle Survey

Barbara Tenning is the lifestyles reporter for the *Springfield Gazette* newspaper. Ever since moving to Springfield to take the job at the *Gazette*, she has wanted to conduct a survey of subscribers to measure various aspects of their lifestyles. Her hope is that by better understanding the lifestyles of readers, she can better identify potential stories of interest to them. She has developed the following list of questions to be asked using an online survey of subscribers. Barbara has asked for your feedback about these questions before she sends the email asking subscribers to complete the online survey. What do you tell her about her survey questions?

1. Marital status   Single   Married   Divorced   Widowed

   If married, what is your spouse's occupation? _____

2. Do you have children? Yes No (If yes, how many? _____)

3. What percent of your monthly income is spent on your children? _____

4. What kind of car do you own? _____

5. What kind of home do you live in? Suburban   Apartment   Country Farm Split-Level Mobile Home   Other _____

6. Approximately what percent of your monthly income do you spend on entertainment/leisure? _____

7. How many times per month do you shop for yourself? _____

8. How style-conscious are you?

_____ Very (I am an avid shopper and I love the retro look)

_____ Somewhat (half of my closet is fashionable and the rest is practical)

_____ Not really (I rarely shop for clothing and my clothes are very affordable)

9. Please list two of the TV shows that you regularly watch: 1. _____

                                           2. _____

10. Please list two magazines that you regularly read: 1. _____

                                          2. _____

11. How many nights per month do you visit restaurants or dance clubs? _____

12. Do you purchase alcohol when dining out?   Yes   No

13. Do you purchase alcohol to drink at home?   Yes   No

14. If yes, what kind of alcoholic beverages do you enjoy?
    Beer   Wine   Liquor   Other _____

15. What is your current job? _____

16. How long have you been on this job? _____

17. How would you categorize your social class?

    Upper Class   Upper Middle Class   Lower Middle Class   Lower Class

---

ENDNOTES

1 J. M. Converse and S. Presser, *Survey Questions: Handcrafting the Standardized Questionnaire* (Beverly Hills, CA: Sage Publications, 1986).

2 Seymour Sudman and N. Bradburn, *Asking Questions: A Practical Guide for Questionnaire Design* (San Francisco: Jossey-Bass, 1982).

3 R. L. Kahn and C. F. Cannell, *The Dynamics of Interviewing* (New York: John Wiley, 1957).

4 B. C. Greenberg, A. L. Adbula, W. L. Simmons and D. G. Horvitz, "The Unrelated Question in Randomized Response Model, Theoretical Framework," *Journal of the American Statistical Association* 64 (1969): 520–539.

5 Cathy Campbell and Brian L. Joiner, "How to Get the Answer without Being Sure You've Asked the Question," *American Statistician* 27 (December 1973): 119–231; see also, James E. Reinmuth and Michael D. Guerts, "The Collection of Sensitive Information Using a Two-Stage Randomized Response Model," *Journal of Marketing Research* 12 (November 1975): 402–407.

CHAPTER $\left(17\right)$

Sampling Procedures

LEARNING OBJECTIVES

1 Define population, population parameter, population element, sample, sample statistic, and sample element.

2 Explain the importance of representative sampling when conducting marketing research surveys and making marketing management decisions.

3 Compare and contrast nonprobability sampling procedures and probability sampling procedures.

4 Describe how marketers can generate samples using convenience sampling procedures, judgment sampling procedures, and referral-based sampling procedures.

5 Define and explain the use of river sampling.

6 Describe how marketers can generate samples using simple random sampling procedures, systematic sampling procedures, stratified sampling procedures, and cluster sampling procedures.

7 Define primary sampling unit and secondary sampling unit

8 Define multiprocedure sampling.

9 Discuss the relative importance of the quality versus the quantity of a sample.

10 Describe the procedures for estimating the required sample size for estimating a proportion and a mean.

11 Define the finite population correction factor.

12 Explain the relationship between sample size and margin of error.

13 Explain the relationship between population variability and sample size.

14 Interpret the ± percent margin of error for a survey.

In most instances, the purpose of a marketing research project (e.g., survey) is to measure a characteristic of a population, such as consumers' attitudes, incomes, perceptions, and even the behaviors of large groups of people (e.g., target markets). These characteristics of a population are called **population parameters**. The entire set of individuals a researcher is interested in is called the **population**. A member of the population is referred to as a **population element**. Surveying every member of the population is called a census. A **census** refers to measuring every member of a population, no matter how large or small the population is. However, it is practically impossible for marketing researchers to survey every person in large populations. A census would take too much time, and it would be too costly.

Sampling. Out of necessity, marketing researchers rely on sampling as a means of estimating characteristics of large populations.[1] Researchers survey a small subset of the larger population, called a **sample**. A member of the sample is referred to as a **sample element**. The **statistics** that are calculated from the sample are then used to estimate the population parameters of interest. However, if a census is never taken, we might never know the true value of a population parameter. Thus, we must use the sample statistic as a best guess of the population parameter.

Many people often wonder how it is possible that a public opinion poll consisting of 1,000 people can accurately represent the characteristics of an entire country containing over 200 million adults. If, in a sample of 1,000 people, 45 percent of people surveyed report that they will vote for candidate Jones, how can we say with any confidence that 45 percent of the entire population will vote for candidate Jones? To most people it seems that a sample of only 1,000 people is simply too small to estimate what a much larger population will do. The answer lies in representative sampling.

Representative Sampling. To illustrate the concept of **representative sampling**, imagine that you have a large box of 1,000 marbles. The box has just been filled with 400 red marbles and 600 blue marbles. Now, imagine that you shake the box so that all of the marbles are mixed and evenly distributed. If you were to close your eyes and randomly draw 100 marbles from the box, what percentage of marbles would you expect to be red? And, what percentage of marbles would you expect to be blue? The answer, of course, is that you expect 40 marbles to be red and 60 marbles to be blue. This is because you know the relative number of red and blue marbles in the entire box.

Similarly, imagine that 45 percent of all Americans own two or more digital televisions. Now, if we took a representative sample of 1,000 Americans randomly drawn from the U.S. population, what percentage of these 1,000 people will have two or more digital televisions? The answer is 45 percent.

This is the logic behind random sampling. If a representative random sample is taken from a population, where every population element has an equal and nonzero chance of being selected, the results from the sample should be an accurate representation of the entire population. If we randomly choose a representative sample of 1,000 Americans and 45 percent of those sampled say that they own two or more digital televisions, the best guess of the percentage of people in the larger population who own two or more digital televisions is also 45 percent. Thus, the characteristics of a sample and the procedure used to select a sample are very important. Researchers must have a representative sample to be able to accurately estimate and predict the larger population.

In most cases it is simply not possible to survey every member of a population. Instead, researchers survey a subset of the population, called a sample.

THE GOAL AND MEANS OF SAMPLING

Many people believe that the goal of sampling is to select a random sample. However, this confuses the goal of sampling with the means by which that goal is achieved. The goal of sampling is to achieve a representative sample. In most cases random sampling procedures are used to help achieve a representative sample. A **random sample** is one in which all population elements have an equal, nonzero chance of being included in the sample. Random sampling is used to eliminate potential sources of sample bias. However, there are times when random sampling is not desirable. For example, if there are more people than necessary for a focus group, it would not be advisable to use random selection to choose the eight consumers who will stay and participate in the focus group and the other consumers who will be sent home. Rather, purposely selecting the focus group participants based on judgment would be recommended. As another example, researchers generally do not randomly select the cities in which they will test market new products. Rather, the cities are often purposely and carefully selected so that their populations will best represent the entire population. In sum, the goal of sampling is to achieve a representative sample. And, the particular situation dictates whether or not random sampling is the best procedure for achieving a representative sample.[2]

> The goal of sampling is to obtain a representative sample of the larger population.

SAMPLING PROCEDURES

All sampling procedures can be classified into one of two main types: probability sampling procedures and nonprobability sampling procedures (see Figure 17.1). Probability sampling procedures include an element of random selection when choosing sample elements. Nonprobability sampling procedures do not include random selection.

FIGURE 17.1 Sampling Procedures

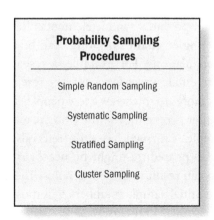

Nonprobability Sampling Procedures	Probability Sampling Procedures
Convenience Sampling	Simple Random Sampling
Judgment Sampling	Systematic Sampling
Referral-Based Sampling	Stratified Sampling
	Cluster Sampling

Nonprobability Sampling Procedures

Nonprobability sampling procedures are not based on a random (probability) selection process. As a result, not all population elements have an equal, nonzero chance of being included in the sample. The three major types of nonprobability sampling procedures are convenience sampling, judgment sampling, and referral-based sampling.

Convenience Sampling. Convenience sampling is used when only the population elements that are the most convenient are selected to be included in the sample. This would be done when there are severe time limits or monetary constraints. An example of convenience sampling would be if a professor conducted a student survey but surveyed only those students in her class. Caution is advised in using this type of sampling procedure. Convenience sampling can result in extremely biased samples.

Convenience sampling can also occur in an online environment. When potential survey respondents are recruited using instant capture promotions such as banner ads and pop-up ads, this is often referred to as **river sampling**.[3] With river sampling, consumers agree to participate in a survey by clicking on a pop-up ad. They are then screened based on demographic variables and subsequently assigned to a survey to complete. This sampling procedure is called river sampling because consumers are caught from the flowing river of people viewing online content. River sampling is essentially a web-based convenience sample of people who happen to be viewing a website on which the pop-up ad appears.

> The quality (representativeness) of a sample is more important than the size of a sample.

Judgment Sampling. Judgment sampling is when a researcher uses judgment to select the sample. An experienced researcher deliberately and purposely selects sample elements based on desired characteristics of the sample. The researcher identifies and determines those characteristics that would make a good sample. For example, a survey of students might be administered in classes that have been selected to intentionally include students at different class levels (freshman, sophomore, junior, senior) and different majors. Choosing participants for a focus group is often a judgment sampling process.

Referral-Based Sampling. Referral-based sampling is when initial sample elements are asked to refer the researcher to other potential sample elements.[4] Referral-based sampling (also called **snowball sampling** or **chain sampling**) can be used to find unusual or otherwise hard-to-find populations. For example, a researcher might seek to survey consumers who are interested in reggae music. The researcher might first go to reggae music clubs or music stores to interview a few people. These people are then asked to provide names of other people they know who are also interested in reggae music. In this way the sample is formed based on referrals from other members of the sample. Although this procedure might be necessary to identify some hard-to-find populations, it too can result in biased samples. The sample can become rather homogeneous because initial sample members will most likely refer the researcher to other people who are similar to themselves.

Probability Sampling Procedures

Probability sampling procedures are based on a random (probability) selection process. All population elements have an equal, nonzero chance of being included in the sample. The four major types of probability sampling procedures are simple random sampling, systematic sampling, stratified sampling, and cluster sampling. Each of these sampling procedures often involves the use of a sampling frame. A **sampling frame** is a list of population elements from which the sample is chosen. For example, a telephone book might be used as a sampling frame. A computer-generated list from a customer database can also be used as a sampling frame. The sampling frame is sometimes referred to as the **working population** because it is the list of population elements with which the researcher is working. However, sampling frame error, where the sampling frame systematically overrepresents or underrepresents certain groups of the population, can lead to a biased sample.

Simple Random Sampling. **Simple random sampling** uses a selection process that assures each member of the population an equal, nonzero chance of being included in the sample. Simple random sampling differs from other probability sampling procedures in that simple random sampling has only one stage of sampling. An example of simple random sampling is when a researcher randomly draws names from a hat. Computer programs can also be used to randomly select sample elements from a computerized database or list.

Simple random sampling has two properties that make it the ideal sampling procedure. First, the sample is **unbiased** in that each member of the population has the same chance of being chosen. Secondly, the sample elements are **independent** in that the selection of one sample element has no effect on the probability of another sample element being selected. Most statistical procedures require the independence and lack of bias of a probability sampling procedure. Without randomized sampling there can be no dependable statistical analysis. Unfortunately, completely unbiased and independent samples are rare in the real world. More common procedures include systematic sampling, stratified sampling, and cluster sampling.

Systematic Sampling. **Systematic sampling** is perhaps the most often used procedure for obtaining a random sample from a large sampling frame. With systematic sampling, a random process selects a starting point, and then every n^{th} number or name on the list is selected. For example, if a customer database contains 2,000 names, the researcher could randomly select the first customer and then systematically select every 10th name after that to generate a sample of 200 customers. The **skip interval** is determined by dividing the total number of population elements in the sampling frame by the desired sample size. Notice that even though the selection process is random, it is not independent because the chance of a customer being selected is dependent upon which customer is initially selected. Caution is advised, however, if there is a pattern to the order in which population elements are listed in the sampling frame.

Stratified Sampling. Stratified sampling is when the population is divided into homogeneous groups, called **stratum**, and random samples are drawn from each stratum. The samples chosen from each stratum may be proportional or disproportional to the number of elements in each stratum. For example, a researcher who knows that 70 percent of a target market is male could randomly select 700 men (from a list of men) and 300 women (from a list of women) to be included in the sample. Stratified sampling is often used to ensure that various subgroups of a population are represented in the sample to the same extent that they are represented in the population.

Cluster Sampling. Cluster sampling is when clusters of population elements, not individual population elements, are selected in one or multiple different stages of sampling.[5] For example, a medical center might first randomly choose 5 days from the previous month, and then randomly choose 10 patients who were treated at the center on each of those 5 days. This would generate a sample of 50 patients. In this example, the days of the month would be referred to as the **primary sampling unit**, and the individual patients would be referred to as **secondary sampling units**. A **sampling unit** is the population element, or group of population elements, subject to being selected in the sample. As an example of a **multistage area sample**, a researcher could randomly choose 5 states, then 5 counties within each of those states, then 3 cities within each county, then 10 people within each city to be included in a sample of 750 people. The advantage of cluster sampling is that it reduces the size of the sampling frame at each stage of sampling. Notice that the sampling units do not have to be individuals. The sampling units can be groups, or clusters of individuals.

ISSUES IN SAMPLING
Multiprocedure Sampling

Multiprocedure sampling is when primary and secondary sampling units are selected and different sampling procedures are used for each stage of sampling. For example, consider a national sample where a researcher wishes to sample 5 states, then 5 counties within those states, then 2 cities within each county, and finally 50 people within each of those cities. If a simple random sampling procedure were used to select the five states, it is possible that Alabama, Tennessee, Georgia, Mississippi, and Arkansas are chosen. However, these five southern states would not represent the entire country. So, the researcher might use a judgment sampling procedure and purposely choose one state in each region of the country. A simple random sampling procedure can then be used to choose the counties and cities, and then a systematic sampling procedure can be used to choose the 50 individuals within each city.

> Many things in life truly are random. Before 2013 the coin toss for the first 46 Super Bowl games resulted in 23 heads and 23 tails.

Using Random Numbers

Many calculators have a **random number generator** that produces a number between 0 and 1 (e.g., 0.9875). All numbers between 0 and 1 are equally likely to be

FIGURE 17.2 Using Random Numbers to Select a Sample

Random Number	Go First to Page	Then, Count Down _____ Names
347521	34	7
136855	13	6

generated. However, the numbers generated by these random number generators are not truly random. An algorithm produces them. As such, they are pseudo-random numbers.

Using Random Numbers. A table of random numbers is provided in the appendix of this book. To use random numbers for sampling, simply adopt a convention with respect to how the random numbers are to be used. For example, when working from a phone book or a computer-generated list, adopt the convention where the first two numbers represent the page number and the next number represents the number of names to be counted down on that page to find the first name to be sampled. This is illustrated in Figure 17.2.

Similarly, random numbers can also be used to select a subset of items from a larger set of items. For instance, retailers who conduct simple customer satisfaction surveys often offer an incentive for completing the survey, such as giving away a prize to 10 randomly selected participants. Random numbers can be used to select such winners. If the survey data can be imported into Microsoft Excel, a random number can be generated as a new variable for each respondent. Then, simply sort the dataset based on this new variable from smallest to largest and choose the respondents who have the smallest random variable. This same procedure can also be used to select even a large number of items or individuals from a computerized database.

Quality vs. Quantity

The quality of a sample is more important than its size. A large sample that does not represent the population will yield meaningless and biased results. As a result, many researchers concentrate on reducing sample bias and response bias more so than on increasing the sample size. Recall that increasing the sample size does not reduce systematic error and bias. Thus, efforts to increase the sample size will be useless if the research methodology contains systematic error or bias.

Sample Size

You might have learned that a sample needs at least 30 members to be large in statistical terms. This does not mean that a sample needs only 30 members to yield accurate results. This actually refers to the sample size needed for the distribution of sample means to become approximately normal, with a mean = μ and standard deviation = $S/\sqrt{n}$. If the sample has at least 30 members, then the **central limit theorem** tells us that the distribution of sample means is approximately normal. However, having only 30 members in a sample is not enough to provide any reasonable level of confidence that the sample is large enough to yield accurate results. In fact, the margin of error for a sample with only 30 members is ±18 percent! And, a sample this small is also subject to many types of error and bias, such as sample selection bias, self-selection bias, and nonresponse error.

DETERMINING SAMPLE SIZE

The size of the sample required for a marketing research project is an important decision. Sample size has a direct effect on the margin of error and accuracy of survey results. In general, larger samples will have smaller margins of error (less random sampling error) and will yield more accurate results. Sample size can be determined based on statistical models, all you can afford, and typical studies.

Statistical Models

Statistical models can be used to calculate the required sample size for estimating an average as well as a proportion.

Sample Size for Estimating an Average. The sample size that is necessary to estimate an average can be calculated with the following formula:

$$n = [Z(S)/E]^2$$

where

Z = the standardized value indicating the desired confidence level
S = sample standard deviation or an estimate of the population standard deviation
    (this is not SE_{mean})
E = acceptable ± magnitude or error (in units being measured)

For example, what sample size is needed to measure the average amount of money people spend on a television set? We want to be 95 percent confident that the estimate is within ± $25 of the true population amount.

Z = 1.96 (Z value for 95 percent confidence level)
S = $100 (estimated)
E = ± $25

$$n = [1.96(100)/25]^2 = 62$$

If we wanted to be 99 percent confident in the estimate, the Z value would be 2.57, and the required sample size would increase to:

$$n = [2.57(100)/25]^2 = 106$$

If we changed E to ±$50 (allowing for more error in the estimate), the required sample size would decrease to:

$$n = [2.57(100)/50]^2 = 27$$

Estimating the Population Standard Deviation. Notice that in the sample size calculations for estimating an average, the standard deviation of the population must be estimated. One way of estimating the population standard deviation is to first estimate a range of 95 percent of the population observations. We know that in a normal distribution (and many naturally occurring distributions are approximately normal) 95 percent of all observations fall within ±1.96 standard deviations of the mean. Thus, we can divide the range by four, and this will estimate the population standard deviation. For example, if we estimate that 95 percent of all consumers spend between $100 and $600 when they purchase a new television set, the range of observations from $100 to $600 accounts for ±1.96 standard deviations in the population distribution. Therefore, there are approximately four standard deviations within this $500 range. We can then estimate that the standard deviation of the population is equal to $125. This value can then be entered into the formula for calculating the desired sample size.

Sample Size for Estimating a Proportion. The sample size that is necessary to estimate a proportion can be calculated with the following formula:

$$n = [Z^2(p)(1 - p)/E^2]$$

where

Z^2 = square of the standardized value indicating the desired confidence level
p = estimated proportion
E^2 = square of the maximum allowance for error (± percent)

Example: A researcher believes that 60 percent of the population is aware of a target brand name. What sample size is needed to be 95 percent confident that the sample proportion is within ± 3 percent of the true population proportion?

$$n = [1.96^2(0.6)(0.4)/(0.03)^2] = 1,024$$

If instead, the researcher believes that 70 percent of the population is aware of the target brand name, the required sample size would decrease to:

$$n = [1.96^2(0.7)(0.3)/(0.03)^2] = 896$$

Notice that the population is now more homogeneous (less variable) because a greater percent of people are aware of the brand name. The less variable the population, the smaller the sample required to estimate it. If we did not know the estimated proportion (p), the most conservative estimate would be based on p = .5. This would make the population the least homogeneous (the most variable) it could possibly be, leading to the largest sample required.

$$n = [1.96^2(0.5)(0.5)/(0.03)^2] = 1,067$$

Notice that the p and $(1 - p)$ components of this equation represent the homogeneity (variability) of the population.

All You Can Afford

In most cases, sample size is determined based on budgetary and time constraints. Sample size can be calculated by dividing the amount budgeted for sampling by the estimated cost per sampling unit.

$$\text{Sample size} = \text{Sampling budget/Cost per sampling unit}$$

Based on Comparable Studies

Sample size can also be determined based on the typical sample sizes for comparable studies. For example, most national surveys have between 1,000 and 2,000 people in the sample. Most regional surveys have between 400 and 1,000 people in the sample. The reason that larger samples are used for national surveys is not due to the larger population from which the sample is taken. In fact, the size of the population from which the sample is taken has little effect on the required sample size. An exception to this is when the sample size represents a large percentage of the total population.

Population Size and Sample Size

The size of the population from which the sample is taken has little effect on the required sample size. To illustrate this, imagine that a researcher wished to estimate the average height of two different populations. Population A has 10,000 members and their heights range from four feet tall to seven feet tall. Population B has 1,000,000 members and they all are exactly six feet tall. Even though population B is larger, population A requires the larger sample to estimate its average height. This is due to the greater variability of heights in population A. In general, the variability of the population is what determines the required sample size. The size of the population has little effect on the required sample size.

Population Variability and Sample Size. Notice that the population size (N) is not included in the previous formulas for calculating sample size. However, the variability of the population is included in both formulas. With respect to calculating the sample size for estimating an average, S in the previous formulas represents the sample standard deviation, which is used to estimate the population standard deviation (the variability of the population). With respect to calculating the required sample size for estimating a proportion, p and (1 − p) in the previous formulas represent the variability of the population.

To further illustrate the relationship between population size and sample size, imagine that you are a judge for a community chili cook-off. John brings his chili in a one-gallon pot. Bill brings his chili in a 10-gallon pot. Must you taste more of Bill's chili because it is in a larger pot? Obviously, the answer is no. You can judge each chili by tasting the same amount from each pot. In the same way, a larger population does not necessarily require a larger sample. The variability of the population determines the required sample size.

When Large Samples are Needed

Large samples are needed when:

- There is a high degree of variability among members of the population from which you are sampling (the population is heterogeneous).

- The population is made up of many different subgroups that will be analyzed individually and separately (many different cross-tabs will be computed).

- Sufficient amounts of time and money are available to cover the costs of increasing the sample size.

- There are potentially severe managerial or financial consequences of making decisions based on a small sample and inaccurate results.

- You need very accurate results and you want to be very confident in the data and estimates from the sample.

- You need a high level of statistical power associated with any statistical tests to be performed.

When Small Samples are Acceptable

Small samples are acceptable when:

- There is little variability among members of the population from which you are sampling (the population is homogeneous).

- The population is not made up of many different subgroups and the data will be analyzed as a single sample (very few cross-tabs will be computed).

- You do not have sufficient time and money to cover the costs of increasing the sample size.

- You will not make many important decisions based on the results from the research.

- You do not need very accurate results and you do not need to be very confident in the data and estimates from the sample.

- You do not need a high level of statistical power associated with any statistical tests to be performed.

FINITE POPULATION CORRECTION FACTOR

In general, the size of the population has no direct effect on the required sample size. This will hold true when the population is essentially infinite (e.g., potential American voters, male Americans). However, when the sample represents a large percentage of the population (a general rule of thumb is if the sample size is greater than 5 percent of the population), the formulas for calculating the variance and standard deviation must be modified using the **finite population correction factor**. If samples are taken from a finite population of size N, the formulas for calculating the variance and standard error of the sample means (the distribution of sample means) are:

$$\sigma^2 \bar{x} = \frac{\sigma^2}{n} \left[\frac{N-n}{N-1} \right] \qquad \sigma \bar{x} = \frac{\sigma}{\sqrt{n}} \sqrt{\frac{N-n}{N-1}}$$

where

N is the population size
n is the sample size
(N – n/N – 1) is the finite population correction factor

For very large populations and very small samples (N is large compared to n), the correction factor reduces to one and can be disregarded. For example, the correction factor for a sample of 1,000 people drawn from a population of 1,000,000 people is 0.9995 ($\sqrt{1,000,000 - 1,000/1,000,000 - 1} = 0.9995$)

SAMPLE SIZE AND MARGIN OF ERROR

The ± percent margin of error for a sample can be calculated using the formula:

$$\pm\,\text{percent margin of error} = 1.96 \sqrt{(0.25 / n)}$$

This formula is used to calculate the margin of error for measuring proportions, not averages. Using 0.25 as the numerator in the equation allows a researcher to calculate the largest possible ± percent margin of error for any given sample size (p = 0.5, 1 – p = 0.5). The chart in Figure 17.3 shows the largest possible ± percent margin of error at a 95 percent confidence level that is associated with various sample sizes.

Figure 17.3 illustrates a number of important relationships between sample size and margin of error. First, notice that margin of error is inversely related to sample size. Larger samples have less sampling error, and smaller samples have more sampling error. Further, as sample size increases, margin of error decreases at a decreasing rate. Although the margin of error will always decrease with increased sample size, the decreases in margin of error become relatively insignificant with sample sizes larger than 1,500. Most public opinion polls designed to measure percentages within ± 3 percent of the true population parameter have samples of

FIGURE 17.3 Relationship between Sample Size and ± Margin of Error

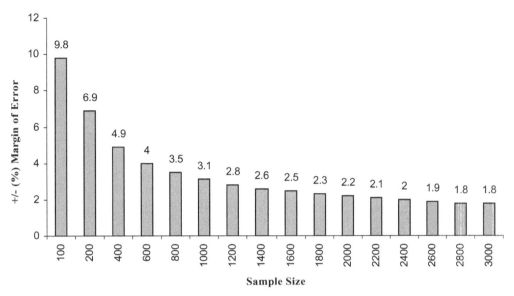

approximately 1,000 people. And, the sample need not be much larger than 1,000 people to obtain accurate results. In fact, the costs associated with increasing the size of a sample that already has 1,000 members will most likely be too great to justify the very small reduction in margin of error. For example, most researchers recognize the value of increasing a sample size from 100 to 1,000. The large reduction in margin of error from ±9.8 percent to ±3.1 percent justifies the monetary and time costs associated with obtaining a larger sample. However, the small reduction in margin of error from ±3.1 percent to ±2.2 percent does not justify the costs associated with increasing the sample size from 1,000 to 2,000. Further, increasing the sample size from 2,000 to 3,000, leads to an insignificant reduction in margin of error from ±2.2 percent to ±1.8 percent. Of course, this discussion assumes that the samples are representative of the population. A researcher need not sample more than 1,000 consumers if the 1,000 consumers already sampled are representative of the population. Additionally, these relationships are between sample size and only random sampling error. Other factors associated with biased samples, such as sampling frame error and sampling procedure error, can require researchers to obtain larger samples to increase the quality and representativeness of samples.

As the variability of the population increases, the sample size must also increase to maintain the same level of acceptable error.

POPULATION VARIABILITY AND SAMPLE SIZE

As previously mentioned, sample size is affected by the variability of the population from which the sample is being chosen. Table 17.1 shows the ± percent margin of error at a 95 percent confidence level for populations of varying degrees of homogeneity. The margins of error for the far right column (p = 0.5, 1 − p = 0.5) are the largest possible ± percent margins of error for a given sample size.

There is a definite relationship between sample size and random error. As the sample size increases, random sampling error decreases. However, as the sample size increases, the margin of error for a survey decreases at a decreasing rate.

TABLE 17.1 Percent Margin of Error at a 95 Percent Confidence Level for Populations of Varying Degrees of Homogeneity

	Population Variability				
	Less Variable ←————————→ More Variable				
	p/(1 − p)				
Sample Size	10/90	20/80	30/70	40/60	50/50
2,500	1.2	1.6	1.8	1.9	2.0
2,000	1.3	1.8	2.0	2.1	2.2
1,500	1.5	2.0	2.3	2.5	2.5
1,000	1.9	2.5	2.8	3.0	3.1
500	2.6	3.5	4.0	4.3	4.4
250	3.7	5.0	5.7	6.1	6.2
100	5.9	7.8	9.0	9.6	9.8
50	8.3	11.1	12.7	13.6	13.8

For example, we can be 95 percent confident that the estimate from a sample of size n = 1,500 is within approximately ±2 percent of the true parameter if p = .2 and 1 − p = .8. Notice that as the variability of the population increases, the sample size must also increase to maintain the same level of acceptable error. The greater the variability of the population from which the sample is taken, the more sampling error will be associated with the estimate.

INTERPRETING THE MARGIN OF ERROR

The margin of error reported for a survey (e.g., ±3 percent) refers to an estimate of a percentage, such as the percent of consumers who wash their cars at least once a month. Such margins of error are not reported when measuring averages, such as the average income of a target market. Further, the margin of error for a survey represents the amount of random sampling error that is associated with an estimate. It does not account for any error that might be present in the results due to systematic error or bias, such as nonresponse error, response bias, sample selection error, or any other administrative error.

For example, with a sample of 500 people, we can say with 95 percent confidence that the amount of survey error due to taking a random sample instead of surveying all members of the population is ±4.4 percent. This means that if they wanted to project the results of the sample onto the larger population, researchers can be 95 percent confident that the percentages for the population will be within ±4.4 percent of the sample result. If researchers survey 500 consumers and find that 37 percent of consumers in a target market wash their cars at least once a month, they can be 95 percent confident that between 32.6 percent and 41.4 percent of consumers in the target market wash their cars at least once a month. However, other factors such as problems with question wording and question interpretation can also lead to additional bias or error being introduced into the results.

If researchers begin with a representative sample derived from random selection, increasing the sample size will lead to greater confidence in the estimates but will not lead to significantly different results. Increasing the sample size will only lead to more of the same types of answers.

SAMPLING AND THE DECISION-MAKING PROCESS

Sampling plays a key role in determining the quality of the results from a marketing research project. As a result, the decisions that marketing researchers make regarding sampling can have a direct effect on the decision-making process. Recall the IDO model of marketing research and the decision-making process, presented in Figure 17.4.

Clearly, the quality, worth, and usefulness of information generated from marketing research can be greatly influenced by the quality and characteristics of the sampling procedures. Nonprobability sampling procedures can have a great deal of sampling error and bias associated with them. Probability sampling procedures are not free from error and bias either. If the researcher has not correctly identified the population of interest, then it does not matter how random the sampling process is, it will not provide useful information. If the sampling frame from which the sample is being drawn is biased, then any sample drawn from that frame will also be biased. And, the size of the sample has a direct relationship to the amount of statistical error associated with survey results. This impacts the degree of confidence that marketing managers can place in the results of the research.

In general, the quality and worth of information generated from a marketing research project will be reduced when:

- The sample is not taken from the correct population.

- The sampling frame from which the sample is selected is not representative of the population, that is, the sampling frame overrepresents some groups of people in the population and underrepresents other groups of people in the population.

- The procedure for selecting the sample systematically overrepresents some groups of people and underrepresents other groups of people.

- The sample is not representative of the larger population.

- The sample is not large enough to yield accurate results due to increased random sampling error.

FIGURE 17.4 The IDO Model of Marketing Research and the Decision-Making Process

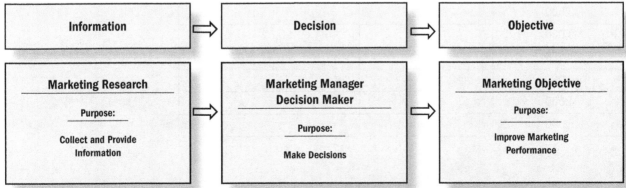

QUESTIONS FOR DISCUSSION

1. What is the primary goal of sampling? Must all samples be randomly selected to achieve this goal?

2. What is the difference between probability sampling procedures and nonprobability sampling procedures?

3. What effect does population size have on sample size?

4. What is the relationship between sample size and the margin of error for a survey?

5. The results from a national poll found that 44% of respondents owned a smartphone. The margin of error for the survey was ±3 percent. This means that the true percentage of people who own a smartphone could be as low as 41 percent and as high as 47 percent. To have a margin of error of ±3 percent, how many people needed to participate in the survey (what was the sample size)?

6. A company approaches you about conducting a national public opinion poll. They tell you that they would like to sample more than 5,000 people. What do you tell them?

7. Which characteristic of a population has the greater effect on determining the size of a sample to be taken from that population?

8. Population A has 90 males and 10 females. Population B has 50 males and 50 females. Which population is more heterogeneous (variable) in terms of the sex of population members?

9. Using the grid below, calculate the decrease in margin of error (at a 95 percent confidence level) associated with increasing the sample size by 500 people.

Sample Size	Margin of Error	Decrease in Margin of Error
500		-----------------
1,000		
1,500		
2,000		
2,500		
3,000		
3,500		
4,000		
4,500		
5,000		

10. How is the representativeness of a sample related to the relationship between sample size and margin of error?

11. What are some of the issues associated with sampling procedures that can have an effect on managerial decision making?

MINICASE 17.1

George Saul for Governor Campaign

You have recently been employed by the George Saul for Governor election campaign. The candidate, George Saul, wants to conduct a mail survey of residents in the state to measure what they think about possibly increasing the state's income tax rate to fund increased health care for the elderly. He has chosen an anonymous mail survey because he wants people to have time to think about the issue and their responses before answering. He will mail 1,000 surveys to randomly selected households across the state. Additionally, he does not want to ask any demographic questions on the survey. He says that demographic questions are boring for respondents to answer, they can make some respondents uncomfortable, and they just make the survey longer than it needs to be.

What do you tell George Saul about asking demographic questions on surveys?

ENDNOTES

1   Seymour Sudman, *Applied Sampling* (New York: Academic Press, 1976).

2   E. Babbie, *Survey Research Methods* (Belmont CA: Wadsworth, 1990).

3   Charles DiSogra, "River Samples: A Good Catch for Researchers?" *Knowledge Networks*, Fall/Winter 2008, **http://www.knowledgenetworks.com/accuracy/fall-winter2008/disogra.html**

4   D. D. Heckathorn, "Respondent-Driven Sampling: A New Approach to the Study of Hidden Populations," *Social Problems* 44 (1997): 174–199; D. D. Heckathorn, "Respondent-Driven Sampling II: Deriving Valid Estimates from Chain-Referral Samples of Hidden Populations," *Social Problems* 49 (2002): 11–34; Matthew J. Salganik and Douglas D. Heckathorn, "Sampling and Estimation in Hidden Populations Using Respondent-Driven Sampling," *Sociological Methodology* 34 (December 2004): 193–240.

5   Seymour Sudman, "Efficient Screening Methods for the Sampling of Geographically Clustered Special Populations," *Journal of Marketing Research* 22 (February 1985): 20–29.

CHAPTER 18

Causal Research and Experimental Design

LEARNING OBJECTIVES

1 Define causal research, experimental design, independent variable, dependent variable, extraneous variable, and confound.

2 Describe and explain the structure of an experimental design using the terms independent variable, dependent variable, and extraneous variable.

3 Explain why researchers cannot prove a causal relationship within the context of statistical hypothesis testing.

4 Explain how researchers can increase their confidence that a causal relationship has been identified.

5 Identify and define the following components of experimental designs: basic experiment, factorial experiment, field experiment, lab experiment, treatments, experimental groups, control groups, and test units.

6 Explain how researchers can control for the effects of extraneous variables using control groups, random assignment, blocking, repeated measures, and counterbalancing the order of presentation.

7 Define and describe a factorial design.

8 Compare and contrast internal validity and external validity.

9 Describe the major threats to the internal validity of experiments.

10 Describe blind and double-blind experiments.

11 Discuss how marketers use test marketing, the advantages and disadvantages of test marketing, and the factors to consider when selecting test market cities.

12 Compare and contrast quasi-experimental designs and true experimental designs.

13 Describe and explain the following quasi-experimental designs: after only design, one group pretest–posttest design, and static group design.

14 Describe and explain the following true experimental designs: pretest–posttest with a control group design, and the posttest only with a control group design.

Causal research is conducted to examine the causal relationship between two or more variables. Marketers might want to examine the causal relationships between marketing mix variables (price, product, place, promotion) and measures of marketing performance (sales, market share, number of customer complaints).[1] **Experimental designs** are used to identify such causal effects. The purpose of an **experiment** is to examine the causal relationship between one or more **independent variables (IV)** and one or more **dependent variables (DV)**, while controlling for the effects of extraneous variables (XV). **Extraneous variables** are those factors that are outside (extraneous to) the control of the experiment. They are sometimes called **confounds** because they confound the relationship between the independent variable and the dependent variable. The presence of extraneous variables often makes it appear that an IV and DV are causally related, even though they are not. In such cases, researchers would say that there is a **spurious association** between the independent and dependent variables (or that they are spuriously related).[2] This general structure for an experiment is illustrated in Figure 18.1.

To illustrate, imagine that a researcher conducted some taste test experiments at a local shopping mall. Consumers tasted either a chocolate chip cookie or a raisin cookie. The taste tests were conducted at two different times during the day. Consumers at the 11 a.m. taste testing session were given the chocolate chip cookie. Consumers at the 1 p.m. taste testing session were given the raisin cookie. Consumers rated the cookie on a 7-point scale, where 1 = dislike very much, and 7 = like very much. If the average rating for consumers tasting the chocolate chip cookie was 6.0, and the average rating for consumers tasting the raisin cookie was 3.0, what does the difference in ratings tell us about the cookies? Did consumers prefer the chocolate chip cookie because it was rated more favorably than the raisin cookie? The structure of this taste test experiment is illustrated in Figure 18.2.

> The purpose of an experiment is to examine the causal relationship between an independent variable and a dependent variable, while controlling for the effects of all other variables.

FIGURE 18.1 Structure of an Experimental Design

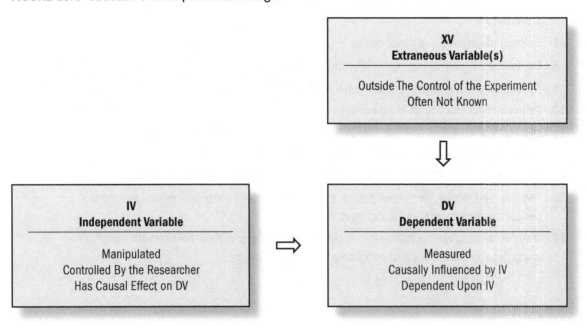

FIGURE 18.2 Structure of a Chocolate Chip Cookie Taste Test Experimental Design

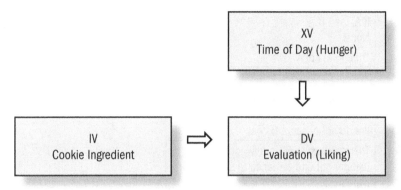

The cookie ingredient is the independent variable (the variable being manipulated by the researcher independently of other variables). Consumers' rating of the cookie on the scale is the dependent variable (the consumers' liking for the cookie is dependent upon, or influenced by, the cookie ingredient). The key question for the researcher is, "What explains the difference in ratings between the two different cookies?" Two possibilities exist. First, it is possible that the chocolate chip cookie actually tasted better than the raisin cookie. This would mean that the differences observed in the dependent variable were attributable to the independent variable. However, an **alternative explanation** results from the presence of an extraneous variable, often referred to as a confound. It is possible that consumers tasting a cookie at 11 a.m. are hungrier than those tasting a cookie at 1 p.m. because they have not yet eaten lunch. And, food naturally tastes better as people become hungrier. This would mean that the differences observed in the dependent variable were attributable to an extraneous variable. Thus, because of this extraneous variable, researchers would not be able to make valid conclusions about the relationship between the independent and dependent variables.

A CAUSAL RELATIONSHIP IS IMPOSSIBLE TO PROVE

Causal research is used to test hypotheses about the causal relationship between an independent variable and a dependent variable. Unfortunately, the structure of the logic by which scientific hypotheses are tested does not allow researchers to either prove or disprove a research hypothesis. There is a logical fallacy. The structure of the logic by which scientific hypotheses are tested is shown in Figure 18.3.

However, imagine the hypotheses shown in Figure 18.4 and the fallacies of this logic to test them.

We cannot make these conclusions, even though they appear to follow logically from the premise and what was observed. Perhaps we did not observe enough dogs (the number of dogs in the sample was too few). Similarly, just because there are clouds present does not always mean it is raining. Because of this logical fallacy (formally referred to as **affirming the consequent**), we cannot say that experimental results

FIGURE 18.3 The Logic of Scientific Hypothesis Testing

If A, then B B
Therefore, A

If A, then B Not B
Therefore, not A

If our hypothesis is true (A), then we should observe B We observe B
Therefore, we accept our hypothesis A (we have no evidence to reject the hypothesis)

If our hypothesis is true (A), then we should observe B We do not observe B
Therefore, we reject our hypothesis A (we did not find evidence to support the hypothesis)

FIGURE 18.4 Fallacies in the Logic of Scientific Hypothesis Testing

If all dogs are brown (A), then we should observe only brown dogs (B) We observe only brown dogs (B)
Therefore, all dogs are brown (A)

If it is raining (A), there will be clouds in the sky (B) There are clouds in the sky (B)
Therefore, it is raining (A)

prove or disprove a research hypothesis. All that we can say is that experimental results support or do not support a research hypothesis.

INCREASING CONFIDENCE IN A CAUSAL RELATIONSHIP

Even though researchers can neither prove nor disprove a research hypothesis with complete certainty, there are three aspects of an experimental design that increase our confidence that the results identify a causal relationship between the independent and dependent variables.

Order of Events

To have any amount of confidence that an experimental design will identify a causal relationship, researchers must show that the change in the dependent variable followed the change in the independent variable. The hypothesized result must occur after the hypothesized cause. For example, a marketer noticed that a product's sales began to increase in January. If the marketer introduced a coupon promotion in June of that same year, the marketer cannot conclude that the coupon promotion was the cause of the increased sales. This is because sales (the dependent variable) began increasing in January, before the introduction of the coupon promotion in June (the independent variable).

Concomitant Variation

Not only must the cause precede the result (effect), but the cause and the result must also occur (vary) together (at about the same time). When the independent and dependent variables occur (vary) at about the same time, this is called **concomitant variation**. For example, if a coupon promotion is introduced in January and sales do not begin to increase until December of that same year, we cannot conclude that the coupon promotion was the cause of the sales increase in December. Even though the coupon was introduced before sales began to increase, the amount of time between the two events is too great. There are too many other factors that could have occurred during the year that could have also had an effect on sales.

No Extraneous Variables

Eliminating **extraneous variables** is perhaps the most difficult task in designing experiments. Researchers must try to eliminate, control for, or hold constant all extraneous variables. If not, a change in the dependent variable might result from multiple causes or multiple variables. In the situation just described, what if a major competitor went out of business in November of that year? The increase in sales in December could be a result of the coupon promotion, or it could also be a result of reduced competition. In this case, there would be multiple explanations for the change in the dependent variable. We could say that the independent and dependent variables are **spuriously related**. This means that the causal relationship is apparent, but not real. We cannot conclude that the change in the dependent variable was the result of only the independent variable manipulated in the experiment.

COMPONENTS OF EXPERIMENTAL DESIGNS

Basic designs are experiments that examine the effect of only one independent variable on the dependent variable. **Basic experiments** are also referred to as **one-factor experiments**.

Factorial designs are experiments that examine the joint effects of two or more variables on the dependent variable. **Factorial experiments** are also referred to as **multifactor experiments**. A full factorial experimental design is one in which all combinations of the independent variables are examined and considered in the experiment. By examining the joint effects of multiple independent variables on a dependent variable, a researcher can examine possible interactions among the independent variables. It is not possible to examine interactions if each independent variable is examined separately in individual experiments (conducting a separate basic experiment for each independent variable).

Field experiments are conducted in the real world. For example, taste tests conducted in real grocery stores and price experiments in real department stores are field experiments. The advantage of field experiments is that they are very realistic.

However, because they are conducted in the real world they do not allow for much internal control over potential extraneous variables.

Lab experiments are conducted in artificial or contrived environments. For example, inviting consumers to a hotel meeting room to view television advertisements would be a lab experiment. Lab experiments allow for a great deal of internal control over potential extraneous variables. However, in making lab experiments so controlled, their results may not be very generalizable. For example, if consumers view an advertisement while sitting in a hotel meeting room (with the researcher observing the consumers), their reactions to the advertisement will probably be different than if they viewed that same advertisement in the privacy of their own home, sitting on their own furniture, with access to their remote control.

Independent variables are the variables that are manipulated by the researcher. They can be changed independently of other variables in the experiment.

Treatments refer to the different levels of the independent variable. If an experiment is designed to manipulate three levels of price (high, medium, and low), then there are three treatments. Each flavor of cookie ingredient in a taste test would be a different treatment.

Experimental groups are the groups or individuals that receive the experimental manipulation.

Control groups are the groups or individuals that do not receive any experimental manipulation. Control groups are so named because they are designed to control for the effects of extraneous variables.

Dependent variables are measured by the researcher. Levels of the dependent variables (e.g., purchase intentions) are dependent on the different treatments (levels of the independent variable). For example, consumers' purchase intentions are most likely dependent upon price of the product (high, medium, or low).

Test units are what get assigned to the different treatments. Consider an advertising experiment where researchers are interested in measuring consumers' reactions to two different advertisements. If they randomly assign half of the consumers to view one advertisement, and randomly assign the other half of the consumers to view a second advertisement, then the consumers are the test units.

IDENTIFYING COMPONENTS OF EXPERIMENTS

To illustrate these components of experimental designs, consider the case of Captain Chips, a potato chip marketer who decided to change the package for their potato chips. Captain Chips developed two new packages and they conducted an experiment to determine which package would be best for their new potato chips. They sold the chips in package A in their stores in Nashville, and they sold the chips in package B in their stores in Memphis. After one month, they measured sales of their chips. This is an example of a basic field experiment. The independent variable is the type of package design. The dependent variable is sales. There are two treatments (two types of package designs) and the cities are the test units (assigned a package design).

Between Subjects Design. This experiment is also a completely randomized, **between subjects design** because the levels of the independent variable (the treatments) are manipulated between the subjects (the test units). Each test unit (city) received only one of the treatments. Consider the total sales of chips in each city for the month after introducing the new package as shown in Table 18.1.

Based on these results, you might conclude that package A led to an increase in sales of $1,000, whereas package B led to an increase in sales of $2,000. But, does this mean that package B is necessarily a better package? Are there any possible extraneous variables in this experiment that might explain these results (see Figure 18.5)?

Using a control group would help to control for the effects of any possible extraneous variables in this design. A control group would be similar in every way to the experimental groups, except it would not receive any experimental manipulation. In this case, a control group would be a store in each city that sold the chips in the old package during the entire experiment. That is, the control group would not get the experimental manipulation—it would not get the new package. Table 18.2 shows the sales for the experimental groups and the control groups.

TABLE 18.1 Results from Between Subjects Design: Potato Chip Package Experiment

	June Monthly Sales before Introducing the New Package	July Monthly Sales after Introducing the New Package
Package A (Nashville)	$1,000	$2,000
Package B (Memphis)	$1,000	$3,000

FIGURE 18.5 Possible Extraneous Variables in a Package Design Experiment

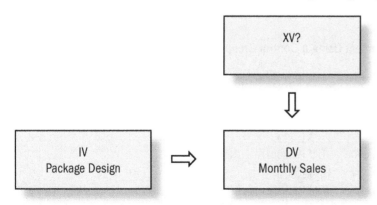

By using a control group (store) in each city, one would conclude that package A led to an increase in sales of $800, whereas package B led to an increase in sales of only $500. Notice that the control group measured what would have happened without the experimental manipulation, that is, without the new package design. In Nashville, sales of potato chips would have increased $200 without the new package. In Memphis, sales would have increased $1,500 without the new package. Thus, only $800 of the $1,000 increase observed in Nashville can be attributed to the new package. Similarly, only $500 of the $2,000 increase observed in Memphis can be attributed to the new package.

Within Subjects Design. As another example of identifying the components of experiments, consider the case of MegaBrew. MegaBrew recently developed a fruit flavored beer. They conducted a 12-month test market in four different cities to determine which of two different promotional campaigns would lead to higher sales. Promotional campaign X was run during the first half of the test market (January through June) whereas promotional campaign Y was run during the last half of the test market (July through December). This same order of campaigns was used in all four test market cities. This is an example of a basic field experiment. The independent variable is the type of promotional campaign. The dependent variable is sales. There are two treatments (two promotional campaigns) and the cities are the test units.

This experiment is considered a **within subjects design** because the levels of the independent variable (the treatments) were manipulated within each city (the test units). This would also be described as a **repeated measures design** because repeated measurements (after the manipulation of each experimental treatment) were taken within each test unit. Consider the graph shown in Figure 18.6 that displays how total sales changed throughout the year. If sales increased during the first six months of the test market, but then decreased during the second six months of the test market, does this mean that campaign X was necessarily the better of the two campaigns?

Based on these results, you might conclude that campaign X had a positive effect on sales, whereas campaign Y had a negative effect on sales. But, are there any potential extraneous variables that might also explain this pattern of results?

One possible extraneous variable involves **seasonal effects**. It is possible that people naturally drink more beer during the summer months. This would explain the increase in sales leading up to the summer months and the decrease in sales

TABLE 18.2 Results from a Package Design Experiment Using a Control Group to Control for Extraneous Variables

	Nashville		Memphis	
	June	July	June	July
Experimental Group	$1,000 (Old Package)	$2,000 (New Package A)	$1,000 (Old Package)	$3,000 (New Package B)
Control Group	$1,000 (Old Package)	$1,200 (Old Package)	$1,000 (Old Package)	$2,500 (Old Package)

FIGURE 18.6 Change in Sales of MegaBrew Fruit-Flavored Beer

after the summer months. It is also possible that other beer marketers noticed the favorable response to the fruit-flavored beer. They might have introduced their own fruit-flavored beer nationally in June before MegaBrew completed their test market. This new competition would lead to decreased sales in the latter half of the year. The extraneous variable (presence of new competition) that was not controlled for in the experiment confounds the relationship between the campaigns and sales. We do not know the true nature of the relationship between these two variables.

CONTROLLING FOR EXTRANEOUS VARIABLES (CONFOUNDS)

There are five major techniques that researchers can incorporate into their experimental designs to control for the effects of extraneous variables (see Figure 18.7).

Control Group

A **control group** is used to measure the effects of extraneous variables. The control group should be similar to the experimental groups in every way except that the control group does not receive any experimental manipulation. The differences in measurements between the control group and the experimental group(s) are presumed to be due to the effects of extraneous variables, even if we do not know what those extraneous variables are. Thus, control groups measure the effects of extraneous variables on the dependent variable.

FIGURE 18.7 Controlling for Extraneous Variables

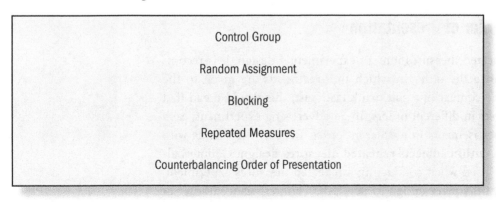

Random Assignment

Randomly assigning treatments to the test units will not eliminate extraneous variables, but it will control for them. With **random assignment** we assume that the effects of extraneous variables are equally spread out over all treatments.[3]

Blocking

If a potential extraneous variable can be identified prior to the experiment, a researcher can block on that variable. With **blocking**, the researcher identifies homogenous subgroups based on that variable. Test units (subjects) are blocked on that variable and then the treatments are randomly assigned to the test units within each matched subgroup.

Blocking test units on an extraneous variable and then randomly assigning treatments within each matched group yields a **randomized block design**. An advantage of a randomized block design is the ability to identify interactions between multiple factors. An **interaction** occurs when the effect of one independent variable on the dependent variable is not the same for all levels of a second independent variable. For example, by blocking on age, a marketer could identify that young consumers prefer advertisement X, whereas older consumers prefer advertisement Y. In this case, age and the type of advertisement are said to interact in determining consumers' preferences. Blocking on potential extraneous variables also allows marketers to identify segments for future targeting.

> Extraneous variables are often called "confounds" because they confound the relationship between the independent variable and the dependent variable.

Repeated Measures

With a **repeated measures design**, repeated measurements are taken on the same test unit. For example, each consumer in a taste test evaluates all flavors of a new soft drink, sees all advertisements that are being tested, or evaluates all products being tested. With a repeated measures design, each test unit is exposed to all treatments. This controls for variations or differences (possible extraneous variables) between the test units. A repeated measures design is also referred to as a **within subjects design**.

Counterbalancing Order of Presentation

When incorporating repeated measures into an experimental design, it is recommended to **counterbalance** the order in which the treatments are given to the different test units. In the context of a soft drink taste test, this would mean that consumers taste the drinks in different orders. In an advertising experiment, each consumer views the advertisements in a different order. Repeated measures with counterbalancing yield a **within subjects repeated measures design**. Counterbalancing should always be used when conducting a repeated measures experiment. Researchers can use a **Latin square** design to develop a counterbalanced order of presentation.

FIGURE 18.8 Between Subjects Randomized Block Design: McDonald's Advertisements

	Dolly Parton	Taylor Swift
Younger than 30	n = 200	n = 200
Older than 30	n = 200	n = 200

DESIGNING AN ADVERTISING EXPERIMENT

To illustrate these techniques, consider the following hypothetical situation:

> McDonald's has hired you as a marketing research consultant. McDonald's has developed two new advertisements, each featuring a different celebrity (Dolly Parton and Taylor Swift). They want you to conduct mall intercept interviews of 800 people and also design an experiment that will help them determine which celebrity leads to more favorable evaluations of the advertisement. That is, they want to determine which advertisement consumers will like more. Within the context of the mall intercept interviews each consumer will have time to view only one of the advertisements.

One possibility would be to use a **between subjects randomized block design**. If we consider age as a possible extraneous variable, we can block on that variable. A 2 × 2 between subjects design, with two levels of celebrity (Dolly Parton and Taylor Swift) and two levels of age (younger than 30 and older than 30), and 200 consumers randomly assigned to each cell would look like the design shown in Figure 18.8. Consumers are thus matched on age to block out the effects of age.

A researcher might also want to block on the sex of the consumer (considering sex as a potential extraneous variable). This would yield a 2 × 2 × 2 between subjects design, with two levels of celebrity (Dolly Parton and Taylor Swift), two levels of age (younger than 30 and older than 30), and two levels of sex (male and female), with 100 consumers randomly assigned to each cell. Consumers would be matched on age and sex to block out the effects of these two potential extraneous variables.

DESIGNING A TASTE TESTING EXPERIMENT

As another example, consider the following hypothetical situation:

> Pizza King has developed two new pizza toppings (fruit and steak). They have reserved a hotel meeting room for four days (Monday, Tuesday, Wednesday, and Thursday) between the hours of 11:30 a.m. and 1:30 p.m. They want to sample a total of 800 people (200 each day). You are to design a taste testing experiment that will allow Pizza King to determine which of the two new toppings consumers are most likely to prefer. Pizza King has determined that to adequately evaluate a pizza topping, a consumer must eat an entire slice of pizza with that topping on it. Also, each subject will be present for only one day of testing. This means that a consumer cannot taste one slice of pizza one day and then come back to taste a different slice on a different day.

FIGURE 18.9 Between Subjects Randomized Block Design: Pizza King

	Fruit Topping	Steak Topping
Lunch	n = 50	n = 50
No Lunch	n = 50	n = 50

FIGURE 18.10 Repeated Measures Design with Counterbalancing across Subjects: Pizza King

	Monday (n = 200)	Tuesday (n = 200)	Wednesday (n = 200)	Thursday (n = 200)
Subject 1	Fruit, Steak	Fruit, Steak	Fruit, Steak	Fruit, Steak
Subject 2	Steak, Fruit	Steak, Fruit	Steak, Fruit	Steak, Fruit
Subject 3	Fruit, Steak	Fruit, Steak	Fruit, Steak	Fruit, Steak
⋮	⋮	⋮	⋮	⋮
Subject 200	Steak, Fruit	Steak, Fruit	Steak, Fruit	Steak, Fruit

One possibility would be to use a **between subjects randomized block design**. If we consider whether or not a consumer has eaten lunch as a possible extraneous variable (hungry consumers are likely to evaluate any piece of pizza more favorably), we can block on that variable. A 2 × 2 between subjects design with two levels of topping (fruit and steak) and two levels of hunger (ate lunch and did not eat lunch), with 50 consumers randomly assigned to each cell each day would look like the design shown in Figure 18.9.

Doing this requires knowing whether or not the consumer has eaten lunch. If this is not known, we could use a **repeated measures design** (**within subjects design**) where all subjects eat both pieces of pizza and the order of presentation is counterbalanced across subjects. This design is shown in Figure 18.10.

FACTORIAL DESIGNS

An experiment that examines the joint effects of two or more independent variables on a dependent variable is called a **factorial design**. In a factorial design the levels of the independent variables (treatments) can be manipulated between subjects or within subjects, and subjects (test units) can be blocked on potential extraneous variables. For example, a company may want to examine the joint effects of the type of advertisement and product price on consumers' purchase intentions for a new product. These two factors can be manipulated jointly in the same experiment to form a factorial design. In a between subjects factorial design, subjects would be randomly assigned to view one advertisement for the product at either a high price or a low price. This design is shown in Figure 18.11.

The researcher could also block on a potential extraneous variable such as sex. In this case, the experiment would be conducted separately for males and for females, as shown in Figure 18.12.

FIGURE 18.11 Between Subjects Factorial Design: Two Factors

	Advertisement 1	Advertisement 2
High Price	Cell 1	Cell 3
Low Price	Cell 2	Cell 4

FIGURE 18.12 Between Subjects Factorial Design with Blocking

	Men		Women	
	Advertisement 1	Advertisement 2	Advertisement 1	Advertisement 2
High Price	Cell 1	Cell 3	Cell 5	Cell 7
Low Price	Cell 2	Cell 4	Cell 6	Cell 8

If the researcher wanted to reduce the number of subjects, the experiment could be conducted as a within subjects design. Each subject could evaluate all four combinations of both advertisements and both prices. In this case, it would be best to counterbalance the order in which the ads are shown. This ordering could be done with a Latin square design as illustrated in Figure 18.13, where A = ad1, high price; B = ad1, low price; C = ad2, high price; and D = ad2, low price.

Latin Square. A Latin square is a $p \times p$ square array of p elements (usually numbers or letters), each repeated p times. Each element appears once in each row and once in each column. Latin squares can be used to control for the effects of two extraneous variables while manipulating an independent variable. The two extraneous variables and the independent variable must be blocked into an equal number of levels to form a square. The rows and columns represent the different levels of the extraneous variables. The individual cells within the Latin square represent the levels of the independent variable. Each level of the independent variable appears once in each row and once in each column. This reduces the number of experimental groups needed for the experiment when the researcher does not wish to examine any potential interactions between the independent variable and the extraneous variables.[4]

FIGURE 18.13 Within Subjects Design Using a Latin Square to Counterbalance Order of Presentation

	Men					Women			
Subject 1	A	B	C	D	Subject 1	A	B	C	D
Subject 2	B	A	D	C	Subject 2	B	A	D	C
Subject 3	C	D	A	B	Subject 3	C	D	A	B
Subject 4	D	C	B	A	Subject 4	D	C	B	A
⋮	⋮	⋮	⋮	⋮	⋮	⋮	⋮	⋮	⋮

INTERNAL AND EXTERNAL EXPERIMENTAL VALIDITY

Experiments should be designed in such a way as to increase the internal and external validity of the experiment.[5]

Internal Validity

Internal validity refers to the ability to make valid conclusions about the relationship between the independent and dependent variables. Controlling for extraneous variables increases the internal validity of experiments. If extraneous variables are present they can confound the relationship between the independent and dependent variables. When extraneous variables are present we cannot be sure that the change in the dependent variable is due to the independent variable that is manipulated, or due to the extraneous variable that is outside the control of the experimental design. Knowing some of the more common sources of potential extraneous variables allows researchers to identify and control for their effects on the dependent variable (see Figure 18.14).[6]

Changes in the External Environment. Changes in the external environment during the course of an experiment can create extraneous variables. Recall the case of MegaBrew and their experiment to test two different promotional campaigns. If new competitors entered the market halfway through the experiment, researchers could not be sure that the decrease in sales observed during the second half of the experiment was due to the second campaign, or due to the presence of new competitors.

FIGURE 18.14 Experimental Validity

Internal Validity

Valid conclusions can be made about the relationship between the independent and dependent variables
All extraneous variables have been controlled for

Threats to Internal Validity
Changes in the environment
Changes in the subject
Prior measurements
Different measures
Subject selection procedures
Differences in experimental groups

External Validity

Results and conclusions can be generalized to a larger population

Changes in the external environment (even changes not foreseen by the researcher) can be controlled for and measured by adding a control group to the experimental design.

Changes in the Subject. A change internal to subjects during the course of the experiment can also create extraneous variables. For example, in repeated measures designs where subjects are exposed to multiple manipulations over a relatively long time period, changes in the subject, such as becoming hungry, bored, irritated, or tired, can affect dependent variables. Such changes can be controlled for by counterbalancing the order in which subjects (test units) receive the manipulations.

Prior Measurements. A prior measurement can cause a subject's exposure to the experimental manipulation to be different than what the exposure to the experimental manipulation would have been without the prior measurement. A prior measurement can lead to heightened awareness or increased attention. This is especially relevant for within subjects (repeated measures) designs. For example, imagine if consumers are called on Monday and asked, "What do you know about Crunchity peanut butter?" Researchers measure whether or not consumers mention that it is low-fat. Then, on Tuesday an advertisement is aired emphasizing the low-fat properties of Crunchity peanut butter. If the same consumers are called again on Wednesday and asked what they know about Crunchity peanut butter, it is possible that they gave greater attention to the advertisement seen on Tuesday because they were asked about Crunchity peanut butter the previous day.

Different Measures. Changes in the measurement scales or survey questions over time can also create extraneous variables. Imagine the problems in interpreting the results from an experiment in which consumers are asked on Monday, "What do you know about Crunchity peanut butter?" and on Wednesday they are asked, "Did you know that Crunchity peanut butter is low-fat?" It is very likely that awareness of low fat will appear to increase from Monday to Wednesday simply because the question asked on Wednesday implies that the peanut butter is low-fat. The leading question asked on Wednesday is likely to lead respondents to say *yes*.

Subject Selection Procedures. Using different selection criteria for different experimental groups can cause extraneous variables. This is especially true if subjects are allowed to self-select which experimental group they would like to be placed in. For example, do not ask subjects, "Which advertisement would you like to see?" or "Which piece of pizza would you like to try first?"

Laboratory experiments tend to have high internal validity and low external validity. Conversely, field experiments tend to have low internal validity and high external validity.

Differences in Experimental Groups. Extraneous variables can also be created if two groups in a between subjects design are systematically different from each other. For between subjects designs it is important that the experimental groups be similar on all variables except for the independent variables (the experimental variables the researcher is manipulating). For example, if hungry consumers are given chocolate chip cookies and consumers who are not hungry are given raisin cookies, the differences in evaluations could be due to differences in hunger across the two experimental groups.

External Validity

External validity refers to the ability to generalize the results and conclusions from an experiment to a larger population, to a different setting, or even to a different context. Typically, experiments in highly realistic contexts have higher external validity with respect to experimental conclusions. Conversely, experiments in less realistic contexts have lower external validity with respect to experimental conclusions. Field experiments tend to have higher external validity than laboratory experiments. However, laboratory experiments tend to have higher internal validity than field experiments. For example, the results and conclusions from a test market where a brand is sold in actual retail stores would stand a better chance of generalizing to other cities than if the experiment were conducted in an artificial laboratory setting.

BLIND AND DOUBLE-BLIND EXPERIMENTS

A **blind experiment** is where subjects (test units) do not know the treatment to which they have been assigned. For example, if researchers are conducting taste tests for Pepsi they might have consumers taste both Pepsi and Coke. If the experiment is blind, the drinks will be in unmarked cups that do not identify a brand name. This is done to eliminate any prior expectations that might influence taste evaluations (subjects' responses to the experimental manipulation).

A **double-blind experiment** is where neither the subject nor the experimenter knows the treatment to which the subject (test unit) has been assigned. Imagine if Pepsi employees were conducting the previously mentioned taste tests. They might intentionally (or even unintentionally or unconsciously) try to influence consumers to rate Pepsi more favorably. The purpose of a double-blind experiment is to eliminate any influences or effects that the experimenter might have on subjects.

However, for companies such as Coca-Cola or Philip Morris that have well-established brands, a blind experiment can actually lead to distorted research results (e.g., taste test results). What happens to brand equity and the emotional attachment that consumers have toward a brand during a blind test? It is eliminated. When Coke conducted their taste tests in the mid-1980s they found that consumers preferred the new formula over the old formula. However, when they introduced the new formula, consumers rebelled and preferred the old formula. Researchers must recognize that consumers make actual purchase decisions knowing full well which brand they are buying. If there is brand equity or emotional attachment for a brand (something marketers spend a great deal of time and money to develop), this brand equity and emotional attachment is disregarded (even eliminated) in a blind experiment.

TEST MARKETING

Test marketing is a large-scale field experiment where marketers introduce a new product in only a few markets. The product is marketed in the test market cities exactly as it would be marketed in full-scale national distribution. The purpose of test marketing is to identify the viability of a new product in a few cities before introducing the product nationally. The cost and risk associated with introducing a new product in only a few cities is much less than introducing it nationally. The majority of products that succeed in test markets tend to succeed in national distribution. Alternatively, the majority of products that are not test marketed tend to fail in national distribution.

Test marketing is a controlled field experiment with relatively high external validity because it is conducted in the real world. Test marketing also has relatively low internal validity because many real-world factors, such as competition and changes in the economy, cannot be controlled. In the context of experimental design, the purpose of test marketing is to examine the causal relationships between marketer-controlled variables, such as the marketing mix, on consumers' responses to new products. This is illustrated in Figure 18.15.

Advantages of Test Marketing

Test marketing offers a number of advantages over surveys and laboratory experiments. It allows marketing researchers to identify potential interactions among marketing mix variables, estimate the future profitability of a new product, and identify potential product cannibalism from new products.

FIGURE 18.15 Test Marketing

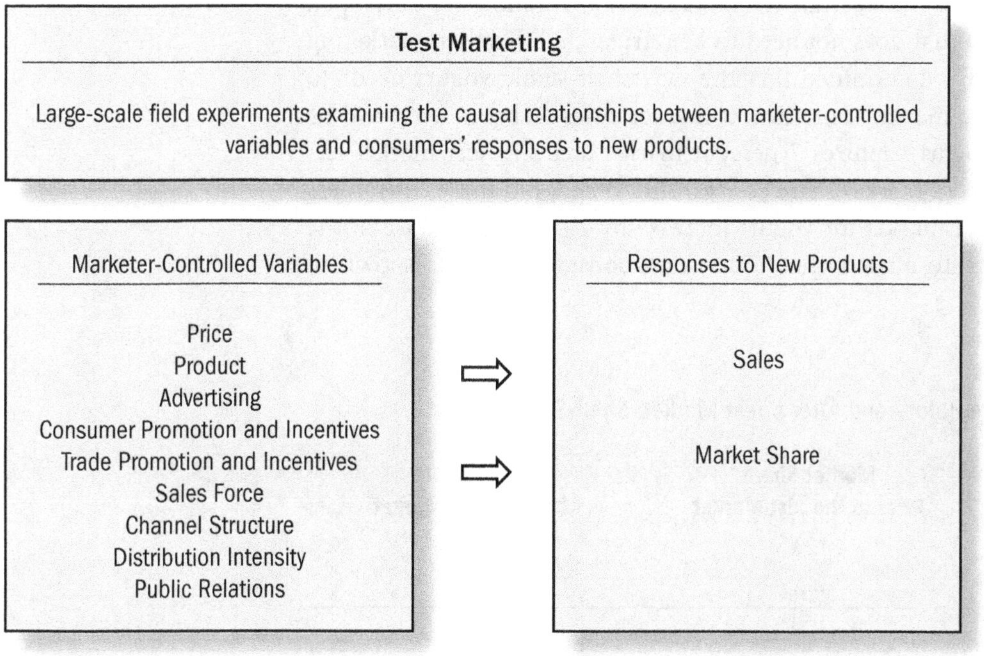

Test Marketing

Large-scale field experiments examining the causal relationships between marketer-controlled variables and consumers' responses to new products.

Marketer-Controlled Variables

Price
Product
Advertising
Consumer Promotion and Incentives
Trade Promotion and Incentives
Sales Force
Channel Structure
Distribution Intensity
Public Relations

Responses to New Products

Sales

Market Share

Interactions among Marketing Mix Variables. Test marketing allows marketing researchers to identify interactions among the elements of the marketing mix. Researchers can examine the joint effects and relationships between pricing, promotion, product characteristics, merchandising displays, distribution, and consumer trial. Such interactions could not be examined with only survey research.

Estimate Profitability. Test marketing allows marketing researchers to measure the future profitability of a new product. The key dependent variable in test marketing is market share, not sales. Market share results from test market cities can be generalized to other cities, whereas per-capita sales cannot. To illustrate this, imagine that a new brand of sunscreen lotion is test marketed in Florida. It is likely that many people living in Florida use sunscreen and are willing to try new brands. If 10 percent of the population becomes loyal repeat customers, does this mean that 10 percent of consumers in other cities are likely to purchase the sunscreen? No. This is because there are a large number of consumers in Florida who purchase sunscreen. Per-capita sales figures cannot be generalized to other cities. Similarly, per-capita sales results from test markets of cheese in Wisconsin, or grits in Alabama, would not generalize to other cities. However, market share results from test marketing experiments will generalize to other cities. Market share figures control for the total size of the market for a product in any given city. If a new sunscreen captures 15 percent of the market for sunscreen products in Florida, it is likely to also capture 15 percent of the market for sunscreen products in Michigan, even though the total market for sunscreen is probably smaller in Michigan.

Potential Product Cannibalism. Test marketing allows researchers to identify potential cannibalism of existing sales that result from introducing new products. **Product cannibalism** means that a new product does not attract new customers. Rather, a new product merely steals away current customers from a marketer's existing brands or product lines. To illustrate this, imagine that Dannon has developed a new shelf-stable yogurt that does not need to be refrigerated. Further, marketing managers at Dannon have determined that the new shelf-stable yogurt needs to capture at least 5 percent market share in test market cities to break even and be profitable. If the new yogurt captures 7 percent market share in test market cities, where did this 7 percent market share come from? Where did these consumers come from? Did the total market for yogurt increase by 7 percent because of the new shelf-stable yogurt? To answer these questions, consider the data shown in Table 18.3.

TABLE 18.3 Market Share Before and After a Test Market: Shelf-Stable Yogurt

	Market Share Prior to the Test Market	Market Share After the Test Market
Existing Yogurt	12%	6%
New Shelf-Stable Yogurt	-----	7%

If the existing brands of Dannon yogurt already had a 12 percent market share prior to test marketing the new shelf-stable yogurt, the conclusion would be that the new yogurt cannibalized 6 percent of the market share from the existing brands, and gained 1 percent market share from either competitors or from new consumers to the yogurt market. The total market share for all Dannon yogurts after the test market is 13 percent. This is only 1 percent higher than their total market share prior to introducing the new yogurt. Marketing managers would then need to decide if this new product is worth introducing. It cannibalized existing market share. But, then again, it might be better to cannibalize existing market share than to let competitors take it away if they introduce their own brand of shelf-stable yogurt. Cannibalizing one's own sales is often better than letting competitors steal away sales.

Disadvantages of Test Marketing

Even though there are many advantages to test marketing, it also has its disadvantages. Test marketing is very expensive, takes a great deal of time, and often provides competitors with ideas and insight into a marketer's strategies.

The Cost of Test Marketing. Test marketing is not cheap. It is often very expensive. However, marketers must decide which is worse, spending a few million dollars to test market a new product and discovering that the new product is likely to be a failure, or not test marketing the product and spending even more money on national distribution and discovering that the new product is definitely a failure. Negative results from marketing research are not always bad. They often save the marketer money in the end. This is easily illustrated with an analogy from real estate. Many potential homebuyers will first pay for a house inspection before agreeing to purchase a house. Imagine that you spend $300 to have a house inspected and the inspector finds numerous problems with the house's foundation, plumbing, electrical wiring, and insulation. Was it worth it to spend the $300 on the home inspection? The answer is obviously yes. In fact, many people would consider that $300 to be the best money they ever spent. It kept them from making a worse financial decision. In the same manner, a negative result from marketing research can keep marketers from making potentially disastrous financial decisions regarding new products. So, the high cost of test marketing can be seen as an insurance policy against even greater financial losses.

Test Marketing Takes Time. Another disadvantage of test marketing is the amount of time it takes to complete the test marketing experiment. The typical length of time for a test market is from nine months to one year. This is because the purpose of a test market is to identify the number of consumers who are loyal, repeat buyers. Many consumers will try new products just for the sake of trying something new. However, many of these **variety seekers** will not become loyal customers. Businesses rely on a small core group of repeat buyers to sustain their business. The 80/20 rule suggests that 80 percent of sales come from 20 percent of customers. The test market should last long enough to allow variety seekers to enter and then leave the market, so marketers can identify the number of consumers on whom they can rely as loyal customers. As a result, the length of a test market often varies by the nature of the purchase, consumption, and repeat purchase cycle for a product. If the purchase, consumption, and repeat purchase cycle for a product is relatively short, then the test market can be completed in less time. However, if this cycle is relatively long, then the test market must last a relatively long time.

Loss of Secrecy. In addition to these disadvantages, marketing managers are keenly aware of the potential loss of secrecy associated with test marketing experiments. Test markets are conducted in the real world. Competitors can easily observe, purchase, and even evaluate for themselves the new product that another marketer is testing. As a result, competitors can easily copy, or match, the new product that is being tested and be the first to introduce their own version of the product for national distribution. Being the first entrant into a market gives the marketer a **pioneering advantage** over later entrants.

When Not to Test Market

It is not necessary to test market all new products. Expensive durables, such as washing machines or industrial drill bits, would probably not need to be test marketed. Due to the high cost of producing just a few expensive durables, it is worth it to go ahead and make enough of the product for national distribution. Also, me-too products, such as unscented or lemon-scented versions of a cleaning product, do not need to be test marketed. The success of similar products in the market indicates their appeal to consumers. Finally, line extensions, such as decaffeinated coffees or caffeine-free soft drinks, also do not need to be test marketed.

Selecting Test Market Cities

One of the most important decisions regarding test marketing is the selection of cities in which a new product will be tested. This is essentially a sampling issue. In general, the cities selected should be representative of the larger population so that conclusions from the test market cities can be generalized to the larger population. There are a number of important considerations in choosing test market cities.

Market Size. The test market city should be large enough to give projectable results, but not so large as to be cost-prohibitive. This is essentially a sample size issue. The sample (population) in the test market city should be large enough to provide valid conclusions about the effects of the marketing strategies on sales and market share. However, the increased costs to distribute, promote, and sell products in very large cities, such as New York City, Los Angeles, or Chicago, make these cities practically too large and expensive for a typical test market.

Representative of the Larger Population. The population in the test market city should be demographically and psychographically similar to the larger population. For example, a new acne facial cleanser should not be test marketed in St. Petersburg, Florida

> A test market city should be large enough to give projectable results, have residents who are representative of the larger population, be self-contained with respect to media and product purchasing, not be overused, and resemble the larger market with respect to marketing variables and the competitive environment.

(which has a high percentage of older residents). The population in St. Petersburg is not representative of the larger population in terms of age. Conversely, a city with an overly large population of young consumers would not be a good test market city for a product targeted toward elderly consumers.

Self-Contained. The city should be self-contained with respect to media viewing and product purchasing. The residents in the city should be exposed to media originating from only the test market city, and do most of their shopping in only the test market city. Further, there should be very few residents from other areas shopping in the city. In other words, the city should be relatively isolated and geographically separated from other large populations. This controls for the effects of promotional messages originating from other nearby cities on consumers' purchasing behaviors. Researchers cannot make valid conclusions about the effects of promotional messages on consumers' behaviors if they do not know what media consumers who are shopping in the city are exposed to. Many marketing researchers consider the self-contained quality of a city to be even more important than the demographic and psychographic representativeness of the city.

Not Over used. A test market city should not be overused. Residents should not be so accustomed to new test market products that they begin to view themselves as professional test market consumers. This might affect their willingness and desire to try new products.

Competitive Environment. The competitive environment in a test market city should resemble that of the larger population. Consumers try and adopt new products in the context of other competing brands. A test market city that does not represent the larger market in terms of the presence of competitors will not yield projectable results.

Product Class Familiarity. The residents in a test market city should be as knowledgeable and familiar with a product class as other consumers across the country. New types of products are sometimes adopted at varying speeds in different parts of the country. Consumers in the Southwest might be very familiar with some products that consumers in the Northeast are less familiar with.

Typical Distribution Channels. The distribution channels in the test market city should be similar to the distribution channels in other cities across the country. Because distribution can be very important to the success of some products, it is necessary to control for this in selecting the test market city.

Frequently Used Test Marketing Cities

Some of the most often used test marketing cities are listed in Figure 18.16. Notice that these cities are not excessively large. Their residents are likely to represent typical American consumers. Further, they are relatively self-contained. They are somewhat isolated and geographically separated from other large populations.

FIGURE 18.16 Frequently Used Test Market Cities

Albany, New York	Fresno, California	Pittsburgh, Pennsylvania
Amarillo, Texas	Indianapolis, Indiana	Portland, Oregon
Buffalo, New York	Jacksonville, Florida	Portland, Maine
Cincinnati, Ohio	Kansas City, Missouri	Providence, Rhode Island
Cleveland, Ohio	Lexington, Kentucky	Rochester, New York
Columbus, Ohio	Lubbock, Texas	Sacramento, California
Davenport, Iowa	Memphis, Tennessee	Salt Lake City, Utah
Dayton, Ohio	Nashville, Tennessee	San Antonio, Texas
Denver, Colorado	Oklahoma City, Oklahoma	South Bend, Indiana

QUASI- AND TRUE EXPERIMENTAL DESIGNS

There are two general classes of experimental designs that marketing researchers can use when conducting experiments. **Quasi-experimental designs** do not control for the effects of extraneous variables. Alternatively, **true experimental designs** do control for the effects of extraneous variables. The most often used quasi-experimental designs and true experimental designs are listed in Figure 18.17 and are detailed in the next section of this chapter.

Quasi-Experimental Designs

The following experimental designs are called **quasi-experimental designs** because they do not control for the effects of extraneous variables.[7] Thus, they tend to have very low internal validity. The symbols used in describing these designs are shown in Figure 18.18.

After Only Design. An **after only design** is perhaps the simplest experimental design (see Figure 18.19). As an example of this design, advertisers often run advertisements and then randomly call consumers to measure **day-after recall** for the advertisement and information contained in the advertisement.

Potential disadvantages of the after only design include:

- There is no measure of what happens to subjects when they are not exposed to the experimental manipulation. There is nothing to compare the measurement to. For advertising, day-after recall scores must be compared to an external benchmark (e.g., day-after recall scores for prime time viewing for typical consumer products are often between 20 percent and 22 percent).

- There is no control for extraneous variables.

FIGURE 18.17 Quasi- and True Experimental Designs

Quasi-Experimental Designs	True Experimental Designs
Do not control for the effects of extraneous variables	Control for the effects of extraneous variables
After Only Design	Pretest–Posttest with a Control Group Design
One Group Pretest–Posttest Design	Posttest Only with a Control Group Design
Static Group Design	

FIGURE 18.18 Symbols Used in Describing Experimental Designs

The Symbol	Means
t_i	Time period
R	Subjects are randomly assigned to a treatment
X	A subject is exposed to an experimental manipulation
M	A measurement or observation is taken on a subject

FIGURE 18.19 After Only Design

After Only Design	
t_1	t_2
X	M_1

One Group Pretest–Posttest Design. In a **one group pretest–posttest design**, the difference between the pretest and posttest provides a measure of the effect of the experimental manipulation (see Figure 18.20). For example, consider an advertiser who measures brand awareness on Monday, runs an advertisement on Tuesday, and then measures brand awareness again on Wednesday. The purpose of the pre and post measurements is to determine the effect of the advertisement on increasing awareness.

FIGURE 18.20 One Group Pretest–Posttest Design

One Group Pretest–Posttest Design		
t_1	t_2	t_3
M_1	X	M_2

Effect of X = $M_2 - M_1$

Some of the disadvantages of this design include:

- If this design is conducted as a within subjects design (a panel design), there is the possibility of extraneous variables created due to changes in the external environment, changes internal to the subject, prior measurement effects, and using different measures for the pre and post measurements.

- If this design is conducted as a between subjects design (a tracking study), there is the possibility of extraneous variables created due to different selection procedures, using different measures for the pre and post measurements, changes in the external environment, and any differences between the two experimental groups.

Static Group Design. A **static group design** uses both an experimental group and a control group (see Figure 18.21). For example, an advertiser runs an advertisement on Monday and randomly calls consumers on Tuesday to measure awareness for the advertised brand. If consumers say they watched the TV show during which the advertisement was run, they are placed in the experimental group. If consumers say they did not watch the TV show during which the advertisement was run, they are placed in the control group. This design solves the problems of the one group pretest–posttest design because there is no pre measurement. So, by definition, there can be no extraneous variables due to changes in the environment, changes in the subject, prior measurements, or the use of different measures. This design also solves the problems of the after only design because it provides a measure of what happens when the subject is not exposed to the experimental manipulation.

Quasi-experimental designs do not control for the effects of extraneous variables. Conversely, true experimental designs do control for the effects of extraneous variables.

Problems with this design include:

- Possible extraneous variables due to selection procedures if subjects are allowed to self-select which group they will be in. Often, the researcher will not know that the two groups are similar in every regard except for the exposure to the experimental manipulation.

- This design assumes that the pretest measurements for experimental and control groups are similar. However, this is not always the case. Imagine if an advertisement for a brand of motor oil is aired during the televised coverage of a NASCAR race. It is possible that consumers who watch NASCAR races are already familiar with brands of motor oil, whereas the consumers who do not watch NASCAR races are less familiar with brands of motor oil. If this is the case, the greater awareness found in the experimental group (consumers who were exposed to the advertisement because they watched the NASCAR race) would not be due solely to the advertisement. It could be due to the fact that the experimental group already had greater awareness for the brand.

FIGURE 18.21 Static Group Design

Static Group Design		
	t_1	t_2
Experimental Group	X	M_1
Control Group		M_2

Effect of X = $M_1 - M_2$

True Experimental Designs

The following are true experimental designs because they control for the effects of extraneous variables. Thus, they tend to have relatively high internal validity.

Pretest–Posttest with a Control Group Design. To illustrate the **pretest–posttest with a control group design** (see Figure 18.22), imagine an advertiser who randomly assigns consumers to either an experimental group or to a control group (consumers do not know which group they are in). The experiment is conducted in a large meeting room of a hotel. Approximately 75 consumers are in the experiment at one time. The consumers in the experimental group are first asked some questions concerning their attitudes toward various brands (one of which is the target brand of interest to the advertiser). They are then shown some TV shows, within which are imbedded some advertisements. And, one of these advertisements is for the target brand. After watching the TV shows, the consumers are again questioned about their attitudes toward various brands (one of which is the target brand). The purpose of the experiment is to measure the effect of the advertisement that was shown during the TV show on changing consumers' attitudes toward the target brand.

FIGURE 18.22 Pretest-Posttest with a Control Group Design

Pretest-Posttest with a Control Group Design				
		t_1	t_2	t_3
Experimental Group	R	M_1	X	M_2
Control Group	R	M_3		M_4

Effect of X = $(M_2 - M_1) - (M_4 - M_3)$

The consumers in the control group are first asked some questions concerning their attitudes toward various brands (one of which is the target brand). They are then shown some TV shows, within which are imbedded some advertisements. However, the control group consumers do not see the advertisement for the target brand. After watching the TV shows, these consumers are again questioned about their attitudes toward various brands (one of which is the target brand).

This is a very popular design. Its major advantage is that the pre and post measurements for the control group control for any extraneous variables created by prior measurements, changes in the external environment, and changes internal to subjects.

Posttest Only with a Control Group Design. The **posttest only with a control group design** is the same as the static group design, except that subjects are randomly assigned to either the experimental group or the control group (see Figure 18.23). As with the static group design, this design assumes that the pre measurements for the experimental and control groups are similar. And, this can be assumed if subjects are randomly assigned to the experimental and control groups.

Some of the major advantages of this design include:

- There is no pre measurement. By definition there can be no extraneous variables caused by changes in the external environment, changes in the subject, prior measurement, or differences in pre and post measures.

- This design provides a measure of what happens when a subject is not exposed to the experimental manipulation (a problem with the after only design).

- There can be no extraneous variables caused by differences in selection procedures because subjects are randomly assigned to the experimental and control groups. Subjects are not allowed to self-select which group they will be in.

FIGURE 18.23 Posttest Only with a Control Group Design

Posttest Only with a Control Group Design		t_1	t_2
Experimental Group	R	X	M_1
Control Group	R		M_2

Effect of X = M_1 – M_2

CAUSAL RESEARCH AND THE DECISION-MAKING PROCESS

Marketing managers often need information about the causal relationships between two or more marketing variables. The results from causal research are frequently used to confirm that decisions to manipulate marketing mix variables, such as price, promotion, place, and product, will lead to the desired changes in important dependent variables, such as sales and market share. The internal validity of an experimental design is of utmost importance. To have any confidence in the results from an experiment, marketing managers must be assured that all extraneous variables have been controlled for or eliminated. If extraneous variables have not been controlled for or eliminated, researchers cannot make valid conclusions about the causal relationship between two or more variables, and decision makers cannot place any confidence in the results from the experiment.

Further, the external validity of an experimental design must also be considered. External validity refers to the ability to generalize the results and conclusions from an experiment to a larger population, to a different setting, or even to a different context. If an experiment is so highly controlled and contrived that it bears no resemblance to real-world conditions, the results from it will be of little use to marketing managers, who are making decisions designed to achieve marketing objectives within the real world.

When marketing researchers conduct causal research they are faced with a dilemma. Efforts to increase the internal validity of an experiment (controlling for extraneous variables) often reduce the external validity of the experiment. Conversely, efforts to increase the external validity of an experiment (conducting an experiment in real-world environments) often reduce the internal validity of the experiment. In either case, decision makers must be informed of the potential presence of extraneous variables and their effects on internal validity, as well as the degree to which the results from the experiment can be generalized to other situations and contexts.

QUESTIONS FOR DISCUSSION

1. Describe the relationship between an independent variable, a dependent variable, and an extraneous variable.

2. What are some of the major techniques researchers can use to control for extraneous variables?

3. Compare and contrast basic and factorial designs.

4. Compare and contrast internal and external validity.

5. What are some of the major threats to the internal validity of an experiment?

6. Discuss blind and double-blind experiments in terms of their internal validity and external validity.

7. What are some of the important factors that marketing researchers should consider when selecting test market cities?

8. Would New York City be a good test market city for testing a new laundry detergent to be sold in grocery stores? Why? Why not?

9. Would the city in which you live be a good test market city? Why? Why not?

10. GE has developed a new heavy-duty kitchen mixer. Should this new product be test marketed?

11. Mama Cataloni (a manufacturer of Italian foods) has developed a new line of shelf-stable pasta salads that do not need to be refrigerated. Should these new products be test marketed?

12. What is the difference between a quasi-experimental design and a true experimental design?

13. What are some of the issues associated with experimental design that can have an effect on the managerial decision-making process?

MINICASE 18.1

Palo Valley Wines

Palo Valley Wines is located in Sacramento, California and has developed three new flavors of wines (peach, apple, and citrus). They have hired your marketing research firm to conduct some taste tests to determine which of the three flavors consumers prefer the most. They would like a total of 600 consumers to participate in the taste test. They have determined that to adequately evaluate a wine flavor, a consumer must drink at least four ounces of the wine. All subjects will be paid $20 for participating. Design this taste testing experiment and be specific about what subjects will do and when they will do it. Identify the following components of this experiment:

1. Independent variable.

2. Dependent variable.

3. Is this a basic or factorial experiment?

4. Is this a lab or field experiment?

5. Number of treatments.

6. Test units.

7. Where should they conduct their taste tests?

8. How should they recruit (sample) the subjects?

9. What should they ask subjects?

10. When should they ask these questions?

11. How should they conduct their taste testing experiment (what will the subjects do)?

SharpCraft Bass Boats

SharpCraft manufacturers and markets their own brand of bass boats. Paul Lemoni, the marketing manager for SharpCraft, recently aired a new advertisement campaign that was shown during a weekend morning hunting and fishing television show. He wanted to test the effectiveness of the television advertisements on increasing consumers' awareness of SharpCraft bass boats. So, he hired a marketing research firm to randomly call local residents to measure their awareness of SharpCraft bass boats. After the first week of the advertisement campaign they randomly called 500 consumers. They first asked whether or not the consumer had seen the hunting and fishing show (whether or not they were exposed to the advertisement). They then asked consumers to list all brands of bass boats that they could think of. Below are the results:

	Percent Mentioning SharpCraft Bass Boats
Saw the TV show (exposed to ads)	84%
Did not see the TV show (not exposed to ads)	12%

Paul Lemoni concluded that the ads were very effective in creating awareness for Sharp-Craft bass boats. He reasons this because the vast majority of people who saw the TV show, and were thus exposed to the advertisement, mentioned SharpCraft bass boats. However, very few of the people who did not see the TV show, and were thus not exposed to the advertisement, mentioned SharpCraft bass boats.

1. If you were consulting with Paul Lemoni about his marketing research efforts, what would you tell him?

2. What are some possible differences in these two groups that might also explain the difference in the percent of consumers mentioning the SharpCraft brand of bass boat?

ENDNOTES

1. B. Sternthal, A. M. Tybout, and B. J. Calder, "Experimental Design: Generalization and Theoretical Explanation," in R. P. Bagozzi (ed.), *Principles of Marketing Research* (New York: Basil Blackwell, 1994), 195–220; see also A. G. Sawyer, P. M. Worthing, and P. E. Sendak, "The Role of Laboratory Experiments to Test Marketing Strategies," *Journal of Marketing* 43 (1979): 60–67.

2. Vernon Ellingstad and Norman W. Heinstra, *Methods in the Study of Human Behavior* (Monterrey, CA: Brooks/Cole, 1974); see also, M. Venkatesan and Robert J. Holloway, *An Introduction to Marketing Experimentation: Methods, Applications and Problems* (New York: Free Press, 1971).

3. Barry F. Anderson, *The Psychological Experiment: An Introduction to the Scientific Method* (Belmont, CA: Brooks/Cole, 1971).

4 B. J. Winer, *Statistical Principles in Experimental Design*, 2nd ed. (New York: McGraw-Hill, 1971).

5 D. T. Campbell and J. C. Stanley, *Experimental and Quasi-Experimental Designs for Research* (Chicago: Rand McNally, 1966).

6 Seymour Banks, *Experimentation in Marketing* (New York: McGraw-Hill, 1965).

7 Campbell and Stanley, *Experimental and Quasi-Experimental Designs for Research* (Chicago: Rand McNally, 1966); see also Thomas D. Cook and Donald T. Campbell, *Quasi-Experimentation: Design and Analysis Issues for Field Settings* (Boston: Houghton Mifflin, 1979).

Preparing and Analyzing Data

LEARNING OBJECTIVES

1 Describe the major steps involved in analyzing survey data.

2 Describe the importance of a coding sheet when entering and analyzing survey data.

3 Discuss the importance of descriptive and unique variable names when entering and analyzing survey data.

4 Describe the process for analyzing the results from open-ended survey questions.

5 Describe the process for identifying coding categories for open-ended survey responses.

6 Describe how word clouds can be used to identify potential categories for coding open-ended responses.

7 Describe the difference between null and alternative hypotheses as it relates to statistical hypothesis testing.

8 Explain what is meant by the *p* value of a statistical test.

9 Discuss the interpretation of *p* values and random sampling error, as opposed to systematic error or bias.

After a survey or other research project has been administered and all responses have been recorded, the data must be converted into a data file to be analyzed. The steps involved in data analysis are listed below:

1. Develop the coding sheet, or code book, for entering the data.

2. Enter the data into a data file spreadsheet or directly into a statistical analysis software package.

3. Convert the data file spreadsheet into a form that can be analyzed by a statistical software package, such as SAS or SPSS.

4. Perform the appropriate statistical analyses.

DEVELOPING THE CODING SHEET

Before any data can be entered and analyzed, researchers must develop a coding sheet. The **coding sheet**, sometimes called a **code book**, identifies the variable name for each survey question and also identifies the scale values that represent each of the possible answers to each question. The coding sheet tells researchers what to enter into the data file spreadsheet to represent each of the possible responses to the survey questions and where to enter it. It also tells researchers which survey question corresponds to a variable name when reading the output from a statistical analysis program. Coding sheets are especially important when surveys are being entered by more than one person. All surveys must be entered the exact same way for the results to have any meaning at all. To illustrate a coding sheet, consider the credit card survey shown below.

1. Do you currently have at least one credit card in your name?   ☐ Yes   ☐ No

2. I have at least one of the following credit cards (check all that apply):

    ☐ Visa   ☐ Department Store Card

    ☐ MasterCard   ☐ Gas Company Card

    ☐ American Express   ☐ Other _____

3. How many bank credit cards (Visa or MasterCard) do you currently have? Write in the number of cards. If none, write in zero. _____ cards.

4. Within the last year, how many months did you have an outstanding balance on your credit card, meaning that you did not pay the full balance at the end of the month? If none, write in zero. _____ months.

5. What do you typically purchase using your credit card? (Check all that apply.)

    ☐ Clothing   ☐ Food/drinks at restaurants, bars, etc.

    ☐ Music (CDs, etc.)   ☐ Gas for your car

    ☐ Groceries   ☐ Other _____

6. Today, what is the approximate amount of your outstanding balance (the amount you will still owe after you pay your monthly payment) on all of your credit cards combined? Write in the dollar amount. If you do not have an outstanding balance, write in zero. $ _____

7. What is your sex?   ☐ Male   ☐ Female

8. What is your age (in years)? I am _____ years old.

9. What is your approximate personal annual income? $_____

10. What is your student classification?   ☐ Freshman   ☐ Sophomore
    ☐ Junior   ☐ Senior   ☐ Grad Student

CODING SHEET FOR CREDIT CARD SURVEY

The coding sheet in Figure 19.1 shows the variable name for each survey question and the codes (or scale values) that correspond to each of the possible answers to the survey question.

FIGURE 19.1 Credit Card Survey Coding Sheet

Question Number	Survey Question	Column in Data File	Variable Name	Coded Scale Values (for all questions, enter a period if the question is left blank.)
1	Do you currently have at least one credit card in your name?	1	Name	1 = Yes 2 = No
2	I have at least one of the following credit cards:	2	Visa	1 = Checked 0 = Not checked
		3	Master	1 = Checked 0 = Not checked
		4	American	1 = Checked 0 = Not checked
		5	Department	1 = Checked 0 = Not checked
		6	Gas	1 = Checked 0 = Not checked
		7	Cardother	1 = Checked 0 = Not checked
3	How many bank credit cards do you currently have?	8	Bank	Enter the number
4	Within the last year, how many months did you have an outstanding balance on your credit card?	9	Outstanding	Enter the number
5	What do you typically purchase using your credit card?	10	Clothing	1 = Checked 0 = Not checked
		11	Music	1 = Checked 0 = Not checked
		12	Groceries	1 = Checked 0 = Not checked
		13	Food	1 = Checked 0 = Not checked
		14	Gas	1 = Checked 0 = Not checked
		15	Buyother	1 = Checked 0 = Not checked
6	Today, what is the approximate amount of your outstanding balance?	16	Balance	Enter the number
7	What is your sex?	17	Sex	1 = Male 2 = Female
8	What is your age?	18	Age	Enter the number
9	What is your approximate personal annual income?	19	Income	Enter the number
10	What is your student classification?	20	Class	1 = Freshman 2 = Sophomore 3 = Junior 4 = Senior 5 = Grad Student

ENTERING DATA INTO A DATA FILE

Before any statistical analysis can be performed on a set of data, it must be entered into a data file in a form that is usable by a statistical analysis software program. Conducting a telephone survey using CATI-based software makes this data entry and data file conversion process especially easy. When telephone interviewers enter a number on the computer to indicate a respondent's answer to a survey question, that data is automatically entered into the data file. It is then a simple matter of exporting the data from the CATI data file into a form that can be analyzed by a statistical program. Similarly, the data entry process is especially easy and automatic when conducting online surveys. When respondents enter their response to an online survey question by checking a button, or they type in either words or numbers to answer a survey question, these responses are automatically entered into the data file. For CATI-based surveys and online surveys the questioning and data entry stages of a survey are essentially combined and completed at the same time. In either case, all that needs to be done for online surveys and CATI-based interviews is to export the data file for analysis.

However, for paper and pencil surveys, such as self-administered surveys, mail surveys, and personal intercept interviews, respondents' answers to the survey questions must be entered manually into a data file or manually entered directly into a statistical analysis software program such as SAS or SPSS.[1] In most cases, the easiest way to enter data that can be exported and used by most statistical analysis programs is to enter the data into a Microsoft Excel spreadsheet. There are a number of guidelines that researchers can follow when developing coding sheets for a survey and when entering survey data into a spreadsheet.

Descriptive Variable Names. Variable names should be as descriptive as possible. To avoid confusion and frustration avoid naming the variables for survey questions based on their question number, for example, *var1*, *var2*, *var3*, and so on. While simply numbering the variables might seem like an efficient and useful coding scheme, it will make interpreting the results from a statistical analysis software program very difficult. Statistical analysis programs can report results about variables only in the form in which they were entered. Perhaps the best way to name a variable is to use a unique or identifying word (or some form of a unique or identifying word) that appears in the question. For example, if the survey question is, "How many bank credit cards do you currently have?" a unique and identifying word in this question is *bank*. As such, the variable could be named *bank*.

> The coding sheet tells a researcher the variable name that corresponds to each survey question, what to enter to represent a respondent's answer to a survey question, and where to enter it in the data file.

To illustrate the importance and usefulness of using descriptive variable names, consider the two outputs in Tables 19.1 and 19.2 for calculating the means for the two variables *bank* and *outstanding* from the credit card survey shown previously. Notice that if the variables were simply named *var1* and *var2* (nondescriptive), the researcher must refer back to the survey and coding sheet to determine the questions to which these results refer. However, using the more descriptive variable names, *bank* and *outstanding*, makes interpreting the output from a statistical analysis much easier. The researcher knows immediately the survey questions to which these results refer.

TABLE 19.1 Output Using Nondescriptive Variable Names

Variable	N	Mean	Std Dev	Minimum	Maximum
var1	10	1.4000000	0.5163978	1.0000000	2.0000000
var2	10	14.7000000	10.1985838	3.0000000	36.0000000

TABLE 19.2 Output Using Descriptive Variable Names

Variable	N	Mean	Std Dev	Minimum	Maximum
Bank	10	1.4000000	0.5163978	1.0000000	2.0000000
Outstanding	10	14.7000000	10.1985838	3.0000000	36.0000000

Notice also that variable names do not need to be complete or proper words. Variable names merely need to be descriptive enough (contain enough information) to allow researchers to identify the survey question to which they refer. In fact, some statistical analysis programs limit the number of characters that can be used to name a variable.

Unique Variable Names. A variable name cannot be used more than once in the same coding sheet or data entry spreadsheet. For example, if multiple questions on a survey each have an *other* category, each of these *other* categories must be identified as different variable names. Notice in the coding sheet for the credit card survey that the *other* category for the second survey question ("I have at least one of the following credit cards") is named *cardother*, whereas the *other* category for the fifth survey question ("What do you typically purchase using your credit card?") is named *buyother*.

Missing Data. Unfortunately, there will often be missing data for any survey research project. Sometimes respondents will choose to skip a question. Sometimes they will accidentally skip over a question. In either case there will be missing data for a survey question from that respondent. The easiest way to indicate missing data is to enter a period (".") in the cell to indicate that a question was not answered.

As another example of how coding sheets are used for entering survey data, consider the following survey questions taken from a car owner survey:

1. Do you own a car?   ☐ Yes   ☐ No

2. Did you take out a loan to purchase your current car?   ☐ Yes   ☐ No

3. Do you think that you will buy a car within the next year?

    ☐ Yes,   probably a new car

    ☐ Yes,   probably a used car

    ☐ No,   I will not buy a car within the next year

4. How many cars have you ever owned (including your current car)? _____

5. If you had to choose, what is more important to you in purchasing a car?

☐ The quality of the car

☐ Where the car is made (Japan, United States, etc.)

6. Indicate your level of agreement with each of the following statements

(1 = Strongly Disagree and 5 = Strongly Agree).

	SD	D	N	A	SA
A car is something to be used.	1	2	3	4	5
A person should get a new car every 2–3 years.	1	2	3	4	5
The style of a car should reflect a person's personality.	1	2	3	4	5
It is perfectly acceptable to borrow money to buy a car.	1	2	3	4	5

7. What is your sex? ☐ Male ☐ Female

8. What is your age (in years)? _____

The coding sheet for entering respondents' answers to these survey questions is shown in Figure 19.2.

FIGURE 19.2 Coding Sheet for Car Owner Survey

Question Number	Survey Question	Column in Data File	Variable Name	Coded Scale Values (for all questions, enter a period if the question is left blank)
1	Do you own a car?	A	Own	1 = Yes 2 = No
2	Did you take out a loan to purchase your current car?	B	Loan	1 = Yes 2 = No
3	Do you think that you will buy a car within the next year?	C	Buy	1 = Yes, a new car 2 = Yes, a used car 3 = No
4	How many cars have you ever owned?	D	Ever	Enter the number
5	If you had to choose, what is more important to you in purchasing a car?	E	Important	1 = Quality of car 2 = Where car made
6	A car is something to be used.	F	Used	Enter the number circled from 1 to 5
6	A person should get a new car every 2–3 years.	G	Get	Enter the number circled from 1 to 5
6	The style of a car should reflect a person's personality.	H	Style	Enter the number circled from 1 to 5
6	It is perfectly acceptable to borrow money to buy a car.	I	Borrow	Enter the number circled from 1 to 5
7	What is your sex?	J	Sex	1 = Male 2 = Female
8	What is your age?	K	Age	Enter the number

The first 10 respondents' answers to these survey questions could be easily entered into an Excel spreadsheet as shown in Figure 19.3. Each respondent's data is entered on a separate row. Missing data is indicated by a period. The fourth respondent did not answer the question, "A car is something to be used" (variable name = *used*), and the eighth respondent did not report her age (variable name = *age*).

FIGURE 19.3 Excel Spreadsheet for Entering Responses to the Car Owner Survey

	A	B	C	D	E	F	G	H	I	J	K
1	*Own*	*Loan*	*Buy*	*Ever*	*Important*	*Used*	*Get*	*Style*	*Borrow*	*Sex*	*Age*
2	1	1	1	1	1	4	5	4	5	1	21
3	2	2	1	3	2	3	3	4	2	2	23
4	2	2	3	6	2	2	2	3	1	2	42
5	1	1	3	2	1	.	4	5	5	1	30
6	1	1	2	3	1	5	3	3	4	1	32
7	1	2	2	1	1	2	4	4	2	1	20
8	1	2	2	1	1	1	4	4	2	2	19
9	2	1	1	2	1	2	3	3	5	2	.
10	2	1	3	4	2	4	4	4	4	2	28
11	1	1	3	3	1	4	2	3	4	1	32

ENTERING DATA INTO MICROSOFT EXCEL

It is very easy to enter survey data into a Microsoft Excel spreadsheet. The Excel spreadsheet below shows the data from 10 respondents' answers to the car owner survey discussed previously in this chapter. Notice that inserting a comment for a variable name can help to reduce data entry error. When the cursor is placed over a cell containing the variable name for which a comment has been added, the comment box appears showing the coding scheme for that survey question.

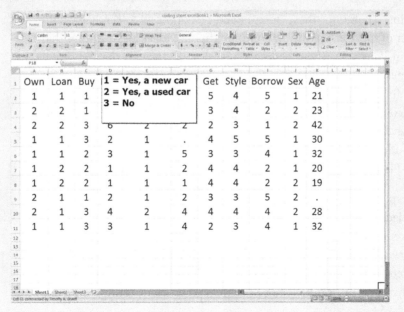

CODING OPEN-ENDED SURVEY QUESTIONS

Coding and entering responses to closed-ended survey questions is a relatively straightforward and easy process. However, coding and entering responses to open-ended survey questions is often less straightforward. Sometimes, marketing managers and decision makers want to be able to read all open-ended responses. As such, all responses must be entered verbatim into a data file and then presented in the research report. This allows them to review all answers that were provided by respondents. However, for large samples this creates a great deal of data that often becomes redundant and unnecessary. In most cases, researchers will identify categories into which the open-ended responses can be coded. When entering an open-ended response, a researcher reads the response, determines which category the response best fits into, and then codes the response as belonging to that category in the data file.

To illustrate this, consider the following open-ended survey question and nine responses to this question.

Survey Question: Why do you shop at Harvey's Market?

Respondents' open-ended responses:

1. I like the vegetables.
2. They have what I like.
3. Weekly specials and sales.
4. Closest store to my house.
5. Meats are fresh and not too fatty.
6. If they don't have something, they will get it for me.
7. Best deals in town.
8. They will cut a large piece of meat into a smaller piece if I ask them to.
9. It's a store.

To develop the coding scheme for these open-ended responses, a researcher would first review a number of surveys looking for common themes, ideas, or meanings that appear in respondents' answers. Then, coding categories are formed that represent these common themes, ideas, or meanings. For example, the first, second, and fifth responses each refer to the selection and quality of the merchandise sold at the market. These could then be combined into a separate coding category named "Selection/Quality." The third and seventh responses refer to weekly specials and low prices, respectively. These could both be combined into a separate category named "Low Price." The categories shown in Figure 19.4 could be formed based on these nine responses.

The open-ended responses would then be coded into the data file as shown in Figure 19.5. The coded scale value shown in the right column would be entered into the spreadsheet to represent that respondent's answer to the open-ended question. Notice also that there will almost always need to be an *other* category. Some respondents will give answers that simply do not relate to anything meaningful and, as such, can only be coded as *other*. This is usually not a problem when interpreting the results

FIGURE 19.4 Open-Ended Coding Categories for the Harvey's Market Survey Question

Category	Code as
Selection/Quality	1
Low Price	2
Convenience	3
People/Service	4
Other	99

FIGURE 19.5 Coding Individual Open-Ended Responses to the Harvey's Market Survey Question

Coding Category	Survey Response	Coded Scale Value
Selection/Quality	I like the vegetables.	1
	They have what I like.	1
	Meats are fresh and not too fatty.	1
Low Price	Weekly specials and sales.	2
	Best deals in town.	2
Convenience	Closest store to my house.	3
People/Service	If they don't have something, they will get it for me.	4
	They will cut a large piece of meat into a smaller piece if I ask them to.	4
Other	It's a store.	99

form surveys as long as the percent of responses coded as *other* is not too large. If more than 20 percent of responses are coded as *other*, the researcher should seek to identify meaningful categories into which at least some of the comments can be coded.

The *other* category is often coded as 99. This leaves room for numbering additional categories that become evident after the coding scheme is developed and the data entry phase has begun. If a new category is seen as important and meaningful, researchers can simply name that category, assign it a code value, and then begin assigning that code value to any additional responses that fit that category.

DEVELOPING OPEN-ENDED CODING SCHEMES AND CATEGORIES

How are coding schemes for open-ended survey questions developed? There are two approaches that researchers can use when developing coding schemes for open-ended questions. The coding schemes and categories can be either predetermined or they can be data-driven.

Predetermined Coding Schemes. Coding schemes for open-ended survey questions can be predetermined prior to beginning the data entry phase of a research project. If researchers know that they are looking for certain types, or categories, of answers to the survey questions, they can use these categories for coding the open-ended responses. If there are certain types of decisions that marketing managers know they will be able to make, or particular actions they know are feasible, they can try to fit the open-ended responses into these categories. For example, if marketing managers have asked for research to identify potential changes to their distribution strategy, researchers can form a coding scheme based on issues related to channels of distribution. However, some researchers are critical of this approach to coding open-ended survey responses. It can give the appearance of forcing the data into what the researcher expected to find, or what the researcher wanted to find, instead of letting the coding scheme emerge from the data as an unbiased representation of the types of comments made by respondents.

Data Driven Coding Schemes. In most cases, researchers will allow the coding categories to be suggested by the data, or to emerge from the data. This is accomplished by examining a subset of the survey responses prior to data entry. Look for the themes, words, elements, or ideas that are common to respondents' answers. Based on these common themes, elements, or ideas, identify a coding category that seems to capture the core meanings of respondents' answers.

Multilabel Codes for Open-Ended Responses. It is often difficult, if not impossible, to code all answers into categories that are each represented by a single word or idea. Sometimes a coding category will include two or more related ideas or concepts. For example, the coding scheme for the Harvey's Market survey above includes the category *people/service*. This category contains comments related to the employees at Harvey's Market, how employees interact with customers, and the services provided by the market.

Develop the coding scheme for entering responses to open-ended survey questions by looking for the common themes, or ideas, that are present in the responses.

Word Clouds for Identifying Categories for Open-Ended Responses. A **word cloud** is a compilation of words representing their frequency of use in the text of a document. A word cloud displays words in an artistic form with words appearing horizontally and/or vertically. Words that are presented in larger and bolder font appear more often in the text, whereas words that appear less often are represented in smaller font, or not at all, because word clouds typically allow the creator to identify words to exclude (e.g., *the, is, an, for*) and limit the number of words to display. A word cloud displaying the most frequently used words in this chapter is displayed in Figure 19.6. This word cloud was created using **www.Tagcrowd.com**.

Word clouds allow for a quick and easy way to display and visualize the results from an open-ended survey question, the verbatim responses from a focus group, or the content of online postings. When analyzing open-ended comments, a word cloud can be used to identify potential category labels representing different ideas, themes, concepts, or topics based on the words that appear most frequently in

FIGURE 19.6 A Word Cloud Showing the Most Frequently Used Words in this Chapter

responses. Then, individual comments can be placed into the separate categories by assigning each a numeric code signifying the category of comment to which it belongs. In this way, open-ended comments can be quantified by examining the number of comments in each category and even relating this to other variables being measured.

However, word clouds are not without their limitations. Word clouds analyze content based on only the frequency of word use. Word clouds do not provide guidance as to the analysis and interpretation of the meaning and intent behind responses to complex topics and issues. For example, the word *bad* might appear prominently in a word cloud; however, this could result from both positive and negative uses of the word, for example, "this product is not bad" and "this is a bad product." Word clouds do not provide insight into the context within which the words are used.

One simple solution to the problem of context is to first sort comments into those that are positive and those that are negative. Then, a word cloud can be created for each set of responses. This will provide at least a sense for the number of times a word such as bad is used to convey a positive evaluation and the number of times it is used to convey a negative evaluation.

Another limitation is that consumers often use varying words or phrases to refer to the same thing. For example, consider the multiple ways in which consumers might refer to a product being too expensive as the reason why they did not purchase it:

- The price was too high.
- They were asking too much for it.
- They wanted too much for it.
- I did not want to spend that much.
- I could not go that high.
- It was not in my budget.

Notice that the word price appears in only one of these comments. As such, the word price might not appear prominently in a word cloud based on only word frequency.

REPORTING OPEN-ENDED RESPONSES IN THE RESEARCH REPORT

When the coded categories for open-ended responses are reported in a research report, it is often helpful to provide examples of the comments that were coded into a category. Decision makers often want to know the specific types of comments that make up a category. For the Harvey's Market survey, decision makers will probably want to know what is meant by *selection/quality*. This can mean different things to different people, so providing specific examples of verbatim comments from respondents helps to provide meaning to the data and the results. Citing specific examples of open-ended comments also helps to convey the tone of respondents' answers and their feelings when answering the survey. Further, the process by which the coding categories were derived should also be reported, that is, either predetermined or data-driven.

ANALYZING QUANTITATIVE DATA

Marketing researchers can use a variety of statistical techniques for analyzing quantitative data. Researchers can perform univariate, bivariate, and multivariate statistical analyses. **Univariate statistical procedures** refer to a class of statistical techniques for analyzing a single variable. **Bivariate statistical procedures** refer to a class of statistical techniques for analyzing two variables. **Multivariate statistical procedures** refer to a class of statistical techniques for analyzing multiple variables (three or more).

Univariate Statistics. When a researcher examines a single variable by itself, this is referred to as a univariate statistic. When working with a single categorical variable measured by a nominal scale or an ordinal scale, the most often performed statistical tests are a **confidence interval for a proportion** and a **hypothesis test of a proportion**. When working with a single continuous variable measured by an interval scale or a ratio scale, the most often performed statistical tests are a **confidence interval for an average** and a **hypothesis test of an average**.

Bivariate Statistics. When researchers examine two variables concurrently to test for a relationship between the two variables or to test for a difference between the two variables, this is referred to as bivariate statistical analysis. The choice of the appropriate statistical procedure for analyzing marketing research data is a function of the type of question to be answered (the stated research objective) and the level of scale (nominal, ordinal, interval, ratio) that was used to measure the data. Nominal and ordinal scales yield **categorical data** that is often referred to as **nonmetric data**. Interval and ratio scales yield **continuous data** that is often referred to as **metric data**. Figure 19.7 shows the most common bivariate statistical analyses based on the level of data for the variables.

FIGURE 19.7 Bivariate Statistical Analyses

Independent Variable	Dependent Variable	Bivariate Analysis
Categorical	Categorical	Cross-Tab, Chi-square (χ^2)
Categorical	Continuous	One-Way ANOVA
Continuous	Continuous	Correlation, Bivariate Regression

FIGURE 19.8 Multivariate Statistical Analyses

Independent Variables	Dependent Variable	Multivariate Analysis
Continuous, Continuous	Continuous	Multiple Regression
Continuous, Categorical	Continuous	Multiple Regression
Categorical, Categorical	Continuous	Two-Way ANOVA

Multivariate Statistics. When researchers examine the relationships between three or more variables concurrently, this is referred to as multivariate statistical analysis. Figure 19.8 shows the most common multivariate statistical analyses based on the level of data for the variables.

Statistical Hypothesis Testing

Most statistical analyses rely on **statistical hypothesis testing** as a method for determining if a statistical result is significant or not. There are two hypotheses that are compared for every statistical test. The **null hypothesis** (denoted as Ho) usually states that a statistical result is not significant, that there is no relationship between the variables being tested, or that there is no difference between the variables being tested. To illustrate, if a researcher wanted to test whether or not men and women have differing attitudes toward a brand, the null hypothesis would state that men's and women's attitudes toward the brand do not differ. The **alternative hypothesis** (denoted as Ha) usually states that a statistical result is significant, that there is a significant relationship between the variables being tested, or that there is a difference between the variables being tested. In the case of men's and women's attitudes toward a brand, the alternative hypothesis would state that there is a difference in men's and women's attitudes toward the brand.

P Values

How do researchers decide whether to accept the null hypothesis or accept the alternative hypothesis? For most statistical analyses researchers base their statistical decisions on *p* values. To understand the meaning of a *p* value, one needs to understand that there are two possible explanations for observed results, or calculated statistics in inferential statistics, such as a χ^2 value, F value, or correlation coefficient.

1. The observed difference between the Ho and the Ha is due to random sampling error, in which case we have no reason to reject the Ho (so we accept the Ho).

2. The observed difference between the Ho and the Ha is because Ho is false, and there is a real difference between Ho and Ha.

The p value for a statistical test indicates the probability that the observed result or calculated statistic is due to random sampling error. With respect to the hypotheses, the p value indicates the probability that the difference between the Ho and the Ha is due to random sampling error. As a general rule, if there is greater than 5 percent probability (p value > .05) that the test statistic could be due to random sampling error, we accept the null hypothesis Ho. In this case, we do not have enough evidence to reject Ho. However, if there is less than 5 percent probability that the test statistic could be due to random sampling error (e.g., p value < .05), we reject the null hypothesis Ho, and accept the alternative hypothesis Ha. In this case, we have sufficient evidence to reject Ho.

Put another way, the p value of a statistical test indicates the probability of finding a test statistic this large, if the Ho is true. Small p values (e.g., p < .05) indicate that there is a very small probability of finding a test statistic this large, if the Ho is true. Therefore, a small p value tells a researcher that they observed something that is very unlikely, if the Ho is true. To illustrate, Figure 19.9 presents p values and their interpretations for various test statistics.

As previously mentioned, the p value of a statistical test indicates the probability of finding a test statistic this large, if the null hypothesis is true. As such, the p value indicates the amount of evidence against the null hypothesis. The amount of evidence against the null hypothesis for various p values is summarized in Figure 19.10.

P Values and Error. Researchers must recognize that p values indicate the probability that an observed result or calculated test statistic is due only to random sampling error. A p value does not account for systematic error or bias that cannot be statistically estimated, such as response bias, nonresponse error, sample bias, or any bias due to question wording. Therefore, researchers must always consider the statistical significance of results within the context of the methodology that was used to generate the data from which the results were calculated. Results that have very high statistical significance (i.e., very low p values) can still contain many other types of error or bias associated with the way the survey was written, the way the data was collected, and even the way the sample was selected.

FIGURE 19.9 Interpreting P Values

Statistical Test	Test Statistic Value	P Value	Decision	Interpretation
Chi-Square	$\chi^2_1 = 6.7$	$p = .01$	Reject Ho	There is only 1 percent probability that a chi-square value this large would occur due to random sampling error. There is only 1 percent probability of finding a chi-square value this large, if the Ho is true. Therefore, since we found something that we were not likely to find if the Ho were true, we reject the Ho.
ANOVA	$F_{1,7} = .13$	$p = .733$	Accept Ho	There is 73.3 percent probability that an F value this large would occur due to random sampling error. There is 73.3 percent probability of finding an F statistic this large, if the Ho is true. Therefore, since we found something that we were likely to find if the Ho were true, we accept the Ho (we have no evidence to reject the Ho).
Correlation	$r = .43$ ($n = 91$)	$p = .0001$	Reject Ho	There is only .01 percent probability that a correlation coefficient this large would occur due to random sampling error. There is only .01 percent probability of finding a correlation coefficient this large, if the Ho is true. Therefore, since we found something that we were very unlikely to find if the Ho were true, we reject the Ho.
Correlation	$r = .059$ ($n = 91$)	$p = .57$	Accept Ho	There is 57 percent probability that a correlation coefficient this large would occur due to random sampling error. There is 57 percent probability of finding a correlation coefficient this large, if the Ho is true. Therefore, since we found something that we were likely to find if the Ho were true, we accept the Ho (we have no evidence to reject the Ho).

FIGURE 19.10 P Values and the Strength of Evidence against the Ho

P Value	Interpretation
$p < .01$	Extremely small probability of finding a test statistic this large, if the Ho is true. Very strong evidence against the Ho.
$.01 \leq p \leq .05$	Very small probability of finding a test statistic this large, if the Ho is true. Strong evidence against the Ho.
$.05 \leq p \leq .10$	Moderate probability of finding a test statistic this large, if the Ho is true. Moderate evidence against the Ho.
$p \geq .10$	Relatively large probability of finding a test statistic this large, if the Ho is true. Little, if any, evidence against the Ho.

NOTE-TAKING SURVEY

A group of students at a large university recently decided to conduct some marketing research to measure potential demand for a note-taking service on their campus. The business would provide a way for students who missed a class to purchase the class notes for the day(s) they were absent. The following survey was designed to measure potential demand for this note-taking service at their university. The results from this survey will be used to illustrate the various statistical tests described in the remaining chapters of this book.

1. How many classes do you miss (due to illness, other priorities, work, etc.) during a typical semester? _____

2. Have you ever borrowed notes from another student when you missed a class?   □ Yes   □ No

3. For those classes that you miss, how many times (where one "time" is for each class, each day) do you borrow notes from another student during a typical semester? _____

4. Do you think that having good (clear, complete) notes is an important part of getting a good grade in a class?   □ Yes   □ No

5. Would you be willing to buy notes from a note-taking service?   □ Yes   □ No

6. How likely would you be to buy notes from a note-taking service?

    Not Likely   1   2   3   4   5   6   7   Very Likely

7. How much would you be willing to pay for one page of notes?

    □ $0   □ $.01–$.24   □ $.25–$.49   □ $.50–$.74   □ $.75–$.99
    □ $1.00 or more

8. What year are you in school?   □ Freshman   □ Sophomore   □ Junior   □ Senior

9. Including this year, how many years have you been in college (taking classes at a university)? _____

10. In which college is your major?   □ Business   □ Liberal Arts

    □ Basic & Applied Science   □ Mass Communications
    □ Education

11. How comfortable would you be buying notes from a note-taking service?

    Very Uncomfortable   1   2   3   4   5   6   7   Very Comfortable

12. How ethical do you think a note-taking service is at a university?

    Very Unethical   1   2   3   4   5   6   7   Very Ethical

13. What is your age? _____

14. What is your sex?   □ Male   □ Female

15. Are you a full-time or a part-time student?   □ Full-Time   □ Part-Time

16. Are you a member of either a fraternity or a sorority?   □ Yes   □ No

FIGURE 19.11 Coding Sheet for the Note-Taking Survey

Question Number	Survey Question	Column in the Data File	Variable Name	Coded Scale Values (for all questions, enter a period if the question is left blank)
1	How many classes do you miss (due to illness, other priorities, work, etc.) during a typical semester?	A	*Number*	Enter the number
2	Have you ever borrowed notes from another student when you missed a class?	B	*Ever*	1 = Yes 2 = No
3	For those classes that you miss, how many times (where one "time" is for each class, each day) do you borrow notes from another student during a typical semester?	C	*Howmany*	Enter the number
4	Do you think that having good (clear, complete) notes is an important part of getting a good grade in a class?	D	*Grade*	1 = Yes 2 = No
5	Would you be willing to buy notes from a note-taking service?	E	*Buy*	1 = Yes 2 = No
6	How likely would you be to buy notes from a note-taking service?	F	*Likely*	Enter the number circled from 1–7
7	How much would you be willing to pay for one page of notes?	G	*Pay*	1 = None 2 = $.01–$.24 3 = $.25–$.49 4 = $.50–$.74 5 = $.75–$.99 6 = $1.00 or more
8	What year are you in school?	H	*Year*	1 = Freshman 2 = Sophomore 3 = Junior 4 = Senior
9	Including this year, how many years have you been in college (taking classes at a university)?	I	*Numyears*	Enter the number
10	In which college is your major?	J	*Major*	1 = Business 2 = Basic & Applied 3 = Education 4 = Liberal Arts 5 = Mass Communication
11	How comfortable would you be buying notes from a note-taking service?	K	*Comfort*	Enter the number circled from 1–7
12	How ethical do you think a note-taking service is at a university?	L	*Ethical*	Enter the number circled from 1–7
13	What is your age?	M	*Age*	Enter the number
14	What is your sex?	N	*Sex*	1 = Male 2 = Female
15	Are you a full-time or a part-time student?	O	*Fullpart*	1 = Full-time 2 = Part-time
16	Are you a member of either a fraternity or a sorority?	P	*Frat*	1 = Yes 2 = No

QUESTIONS FOR DISCUSSION

1. What is a coding sheet, and why is it important to marketing researchers?

2. How can researchers develop coding categories for open-ended survey questions?

3. Why should variable names be descriptive and unique?

4. What is a word cloud and how can word clouds be used to develop categories for coding open-ended responses to surveys?

5. When would univariate statistical analysis be performed?

6. When would bivariate statistical analysis be performed?

7. When would multivariate statistical analysis be performed?

8. If the p value for a statistical test is 0.029, what is the probability of finding a test statistic this large, if the Ho is true?

9. What source of error is indicated by the p value of a statistical test?

10. What source(s) of error are not indicated by the p value of a statistical test?

11. If you wanted to examine the potential relationship between age and personal annual income, what analysis would be most appropriate: chi-square, correlation analysis, ANOVA, or regression?

12. To examine whether there is a statistical relationship between a person's sex (male or female) and whether or not they shop at a particular store (yes or no), what analysis would be most appropriate: chi-square, correlation analysis, ANOVA, or regression?

MINICASE 19.1

Mount Granite College Student Health Services

Dianne Rothman is the health services director at Mount Granite College. She recently attended a conference and was disturbed to learn that many college students do not engage in health care and health maintenance activities on a regular basis. One disturbing statistic that Dianne learned is that American college students exercise an average of only 4.5 hours per month. Dianne decided to conduct some marketing research to compare the amount of time that students at Mount Granite College exercise to this national average. An email was sent to 1,000 randomly selected students. In the email, students were asked to come to the Student Health Services office to participate in an interview about health and exercise. They were also told that five randomly selected participants would each receive a $25 grocery story gift card.

A total of 128 students agreed to participate and came to the Student Health Services office to complete the interview. The average number of hours that these students reported exercising per month was 12.2. Dianne performed a simple t-test to compare this average to the average number of hours that American college students exercise (4.5). The p value for the test comparing the two averages was $p < .001$. She asked a statistics professor to interpret the p value, and she was happy to hear that students at Mount Granite College actually exercise significantly more than the average for all American college students. In fact, Dianne is considering publishing this finding in upcoming marketing pieces to promote Mount Granite College.

What do you tell Dianne Rothman? Do you agree that students at Mount Granite College exercise significantly more than the rest of American college students? If she had asked you, how would you interpret the p value for the test comparing these two averages?

MINICASE 19.2

Pine Tree Mobile Homes

Pine Tree Mobile Homes has been in business for 10 years selling mobile homes of various sizes and price levels. Pine Tree Mobile Homes is located in a town with a population of 200,000 that includes a public university with an enrollment of 10,000 students. Billy Kendall, the owner of Pine Tree Mobile Homes, has recently been searching for new target markets and customers for mobile homes. He has noticed that many college students live off campus. So, he has been considering marketing mobile homes to college students. Billy has developed the following survey that he used for measuring various issues related to students' attitudes toward mobile homes. Even though you had no say in creating the survey, he would like your help with coding and entering the data.

Create a coding sheet for the Pine Tree Mobile Home survey. What variable name would you use for each question? What scale values would you use to represent the possible responses to the survey questions? Use the blank coding sheet that is provided.

1. Where do you currently live?
   - ☐ Apartment   ☐ With my parents
   - ☐ House   ☐ Mobile home
   - ☐ Dorm   ☐ Other _____

2. How much do you currently pay for rent (per month)? (If none, leave this question blank.)
   - ☐ Less than $100   ☐ $300–$399
   - ☐ $100–$199   ☐ $400–$499
   - ☐ $200–$299   ☐ $500 or more

3. How much is the maximum you would be willing to pay (could afford to pay) for monthly rent (housing)?
   - ☐ Less than $100   ☐ $300–$399
   - ☐ $100–$199   ☐ $400–$499
   - ☐ $200–$299   ☐ $500 or more

4. Where do you look for information about housing options? (Check all that apply.)
   - ☐ Newspaper   ☐ Roadside signs
   - ☐ Housing magazine   ☐ Online
   - ☐ Word of mouth   ☐ Other _____

5. Would your family approve of you living in a mobile home?   ☐ Yes   ☐ No

6. Would your friends approve of you living in a mobile home?   ☐ Yes   ☐ No

7. If you lived in a mobile home while you were a college student, would you want to move your mobile home after school, if you got a job in a different city?   ☐ Yes   ☐ No

8. Are you currently employed?   ☐ Yes   ☐ No

9. Which of the following would influence you to <u>not</u> purchase a mobile home? (Check all that apply.)
   ☐ Price   ☐ Neighbor quality
   ☐ Image   ☐ Campus accessibility
   ☐ Safety/security   ☐ Access to utilities, cable, etc.
   ☐ Size (square footage)   ☐ Stability/durability
   ☐ Other _____

10. What is your current annual (personal) income? $_____

Survey Coding Sheet

Question Number	Survey Question	Column in Data File	Variable Name	Coded Scale Values

ENDNOTE

1   SAS Institute Inc., Cary, NC, USA 27513. For more information about SAS and SAS/STAT statistical software, go to **www.sas.com**. SPSS, 233 Wacker Drive, 11th Floor, Chicago Illinois 60606. For more information about SPSS statistical software, go to **www.spss.com**.

Distributions and Statistics

LEARNING OBJECTIVES

1 Describe the three measures of central tendency: mode, median, and mean.

2 Describe what is meant by the dispersion of a distribution.

3 Describe a normal distribution.

4 Describe a standardized normal distribution.

5 Define and calculate a Z score.

6 Define, and then describe the relationship between the population distribution, the sample distribution, and the sampling distribution of the mean.

7 Explain the central limit theorem and its importance to marketing researchers when calculating estimates of population parameters.

8 Describe and explain how researchers use normal distributions to make managerial decisions based on probabilities.

Marketing research data must be analyzed after it has been collected. Researchers work with distributions of variables to perform statistical analysis of marketing research data. For example, if we measured the age of 400 consumers, these 400 ages would form a distribution of ages. Distributions are described in terms of their central tendency (the middle of the distribution) as well as their dispersion (how spread out the distribution is). Statistical procedures that compare two or more means do so by analyzing the means of the distributions as well as the dispersion of the distributions.

CENTRAL TENDENCY

Measures of central tendency indicate where the center (or middle) of a distribution is. The three most often used measures of central tendency are the **mode**, the **median**, and the **mean** (see Figure 20.1).

DISPERSION

Measures of dispersion indicate how spread out a distribution is. The **population variance** (σ^2), **sample variance** (s^2), **population standard deviation** (σ), and the **sample standard deviation** (s) are the most often used measures of a distribution's

FIGURE 20.1 Measures of Central Tendency

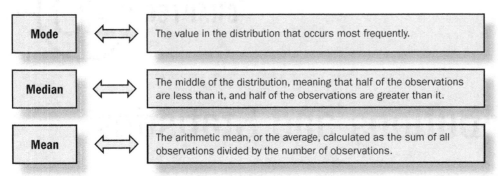

dispersion. Notice in the following formulas that $(n - 1)$ is used to calculate the sample variance and the sample standard deviation. By using $(n - 1)$, the expected value of the sample variance equals the population variance. If $(n - 1)$ were not used, the sample variance would underestimate the population variance. By using $(n - 1)$, the sample variance becomes an unbiased estimator of the population variance.

Population Distribution   **Sample Distribution**

$$\sigma^2 = \frac{\Sigma(x - \mu)^2}{n}$$ $$s^2 = \frac{\Sigma(x - \bar{x})^2}{n - 1}$$

$$\sigma = \sqrt{\frac{\Sigma(x - \mu)^2}{n}}$$ $$s = \sqrt{\frac{\Sigma(x - \bar{x})^2}{n - 1}}$$

STATISTICS AND DISTRIBUTIONS

A fundamental purpose of using statistics in business is to minimize the risk associated with managerial and marketing decisions. Before spending any money, managers want to know the probability that a decision (investment, project) will succeed or be profitable.

Probability of Success. To illustrate this, consider the case of RazorCorp, a company wishing to introduce a new razor into the market. Marketing managers at RazorCorp have determined that to be profitable at least 10 percent of the target market must be willing to purchase the razor. Imagine that RazorCorp interviews a sample of 500 people from their target market. If only 8 percent of those people interviewed reported that they would be willing to purchase the razor, should RazorCorp begin marketing the new razor? Even though the sample statistic is the best estimate (guess) of the true population parameter, the true population parameter might be slightly different than the calculated sample statistic. The question that RazorCorp must answer is, "Given that we calculated a sample statistic of 8 percent, what is the probability (chance) that the true population parameter could be as large as 10

Statistical inferences are based on normal distributions and the idea that observations that are similar to the mean should occur more frequently than observations that are less similar to the mean.

percent?" Marketing researchers can determine such probabilities by using the normal distribution and the standardized normal distribution.

THE NORMAL DISTRIBUTION

Probability and Distance from the Mean. The decisions that researchers make in performing statistical analyses are based upon the distributions of the variables being measured. A special type of distribution is the normal distribution. And, many naturally occurring distributions are approximately normally distributed. In a **normal distribution**, the probability of observing a particular value is a function of how many standard deviations that value is from the mean of its distribution. In other words, probabilities in a normal distribution can be determined by calculating how far a value is from the mean of its distribution. In normal distributions, probability is related to distance from the mean. If a variable is normally distributed, we expect to find values that are close to (similar to) the mean of the distribution more often than we expect to find values that are very different from the mean of the distribution. The probability of observing something one standard deviation from the mean of its normal distribution is greater than the probability of observing something three standard deviations from the mean of its normal distribution. Put another way, things that are similar to the norm should occur more frequently than things that are very different from the norm. Some important characteristics of a normal distribution are:

- A normal distribution is symmetrical about its mean.

- The mean of a normal distribution is its highest point.

- Approximately 68 percent of the observations in a normal distribution are within ±1 standard deviation (σ) of the mean.

- Approximately 95 percent of the observations in a normal distribution are within ±2 standard deviations (σ) of the mean.

- Approximately 99 percent of the observations in a normal distribution are within ±3 standard deviations (σ) of the mean.

Consider the example of a normal distribution of annual salaries for part-time musicians shown in Figure 20.2. The mean of this distribution (μ) = $22,000, and the standard deviation (σ) = $2,000. Notice that this is a normal distribution of annual salaries.

By working with a normal distribution we can answer questions concerning the probability of certain events occurring. For example, we can answer such questions as:

1. What is the probability of randomly choosing a part-time musician with an annual salary between $20,000 and $24,000?

2. What is the probability of randomly choosing a part-time musician with an annual salary greater than $26,000?

Many naturally occurring distributions are approximately normal.

FIGURE 20.2 Normal Distribution and Standardized Normal Distribution

A Normal Distribution of Annual Salaries (μ = $22,000; σ = $2,000)

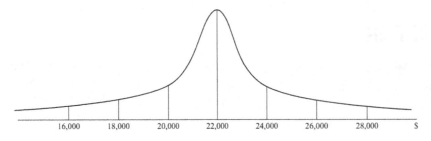

The Standardized Normal Distribution of Z Scores (μ = 0; σ = 1)

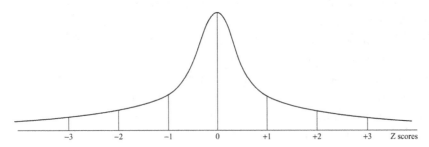

3. What is more likely, randomly choosing a part-time musician with an annual salary greater than $26,000, or randomly choosing a part-time musician with an annual salary greater than $28,000?

Because we work with a normal distribution, these questions can be answered by first calculating distances from the mean of the distribution. To answer question 1, first calculate how far (in number of standard deviations) $20,000 and $24,000 are from the mean. Since they are both one standard deviation from the mean ($20,000 is one standard deviation below the mean, and $24,000 is one standard deviation above the mean), we can estimate that there is a 68 percent chance of randomly selecting a part-time musician with an annual salary within this range. This is because approximately 68 percent of the observations in a normal distribution are within ±1 standard deviation (σ) of the mean.

To answer question 2, calculate how far $26,000 is from the mean. It is two standard deviations above the mean. Since approximately 95 percent of the observations in a normal distribution are within ±2 standard deviations (σ) of the mean, and a normal distribution is symmetrical about the mean, this means that there is a 2.5 percent chance of randomly selecting a part-time musician with an annual salary greater than $26,000. If 50 percent of the observations are above the mean (to the right of the mean), and 47.5 percent of the observations are between the mean and two standard deviations above the mean (half of 95 percent is 47.5 percent), this

> To standardize a variable, simply calculate the number of standard deviations that an observed value is from the mean of its distribution. A Z score is nothing more than a calculation to determine how many standard deviations a variable is from the mean of its distribution.

means that 2.5 percent of the observations are greater than two standard deviations above the mean.

Question 3 is also answered based on distance from the mean. Since $26,000 is closer to the mean than is $28,000, we are more likely to randomly select a part-time musician with an annual salary greater than $26,000.

THE STANDARDIZED NORMAL DISTRIBUTION

The distribution shown directly below the normal distribution of annual salaries in Figure 20.2 is a **standardized normal distribution**. It is not a distribution of annual salaries. Rather, it is a distribution of standardized values. The standardized normal distribution is formed by calculating the number of standard deviations each observation is from the mean. Since $20,000 is one standard deviation below the mean (less than the mean) its standardized value is −1. Similarly, since $26,000 is two standard deviations above the mean (greater than the mean) its standardized value is +2. These standardized values are usually referred to as **Z scores**. Thus, the Z score for $20,000 is −1, and the Z score for $26,000 is +2. A Z score is nothing more than a calculation of how many standard deviations an observation is from the mean of its distribution. A Z score is also referred to as a **standardized variable** because it is a measure of how many standard deviations a normal variable is from the mean of its distribution. In contrast, annual part-time salaries (the variable being measured) are referred to as **normal variables**. To estimate probabilities, first calculate a Z score because a Z score is the measure of how far an observation is from the mean of its distribution.

Calculating Z Scores. The formula for calculating a Z score is:

$$Z \text{ score} = (x - \mu)/\sigma$$

Notice that this formula calculates how many standard deviations (σ) an observation (x) is from the mean of its distribution (μ).

Some important characteristics of the standardized normal distribution are:

- A standardized normal distribution is symmetrical about its mean.

- The mean of a standardized normal distribution is its highest point.

- Approximately 68 percent of the observations in a standardized normal distribution are within ±1 standard deviation (σ) of the mean.

- Approximately 95 percent of the observations in a standardized normal distribution are within ±2 standard deviations (σ) of the mean.

- Approximately 99 percent of the observations in a standardized normal distribution are within ±3 standard deviations (σ) of the mean.

- The mean of a standardized normal distribution is 0 (the mean of a normal distribution is zero standard deviations from itself), and the standard deviation = 1.

- The area under the standardized normal distribution has a probability density function = 1.

This fact that the area under the standardized normal distribution has a **probability density function** = 1 allows researchers to calculate probabilities. For example, the area under 50 percent of the curve corresponds to 50 percent probability. And, the area under 95 percent of the curve corresponds to 95 percent probability. Thus, if we can standardize a normal variable to determine the number of standard deviations that a value is from the mean of its normal distribution (calculate a Z score), we can determine the probability of it occurring. The values that are close to the mean of the distribution should occur with a greater probability than those values that are farther away from the mean of the distribution. By standardizing we answer the question, "What is the probability of observing a certain value?" This enables us to answer managerial questions such as:

- What is the probability that monthly sales will be greater than $30,000?

- What is the probability that the percentage of our target market likely to buy our new product is greater than 20 percent?

The Z Table. The probability table for a standardized normal distribution is included in the appendix. It is usually referred to as the **Z table** because it is a table of probabilities associated with different Z scores. An advantage of using a standardized normal distribution is that it allows us to work with only one distribution, instead of many. Without the standardized normal distribution we would have to estimate probabilities by using a different probability table for every possible distribution. Imagine the infinite number of possible probability tables that would need to be created for every possible combination of means and standard deviations.

THE THREE DISTRIBUTIONS OF STATISTICAL INFERENCE

Statistical inference is the process of making inferences about population parameters based on the sample statistics that are calculated from a sample. To make valid inferences about population parameters researchers rely on three very important distributions: the population distribution, the sample distribution, and the sampling distribution of the mean (the distribution of sample means). The relationship between these three distributions is shown in Figure 20.3 (illustrated for estimating a mean).

The Population Distribution

The **population distribution** is the distribution of all elements (observations) in the population. For example, if researchers measured the age of every consumer in a target market, these ages would be distributed in the form of the population distribution.

FIGURE 20.3 The Three Distributions of Statistical Inference

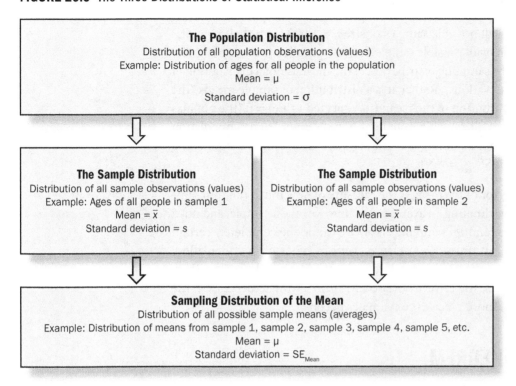

Recall that distributions are described by their central tendency (mean), as well as their dispersion (standard deviation). The population distribution is described by its mean = μ and standard deviation = σ.

The Sample Distribution

Researchers rarely know the characteristics of the population distribution. Because we are usually not able to take a census of every member of the population, we take a sample. For example, if 1,000 consumers are randomly sampled, the ages of these 1,000 consumers would be distributed in the form of the **sample distribution**. The sample distribution is described by its mean = $\overline{X}$ and standard deviation = S.

Because a random sample is only a subset of the entire population, the true population parameter is likely to be slightly different than the sample statistic. This is the result of random sampling error. If we take a second random sample of 1,000 different consumers, this second sample average will likely be slightly different than the average from the first sample. In fact, there are many different samples of size n = 1,000 that can be taken from the population. And, these samples will yield sample averages that are slightly different from each other. Each sample distribution will be defined by its own sample average and sample standard deviation. Because of random sampling error, some sample distributions will have sample averages that are greater than the population parameter, and some sample distributions will have sample averages that are less than the population parameter.

Even if the population distribution is not normal, the central limit theorem tells us that the distribution of all possible sample means taken from almost any population will form a distribution that is approximately normal. This distribution, called the sampling distribution of the mean, is what researchers use for making statistical inferences about population parameters.

The Sampling Distribution of the Mean

The sample averages from all possible samples of size $n = 1,000$ form their own distribution. The distribution of all possible sample averages is called the **sampling distribution of the mean**. The sampling distribution of the mean is not a distribution of individual responses (observations). Rather, it is a distribution of sample means. The mean of the sampling distribution of the mean (its expected value) = μ (the population mean). The average of all possible sample averages drawn from a population should be the same as the population mean. The standard deviation of the sampling distribution of the mean is $SE_{mean} = S/\sqrt{n}$.

Recall that the standard error of the mean is the measure of how much random sampling error there is when estimating an average. Anytime we take a sample, and not a census, there will be some random sampling error. We cannot be completely certain of the true population mean unless we measure every member of the population. As the size of the sample increases, the standard error of the mean decreases. Thus, as the sample size increases, the error associated with the estimate decreases. The larger the sample size, the more precise the estimates become.

CENTRAL LIMIT THEOREM

As the sample size (n) increases, the distribution of sample means taken from practically any population approaches a normal distribution with mean = μ and standard deviation $SE_{mean} = S/\sqrt{n}$. This is referred to as the **central limit theorem**. Because we do not know the mean and standard deviation of the population, we estimate μ with $\overline{X}$ and estimate σ with S. Because the distribution of sample means approaches a normal distribution, it can be used to make conclusions about the probability of certain events occurring.

More formally, the central limit theorem states that if sample sizes are sufficiently large (greater than 30), and samples are randomly drawn, the distribution of sample means will be approximately normally distributed with mean = μ and standard deviation $SE_{mean} = S/\sqrt{n}$. Because the distribution of sample means becomes approximately normal, it can be used to form confidence intervals for point estimates where:

- Confidence interval for estimating a mean: $\mu = \overline{X} \pm Z\,(SE_{mean})$
- Confidence interval for estimating a proportion: $\pi = p \pm Z\,(SE_{prop})$

where

$SE_{mean} = S/\sqrt{n}$

$SE_{prop} = \sqrt{p(1-p)/n}$

These confidence intervals are based on the idea that the population parameter is equal to the sample statistic plus or minus some random sampling error (see Figure 20.4).

FIGURE 20.4 Calculating a Confidence Interval

Population Parameter	=	Sample Statistic	±	Sampling Error
Population Mean	=	Sample Mean	±	$Z\,(SE_{mean})$
Population Proportion	=	Sample Proportion	±	$Z\,(SE_{prop})$

QUESTIONS FOR DISCUSSION

1. How are distributions of observations described?

2. What is meant by a measure of central tendency?

3. What is meant by a measure of dispersion?

4. Describe a normal distribution.

5. Describe a standardized normal distribution.

6. What is the population distribution?

7. What is the sample distribution?

8. What is the sampling distribution of the mean?

9. What is the central limit theorem and why is it important to marketing researchers?

10. Imagine that the ages of all of the people in a particular population are not normally distributed. If 1,000 random samples are taken from this population, and the average age from each sample is calculated, what will the distribution of these 1,000 sample averages look like?

MINICASE 20.1

Central Limit Theorem

The purpose of this MiniCase is to demonstrate sampling from a population distribution that is not normally distributed. The central limit theorem states that if sample sizes are sufficiently large (e.g., larger than 30) and samples are randomly drawn, the distribution of sample means will be approximately normally distributed with a mean equal to the population mean. As the sample size increases, the distribution of means of random samples taken from any population approaches a normal distribution.

To illustrate this, imagine that you are the owner of a company that sells widgets. You have eight different regional sales offices. Each sales office has 25 salespeople, making a total of 200 salespeople selling your widgets. You want to know the average number of sales calls your salespeople make in a month. You cannot measure each salesperson, so you decide to take a sample. Below are the actual numbers of sales calls for each of your 200 salespeople for last month. The first number is the salesperson number, and the second number is the number of sales calls that person made.[1]

Sales Office 1	Sales Office 2	Sales Office 3	Sales Office 4	Sales Office 5	Sales Office 6	Sales Office 7	Sales Office 8
1. 30	26. 25	51. 30	76. 25	101. 30	126. 25	151. 30	176. 25
2. 27	27. 29	52. 27	77. 29	102. 27	127. 29	152. 27	177. 29
3. 30	28. 21	53. 30	78. 21	103. 30	128. 21	153. 30	178. 21
4. 28	29. 27	54. 28	79. 27	104. 28	129. 27	154. 28	179. 27
5. 30	30. 29	55. 30	80. 29	105. 30	130. 29	155. 30	180. 29
6. 29	31. 29	56. 29	81. 29	106. 29	131. 29	156. 29	181. 29
7. 26	32. 24	57. 26	82. 24	107. 26	132. 24	157. 26	182. 24
8. 19	33. 28	58. 19	83. 28	108. 19	133. 28	158. 19	183. 28
9. 26	34. 30	59. 26	84. 30	109. 26	134. 30	159. 26	184. 30
10. 24	35. 26	60. 24	85. 26	110. 24	135. 26	160. 24	185. 26
11. 28	36. 25	61. 28	86. 25	111. 28	136. 25	161. 28	186. 25
12. 20	37. 29	62. 20	87. 29	112. 20	137. 29	162. 20	187. 29
13. 18	38. 26	63. 18	88. 26	113. 18	138. 26	163. 18	188. 26
14. 23	39. 22	64. 23	89. 22	114. 23	139. 22	164. 23	189. 22
15. 27	40. 29	65. 27	90. 29	115. 27	140. 29	165. 27	190. 29
16. 24	41. 28	66. 24	91. 28	116. 24	141. 28	166. 24	191. 28
17. 30	42. 23	67. 30	92. 23	117. 30	142. 23	167. 30	192. 23
18. 26	43. 17	68. 26	93. 17	118. 26	143. 17	168. 26	193. 17
19. 28	44. 27	69. 28	94. 27	119. 28	144. 27	169. 28	194. 27
20. 23	45. 30	70. 23	95. 30	120. 23	145. 30	170. 23	195. 30
21. 28	46. 24	71. 28	96. 24	121. 28	146. 24	171. 28	196. 24
22. 25	47. 29	72. 25	97. 29	122. 25	147. 29	172. 25	197. 29
23. 30	48. 30	73. 30	98. 30	123. 30	148. 30	173. 30	198. 30
24. 22	49. 25	74. 22	99. 25	124. 22	149. 25	174. 22	199. 25
25. 27	50. 16	75. 27	100. 16	125. 27	150. 16	175. 27	200. 16

The distribution of these 200 sales calls is shown in the table below. Notice that this distribution is not normally distributed. In fact, it is negatively skewed.

Frequency (number of people making this many calls, X = 4 people)
μ = 25.92; σ = 3.624

```
                                                                      X
                                                                 X    X
                                                            X    X    X
                                                  X    X    X    X    X
                                        X    X    X    X    X    X    X
                                   X    X    X    X    X    X    X    X
                              X    X    X    X    X    X    X    X    X
 X    X    X    X    X    X    X    X    X    X    X    X    X    X    X
 16   17   18   19   20   21   22   23   24   25   26   27   28   29   30
```
Number of Sales Calls

CHAPTER 20 DISTRIBUTIONS AND STATISTICS

From the population of 200 salespeople, choose a sample of 40 salespeople using three different sampling techniques: simple random sampling, systematic sampling, and cluster sampling. For each sampling technique, calculate the sample average and sample standard deviation. Record the sample averages and sample standard deviations in the table below.

1. Simple Random Sample

   Use a random number generator on a calculator or a random number table to randomly choose a sample of 40 people. Or, enter the numbers 1 to 200 in Microsoft Excel in column A. Then create 200 random numbers in column B using the formula = RAND(). Sort the two columns by column B, and then select the 40 top numbers listed in column A.

2. Systematic Sampling

   Use a random number generator on a calculator or a random number table to rOandomly choose the first person. Then systematically choose every fifth person.

3. Cluster Sampling

   Use a random number generator on a calculator or a random number table to randomly choose four of the sales offices. Then, randomly choose 10 people from each of these sales offices.

	Sample Average	Sample Standard Deviation
Simple Random Sample		
Systematic Sampling		
Cluster Sampling		

On the scales below, plot all of the averages from each sampling technique that were calculated from other students in your class. Place an X above the scale value for each sample average. Then, calculate the mean of the sample averages for each sampling technique.

1. Simple Random Sample: Mean of Sample Averages = _____

   21   22   23   24   25   26   27   28   29   30   31   32

2. Systematic Sampling: Mean of Sample Averages = _____

   21   22   23   24   25   26   27   28   29   30   31   32

3. Cluster Sampling: Mean of Sample Averages = _____

   21   22   23   24   25   26   27   28   29   30   31   32

What do these distributions look like? How would you describe these distributions of sample averages? Do these distributions look like the population distribution? Why, or why not? What is the central limit theorem?

ENDNOTE

1   This exercise is adapted from Scott Burton and George M. Zinkhan, "An In-Class Exercise Which Demonstrates Some of the Benefits and Problems Associated with Probability-Based Sampling in Marketing Research," *Journal of Marketing Education* (Spring 1986): 39–43.

CHAPTER 21

Confidence Intervals

LEARNING OBJECTIVES

1 Describe confidence intervals.

2 Explain how marketers and marketing researchers use confidence intervals to help make managerial decisions.

3 Calculate and interpret a confidence interval for an average.

4 Calculate and interpret a confidence interval for a proportion.

5 Describe how marketing researchers can increase their level of confidence in a statistical estimate.

CONFIDENCE INTERVAL FOR AN AVERAGE

Often, a research objective is to measure the average of a single variable of interest. To do this, the average that is calculated for the sample is used to estimate the population average. However, as discussed in previous chapters, researchers must always allow for some random sampling error in the estimate. A **confidence interval** is a way of reporting the estimate and the accompanying margin of error. A confidence interval for an average is stated as:

$$\mu = \overline{X} \pm Z\,(\mathrm{SE}_{mean})$$

where:

$\overline{X}$ is the average from the sample

Z is the Z value reflecting the level of confidence in the estimate

SE_{mean} is the standard error of the mean $= S/\sqrt{n}$

The quantity $Z\,(\mathrm{SE}_{mean})$ is often referred to as the **margin of error**. Thus, the confidence interval reports the sample average plus or minus ($\pm$) a margin of error.

For example, imagine that we wanted to estimate the average age of women in a market area. From a sample of 100 women, the sample average age is found to be 37.5, and the sample standard deviation is 12 years. Because this is a sample, and not a census, there will be some random sampling error. The true average age might be less

FIGURE 21.1 Distribution of Z Scores

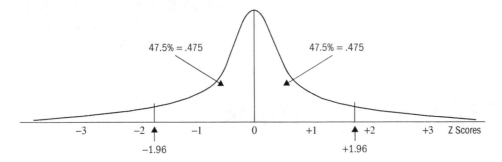

than 37.5, or it might be greater than 37.5. We would like to determine the interval, or range of ages, within which most (95 percent) of the sample averages we could observe will fall. In other words, we would like to determine how probable it is that the population mean would fall within a certain range of values (ages).

For this example the standard error of the mean (SE_{mean}) = 12 divided by the square root of 100. Thus, the standard error of the mean = 1.2. The sample average comes from a distribution of all possible averages from samples of size 100. The mean of this distribution of sample averages is 37.5, and the standard deviation of this distribution of sample averages is 1.2. From the **Z table** (found in the appendix), we find that 95 percent of all observations fall within 1.96 standard deviations from the mean of their normal distribution (see Figure 21.1).

Looking in the Z table, we see that 1.96 is the Z score corresponding to a 95 percent confidence level (1.96 is the Z score corresponding to 0.475 in the Z table). Next, simply calculate the ages that are 1.96 standard deviations (standard errors) from 37.5. The confidence interval is thus:

$$37.5 \pm 1.96\,(1.2)$$

$$37.5 \pm 2.352$$

Reporting the Results from a Confidence Interval

The results from the confidence interval calculated for this average can be reported as follows:

- We are 95 percent confident that the population mean is between 35.15 and 39.85.

- We are 95 percent confident that $35.15 \leq \mu \leq 39.85$.

- 95 percent of all samples of size $n = 100$ that could be taken from this same population will produce sample averages between 35.15 and 39.85.

- If we took 1,000 samples of size $n = 100$ from this same population, 950 of the sample averages will be between 35.15 and 39.85.

- Given that the sample average is our best estimate of the population mean, we can be 95 percent confident that the mean age of the women in the target area is between 35.15 and 39.85.

CONFIDENCE INTERVALS (AVERAGES) FOR THE NOTE-TAKING SURVEY

A confidence interval for an average can be used to address the following research objectives from the note-taking survey:

A confidence interval is a way of reporting the estimate of a population parameter and the accompanying margin of error.

- Measure the average number of classes that students miss during a typical semester (*number*).

- Measure the average number of classes missed for which students borrow notes in a typical semester (*howmany*).

The averages for the two variables *number* and *howmany* are shown in Table 21.1. Using these averages the confidence intervals can be calculated as shown in Table 21.2.

Therefore, we can conclude that:

- We are 95 percent confident that the average number of classes that students miss during a typical semester is between 8.24 and 9.96.

- We are 95 percent confident that the average number of classes missed for which students borrow notes in a typical semester is between 3.93 and 5.18.

TABLE 21.1 Means for the Variables *Number, Howmany*

Variable	N	Mean	Minimum	Maximum	Std Dev	Std Error
Number	109	9.1009174	4.0000000	20.0000000	4.5824645	0.4389205
Howmany	109	4.5688073	1.0000000	16.0000000	3.3399018	0.3199046

TABLE 21.2 Confidence Interval for an Average: Variables *Number, Howmany*

Variable	95 percent of samples will yield results between:			
	$\bar{X} - 1.96(SE_{mean})$	(μ)	$\bar{X} + 1.96(SE_{mean})$	$1.96\,(SE_{mean})$
Number	8.24	9.10	9.96	0.86
Howmany	3.93	4.56	5.18	0.625

CONFIDENCE INTERVAL FOR A PROPORTION

A **confidence interval for a proportion** is stated as:

$$\pi = p \pm Z\,(\text{SE}_{\text{prop}})$$

where

π is the population proportion

p is the sample proportion (calculated)

SE_{prop} is the standard error of the proportion $= \sqrt{p(1-p)/n}$

For example, in a telephone survey of 1,000 consumers in a test market, 20 percent of consumers said that they recalled seeing a particular advertisement. What interval lets us be 95 percent confident that the true population proportion, π (the percentage of all people in the population who recall seeing a particular advertisement), is in that interval? Since $p = .20$, the standard error of the proportion equals the square root of 0.2 times 0.8, divided by 1,000.

The margin of error reported with a confidence interval accounts for only random sampling error. It does not account for any systematic error or bias resulting from the data collection methodology or response bias.

$$\pi = p \pm Z\,(\text{SE}_{\text{prop}})$$

$$\pi = .20 \pm 1.96\sqrt{.2(.8)/1{,}000}$$

$$\pi = .20 \pm .0248$$

$$17.52\% \leq \pi \leq 22.48\%$$

Reporting the Results from a Confidence Interval

The results from the confidence interval calculated for this proportion can be reported as follows:

- We are 95 percent confident that the population proportion is between 17.52 percent and 22.48 percent.

- We are 95 percent confident that 17.52 percent $\leq \pi \leq$ 22.48 percent.

- We can say that we are 95 percent confident of this because if we were to take 100 samples of size $n = 1,000$ from this same population, 95 of them would produce sample proportions between 17.52 percent and 22.48 percent.

- Thus, if almost all of our sample proportions are within this interval, we can be very confident that the true population parameter is also in this interval.

CONFIDENCE INTERVALS (PROPORTIONS) FOR THE NOTE-TAKING SURVEY

A confidence interval for a proportion can be used to address the following research objectives from the note-taking survey:

- Measure the percentage of students who have ever borrowed notes (*ever*).

- Measure the percentage of students who think that having good notes is an important part of getting a good grade in a class (*grade*).

- Measure the percentage of students who would buy notes from a note-taking service (*buy*).

The calculated proportions for the variables *ever*, *grade*, and *buy* are shown in Table 21.3.

Using these percentages the confidence intervals can be calculated as shown in Table 21.4.

TABLE 21.3 Proportions for the Variables *Ever*, *Grade*, and *Buy*

	Frequency	Percent	Cumulative Frequency	Cumulative Percent
Ever				
1	79	72.5	79	72.48
2	30	27.5	109	100.00
Grade				
1	81	74.3	81	74.31
2	28	25.7	109	100.00
Buy				
1	67	61.5	67	61.47
2	42	38.5	109	100.00

TABLE 21.4 Confidence Interval for a Proportion: Variables *Ever*, *Grade*, and *Buy*

	95 percent of samples will yield results between:			
Variable	$p - 1.96(SE_{prop})$	(π)	$p + 1.96(SE_{prop})$	$1.96(SE_{prop})$
Ever	0.645	0.725	0.805	0.08
Grade	0.663	0.743	0.823	0.08
Buy	0.525	0.615	0.705	0.09

Therefore, we conclude that:

- We are 95 percent confident that the percentage of students who have ever borrowed notes is between 64.5 percent and 80.5 percent.

- We are 95 percent confident that the percentage of students who think that having good notes is an important part of getting a good grade in a class is between 66.3 percent and 82.3 percent.

- We are 95 percent confident that the percentage of students who would buy notes from a note-taking service is between 52.5 percent and 70.5 percent.

INCREASING CONFIDENCE IN ESTIMATES

Although 95 percent confidence is usually good enough for most surveys and public opinion polls, researchers sometimes want to be even more confident in their estimates. There are two methods for increasing the confidence in statistical estimates: increasing the size of the interval and increasing the accuracy of the estimate.

Increasing the Size of the Interval

The first method is to increase the size of the confidence interval. The greater the margin of error we are willing to accept, the more certain we can be that the true value of either π or μ is in that interval. In the extreme, we can always say that we are 100 percent confident that the population proportion is between 0 and 100 percent. The size of the confidence interval can be increased by changing the Z value used in the confidence interval formula.

$$\mu = \overline{X} \pm Z\,(\mathrm{SE}_{mean}) \qquad \pi = p \pm Z\,(\mathrm{SE}_{prop})$$

For example, set:

$Z = 1.28$, for 80 percent confidence in the estimate (80 percent of observations are within 1.28 standard deviations of the mean).

$Z = 1.64$, for 90 percent confidence in the estimate (90 percent of observations are within 1.64 standard deviations of the mean).

$Z = 1.96$, for 95 percent confidence in the estimate (95 percent of observations are within 1.96 standard deviations of the mean).

$Z = 2.58$, for 99 percent confidence in the estimate (99 percent of observations are within 2.58 standard deviations of the mean).

The 95 Percent Confidence Level. Even though the confidence level can be adjusted to reflect a small margin of error for any sample size, the generally accepted confidence level that is most often used is 95 percent, with a corresponding Z score = 1.96. Thus, for most surveys and public opinion polls that report only the margin of error, it is usually safe to assume that the margin of error was calculated based on a 95 percent confidence level. Interestingly, the standard of setting alpha equal to 0.05 or 0.01 is actually a carryover from the days before computers. Before computers were available, statisticians had to refer to statistical tables, like the Z table shown in the appendix of this book. To avoid having to calculate and print many different tables, most textbooks provided only those tables corresponding to alpha values of 0.05 and 0.01.

Increasing the Accuracy of the Estimate

The second method is to increase the accuracy of the estimate. This is done by increasing the sample size. The width of the confidence interval depends upon the size of the sample. As the sample size gets larger, the standard error of the mean and the standard error of the proportion will both become smaller. As the sample size increases, the amount of random sampling error decreases. Recall that the sample size is the denominator in the equations used to calculate the standard error of the mean, as well as the standard error of the proportion. If the sample size is increased, the standard error will decrease. And, if the standard error decreases, the confidence interval will become narrower.

QUESTIONS FOR DISCUSSION

1. What is a confidence interval?

2. How can researchers increase confidence in their estimates?

3. Interpret the following confidence interval that was calculated using $\mu = 56.0$ and $Z = 1.96$:

$$47.5 \leq \mu \leq 64.5$$

4. How would the confidence interval shown in question 3 change if the sample size remained the same, but the confidence level (and corresponding Z value) were changed to:
   a. 90 percent
   b. 99 percent

5. How would the confidence interval shown in question 3 change if the confidence level remained the same, but the estimate was based on a:
   a. Smaller sample
   b. Larger sample

RazorCorp Heated Razor

RazorCorp has recently developed a new men's razor. The handle of the razor contains one AA battery that is used to heat the razor blades. Thus, a man can shave with hot water as well as hot blades. Marketing managers at RazorCorp have employed you as a marketing research consultant to help them interpret the results from some research. They recently conducted some market testing to see how well this new heated razor would be received by men. They randomly selected 300 men to receive a free heated razor. These men were to use the razor for one week and then respond to a short phone interview measuring their reactions and possible desire to purchase a RazorCorp heated razor. Marketing managers at RazorCorp have performed some cost accounting and determined that the heated razor needs to achieve a 10 percent market share to be profitable to manufacture and market. However, only 6 percent of men in their market test said that they like the razor and intend to purchase it. Based on this sample, the margin of error that they calculated for the confidence interval to estimate the percent of men in the entire population who intend to purchase the heated razor is ± 2.7 percent. They interpret this to mean that between 3.3 and 8.7 percent of men in the population intend to purchase the heated razor. However, they are concerned because they need at least 10 percent of men to purchase it. They believe that this low percentage of men in their market test who intend to purchase the razor is due to a small sample size. They ask you if increasing the sample size will possibly result in a larger percentage of men willing to purchase the razor. What do you tell them?

CHAPTER 22

Hypothesis Testing

LEARNING OBJECTIVES

1   Define statistical hypothesis testing.

2   List and explain the steps involved in conducting a statistical hypothesis test.

3   Define and explain the alpha significance level.

4   Define critical value, observed value, acceptance region, and rejection region.

5   Define and explain type I errors in statistical hypothesis testing.

6   Explain the relationship between the alpha significance level and the probability of making a type I error in statistical hypothesis testing.

7   Define and explain type II errors in statistical hypothesis testing.

8   Define the power of a statistical test.

9   Explain the relationship between statistical power and sample size.

10   Discuss why researchers are often reluctant to hypothesize no effects (or the lack of a statistical effect).

11   Conduct and interpret a hypothesis test for an average.

12   Conduct and interpret a hypothesis test for a proportion.

Hypothesis testing is a statistical procedure for comparing what a researcher expected to find to what was actually found from the survey results. An outline of the logic of hypothesis testing is shown in Figure 22.1.

For example, if we believe that all dogs are brown (A), we expect to observe only brown dogs (B). Imagine that when we go out to observe dogs we see a black dog (not B). Since this is not what we expected to find if our hypothesis were true, we conclude that the hypothesis is not true. Alternatively, if we observe only brown dogs (B), then we accept the hypothesis. Realize, however, that this evidence (observing only brown dogs) alone does not prove the hypothesis. We accept the hypothesis because we have no reason to reject it. We did not observe any dogs that were any color other than brown.

Steps in Hypothesis Testing. The following steps are used to conduct a statistical hypothesis test:

1.   Determine a statistical null hypothesis (Ho).

2.   Determine what the sampling distribution (the distribution of sample means or sample proportions) would be if the hypothesis were true.

FIGURE 22.1 The Logic of Statistical Hypothesis Testing

If A, then we expect to observe B.
We observe B.
Therefore, A must be true.
(Observations and data support A.)

If A, then we expect to observe B.
We do not observe B (not B).
Therefore, A must not be true.
(Observations and data do not support A.)

3. Take a sample and calculate the sample statistics (sample mean, sample proportion, SE_{mean}, SE_{prop}).

4. Determine if the sample statistic (sample mean or sample proportion) deviates from the mean of the hypothesized sampling distribution (μ or π) by a value large enough to conclude that a deviation this large would be somewhat rare if the statistical hypothesis (Ho) were true.

Without using statistical terminology, the steps involved in a hypothesis test are described as:

1. Determine: What is the hypothesis? What do we expect to be true?

2. Determine what you would expect to observe if the hypothesis were true.

3. Take a sample and make an observation.

4. Determine if what you observed is similar to what you expected to observe if the hypothesis were true.
   a. If yes, you observed something similar to what you expected to observe if the hypothesis were true. Therefore, you should accept the hypothesis because you have no evidence or reason to reject it. Everything that was observed supports the hypothesis.
   b. If no, you observed something different from what you expected to observe if the hypothesis were true. Therefore, you should reject the hypothesis because you have evidence or reason to reject it. You observed something you should not have observed if the hypothesis were true.

The **alpha significance level (α)** determines the probability (e.g., 0.05) that is considered too low to warrant support of the null hypothesis. Recall that the sampling distribution is the distribution of all possible sample averages or proportions. In the case of an average, the sampling distribution has a mean = μ (the hypothesized population mean) and a standard deviation = SE_{mean}. If the null hypothesis is true, 95 percent of the possible sample means will be within ± 1.96 standard deviations (Z scores) of the mean of this distribution. This is illustrated in Figure 22.2.

The purpose of a statistical hypothesis test is to determine whether or not the observed sample mean is within ± 1.96 standard deviations (Z scores) of the

FIGURE 22.2 The Distribution of All Possible Sample Means

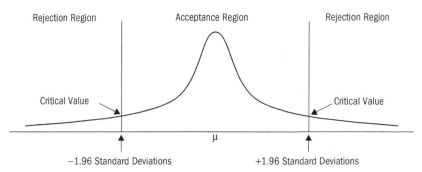

hypothesized population mean. If the observed sample mean is more than 1.96 standard deviations from the hypothesized population mean, we conclude with 95 percent confidence that μ does not equal the hypothesized value under the null hypothesis.

CRITICAL VALUES, ACCEPTANCE REGIONS, AND REJECTION REGIONS

Those values that are 1.96 standard deviations from the hypothesized mean (the value of μ under the Ho) are called the **critical values**. The **observed value** that is calculated from the sample is compared to these critical values. If the calculated mean from the sample is inside, or within, these critical values (it is within the **acceptance region**), accept the null hypothesis (Ho). If the calculated mean is outside, or beyond, these critical values (it is in the **rejection region**), reject the null hypothesis (Ho).

In most cases, even if the null hypothesis is in fact true, the mean of the sample will not be exactly the same as the hypothesized mean. Even if the null hypothesis is accepted, the calculated sample mean will probably be slightly different than the hypothesized mean. The question becomes, if the calculated mean is different than the hypothesized mean, what is the reason for the difference?

Difference Due to Random Error. If the null hypothesis is accepted (the calculated value is within the acceptance region defined by the critical values), we conclude that the calculated value is within the range of what we should have found if the null hypothesis were true. In this case, we conclude that the difference between the calculated mean and the hypothesized mean is due simply to random sampling error.

Difference Due to a False Null Hypothesis. If, however, the null hypothesis is rejected (the calculated mean is in the rejection region defined by the critical values), we conclude that the calculated mean is not within the range of what we should have found if the null hypothesis were true. In this case, we conclude that the difference between the calculated mean and the hypothesized mean is due to

There are two types of errors that researchers can make when performing statistical hypothesis tests. They can reject a null hypothesis that is actually true (Type I error), and they can accept a null hypothesis that is actually false (Type II error).

something other than random sampling error. We conclude that the null hypothesis is actually false.

A LEGAL EXAMPLE OF HYPOTHESIS TESTING

A legal example can be used to illustrate the logic of statistical hypothesis testing.[1] In several legal cases argued in the southern United States between 1960 and 1980, a number of expert witnesses presented evidence for racial bias in selecting jury members. Jury panels are presumably chosen at random from a list of eligible citizens. However, very few African Americans living in southern states were being selected for jury panels. As a result, many defendants challenged the verdicts. On one appeal, an expert statistician witness highlighted two key pieces of evidence:

> A statistical hypothesis test is a way to compare what was observed from a sample to what was expected, if the hypothesis were true.

1. Fifty percent of eligible citizens in these southern states were African Americans.

2. On an 80-person panel of potential jurors, only four were African Americans.

Could this low number of African Americans on the 80-person jury panel be the result of pure chance? If jury members were selected randomly, the number of African Americans on the 80-person panel would be the result of 80 different random selections, each with a 50 percent chance of selecting an African American. Based on standard laws of probability, the probability of getting a jury panel with only four African Americans is equal to 0.0000000000000000014!

Because this probability of finding an 80-person panel with only four African Americans is so small, this was strong evidence against the hypothesis that the jury members were selected purely by random. Further, the statistician noted that this probability is less than the chances of getting three consecutive royal flushes in poker. As a result, the judge rejected the hypothesis of random selection.

The Jury Selection Case in Statistical Terms. In statistical hypothesis testing, the null hypothesis states that the observations are the result of random chance.

> Ho: Jury panels are randomly selected from the whole population.

The alternative hypothesis states that there is a real effect.

> Ha: Jury panels are not randomly selected from the whole population. African Americans are less likely than their proportion in the population to be selected for a jury panel.

The probability of selecting a jury panel with only four African Americans is equal to 0.0000000000000000014. This probability serves as the p value for the statistical hypothesis test. The p value indicates the probability that the observed result (or test statistic) would be found if the null hypothesis is true. If Ho is true, and all jurors are randomly selected, the probability of finding an 80-person jury panel with only four African Americans is 1.4×10^{-18}. We usually fix alpha at 0.05. **Alpha (α)** acts as a cut-off point below which we agree that an observed result is statistically significant. That is, if the *p* value is less than alpha, we reject the null hypothesis and conclude that the observed result could not have occurred by pure chance, if the null hypothesis is true. The smaller the *p* value, the stronger the evidence against the null hypothesis.

In general, if we set alpha equal to 5 percent ($\alpha = .05$), we accept the null hypothesis if we observe something that should occur more than 5 percent of the time if the null hypothesis is true. Conversely, we reject the null hypothesis if we observe something that should occur less than 5 percent of the time, if the null hypothesis is true. Is an 80-person jury panel with only four African Americans something that should have occurred more than 5 percent of the time, if Ho is true? No. It should only occur with probability = 1.4×10^{-18} if Ho is true. Therefore, because we found something we should not have found if the null hypothesis is true, we reject the null hypothesis.

ERRORS IN STATISTICAL HYPOTHESIS TESTING

Whenever a decision is made to either accept or reject a statistical hypothesis, there is always a chance that the decision is wrong. There are two types of errors that are possible when decisions are made regarding statistical hypotheses. To illustrate these two types of decision errors, image that your professor has accused you of cheating on an exam. However, you are assumed to be innocent until proven guilty. As such, the null hypothesis is Ho: You are innocent. The alternative hypothesis is Ha: You are guilty. Given this, there are four possible situations and two possible decision errors, as shown in Figure 22.3.

If we conclude that an innocent person is guilty, we make a **type I error**. The probability of this occurring is α (alpha). Typically, α is set at 0.05. This means that we allow a 5 percent probability of making this type of error. Alternatively, if we conclude that a guilty person is innocent, we make a **type II error**. The probability of this occurring is β (beta).

To illustrate the relationship between α and β, consider the following example. We wish to test the null hypothesis that the average age of consumers in a target market is 30 (Ho: $\mu = 30$) versus the alternative hypothesis that the average age of consumers in a target market is greater than 30 (Ha: $\mu > 30$). The top curve shown in Figure 22.4

FIGURE 22.3 Correct Decisions and Errors in Statistical Hypothesis Testing

Verdict	True Situation You Are:	
	Innocent	Guilty
Innocent: Accept Ho	Correct Decision Probability = $1 - \alpha$	Error (Type II) Probability = β
Guilty: Reject Ho	Error (Type I) Probability = α	Correct Decision Probability = $1 - \beta$

FIGURE 22.4 The Relationship between Alpha and Beta

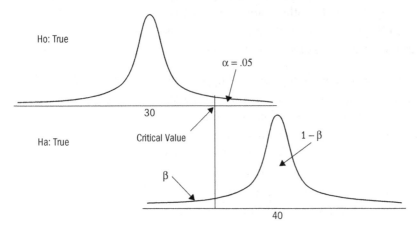

depicts what the distribution of sample means would look like if the null hypothesis were true. The bottom curve depicts what the distribution of sample means would look like if the alternative hypothesis were true (the true average age of our target market is greater than 30, e.g., it is actually 40).

As shown in the bottom curve, $1 - \beta$ refers to the probability of correctly rejecting a false null hypothesis. This is referred to as the **power** of a statistical test. Notice also that as α gets larger, β gets smaller. And, as α gets smaller, β gets larger. However, we would rather have a large β than a large α. We would rather let a guilty person go free than convict an innocent person. It is also important to note that α and β do not sum to one ($\alpha + \beta \neq 1$).

INCREASING STATISTICAL POWER BY INCREASING SAMPLE SIZE

The **power of a statistical test** refers to the probability of rejecting the null hypothesis when it is false. In other words, the higher the power of a test, the more likely we are to conclude that a statistic is significant, when in fact it is significant. One of the easiest ways to increase statistical power is to increase the sample size. For example, consider the case of a marketer who believes that 50 percent of consumers in a market area are aware of the brand name for his company's product. The null hypothesis is then stated as Ho: $\pi = .50$. But, what if only 45 percent of consumers in the market area are actually aware of the brand name? In this case, rejecting the null hypothesis would be the correct decision. Now, imagine that 100 consumers are randomly sampled and 45 percent of these consumers are aware of the brand name. If α is set at 0.05, what is the probability that we will make a correct decision and reject the false null hypothesis?

> Statistical power refers to the probability of rejecting a null hypothesis, when the null hypothesis is indeed false (i.e., when it should be rejected).

Increasing Statistical Power by Increasing the Sample Size. The probability of making this correct decision (the power of the test) can be increased by increasing the sample size. Increasing the sample size reduces the standard deviation of the

FIGURE 22.5 Increasing Sample Size and Increased Statistical Power

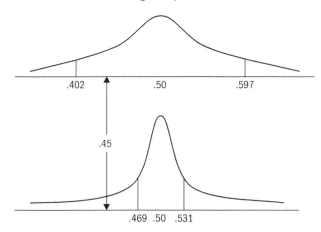

distribution of sample proportions (making it narrower). Therefore, increasing the sample size increases the power of the test without having to increase alpha. Recall the formulas for calculating the standard error of the mean and the standard error of the proportion. Increasing the sample size (n) reduces the standard errors.

$$SE_{mean} = S/\sqrt{n} \qquad SE_{prop} = \sqrt{p(1-p)/n}$$

The curves shown in Figure 22.5 illustrate how increasing the sample size from 100 to 1,000 decreases the standard error, and thus increases the power of the test. The top curve illustrates the distribution of sample proportions under the null hypothesis based on a sample of 100 consumers. The bottom curve illustrates the distribution of sample proportions under the null hypothesis based on a sample of 1,000 consumers. Notice that the distribution of sample proportions based on a sample of 1,000 consumers is much narrower because of the reduced standard error.

If we set α = .05 and surveyed only 100 consumers, the lower critical value would be 0.402 and the upper critical value would be 0.597. This is shown on the top curve in Figure 22.5. Since 0.45 falls within the acceptance region, we would accept the false null. This would be a type II error. However, if we surveyed 1,000 consumers, the lower critical value would be 0.469 and the upper critical value would be 0.531. Since 0.45 now falls outside of the acceptance region, we would reject the false null. This would be the correct decision. In general, as the sample size increases, the probability (β) of making a type II error decreases, and the power of the test (1 – β) increases.

CAUTIONS WITH HYPOTHESIZING NO EFFECTS

Null hypotheses usually state that there are no statistical effects, for example, there is no difference between two means, there is no relationship between two variables, there is no significant correlation between two variables, or a regression coefficient is not significant. Alternative hypotheses usually state the presence of statistical effects, for example, there is a difference between variables, there is a relationship between variables, there is a significant correlation between variables, a regression coefficient is significant.

It is not advisable for the null hypothesis to be the hypothesis of interest that is being tested. In other words, avoid having the lack of a statistical effect, such as the lack of a difference between two groups, as the hypothesis that will hopefully be demonstrated by the research. The following statements hypothesize the lack of a statistical effect.

- Women can run as fast as men, and I can statistically show it!

- Saleswomen can generate just as much sales as salesmen, and I can statistically show it!

- Men perform as well as women in nursing classes, and I can statistically show it!

The hypothesis of interest should be the presence of a statistical effect. Then, if there is insufficient statistical evidence, the null hypothesis of no statistical effect will be accepted. The problem with hypothesizing, or trying to demonstrate, the absence of a statistically significant finding is that such hypotheses can be supported merely through low statistical power. Recall that statistical power is the probability of rejecting the null hypothesis when it is false (e.g., concluding that there is a difference between two groups when in fact there is a difference between the groups). For example, consider a researcher who believes that men and women have equal evaluations of a brand and wants to test this hypothesis. Since the null hypothesis is usually stated as the lack of an effect, the hypotheses are as follows:

Ho: Men and women have equal evaluations of the brand ($\mu_{men} = \mu_{women}$).

Ha: Men and women have different evaluations of the brand ($\mu_{men} \neq \mu_{women}$).

Ten people are sampled (five males and five females) and their responses on a 7-point scale (1 = unfavorable, 7 = favorable) are shown in Table 22.1.

TABLE 22.1 EVALUATIONS FROM TEN CONSUMERS

Sex	Evaluation
m	4
m	5
m	6
m	5
m	6
f	4
f	5
f	7
f	2
f	3

The mean rating for the five men is 5.2, whereas the mean rating for the five women is 4.2. Based on an F-test to compare the two means, the null hypothesis is accepted and the researcher concludes that there is no difference between the evaluations of men and women. The test statistic is $F_{1,8} = 1.14$, $p = .31$. However, if 30 more consumers who were exactly the same as the first 10 consumers were also sampled, the responses of these 40 consumers would be as shown in Table 22.2.

The mean rating for the 20 men is again 5.2, and the mean rating for the 20 women is again 4.2. Notice that the means are exactly the same as they were with a sample of only 10 people. The only difference is the larger sample. With the larger sample, the null hypothesis is now rejected. The conclusion is that men and women do in fact differ in their evaluations. The test statistic is $F_{1,38} = 5.4$, $p = .02$. The Ho is rejected with a larger sample because of the greater statistical power of a test with $n = 40$, compared to $n = 10$. In this case, there really is a difference between the evaluations of men and women. But, this difference could not be seen statistically due to the lack of statistical power associated with a sample of only 10 consumers.

The easiest way to demonstrate that men and women have the same evaluations of the brand is to use a very small sample. A small sample will result in very low statistical power. The lower the statistical power, the less likely a difference between men

TABLE 22.2 EVALUATIONS FROM 40 CONSUMERS

Sex	Evaluation	Sex	Evaluation
m	4	m	4
m	5	m	5
m	6	m	6
m	5	m	5
m	6	m	6
f	4	f	4
f	5	f	5
f	7	f	7
f	2	f	2
f	3	f	3
m	4	m	4
m	5	m	5
m	6	m	6
m	5	m	5
m	6	m	6
f	4	f	4
f	5	f	5
f	7	f	7
f	2	f	2
f	3	f	3

and women will be found, when in fact there is a difference. Therefore, a common criticism of conclusions that support a hypothesized lack of statistical effects is that the power of the statistical test was not sufficient to observe the effects.

HYPOTHESIS TEST OF AN AVERAGE

To demonstrate a **hypothesis test of an average**, imagine that managers for a company that sells running shoes believe that the consumers in their target market exercise an average of five days a week. From a sample of 100 consumers, these researchers found that the average number of days these consumers exercise per week was 3.5, and the standard deviation for the sample was 1.2. To test the hypothesis, first determine what the distribution of sample means would look like if the null hypothesis were true (at a 95 percent confidence level).

Ho: $\mu = 5.0$

Ha: $\mu \neq 5.0$

Assuming the Ho is true, the distribution of sample means would look like the curve shown in Figure 22.6. And, 95 percent of all sample averages would fall within ± 1.96 standard deviations of the mean.

This curve shows what the distribution of all possible sample means would look like if the null hypothesis were true. In this case the observed sample mean lies outside of the acceptance region. It is outside the range of sample means that should have been observed if the null hypothesis were true. What we observed in the sample is more than 1.96 standard deviations from the hypothesized mean (what we should have found if the null hypothesis were true). Therefore, we reject the Ho, and conclude that $\mu \neq 5.0$.

We can say that the sample result is statistically significant beyond the 0.05 level. Fewer than 5 out of 100 samples (of size $n = 100$) will yield results that deviate this much from the hypothesized null hypothesis, when in fact the null hypothesis is true. Thus, there are less than 5 in 100 chances that this result would occur because

FIGURE 22.6 Distribution of Sample Means

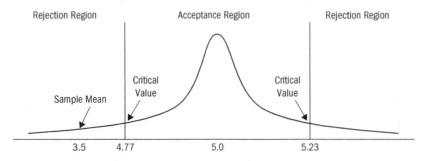

of random sampling error. Therefore, it must have occurred because the true population mean does not equal 5.

HYPOTHESIS TEST OF AN AVERAGE: NOTE-TAKING SURVEY

Hypothesis testing procedures can be used to determine the representativeness of a sample. By comparing the characteristics of the sample respondents to those of the larger population, researchers can determine whether or not the sample is representative of the larger population. For example, if a university has 40 percent female students, a sample taken from this population should include approximately 40 percent females. In this case, the null hypothesis is that the sample is representative.

Ho: The sample is representative (the sample mean/proportion = the population mean/proportion).

Ha: The sample is not representative (the sample mean/proportion ≠ the population mean/proportion).

If the sample is representative of the larger population, the sample characteristics should be similar to the characteristics of the larger population.

For the note-taking survey, we can compare the age, sex, whether students are full-time or part-time, and their fraternity affiliation with the known values for these variables in the larger population of all students at this university. Notice that age is a continuous variable (metric variable) measured on a ratio scale. Thus, age will be examined by using a hypothesis test of an average. The other three variables were measured on nominal scales and will be examined by using a hypothesis test of a proportion. If the true average age of students at the university is 22.2 years old, is the sample representative? The average age of students in the sample was found to be 24.9. Therefore, if the sample is representative of the larger population then 95 percent of samples will yield sample averages between 21.8 and 22.5 (see Table 22.3).

The average age found in the sample is outside the range of what we should have found, given that the true average age of the population is 22.2 years old. Therefore, we conclude that the sample is not representative of the population on the variable age.

TABLE 22.3 Comparing the Average Age in the Sample to the Average Age in the Population

| Variable | If the Null Hypothesis is True, 95 Percent of Samples will Yield Results Between | | | Result from the Survey |
	$\bar{X} - 1.96\ (SE_{mean})$	(μ)	$\bar{X} + 1.96\ (SE_{mean})$	Sample Mean
Age	21.8	22.2	22.5	24.9

HYPOTHESIS TEST OF A PROPORTION

A **hypothesis test of a proportion** is conceptually similar to the hypothesis test of a mean, except that the formulation of the standard error of the proportion differs from the formulation of the standard error of the mean.

$$\text{Recall:} \quad SE_{prop} = \sqrt{p(1-p)/n}$$

For example, we believe that 70 percent of consumers purchasing our product are men.

Ho: $\pi = .70$

Ha: $\pi \neq .70$

In a sample of 100 customers, 62 percent are males.

$$p = .62$$

$$(1 - p) = .38$$

$$SE_{prop} = \sqrt{.62(.38)/100} = .048$$

Assuming the Ho is true, the distribution of sample proportions would look like the curve shown in Figure 22.7. And, 95 percent of all sample proportions would fall within ± 1.96 standard deviations of the mean.

This curve in Figure 22.7 shows what the distribution of all possible sample proportions would look like if the null hypothesis were true. The observed sample proportion lies within the acceptance region. What we observed in the sample is within 1.96 standard deviations from the hypothesized proportion (what we should have found if the null hypothesis were true). Therefore, we accept the Ho and conclude that $\pi = .70$. The difference between the hypothesized proportion and the sample proportion could be due to random sampling error.

FIGURE 22.7 Distribution of Sample Proportions

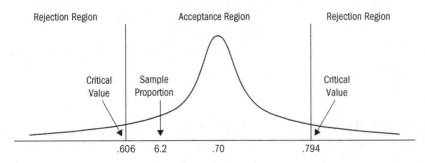

HYPOTHESIS TEST OF A PROPORTION: NOTE-TAKING SURVEY

We can use a hypothesis test of a proportion to examine whether or not the sample is representative of the population with regard to sex, full-time or part-time status, and fraternity affiliation. From university records we know that there are:

- 53 percent males at the university (47 percent females).

- 90 percent of students are considered full-time students.

- 24 percent of the students are members of either a fraternity or a sorority.

These percentages are the null hypotheses. The results from the sample are as follows:

- 59.6 percent of students in the sampler are male (40.4 percent are female).

- 85.3 percent of students in the sample are full-time students.

- 22.2 percent of students in the sample are members of either a fraternity or a sorority.

Therefore, if the sample is representative of the larger population, then 95 percent of samples will yield percentages for these variables as shown in Table 22.4.

Since all three of the sample proportions are within the range of what we expected to find, we conclude that the sample is representative of the population with regard to sex, full-time or part-time status, and membership in either a fraternity or a sorority.

QUESTIONS FOR DISCUSSION

1. Describe the steps involved in a statistical hypothesis test.

2. Do researchers want to make type I errors?

3. How can researchers reduce the chance of making type I errors?

4. What happens to the power of a statistical test if alpha (α) is reduced?

TABLE 22.4 COMPARING PROPORTIONS IN THE SAMPLE TO PROPORTIONS IN THE POPULATION

Variable	If the null hypothesis is true, 95 percent of samples will yield results between			Result from the survey
	$p - 1.96 \, (SE_{prop})$	(π)	$p + 1.96 \, (SE_{prop})$	Sample Proportion
Sex (male)	.438	.53	.622	.596
Fullpart (full time)	.834	.90	.966	.853
Frat (in frat or sorority)	.163	.24	.317	.220

5. How can researchers increase the power of a statistical test without increasing the chance of making a type I error?

6. If α = .05, how often will type I errors occur?

7. If α = .05, and the true average age of the population is 35, how often will we take a random sample from the population and conclude that the true average age is not 35?

MINICASE 22.1

Marvin's Neighborhood Market

Calvin Bart is the owner of Marvin's Neighborhood Market, which is an independent grocery store located in a suburban area of Topeka, Kansas. Marvin's Neighborhood Market has been in business for 27 years and has been able to remain competitive with other larger grocery stores through excellent service and friendly employees. Marvin's Neighborhood Market has a number of different departments (e.g., dairy, bakery, meats and fish, produce, frozen foods, pharmacy, and florist). Each department has a separate department manager who is responsible for overseeing the quality of service and merchandise in his or her department.

Recently, two new florists have opened in the neighborhood. This, along with decreased sales from the Marvin's florist department, has caused Calvin to wonder if he can still remain competitive in this area. So, Calvin decided to conduct some customer satisfaction surveys to measure customers' evaluations of the different departments in the grocery store. He asked Melodie Toner, who is the florist department manager, to conduct the customer satisfaction survey. He has also informed her that if the florist department is evaluated significantly lower than the other departments, he will consider getting rid of that department.

The surveys were given to customers as they finished paying for their groceries and other purchases. The survey was very short and customers were asked to complete it and place it in the survey collection box before leaving the store. A key question on the survey asked customers to rate how much each department contributed to their overall level of satisfaction with Marvin's Neighborhood Market. This was measured on a 7-point scale, where 1 = not at all and 7 = a great deal. When Melodie finished conducting the survey and compiling the results, she informed Mr. Bart that for this question, the florist department received an average rating of 3.9, which statistically was not significantly lower than the average rating for any of the other departments.

a. If you were Calvin Bart, what questions would you ask Melodie Toner?

b. If you were Calvin Bart, how would you conduct these surveys?

ENDNOTES

1 Larry Gonick & Woollcott Smith, *The Cartoon Guide to Statistics* (New York, NY: Harper Perennial, 1993).

CHAPTER 23

Cross-Tabulating Survey Data

LEARNING OBJECTIVES

1 Define contingency table, frequency table, and percentage table.

2 Describe how frequencies can be converted to percentages within a bivariate cross-tab table.

3 List and explain some of the guidelines for cross-tabulating survey data.

4 Interpret the output from a cross-tab analysis.

Cross-tabulating survey data allows researchers to examine the relationship between two or more variables. This allows marketing researchers to examine the differences in survey responses across two or more groups of people. Rarely, if ever, do all consumers in a sample respond the same way to a survey question. So, cross-tabulating survey data allows marketers to identify, or confirm, differences in thoughts, perceptions, or beliefs across various market segments.

Contingency Tables. Survey data is often analyzed by arranging the data into contingency tables. **Contingency tables** show how responses to one survey question (variable) differ across levels of a second survey question (variable). As such, they show the joint distribution of two or more variables. Contingency tables can be in the form of frequencies or percentages. A **frequency table** shows the number of people who answered a survey question in a given manner. A **percentage table** is formed by converting these frequencies to percentages. Usually, frequency tables are converted to percentage tables because percentages are easier to interpret.

> A cross-tab contingency table shows how responses to one survey question (variable) differ across levels of a second survey question (variable).

Bivariate Cross-Tab Tables. A **bivariate cross-tab table** for two variables is shown in Table 23.1. One hundred people were asked to watch and evaluate a new movie prior to its release in movie theaters. The number of men and women who rated the movie as *good*, *average*, or *bad* is shown as frequencies in Table 23.1.

TABLE 23.1 Frequency Cross-Tabs: Evaluations of a New Movie

	Men	Women	Total
Good	30	20	50
Average	10	5	15
Bad	30	5	35
Total	70	30	100

Thirty men rated the movie *good*, whereas only 20 women rated the movie *good*. Does this mean that men liked the movie more than the women did? To answer this question, it is helpful to convert the frequencies to percentages. When there are two variables, the individual **cell frequencies** should be divided by the **margin total** for the independent variable. In this case, it makes more sense to say that consumers' sex has an influence on their evaluation of a movie than to say that consumers' evaluation of a movie has an influence on their sex. Thus, sex is considered to be the independent variable. Dividing by the margin totals for the independent variable controls for differences in sample size across the different levels of that variable. For this situation, each of the individual cell frequencies for men should be divided by the margin total for men, and each of the individual cell frequencies for women should be divided by the margin total for women. For example, to convert the 30 men who rated the movie as *good* to a percentage, 30 should be divided by 70, which is the margin total for men. Similarly, to convert the 20 women who rated the movie as *good* to a percentage, 20 should be divided by 30, which is the margin total for women. The percentages shown in Table 23.2 clearly indicate that women liked the movie more than men did, even though more men rated the movie positively. Whereas 42.8 percent of men rated the movie *good*, 66.6 percent of women rated the movie *good*.

TABLE 23.2 Percentage Cross-Tabs

	Men	Women	Total
Good	42.8%	66.6%	50%
Average	14.2%	16.7%	15%
Bad	42.8%	16.7%	35%
Total	100%	100%	100%

The Value of Cross-Tabulating Survey Data. Cross-tabulating survey data can be a very useful tool for researchers. A cross-tab can identify relationships among variables that might otherwise go unnoticed if the survey data were analyzed in total, as a single group. To illustrate the value of cross-tabulating survey data, consider the results shown in Table 23.3. One hundred consumers were asked to indicate their preferred fast food restaurant, either Burger King or McDonald's.

TABLE 23.3 Fast Food Preference: Total Sample

Burger King	45%
McDonald's	55%
Total	100%

The results clearly suggest that McDonald's is the preferred restaurant among consumers in this sample. However, the data can be cross-tabulated to analyze additional variables that might provide further insight into the results. The frequency table in Table 23.4 shows the restaurant preferences cross-tabulated by consumers' sex.

TABLE 23.4 Fast Food Preference: Frequency Cross-Tabs

	Burger King	McDonald's	Total
Men	15	35	50
Women	30	20	50
Total	45	55	100

Usually, frequencies are converted to percentages because percentages are easier for people to interpret and understand. Table 23.5 shows these frequencies converted to percentages. Each frequency is divided by the margin total for sex (the number of men in the sample or the number of women in the sample). Notice also that sometimes you will divide by the margin totals for rows, and sometimes you will divide by the margin totals for columns. In some tables the independent variable will be presented in the rows, and in some tables the independent variable will be presented in the columns.

TABLE 23.5 Fast Food Preference: Percentage Cross-Tabs

	Burger King	McDonald's	Total
Men	30%	70%	100%
Women	60%	40%	100%
Total	45%	55%	100%

These percentages suggest that women prefer Burger King, whereas men prefer McDonald's. The data can also be cross-tabulated to analyze three variables. The frequency table in Table 23.6 shows the restaurant preferences cross-tabulated by consumers' sex and marital status.

TABLE 23.6 Fast Food Preference: Frequency Cross-Tabs for Three Variables

	Single		Married		
	Men	Women	Men	Women	Total
Burger King	7	14	8	16	45
McDonald's	28	8	7	12	55
Total	35	22	15	28	100

Notice that as additional variables are included in the analysis, the frequency table becomes more and more difficult to interpret. Converting frequencies to percentages aids in the interpretation of such multivariable cross-tabs. Table 23.7 shows these frequencies converted to percentages. Notice that these frequencies are converted to percentages by again dividing by the margin total for each sex. However, in this case each cell frequency is divided by either the margin total for single men, the margin total for married men, the margin total for single women, or the margin total for married women. For the 14 single women who prefer Burger King, the 14 is divided by 22, which is the margin total for single women. As such, the percentages for each column in this percentage table sum to 100 percent.

A cross-tab table allows researchers to examine the differences in survey responses across two or more groups of people.

TABLE 23.7 Fast Food Preference: Percentage Cross-Tabs for Three Variables

	Single		Married		
	Men	**Women**	**Men**	**Women**	**Total**
Burger King	20%	64%	53%	57%	45%
McDonald's	80%	36%	47%	43%	55%
Total	100%	100%	100%	100%	100%

Based on these cross-tabs we can conclude that:

- In general, McDonald's is preferred over Burger King.

- In general, men prefer McDonald's, whereas women prefer Burger King.

- Marital status has a relatively large effect on men's preferences, and a relatively smaller effect on women's preferences. Married men prefer Burger King, whereas single men prefer McDonald's.

- The general preference of McDonald's over Burger King is due to the relatively large number of single men in the sample, and the relatively small number of married men in the sample.

As this example illustrates, cross-tabulated survey data can provide marketing researchers with insights into the relationships between variables that are not provided when survey data are analyzed as a single group. The relationships that a cross-tab identifies can be very useful in terms of identifying and marketing to individual target markets.

> Calculate percentages in a cross-tab table by dividing by the margin totals for the independent variable. This controls for differences in sample size across levels of that variable.

GUIDELINES FOR CROSS-TABULATING SURVEY DATA

It is relatively easy to cross-tabulate survey data. Some guidelines for cross-tabulating survey data are listed below:

- The variables should be meaningful and related to the research purpose. For example, data from a survey on consumers' preferences for pizza toppings should not be cross-tabulated based on the height of consumers.

- The categories created by cross-tabs should be mutually exclusive and collectively exhaustive. For example, cross-tabulating based on sex is mutually exclusive because a person can be only one sex. It is also collectively exhaustive because all people can be categorized as either male or female.

- Dividing by the margin total for each level of the independent variable controls for differences in sample size across levels of that variable.

- The results from a cross-tab are usually reported by first stating the percent for the independent variable followed by the percent for the dependent variable. For example, "20 percent of single men prefer Burger King."

CROSS-TABS AND STATISTICAL SIGNIFICANCE

As discussed in this chapter, cross-tabulating survey data can lead to important insights about the potential relationships between two or more variables. However, a cross-tab alone does not provide evidence regarding the statistical significance of a relationship between variables. A chi-square analysis, discussed in the next chapter, tests statistical hypotheses regarding the strength of the relationship between variables.

INTERPRETING CROSS-TAB OUTPUTS FROM STATISTICAL ANALYSIS PROGRAMS

Interpreting the cross-tab output from a statistical program can be a bit confusing. This is because the statistical program usually does not know how the researcher intends to interpret the data and the results. It does not know which one of the two variables is the independent variable, and which one of the two variables is the dependent variable. As such, most statistical programs will provide cross-tab results showing three different percentages that have been calculated for a single cell frequency. To illustrate this, consider the cross-tab output shown in Table 23.8 that was produced from the SAS statistical analysis program. It shows a cross-tab table generated for two variables: *sex* (M = male, F = female) and *shop* (Do you shop at our store? Y = yes, N = no). The top left cell of the table describes the numbers that appear within each of the other individual cells.

TABLE 23.8 Cross-Tab Table of *Shop* by *Sex*

		Table of *Shop* by *Sex*		
		Sex		
Shop		M	F	Total
Frequency Percent Row Pct Col Pct	Y	4 20.00 33.33 40.00	8 40.00 66.67 80.00	12 60.00
	N	6 30.00 75.00 60.00	2 10.00 25.00 20.00	8 40.00
Total		10 50.00	10 50.00	20 100.00

Frequency refers to the number of people within a cell. For example, four men reported that they shop at the store (*sex* M, *shop* Y), and two women reported that they do not shop at the store (*sex* F, *shop* N).

Percent refers to the percentage calculated by dividing each cell frequency by the total number of people answering the question, that is, each cell mean divided by the total sample size (in this case, 20). This means that 20 percent of the people in the sample are men who shop at the store.

Row pct (row percent) refers to the percentage calculated by dividing each cell frequency by its respective row margin total. Since the different levels of the variable *shop* are represented in the rows (consumers who shop at the store are in the top row and consumers who do not shop at the store are in the bottom row), using this percentage would lead to the following conclusions:

- 33.3 percent of the consumers in the sample who shop at the store are men.
- 25 percent of the consumers in the sample who do not shop at the store are women.

And, in this case, using the row percentages would be misleading and somewhat difficult to understand. This is because the variable *shop* is more likely to be considered the dependent variable. The variable *sex* is more likely to be considered the independent variable. It makes more sense to say that shopping at a store is influenced by a consumer's sex than to say that a consumer's sex is influenced by whether or not they shop at a store.

Col pct (column percent) refers to the percentage calculated by dividing each cell frequency by its respective column margin total. Since the different levels of the variable sex are represented in the columns (males are in the left column and females are in the right column), using this percentage would lead to the following conclusions:

- 40 percent of males in the sample shop at the store.
- 80 percent of females in the sample shop at the store.

And, because sex is more likely to be the independent variable in this case, using the column percentages would be appropriate.

QUESTIONS FOR DISCUSSION

1. Based on the frequency table shown below, does it appear that consumers' level of household income is related to the number of cars they own?

Level Of Income	1 Car	2 or More Cars	Total
Less Than $45,000	480	60	540
More Than $45,000	270	190	460
Total	750	250	1,000

2. Based on the frequency table shown below, does it appear that consumers' sex is related to willingness to purchase a new style of car? Who is more willing to purchase the new style of car, men or women?

Willing To Purchase?	Male	Female	Total
Yes	40	300	340
No	10	650	660
Total	50	950	1,000

Treasure Box

Researchers working for Treasure Box, a retail store that sells women's clothing, recently surveyed residents of a small town to see if their proximity to the store is related to whether or not they shop at the store. A random telephone survey was used to measure how far consumers live from the store (*live*, <10 = within 10 miles of the store, >10 = more than 10 miles from the store), as well as whether or not they shop at the store (*shop*, Y = yes, N = no). A total of 400 consumers agreed to participate and answer the survey questions. Below are the results from a cross-tab analysis of participants' responses to these two survey questions.

Table of *Live* by *Shop*

			Shop	
	Live	Y	N	Total
Frequency Percent Row Pct Col Pct	<10	140 35.00 63.64 73.68	80 20.00 36.36 38.10	220 55.00
	>10	50 12.50 27.78 26.32	130 32.50 72.22 61.90	180 45.00
	Total	190 47.50	210 52.50	400 100.00

1. Based on these cross-tab results, does there appear to be a relationship between how far consumers live from the store and whether or not they shop at the store? What percentages would be appropriate to use in answering this question?

2. If managers for Treasure Box wanted to conduct some intercept surveys to gain more understanding of why consumers do not shop at Treasure Box, where should they conduct these intercept interviews?

3. If you wanted to gain even further understanding of these results, what other variable(s) might you want to consider examining and including in the cross-tab analysis?

CHAPTER 24

Chi-Square Goodness of Fit Test

LEARNING OBJECTIVES

1 Describe the relationship between a cross-tab table and a chi-square test.

2 Describe the degrees of freedom associated with a chi-square test for the relationship between two variables.

3 Describe how expected values and observed values are used to calculate a chi-square statistic.

4 Write and explain the null hypothesis and the alternative hypothesis for a chi-square test.

5 Describe the decision rules based on the p value for a calculated chi-square test.

6 Calculate a chi-square test statistic for examining the relationship between two variables.

7 Interpret the output from a chi-square test performed by a statistical analysis program.

A **chi-square (χ^2) test** is used for determining if there is a statistically significant relationship between two categorical variables. The cross-tabulated data in the previous chapter could be analyzed statistically with a chi-square test. A chi-square test is calculated based on contingency tables that are joint frequency distributions of observations on two or more variables.

The hypotheses for a chi-square test will usually be:

Ho: There is no relationship between the variables; the variables are independent of one another.

Ha: There is a relationship between the variables; the variables are dependent on one another.

The decision rules for a chi-square test are:

$p > .05$, calculated χ^2 value < critical value; accept Ho; there is no relationship between the variables; they are independent of one another.

$p \leq .05$, calculated χ^2 value > critical value; reject Ho; there is a statistically significant relationship between the variables; the variables are dependent on one another.

To illustrate a chi-square test, imagine that we are interested in examining the potential relationship between a consumer's sex and whether or not they are aware of a store location. The null and alternative hypotheses for this chi-square test are:

Ho: Men and women are equally aware of the store location (i.e., there is no relationship between sex and awareness).

Ha: Awareness differs by sex (i.e., there is a relationship between sex and awareness).

As these hypotheses indicate, the chi-square will test for a significant relationship between sex and awareness of the store. In other words, the chi-square will test whether men and women have equal levels of awareness for the store location.

Degrees of Freedom. The **degrees of freedom (df)** for two variables in a contingency table $= (r - 1)(c - 1)$, where r is the number of rows and c is the number of columns in the contingency table. With a 2×2 contingency table, there is one degree of freedom. With a 2×4 contingency table there are three degrees of freedom. For the hypotheses stated above, imagine that we sample 100 consumers and the results are as shown in Table 24.1.

First, let's imagine that we know the margin totals for each variable. That is, we know that out of the total 100 respondents in the sample, 50 of them are men and 50 of them are women. We also know that 70 of them are aware of the store and 30 of them are unaware of the store. Given these margin totals, we need to know only one of the individual cell frequencies to be able to calculate the remaining three cell frequencies. Therefore, there is one degree of freedom. Only one of the cell frequencies is free to vary.

Calculating the Chi-Square Statistic. The chi-square statistic is calculated by comparing the **observed value** for each cell in the contingency table to its **expected value**. The calculation of a chi-square statistic is shown below.

$$\chi^2 = \Sigma \, [(\text{observed value} - \text{expected value})^2/\text{expected value}]$$

The expected frequency of each cell in the contingency table is calculated as:

$$E_{ij} = R_i(C_j)/n$$

where

R_i = total observed for the ith row (margin total for the ith row)
C_j = total observed for the jth column (margin total for the jth column)
n = total sample size

Thus, for the data in Table 24.1, the expected value of each cell in the contingency table is shown in Table 24.2 in parentheses.

A chi-square test is used to determine if there is a statistically significant relationship between two categorical variables.

TABLE 24.1 A 2 × 2 Contingency Table of Store Awareness by Respondent Sex

	Male	Female	Total
Aware	40	30	70
Unaware	10	20	30
Total	50	50	100

TABLE 24.2 Observed and (Expected) Values for Store Awareness by Respondent Sex

	Male	Female	Total
Aware	40 (35)	30 (35)	70
Unaware	10 (15)	20 (15)	30
Total	50	50	100

The chi-square statistic is calculated as $\chi^2 = \Sigma\,[(\text{observed value} - \text{expected value})^2/\text{expected value}]$

For the data in Table 24.2:

$$\chi^2 = \frac{(40-35)^2}{35} + \frac{(10-15)^2}{15} + \frac{(30-35)^2}{35} + \frac{(20-15)^2}{15}$$
$$= .714 + 1.67 + .714 + 1.67$$
$$= 4.77$$

The χ^2 distribution is shown in Figure 24.1.

Critical Values and Statistical Decisions. The critical value for a chi-square test statistic with one degree of freedom and alpha (α) = .05 is 3.84. This can be found by referring to the chi-square table provided in the appendix of this book. Since the calculated value (4.77) is greater than the critical value (at α = .05), we conclude that there is a statistically significant difference between men and women in terms of awareness. Thus, we conclude that there is a relationship between sex and awareness (reject Ho) at a 95 percent confidence level.

FIGURE 24.1 The Chi-Square (χ^2) Distribution

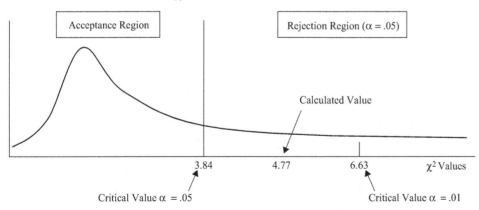

However, if alpha (α) = .01, the critical value is 6.63. In this case, we would conclude that there is no statistically significant difference between men and women in terms of awareness. Thus, we would conclude that there is no relationship between sex and awareness (accept Ho) at a 99 percent confidence level.

INTERPRETING THE CHI-SQUARE ANALYSIS OUTPUT

Interpreting the output from a chi-square analysis can be a bit confusing. This is because the proper interpretation of a chi-square analysis requires that the researcher know which of the two variables is to be treated as the independent variable, and which of the two variables is to be treated as the dependent variable. A statistical analysis program (such as SAS or SPSS) usually does not know how the researcher intends to interpret the data and the results. It does not know which one of the two variables is the independent variable and which one of the two variables is the dependent variable. As such, the output from a chi-square analysis will also provide a cross-tab table showing three different percentages that have been calculated for a single cell frequency. It is up to the researcher to select the appropriate percentage for the correct interpretation of the results. To illustrate this, consider the following survey questions and the coding scheme shown in Figure 24.2.

Do you consider yourself to be "in shape"?   ☐ Yes   ☐ No

What is your marital status?   ☐ Single   ☐ Married

The output from the chi-square analysis is show in Table 24.3, including the cross-tab table of frequencies and percentages, as well as the calculated chi-square statistic. The *p* value is shown under the column labeled *Prob*, which refers to the probability of finding a chi-square statistic this large, if the null hypothesis is true. The top left cell of the table describes the numbers that appear within each of the other individual cells.

Frequency refers to the number of people within a cell. For example, 38 single people in the sample reported that they consider themselves to be in shape (*inshape* = Y, *marital* = S), and 30 married people in the sample reported that they do not consider themselves to be in shape (*inshape* = N, *marital* = M). **Percent** refers to the percentage calculated by dividing each cell frequency by the total number of people answering the question, that is, each cell mean divided by the total sample size (in this case, 100). This means that 14 percent of the sample are single people who do not consider themselves to be in shape.

FIGURE 24.2 Coding Scheme for the Variables

Variable Name	Coded As
Inshape	Y = Yes N = No
Marital	S = Single M = Married

TABLE 24.3 Chi-Square Output

Table of *Inshape* by *Marital*

	Inshape	Marital S	M	Total
Frequency Percent Row Pct Col Pct	Y	38 38.00 67.86 73.08	18 18.00 32.14 37.50	56 56.00
	N	14 14.00 31.82 26.92	30 30.00 68.18 62.50	44 44.00
	Total	52 52.00	48 48.00	100 100.00

Statistic	DF	Value	Prob
Chi-Square	1	12.8216	0.0003

Row pct (row percent) refers to the percentage calculated by dividing each cell frequency by its respective row margin total. Since the different levels of the variable *inshape* are represented in the rows (people who consider themselves to be in shape are in the top row, and people who do not consider themselves to be in shape are in the bottom row), using this percentage would lead to the following conclusions:

- 32.14 percent of those people who consider themselves to be in shape are married.

- 31.82 percent of those people who do not consider themselves to be in shape are single.

In this case, using the row percentages would not be appropriate. This is because the variable *inshape* is more likely to be considered the dependent variable. The variable *marital* is more likely to be considered the independent variable. It makes more sense to say that perceptions of being in shape are influenced by a person's marital status than to say that a person's marital status is influenced by whether or not they perceive themselves to be in shape.

Col pct (column percent) refers to the percentage calculated by dividing each cell frequency by its respective column margin total. Since the different levels of the variable *marital* are represented in the columns (single people are in the left column and married people are in the right column), using this percentage would lead to the following conclusions:

- 73.08 percent of single people in the sample say that they are in shape.

- 37.5 percent of married people in the sample say that they are in shape.

A calculated chi-square statistic with an accompanying small p value (e.g., $p < .05$) indicates that there is a statistically significant relationship between the variables.

And, because marital status is more likely to be the independent variable in this case, using the column percentages would be appropriate.

The Calculated Chi-Square Statistic The calculated chi-square statistic (χ^2) = 12.82. Since the p value is very small (p = .0003, shown under the column labeled "Prob"), we conclude that the test statistic is significant and that the two variables are related. Compared to married people, single people are more likely to say that they are in shape.

CHI-SQUARE GOODNESS OF FIT TEST FOR THE NOTE-TAKING SURVEY

A chi-square test is appropriate for examining the relationship between whether or not a student would buy notes from a note-taking service (*buy*; 1 = yes, 2 = no) and

- Whether or not they have ever borrowed notes from another student (*ever*; 1 = yes, 2 = no).

- Whether or not they think having good notes is important to getting a good grade in a class (*grade*; 1 = yes, 2 = no).

- Their year in school (*year*; 1 = freshman, 2 = sophomore, 3 = junior, 4 = senior).

- Their major (*major*; 1 = business, 2 = basic and applied sciences, 3 = education, 4 = liberal arts, 5 = mass communication).

- Their sex (*sex*; 1 = male, 2 = female).

- Whether or not they are a full-time or a part-time student (*fullpart*; 1 = full-time, 2 = part-time).

- Whether or not they are a member of either a fraternity or a sorority (*frat*; 1 = yes, 2 = no).

The results from these analyses are shown in Tables 24.4 through 24.10.

Based on these chi-square analyses, we conclude that students' willingness to purchase notes from a note-taking service is significantly related to:

- Whether or not students have ever borrowed notes from another student. Those who have borrowed notes were more likely to say that they would buy notes.

- Whether or not students thought having good notes was important to getting a good grade in a class. Those who thought it was important were more likely to say that they would buy notes.

- Students' year in school. Sophomores and seniors were more likely to say that they would buy notes.

- Students' major. Students majoring in business, education, and liberal arts were more likely to say that they would buy notes.

- Students' full-time/part-time status. Full-time students were more likely to say that they would buy notes.

TABLE 24.4 Chi-Square Results for *Buy* by *Ever*

		Table of Buy by Ever		
		Ever		
Buy		**1**	**2**	**Total**
Frequency Percent Row Pct Col Pct	1	61 55.96 91.04 77.22	6 5.50 8.96 20.00	67 61.47
	2	18 16.51 42.86 22.78	24 22.02 57.14 80.00	42 38.53
Total		79 72.48	30 27.52	109 100.00

Statistic	DF	Value	Prob
Chi-Square	1	30.0520	<.0001

TABLE 24.5 Chi-Square Results for *Buy* by *Grade*

		Table of Buy by Grade		
		Grade		
Buy		**1**	**2**	**Total**
Frequency Percent Row Pct Col Pct	1	63 57.80 94.03 77.78	4 3.67 5.97 14.29	67 61.47
	2	18 16.51 42.86 22.22	24 22.02 57.14 85.71	42 38.53
Total		81 74.31	28 25.69	109 100.00

Statistic	DF	Value	Prob
Chi-Square	1	35.4148	<.0001

TABLE 24.6 Chi-Square Results for *Buy* by *Year*

| | | | | Table of *Buy* by *Year* | | |
| | | | | **Year** | | |

Buy		1	2	3	4	Total
Frequency Percent Row Pct Col Pct	1	12 11.01 17.91 54.55	21 19.27 31.34 77.78	14 12.84 20.90 41.18	20 18.35 29.85 76.92	67 61.47
	2	10 9.17 23.81 45.45	6 5.50 14.29 22.22	20 18.35 47.62 58.82	6 5.50 14.29 23.08	42 38.53
Total		22 20.18	27 24.77	34 31.19	26 23.85	109 100.00

Statistic	DF	Value	Prob
Chi-Square	3	12.0103	0.0073

TABLE 24.7 Chi-Square Results for *Buy* by *Major*

| | | | | Table of *Buy* by *Major* | | | |
| | | | | **Major** | | | |

Buy		1	2	3	4	5	Total
Frequency Percent Row Pct Col Pct	1	20 18.35 29.85 90.91	6 5.50 8.96 27.27	17 15.60 25.37 73.91	16 14.68 23.88 72.73	8 7.34 11.94 40.00	67 61.47
	2	2 1.83 4.76 9.09	16 14.68 38.10 72.73	6 5.50 14.29 26.09	6 5.50 14.29 27.27	12 11.01 28.57 60.00	42 38.53
Total		22 20.18	22 20.18	23 21.10	22 20.18	20 18.35	109 100.00

Statistic	DF	Value	Prob
Chi-Square	4	25.4858	<.0001

TABLE 24.8 Chi-Square Results for *Buy* by *Sex*

		Sex		
Buy		**1**	**2**	**Total**
Frequency Percent Row Pct Col Pct	1	41 37.61 61.19 63.08	26 23.85 38.81 59.09	67 61.47
	2	24 22.02 57.14 36.92	18 16.51 42.86 40.91	42 38.53
Total		65 59.63	44 40.37	109 100.00

Table of *Buy* by *Sex*

Statistic	DF	Value	Prob
Chi-Square	1	0.1760	0.6748

TABLE 24.9 Chi-Square Results for *Buy* by *Fullpart*

		Fullpart		
Buy		**1**	**2**	**Total**
Frequency Percent Row Pct Col Pct	1	65 59.63 97.01 69.89	2 1.83 2.99 12.50	67 61.47
	2	28 25.69 66.67 30.11	14 12.84 33.33 87.50	42 38.53
Total		93 85.32	16 14.68	109 100.00

Table of *Buy* by *Fullpart*

Statistic	DF	Value	Prob
Chi-Square	1	18.9852	<.0001

TABLE 24.10 Chi-Square Results for *Buy* by *Frat*

		Frat		
Buy		1	2	Total
Frequency Percent Row Pct Col Pct	1	18 16.51 26.87 75.00	49 44.95 73.13 57.65	67 61.47
	2	6 5.50 14.29 25.00	36 33.03 85.71 42.35	42 38.53
Total		24 22.02	85 77.98	109 100.00

Statistic	DF	Value	Prob
Chi-Square	1	2.3795	0.1229

We also conclude that students' willingness to purchase notes from a note-taking service is not significantly related to:

- Students' sex.

- Whether or not students are in either a fraternity or a sorority.

QUESTIONS FOR DISCUSSION

1. Based on the chi-square results for the note-taking survey presented in this chapter, what marketing recommendations would you offer to someone seeking to open this type of business?

2. Describe the difference between a cross-tab analysis, described in the previous chapter, and a chi-square analysis, described in this chapter.

3. How many degrees of freedom are associated with the following cross-tab tables for a chi-square analysis:
   a. 2×3 table
   b. 4×5 table
   c. 3×6 table

MINICASE **24.1**

Fur on the Floor Dog Grooming

Janet Culbertson loves dogs. Last year she decided to open her own dog grooming business, called Fur on the Floor Dog Groomers. Business has been acceptable, but not what she had hoped for. So, she recently conducted some simple marketing research surveys of her customers. As a customer finished paying for the dog grooming service, he or she was given a short survey to complete measuring satisfaction with the service received at Fur on the Floor. Two of the questions on the survey asked for the respondent's sex (M = male; F = female), and whether or not they intended to return to Fur on the Floor Dog Groomers (Y = intend to return again, N = do not intend to return again). Below is a cross-tab table showing how men and women responded to the question about returning to Fur on the Floor Dog Groomers.

Table of Sex by Return

| | Sex | Return | | Total |
		Y	N	
Frequency	M	120	80	200
	F	90	110	200
	Total	210	190	400

Based on these results:

1. Determine the Ho and Ha for a chi-square test.

2. Calculate the expected value of each cell.

3. Calculate the chi-square statistic.

4. Determine if the chi-square statistic is statistically significant at $\alpha = .05$.

5. Determine if the chi-square statistic is statistically significant at $\alpha = .01$.

6. Interpret the results. What type of customers like the service and intend to return again?

MINICASE 24.2

Maple Street JazzFest

The Maple Street JazzFest is a two-day music festival featuring jazz music and local food vendors. Organizers of the Maple Street JazzFest recently conducted some customer satisfaction surveys of people who attended this past year's JazzFest. The coding sheet below shows the variable names and codes assigned to response alternatives for selected questions from the survey. Using the chi-square analysis outputs, answer the following questions:

1. Is there a significant relationship between the number of people in a group and the amount of time that people stay at the JazzFest? If so, what is the nature of this relationship?

2. Is there a significant relationship between the amount of time someone stays at the JazzFest and the amount of money they spend there? If so, what is the nature of this relationship?

3. Is there a significant relationship between the number of people in a group and the amount of money spent at the JazzFest? If so, what is the nature of this relationship?

4. Is there a significant relationship between how much people enjoy the music at the JazzFest and intention to attend next year's JazzFest? If so, what is the nature of this relationship?

5. Is there a significant relationship between how much people enjoy the food at the JazzFest and intention to attend next year's JazzFest? If so, what is the nature of this relationship?

6. What marketing recommendations would you offer if organizers of the JazzFest are hoping to increase the amount of time and money that people spend at next year's JazzFest?

MAPLE STREET JAZZFEST SURVEY CODING SHEET

Survey Question	Variable Name	Coding Scheme
How many people (friends, family members) are with you today (including yourself)?	People	1, 2 = 1 or 2 people >2 = More than 2 people
How many hours will you spend at this year's JazzFest?	Hours	1-3 = 3 hours or less >3 = More than 3 hours
Approximately how much money will you spend per person at this year's JazzFest?	Money	<10 = $10 or less >10 = More than $10
How enjoyable was the music at this year's JazzFest?	Music	1 = Not enjoyable 2 = Somewhat enjoyable 3 = Very enjoyable
How enjoyable was the food at this year's JazzFest?	Food	1 = Not enjoyable 2 = Somewhat enjoyable 3 = Very enjoyable
Do you plan on attending next year's JazzFest?	Nextyear	1 = Yes 2 = No

Table of *Hours* by *People*

	Hours	People 1, 2	>2	Total
Frequency Percent Row Pct Col Pct	1-3	324 36.20 57.86 69.38	236 26.37 42.14 55.14	560 62.57
	>3	143 15.98 42.69 30.62	192 21.45 57.31 44.86	335 37.43
	Total	467 52.18	428 47.82	895 100.00

Statistic	DF	Value	Prob
Chi-Square	1	19.3330	<.0001

Table of *Money* by *Hours*

		Hours		
	Money	1–3	>3	Total
Frequency Percent Row Pct Col Pct	<10	421 47.04 70.28 75.18	178 19.89 29.72 53.13	599 66.93
	>10	139 15.53 46.96 24.82	157 17.54 53.04 46.87	296 33.07
	Total	560 62.57	335 37.43	895 100.00

Statistic	DF	Value	Prob
Chi-Square	1	46.0180	<.0001

Table of *Money* by *People*

		People		
	Money	1, 2	>2	Total
Frequency Percent Row Pct Col Pct	<10	326 36.42 54.42 69.81	273 30.50 45.58 63.79	599 66.93
	>10	141 15.75 47.64 30.19	155 17.32 52.36 36.21	296 33.07
	Total	467 52.18	428 47.82	895 100.00

Statistic	DF	Value	Prob
Chi-Square	1	3.6592	0.0558

Table of *Music* by *Nextyear*

	Music	Nextyear 1	Nextyear 2	Total
Frequency Percent Row Pct Col Pct	1	11 1.32 78.57 1.39	3 0.36 21.43 7.14	14 1.67
	2	108 12.92 87.80 13.60	15 1.79 12.20 35.71	123 14.71
	3	675 80.74 96.57 85.01	24 2.87 3.43 57.14	699 83.61
Total		794 94.98	42 5.02	836 100.00

Statistic	DF	Value	Prob
Chi-Square	2	24.8581	<.0001

Table of *Food* by *Nextyear*

	Food	Nextyear 1	Nextyear 2	Total
Frequency Percent Row Pct Col Pct	1	10 1.43 66.67 1.52	5 0.71 33.33 12.50	15 2.14
	2	165 23.57 89.67 25.00	19 2.71 10.33 47.50	184 26.29
	3	485 69.29 96.81 73.48	16 2.29 3.19 40.00	501 71.57
Total		660 94.29	40 5.71	700 100.00

Statistic	DF	Value	Prob
Chi-Square	2	34.4093	<.0001

CHAPTER 25

Analysis of Variance (Anova)

LEARNING OBJECTIVES

1 Define ANOVA.

2 Describe the purpose and use of ANOVA.

3 Explain the differences between within group variability and between group variability.

4 Write and explain the null hypothesis and the alternative hypothesis for an ANOVA.

5 Describe the decision rules for an ANOVA based on the calculated p value for an F-test.

6 Interpret the output from an ANOVA performed by a statistical analysis program.

7 Explain what is meant by multiple comparison procedures and when they would be used.

One-way **analysis of variance (ANOVA)** is used to test for differences among the mean values of a single dependent variable across two or more levels of a single independent variable. For example, we might want to examine whether or not the average number of DVDs that students rent per month varies by their year in school, either freshman, sophomore, junior, or senior.

The null hypothesis for ANOVA will usually be that the means for the different levels of the independent variable (the means for each treatment) are the same. The alternative hypothesis will usually be that the means for the different levels of the independent variable (the means for each treatment) are different, or, one of the treatment means is different from another mean.

Ho: $\mu_1 = \mu_2 = \ldots = \mu_n$, the means for the groups do not differ (all group means are the same).

Ha: $\mu_1 \neq \mu_2 \neq \ldots \neq \mu_n$, the means for the groups differ (at least one group mean is significantly different from another group mean).

The decision rules for ANOVA are:

$p > .05$, calculated F value < critical value; accept Ho; the group means do not differ.

$p \leq .05$, calculated F value > critical value; reject Ho; the group means differ (at least one group mean is significantly different from another group mean).

Means and Variability. In making comparisons across the different levels of an independent variable, ANOVA considers both the means of each treatment and the variability of the observations that make up each mean. With ANOVA, an F-test is used to examine the total amount of variation in the sample. There are two forms of variation:

1. Variation of scores due to random error, or **within group variation** due to individual differences.

2. Systematic variation of scores across the groups, or **between group variation** as a result of manipulating an independent variable, or due to characteristics of the independent variable.

The total variation is equal to the sum of the variation within groups plus the variation between groups. The F-statistic is the ratio of variation between groups divided by the variation within groups.

F = between group variation/within group variation

The larger the F-statistic, the greater the evidence that the means for the groups do in fact differ. To illustrate this, consider the graphical representation of four group means presented in Figure 25.1.

In Figure 25.1, groups 1 and 3 have the same mean and groups 2 and 4 have the same mean. However, the variation within groups 1 and 2 is much greater than the variation within groups 3 and 4. As a result, the comparison between the means of group 1 and group 2 is not likely to result in a statistically significant difference. This is due to the large within group variability in these two groups. But, the comparison between the means of group 3 and group 4 is very likely to result in a statistically significant difference. This is because of the small within group variability in these two groups.

ANOVA Summary Table. The results from a one-way ANOVA are usually presented in an **ANOVA summary table**, as shown in Table 25.1. The term **sum of squares** refers to variability. **Sum of squares between groups** (SSB) refers to the variability between groups. **Sum of squares within groups** (SSE) refers to variability within groups.

> One-way analysis of variance (ANOVA) is used to test for differences among the mean values of a dependent variable across two or more levels of a single independent variable.

FIGURE 25.1 Graphical Representation of Between Group and Within Group Variation

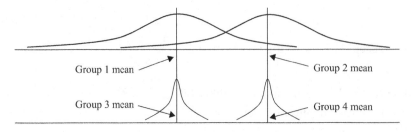

Group 1 mean
Group 2 mean
Group 3 mean
Group 4 mean

TABLE 25.1 ANOVA Summary Table

Source of Variation	Degrees of Freedom	Sum of Squares	Mean Square	F-Ratio
Between Groups	$c-1$	SSB	$SSB/c-1$	MSB/MSE
Within Groups	$cn-c$	SSE	$SSE/cn-c$	
Total	$cn-1$	SST		

where
c = number of groups
n = number of observations in a group

EXPLAINING VARIABILITY

To illustrate ANOVA, consider the example shown in Table 25.2, in which 10 people completed a survey measuring their income, sex, and marital status.

Imagine that we were to survey an 11th person and we wanted to know if that person's income was above or below the average income of $35,500. If we were not able to measure that person's income, which of the following questions would you ask?

1. What is your sex?

2. What is your marital status?

In other words, which of these two variables (sex or marital status) will best predict whether the 11th person's income is above or below the average income? Of the variables sex and marital status, which one best explains more of the variation in incomes?

TABLE 25.2 Income, Sex, and Marital Status of 10 People

Annual Personal Income ($)	Sex	Marital Status
10,000	F	M
60,000	M	S
30,000	F	S
20,000	F	M
15,000	F	S
55,000	M	M
10,000	F	M
45,000	M	S
40,000	M	S
70,000	M	M
Average annual income = $35,500	5 male, 5 female	5 married, 5 single

By looking at the data in Table 25.2, it appears that some of the married people have low incomes and some have high incomes. The same can be said of the single people. Thus, marital status does not seem to explain the variation in incomes. However, it appears that there is a systematic difference in incomes for men and women. For the people in this sample, women tend to have lower incomes whereas men tend to have higher incomes. Thus, a person's sex seems to explain the variation in incomes.

The ANOVA output analyzing the average incomes of men versus women and married versus single people in this example is shown in Table 25.3. The F statistic is shown under the column labeled "F Value." The p value for the test is shown under the column labeled "Pr > F." This indicates the probability of finding an F statistic this large, if the null hypothesis is true.

This output indicates that the overall ANOVA model is significant ($F_{2,7} = 14.41$, $p = .0033$). However, only the variable sex is statistically significant in terms of explaining the variability of incomes ($F_{1,7} = 28.29$, $p = .0011$). From this analysis we would conclude that:

> When performing an ANOVA, a large F statistic and a small p value (e.g., p < .05) indicate that the mean scores for the dependent variable are significantly different across levels of the independent variable.

- Men have higher incomes than women.

- The difference in sample mean incomes across the two sexes ($mean_{male} = \$54,000$, $mean_{female} = \$17,000$) is due to actual differences in average incomes for men and women in the population.

TABLE 25.3 ANOVA Output: Dependent Variable *Income*

Source	DF	Sum of Squares	Mean Square	F Value	Pr > F
Model	2	3437500000	1718750000	14.41	0.0033
Error	7	835000000	119285714		
Corrected Total	9	4272500000			

Source	DF	Sum of Squares	Mean Square	F Value	Pr > F
Sex	1	3375000000	3375000000	28.29	0.0011
Marital	1	15000000	15000000	0.13	0.7333

Level of Sex	N	Income Mean	Income SD
F	5	17000.00	8366.6
M	5	54000.00	11937.3

Level of Marital	N	Income Mean	Income SD
M	5	33000.00	27748.9
S	5	38000.00	16807.7

- Single people do not have significantly higher incomes than married people.

- The higher average income for single people (mean$_{single}$ = $38,000) compared to married people (mean$_{married}$ = $33,000) is due to random sampling error.

ANOVA FOR THE NOTE-TAKING SURVEY

ANOVA can be used to examine the following research objectives for the note-taking survey. Measure whether the likelihood of students buying notes from a note-taking service (*likely*) differs for:

- Those who have and those who have not borrowed notes in the past (*ever*).

- Students at different years in their college education (*year*).

- Students in different majors (*major*).

- Students who are in fraternities or sororities compared to those who are not (*frat*).

The output from the ANOVA examining these research objectives is shown in Table 25.4.

TABLE 25.4 ANOVA OUTPUT: DEPENDENT VARIABLE *LIKELY*

Source	DF	Sum of Squares	Mean Square	F Value	Pr > F
Model	9	239.5347303	26.6149700	11.67	<.0001
Error	99	225.7313248	2.2801144		
Corrected Total	108	465.2660550			

Source	DF	Sum of Squares	Mean Square	F Value	Pr > F
Ever	1	97.8234390	97.8234390	42.90	<.0001
Year	3	36.5743161	12.1914387	5.35	0.0019
Major	4	104.5317564	26.1329391	11.46	<.0001
Frat	1	0.6052188	0.6052188	0.27	0.6076

Level of Ever	N	Likely Mean	SD
1	79	4.35	1.97
2	30	2.23	1.47

Level of Year	N	Likely Mean	SD
1	22	3.59	1.89
2	27	4.48	2.17
3	34	2.88	1.87
4	26	4.34	2.01

Level of *Major*	N	Likely Mean	SD
1	22	5.63	1.70
2	22	2.86	2.05
3	23	4.17	2.10
4	22	2.90	1.41
5	20	3.20	1.70

Level of *Frat*	N	Likely Mean	SD
1	24	4.75	2.40
2	85	3.49	1.90

The F values for *ever*, *year*, and *major* were significant. Based on this analysis, we conclude that:

- Students who have borrowed notes in the past are more likely to buy notes.

- The average purchase likelihood varies by students' year in school.

- There is a significant difference in purchase likelihood across majors.

- Even though the average likelihood for those students who are in fraternities or sororities is higher than the average likelihood for those students who are not in fraternities or sororities, this difference is not statistically significant. The observed difference could be due to random sampling error.

Notice that for students' *year* in school and students' *major*, we know only that there is a significant difference in means across groups. We are not able to say which levels of these variables have significantly different purchase likelihood. ANOVA indicates whether or not there is a difference in the levels of the variable, but it does not indicate which levels of the variable are significantly different from each other. To do that, we need to use a multiple comparison procedure.

MULTIPLE COMPARISON PROCEDURES

When the null hypothesis is rejected in a one-way analysis of variance, this indicates that the treatment means are different. But, which treatment means are responsible for the difference among treatment means? One way of answering this question is to perform a series of *t*-tests on all pairs of treatment means to determine which are significantly different. For example, if we were testing for differences in the average age across seven separate market segments, there would be $k = 7$ different groups. With 7 groups, there would be 21 possible hypotheses to test concerning the difference between the individual group means (e.g., group 1 versus group 2, group 1 versus group 3, etc.). In general, with k groups, there will be $k(k − 1)/2$ separate comparisons.

Problems with Multiple t-Tests. The problem with performing these multiple tests is that for each test there will be a 5 percent probability of making a type I error (if α = .05). Thus, if we perform 100 tests with α = .05, we can expect to incorrectly reject five null hypotheses (where the null is that the groups are the same) that in fact are correct. We would falsely conclude that the groups are different. This means that we will falsely conclude that some of the treatment means differ when they really do not differ. The α level applies only to a single test, not to a series of tests.

Data snooping is the tendency to investigate group comparisons where the differences in group means appear to be large from the sample data. This should be avoided. With a greater number of factor levels, the likelihood of a false indication of a real effect is increased.

Multiple Comparison Procedures. One way to avoid this problem is to perform each test at a significance level of $\alpha/[k(k − 1)/2]$. This method is referred to as the **least significant difference method (LSD)**, which ensures that the overall significance level does not exceed α. However, by doing this the overall power of the test is lowered, making the probability of a type II error relatively higher. More powerful and more commonly used procedures are **Tukey's multiple comparison procedure**, **Scheffe's multiple comparison procedure**, or **Bonferroni's multiple comparison procedure**.

These three procedures allow for a family confidence coefficient for the family of comparisons to be controlled. As such, they provide assurance that all comparisons in the family are correct. The Tukey and Scheffe methods allow for data snooping without affecting the confidence coefficient. Tukey's procedure is probably the most often used. All of these procedures can be easily requested within the context of the ANOVA procedure in most statistical analysis programs.

> A multiple comparison procedure is used to answer the question, "Which treatment means are significantly different from each other?"

MULTIPLE COMPARISON PROCEDURE FOR THE NOTE-TAKING SURVEY

The results from the Tukey multiple comparison analysis for the note-taking survey are shown in Table 25.5.

TABLE 25.5 Results from the Multiple Comparison Procedure: Dependent Variable *Likely*

Source	DF	Sum of Squares	Mean Square	F Value	Pr > F
Model	4	121.2617072	30.3154268	9.17	<.0001
Error	104	344.0043478	3.3077341		
Corrected Total	108	465.2660550			

	Comparisons significant at the 0.05 level are indicated by ***			
Major Comparison	**Difference Between Means**	**Simultaneous 95% Confidence Limits**		
1 - 3	1.4625	−0.0433	2.9682	
1 - 5	2.4364	0.8764	3.9963	***
1 - 4	2.7273	1.2049	4.2497	***
1 - 2	2.7727	1.2503	4.2951	***
3 - 1	−1.4625	−2.9682	0.0433	
3 - 5	0.9739	−0.5698	2.5177	
3 - 4	1.2648	−0.2409	2.7706	
3 - 2	1.3103	−0.1955	2.8160	
5 - 1	−2.4364	−3.9963	−0.8764	***
5 - 3	−0.9739	−2.5177	0.5698	
5 - 4	0.2909	−1.2691	1.8509	
5 - 2	0.3364	−1.2236	1.8963	
4 - 1	−2.7273	−4.2497	−1.2049	***
4 - 3	−1.2648	−2.7706	0.2409	
4 - 5	−0.2909	−1.8509	1.2691	
4 - 2	0.0455	−1.4769	1.5678	
2 - 1	−2.7727	−4.2951	−1.2503	***
2 - 3	−1.3103	−2.8160	0.1955	
2 - 5	−0.3364	−1.8963	1.2236	
2 - 4	−0.0455	−1.5678	1.4769	

From this analysis we conclude that there are significant differences between group means 1 and 2, between group means 1 and 4, and between group means 1 and 5. This means that students majoring in business (group 1) are more likely to use the note-taking service than are students majoring in basic and applied sciences (group 2), liberal arts (group 4), and mass communication (group 5).

QUESTIONS FOR DISCUSSION

1. What is between subjects variability?

2. What is within subjects variability?

3. How are between subjects variability and within subjects variability compared in an ANOVA?

4. Imagine that you sampled men and women and found that the average age for men was 32, whereas the average age for women was 27. If you were testing to see whether the average age for men in the population is different from the average age of women in the population, and the results from the ANOVA were:

$$F_{1,176} = 1.45, p = .29$$

a. What is the null hypothesis (Ho)?

b. What is the alternative hypothesis (Ha)?

c. What do you conclude regarding the null and alternative hypotheses? What do you accept? What do you reject?

d. What is the probability of finding a difference in ages between men and women this large (32 compared to 27), if there is actually no difference in average ages for men and women in the population?

5. Based on the ANOVA results for the note-taking survey presented in this chapter, what marketing recommendations would you offer to someone seeking to open this type of business?

6. What are multiple comparison procedures? When are they used in marketing research?

MINICASE 25.1

Super Speedway

A nationally known Super Speedway recently conducted a customer satisfaction survey of 422 fans who attended a NASCAR-sponsored race at the Speedway. The coding sheet below shows the variable names and codes assigned to the response alternatives for selected questions from the survey. Using the ANOVA analysis outputs, answer the following questions:

1. Is there a difference between men and women in terms of their level of satisfaction with:

a. The location of concession stands?

b. The quality of the concessions?

c. The amount of children's/family activities at the Speedway?

d. The experience offered by the Fan Walk? (Note: The Fan Walk provides fans with an opportunity to walk by the garage area prior to the race for an up-close experience with the drivers, cars, pit crews, and teams.)

2. If so, what is the nature of the difference?

SUPER SPEEDWAY SURVEY CODING SHEET

Survey Question	Variable name	Coding Scheme
Indicate your level of satisfaction with the following, where 1 = Very Dissatisfied and 7 = Very Satisfied.		
Location of Concession Stands	*locconces*	Enter the number from 1–7
Quality of the Concessions	*qualconces*	Enter the number from 1–7
Amount of Children's/Family Activities	*childfam*	Enter the number from 1–7
Experience Offered by the Fan Walk Area	*fanwalk*	Enter the number from 1–7
What is your sex?	*sex*	1 = Male; 2 = Female

RESULTS FROM THE ANOVA: SUPER SPEEDWAY

Source	DF	Sum of Squares	Mean Square	F Value	Pr > F
Locconces	1	4.3811935	4.3811935	3.15	0.0767
Qualconces	1	3.4078663	3.4078663	1.82	0.1786
Childfam	1	19.8977356	19.8977356	9.88	0.0018
Fanwalk	1	14.0742710	14.0742710	6.27	0.0127

		Locconces	
Level of *Sex*	N	Mean	SD
1	272	6.11	1.18
2	156	6.32	1.16

		Qualconces	
Level of *Sex*	N	Mean	SD
1	263	6.05	1.34
2	156	6.24	1.41

		Childfam	
Level of *Sex*	N	Mean	SD
1	264	6.28	1.45
2	156	6.73	1.36

		Fanwalk	
Level of *Sex*	N	Mean	SD
1	267	6.29	1.53
2	155	6.67	1.42

CHAPTER (26)

Correlation Analysis

LEARNING OBJECTIVES

1 Explain the difference between correlation analysis, chi-square analysis, and ANOVA in terms of the information they provide researchers about the relationship between two variables.

2 Interpret the nature of the relationship between two variables if the correlation between them is zero ($r = 0$).

3 Interpret the nature of the relationship between two variables if the correlation between them is negative ($-1 \leq r < 0$).

4 Interpret the nature of the relationship between two variables if the correlation between them is positive ($0 < r \leq +1$).

5 Describe the relationship between correlation and causation.

6 Define and explain the coefficient of determination (r^2).

7 Write and explain the null hypothesis and the alternative hypothesis for a correlation analysis.

8 Describe the decision rules for a correlation analysis based on the calculated p value for a correlation coefficient.

9 Interpret the output from a correlation analysis performed by a statistical analysis program.

A chi-square analysis provides information about whether or not there is a relationship between two variables. An ANOVA provides information about whether or not there is a significant difference between group means. In contrast, the simple **correlation coefficient** (**Pearson product-moment correlation coefficient**) provides information about the strength or degree of relationship between variables. The simple correlation coefficient requires interval-scaled or ratio-scaled data.

Correlation and Covariation. The correlation coefficient (r) is a statistical measure of the **covariation**, or degree of **association**, between two variables. The correlation coefficient ranges from -1.0 to $+1.0$ (see Figure 26.1). The correlation coefficient (r) is the sample correlation coefficient, which is calculated to estimate ρ (rho) the population correlation coefficient. The correlation coefficient measures both the direction and magnitude of the relationship between two variables. If $r = +1.0$, there is a perfect positive relationship between two variables. Conversely, if $r = -1.0$, there is a perfect negative relationship between two variables. Correlation values between $+1.0$ and -1.0 indicate the degree to which two variables either vary in the same direction

FIGURE 26.1 Correlation Coefficients and the Relationship between Two Variables

r = +1. There is a perfect positive relationship between the two variables.

The two variables vary in the same direction.

r = 0   There is no correlation (relationship) between the variables.

The two variables vary in opposite directions.

r = −1. There is a perfect negative relationship between the two variables.

or vary in opposite directions. A zero correlation coefficient indicates that the two variables do not vary with each other in any consistent direction, and as such, are not related.

For example, there is likely to be a positive correlation between a salesperson's years of experience in sales and their annual sales commissions. Salespeople who have more years of experience in sales will likely earn relatively higher annual commissions. Salespeople who have very few years of sales experience will likely earn relatively lower commissions. Conversely, there is likely to be a negative correlation between a salesperson's years of experience in sales and the amount of errors on their written sales orders. More experienced salespeople will likely have fewer errors on their written sales orders, whereas less experienced salespeople will likely have more errors on their written sales orders. And finally, there is likely to be no correlation between a salesperson's years of experience in sales and their height. The interpretations of various correlation coefficients are illustrated in Figure 26.2.

A *t*-test is used to determine if a correlation is statistically significant.

$$t = (r - \rho)/S_r$$

FIGURE 26.2 Interpreting the Correlation between Two Variables (*X* and *Y*)

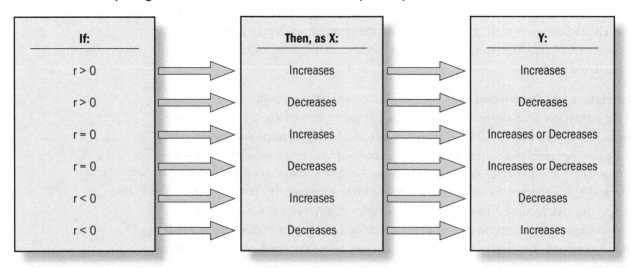

If:	Then, as X:	Y:
r > 0	Increases	Increases
r > 0	Decreases	Decreases
r = 0	Increases	Increases or Decreases
r = 0	Decreases	Increases or Decreases
r < 0	Increases	Decreases
r < 0	Decreases	Increases

In this test, ρ = the hypothesized correlation. Typically, the null hypothesis is that there is no correlation between the variables. The alternative hypothesis is that there is a significant correlation between the variables.

Ho: $\rho = 0$ (there is no correlation between the variables, there is no significant relationship between the variables).

Ha: $\rho \neq 0$ (there is a correlation between the variables, there is a significant relationship between the variables).

The decision rules for testing these hypotheses are:

$p > .05$, calculated t-value < critical value; accept Ho; the correlation is not significantly different from 0; there is no statistically significant relationship between the variables.

$p \leq .05$, calculated t-value > critical value; reject Ho; the correlation is significantly different from 0; there is a statistically significant relationship between the variables.

Correlation and Causation. It is important to note that a significant correlation between two variables does not mean that there is a significant causal relationship between the two variables. Correlation does not mean causation. Just because two variables are correlated, or are associated with each other, does not mean that one causes the other. For instance, a significant correlation between the level of the U.S. Stock Market and the length of women's skirts does not mean that there is a causal relationship between the two variables.

Percentage of Variation Explained. The **coefficient of determination (r^2)** is the proportion of variance in one variable (Y) explained by another variable (X). As such, r^2 is equal to the ratio of explained variance divided by the total variance. For example, the r^2 between students' grade point average and the number of hours they spend studying will most likely be larger than the r^2 between students' grade point average and their shoe size. The number of hours students spend studying will most likely explain a greater amount of the variation in grade point averages than will students' shoe sizes.

Whereas chi-square and ANOVA can provide evidence as to whether or not two variables are related, the correlation coefficient provides evidence about the strength and direction of the relationship between two variables.

CORRELATION ANALYSIS FOR THE NOTE-TAKING SURVEY

A correlation analysis can be used to determine whether or not there are any significant relationships between:

- The number of classes that a student misses during a typical semester (*number*).

- The number of times that a student borrows notes during a typical semester (*howmany*).

- How likely a student is to buy notes from a note-taking service (*likely*).

- The number of years that a student has been in college (*numyears*).

- How comfortable a student is in buying notes from a note-taking service (*comfort*).

- How ethical a student thinks that a note-taking service is (*ethical*).

- A student's age (*age*).

The results from the correlation analysis for these variables are shown in Table 26.1. Two numbers are reported for each cell in the correlation matrix shown below. The top number is the correlation coefficient (r). The bottom number is the p value for the test that the correlation coefficient equals zero. The p value is referred to by Prob > |r| under Ho: Rho = 0 (indicating the probability of finding a correlation coefficient this large, if the null is true). A very small p value indicates that the correlation coefficient is significantly different from zero, that is, there is a significant correlation between the variables. Notice that the correlations along the diagonal = 1.0. This is because every variable correlates perfectly with itself.

The correlations for a number of important relationships in this analysis are summarized in Table 26.2.

From this analysis we conclude that:

- The more often students miss class, the more often they borrow notes.

- Likelihood of buying notes is positively related to the number of classes students miss and their level of comfort in buying notes.

TABLE 26.1 Results from the Correlation Analysis: Note-Taking Survey

| | | | Pearson Correlation Coefficients, $N = 109$ | | | | |
| | | | Prob > \|r\| under Ho: Rho = 0 | | | | |
	Number	**Howmany**	**Likely**	**Numyears**	**Comfort**	**Ethical**	**Age**
Number	1.00000	0.64355 <.0001	0.46584 <.0001	0.30680 0.0012	0.56225 <.0001	−0.01416 0.8838	0.74133 <.0001
Howmany	0.64355 <.0001	1.00000	0.64009 <.0001	0.04326 0.6552	0.42346 <.0001	0.18062 0.0602	0.44287 <.0001
Likely	0.46584 <.0001	0.64009 <.0001	1.00000	−0.10026 0.2996	0.59047 <.0001	0.07621 0.4309	0.19710 0.0399
Numyears	0.30680 0.0012	0.04326 0.6552	−0.10026 0.2996	1.00000	0.15684 0.1034	0.19108 0.0466	0.73371 <.0001
Comfort	0.56225 <.0001	0.42346 <.0001	0.59047 <.0001	0.15684 0.1034	1.00000	−0.00122 0.9900	0.47582 <.0001
Ethical	−0.01416 0.8838	0.18062 0.0602	0.07621 0.4309	0.19108 0.0466	−0.00122 0.9900	1.00000	0.22235 0.0201
Age	0.74133 <.0001	0.44287 <.0001	0.19710 0.0399	0.73371 <.0001	0.47582 <.0001	0.22235 0.0201	1.00000

TABLE 26.2 Summary of Correlations: Note-Taking Survey

Variable	Variable	Correlation Coefficient	P Value
The number of classes students miss	How many times they borrow notes	.64	.0001
Students' likelihood of buying notes	The number of classes students miss	.46	.0001
Students' likelihood of buying notes	Number of years they have been in school	−.10	.29
Students' likelihood of buying notes	How ethical they feel the service is	.07	.43
Students' likelihood of buying notes	Level of comfort in buying notes	.59	.0001

QUESTIONS FOR DISCUSSION

1. What is the difference between correlation analysis, chi-square analysis, and ANOVA?

2. What does it mean if the correlation between two variables is:
   a. $r = .67$
   b. $r = -.52$
   c. $r = .00$

3. Does a significant correlation between two variables mean that there is a causal relationship between the two variables?

4. If the correlation coefficient between two variables is $r = .36$, what is the coefficient of determination between the two variables?

5. If the coefficient of determination between two variables $= .42$, what does this mean?

6. Based on the results from the correlation analysis for the note-taking survey presented in this chapter, what promotional messages would you recommend to someone who wanted to increase the likelihood of students buying notes from a note-taking service?

MINICASE 26.1

Super Speedway

A nationally known Super Speedway recently conducted a customer satisfaction survey of fans who attended a NASCAR-sponsored race at the Speedway. The coding sheet below shows the variable names and codes assigned to the response alternatives for selected questions from the survey. A total of 422 race fans completed the survey. Using the correlation analysis output, answer the following questions:

1. Is there a significant relationship between a fan's age and their level of satisfaction with:
   a. The quality of concessions?
   b. The value received from the concessions?

c. The location of restrooms?

d. The experience offered by the Fan Walk? (Note: The Fan Walk provides fans with an opportunity to walk by the garage area prior to the race for an up-close experience with the drivers, cars, pit crews, and teams.)

2. If so, what is the nature of the relationship?

3. If the Super Speedway wanted to attract and retain older fans, in what areas should they try to improve, and then what marketing or promotional messages could be created to promote these improvements to older fans?

Super Speedway Survey Coding Sheet		
Survey Question	**Variable Name**	**Coding Scheme**
Indicate your level of satisfaction with the following, where 1 = Very Dissatisfied and 7 = Very Satisfied.		
Quality of the Concessions	*qualconces*	Enter the number from 1–7
Value Received from Concessions	*valconces*	Enter the number from 1–7
Location of Restrooms	*locrest*	Enter the number from 1–7
Experience Offered by the Fan Walk Area	*fanwalk*	Enter the number from 1–7
In what year were you born?	*age*	Enter the year. Age = current year minus year entered.

Pearson Correlation Coefficients Prob > |r| under Ho: Rho = 0 Number of Observations					
	age	*qualconces*	*valconces*	*locrest*	*fanwalk*
age	1.00000	−0.13285 0.0076	−0.13733 0.0056	−0.02733 0.5815	0.00516 0.9174
qualconces	−0.13285 0.0076	1.00000	0.70003 <.0001	0.58899 <.0001	0.45672 <.0001
valconces	−0.13733 0.0056	0.70003 <.0001	1.00000	0.41255 <.0001	0.34032 <.0001
locrest	−0.02733 0.5815	0.58899 <.0001	0.41255 <.0001	1.00000	0.52823 <.0001
fanwalk	0.00516 0.9174	0.45672 <.0001	0.34032 <.0001	0.52823 <.0001	1.00000

CHAPTER 27

Two-Way ANOVA

LEARNING OBJECTIVES

1 Describe the purpose of a two-way analysis of variance (ANOVA).

2 Describe a factorial design.

3 Define main effect and interaction effect.

4 Identify main effects and interaction effects from cell means and margin means for survey data.

5 Graph and interpret an interaction effect between two variables.

6 Write and explain the null hypothesis and the alternative hypothesis for a two-way ANOVA.

7 Describe the decision rules for a two-way ANOVA based on the calculated p value for the F-test.

8 Interpret the output from a two-way ANOVA performed by a statistical analysis program.

MAIN EFFECTS AND INTERACTIONS

As discussed in a previous chapter, one-way analysis of variance (ANOVA) tests for differences among the mean values for a single dependent variable across levels of a single independent variable. In contrast, a **two-way ANOVA** allows researchers to test for differences among the mean values for a dependent variable across levels of two or more independent variables. This is accomplished by using a factorial design. A **factorial design** is one that allows the researcher to investigate possible interactions, or joint effects, of two or more independent variables (factors) on a single dependent variable. For example, consider the case of a marketer who has developed a new laundry detergent. There are two possible packages for this detergent (packages A and B) and two possible levels of price (high price and low price). Instead of conducting two separate experiments to examine the individual effect of each variable on the dependent variable, the researcher can examine the joint effects of both variables on the dependent variable within the context of a single experiment.

To perform the two-way ANOVA, the researcher randomly assigns 100 people to evaluate the detergent. Consumers evaluate only one particular combination of package and price and then indicate their likelihood of purchasing the product on a 7-point scale, where 1 = not likely to purchase and 7 = very likely to purchase. This is a 2 × 2 between subjects design because there are two levels of package and two

TABLE 27.1 Mean Evaluations by Package Design and Price Level

	Package A	Package B	Mean for Each Level of Price
High Price	1.0	3.0	2.0
Low Price	3.0	5.0	4.0
Mean for Each Level of Package	2.0	4.0	

levels of price, and both variables are manipulated across (between) the subjects. The average ratings for the 25 consumers in each of the four cells are shown in Table 27.1.

Main Effects. These results suggest that there is a significant main effect for price. A **main effect** refers to the effect of a single independent variable on the dependent variable. Each independent variable in a two-way ANOVA has a main effect, although it might not be statistically significant. A significant main effect means that averaged across all other variables, an independent variable has a significant effect on the dependent variable. When there is a significant main effect, the **margin means** for the different levels of an independent variable will be significantly different. For main effects, look at the margin means for the different levels of a variable, not the individual cell means.

Averaged across the two levels of package there is greater purchase likelihood for the lower price. There also appears to be a significant main effect for package. Averaged across the two levels of price there is greater purchase likelihood for package B.

Interactions. An **interaction** refers to the joint effect of a combination of two or more variables on the dependent variable. A significant interaction means that the effect of one independent variable on the dependent variable is not the same for all levels of a second independent variable. To identify interactions, look at the individual cell means.

In this case, price and package do not appear to interact in affecting purchase likelihood. This is because the effect of price on purchase likelihood is the same for both levels of package, and the effect of package on purchase likelihood is the same for both levels of price.

IDENTIFYING MAIN EFFECTS AND INTERACTIONS

Main effects and interactions are easily identified by examining margin means for each independent variable and plotting individual cells means. Imagine that consumers evaluate a new brand that has either a high price or a low price and is packaged in either package A or package B. They evaluate the brand on a 7-point scale, where 1 = dislike and 7 = like. Below are the results from three different situations.

Situation 1: Two Main Effects, No Interaction

The mean ratings for the consumers who evaluated the brand in the first situation are shown in Table 27.2 and shown graphically in Figure 27.1.

In this first situation, there appears to be a significant main effect for package. Averaged across both levels of price, evaluations are more positive for package B (mean$_B$ = 5.5) than for package A (mean$_A$ = 2.5). There also appears to be a significant main effect for price. Averaged across both levels of package, evaluations are more positive for the low price (mean$_{low}$ = 5.5) compared to the high price (mean$_{high}$ = 2.5). However, there does not appear to be a significant interaction. The effect of price on consumers' evaluations is the same for both packages. Likewise, the effect of package on consumers' evaluations is the same for both levels of price.

> A main effect refers to the effect of a single independent variable on the dependent variable.

Situation 2: Two Main Effects and Interaction

The mean ratings for the consumers who evaluated the brand in this second situation are shown in Table 27.3 and shown graphically in Figure 27.2.

As with the previous situation, there appears to be a significant main effect for package. Averaged across both levels of price, evaluations are more positive for package B (mean$_B$ = 4.0) than for package A (mean$_A$ = 1.5). There also appears to be a

TABLE 27.2 Mean Evaluations for Situation 1: Two Main Effects, No Interaction

	Package A	Package B	Mean for Each Level of Price
Low Price	4	7	5.5
High Price	1	4	2.5
Mean for Each Level of Package	2.5	5.5	

FIGURE 27.1 Mean Evaluations for Situation 1: Two Main Effects, No Interaction

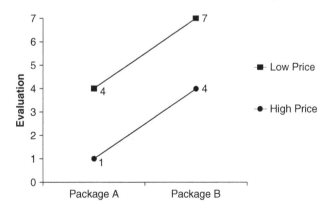

TABLE 27.3 Mean Evaluations for Situation 2: Two Main Effects and Interaction

	Package A	Package B	Mean for Each Level of Price
Low Price	2	7	4.5
High Price	1	1	1.0
Mean for Each Level of Package	1.5	4.0	

FIGURE 27.2 Mean Evaluations for Situation 2: Two Main Effects and Interaction

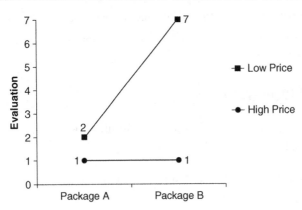

significant main effect for price. Averaged across both packages, evaluations are more positive for the low price (mean$_{low}$ = 4.5) compared to the high price (mean$_{high}$ = 1.0). Further, there also appears to be a significant interaction between price and package. Differences in package design appear to have a large effect on evaluations for the low price. Conversely, differences in package design appear to have no effect on evaluations for the high price. Thus, the effect of package on evaluations is not the same across both levels of price.

> A significant interaction means that the effect of one independent variable on the dependent variable is not the same for all levels of a second independent variable.

Situation 3: Interaction with No Main Effects

The mean ratings for the consumers who evaluated the brand in this third situation are shown in Table 27.4 and shown graphically in Figure 27.3.

In this third situation, there does not appear to be a significant main effect for either price or package. Averaged across both levels of package, the average evaluation for the low price (mean$_{low}$ = 4.0) is the same as the average evaluation for the high price (mean$_{high}$ = 4.0). Similarly, averaged across both levels of price, the average evaluation for package A (mean$_A$ = 4.0) is the same as the average evaluation for package B (mean$_B$ = 4.0). However, there does appear to be a significant interaction between price and package. The effect of price on evaluations is not the same for both package designs, and the effect of package on evaluations is not the same for both levels of price. In general, when results are graphed as in the above examples, lines that are not parallel to each other indicate an interaction between variables.

TABLE 27.4 Mean Evaluations for Situation 3: Interaction with No Main Effects

	Package A	Package B	Mean for Each Level of Price
Low Price	1	7	4.0
High Price	7	1	4.0
Mean for Each Level of Package	4.0	4.0	

FIGURE 27.3 Mean Evaluations for Situation 3: Interaction with No Main Effects

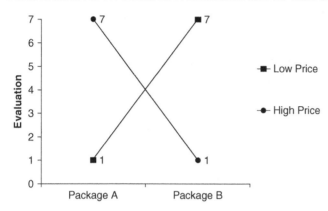

PREFERENCE FOR INTERACTIONS OVER MAIN EFFECTS

Compared to hypothesizing main effects, many researchers consider hypothesizing interactions to be stronger tests of theories. This is because it is usually easier to identify alternative plausible explanations for a main effect than it is for an interaction. Most of the articles published in academic research journals (*Journal of Marketing Research*, *Journal of Consumer Research*) present hypotheses concerning interactions. Very few of these articles present hypotheses concerning only main effects. Main effects are very easily explained away with alternative plausible explanations, and most researchers consider interactions to be more interesting than simple main effects.

INTERPRETING MARGIN MEANS

A difference in sample means does not always indicate that a main effect or an interaction effect is actually present. Differences in sample means could be merely the result of random sampling error. An analysis of variance (ANOVA) can be performed to determine if the observed effects are statistically significant.

TWO-WAY ANOVA HYPOTHESES AND DECISION RULES

The null hypothesis, alternative hypothesis, and the accompanying decision rules for a two-way ANOVA are as follows.

Main Effect for Factor A

Null and Alternative Hypotheses.

Ho: $\mu_{1.} = \mu_{2.} = \ldots = \mu_{a.}$, there is no significant main effect for factor A; all margin means for factor A are equal.

Ha: not all $\mu_{i.}$ are equal, there is a significant main effect for factor A; at least one margin mean for factor A is significantly different from the others.

The decision rules to test these hypotheses are:

$p > .05$, calculated F value < critical value; accept Ho; there is no significant main effect for factor A; the margin means for factor A do not differ.

$p \leq .05$, calculated F value > critical value; reject Ho; there is a significant main effect for factor A; the margin means for factor A differ.

Main Effect for Factor B

Null and Alternative Hypotheses.

Ho: $\mu_{.1} = \mu_{.2} = \ldots = \mu_{.b}$, there is no significant main effect for factor B; all margin means for factor B are equal.

Ha: not all $\mu_{.j}$ are equal, there is a significant main effect for factor B; at least one margin mean for factor B is significantly different from the others.

The decision rules to test these hypotheses are:

$p > .05$, calculated F value < critical value; accept Ho; there is no significant main effect for factor B; the margin means for factor B do not differ.

$p \leq .05$, calculated F value > critical value; reject Ho; there is a significant main effect for factor B; the margin means for factor B differ.

Interaction Between Factors A and B

Null and Alternative Hypotheses.

Ho: all $(\alpha\beta)_{ij} = 0$, there is no significant interaction between factors A and B.

Ha: not all $(\alpha\beta)_{ij} = 0$, there is a significant interaction between factors A and B.

The decision rules to test these hypotheses are:

$p > .05$, calculated F value < critical value; accept Ho; there is no significant interaction between factors A and B; the effect of factor A on the dependent variable is the same for all levels of factor B (and vice versa).

$p \leq .05$, calculated F value > critical value; reject Ho; there is a significant interaction between factors A and B; the effect of factor A on the dependent variable is not the same for all levels of factor B (and vice versa).

TWO-WAY ANOVA FOR THE NOTE-TAKING SURVEY

Two-way ANOVA is appropriate for examining the joint effects of students' sex (*sex*; 1 = male, 2 = female) and their year in school (*year*; 1 = freshman, 2 = sophomore, 3 = junior, 4 = senior) on their rating of how ethical a note-taking service is. The results of the ANOVA are shown in Table 27.5. The calculated F statistic is shown under the column labeled "F Value." The *p* value for the test is shown under the column labeled "Pr > F," which indicates the probability of finding an F statistic this large, if the null hypothesis is true.

Table 27.6 shows the individual cell means and the margin means for each of the two independent variables. Figure 27.4 graphically shows these individual cell means. The results from the analysis and the graph of cell means shown in Figure 27.4 indicate that there is a significant main effect for sex. The margin mean for males (4.26) is significantly greater than the margin mean for females (3.18). Similarly, there is a main effect for year in school. The margin mean for senior (5.07) is significantly greater than the other means. There is also a significant interaction. The graph in Figure 27.4 displays the nature of this interaction. The difference in ethical ratings between males and females is greater for seniors than for the other classes.

TABLE 27.5 Results for the ANOVA: Joint Effects of Sex and Year in School on Ethical Ratings

Source	DF	Sum of Squares	Mean Square	F Value	Pr > F
Model	7	148.4787600	21.2112514	4.34	0.0003
Error	101	493.2093134	4.8832605		
Corrected Total	108	641.6880734			

Source	DF	Type I SS	Mean Square	F Value	Pr > F
Sex	1	30.58877270	30.58877270	6.26	0.0139
Year	3	65.32976209	21.77658736	4.46	0.0055
Sex*Year	3	52.56022522	17.52007507	3.59	0.0163

TABLE 27.6 Mean Scores (Ethical) by Sex and Year in School

Source	Freshman	Sophomore	Junior	Senior	Total
Male	2.85	4.23	3.63	6.40	4.26
Female	4.00	3.50	2.47	3.27	3.18
Total	3.27	3.96	3.12	5.07	

FIGURE 27.4 Mean Scores (Ethical) by Sex and Year in School

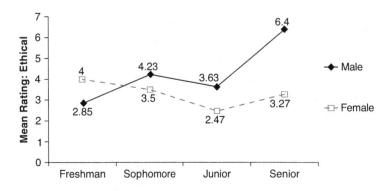

QUESTIONS FOR DISCUSSION

1. What is the purpose of a two-way ANOVA?

2. What is a factorial design and what is the purpose of a factorial design?

3. What do researchers look at to determine if there is a significant interaction between two variables?

4. If there is a significant interaction between two variables, and the means for the two variables are plotted graphically, what defining characteristic of the graph will be evident?

5. If there is a significant interaction between two variables, what does this mean? What is the interpretation of a significant interaction?

MINICASE 27.1

The Caballero Grill

The Caballero Grill is a restaurant that specializes in unique and authentic Mexican dishes. Researchers working for The Caballero Grill recently conducted a study to examine the effects of ambient lighting and music played in the restaurant on the length of time that customers stay at a table after being served their food. Two levels of music were examined: *fast*-paced music and *slow*-paced music. Two levels of lighting were examined: *low* lighting and *bright* lighting. These two factors were examined jointly within the context of a two-way ANOVA. Since most customers at a table tend to leave at the same time, a table of customers was treated as one customer. A total of 52 tables of customers were included in the study. The length of *time* that these customers remained at their table after being served their food was measured (in minutes). Customers were served in one of four possible conditions:

   i. *Low* lighting with *slow* music.

   ii. *Low* lighting with *fast* music.

   iii. *Bright* lighting with *slow* music.

   iv. *Bright* lighting with *fast* music.

Below are the results from the two-way ANOVA along with the individual cell means for the mean time spent at a table by pace of music and level of lighting.

Source	DF	Sum of Squares	Mean Square	F Value	Pr > F
Model	3	2440.076923	813.358974	53.50	<.0001
Error	48	729.692308	15.201923		
Corrected Total	51	3169.769231			

Source	DF	Type I SS	Mean Square	F Value	Pr > F
Music	1	784.692308	784.692308	51.62	<.0001
Light	1	1340.307692	1340.307692	88.17	<.0001
Music*Light	1	315.076923	315.076923	20.73	<.0001

Mean Time at Table by Pace of Music and Lighting	Slow Music	Fast Music	Mean for Each Level of Lighting
Low Lighting	46.8 (n = 13)	34.1 (n = 13)	40.4 (n = 26)
Bright Lighting	31.7 (n = 13)	28.8 (n = 13)	30.3 (n = 26)
Mean for Each Level of Music	39.2 (n = 26)	31.5 (n = 26)	

Graph the individual cell means to help you interpret the effects of lighting and pace of music on the length of time that customers remained at their table after being served their food. Draw a line representing the cell means for the low lighting condition. Then draw a separate line representing the cell means for the bright lighting condition.

1. Is there a significant main effect for lighting on the length of time that customers remained at their table after being served their food? If so, describe this effect.

2. Is there a significant main effect for the pace of music on the length of time that customers remained at their table after being served their food? If so, describe this effect.

3. Is there a significant interaction effect between lighting and the pace of music on the length of time that customers remained at their table after being served their food? If so, describe this interaction.

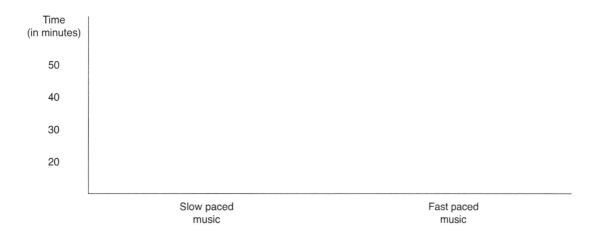

4. Did differences in the pace of music have a large effect or a small effect on the length of time that customers remained at their table after being served their food in the bright lighting condition?

5. Did differences in the pace of music have a large effect or a small effect on the length of time that customers remained at their table after being served their food in the low lighting condition?

6. What would you recommend if managers at The Caballero Grill wanted to:

   a. Decrease the amount of time that guests stay at their tables during times of day when the restaurant is very busy and customers are waiting for tables?

   b. Increase the amount of time that guests stay at their tables during times of day when the restaurant is not busy?

CHAPTER 28

Multiple Regression Analysis

LEARNING OBJECTIVES

1 Describe multiple regression analysis.

2 Interpret a main effect and an interaction effect within a multiple regression analysis.

3 Define and explain the coefficient of multiple determination (R^2) and the adjusted R^2.

4 Explain the rationale for calculating and using standardized variables within a multiple regression analysis.

5 Define and explain the coefficient of partial determination.

6 Define beta coefficient.

7 Write and explain the null hypothesis and the alternative hypothesis for a multiple regression analysis.

8 Describe the decision rules for a multiple regression analysis based on the calculated p value for the regression estimates.

9 Interpret the output from a multiple regression analysis performed by a statistical analysis program.

10 Explain the use of selection procedures in multiple regression analysis.

11 Compare and contrast forward selection procedures, backward selection procedures, and stepwise selection procedures.

12 Interpret the output from a multiple regression analysis performed by a statistical analysis program that uses a selection process.

A regression analysis is a statistical procedure for examining the relationship between an independent variable and a dependent variable. With **bivariate regression**, variations in the dependent variable are attributed to changes in only a single independent variable. However, in many real-life situations there are actually multiple factors that can have an effect on a dependent variable. As with two-way ANOVA, researchers using multiple regressions can examine the effects of more than one independent variable on the dependent variable. **Multiple regression** analysis allows a researcher to simultaneously investigate the individual and joint effects of two or more independent variables on a single dependent variable. With multiple regression analysis, researchers can determine whether or not a given set of independent variables is a significant predictor of a dependent variable. A multiple regression also allows researchers to examine which individual independent variables are significant predictors of a dependent variable.

The Overall Regression Model. A multiple regression analysis calculates whether or not a given set of independent variables is a significant predictor of the dependent variable. A significant F test for the overall regression model indicates that the combined set of independent variables is a significant predictor of the dependent variable.

Individual Regression Estimates. A multiple regression analysis also calculates a regression parameter estimate for each independent variable included in the regression model. The regression parameter estimate is a measure of the slope of a line that best fits (describes, explains) the level of the dependent variable at varying levels of the independent variable. A significant regression parameter estimate indicates that the slope of the relationship between the independent variable and the dependent variable is significantly different from zero, that is, the independent variable is a significant predictor of the dependent variable.

Interactions in Multiple Regression. In two-way ANOVA, a significant interaction term indicated that the effect of one independent variable on the dependent variable was not the same for all levels of a second variable. Recall that in two-way ANOVA the independent variables were categorical. However, in multiple regression analysis the independent variables can be either categorical or continuous. If researchers test for the interaction between two independent variables that are continuous variables (interval-scaled or ratio-scaled) in a multiple regression analysis, a significant **interaction** term means that the slope of the relationship between one independent variable (X_1) and the dependent variable (Y) changes across values of the second independent variable (X_2). In this case, the second independent variable (X_2) is called a **moderator variable**. In general, an interaction is also referred to as a **moderator effect**. And, a moderator effect occurs when one independent variable (a moderator variable) changes the form (slope) of the relationship between a second independent variable and the dependent variable.

Logistic Regression. **Logistic regression** (also called **linear probability models** and **logit analysis**) is a combination of multiple regression and **multiple discriminant analysis**. Both multiple regression and logistic regression examine the effects of multiple independent variables predicting a single dependent variable. However, in multiple regression, the dependent variable is a metric variable (interval-scaled or ratio-scaled), and in logistic regression the dependent variable is nonmetric (nominal-scaled or ordinal-scaled).

Coefficient of Multiple Determination. The **coefficient of multiple determination** (R^2) measures the proportion of variation in the dependent variable (Y) explained by the entire set of independent variables (X) included in the model. However, the R^2 will increase as more independent variables are added to a regression model. The coefficient of multiple determination can never decrease when more independent variables are added to the multiple regression model. Since R^2 can be made larger by

> By using multiple regression analysis, researchers can determine whether or not a given set of independent variables is a significant predictor of a dependent variable. A multiple regression also allows researchers to examine which of the individual independent variables are significant predictors of a dependent variable.

adding more variables, it is sometimes suggested that the researcher work with the adjusted R^2. The **adjusted R^2** recognizes the number of independent variables in the model, and can actually go down with additional variables.

The adjusted $R^2_a = 1 - [(n - 1)/(n - p)]$ [SSerror/SStotal]

where n = number of observations and p = the number of independent variables.

WHY STANDARDIZE VARIABLES?

Sometimes, the variables included in a multiple regression are not measured on the same scale. As a result, scale values for one variable do not mean the same thing as scale values for a second variable. This can cause problems when trying to interpret the results from the regression analysis. Standardizing all of the variables solves these problems of different scales for different variables. It converts all variables to comparable scales. A variable is **standardized** by calculating the number of standard deviations each observation is from the mean of its distribution. An observation (**raw score**) that is one standard deviation greater than the mean of its distribution has a **standardized score** of +1.0. Similarly, an observation (raw score) that is three standard deviations less than the mean of its distribution has a standardized score of -3.0.

Using Standardized Variables. To illustrate the usefulness of standardized variables, imagine that 1,000 consumers are surveyed to measure their level of expertise with respect to photography and using cameras. A two-item index comprised of two separate survey questions is used to measure their expertise. The first question measures objective experience, that is, the number of pictures that person actually takes in a typical month. The second question measures subjective experience, that is, a person's own perception of how experienced he or she is with respect to cameras and photography. The means and standard deviations for each of these two variables are shown in Table 28.1.

When multiple items (survey questions) are used to measure a single construct, the scores for all items in the index are summed or averaged to form the single measure of that construct. In this case, consumers' scores on both questions can be summed to form the composite measure of their overall level of expertise. Imagine that two consumers (Ann and Bill) responded to these two questions in the manner shown in Table 28.2. Based on the two-item index, which of these two consumers is more experienced with cameras and photography?

TABLE 28.1 Means and Standard Deviations: Expertise with Photography Survey

Survey Question	Sample Mean	Sample Standard Deviation
1. Approximately how photographs do you take in a typical month?	20	10
2. On a 7-point scale, where 1 = very little experience and 7 = very much experience, how much experience have you had with cameras and photography?	4	1

TABLE 28.2 Index Based on Raw Scores: Photography Survey

Raw Scores (answers to the survey questions)	Number of Photos	Experience 1–7 scale	Total (Sum)
Ann	30	6	36
Bill	34	4	38

TABLE 28.3 Index Based on Standardized Scores: Photography Survey

Standardized Scores	Number of Photos	Experience 1–7 scale	Total (Sum)
Ann	+ 1	+ 2	+ 3
Bill	+ 1.4	0	+ 1.4

Based on the raw scores (answers to the survey questions), we might conclude that Bill is more experienced because he has a larger combined score. But, this would actually be incorrect. Because the two scales are so very different in terms of their units of measurement (different ranges and different standard deviations), combining the raw scores would be misleading. Standardizing each raw score, and then summing the standardized scores, provides a better representation of which consumer actually has more experience with cameras and photography. These standardized scores are shown in Table 28.3.

The number of photos that Ann takes (30) is one standard deviation (10) above the mean number of photos for the sample (20). Similarly, the number or photos that Bill takes (34) is 1.4 standard deviations above the mean number of photos for the sample. The standardized scores for both consumers' answers on the 1–7 experience scale are calculated in a similar manner. Based on the standardized scores we would correctly conclude that Ann has more experience with cameras and photography.

STANDARDIZED REGRESSION ESTIMATES (BETA COEFFICIENTS)

Beta coefficients are **standardized estimates** that allow for a direct comparison between regression coefficients as to the relative explanatory power of the dependent variable. Although regression coefficients are expressed in terms of the original units of the associated variables (making comparisons between independent variables inappropriate in many cases), beta coefficients use standardized data and can be directly compared. Beta coefficients are calculated by standardizing each variable to a mean = 0 and standard deviation = 1 before estimating the regression equation. They eliminate the problem of dealing with different units of measurement and they reflect the relative impact of a change in one standard deviation of the independent variable on the dependent variable. A beta coefficient equal to 0.5 indicates that

Beta coefficients are standardized estimates that allow for a direct comparison between regression coefficients as to their relative explanatory power of the dependent variable.

a one standard deviation change in the independent variable is associated with a 0.5 standard deviation change in the dependent variable.

There are, however, a few cautions associated with using and interpreting beta coefficients. Beta coefficients should be used as a guide to the relative importance of individual independent variables only when the independent variables are not highly correlated with each other. Also, the beta coefficients can be interpreted only in the context of the other variables in the regression equation. It is not appropriate to compare beta coefficients of variables included in the model to beta coefficients not included in the model, or to beta coefficients for variables in different models estimated from different samples. Finally, beta coefficients should be used to measure the predictive power of variables only within the range of values actually measured in the sample.

MULTIPLE REGRESSION HYPOTHESES AND DECISION RULES

The null hypothesis, alternative hypothesis, and the accompanying decision rules for a multiple regression analysis are as follows.

Overall Regression Model

Null and Alternative Hypotheses.

Ho: $\beta_1 = \beta_2 = \ldots = \beta_n = 0$, there is no significant regression relationship between the set of independent variables and the dependent variable.

Ha: not all $\beta_n = 0$, there is a significant regression relationship between the set of independent variables and the dependent variable.

The decision rules for testing these hypotheses are:

$p > .05$, calculated F value < critical value; accept Ho; there is no significant regression relationship between the set of independent variables and the dependent variable.

$p \leq .05$, calculated F value > critical value; reject Ho; there is a significant regression relationship between the set of independent variables and the dependent variable.

Individual Regression Estimates

Null and Alternative Hypotheses.

Ho: $\beta_n = 0$, the individual regression parameter estimate is not significant; its slope = 0.

Ha: $\beta_n \neq 0$, the individual regression parameter estimate is significant; its slope is different from 0.

The decision rules for testing these hypotheses are:

$p > .05$, calculated F value < critical value; accept Ho; there is no significant regression relationship between the independent variable and the dependent variable; the independent variable is not a significant predictor of the dependent variable.

$p \leq .05$, calculated F value > critical value; reject Ho; there is a significant regression relationship between the independent variable and the dependent variable; the independent variable is a significant predictor of the dependent variable.

MULTIPLE REGRESSION WITH STANDARDIZED REGRESSION ESTIMATES FOR THE NOTE-TAKING SURVEY

The following research objectives can be examined with multiple regression and standardized regression estimates:

- Measure which of the following variables is a significant predictor of students' likelihood of buying notes from a note-taking service (*likely*):

    - Number of classes a student misses in a typical semester (*number*).

    - Whether or not a student has ever borrowed notes from another student (*ever*).

    - How many times in a typical semester a student borrows notes from another student (*howmany*).

    - Whether or not students think that having good notes is important to getting a good grade (*grade*).

    - A student's year in school (*year*).

    - The total number of years that a student has been in school (*numyears*).

    - How comfortable a student would be in buying notes from a note-taking service (*comfort*).

    - How ethical a student thinks that a note-taking service is (*ethical*).

- Determine which of the above variables has the greatest effect on students' likelihood of buying notes from a note-taking service.

The output from the regression analysis is shown in Table 28.4. An F test is used to test for the significance of the overall regression model. The calculated F statistic is shown under the column labeled "F Value." The p value for the F test is shown under the column labeled "Pr > F," which indicates the probability of finding an F statistic this large, if the null hypothesis is true. The output also shows the individual parameter estimates for each of the independent variables. A *t*-test is used to test for the significance of each parameter estimate. The p values for the individual *t*-tests are

TABLE 28.4 Results from the Regression Analysis: Note-Taking Survey

		Analysis of Variance (Dependent Variable: *Likely*)			
Source	**DF**	**Sum of Squares**	**Mean Square**	**F Value**	**Pr > F**
Model	8	285.11763	35.63970	19.78	<.0001
Error	100	180.14843	1.80148		
Corrected Total	108	465.26606			
R-Square		0.6128	Adj R-Square		0.5818

		Parameter Estimates				
Variable	**DF**	**Parameter Estimate**	**Standard Error**	**t Value**	**Pr > |t|**	**Standardized Estimate**
Intercept	1	3.15867	0.79263	3.99	0.0001	0
Number	1	0.00699	0.04571	0.15	0.8788	0.01542
Ever	1	−0.88399	0.36723	−2.41	0.0179	−0.19110
Howmany	1	0.24686	0.05718	4.32	<.0001	0.39723
Grade	1	−0.29063	0.40978	−0.71	0.4798	−0.06146
Year	1	0.00401	0.14772	0.03	0.9784	0.00206
Numyears	1	−0.21580	0.09150	−2.36	0.0203	−0.18071
Comfort	1	0.42486	0.09508	4.47	<.0001	0.36332
Ethical	1	0.02190	0.05807	0.38	0.7069	0.02572

shown under the column labeled "Pr > $|t|$," which indicates the probability of finding a t-test this large, if the null hypothesis is true. The output also shows the standardized estimate for each of the independent variables.

From this analysis, we conclude that the variables *ever, howmany, numyears*, and *comfort* are significant predictors of students' likelihood of purchasing notes. The betas (standardized estimates) indicate that *howmany* and *comfort* have the greatest explanatory power in predicting students' likelihood of purchasing notes. Further, the fact that the regression estimates for both *howmany* and *comfort* are positive indicates that purchase likelihood increases with the number of times that a student has previously borrowed notes (*howmany*), and also increases with the degree to which a student feels comfortable about buying notes from a note-taking service (*comfort*).

MODEL BUILDING AND SELECTION PROCEDURES

When dealing with a large number of independent variables, researchers often want to identify only those variables that have significant effects on the dependent variable to include in future regression models and research. The **coefficient of multiple determination (R^2)** measures the proportion of variation in the dependent variable (Y) explained by the entire set of independent variables (X) in the regression equation. In contrast, the **coefficient of partial determination** measures the marginal contribution of one independent variable (X) when all other independent variables are already included in the model.

The coefficient of partial determination between Y and X_2, given that X_1 is already in the model, is denoted by $r^2_{y2.1}$. Thus, $r^2_{y2.1}$ measures the proportionate reduction in the variation of Y remaining after X_1 is included in the model that is gained by also including X_2 in the model.

Selection Procedures. Sequential selection procedures provide a way for selecting the set of independent variables that combine to form the regression model that best accounts for (explains) the variation in the dependent variable. The independent variables are either entered or removed from the regression model one at a time. The three most often used sequential selection procedures are forward selection, backward selection, and stepwise selection.

Forward Selection. With a **forward selection procedure**, no independent (predictor) variables are initially in the regression equation. Predictor variables are entered one at a time only if they meet certain criteria specified in terms of the F ratio. The order in which the variables are included in the model depends on how much variation in the dependent variable (Y) is explained by each variable (coefficient of partial determination). Once a variable is included in the model it is never removed from the model.

Backward Selection. With a **backward selection procedure**, all of the predictor variables are initially included in the regression model. Predictor variables are removed one at a time based on the F ratio for removal. Once a variable has been removed from the model it is never added back into the model.

Stepwise Selection. With a **stepwise selection procedure**, the forward addition process is combined with the potential removal of predictors that no longer meet the specified criterion at each step. This stepwise selection process is probably the most frequently used sequential search procedure.

STEPWISE REGRESSION FOR THE NOTE-TAKING SURVEY

A stepwise regression procedure can be used to determine which of the previous variables combine to form the best set of predictors of students' likelihood of buying notes from a note-taking service. The results from the stepwise regression procedure are shown in Tables 28.5 and 28.6.

Based on this analysis, we conclude that the variables *ever*, *howmany*, *numyears*, and *comfort* are the independent variables that best predict students' likelihood of purchasing notes. Further, the betas (standardized estimates) indicate that *howmany* and *comfort* have the most explanatory power in predicting students' likelihood of purchasing notes.

TABLE 28.5 Summary of Variables Entered and Removed in the Stepwise Selection Process

Step	Variable Entered	Variable Removed	Number Vars In	Partial R-Square	Model R-Square	C(p)	F Value	Pr > F
1	Howmany	---	1	0.4097	0.4097	47.4528	74.27	<.0001
2	Comfort	---	2	0.1243	0.5340	17.3452	28.28	<.0001
3	Ever	---	3	0.0490	0.5831	6.6814	12.35	0.0007
4	Numyears	---	4	0.0267	0.6097	1.7923	7.11	0.0089

TABLE 28.6 Summary of the Regression Model Resulting from the Stepwise Selection Process

		Analysis of Variance			
Source	DF	Sum of Squares	Mean Square	F Value	Pr > F
Model	4	283.69025	70.92256	40.62	<.0001
Error	104	181.57581	1.74592		
Corrected Total	108	465.26606			
R-Square	0.6097		Adj R-Square	0.5947	

		Parameter Estimates				
Variable	DF	Parameter Estimate	Standard Error	t Value	Pr > |t|	Standardized Estimate
Intercept	1	2.90916	0.60757	4.79	<.0001	0
Ever	1	−1.01133	0.30311	−3.34	0.0012	−0.21863
Howmany	1	0.26143	0.04303	6.08	<.0001	0.42068
Numyears	1	−0.19850	0.07445	−2.67	0.0089	−0.16622
Comfort	1	0.44273	0.08136	5.44	<.0001	0.37861

QUESTIONS FOR DISCUSSION

1. What is the purpose of conducting a multiple regression analysis?

2. How do you interpret a significant interaction between two continuous variables in a multiple regression analysis?

3. What is the coefficient of multiple determination?

4. How is the adjusted R^2 different from the R^2 for a multiple regression analysis?

5. Why do researchers sometimes standardize variables when conducting a multiple regression analysis?

6. What is a beta coefficient?

7. What is the difference between forward, backward, and stepwise selection procedures used in multiple regression analysis?

8. Given the multiple regression results for the note taking survey presented in this chapter, what marketing recommendations would you offer to someone who wanted to open this type of business? What message(s) should be emphasized in promotions to increase the likelihood of students buying notes?

MINICASE 28.1

Super Speedway

A nationally known Super Speedway recently conducted a customer satisfaction survey of fans who attended a NASCAR-sponsored race at the Speedway. The coding sheet below shows the variable names and codes assigned to the response alternatives for selected questions from the survey. Using the multiple regression analysis output, answer the following questions:

1. Which of the following (if any) are significant predictors of a fan's overall level of satisfaction with attending the race at the Super Speedway:

   a. Cleanliness of the Speedway facility.

   b. Courteousness of ushers.

   c. Location of concession stands.

   d. Quality of the concessions.

   e. Value received from the concessions.

   f. Availability of vendors in the grandstands.

   g. Location of restrooms.

   h. Number of restrooms.

   i. Amount of children's/family activities.

   j. Public safety and crowd control.

   k. Parking.

   l. The experience offered by the Fan Walk. (Note: The Fan Walk provides fans with an opportunity to walk by the garage area prior to the race for an up-close experience with the drivers, cars, pit crews, and teams.)

2. Which of the above are the best predictors of a fan's overall level of satisfaction with attending the race at the Super Speedway?

3. How could managers of the Super Speedway use this information to help them promote and market the Super Speedway? What should they emphasize in their promotions? Should they promote the fan walk, or should they promote the children's/family activities at the Super Speedway?

Survey Question	Variable Name	Coding Scheme
Indicate your level of satisfaction with the following, where 1 = Very Dissatisfied and 7 = Very Satisfied.		
Cleanliness of the Speedway facility	Clean	Enter the number from 1–7
Courteousness of ushers	Courteous	Enter the number from 1–7
Location of concession stands	Locconces	Enter the number from 1–7
Quality of the concessions	Qualconces	Enter the number from 1–7
Value received from concessions	Valconces	Enter the number from 1–7
Availability of vendors in the grandstands	Vendors	Enter the number from 1–7
Location of restrooms	Locrest	Enter the number from 1–7
Number of restrooms	Numrest	Enter the number from 1–7
Amount of children's/family activities	Childfam	Enter the number from 1–7
Public safety and crowd control	Safety	Enter the number from 1–7
Parking	Parking	Enter the number from 1–7
Experience offered by the Fan Walk area	Fanwalk	Enter the number from 1–7
Overall experience at the Super Speedway	Overall	Enter the number from 1–7

Analysis of Variance

Source	DF	Sum of Squares	Mean Square	F Value	Pr > F
Model	12	398.55453	33.21288	65.53	<.0001
Error	377	191.08906	0.50687		
Corrected Total	389	589.64359			
R-Square		0.6759	Adj R-Sq	0.6656	

Parameter Estimates

Variable	DF	Parameter Estimate	Standard Error	t Value	Pr > |t|	Standardized Estimate
intercept	1	0.61331	0.21932	2.80	0.0054	0
clean	1	0.21167	0.05595	3.78	0.0002	0.21781
courteous	1	0.02461	0.05213	0.47	0.6371	0.02644
locconces	1	0.03768	0.05098	0.74	0.4603	0.03620
qualconces	1	0.06264	0.04670	1.34	0.1806	0.06994
valconces	1	0.03126	0.03318	0.94	0.3466	0.04269
vendors	1	−0.01382	0.03898	−0.35	0.7232	−0.01618
locrest	1	0.16039	0.06708	2.39	0.0173	0.15741
numrest	1	−0.04205	0.06206	−0.68	0.4985	−0.04217
childfam	1	−0.01669	0.03483	−0.48	0.6320	−0.01977
safety	1	0.14306	0.04887	2.93	0.0036	0.15649
parking	1	0.06416	0.02395	2.68	0.0077	0.09234
fanwalk	1	0.25542	0.03262	7.83	<.0001	0.31446

The Research Report

LEARNING OBJECTIVES

1 Describe the role that the marketing research report plays in the marketing research process.

2 Describe the major sections and/or topics that should be included in a marketing research report.

3 Describe how research results can be presented by using charts.

4 Make a pie chart, a bar chart, and a line chart to present the results from a marketing research survey.

5 Describe situations when a pie chart is appropriate and when a pie chart is not appropriate.

6 Describe situations when a bar chart is appropriate and when a bar chart is not appropriate.

7 Describe situations when a line chart is appropriate and when a line chart is not appropriate.

8 Interpret charts that present the results from a marketing research survey.

A marketing research project is not complete until the results from the research are effectively communicated to decision makers. The **research report** should be designed to easily, effectively, and concisely communicate the purpose of the research project, the managerial reasons for conducting the research, the methodology used, the research results, any limitations of the research, and the conclusions and recommendations from the research.

THE RESEARCH REPORT AND MARKETING OBJECTIVES

Recall the IDO model of marketing research and decision making, presented in Figure 29.1. Keep this model in mind when preparing a research report. The purpose of marketing research is to collect information that marketing managers can use to make decisions. As such, present the information in a way that is useful, helpful, and informative to decision makers. Consider their level of experience with statistics. They might not be very familiar with statistics and the way that different statistical tests are calculated, used, and interpreted. Consider their familiarity with research methodologies and the various sources of error associated with research results. They might not be familiar with the terms used to describe sources of error, such as random sampling error, nonresponse error, and response bias. As such, these terms should be explained fully using words and examples that decision

FIGURE 29.1 The IDO Model of Marketing Research and the Decision-Making Process

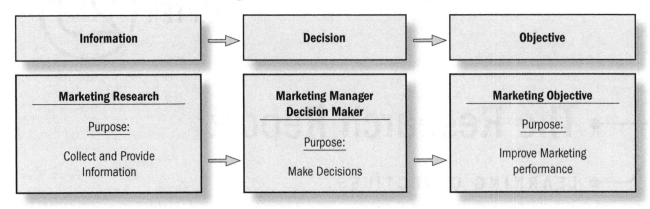

makers can understand. In the final analysis, a research report is worth only what a decision maker can take out of it to help him or her make decisions. A research project that requires a great deal of time, effort, and money to complete will be worthless if the results from it cannot be used effectively to help marketing managers make decisions.

OUTLINE OF A RESEARCH REPORT

Not all marketing research reports will look the same. Obviously, a report summarizing the results from a focus group or other qualitative research will include very few charts and tables summarizing the results from statistical analyses. Instead, it might include more verbatim comments made by respondents that are used to illustrate various themes or concepts that emerged from the research. Conversely, a research report summarizing the results from a survey will almost always include tables of numbers, charts that summarize respondents' answers to various survey questions, and even tables showing the results from statistical analyses of the data. The specific form of the report and the nature of the information that is presented in the report will be a function of the specific research purpose and the research techniques used.

Marketing Decisions and the Research Report. When writing a research report, it is often helpful to consider the types of decisions that managers must make. Structure the report around these decisions. Help the decision maker by organizing the report so that the results from the research correspond with the decisions that need to be made. A marketing manager will undoubtedly have questions that he or she will want to have answered while reading the report. These questions should be anticipated as you prepare the report. A generic outline of the topics that are most often included in a research report as well as some of the most common questions that should be answered in a research report are listed below.

1. **Title page** that includes the name(s) of the organization(s) for whom the research is being conducted, the name(s) of the organization(s) conducting the research, the name(s) of the researcher(s), and the date.

2. **Executive summary**, which is a one- to two-page summary of the project, including brief descriptions of:

  - The overall purpose/objective of the research.

  - Approach or methodologies used.

  - Nature of the sample and a brief statement about how the sample was selected.

  - Major findings/results.

  - Major conclusions/recommendations.

  The executive summary is a synopsis of the research that allows a reader to quickly understand the purpose of the research and the main findings and conclusions from the research. Remember, many people who read research reports are not familiar with research methods and analysis procedures. Avoid technical language in the executive summary.

3. **Table of contents**, which lists all of the information that is included in the report and the pages on which this information can be found.

4. **Introduction and research purpose**, which describes in detail the purpose of the research, the managerial problems or goals that were addressed by the research, and the rationale for conducting the research.

  - What was the purpose of this research?

  - Why was the research conducted?

  - What management decisions must be made that will be aided by this research?

  - What were the specific research objectives?

  - What was measured and why was this important?

  - How will measuring this help managers make decisions?

5. **Secondary data research**, which summarizes any data and information that was obtained from secondary data sources prior to any primary data collection. Are these secondary data sources credible? How was the information in the secondary data collected?

6. **Qualitative research**, if any, that was conducted. Because qualitative research (such as focus groups, mystery shoppers, or observation) is often conducted at earlier stages in the research process, the results from this exploratory research should be presented first. This is especially true if the results from qualitative research were used to help design and guide subsequent quantitative research, such as surveys or causal research.

Focus Groups:

- When was the focus group conducted?

- Who participated in the focus group?

- How were participants chosen?

- Who conducted the focus group?

- What questions were asked in the focus group (the moderator's guide)?

- What were the main findings from the focus group?

- Was there any bias in the sample of people participating in the focus group?

- Were focus group participants representative of the larger population (target market)?

- If not, how does this affect the results and conclusions from the focus group?

- How do the results from the focus group contribute to the rest of the results in this report?

Observation/Mystery Shoppers:

- Why was observation used as a research technique?

- Who was observed, where were they observed, when were they observed, and under what conditions were they observed?

- How, and why, were these people selected to be observed?

- What was observed and recorded?

- How was this recorded (human observation, mechanical observation), and why?

- How were the observations analyzed and interpreted?

- What conclusions can be made based on these observations?

- How do these observations contribute to the rest of the results in this report?

7. **Quantitative research and sampling**, which summarizes how the quantitative research was conducted and how the respondents were selected to participate in the research.

Surveys:

- How and when were surveys administered and the data collected?

- Why was the data collected this way?

- Was there any bias in the way that the data was collected?

- What was done to avoid bias in collecting the data?

- What issues were addressed on the survey?

- Where did the survey questions come from (how were they developed, designed, written)?

Sampling:

- Who was in the sample?

- How were people selected to be included in the sample?

- Why were these people selected to be included in the sample?

- Is the sample representative of the larger population (target market)?

- How do the characteristics of the sample compare to the characteristics of the population?

- If the sample is not representative of the larger population, what does this mean with respect to interpreting the results?

- How large was the sample?

- What is the margin of error for a sample this size?

- What does this margin of error mean?

Causal Research/Experimentation:

- Why was experimentation needed?

- What questions will the results from experimentation answer?

- What variables were manipulated?

- What variables were measured?

- What were the conditions under which the experiment was conducted?

- Do the experimentation procedures provide for high internal and external validity of results?

8. **Data analysis and results**, which describe the methods for analyzing the data and the main findings from the research. Again, remember that many people who read research reports are not familiar with research methods and analysis procedures. If technical language is used, it should be clearly defined and explained for such readers.

Data Analysis:

- What methods of analysis were used? Why?

- How can the significance of these analysis methods be determined?

Results:

- What were the main findings from the research?

- Are all of the results presented in tables or charts that are either in the text of the report or at the end of the report in an appendix?

- How can the results be interpreted?

- What do these results mean with respect to the managerial decisions that must be made?

- What statistical analyses were performed on the data from this research?

- Why were these statistical analyses performed?

- How can (should) a marketing manager interpret the results from these statistical analyses?

- Are these results reliable and valid?

9. **Conclusions**, which summarize the main findings from the research and also offer recommendations based on these results. Be careful to not offer conclusions that are not supported by the data and the research.

- What can be concluded based on the results?

- What conclusions cannot be supported by the results and the research?

- What managerial decisions are recommended, and how do the results support these recommendations?

10. **Limitations and suggestions for future research**, which address any limitations in the research that might introduce error or bias and therefore make it difficult to draw valid conclusions from the research. No research project is perfect, and there may be limitations due to factors that are beyond the control of the researcher (e.g., budget constraints, market changes, external events, economic changes during the course of the research, natural disasters). This section should also highlight potential questions for subsequent research and possible research approaches for answering those research questions.

- What were the main limitations of the research? Was there any methodological bias, sample bias, error due to question wording or not asking particular questions, and so on?

- What limitations were outside the control of the researcher?

- How do these limitations affect the results and conclusions?

- What should be done differently if further research is to be conducted?

- Did any of the findings raise questions to be addressed in future research?

- Is further research recommended?

- What topics or issues should be addressed in subsequent research?

- How should these issues be addressed?

- What research methodologies are best suited for addressing these issues?

11. **References**, which list all sources of information for secondary data or other sources of information used in the research project.

12. **Appendices**, which include all supporting documents or information that was not included in the body of the report. For example, the appendix should include all surveys, focus group moderator's guides, observation forms, or other materials used in the research. The appendix should also contain all tables and charts used in complex statistical analyses that were too detailed to include in the body of the report. Remember, most managers who read marketing research reports simply want to know what you did, what your found, and what that might mean for them. However, some readers might be interested in the details behind some of the more complex analyses and procedures used in the research. Including such complex information in the body of the report would simply make reading it too cumbersome and difficult.

THE RESEARCH PRESENTATION

In some cases it will be necessary to make a formal presentation of the research results, in addition to submitting a written report. Most often this involves some form of presentation software, such as PowerPoint. The slides used for a formal presentation should be attractive, descriptive, easy to read, concise, and informative. But, do not feel compelled to include everything in the presentation slides. People in the audience can always be referred to the written report if detailed or technical information is needed. The purpose of a formal presentation is to summarize the key points of the research. Some of the information that is most often included in formal presentations using PowerPoint is listed below. Most of this information can be conveyed effectively using bullet points, rather than complete sentences and paragraphs. Of course, a presentation need not be exactly as outlined below. The best approach is to design a presentation that is most appropriate for the situation and the audience. In most cases, however, it is best to emphasize the managerial relevance and usefulness of the research whenever possible.

1. **Title slide and introduction**. Use an introductory slide to begin the presentation and introduce the research team members.

2. **Purpose of the research**. Introduce the presentation in more detail. What was the purpose of the research? Why did you do this research?

3. **The research objectives**. List and discuss the major objectives of the research. What was measured and why was it measured? How will measuring these objectives help make managerial decisions?

4. **The research process**. What types of research did you do? In what stages did you conduct this research project? Why did you do more than one type of research? Who were the participants at each stage in the research project? What did you measure in this research and how will measuring this help managers make decisions?

5. **The focus group**. Describe the focus group. Why did you conduct a focus group? What did you hope to learn from the focus group? Who participated in the focus group? Who led the focus group? How were participants screened, identified, selected, and compensated? What was the procedure for conducting the focus group? Were focus group participants representative of the larger population of consumers? If not, how does this affect your results from the focus group? List the major topics discussed in the focus group. What questions were asked during the focus group? Why were these topics or questions discussed? What did you hope to learn from asking these questions or from discussing these topics? What did participants say in the focus group? What were the main conclusions from the focus group? What did you learn from the focus group? What do you know now that you did not know before conducting the focus group? How will the results from this focus group help managers make decisions?

6. **The survey**. Why did you need to do a survey? What type of survey did you do? Describe the methodology for conducting the survey. Whom did you survey? What did you ask them? When did you conduct the survey? How did you administer the survey? Where did you conduct the survey? Why did you conduct the survey in this manner? Was there any bias in the way you collected the survey data? What did you do to eliminate or reduce the possibility of bias or error in your results? If possible, show a copy of the survey. If the survey is too long, you might want to give a brief overview of the structure of the survey, the major sections on the survey, and the types of questions asked on the survey.

7. **The sample**. Describe the sample and the sampling procedures. Who was in the sample? How did you choose these people to be in the sample? Why were these people chosen to be in the sample? How large was the sample? What is the margin of error for a sample this size? What does this margin of error mean? Is the sample representative of the larger population? What variables did you measure on the survey that will allow you to determine whether or not the sample is representative of the population? If the sample is not representative, what does this mean in terms of interpreting the results and making managerial decisions? If possible, use charts to show whether or not the sample is representative of the larger population by comparing the sample demographics to the population demographics. Discuss the impact that the

sample characteristics might have on interpreting the results from the survey and making managerial decisions.

8. **Results**. Use charts to show the results from the survey. Interpret the charts. What do the results presented in the charts mean?

9. **Conclusions and recommendations**. After presenting the important results, discuss the conclusions from the research. What do you conclude based on your results? What managerial decisions can be made or should be made based on the results? What recommendations can you offer to decision makers? How do the results from the research support your conclusions and recommendations?

10. **Limitations and future research**. Be prepared to discuss limitations of the research. What were the main limitations of your research (methodological bias, sample bias, question wording bias, questions not asked on the survey, etc.)? How do these limitations affect the results and your conclusions and recommendations? What would you do differently next time? Where there any findings that raise questions to be addressed in future research? What topics or issues should be addressed in subsequent research?

11. **Questions**. Conclude the presentation by asking for questions from the audience.

Presenting the Written Report Using PowerPoint Slides. Recently, some marketing researchers have begun preparing written research reports using PowerPoint slides as opposed to a more traditional paragraph (text) format. Researchers will often present their research in the form of an oral presentation using PowerPoint anyway. And, many managers and decision makers actually prefer receiving the printed copy of the PowerPoint slides (in addition to the electronic file) as the research report itself. The ability of PowerPoint slides to present and convey information quickly, concisely, and visually is seen as a major advantage to this form of research report. A reader need not search through massive amounts of text to find the information for which he or she is looking. And, commentary can be easily added to slides containing charts. This helps to summarize the results and to convey important points and conclusions. However, it is important that all relevant information still be presented within the report. If need be, researchers can include appendices that contain written descriptions of details related to the research.

REPORTING RESULTS WITH CHARTS

Often, the easiest and best way to report research results is to present them in the form of a chart. Bar charts, line charts, and pie charts can convey a great deal of information. Furthermore, the graphical nature of such charts makes them easy to read and understand, even by readers with very little experience with research and very little knowledge of statistics. Readers can visually compare the height of two different bars, the shape and trend of a line, and even the relative sizes of the sections of a pie chart. In fact, many managers will quickly scan through a research report looking first for the charts and graphs. Bar charts, line charts, and pie charts can be easily created using Microsoft Excel and Microsoft PowerPoint.

Pie Charts

Pie charts can be a very effective means of presenting the results from a marketing research project. Pie charts are good at comparing percentages across a small set of response options. Pie charts are sometimes less effective when the number of response options is very large. For a pie chart to be appropriate, the percentages must sum to 100 percent. As such, pie charts are not effective when presenting the results from checklist questions, or for presenting means or averages. The pie chart in Figure 29.2 effectively and easily shows the percent of male and female respondents in a sample.

Bar Charts

Bar charts are very effective at displaying relative percentages and relative means. And, they can be used for restricted choice questions (where the percentages for all response options sum to 100 percent) as well as for checklist questions (where the percentages for all response options sum to more than 100 percent). The **horizontal bar chart** shown in Figure 29.3 is a very efficient way to convey

FIGURE 29.2 Pie Chart: Sex of Respondents

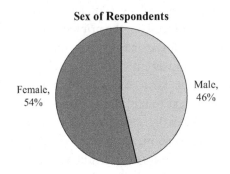

FIGURE 29.3 Horizontal Bar Chart

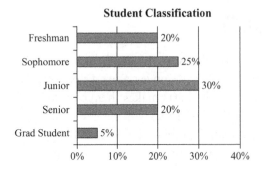

the percent of students in a sample who are in different years of their college career. Many people like bar charts because they can easily compare the length (or height) of a bar.

The **vertical bar chart** (sometimes called a **column chart**) shown in Figure 29.4 is used to report the percentages from a checklist question. Notice that the percentages sum to more than 100 percent. This is because respondents could choose more than one response option. When making charts for checklist questions, the fact that respondents could choose more than one response option should be made clear in the chart. If not, a reader could easily become confused and misinterpret the meaning of the percentages shown in the chart. Showing the percentage above each vertical bar also makes it easier to read and interpret a chart like the one shown.

Bar charts can also be used to show how responses vary across two or more groups, or how a single group of respondents answered two or more questions. The vertical bar chart in Figure 29.5 can be used for conducting a gap analysis where researchers compare respondents' ratings of importance to their evaluations for a number of different product features.

FIGURE 29.4 Vertical Bar Chart

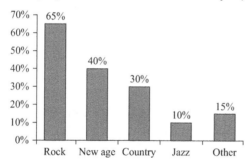

Type(s) of Music CD's that Respondents Purchase
(Respondents could choose more than one option)

FIGURE 29.5 Vertical Bar Chart for Conducting a Gap Analysis

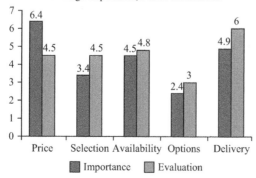

**Gap Analysis Comparing Importance of
Feature to Evaluation of Feature**
1 = Low Importance; Negative Evaluation
7 = High Importance; Positive Evaluation

Defining Scale Values. When charts are used to present the results for percentages, there is usually no need to define or interpret the meaning of the scale values. Most people understand percentages. For example, most people know what 60 percent means, regardless of what is being measured. However, when a chart presents the results for means, it is very important that a definition, description, or an interpretation of the scale values be clearly shown somewhere on the chart. Notice that in the gap analysis chart shown in Figure 29.5, the subtitle for the chart defines the meaning of "1" on both of the scales, as well as the meaning of "7" on both of the scales. Reporting that the mean rating for *price* was 6.4 does very little good if readers do not know the scale on which *price* was measured. Readers must be told what 6.4 means.

Scale Values on Charts and Graphs. The manner in which a chart or graph is interpreted can be greatly influenced by the range of scale values used for the horizontal and vertical axes. This is especially so for charts displaying relative percentages. Consider the bar chart shown in Figure 29.6.

At first glance, it appears that there is a very large difference between the percent of customers who purchase shoes versus the percent of customers who purchase either clothing or sports equipment. However, this apparent large difference is due to the small range of scale values used for the vertical axis. The chart shows percentages only from 42 percent to 54 percent. This small range of scale values will exaggerate even small differences in percentages shown on the chart, especially when the percentages are not shown above each bar (column).

The chart shown in Figure 29.7 presents the same data, except this chart has a vertical axis with a much wider range of values (from 0 percent to 100 percent). This wider range of scale values makes the differences in percentages for the three types of products seem small and insignificant. In general, a narrow range of scale values will make even small differences in responses appear large (or more significant). Conversely, a wide range of scale values will make even large differences in responses appear small (or less significant).

FIGURE 29.6 Bar Chart with Small Range of Scale Values

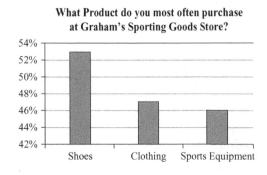

FIGURE 29.7 Bar Chart with Wide Range of Scale Values

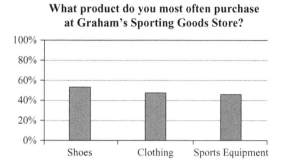

What product do you most often purchase
at Graham's Sporting Goods Store?

Line Charts

Line charts are good for presenting results related to longitudinal variables that reflect an element of time. They are also good for presenting results related to variables for which there is an ordinal relationship between the response options. The line chart in Figure 29.8 shows how the number of digital music downloads for a sample of consumers varies during the year.

Line charts should be avoided when there is no longitudinal nature to the variables being represented, when the response options are distinct and unrelated with respect to time, and when there is no ordinal relationship between the response options. To illustrate this, the line chart shown in Figure 29.9 does not properly represent the variable being reported. The line connecting the categories indicates that there is a relationship between the types of music, or that there is a connection between the types of music. Given that there is no longitudinal relationship between the types of music and there is no ordinal relationship between the types of music, a bar chart would be a better choice to present these results.

FIGURE 29.8 Line Chart

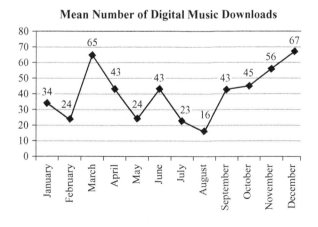

Mean Number of Digital Music Downloads

FIGURE 29.9 Inappropriate Use of a Line Chart

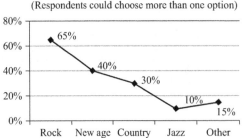

SURVEY QUESTIONS AS CHART TITLES

Researchers often write titles for charts by trying to come up with very short phrases or labels that are condensed versions of survey questions. However, this can often lead to confusion on the part of the reader if the chart title is not very descriptive. In most cases, the best approach to writing a title for a chart or graph is to simply restate the survey question. This way the reader knows exactly what was asked in the survey question to which the results in the chart refer. Do not be afraid to make the title of a chart a complete sentence, or even a paragraph, if necessary. Chart titles should be very descriptive. They should tell the reader everything that he or she needs to know to completely understand the results presented in the chart and the survey question that was asked to generate the results. A chart should be self-contained. A reader should not have to read the text portion of the results section to be able to understand a chart or graph. The chart should provide information about the exact wording of the survey question, the potential response options, and the results related to the number (percent) of respondents providing a particular response. To illustrate this, consider the chart title shown in Figure 29.10.

Unfortunately, the title, "Purchase Likelihood," provides very little guidance when it comes to interpreting the results presented in the chart. Notice how the chart title shown in Figure 29.11 is much more descriptive. A reader could look at this chart, and only this chart, and be able to interpret the results.

FIGURE 29.10 Bar Chart with Nondescript Title

FIGURE 29.11 Bar Chart with Descriptive Title

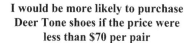

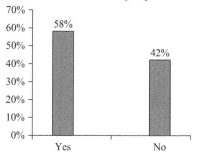

An exception to this recommendation regarding chart titles is when presenting results related to demographic variables. Results related to demographic variables can be easily and effectively presented in charts with condensed titles such as "Sex," "Annual Personal Income," "Number of Children Younger than 18 Living at Home," "Marital Status," and so on. It would not be necessary to make the chart title "What Is Your Sex?" A reader could be expected to accurately interpret the chart without repeating the entire demographic survey question.

KEEP CHARTS AND GRAPHS SIMPLE AND UNCLUTTERED

Researchers will sometimes try to present too much information on a single chart or graph. This is especially problematic if the research report is being prepared using PowerPoint slides. Slides with too much information become cluttered and very difficult to read and interpret. There is only so much information that can be shown on a single PowerPoint slide.

INTERPRETING RESULTS IN CHARTS AND TABLES

It is not enough to simply present the results of research in the form of charts and tables. A researcher must also interpret, and attempt to give meaning to, the information contained in the charts and tables. Often, managers do not know much about statistics and how statistical information is presented. So, it is very helpful to interpret the information that the charts or tables are conveying about the data. This means more than merely repeating the numbers from a chart or table in the text of the results section. The numbers should be distilled to identify the main point of what they are saying about the data and the results.

Interpreting results is not difficult, but many researchers fall into the trap of merely repeating the numbers from a chart or table when interpreting results. For example, consider the chart in Figure 29.12 regarding the items that consumers purchase at convenience stores.

FIGURE 29.12 Horizontal Bar Chart

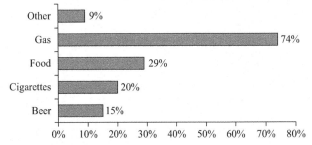

Which of the following items do you purchase at least once a week at convenience stores? (Check all that apply)

A researcher might simply describe these results by stating:

> When asked about the items they purchase at convenience stores, 15 percent said they buy beer, 20 percent said they buy cigarettes, 29 percent said they buy food, 74 percent said they buy gas, and 9 percent said they buy other items.

Unfortunately, this does nothing more than repeat the information that is already presented in the chart. Avoid repeating numbers that are already presented in charts. In fact, the purpose of the chart is to present all of the numbers so that they do not need to be reported in the text portion of the report. This chart is better summarized by stating:

> By far, the most often purchased item at convenience stores is gas (74 percent of consumers), followed by food (29 percent of consumers).

It is sometimes useful to report a few key numbers while interpreting charts. But, avoid reporting too many numbers in the chart interpretations.

As another example, the chart in Figure 29.13 could be easily summarized by stating, "Compared to females, males are more likely to be willing to pay for the service."

The chart in Figure 29.14 could be summarized by stating, "Likelihood of using the service does not vary much from day to day during the week."

The chart in Figure 29.15 could be summarized by stating, "Willingness to use the service is positively related to age of consumers—older consumers are more likely to use the service than are younger consumers."

FIGURE 29.13 Horizontal Bar Chart with Two Variables

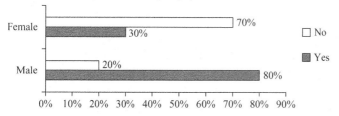

Would you be willing to pay for our service?

FIGURE 29.14 Vertical Bar Chart

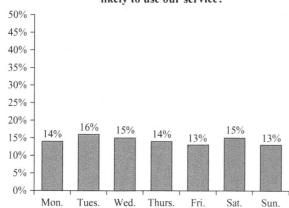

What day of the week would you be most likely to use our service?

FIGURE 29.15 Column Chart

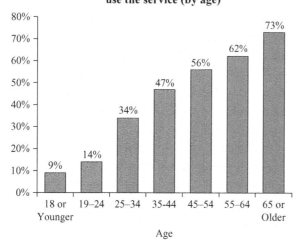

Percent of consumers who would use the service (by age)

MARKETING RESEARCH AND MANAGERIAL DECISION MAKING

Notice that the purpose of marketing research is to collect *and* provide information. It is not enough to merely collect information. The information that is collected is useful to the decision-making process only when that information is communicated to decision makers in a way that is useful and informative to them. A complete marketing research project involves more than merely collecting information. As such, an important consideration for researchers is how the results from a research project are communicated to marketing managers. When effectively communicated to decision makers, the results from marketing research projects can have a profound impact on the success of a business or organization.

The Importance of Marketing Research. Marketing research is one of the most important business functions. As highlighted throughout this book, marketing managers need information to make decisions and to compete in the marketplace. Marketing research is a vital input into the marketing managerial decision-making process. The purpose of marketing research is to collect information that marketing managers need to make decisions designed to achieve marketing objectives. Moreover, given that all managers, no matter what the business, industry, or service, must routinely make decisions, understanding marketing research and the processes involved in collecting information that is used to make decisions is vitally important to any business manager. As such, both researchers and managers must have a clear understanding of the role that marketing research plays in the entire decision-making process.

FINAL THOUGHTS

Marketing research is an exciting field of discovery that can be applied to any marketing situation. This book has examined the role of marketing research projects in helping marketing managers make marketing decisions. I hope that by reading this book you have come to appreciate the many benefits that marketing research has to offer. Even if you are not considering a career in marketing research, any marketing professional will undoubtedly be exposed to the results from marketing research when making marketing and business decisions. A basic understanding of the marketing research process, the techniques and methodologies used in marketing research, and even the limitations and possible sources of error associated with various research techniques will aid a marketing manager when making decisions. Not only must a marketing manager know the results of the research that he or she is using to make decisions, the manager must also fully understand the process by which that information was collected to be able to judge the usefulness of the information for making marketing decisions.

QUESTIONS FOR DISCUSSION

1. What role does the marketing research report play in the managerial decision-making process?

2. What topics/sections should be included in a marketing research report?

3. What topics should be discussed in a marketing research presentation?

4. Should a researcher merely read the research report when making a research presentation?

5. In what situations are the following chart types appropriate/inappropriate:
   a. Bar chart.
   b. Column chart.
   c. Pie chart.
   d. Line chart.

6. What effect can the range of scale values have on interpreting the data presented in a chart?

7. What are some general strategies for developing titles for charts?

8. What are some general strategies for interpreting the results presented in charts?

STRICKLAND COLLEGE STUDENT DRINKING SURVEY

Katherine Brenton is vice president for student affairs at Strickland College, which is a private, liberal arts college located in the Midwest United States. Strickland College is a relatively small school, with an enrollment of 3,300 students. She recently attended a conference for university administrators where the topic of college drinking was discussed. After hearing about some disturbing data related to the amount of drinking that is occurring on college campuses across the country, she decided to conduct a survey of her students to measure the amount of drinking that was occurring on the campus of Strickland College.

An email with a link to the online survey was sent to every student enrolled at Strickland College. Students were assured of their anonymity and a number of incentives were offered to encourage students to participate in the survey (e.g., iTunes gift cards, gift cards to local grocery stores, etc.). A total of 93 students completed the survey. The research objectives for the survey are listed below. This is followed by a copy of the survey, the coding sheet, and a list of analysis questions. The outputs from the statistical analyses are also given.

Katherine Brenton has asked for your help with analyzing the data and answering the analysis questions.

RESEARCH OBJECTIVES FOR THE DRINKING SURVEY

1. Measure the percent of Strickland College (SC) students who drink alcohol.

2. Measure the average number of 12-ounce beers and regular-sized mixed drinks SC students drink in a typical week and compare these amounts to national averages.

3. Measure aspects of SC students' drinking behavior, including:
    a. The percent of SC students who drink alcohol.

b. Average number of 12-ounce beers that SC students drink in a typical week.

c. Average number of regular-sized mixed drinks that SC students drink in a typical week.

And, examine whether these aspects of drinking behavior vary by (are related to):

a. Sex (male versus female students).

b. Fraternal affiliation (members versus nonmembers of fraternal organizations).

c. Marital status (married versus single students).

d. Age.

4. Examine the nature of the relationship between the number of beers that SC students drink in a typical week and the number of mixed drinks that SC students drink in a typical week.

5. Measure the types of alcoholic beverages that SC students drink regularly.

6. Measure the frequency with which SC students drink so much that they become intoxicated.

7. Measure the relationship between age and:

a. The number of beers that SC students drink in a typical week.

b. The number of mixed drinks that SC students drink in a typical week.

STRICKLAND COLLEGE DRINKING SURVEY

1. Do you drink alcohol?

☐ Yes (go to question #2)

☐ No (go to question #7)

2. When was the last time you drank an alcoholic beverage?

Within the last:

☐ 24 hours

☐ Week

☐ 2 weeks

☐ Month

☐ More than one month

3. What types of alcohol do you regularly drink? (Check all that you regularly drink.)

☐ Beer

☐ Straight liquor (scotch, bourbon)

☐ Mixed drinks (cocktails)

☐ Frozen alcoholic drinks (daiquiris)

☐ Other _____

4. How many 12-ounce servings (cans, bottles) of beer do you drink in a typical week?

____ 12-ounce servings (cans, bottles)

5. How many regular-sized "mixed drinks" do you drink in a typical week?

____ regular-sized mixed drinks

6. How often do you drink so much that you become intoxicated?

☐ About every day

☐ About once a week

☐ About once every two weeks

☐ About once a month

☐ About once every three months

☐ About once a year

☐ Never

7. Are you a member of either a fraternity or a sorority?   ☐ Yes   ☐ No

8. What is your sex?   ☐ Male   ☐ Female

9. Are you married or single?   ☐ Married   ☐ Single

10. What is your age (in years)?   I am ____ years old.

11. What is your approximate (personal) annual income? $_____

TABLE C1.1 Strickland College Drinking Survey Coding Sheet

Question Number	Survey Question	Variable Name	Coded Scale Values
1	Do you drink alcohol?	Drink	y = Yes n = No
2	When was the last time you drank an alcoholic beverage?	Last	. = no answer 1 = 24 hours 2 = week 3 = 2 weeks 4 = month 5 = more than one month
3	What types of alcohol do you regularly drink?	Typebeer	1 = checked 0 = not checked
		Typestraight	1 = checked 0 = not checked

Question Number	Survey Question	Variable Name	Coded Scale Values
		Typemixed	1 = checked 0 = not checked
		Typefrozen	1 = checked 0 = not checked
		Typeother	1 = checked 0 = not checked
4	How many 12-ounce servings of beer do you drink in a typical week?	Beers	Enter the number
5	How many regular-sized mixed drinks do you drink in a typical week?	Mixed	Enter the number
6	How often do you drink so much that you become intoxicated?	Often	. = no answer 1 = every day 2 = once a week 3 = once every two weeks 4 = once a month 5 = once every three months 6 = once a year 7 = never
7	Are you a member of either a fraternity or a sorority?	Frat	y = Yes n = No
8	What is your sex?	Sex	m = Male f = Female
9	Are you married or single?	Married	m = Married s = Single
10	What is your age?	Age	Enter the number
11	What is your approximate personal annual income?	Income	Enter the number

ANALYSIS QUESTIONS BASED ON THE RESEARCH OBJECTIVES

The following information was obtained from the Strickland College Records Office:

The true average age of SC students is 24.2.

The true average annual income of SC students is $12,000.

The true percentage of SC students in fraternal organizations is 25 percent.

The true percentage of married SC students is 35 percent.

The true percentage of male SC students is 40 percent.

1. Is the sample representative of the university student population based on age, income, fraternal affiliation, marital status, and sex?

2. Based on the survey results, what percent of SC students drink alcohol?

3. Based on the survey results, what is the average number of 12-ounce beers that SC students drink in a typical week?

4. A recent national survey found that on average, college students drink:
    a. 1.5 regular-sized mixed drinks in a typical week.
    b. Three 12-ounce beers in a typical week.

How does SC compare to these national averages?

5. Do:
    a. Male and female students
    b. Fraternal organization members and nonmembers
    c. Married and single students

Differ with respect to whether or not they drink alcohol?

6. Do male and female students differ with respect to:
    a. The number of 12-ounce beers that they drink in a typical week?
    b. The number of regular-sized mixed drinks that they drink in a typical week?

7. Do fraternal organization members and nonmembers differ with respect to:
    a. The number of 12-ounce beers that they drink in a typical week?
    b. The number of regular-sized mixed drinks that they drink in a typical week?

8. Do married and single students differ with respect to:
    a. The number of 12-ounce beers that they drink in a typical week?
    b. The number of regular-sized mixed drinks that they drink in a typical week?

9. What is the relationship between the number of 12-ounce beers that SC students drink in a typical week and the number of regular-sized mixed drinks that SC students drink in a typical week? Are they related?

10. What is the relationship between age and:
    a. The number of 12-ounce beers that students drink in a typical week?
    b. The number of regular-sized mixed drinks that students drink in a typical week?

11. Are there any potential sources of error associated with this survey? If so, what are they, and how might these sources of error affect the results and/or the ability of administrators at Strickland College to interpret the results?

RESULTS FROM THE STRICKLAND COLLEGE STUDENT DRINKING SURVEY

TABLE C1.2 Means for the Variables: Beers, Mixed, Age, Income

Variable	N	Mean	Std Dev	Std Error
Beers	93	5.58	7.32	0.76
Mixed	93	0.98	2.17	0.22
Age	93	23.72	3.72	0.38
Income	93	11539.81	8540.48	885.60

TABLE C1.3 Frequency Distributions for the Variables

Drink	Frequency	Percent	Cumulative Frequency	Cumulative Percent
N	23	24.73	23	24.73
Y	70	75.27	93	100.00

Last	Frequency	Percent	Cumulative Frequency	Cumulative Percent
.	23	24.73	23	24.73
1	22	23.66	45	48.39
2	26	27.96	71	76.34
3	5	5.38	76	81.72
4	4	4.30	80	86.02
5	13	13.98	93	100.00

Typebeer	Frequency	Percent	Cumulative Frequency	Cumulative Percent
0	39	41.94	39	41.94
1	54	58.06	93	100.00

Typestraight	Frequency	Percent	Cumulative Frequency	Cumulative Percent
0	79	84.95	79	84.95
1	14	15.05	93	100.00

Typemixed	Frequency	Percent	Cumulative Frequency	Cumulative Percent
0	58	62.37	58	62.37
1	35	37.63	93	100.00

Typefrozen	Frequency	Percent	Cumulative Frequency	Cumulative Percent
0	76	81.72	76	81.72
1	17	18.28	93	100.00

(continued)

Typeother	Frequency	Percent	Cumulative Frequency	Cumulative Percent
0	83	89.25	83	89.25
1	10	10.75	93	100.00

Often	Frequency	Percent	Cumulative Frequency	Cumulative Percent
.	23	24.73	23	24.73
1	1	1.08	24	25.81
2	18	19.35	42	45.16
3	10	10.75	52	55.91
4	11	11.83	63	67.74
5	13	13.98	76	81.72
6	8	8.60	84	90.32
7	9	9.68	93	100.00

Frat	Frequency	Percent	Cumulative Frequency	Cumulative Percent
N	53	56.99	53	56.99
Y	40	43.01	93	100.00

Sex	Frequency	Percent	Cumulative Frequency	Cumulative Percent
F	37	39.78	37	39.78
M	56	60.22	93	100.00

Married	Frequency	Percent	Cumulative Frequency	Cumulative Percent
M	24	25.81	24	25.81
S	69	74.19	93	100.00

IS THE SAMPLE REPRESENTATIVE OF THE POPULATION OF AMERICAN COLLEGE STUDENTS?

Use Table C1.4 to determine if the sample is representative of the population of American college students.

TABLE C1.4 Hypothesis Test Worksheet

Variable	95 Percent of Samples Should Yield Results Between			Result from the SC Survey
	$\bar{X} - 1.96(SE)$	(μ)	$\bar{X} + 1.96(SE)$	$(\bar{X})$
Number of mixed drinks per week	←		→	
Number of beers per week	←		→	

IS THE SAMPLE REPRESENTATIVE OF THE LARGER SC POPULATION?

Use Table C1.5 to determine if the sample is representative of the larger SC population.

TABLE C1.5 Hypothesis Test Worksheet

Variable	95 Percent of Samples Should Yield Results Between			Result from the SC Survey
	$(\bar{X}, p) - 1.96(SE)$	(μ, π)	$(\bar{X}, p) + 1.96(SE)$	$(\bar{X}, p)$
Age	←———		———→	
Income	←———		———→	
Frat member	←———		———→	
Married	←———		———→	
Sex (male)	←———		———→	

TABLE C1.6 Chi-Square Analysis: Drink by Sex

Table of Drink by Sex				
		Sex		
	Drink	F	M	Total
Frequency Percent Row Pct Col Pct	N	13 13.98 56.52 35.14	10 10.75 43.48 17.86	23 24.73
	Y	24 25.81 34.29 64.86	46 49.46 65.71 82.14	70 75.27
	Total	37 39.78	56 60.22	93 100.00

Statistic	DF	Value	Prob
Chi-Square	1	3.5730	0.0587

TABLE C1.7 Chi-Square Analysis: Drink by Frat

Table of Drink by Frat			
	Frat		
Drink	**N**	**Y**	**Total**
Frequency N Percent Row Pct Col Pct	18 19.35 78.26 33.96	5 5.38 21.74 12.50	23 24.73
Y	35 37.63 50.00 66.04	35 37.63 50.00 87.50	70 75.27
Total	53 **56.99**	40 **43.01**	93 **100.00**

Statistic	DF	Value	Prob
Chi-Square	1	5.6408	0.0175

TABLE C1.8 Chi-Square Analysis: Drink by Married

Table of Drink by Married			
	Married		
Drink	**M**	**S**	**Total**
Frequency N Percent Row Pct Col Pct	14 15.05 60.87 58.33	9 9.68 39.13 13.04	23 24.73
Y	10 10.75 14.29 41.67	60 64.52 85.71 86.96	70 75.27
Total	24 **25.81**	69 **74.19**	93 **100.00**

Statistic	DF	Value	Prob
Chi-Square	1	19.6209	<.0001

TABLE C1.9 ANOVA Results Testing for Differences in Beers and Mixed by Level of Sex

Dependent Variable: Beers

Source	DF	Sum of Squares	Mean Square	F Value	Pr > F
Model	1	1085.085316	1085.085316	25.60	<.0001
Error	91	3857.559846	42.390768		
Corrected Total	92	4942.645161			

Source	DF	Type I SS	Mean Square	F Value	Pr > F
sex	1	1085.085316	1085.085316	25.60	<.0001

Dependent Variable: Mixed

Source	DF	Sum of Squares	Mean Square	F Value	Pr > F
Model	1	13.9067184	13.9067184	2.99	0.0871
Error	91	423.0825290	4.6492586		
Corrected Total	92	436.9892473			

Source	DF	Type I SS	Mean Square	F Value	Pr > F
sex	1	13.90671835	13.90671835	2.99	0.0871

Level of sex	N	Beers		Mixed	
		Mean	Std Dev	Mean	Std Dev
f	37	1.37	2.60	0.51	0.93
m	56	8.35	8.10	1.30	2.66

TABLE C1.10 ANOVA Results Testing for Differences in Beers and Mixed by Level of Frat

Dependent Variable: Beers

Source	DF	Sum of Squares	Mean Square	F Value	Pr > F
Model	1	232.328180	232.328180	4.49	0.0369
Error	91	4710.316981	51.761725		
Corrected Total	92	4942.645161			

Source	DF	Type I SS	Mean Square	F Value	Pr > F
frat	1	232.3281802	232.3281802	4.49	0.0369

(continued)

Dependent Variable: Mixed

Source	DF	Sum of Squares	Mean Square	F Value	Pr > F
Model	1	0.1081152	0.1081152	0.02	0.8810
Error	91	436.8811321	4.8008916		
Corrected Total	92	436.9892473			

Source	DF	Type I SS	Mean Square	F Value	Pr > F
Frat	1	0.10811524	0.10811524	0.02	0.8810

Level of frat	N	Beers		Mixed	
		Mean	Std Dev	Mean	Std Dev
n	53	4.20	7.38	1.01	2.67
y	40	7.40	6.93	0.95	1.29

TABLE C1.11 ANOVA Results Testing for Differences in Beers and Mixed by Level of Married

Dependent Variable: Beers

Source	DF	Sum of Squares	Mean Square	F Value	Pr > F
Model	1	12.527408	12.527408	0.23	0.6318
Error	91	4930.117754	54.177118		
Corrected Total	92	4942.645161			

Source	DF	Type I SS	Mean Square	F Value	Pr > F
Married	1	12.52740767	12.52740767	0.23	0.6318

Dependent Variable: Mixed

Source	DF	Sum of Squares	Mean Square	F Value	Pr > F
Model	1	0.4222183	0.4222183	0.09	0.7674
Error	91	436.5670290	4.7974399		
Corrected Total	92	436.9892473			

Source	DF	Type I SS	Mean Square	F Value	Pr > F
Married	1	0.42221833	0.42221833	0.09	0.7674

Level of Married	N	Beers		Mixed	
		Mean	Std Dev	Mean	Std Dev
m	24	4.95	8.84	0.87	3.69
s	69	5.79	6.78	1.02	1.33

TABLE C1.12 Correlation Analysis

Pearson Correlation Coefficients, N = 93 Prob > |r| Under H0: Rho = 0				
	Beers	**Mixed**	**Age**	**Income**
beers	1.00000	0.45628 <.0001	0.05414 0.6063	0.02409 0.8187
mixed	0.45628 <.0001	1.00000	-0.01910 0.8558	-0.05376 0.6088
age	0.05414 0.6063	-0.01910 0.8558	1.00000	0.53434 <.0001
income	0.02409 0.8187	-0.05376 0.6088	0.53434 <.0001	1.00000

THE RED HILLS MALL

The Red Hills Mall (RHM) is a shopping mall located near the center of a large Midwest town. When the mall was built in 1983, it was the largest shopping mall in the surrounding five-county area. However, newer shopping centers have opened in and around town and there are plans to begin renovating the Red Hills Mall within the next year. To help plan for the physical renovations, the owners of the mall recently commissioned a telephone survey of local residents to learn about possible stores and incentives that would draw attention and customers to the mall, and to learn about consumers' shopping and spending habits.

The Red Hills Mall is a single-story mall with 48 stores. The mall offers a variety of store types, including apparel, shoes, electronics and wireless, entertainment and music, jewelry and accessories, specialty stores, crafts, specialty foods, health and beauty, and services (e.g., hair and nail salons). Currently, the mall has only one sit down–style restaurant, which is a cafeteria offering a variety of food options. The cafeteria is located in the southeast corner of the mall. There is also a food court with seating for 52 people. The fast food restaurants in the food court include Sbarro, Auntie Anne's Pretzels, Great American Cookies, The Cajun Café, and Sarku Japan. There is no movie theater in the mall.

In addition to the stores, the cafeteria, and the food court, the mall also offers the following services for its customers: children's play area, family restrooms, lost and found, stroller rental, wheelchair rental, safety escorts, ATMs, U.S. Mail Box, and multiple soft seating areas located throughout the interior of the mall.

The mall is located near one of four different exits off of an interstate highway that leads to the town. There are no other shopping malls located near any of the other interstate exits. When the mall was built, there was very little development to inhibit building the mall and the parking lot. As a result, the parking lot for the mall is very large compared to parking lots for other similar-sized shopping centers. The parking lot could easily be developed into other shops or restaurants while still leaving ample parking spaces for customers.

There are three anchor department stores in the Red Hills Mall. JCPenney is at the east end of the mall, Macy's is at the west end of the mall, Belk is in the middle of the mall on the north side, and the food court is directly across from Belk in the middle of the mall on the south side. The mall maintains standard hours for shopping centers.

The mall is open Monday through Saturday from 10am to 9pm; and on Sunday from noon to 6pm.

There are a number of other shopping malls and shopping centers that have opened in the town that are in direct competition with the Red Hills Mall. However, the most direct competition has come from The Shops at The Glen, which is a newly opened lifestyle shopping center that offers outdoor entrances to its stores. The Shops at The Glen also offers four full-service sit-down restaurants and ample parking for its customers. While The Shops at The Glen does not offer a movie theater, it does offer 20 more stores than the Red Hills Mall.

In terms of marketing, there has been very little concerted effort to market the Red Hills Mall. In the past, each store was responsible for most of its own advertising. However, the mall does have a website that provides general information, including a directory of stores, list of services, hours, and contact information.

Philip Marten is the newly hired marketing manager of the Red Hills Mall. Ironically, Philip does not have much experience with marketing research and understanding the results from research reports. His background is in the area of personal selling. He is a very personable man who is able to talk with almost anyone. However, his analytical skills are lacking. He has been heard saying, "I can talk to anyone, but numbers have never spoken to me."

Philip Marten has asked you to meet with him to review the results from the telephone surveys that were recently conducted for the mall. His predecessor had commissioned the research and worked with the research firm that conducted the phone surveys. Unfortunately, Philip was not involved with the design of the surveys or any discussions with the research firm following the completion of the research. So, he needs someone to help him interpret the results and form some conclusions based on them. Below are the results from the telephone surveys.

TABLE C2.1 Demographics of the Sample

Demographics of Survey Respondents	Nonshoppers (n = 142) [Have not shopped at RHM in the last 90 days]	Infrequent Shoppers (n = 168) [Shopped at RHM 1–2 times in last 90 days]	Frequent Shoppers (n = 195) [Shopped at RHM 3 or more times in last 90 days]
Percent male	57%	51%	42%
Percent female	43%	49%	58%
Average age	42.8	39.7	28.2
Live within 10 miles of RHM	21%	37%	42%
Live more than 10 miles from RHM	38%	37%	25%

TABLE C2.2 Shopping Frequency

In the <u>Past 90 Days</u>, How Many Times Have You Visited Each of the Following Malls/Shopping Centers?	Never	1 to 3 Times	4 to 9 Times	10 or More
Austin Heights	51%	41%	5%	3%
The Shops at The Glen	23%	47%	21%	9%
Bradford Gap Mall	84%	12%	2%	2%
East Lake Galleria	69%	26%	3%	2%
Mall at Gregory Park	77%	18%	3%	2%
Prestige Outlets, Limberton	83%	12%	4%	1%
Red Hills Mall	27%	44%	18%	11%
The Warehouse, Brighton	84%	9%	6%	1%

TABLE C2.3 Shopping Duration

How Much Time Do You Spend on a Typical Shopping Trip to Each of the Following Malls/Shopping Centers?	Less Than 30 Minutes	30 Min. to 1 Hour	1–2 Hours	2 Hours or More
Austin Heights	21%	19%	31%	29%
The Shops at The Glen	11%	19%	34%	36%
Bradford Gap Mall	24%	26%	28%	22%
East Lake Galleria	27%	27%	27%	19%
Mall at Gregory Park	16%	25%	44%	15%
Prestige Outlets, Limberton	20%	25%	38%	17%
Red Hills Mall	23%	39%	26%	12%
The Warehouse, Brighton	29%	38%	29%	4%

TABLE C2.4 Shopping Importance

When You Decide to Go Shopping for <u>Clothes and Accessories</u>, How Important is Each of the Following Factors in Determining Where You Like to Go Shopping? [1 = Not Important; 7 = Very Important]	
Convenient Location	4.85
Food/Restaurants Near the Mall	3.18
Food/Restaurants in the Mall	2.6
Fun Experience	4.78
Low Prices	5.45
Number of Stores in a Mall/Shopping Center	4.19
Other	3.28
Selection of Stores	5.37
Uniqueness of Stores	5.99
Value for My Money	5.83
Variety of Merchandise	5.54

TABLE C2.5 Shopping Expenditures

On a Typical Visit to <u>Any Shopping Mall</u>, Approximately How Much Do You Spend (Per Visit) on Apparel, Shoes, and Accessories?	
Nothing	6%
$1–$20	13%
$21–$40	16%
$41–$60	19%
$61–$75	12%
$76–$100	14%
$101–$200	15%
$201–$500	4%
More than $500	1%

TABLE C2.6 Shopping Expenditures: Red Hills Mall

On a Typical Visit to <u>Red Hills Mall</u>, Approximately How Much Do You Spend (Per Visit) on Apparel, Shoes, and Accessories?	
Nothing	25%
$1–$20	18%
$21–$40	22%
$41–$60	14%
$61–$75	8%
$76–$100	6%
$101–$200	5%
$201–$500	1%
More than $500	1%

TABLE C2.7 Food Court Frequency

How Many Times in the <u>Past 90 Days</u> Have You Eaten at the <u>Red Hills Mall Food Court</u>?	
Never	70.6%
1–3 times	24.9%
4–6 times	2.1%
7–9 times	1.2%
10–12 times	0.3%
13–15 times	0.2%
More than 15 times	0.4%
Did not know it had a food court	0.3%

TABLE C2.8 Food Court Intentions

What Would Make You Eat at the <u>Red Hills Mall Food Court</u> More Often? [Check All That Apply.]	
Cleaner	18%
Lower Prices	35%
More Places to Sit	33%
None of These	13%
More Food Choices	56%
Other	5%

TABLE C2.9 Store Preferences

Which of the Following <u>Store Types</u> Would You Like to See More of at Red Hills Mall? [Check All That Apply.]	
Affordable Fashion	29%
Athletic Shoe Stores	17%
Children's Apparel	3%
Computer	24%
Cosmetics	21%
Department Stores	11%
Electronics	14%
Entertainment	23%
Fast Food	24%
Men's Clothing	29%
Music/Games/Movies	25%
None	10%
Other	5%
Women's Apparel	31%
Women's Shoes	21%
Younger Apparel	28%

TABLE C2.10 Promotional Preferences

Which of the Following Types of <u>Promotions</u> Would Make You More Likely to Shop at Red Hills Mall? [Check All That Apply.]	
Free Gift Card with Purchase	49%
Free Gift With Purchase	18%
None	16%
Stores Sales/Discounts	62%

TABLE C2.11 Mall Features and Shopping Intentions

Which of the Following Mall Features Would Make You More wLikely to Shop at Red Hills Mall? [Check All That Apply.]	
Community Presence	10%
Game Room/Activity Center	12%
More "Unique" Stores	57%
More Department Stores	31%
More Food Choices in the Food Court	23%
More Full-Service Restaurants	46%
Movie Theater	39%
Other	5%
Special Events	33%

TABLE C2.12 Information Preferences

What is Your Preferred Method of Receiving Information About Upcoming Sales, Special Events, or Special Offers From Red Hills Mall? [Check All That Apply.]	
Banner Ads (Online)	7%
Billboard Ads	22%
Direct Mail to Home Address	10%
Emails from Specific Stores	37%
Emails Promoting the Entire Mall	32%
Facebook	24%
Mall Website	13%
Newspaper Ads	16%
Other	4%
Radio Ads	19%
Signs in Mall	16%
Television Ads	29%
Text Messaging	8%
Twitter	6%

RED HILLS MALL CASE ANALYSIS QUESTIONS

1. One of the first questions that Philip Marten asks has to do with the methodological aspects of the research. Philip is not sure how to interpret the margin of error and what it means when the research report states:

   > A randomly selected sample of local residents was selected to participate in a telephone survey. A total of 2,046 residents were contacted and asked to participate in the survey. Of these, 505 residents agreed and completed the survey. With a sample of 505 people we can say with 95% confidence that the amount of survey error due to taking a random sample instead of surveying all members of the population is ± 4.4%.

2. What is the profile of the typical Red Hills Mall shopper?
    a. What is the demographic profile of a frequent Red Hills Mall shopper?
    b. Where do they live, in comparison to the mall?
    c. Would you describe the typical Red Hills Mall shopper as a "big ticket" shopper, or as a "small ticket" shopper?

3. If the Red Hills Mall were to add stores as part of the renovation, what types of stores or restaurants should they add, and why?

4. What should be a marketing goal for Red Hills Mall: increase the frequency with which shoppers visit the mall, or increase the duration of each shopping visit (i.e., the length of time each shopper spends at the Red Hills Mall)?

5. What types of marketing communications and promotions would you recommend?

6. What promotional messages would you recommend?

7. What other information would you like to have for making marketing decisions regarding the Red Hills Mall?

8. What other analysis would be helpful in making marketing decisions regarding the Red Hills Mall?

9. What questions would you ask the research firm to help you better understand and interpret the results from the telephone surveys?

ROCKVILLE MEDICAL CENTER

The Rockville medical center is a multiservice medical center located in a large city in the northeast United States. The center offers comprehensive diagnostic and treatment care for its patients. Along with traditional medical services, the center offers facilities for diagnosis, treatment, and consultations with physicians, nurses, and surgeons. The center is a certified American College of Radiology accredited facility and takes pride in being able to offer the most current diagnostic imaging and scanning capabilities. The diagnostic imaging technologies for testing that are offered at Rockville Medical Center include PET/CT scan, radiology, cardiac scoring, ultrasound, MRI, echocardiography, digital mammography, angiography, diagnostic imaging, vascular imaging, bone densitometry (osteoporosis screening), stereotactic breast unit, and X-ray.

The center is home to eight physicians, five physicians' assistants, nine registered nurses, and eight administrative staff. Julie Johnson is the chief operating officer, and Marcus Oppenheim is the marketing and public relations director for the center.

The Rockville Medical Center facility has a waiting room capable of seating 40 people comfortably on cushioned chairs arranged in small groups with end tables, coffee tables, lamps, magazines, and plenty of outlets for charging mobile communication devices. There are eight treatment rooms in addition to the testing rooms that house the diagnostic imaging equipment.

Four medical receptionists work at the front desk and are responsible for greeting patients and visitors as they enter the facility and directing them to appropriate locations. The receptionists are responsible for scheduling patients' appointments, answering the phones, answering patients' and visitors' questions, and assisting patients with insurance forms.

Julie Johnson and Marcus Oppenheim recently attended a conference where the issue of marketing research for health care services was discussed. In the past, the physicians who work at the Rockville Medical Center have been reluctant to conduct any form of marketing research. Most of the physicians at Rockville believe that good quality medical care should not need to be marketed. However, in the past two years Julie Johnson has noticed a small decrease in the year-to-year number of patients coming to the Rockville Medical Center. So, working with Marcus Oppenheim, they developed a survey that was given to every patient who came to the center for either a consultation, treatment, or testing during the last month. Each patient was given a survey as he or she was leaving the center and was asked to return the completed survey in the postage paid envelope. No incentive for completing the survey was offered. Julie and Marcus decided that doing so might cause patients to question the anonymity of their responses (if their name and contact information were associated with the survey). The first part of the survey asked patients to record the length of time that they had to wait in the waiting room and then in the treatment/test room. Patients were then asked to respond to 19 separate questions that measured their opinions regarding the specific aspects of the health care service they received. All of these 19 questions were measured on 5-point scales, where 1 = very poor and 5 = very good. A total of 114 patients completed the survey and returned it. Twelve patients returned incomplete surveys. The results from these 12 incomplete surveys were not included in the analysis.

Neither Julie Johnson nor Marcus Oppenheim has much experience working with results from marketing research, especially the results from customer satisfaction survey research. Most of their marketing experience has centered on working with medical supply firms or negotiating with medical supply vendors. They have entered the results from the survey into Excel and performed some simple analyses. The mean responses to the survey questions are shown in Table C3.1. From the conference they attended, both Julie and Marcus learned that correlations can be very useful when trying to interpret the results from surveys. The results from various correlation analyses are shown in Tables C3.2 through C3.5. Julie and Marcus have asked you to help them interpret these results and develop some strategies for marketing the medical center.

TABLE C3.1 Mean Responses to the Survey Questions

Survey Question (*Variable Name*)	N	Mean	Std Dev	Min	Max
How many minutes did you wait in the lobby after your scheduled appointment time before you were called to the test or treatment area? (*lobby wait*)	114	14.7	6.7	5.0	30.0
How many minutes did you wait in the test or treatment area before your test or treatment began? (*treat wait*)	114	24.3	7.2	7.0	45.0
The following survey questions were answered on a 5-point scale, where 1=very poor and 5 = very good					
Registration					
Helpfulness of the person at the registration desk (*helpful reg*)	114	4.1	1.0	1.0	5.0
Ease of the registration process (*ease reg*)	114	3.3	1.3	1.0	5.0
Waiting time in registration (*wait reg*)	114	2.6	1.0	1.0	5.0
How well billing and insurance questions were handled (*billing quest*)	114	3.8	1.1	1.0	5.0

Survey Question (*Variable Name*)	N	Mean	Std Dev	Min	Max
Facility					
Comfort of the waiting area (*comfort wait*)	114	3.7	1.3	1.0	5.0
Ease of finding your way around (*way around*)	114	2.5	1.3	1.0	5.0
Cleanliness of the facility (*cleanliness*)	114	3.0	1.1	1.0	5.0
Test & Treatment Area					
Friendliness of the staff who provided your test (*friendly staff*)	114	3.0	1.3	1.0	5.0
Explanations from the staff about your test (*explain staff*)	114	2.8	1.2	1.0	5.0
Test staff's concern for your comfort (*concern comfort*)	114	2.5	1.2	1.0	5.0
Time you spent waiting in the test area (*test wait*)	114	2.4	1.0	1.0	5.0
Explanations of/for tests provided by the doctor (*doc explain*)	114	2.9	1.0	1.0	5.0
Personal Issues					
Our concern for your privacy (*privacy*)	114	3.6	1.2	1.0	5.0
Our sensitivity to your needs (*sensitivity*)	114	3.1	1.3	1.0	5.0
Response to your concerns made during your visit (*concerns*)	114	3.0	1.1	1.0	5.0
Staff courtesy toward your family (*courtesy family*)	114	3.0	1.0	1.0	5.0
Staff concern for keeping your family informed (*family informed*)	114	3.1	1.0	1.0	5.0
Overall Assessment					
Overall rating of the care received during your visit (*overall*)	114	3.4	1.4	1.0	5.0
Likelihood of recommending our facility to others (*recommend*)	114	3.3	1.2	1.0	5.0

TABLE C3.2 Correlation Analysis Relating Overall Evaluations with <u>Registration</u>

	Overall	Recommend	Lobby Wait	Treat Wait	Helpful Reg.	Ease Reg.	Wait Reg.
Recommend	0.79**	----------					
Lobby Wait	−0.24**	−0.21*	----------				
Treat Wait	−0.38**	−0.35**	0.18	----------			
Helpful Reg	0.15	0.12	0.06	0.04	----------		
Ease Reg	0.27**	0.29**	0.11	−0.01	0.24*	----------	
Wait Reg	0.31**	0.34**	0.17	−0.04	0.14	0.18	----------
Billing Quest	0.16	0.09	0.12	0.03	0.20	0.15	0.09

*$p < .05$ **$p < .01$

TABLE C3.3 Correlation Analysis Relating Overall Evaluations with <u>Facility</u>

	Overall	Recommend	Comfort Wait	Way Around
Recommend	0.79**	----------		
Comfort Wait	0.26**	0.32**	----------	
Way Around	0.06	0.09	−0.04	----------
Cleanliness	0.31**	0.27**	0.21*	0.06

*p < .05   **p < .01

TABLE C3.4 Correlation Analysis Relating Overall Evaluations with <u>Test & Treatment Area</u>

	Overall	Recommend	Friendly Staff	Explain Staff	Concern Comfort	Test Wait
Recommend	0.79**	----------				
Friendly Staff	0.16	0.19*	----------			
Explain Staff	0.14	0.20*	0.13	----------		
Concern Comfort	0.08	0.16	0.19*	0.12	----------	
Test Wait	0.29**	0.31**	0.09	0.02	0.10	----------
Doc Explain	0.27**	0.25**	0.07	0.15	0.16	−0.01

*p < .05   **p < .01

TABLE C3.5 Correlation Analysis Relating Overall Evaluations with <u>Personal Issues</u>

	Overall	Recommend	Privacy	Sensitivity	Concerns	Courtesy Family
Recommend	0.79**	----------				
Privacy	0.12	0.14	----------			
Sensitivity	0.19*	0.26**	0.21*	----------		
Concerns	0.18	0.11	0.09	0.17	----------	
Courtesy Family	0.20*	0.25**	0.12	0.19*	0.14	----------
Family Informed	0.07	0.06	0.06	0.09	0.11	0.19*

*p < .05   **p < .01

ROCKVILLE MEDICAL CENTER ANALYSIS QUESTIONS

1. What do the means indicate about patients' evaluations of the medical center?

2. Based on the means, where is the medical center doing well and where is the medical center doing poorly?

3. The average rating for some of the factors was below the midpoint of the scale (i.e., less than 3 on the 5-point scale). Should Julie and Marcus try to improve the medical center's service in all of these areas if they want to significantly affect patients' overall evaluations of the medical center? If not, which factors should they emphasize?

4. Did the survey measure actual performance of the medical center and its staff, or did it merely ask for patients' perceptions of the medical center and its staff? What difference does this make in terms of interpreting the results?

5. Do the means alone provide adequate information for making managerial decisions in this case?

6. Does the correlation analysis provide any additional insight into the relationships between these variables?

7. Which factor(s) seem to be related to patients' overall evaluation and their likelihood of recommending the medical center?

8. What other analyses might be useful for interpreting the current data?

9. What other questions could be asked on the survey and included in the analysis to give a more complete picture of patients' evaluations of the medical center and areas where the medical center might seek to improve their service?

10. In addition to surveying patients, who else might be surveyed, and what questions might you ask these people?

11. If you were offering marketing advice to Julie Johnson and Marcus Oppenheim, what would you recommend to them?

12. Which areas of the medical center's service would you concentrate on if you wanted to hopefully increase patients' evaluations of the center and their willingness to recommend it?

13. Are there any potential sources of error associated with these results and the methodology by which the survey was administered? If so, what effect might these sources of error have on the results and the ability of someone to interpret the results from the research?

14. The patients were asked to take the survey home and then mail it back to the medical center. Would the results from the survey be different if all patients were asked to complete the survey before leaving the medical center?

15. If patients were asked to complete the survey before leaving the medical center, would this have any effect on:
    a. Patients' perceived anonymity?
    b. The number of patients who complete the survey (i.e., the response rate)?
    c. Patients' responses to the survey questions?

16. What other information about the medical center would you like to know?

17. What other analysis might be helpful in interpreting the results and developing marketing recommendations?

Appendices

APPENDIX 1

Table of Random Numbers   **555**

APPENDIX 2

Area under the Normal Curve (Z Values)   **557**

APPENDIX 3

Chi-Square (x^2) Distribution   **559**

APPENDIX 4

The Group Research Project   **561**

APPENDIX 1

Table of Random Numbers

773766	288064	288834	848508	400343	977035	666050	484631	751592
172343	793475	923818	122425	452648	664623	469237	592166	589233
868383	601023	858766	152398	918280	631135	582452	471678	565905
565911	927262	956534	331783	651626	827221	343591	619010	465729
502482	891511	947783	382477	521568	525534	477013	955931	134789
402098	217239	715171	903942	825900	372987	322212	656689	973532
553626	370151	469012	375149	551030	872577	791289	460326	263345
277240	792273	116937	653700	200994	172526	592117	388465	526166
327182	470299	120877	249544	983310	294748	937859	924946	684848
105086	267111	511664	267671	611020	444380	465420	103191	106573
652870	750287	283770	917650	446354	857928	919720	775352	863978
940561	459588	826759	804904	171783	293319	901637	182177	339174
376135	234568	903350	798182	570682	879766	391786	943128	239994
663624	664081	150985	841760	337762	376772	493374	641634	191450
694836	198226	989984	842550	893493	205490	327484	430595	440714
384932	333650	993565	511534	489495	541434	637789	939455	464979
593281	823112	987293	408142	573662	141194	885666	331975	769622
537693	891489	517084	497308	277160	197297	872045	561958	663685
200624	538082	717159	428075	335067	906119	205413	577642	262497
229435	493253	453486	896716	855892	922058	738492	939544	194424
469051	764791	216821	610228	263822	210592	435137	692545	650078
691532	742954	762820	860926	365737	112094	191809	867612	625812
422447	663234	828207	324272	596176	252512	133923	470219	305715
236607	929264	511953	105357	922370	802622	758269	170331	642220
431817	691136	851367	487928	147851	256597	252530	306895	455118
233147	951861	429998	220226	455799	213243	472488	517335	925399
961376	882624	459846	356945	770836	592556	701418	830981	549076
269068	727755	491571	926666	990722	284274	867692	812360	687451
400700	486833	394123	894821	242297	809605	343408	827533	669520
413482	621368	373538	431734	272779	172486	201869	772536	565926
316060	239718	480271	951065	613743	784806	792434	701304	711287
755354	541644	699054	620548	612060	255760	631225	876796	216633
768440	454618	623307	708659	945819	997722	943973	967482	851727
618472	634167	367012	635650	926815	461302	656472	417847	891082
945494	905048	682615	170172	473524	690264	288196	582172	723820
849024	470189	937861	939296	530072	553569	815946	610174	726227
482230	190310	253360	461052	202309	592120	921434	611199	790961
240126	494593	609849	539969	242732	482878	159905	641655	905914
190238	540970	480663	405809	662424	879849	208052	489342	439424
394603	607765	568455	510077	679826	785563	226524	907836	369534
108118	946595	825500	441348	686898	232168	339471	159283	535342
802766	172974	992450	254322	713706	515124	246644	504700	870782
153042	239482	167010	423618	562358	126208	706671	428930	730635
779365	348697	768695	564275	957043	321409	775424	647887	104321

APPENDIX 2

Area Under the Normal Curve (Z Values)

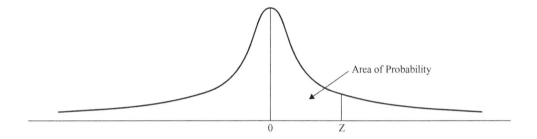

Area of Probability

0   Z

Example: The area under the curve between the mean and $Z = 2.53$ is .4943.

Example: The area under the curve between $Z = -1.25$ and $Z = 1.25$ is $(.3944 \times 2) = .7888$.

Z score	.00	.01	.03	.05	.07	.09
.0	.0000	.0040	.0120	.0199	.0279	.0359
.1	.0398	.0438	.0517	.0596	.0675	.0753
.2	.0793	.0832	.0910	.0987	.1064	.1141
.3	.1179	.1217	.1293	.1368	.1443	.1517
.4	.1554	.1591	.1664	.1736	.1808	.1879
.5	.1915	.1950	.2019	.2088	.2157	.2224
.6	.2257	.2291	.2357	.2422	.2486	.2549
.7	.2580	.2612	.2673	.2734	.2794	.2852
.8	.2881	.2910	.2967	.3023	.3078	.3133
.9	.3159	.3186	.3238	.3289	.3340	.3389
1.0	.3413	.3438	.3485	.3531	.3577	.3621
1.1	.3643	.3665	.3708	.3749	.3790	.3830
1.2	.3849	.3869	.3907	.3944	.3980	.4015
1.3	.4032	.4049	.4082	.4115	.4147	.4177
1.4	.4192	.4207	.4236	.4265	.4292	.4319
1.5	.4332	.4345	.4370	.4394	.4418	.4441
1.6	.4452	.4463	.4484	.4505	.4525	.4545
1.7	.4554	.4564	.4582	.4599	.4616	.4633
1.8	.4641	.4649	.4664	.4678	.4693	.4706
1.9	.4713	.4719	.4732	.4744	.4756	.4767
2.0	.4772	.4778	.4788	.4798	.4808	.4817
2.1	.4821	.4826	.4834	.4842	.4850	.4857

Z score	.00	.01	.03	.05	.07	.09
2.2	.4861	.4864	.4871	.4878	.4884	.4890
2.3	.4893	.4896	.4901	.4906	.4911	.4916
2.4	.4918	.4920	.4925	.4929	.4932	.4936
2.5	.4938	.4940	.4943	.4946	.4949	.4952
2.6	.4953	.4955	.4957	.4960	.4962	.4964
2.7	.4965	.4966	.4968	.4970	.4972	.4974
2.8	.4974	.4975	.4977	.4978	.4979	.4981
2.9	.4981	.4982	.4983	.4984	.4985	.4986
3.0	.4986	.4987	.4988	.4989	.4989	.4990

APPENDIX 3
Chi-Square (*x²*) Distribution

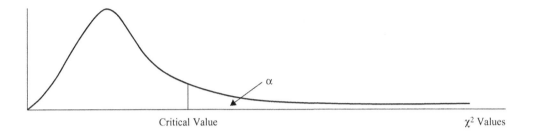

Critical Value χ^2 Values

Example: The critical value for $\alpha = .05$ and 1 degree of freedom is 3.841.

Example: The critical value for $\alpha = .01$ and 4 degree of freedom is 13.277.

Degrees of Freedom	Area in Right Tail (α)		
	.10	.05	.01
1	2.706	3.841	6.635
2	4.605	5.991	9.210
3	6.251	7.815	11.345
4	7.779	9.488	13.277
5	9.236	11.070	15.086
6	10.645	12.592	16.812
7	12.017	14.067	18.475
8	13.362	15.507	20.090
9	14.684	16.919	21.666
10	15.987	18.307	23.209
11	17.275	19.675	24.725
12	18.549	21.026	26.217
13	19.812	22.362	27.688
14	21.064	23.685	29.141
15	22.307	24.996	30.578
16	23.542	26.296	32.000
17	24.769	27.587	33.409
18	25.989	28.869	34.805
19	27.204	30.144	36.191
20	28.412	31.410	37.566
21	29.615	32.671	38.932
22	30.813	33.924	40.289
23	32.007	35.172	41.638
24	33.196	36.415	42.980

	Area in Right Tail (α)		
Degrees of Freedom	.10	.05	.01
25	34.382	37.652	44.314
26	35.563	38.885	45.642
27	36.741	40.113	46.963
28	37.916	41.337	48.278
29	39.087	42.557	49.588
30	40.256	43.773	50.892

APPENDIX 4

The Group Research Project

This semester-long project has been designed to help students learn and apply the marketing research concepts discussed in this book. The overall purpose of this project is to illustrate how marketing research is used to collect information that managers need to make decisions. The project is to be conducted by groups of three to four students. Each group will work on one small-business marketing research project. As students learn about marketing research topics and the stages in the research process throughout the semester, they will work on their group project and review the projects from other groups. For a more detailed description of the project see Timothy R. Graeff, "Bringing Reflective Learning to the Marketing Research Course: A Cooperative Learning Project Using Inter-Group Critique," *Journal of Marketing Education* 19 no. 1 (1997): 53–64.

Small-Business Investment Decision This project is designed to give students hands-on experience with using marketing research to deal with a small-business investment decision. Students should place themselves in the position of an entrepreneur who is considering opening a new business, but is not sure what to do, who to target, where to locate the store or retail outlet, or even if there is a good chance that the business will succeed. The primary target market for the small business should consist of students. This will allow students to collect data from the target market relatively quickly and easily.

Assume that the new business requires an initial investment of $25,000. Design the research project with the following in mind: Before I invest my $25,000 in this business, what do I want to know about students who will be in my target market? The overall purpose of the project is to collect the information that will help a marketer make a managerial decision regarding opening this business.

Example Projects. Example group projects include:

- You are considering opening a food delivery service on campus that delivers to dorms.

- You are considering opening a dorm cleaning service.

- You are considering starting a note-taking service on campus.

- You are considering opening a florist.

- You are considering opening an ice cream shop.

- You are considering opening a car wash.

Intergroup Critique. There are nine major sections of this project corresponding to the major stages in the research process. After completing each of these nine sections of the project, your group (called the **research group**) will give your project materials (e.g., list of research objectives, draft of the survey) to another group (called the **critique group**). The critique group will review your project materials and offer suggestions for improving your project. After you have received a critique from another group, reflect on this critique. For example, each group will critique a different group's research objectives. Comments and suggestions made by the critique group will then be given back to the research group. Based on these comments, the research group can revise this part of their project and begin work on the next part of their project, which will later be critiqued by a different group. Your instructor might also want to review each group's work with the entire class. This will inform other students of your group project and will give all students a chance to comment on the research projects. Hopefully, everyone will learn from these in-class exercises.

Research Instructions. As you work on this project, consider the materials that you submit to the critique group as detailed research instructions. This means that another person who is not in your group should be able to read your project materials and conduct the research exactly as you intended. Each part of your project should be specific and detailed, not vague and ambiguous. For instance, do not state that you will conduct personal interviews of students on campus. This needs to be more specific. You must specify exactly who, what, where, when, and how these students will be interviewed. As another example, do not simply state that you will sample 500 students. You must be specific in detailing exactly how these 500 students are to be selected, the exact nature of the sampling procedure, and even the sampling frame.

OUTLINE OF THE GROUP PROJECT

1. Description of the Business and Target Market

Write a preliminary description of your business and target market. What will your business be? What will you sell? What services will you offer? Where will your business be located? Why might this new business be successful? Who are your primary customers? This is preliminary because the results from subsequent research (the focus group) might help you better define your business and target market (who you will target, what services you will offer, where you will be located, etc.).

Preliminary Survey. Many people believe that writing a survey is very easy. They believe that anyone can do it. However, writing a survey and conducting marketing research that measures precise variables to aid in making managerial or marketing decisions involves more than most people think it does. To illustrate this, it is instructive to try to write a survey before beginning the class or reading through this book. Write a survey that you think will help you measure demand for this new business. To help you with this, ask yourself, "What do I want to know about potential customers?" At the end of the semester, refer back to this and compare your final survey to this survey. You might be surprised at how much you have learned from your marketing research class and from reading this book.

Critique. Does the description provide information about the target market, the services that the business will provide, how much these services will cost, and when students can use the services of the business?

Reflection. What information is missing from the description? What information is necessary to describe a new business?

2. Focus Group

Conduct a focus group on a group of students that you have recruited to represent the market you are targeting for your business. Use the results from this focus group to help you define your business. Keep note of what the focus group participants say about their desire, or lack of desire, to use your business/service. What ideas do they offer that might help you to refine your business description and increase your chances for financial success? Most focus groups are videotaped or audio recorded so that verbatim transcripts can be made later. For your focus group, you might be able to videotape it, or at least record it. This will come in handy later when you are reviewing the results from the focus group. After conducting the focus group, determine what the most important results were from the session. What were respondents saying? What were the major themes of their comments? Did they offer any new ideas for your business? Did they offer any criticisms about your business idea?

Critique. Does the moderator's guide provide adequate guidance to the moderator? Will the questions on the moderator's guide obtain the information that is needed? Are questions asked using the funneling technique? Are questions written to allow for participant-generated ideas to emerge during the group session?

Reflection. How should a moderator's guide be written? What is the purpose of a moderator's guide for a focus group? How should questions be asked during a focus group?

3. Quantitative Research Objectives

Develop the list of specific and measurable research objectives to be measured on your survey. Note, you are not writing questions at this stage—that will come later. At this stage you are merely writing statements of what you want to know about students (your target market). Identify research objectives that can be met with secondary data. Identify research objectives that must be met with primary data. You might also want to develop decision criteria for those research objectives that are related to measuring demand for your new business, and thus your decision to either open this business or to not open this business.

Critique. Do these research objectives specify what is to be measured and how it is to be measured? Can a survey question be written to achieve each of these objectives?

Do the objectives need to be more specific? Vague objectives usually lead to vague results. Are there other important research objectives that are not identified (other relevant variables to be measured)? Can the research objectives be met with just one survey? Are two or more surveys required (sent to different segments, i.e., faculty and students)?

Reflection. Which of the objectives are good (specific and measurable)? Which of the objectives are bad (not specific and not measurable)? As a rule, how should research objectives be written? What is the difference between good and bad research objectives?

4. Data Collection Procedures

Design the data collection procedures for your group project. Considering the research objectives you have previously developed and the types of survey error described in this book, you must decide how you will collect your data. How will you administer the survey? How will you get the survey to potential respondents? Will you use a telephone survey, an online survey, or an intercept survey? Be specific in describing your data collection procedures. Do not merely state that you will conduct intercept interviews on campus. You must specify when, where, how, and how often you will conduct intercept interviews on campus. Consider these data collection procedures as a set of specific instructions. If given to someone else, that person should be able to read your data collection procedures and collect the data exactly as you intended. There should be no question about exactly how you will collect the data.

Critique. Is the procedure for administering the survey complete? Are there any sources of error or bias that might be associated with the data collection procedures?

Reflection. What was wrong with the data collection procedures? Why is it important that the description of data collection procedures be specific? What sources of error or bias are associated with the data collection procedures? What are the major sources of error or bias associated with the data collection procedures? How can these sources of error be reduced or be eliminated? What must be considered when designing data collection procedures for a survey?

5. Design the Survey

Write the survey that you will use to measure the information that will be used to make your business investment decision. All surveys need some sort of introduction. The introduction to a survey is used to encourage respondents to complete the survey. Keep in mind the way in which you will be collecting the data. Are you conducting a phone survey, are you conducting a personal intercept survey, or are you conducting an online survey? If you are conducting a phone survey or a personal intercept survey, you must still develop an introductory statement introducing yourself to respondents.

To write your survey, refer back to your research objectives. Your research objectives will identify what to ask on your survey. Be sure that your survey achieves all of your objectives, asks all questions identified in your objectives, and asks questions on the appropriate scales. For example, if one of your objectives is to measure the average age of students, you must use a scale that will allow you to calculate the average.

Critique. Is there a cover letter or scripted oral introduction to the survey? Does the introduction answer all of the questions that a potential respondent might ask about the survey and their participation in it? (For example, What is this? Who wants to know? Why do they want to know this? Why was I chosen? How important is this? Will this be difficult? How long will this take? Will this cost me anything? What do I get out of this? Will I be identified with my answers? How will this be used? When should I do this?) Does the survey have any biased or poorly worded questions that are loaded, leading, ambiguous, vague, taxing, or double-barreled? Is the ordering of questions on the survey appropriate? Does the survey require any skip, filter, or branching questions? If so, are they in the appropriate location on the survey? Does the survey use the appropriate scales for measuring the issues and variables as they are stated in the list of research objectives? Does the survey fulfill all of the stated research objectives? Does the survey provide a means for determining the representativeness of the respondents?

Reflection. What is the purpose of the introduction to a survey and what important information should be included in the introduction? What was wrong with the survey? Why did the critique group not answer the survey question as we had intended? How does the wording of questions on the survey influence the way that respondents answer them? What is the appropriate ordering of questions on a survey, and why is this important? Why is it important to consider the range of all possible answers to a survey question?

6. Design the Sampling Procedures

What is the population of interest for your survey? Can you obtain a list of all members of the population? What list of population members (sampling frame) will you use to choose the sample? How many people will you survey? What will be your expected sample size? How will you choose the people from the sampling frame to be in your sample? Will you use a nonprobability sampling procedure or a probability sampling procedure? Will there be only one stage of sampling or multiple stages of sampling? What sampling procedures will you use at each stage in the sampling process? What characteristics of respondents must be considered (measured) to determine the representativeness of the sample?

Critique. Will the sampling procedure yield a representative and unbiased sample of the stated target market? Does the sampling procedure systematically eliminate any member(s) of the target market from being included in the sample?

Reflection. What was wrong with the sampling procedures? Why is it important that the description of the sampling procedures be specific? What sources of error or bias are associated with the sampling procedures? How can these sources of error be reduced or eliminated? Why is representative sampling important? What must be considered when designing sampling procedures?

7. Collect the Data

Administer your survey and collect the data.

Critique. Was the data collected in an unbiased manner? Did the manner in which the data was collected have any influence on subjects' responses to the survey questions? Did the manner in which the data was collected systematically eliminate any member(s) of the target market from being included in the sample?

Reflection. How should a research project be designed so that there is no bias associated with the data collection procedures? What aspects of the data collection procedures might bias potential responses? What aspects of the data collection procedures might systematically eliminate any member(s) of the target market from being included in the sample?

8. Enter and Analyze the Data

If you conducted a CATI phone interview or an online survey, your data is most likely already in the form of a data file that can be easily exported and analyzed using a statistical analysis program. However, if you conducted an intercept survey or a self-administered survey, you must enter the results from the survey into a data file (e.g., using Microsoft Excel) and then perform the analysis. You must also identify the appropriate statistical analysis for each of your research objectives. A blank coding sheet is provided at the end of this appendix for you to use when entering the results from your surveys. Worksheets for calculating confidence intervals and for conducting hypothesis tests are also provided at the end of this appendix for you to use.

Critique. Was the appropriate data analysis performed for each objective? Are the results from the data analyses stated clearly and correctly?

Reflection. What level scales were used to measure the variables? For a given research objective and a given set of variables, what is the appropriate analysis? What are all the possible explanations for the results that were observed? Are the results due to random sampling error, bias, or real effects?

9. Prepare the Research Report

Before managers can make decisions based on the results from a marketing research project, the research results must be presented in the form of a marketing research report. The marketing research report summarizes the research techniques that were used, the methodology that was employed, the information that was collected, and the usefulness of this information to the decision-making process. Your group project is not complete until the results from it are presented in the form of a marketing research report.

Critique. Is the report well written? Does the report address all major issues associated with the research? Does the report present the results from the research project in a manner that is useful to marketing managers?

Reflection. How can the report be written so that it is easier to read? How knowledgeable is the target audience in terms of research methodology and statistical analysis?

BLANK CODING SHEET

Below is a blank coding sheet that can be used for entering data from a survey.

Question Number	Survey Question	Column in Data File	Variable Name	Coded Scale Values

CONFIDENCE INTERVAL WORKSHEET

Confidence Interval for an Average

Variable	$\bar{X} - 1.96(SE_{mean})$	95 percent of samples will yield results between (μ)	$\bar{X} + 1.96(SE_{mean})$	$1.96(SE_{mean})$
	←	→		
	←	→		
	←	→		
	←	→		
	←	→		
	←	→		
	←	→		
	←	→		
	←	→		
	←	→		

Confidence Interval for a Proportion

Variable	$p - 1.96(SE_{prop})$	95 percent of samples will yield results between (π)	$p + 1.96(SE_{prop})$	$1.96(SE_{prop})$
	←	→		
	←	→		
	←	→		
	←	→		
	←	→		
	←	→		
	←	→		
	←	→		
	←	→		
	←	→		

HYPOTHESIS TEST WORKSHEET

Variable	If the null hypothesis (Ho) is true, 95 percent of samples will yield results within			Result from the survey Sample Average or Proportion
	-1.96(SE)	(μ or π)	+1.96(SE)	
	←		→	
	←		→	
	←		→	
	←		→	
	←		→	
	←		→	
	←		→	
	←		→	
	←		→	
	←		→	
	←		→	
	←		→	
	←		→	
	←		→	
	←		→	

Index

80 percent rule, 47
80/20 rule, 110

Absolute zero, 261
ACASI (audio computer aided self-administered interviewing), 208
Acceptance region, 435
Acquiescence bias, 229
Active Group, 136
Adjusted R^2, 497
Administrative error, 6, 235
Adoption process models (consumer), 175
Affirming the consequent, 365
After only design, 384
Alpha (significance level), 434, 437
Alternative explanation, 365
Alternative hypothesis, 405
Ambiguous questions, 306
American Association for Public Opinion Research (AAPOR), 16
American Marketing Association (code of ethics), 16, 133
Analysis paralysis, 56
Anchoring and adjustment, 231
Annual survey of manufacturers (ASM), 105
ANOVA (one-way), 469
ANOVA (two-way), 485
ANOVA summary table, 470
Apathy bias, 232, 323
Applied research, 4
Apps-based research, 45
Articulation questions, 139
Association, 479
Attitudes, 184
Attributes (product), 157
Audio SAQ (audio self-administered questionnaire), 208

Background analysis, 64, 84
Backward selection procedure, 502
Bandwagon effect, 127
Bar charts, 516
Basic experiments, 367
Basic research, 3
Behavior (consumers'), 98
Behavioral constructs, 251

Behavioral intentions, 184, 185
Benefits (product), 157
Beta coefficients, 498
Beta, 437
Between group variation, 470
Between subjects design, 369
Between subjects randomized block design, 373, 374
Bias, 223
Big data, 56
Biometrics, 51
Bipolar adjectives, 294
Bivariate analysis, 268
Bivariate cross-tab table, 447
Bivariate regression, 495
Bivariate statistical procedures, 404
Blind experiments, 378
Blocking, 372
Bonferroni's multiple comparison procedure, 475
Bounce rate, 49
Branching questions, 320
Brand community, 43
Brand personality, 161
Brand sensitivities, 140
Brands (as social objects), 38
Broadcasting, 110
Bureau of Labor Statistics (BLS), 11, 105
Burke Institute, 133

Cannibalism (product), 380
CAPI (computer assisted personal interview), 209
CASI (computer assisted self-administered interview), 209
Categorical data, 404
Categories (combining), 259
Category ranges (and ordinal scales), 263
CATI (computer assisted telephone interview), 209
Causal research, 66, 363
Cell frequencies, 448
Census (U.S.), 103
Census, 219, 345
Central limit theorem, 351, 420
Central tendency (measures of), 254, 413
Chain sampling, 348

Challenges (facing marketing research), 55
Changes in the subject (and validity), 377
Chart titles, 520
Charts (interpreting), 521
Checklist question, 292
Chi-Square distribution (table), 457, 559
Chi-Square test, 455
Client (meeting with), 28
Client lounge, 135
Clients (satisfying), 33
Client-side researchers, 12
Closed-ended questions, 289
Cluster sampling, 350
Code book, 393
Coding schemes (data driven), 402
Coding schemes (pre-determined), 402
Coding sheet (blank), 567
Coding sheet, 393
Coefficient alpha, 279
Coefficient of determination (r^2), 481
Coefficient of multiple determination (R^2), 496, 501
Coefficient of partial determination, 501
Collages, 162
Collectively exhaustive, 288, 290
Column chart, 517
Column percent, 452, 459
Communities (managed), 44
Communities (open), 44
Company data, 104
Comparative rating scale, 291
Competitors (identifying with reverse laddering), 159
Compiled lists, 117
Completion rate, 197
Computer Assisted Telephone Interviewing (CATI), 199
Computer based interviewing, 208
Conceptual definition, 252
Concomitant variation, 367
Concurrent validity, 281
Confidence in estimates (increasing), 430
Confidence interval for a proportion, 428
Confidence interval for an average, 425
Confidence interval worksheet (blank), 568
Confounds, 363

Constant sum scale, 297
Construct validity, 281
Constructs (abstract), 252
Constructs (concrete), 252
Constructs, 251
Consumer generated media (CGM), 38
Consumer packaged goods (CPG), 106
Consumer panels, 105
Content validity, 280
Contingency tables, 447
Continuous data, 404
Continuous rating scale, 294
Control group, 368, 371
Convenience sampling, 348
Convergent validity, 281
Conversion, 49
Corporate researchers, 12
Correlation (and causation), 481
Correlation coefficient (r), 479
Counter balancing order of
    presentation, 372
Counter biasing statement, 234, 310
County business patterns (CBP), 105
Covariation, 479
Cover letter, 316
Covert observation, 92
Criterion validity, 280
Critical value, 435
Cronbach's alpha, 279
Cross cultural marketing mistakes, 211
Cross-sectional survey, 237
Cross-tabulating survey data, 447
Customer contact (service) audit, 182
Customer relationship management, 4
Customer satisfaction (surveys), 180
Customer service, 180

Data collection (surveys), 195
Data processing error, 236
Data snooping, 475
Database (creating), 110
Database marketing, 108
Day-after recall, 384
Debate sessions, 163
Decision maker, 180
Decision support system, 4
Decisions (identifying), 30
Decisions (making informed), 8
Degrees of freedom, 456
Demand effect, 230
Demographic constructs, 251
Demographic questions (placement on a
    survey), 319
Demographics (consumer), 103
Dependent variable, 66, 173, 363
Descriptive research, 65
Diary media panel, 106

Diary purchase panel, 105
Direct marketing, 108
Direct traffic, 49
Discriminant validity, 281
Discussion guide, 138
Dispersion (measures of), 403
Distributions, 413
Do-it-yourself (DIY) research, 55
Don't know / no opinion
    (and validity), 281
Do-not-call, 200, 329
Door-to-door interviews, 197
Double blind experiments, 378
Double negatives (questions
    containing), 313
Double-barreled question, 311

Economic census, 104
Electroencephalography (EEG), 53
Emerging technologies, 42
Employee interviews and focus
    groups, 85
EMS (electronic mail survey), 209
Equivalent forms method, 278
Ethics (in marketing research), 16, 57
Ethnography, 93
Executive summary, 509
Expectations, 181
Expected value, 456
Experimental designs, 363
Experimental group, 368
Explaining variability (ANOVA), 471
Exploratory research, 63
External environment (and validity), 376
External searches, 48
External validity, 378
Extraneous variables, 66, 363, 367, 371
Extrapolating (and non-response
    error), 228
Extremity bias, 231
Eye tracking, 51

Face validity, 280
Facebook, 40
Facial analysis, 52
Factorial design, 367, 374, 485
False comparisons (questions
    containing), 313
FASI (fully automated
    self-interview), 209
FATI (fully automated telephone
    interview), 209
Field experiments, 367
Filter questions, 320
Finite population correction factor, 356
Focus group evaluation, 165
Focus group facilities, 131
Focus group room, 135

Focus groups (online), 163
Focus groups, 97, 125, 130
Focus Vision, 136
Forced choice scale, 294
Forward selection procedure, 502
Frequency tables, 447
Frequency, 119
Frugging, 200
Full service research firms, 11
Functional magnetic resonance imaging
    (fMRI), 53
Funneling, 142, 152, 233, 318

Gamification, 56
Gap analysis, 181
Gaze motion, 51
Gaze plot, 52
Geolocation, 92
Global survey research, 210
Goal conversion rate, 50
Goals (personal), 157
Google analytics, 48
Google consumer surveys, 205
GPS, 92
Graphic rating scale, 294
Green Book, 131
Ground rules (for focus groups), 144
Group research project, 561

Halo effect, 323
Heat map, 52
Hostility bias, 230, 323
Hypotheses, 190
Hypothesis test of a proportion, 444
Hypothesis test of an average, 442
Hypothesis test worksheet (blank), 569
Hypothesis testing, 433

Identify preserving transformations, 257
IDO model, 26, 74
Image profile, 295
Importance, 181
Impulse Survey, 131
Independent (sampling), 349
Independent variable, 66, 173, 363, 368
Index of items, 278, 298
Industry data, 104
Information (identifying), 30
In-home interviews, 197
Instability of true scores
    (and reliability), 277
Interaction (ANOVA), 486
Interaction (in multiple regression), 496
Interactions (among marketing mix
    variables), 372, 380
Intergroup critique (group project), 562
Internal consistency, 278

Internal searches, 49
Internal validity, 376
Interval preserving transformations, 260
Interval scale, 260
Interviewer cheating error, 236
Interviewer error (bias), 231, 236
Interviewer guidelines, 328
Introduction (to a survey), 316
Irrelevance (of the decision maker), 7
Item response rate, 197

Jargon (questions containing), 312
Judgment sampling, 348

Lab experiments, 368
Laddering (interviews), 155, 157
Landing page, 49
Latin square, 372, 375
Leading questions, 234, 309
Least significance difference method
   (LSD), 475
Lifestyles (consumer), 103
Likert scale, 293
Line charts, 519
Linear probability models, 496
Linear transformations (of scale), 260
List providers, 116
Loaded questions, 309
Logistic regression, 496
Logit analysis, 496
Longitudinal survey, 238
Loyalty programs, 113
Loyalty, 50

Mail surveys, 201
Mailed regression, 117
Main effect (ANOVA), 486
Mall intercept interviews, 198
Margin means, 486
Margin of error, 358, 425
Margin totals, 448
Market intelligence, 104
Marketing information system, 4
Marketing research analyst, 12
Marketing Research Association, 14, 16
Marketing research contacts, 15
Marketing research jobs, 13
Marketing research online communities
   (MROC), 45
Marketing research process, 71
Marketing research salaries, 13
Marketing research, 1
Master's in Marketing Research (MMR), 13
MCAPI (mobile computer assisted
   personal interview), 209
Mean, 254, 403
Means-end chains (MEC), 156

Measurement, 251
Media monitoring, 48
Median, 254, 403
Memory bias, 231
Memory effects (and reliability), 277
Metric data, 404
Micro marketing, 110
Mini-groups, 137
Missing data (entering), 397
Mobile surveys, 45, 204
Mobile ethnography, 96
Mode, 254, 403
Model building and selection
   procedures, 501
Moderator (focus group), 133
Moderator variable (effect), 496
Moderator's guide, 138
Monadic rating scale, 291
Monetary, 119
Multicultural (surveys), 210
Multicultural research (and
   ethnography), 96
Multi-dimensional constructs, 298
Multi-factor experiments, 367
Multi-item index, 278, 298
Multi-label codes, 402
Multiple comparison procedures, 474
Multiple regression analysis, 495
Multi-procedure sampling, 350
Multi-stage area sample, 350
Multivariate analysis, 268, 405
Mutually exclusive, 290
Mystery shopper, 87
Mystery Shopping Providers Association
   (MSPA), 89

Narrowcasting, 110
Natural language processing
   algorithms, 57
Negative gap, 181
Neuromarketing, 53
Niche marketing, 110
Nielsen Television Index, 106
Nominal scale, 256
Non-customers, 180
Nonmetric data, 404
Non-probability sampling procedures, 348
Non-response error, 225
Normal distribution, 415
Normal variable, 417
Null hypothesis, 405

Objectives (identifying), 28
Objectives (managerial), 72 , 73
Objectives (research), 72, 74
Observation (human), 91

Observation (mechanical), 91
Observation research, 90
Observed value, 456
Omnibus surveys, 2066
One group pretest-posttest design, 385
One-factor experiments, 367
One-way mirror, 135
Online ethnography, 96
Online (internet) surveys, 45, 202
Online communities, 43
Online community manager, 45
Open-ended questions, 289
Open-ended questions coding
   schemes, 400
Operational definition, 252
Operationalized (variable), 172
Opinion leader, 141, 128
Opt-in email, 117
Oral introduction (survey), 316
Order of events, 366
Order preserving transformations, 258
Ordinal scale, 257
Other (response category), 292
Outliers, 265
Overt observation, 92

P values, 244, 405
Page view, 49
Panel study, 238
Participant observer, 93
Paywall, 205
Pearson product-moment correlation
   coefficient (r), 479
People Meters™, 106
Percentage table, 447
Personal interviews, 196
Photo sort, 162
Pie charts, 516
Pilot testing, 34
Pin-point marketing, 110
Pioneering advantage, 382
Point-of-sale interviews, 198
Population distribution, 418
Population element, 345
Population mean, 220
Population parameter, 219, 345
Population proportion, 220
Population selection error, 235
Population standard deviation
   (estimating), 353
Population standard deviation, 220, 403
Population variability
   (and sample size), 357
Population variance, 220, 403
Population, 345
Portable people meter (PPM™), 106

Positioning data collection efforts, 113
Positive gap, 181
Posttest only with a control group
    design, 388
Precise measurement, 65, 66
Precision marketing, 110
Predictive targeting, 115
Predictive validity, 281
Predictor variables, 178
Prestige bias, 230
Pretest – posttest with a control group
    design, 387
Primary data, 3
Primary sampling unit, 350
Prior measurements, 377
Privacy concerns, 55
Probability sampling procedures, 349
Problems (defining marketing), 71
Problems (identifying marketing), 83
Product registration cards, 116
Professional Researcher Certification
    (PRC), 14
Project director, 12
Projective techniques, 146, 160
Prompters, 233, 319
Proprietary credit cards, 114
Psycho-drawing, 162
Psychographic constructs, 251
Psychographics (consumer), 103
Publisher (Google Consumer
    Survey), 205
Purchase process models (consumer), 175
Push poll, 19, 213

Qualitative data, 65
Qualitative Research Consultants
    Association (QRCA), 128
Quantitative research objectives, 172
Quasi-experimental design, 384
Question order bias, 230
Quick response (QR) codes, 46
Quirk's Marketing Research Source
    Book, 131

Random assignment, 372
Random digit dialing (RDD), 200
Random number generator, 350
Random numbers (table of), 351, 555
Random sample, 347
Random sampling error, 7, 221
Randomized block design, 372
Randomized response questions, 325
Ranking questions, 298
Ratio scale, 261
Recency, 118
Referral based sampling, 348
Rejection region, 435

Reliability, 276
Repeated measures design, 370, 372, 374
Repeated questions, 324
Representative sampling, 346
Research presentation, 513
Research report, 507
Research techniques (identifying), 31
Respondent cooperation, 55
Respondents' intent, 306
Response bias (reducing), 232
Response bias, 7, 229, 283
Response categories (defining), 309
Response lists, 117
Response rates (increasing), 326
Restricted choice question, 290
Retail audit, 106
Reverse laddering interview, 160
Reverse-scored (questions), 233,
    298, 313, 323
Reward credit cards, 115
RFM analysis, 118
River sampling, 348
Role playing, 161
Root causes, 77
Row percent, 452, 459

Sample distribution, 419
Sample element, 346
Sample mean, 220
Sample proportion, 220
Sample selection error, 235
Sample size (and margin of error), 356
Sample size (determining), 352
Sample standard deviation, 220, 403
Sample statistic, 219
Sample variance, 220, 403
Sampling (statistical) error, 7, 221
Sampling distribution of the mean, 420
Sampling frame error, 235
Sampling frame, 235, 349
Sampling procedure error, 235
Sampling procedures, 347
Sampling units, 350
Sampling, 345
Satisfaction, 181
Scale (measurement), 253
Scale points (number of), 296
Scale range, 518
Scales (levels of), 254
Scheffe's multiple comparison
    procedure, 475
Screening survey, 134, 139,
Seasonal effects, 370
Secondary data, 3, 102, 107
Secondary sampling unit, 350
Self-administered survey, 201
Self-contained (test market), 383

Self-selection bias, 225
Semantic differential scale, 294
Senior project director, 12
Sensitivity, 276, 279
Sentiment score, 50
Sequences of causes, 77
Short message service (SMS), 40
Simple random sampling, 349
Simulated shopping
    environments, 92, 135
Situation analysis, 84
Skip interval, 349
Skip questions, 320
Snake diagram, 295
Snowball sampling, 348
Social desirability bias, 229
Social media (analytics), 48
Social media (monitoring), 42, 46, 98
Social media, 38
Socially acceptable, 229
Split half method, 278
Sponsorship bias, 230
Spurious association, 363, 367
Standard error of the mean, 222
Standard error of the proportion, 222
Standardized estimates, 498
Standardized normal distribution, 417
Standardized variable (score), 417, 497
Stapel scale, 297
Static group design, 386
Statistic (sample), 346
Statistical analysis, 267
Statistical hypothesis testing, 405
Statistical inference, 418
Statistical power, 328, 438
Stepwise selection procedure, 502
Store audit, 106
Store credit cards, 114
Story / sentence completion, 161
Straight line (column)
    responding, 233, 323
Stratified sampling, 350
Straw polls, 208
Structured data, 57
Subscribers (to syndicated surveys), 206
Successive waves (and non-response
    error), 228
Sugging, 200
Sum of squares, 470
Survey error, 219
Surveywall, 205
SWOT analysis, 85
Symptoms (marketing), 72
Synchronized marketing, 110, 111
Syndicated surveys, 206
Systematic error, 223
Systematic sampling, 349

TATI (touch-tone aided telephone interview), 209
Taxing questions, 311
Technical language (questions containing), 312
Telemarketing (versus telephone surveying), 200
Telemarketing and Consumer Fraud and Abuse Prevention Act, 200
Telephone Consumer Protection Act, 200
Telephone surveys, 199
Telescoping (backward), 231
Telescoping (forward), 231
Test kitchen, 135
Test marketing, 379
Test units, 368
Test-retest method, 277
Text analytics, 50
Text mining, 48
Thematic Apperception Test, 162
Third person technique, 161
Threat bias, 230
Time on site, 50
Time trends (and non-response error), 229

Top exit pages, 50
Tracking study, 238
Traffic, 49
Transformations (allowable scale), 256
Treatments, 368
Triad, 137
True experimental design, 384, 387
Tukey's multiple comparison procedure, 475
Twitter, 40
Type I error, 437
Type II error, 437

Unbiased (sampling), 349
Unethical practices (in marketing research), 16
Uninformed response bias, 7, 232, 323
Univariate analysis, 268
Univariate statistical procedures, 404
Unstructured data, 57

Validity, 276, 280
Values (personal), 157
Variable (categorical), 172
Variable (continuous), 172

Variable names, 396
Variety seekers, 381
Verbal labels (on scales), 262
Vertical bar chart, 517
Video streaming (of focus groups), 136
Viewing room, 135
Virtual straw poll, 208

Warranty cards, 116
Wholesale audit, 107
Within group variation, 470
Within subjects repeated measures design, 370, 372
Word association, 161
Word clouds, 402
Working population, 235, 349

Yea-saying bias, 230
YouTube, 40

Z scores, 417
Z table, 418, 425, 557
Zero (as a response category), 321
Zero (on scales), 262